W9-DCI-533

Foreign Relations of the United States, 1958–1960

Volume XVII

Indonesia

Editor	Robert J. McMahon
General Editor	Glenn W. LaFantasie

United States Government Printing Office
Washington
1994

DEPARTMENT OF STATE PUBLICATION 10158

OFFICE OF THE HISTORIAN

BUREAU OF PUBLIC AFFAIRS

For sale by the U.S. Government Printing Office
Superintendent of Documents, Mail Stop: SSOP, Washington, DC 20402-9328
ISBN 0-16-041836-4

Preface

The *Foreign Relations of the United States* series presents the official documentary historical record of major foreign policy decisions and significant diplomatic activity of the United States Government. The series documents the formulation of policies, including the events which contributed to that process, and includes evidence of supporting and alternative views to the policy positions ultimately adopted.

The Historian of the Department of State is charged with the responsibility for the preparation of the *Foreign Relations* series. The staff of the Office of the Historian, Bureau of Public Affairs, plans, researches, compiles, and edits the volumes in the series. This documentary editing proceeds in full accord with the generally accepted standards of historical scholarship. Official regulations codifying specific standards for the selection and editing of documents for the series were first promulgated by Secretary of State Frank B. Kellogg on March 26, 1925. These regulations, with minor modifications, guided the series through 1991.

A new statutory charter for the preparation of the series was established by Public Law 102–138, the Foreign Relations Authorization Act, Fiscal Years 1992 and 1993, which was signed by President George Bush on October 28, 1991. Section 198 of P.L. 102–138 added a new Title IV to the Department of State's Basic Authorities Act of 1956 (22 USC 4351, *et seq.*).

The statute requires that the *Foreign Relations* series be a thorough, accurate, and reliable record of major United States foreign policy decisions and significant United States diplomatic activity. The volumes of the series should include all records needed to provide comprehensive documentation of major foreign policy decisions and actions of the United States Government, including facts that contributed to the formulation of policies and records that provided supporting and alternative views to the policy positions ultimately adopted.

The statute confirms the editing principles established by Secretary Kellogg: the *Foreign Relations* series is guided by the principles of historical objectivity and accuracy; records should not be altered or deletions made without indicating in the published text that a deletion has been made; the published record should omit no facts that were of major importance in reaching a decision; and nothing should be omitted for the purposes of concealing a defect in policy. The statute also requires that the *Foreign Relations* series be published not more than 30 years after the events recorded.

The General Editor of the series and the editor of this volume, which was compiled in 1980–1981, are convinced that it meets all regulatory, statutory, and scholarly standards of selection and editing. Although this volume records policies and events of more than 30 years ago, the statute of October 28, 1991, allows the Department until 1996 to reach the 30-year line in the publication of the series.

Structure and Scope of the Foreign Relations Series

This volume is part of a triennial subseries of volumes of the *Foreign Relations* series. This subseries documents the most important issues in the foreign policy of the final three years (1958–1960) of the administration of Dwight D. Eisenhower. Within the 1958–1960 subseries, six volumes and four microfiche supplements present the record of U.S. policy toward East Asia. This volume presents documentation on U.S. policy toward Indonesia. Volume XVIII covers Japan and Korea and Volume XIX documents U.S. policy toward China and the related question of the rebellion in Tibet. Volume I is devoted exclusively to Vietnam. Volume XVI includes an overview of U.S. regional policy for East Asia as well as extensive material on policy toward Cambodia and Laos. Volume XV includes material on the rest of Southeast Asia.

Additional documents on Indonesia are presented in a microfiche supplement to this volume (which also includes documents from Volume XVIII) and additional material on the rest of Asia is in microfiche supplements to Volumes XV, XVI, and XIX.

The statute of October 28, 1991, requires that the published record in the *Foreign Relations* series include all records needed to provide comprehensive documentation on all the major foreign policy decisions and actions of the U.S. Government. It further requires that government agencies, departments, and other entities of the U.S. Government cooperate with the Department of State Historian by providing full and complete access to records pertinent to foreign policy decisions and actions and by providing copies of selected records. The editors believe that in terms of access to documentation this volume meets the standards and mandates of this statute.

Sources for the Foreign Relations Series

The editor responsible for research, selection, and annotation of this volume, Robert J. McMahon, had complete access to all the retired records and papers in the Department of State: the central files of the Department; the decentralized ("lot files") of the Department at the bureau, office, and division levels; the files of the Department's Executive Secretariat, which contain the records of international conferences and high-level official visits, correspondence with foreign leaders by the President and Secretary of State, and memoranda of conversations between the President and Secretary of State and foreign officials; and the files of overseas diplomatic posts. Any failure to include a complete Department of State record in the *Foreign Relations* series cannot be attributed to constraints or limitations placed upon the Department historians in their access to Department records, information security regulations and practices notwithstanding.

The editor of this volume fully researched the papers of President Eisenhower and other White House foreign policy records. Presidential papers maintained and preserved at the Presidential libraries include some of the most significant foreign affairs-related documentation from other federal agencies including the National Security Council, the Central Intelligence Agency, the Department of Defense, and the Joint Chiefs of Staff. All of this documentation has been made available for use in the *Foreign Relations* series thanks to the consent of these agencies and the cooperation and support of the National Archives and Records Administration.

Department of State historians have also enjoyed steadily broadened access to records of the Department of Defense, particularly the records of the Joint Chiefs of Staff and the Secretary of Defense and his major assistants.

As noted above, the statute of October 28, 1991, requires that the editors have full and complete access to all records pertinent to foreign policy decisions and actions. The research, compiling, and editing of this volume, however, were completed in 1981, with limited, background only, access to Central Intelligence Agency records. Since early 1991, the Central Intelligence Agency, in cooperation with the Department of State, has provided expanded access to Department historians to high-level intelligence documents from those records still in the custody of that Agency. Submitting such documents for declassification review would have necessitated considerable delay in the publication of the volume, however, and the Department chose not to postpone publication. The Department of State historians' expanded access was arranged by the History Staff of the Center for the Study of Intelligence, Central Intelligence Agency.

Apart from this exception, this volume was prepared in a manner consonant with the standards and mandates of the statute. The List of Sources, pages XIII–XVI, identifies the particular files and collections used in the preparation of this volume.

Principles of Selection for Foreign Relations, 1958–1960, Volume XVII

In selecting documents for inclusion in Volume XVII, the editor gave primary consideration to the formulation of policy within the U.S. Government and the most significant aspects of U.S. relations with Indonesia and the Netherlands. Indonesian claims to West New Guinea-West Irian made the Netherlands Government a more than interested observer in U.S.-Indonesian relations. Policy recommendations to President Eisenhower and his decisions with respect to government policies and actions are documented as fully as possible. Discussions and actions of the National Security Council and Presidential discussions of policy with Cabinet-level officers are included.

During the years 1958–1960, the Department of State played a leading role in the formulation of U.S. foreign policy. Secretaries of State John Foster Dulles and Christian A. Herter drew upon the Department's expertise in advising the President and taking leading roles in the deliberations of the National Security Council. The editor sought to include material documenting their roles and, where relevant, the interaction of the Department of State with the Department of Defense or other government agencies. Reportage and intelligence estimates that were seen by high-level policymakers and may have influenced their policy decisions have also been included.

The editor sought to document as comprehensively as possible the implementation of U.S. policies toward Indonesia through exchanges between high-level U.S. officials and foreign government officials on key issues that were of primary concern to the policymakers at the time. The editor made no attempt to document the whole range of day-to-day relationships, issues, and contacts between the United States and Indonesia.

Editorial Methodology

The documents are presented chronologically according to Washington time. Incoming telegrams from U.S. Missions are placed according to time of receipt in the Department of State or other receiving agency, rather than the time of transmission; memoranda of conversation are placed according to the time and date of the conversation, rather than the date the memorandum was drafted.

Editorial treatment of the documents published in the *Foreign Relations* series follows Office style guidelines, supplemented by guidance from the General Editor and the chief technical editor. The source text is reproduced as exactly as possible, including marginalia or other notations, which are described in the footnotes. Texts are transcribed and printed according to accepted conventions for the publication of historical documents in the limitations of modern typography. A heading has been supplied by the editor for each document included in the volume. Spelling, capitalization, and punctuation are retained as found in the source text, except that obvious typographical errors are silently corrected. Other mistakes and omissions in the source text are corrected by bracketed insertions: a correction is set in italic type; an addition in roman type. Words or phrases underlined in the source text are printed in italics. Abbreviations and contractions are preserved as found in the source text, and a list of abbreviations is included in the front matter of each volume.

Bracketed insertions are also used to indicate omitted text that deals with an unrelated subject (in roman type) or that remains classified after declassification review (in italic type). The amount of material not declassified has been noted by indicating the number of lines or pages of source text that were omitted. Entire documents withheld for declassification purposes have been accounted for and are listed by headings, source notes, and number of pages not declassified in chronological order. The amount of material omitted because it was unrelated to the subject of the volume, however, has not been delineated. All ellipses and brackets that appear in the source text are so identified by footnotes.

The unnumbered first footnote to each document indicates the document's source, original classification, distribution, and drafting information. The source footnote also provides the background of important documents and policies and indicates if the President or his major policy advisers read the document. Every effort has been made to determine if a document has been previously published, and this information has been included in the source footnote.

Editorial notes and additional annotation summarize pertinent material not printed in the volume, indicate the location of additional documentary sources, provide references to important related documents printed in other volumes, describe key events, and provide summaries of and citations to public statements that supplement and elucidate the printed documents. Information derived from memoirs and other firsthand accounts have been used when appropriate to supplement or explicate the official record.

Advisory Committee on Historical Diplomatic Documentation

The Advisory Committee on Historical Diplomatic Documentation, established under Title IV of the Department of State's Basic Authorities Act, amended on October 28, 1991, reviews records, advises, and makes recommendations concerning the *Foreign Relations* series. The Advisory Committee monitors the overall compilation and editorial process of the series and assists with any access and/or clearance problems that arise. Time constraints prevent the Advisory Committee from reviewing all volumes in the series. The Advisory Committee did not review this volume.

Declassification Review

The declassification review of this volume, which was completed in 1993, resulted in the decision to withhold 1.7 percent of the documents originally selected by Department of State historians and proposed for publication in this volume. The most important portions of the documents withheld from publication as a result of the declassification review were those relating to the details of U.S. covert support of the Indonesian rebellion in Sumatra and Sulawesi (Celebes) and to liaison with other countries interested and involved in this operation. For the first time since the *Foreign Relations* volumes on Vietnam for 1963 were published, the U.S. Government has acknowledged the existence of and policy deliberations about a major covert operation. In this respect, Volume XVII is a transitional volume on the road to fuller release of information of important intelligence operations. Although the details are lacking, there is ample evidence that the United States encouraged and supported the rebellion until it was clear that it was failing. Then the United States shifted its policy toward support of the Indonesian military as the best bulwark against communism in Indonesia. In its general outline of these policies, the published record regarding policy toward Indonesia meets generally accepted scholarly standards of accuracy and completeness.

Although the details of U.S. intelligence operations in Indonesia cannot be published here, the editors regard the record as important to a public understanding of U.S. foreign policy toward an important country of East Asia. The statute of 1991 establishes a 30-year publication line for the series, and thus the foreign affairs record for the administration of Dwight D. Eisenhower must now be published. At such time as the remainder of the details of intelligence operations in Indonesia can be declassified as promised by the Central Intelligence Agency, consistent with national security criteria, the Department will take steps to disclose and publish it in an appropriate format.

The Department of State's Advisory Committee on Historical Diplomatic Documentation has been apprised of the Department's decisions regarding declassification review of this volume.

Those documents omitted in their entirety from this volume are identified (by description, date, and archival provenance) in the text where they would have been printed. Excisions from printed texts are identified by suitable editorial devices.

The Division of Historical Documents Review of the Office of Freedom of Information, Privacy, and Classification Review, Bureau of Administration, Department of State, conducted the declassification review of the documents published in this volume. The review was conducted in accordance with the standards set forth in Executive Order 12356 on National Security Information and applicable laws.

Under Executive Order 12356, information that concerns one or more of the following categories, and the disclosure of which reasonably could be expected to cause damage to the national security, requires classification:

1) military plans, weapons, or operations;
2) the vulnerabilities or capabilities of systems, installations, projects, or plans relating to the national security;
3) foreign government information;
4) intelligence activities (including special activities), or intelligence sources or methods;
5) foreign relations or foreign activities of the United States;
6) scientific, technological, or economic matters relating to national security;
7) U.S. Government programs for safeguarding nuclear materials or facilities;
8) cryptology; or
9) a confidential source.

The principle guiding declassification review is to release all information, subject only to the current requirements of national security and law. Declassification decisions entailed concurrence of the appropriate geographic and functional bureaus in the Department of State, other concerned agencies of the U.S. Government, and the appropriate foreign governments regarding specific documents of those governments.

Acknowledgements

The editors wish to acknowledge the assistance of officials at the National Archives and Records Administration's Dwight D. Eisenhower Library, in particular David Haight, who provided invaluable help in the collection of documents for this volume. Others who deserve special thanks include Sandra Meagher at the Department of Defense and officials at the United States Military History Institute.

Robert J. McMahon collected, selected, and edited the documents in this volume under the supervision of former Editor in Chief John P. Glennon. David W. Mabon provided planning and direction. General Editor Glenn W. LaFantasie and Edward C. Keefer supervised the final steps in the editorial and publishing process. Jeffrey Soukup prepared lists of persons, abbreviations, and sources. Vicki E. Futscher performed copy and technical editing. Barbara A. Bacon of Publishing Services Division (Natalie H. Lee, Chief) oversaw the production of the volume. Breffni Whelan prepared the index.

William Z. Slany
The Historian
Bureau of Public Affairs

June 1994

Contents

Page

Preface III

List of Sources XIII

List of Abbreviations XIV

List of Persons XIX

Indonesia

January–May 1958: U.S. concern over the political orientation of
Indonesia and the regional rebellions in Sumatra and Sulawesi 1

June–December 1958: Establishment of a token Military Assistance
Program for the Indonesian armed forces and U.S. encourage-
ment of the anti-Communist elements within the Indonesian
Government 213

January–July 1959: NSC consideration of U.S. policy on Indonesia;
augmentation of U.S. military assistance to Indonesia; concern
of the Netherlands over U.S. military aid; U.S. policy toward the
West Irian-West New Guinea dispute; and establishment of
Sukarno's "Guided Democracy" government 316

August 1959–August 1960: President Sukarno's invitation to President
Eisenhower to visit Indonesia; Khrushchev's visit to Indonesia; and
heightened Indonesian-Netherlands tension over the West Irian-
West New Guinea dispute occasioned by the cruise of the *Karel
Doorman* 417

September–December 1960: Visits of President Sukarno and Army Chief
of Staff Nasution to the United States; U.S. reexamination of policy
toward Indonesia and the West Irian-West New Guinea dispute 531

Index 593

List of Sources

Department of State

Indexed Central Files: The principal source of documentation for this volume was the indexed central files of the Department of State. Many of the documents were selected from the following files:

033.1100–PI: Congressional visits abroad
033.4356: official visits of Australian officials to the Netherlands
033.56D11: official visits of Indonesian officials to the United States
033.5611: official visits of Netherlands officials to the United States
033.9811: official visits of Indonesian officials to the United States
123, Allison, John Moore: post personnel files
123, Jones, Howard P.: post personnel files
256F.1122: protection of U.S. interests in Sumatra
298.112, Pope: protection in Indonesia of Allen L. Pope against unofficial acts
320: General Assembly files
411.56D41: U.S.-Indonesian trade relations
601.9811: Indonesian diplomatic representation in the United States
611.56D: U.S.-Indonesian relations
611.98: U.S.-Indonesian relations/arbitration
656.56D: Netherlands-Indonesian relations
656.56D13: Netherlands-Indonesian relations/transfer or dispute of territory
656.98: Netherlands-Indonesian relations
656.9813: Netherlands-Indonesian relations/transfer or dispute of territory
656.56D: West New Guinea-Indonesian relations
656C.98: West New Guinea-Indonesian relations
711.11–EI: political affairs of President Eisenhower
711.56C: U.S. political affairs regarding West New Guinea
741.5622: sale of British aircraft
756.D13: cabinet and ministerial politics in Indonesia
756C.00: political affairs in West New Guinea
756C.5: defense affairs in West New Guinea
756D.00: political affairs in Indonesia
756C.5: defense affairs in West New Guinea
756D.00: political affairs in Indonesia
756D.001: communism in Indonesia
756D.07: political rights in Indonesia
756D.11: chief executive political affairs in Indonesia
756D.03: constitutional politics in Indonesia
756D.5–MSP: defense affairs in Indonesia/Mutual Security Programs
756D.551: defense affairs in Indonesia/personnel
756D.56: defense affairs in Indonesia/equipment and supplies
756D.5621: defense affairs in Indonesia/military ships
756D.5622: defense affairs in Indonesia/military aircraft
756 D.58: defense affairs in Indonesia/missions
790.5856: Far East military visits to the Netherlands
793.00: political affairs in China
798.00: political affairs in Indonesia

798.11: chief executive political affairs in Indonesia
798.5: defense affairs in Indonesia
798.5–MSP: defense affairs in Indonesia/Mutual Security Programs
798.56: defense affairs in Indoensia/equipment and supplies
798.5621: defense affairs in Indonesia/military ships
856D.2395: rubber industry in Indonesia
856D.2553: petroleum industry in Indonesia
856D10: financial matters in Indonesia
856D.424: commemorative celebrations in Indonesia
861.0098: Soviet economic matters in Indonesia
856F.2553: petroleum industry in Indonesia

Lot Files: Documents from the central files have been supplemented by materials from decentralized office files, the lot files of the Department of State. A list of the major lot files used or consulted follows:

Conference Files: Lot 63 D 123

Collection of documentation on visits to the United States by foreign heads of state and ministers, and major international conferences attended by the Secretary of State for 1955–1958, maintained by the Executive Secretariat.

Conference Files: Lot 64 D 560

Visits to the United States by high-ranking foreign officials and major conferences attended by the Secretary of State for 1958–1959, maintained by the Executive Secretariat.

Current Economic Developments: Lot 70 D 467

Master file of the National Advisory Council on International Monetary and Financial Problems for 1945–1958, maintained by the Bureau of Economic and Business Affairs, Department of State.

Djakarta Embassy Files: Lot 63 F 50

Files of the Embassy in Djakarta for 1958–1960.

EUR/WE Files: Lot 63 D 106

Swiss-Benelux desk files for Netherlands-Indonesian relations for 1957–1961.

FE Files: Lot 62 D 26

Files of the Bureau of Far Eastern Affairs for 1960.

INR–NIE Files

Files retained by the Bureau of Intelligence and Research containing copies of National Intelligence Estimates and Special National Intelligence Estimates, including NIEs and SNIEs for 1958–1960.

Secretary's Memoranda of Conversation: Lot 64 D 199

Chronological collection of the Secretary's memoranda for 1953–1960, maintained by the Executive Secretariat.

Secretary's Staff Meetings: Lot 63 D 75

Chronological collection of the minutes of the Secretary's Staff meetings for 1952–1960, maintained by the Executive Secretariat.

SPA Files: Lot 62 D 409

Indonesian desk files for 1952 (partial) and for 1958–1959.

SPA Files: Lot 63 D 436

Indonesia political and economic desk files for 1960.

SPA Files: Lot 64 D 469

Correspondence of the Office of Southwest Pacific Affairs for 1959–1961.

S/P–NSC Files: Lot 62 D 1

Master file of National Security Council records for 1948–1961, maintained by the Policy Planning Staff.

S/S–NSC Files: Lot 63 D 351

Master file of NSC records and related Department of State memoranda for 1947–1961, maintained by the Executive Secretariat.

S/S–OCB Files: Lot 61 D 385

Master files of the Operations Coordinating Board for 1953–1960, maintained by the Operations Staff.

S/S–OCB Files: Lot 62 D 430

Master files of the Operations Coordinating Board for 1953–1960, maintained by the Executive Secretariat.

State–JCS Meetings: Lot 61 D 417

Top Secret records of meetings between the JCS and Department of State for 1951–1959, maintained by the Executive Secretariat.

WE Files: Lot 63 D 136

Subject files of the Office of Swiss-Benelux Affairs for 1960–1961.

WE Files: Lot 63 D 221

Subject files for the Netherlands and Indonesia for 1956–1961.

Eisenhower Library

Dulles Papers

Records of John Foster Dulles, 1952–1959.

Herter Papers

Papers of Christian A. Herter, Under Secretary of State and then Secretary of State, 1957–1961. The collection includes the Chronological File, Miscellaneous Memoranda, and Telephone Coversations.

White House Office Files

White House Office collections, including Project Clean Up, and the records of Gordon Gray, Robert Cutler, Henry McPhee, and Andrew J. Goodpaster for 1953–1961.

Whitman File

Papers of Dwight D. Eisenhower as President of the United States, 1953–1961, maintained by his personal secretary, Ann C. Whitman. The Whitman File includes the following elements: Name Series, Dulles–Herter Series, Eisenhower Diaries, Ann Whitman (ACW) Diaries, National Security Council Records, Miscellaneous Records, Cabinet Papers, Legislative Meetings, International Meetings, Administration Series, and International File.

National Archives and Records Administration, Washington, D.C.

Record Group 218, Records of the Joint Chiefs of Staff and the Chairman of the Joint Chiefs of Staff

CCS 092 Asia

Washington National Records Center, Suitland, Maryland

Record Group 330, Records of the Office of the Secretary of Defense

OASD/ISA Files: FRC 62 A 1698

Country and general files for the Assistant Secretary of Defense (International Security Affairs) for 1958.

OSAD/ISA Files: FRC 63 A 1672

Country and general files for the Assistant Secretary of Defense (International Security Affairs) for 1959.

OSAD/ISA Files: FRC 64 A 2170

Country and general files for the Assistant Secretary of Defense (International Security Affairs) for 1960.

List of Abbreviations

ACS, Army Chief of Staff
AEC, Atomic Energy Commission
AF, Bureau of African Affairs, Department of State
AFCIN, Air Force Chief of Intelligence
ALFA, Air-Land Forces Agency
ALRI, Indonesian Navy
ALUSNA, American Legation, U.S. Naval Attaché
ANZAM, Australia, New Zealand, Malaya
ANZUS, Australia, New Zealand, United States
ARMA, U.S. Army Attaché
ASCI, Assistant Chief of Staff for Intelligence, Department of the Army
ASTARMA, Assistant U.S. Army Attaché
AURI, Angkatan Udara Republic Indonesia (Indonesian Air Force)
BNA, Office of British and North European Affairs, Department of State
CALTEX, California Texas Oil Company
ChiCom, Chinese Communist
ChiNat, Chinese Nationalist
CHMILTAG, Chief, Military Technical Advisory Group
CIA, Central Intelligence Agency
CINCPAC, Commander in Chief of the Pacific
CINCPACFLT, CINCPAC Fleet
CNO, Chief of Naval Operations
Codel, Congressional delegation
COMNAPHIL, Commander, U.S. Naval Forces in the Philippines
CP, Communist Party
CPR, Chinese People's Republic
CX, telegraphic indicator for ARMAs
DCM, Deputy Chief of Mission
DDE, antisubmarine destroyer
DEPTAR, Department of the Army
DI, Darul Islam (House of Islam), Indonesian political movement
DLF, Development Loan Fund
DNI, Director, Naval Intelligence
DWI, Dutch West Indies

EUR, Bureau of European and Canadian Affairs, Department of State
EXIM, Export-Import Bank
FBI, Federal Bureau of Investigation
FE, Bureau of Far Eastern Affairs, Department of State
FO, Foreign Office
fon, foreign
FY, fiscal year
G, Bureau of Management, Department of State
Garuda, Indonesian government-owned flagship airline
GRC, Government of the Republic of China
IAC, Intelligence Advisory Committee
IBU, Ikatan Buruh Umum (General Workers' Union, Indonesia)
ICA, International Cooperation Administration
ICATO, series indicator for telegrams going to the ICA
IMG, Information Media Guarantee Agreement
INR, Bureau of Intelligence and Research, Department of State
IPKI, Ikatan Pendulung Kemerdekaan Indonesia (Association of Defenders of Indonesian Independence)
JCS, Joint Chiefs of Staff
KLM, airline company of the Netherlands
KMT, Kuomintang (Chinese Nationalist Party)
L, Office of the Legal Advisor, Department of State
LCVP, landing craft vehicle/personnel
LST, landing ship transport
MAAG, Military Advisory Assistance Group
MAP, Military Assistance Program
Masjumi, Madjelis Sjuro Muslimin Indonesia (Council of the Indonesian Moslem Association)
MC, memorandum of conversation
MiG, Soviet military fighter aircraft
MILREP, military representative

MILTAG, military technical advisory group
MSA, mutual security assistance
MSP, Mutual Security Program
MTB, motor torpedo boat
MTTS, marine terminal tankage system
NAC, North Atlantic Council; National Advisory Council on Monetary and Financial Problems
NATO, North Atlantic Treaty Organization
NIE, National Intelligence Estimate
NSC, National Security Council
NU, Nahdatul Ulama (Association of Orthodox Muslims), Indonesia
OASD, Office of the Assistant Secretary of Defense
OCB, Operations Control Board
PKI, Indonesian Communist Party
PL, public law
PNI, Partai Nasionalis Indonesia (Indonesian Nationalist Party)
POLAD, political advisor
Polto, series indicator for telegrams from the U.S. Permanent Representative to NATO
PRRI, Revolutionary Government of the Republic of Indonesia
PSI, Partai Sosialis Indonesia (Indonesian Socialist Party)
RA, Office of Regional Affairs, Bureau of European and Canadian Affairs, Department of State
SEA, Office of Southeast Asian Affairs, Bureau of Far Eastern Affairs, Department of State
SEATO, Southeast Asian Treaty Organization
Sec, Secretary
SNIE, Special National Security Estimate
SOBSI, Sentral Organiasi Buruh Seluruh Indonesia (Central

Organization of All Indonesian Labor)
SPA, Office of Southwest Pacific Affairs, Bureau of Far Eastern Affairs, Department of State
S/S, Executive Secretariat of the Department of State
STANVAC, Standard Vacuum Oil Company
TOICA, series indicator for telegrams going to the ICA
UK, United Kingdom
U/MSC, Office of the Deputy Coordinator of Mutual Security for the Under Secretary of State
UN, United Nations
UNP, Office of United Nations Political and Security Affairs, Bureau of International Organizations Affairs, Department of State
UP, United Press International
US, United States
USA, United States Army
USAF, United States Air Force
USIA, United States Information Agency
USIS, United States Information Service
USN, United States Navy
USRO, United States Mission to the North Atlantic Treaty Organization and European Regional Organizations
USS, United States ship
UST, United States treaty
WE, Office of West European Affairs, Department of State
W/MSC, Office of the Special Assistant for Mutual Security Coordination, Office of the Deputy Under Secretary of State for Economic Affairs
WNG, West New Guinea

List of Persons

Abdul Rahman, Tunku ibni Al-Marhum, first Prime Minister of the Malay Federation until April 1959; Prime Minister from August 1959

Abdulgani, Roeslan, Vice Chairman and Secretary General of the Indonesian National Council

Aidit, Dipa N., Chairman of the Communist Party of Indonesia (PKI)

Allen, George V., Director, U.S. Information Agency

Allison, John M., Ambassador to Indonesia from March 1958

Baird, Julian B., Under Secretary of the Treasury

Beale, Howard, Australian Ambassador to the United States

Becker, Loftus E., Legal Advisor, Department of State, until August 1959

Bell, James D., Director, Office of Southwest Pacific Affairs, Bureau of Far Eastern Affairs, Department of State, from June 1960

Berlin, Colonel Jack, STANVAC representative in Indonesia

Bernau, Phyllis D., Personal Assistant to the Special Consultant to the President

Bernhard, Prince of the Netherlands

Boggs, Marion W., Deputy Executive Secretary of the NSC

Bohlen, Charles E., Ambassador to the Philippines until October 1959; Special Assistant to the Secretary of State from December 1959

Booker, Malcolm R., Counselor in the Australian Embassy in Washington

Burgess, Warren R., Permanent Representative to NATO

Burke, Admiral Arleigh A., Chief of Naval Operations

Cabell, General Charles P., Director of Intelligence, U.S. Air Force

Caccia, Sir Harold, British Ambassador to the United States

Cameron, Turner C., Jr., Deputy Director, Office of Western European Affairs, Bureau of European and Canadian Affairs, Department of State, from September 1958

Casey, Richard G., Australian Minister of External Affairs

Chadbourn, Philip H., Office of West European Affairs, Bureau of European and Canadian Affairs, Department of State

Chalid, Idham, Deputy Premier of Indonesia

Chiang Kai-shek, General, President of Republic of China

Chou En-lai, Prime Minister and Minister of Foreign Affairs, People's Republic of China

Cole, Colonel William R., U.S. Army Attaché in Djakarta

Cottrell, Sterling J., Counselor, U.S. Embassy in Djakarta from January 1958; thereafter Counselor, U.S. Embassy in Taipei

Cumming, Hugh S., Jr., Director of the Bureau of Intelligence and Research, Department of State

Cutler, Robert, Special Assistant to President Eisenhower for National Security Affairs

Dillon, C. Douglas, Deputy Under Secretary of State for Economic Affairs until June, 1958; thereafter Under Secretary of State

Djuanda, Dr. Kartawidjaja, Indonesian Prime Minister and Minister of Defense from April 1957

Drumright, Everett F., Ambassador to the Republic of China

Dulles, Allen W., Director of Central Intelligence

Dulles, John Foster, Secretary of State until April 1959

Eisenhower, Dwight D., President of the United States

Elbrick, C. Burke, Assistant Secretary of State, Bureau of European and Canadian Affairs, Department of State

Fales, Herbert P., Counselor at the U.S. Embassy in The Hague
Felt, Admiral Harry D., Commander in Chief of U.S. Forces in the Pacific (CINCPAC) from July 1958
Frost, Rear Admiral Laurence H., Assistant Chief of Naval Operations

Gates, Thomas S. Jr., Secretary of Defense from December 1959
Gleason, S. Everett, Deputy Executive Secretary of the NSC until July 1959
Goodpaster, Brigadier General Andrew J., Jr., Staff Secretary to President Eisenhower
Gray, Gordon, Assistant Secretary of Defense for International Security Affairs
Green, Marshall, Acting Deputy Assistant Secretary of State for Far Eastern Affairs, Department of State, July–October 1959

Hare, Raymond A., Deputy Under Secretary of State for Political Affairs from January 1960
Hatta, Dr. Mohammad, former Indonesian Prime Minister
Henderson, John W., Counselor, U.S. Embassy in Djarkarta from June 1958
Henderson, Loy W., former Under Secretary of State for Management
Herter, Christian A., Under Secretary of State until April 1959; thereafter Secretary of State
Hood, Vicount Samuel, British Foreign Minister
van Houten, Hans R., Netherlands State Secretary for Foreign Affairs
Hussein, Ahmad, Lieutenant Colonel, Indonesian Army territorial commander in West Sumatra
Huydecoper, Jonkheer J.L.R., First Secretary of the Netherlands Embassy in Washington

Irwin, John N. II, Assistant Secretary of Defense for International Security Affairs from September 1958

Jandrey, Fred W., Deputy Assistant Secretary of State for European and Canadian Affairs, Department of State
Jani, Colonel and later General, First Deputy Chief of Staff, Indonesian Army
Jones, Howard P., Deputy Assistant Secretary of State for Far Eastern Affairs until March 1958; thereafter Ambassador to Indonesia
Juliana, Queen of the Netherlands

Ketel, D., First Secretary of the Embassy of the Netherlands in Washington
Khrushchev, Nikita S., Chairman of the Council of Ministers of the Soviet Union
Kohler, Foy D., Deputy Assistant Secretary of State for European and Canadian Affairs until April 1958; Assistant Secretary of State for European and Canadian Affairs from December 1959
Knight, Robert, Deputy Assistant Secretary of Defense for International Security Affairs 1959–1960
Kusumasumantri, Iwa, Indonesian Minister of Defense, 1953–1955

Lay, James S., Executive Secretary of the National Security Council
Leimena, Johannes, Deputy Prime Minister of Indonesia
Lloyd, J. Selwyn, British Secretary of State for Foreign Affairs
Luns, Dr. Joseph, Foreign Minister of the Netherlands

McBride, Robert H., Director, Office of West European Affairs, Bureau of European and Canadian Affairs, Department of State from September 1958
McCartney, Lieutenant Colonel Henry A., Naval Attaché in Indonesia
McIntyre, Sir Laurence R., Australian Ambassador to Indonesia

Mein, John Gordon, Director, Office of Southwest Pacific Affairs, Bureau of Far Eastern Affairs, Department of State, until May 1960

Menzies, Robert Gordon, Australian Prime Minister

Merchant, Livingston T., Assistant Secretary of State for European and Canadian Affairs November 1958–August 1959; Deputy Under Secretary of State for Political Affairs August 1959–December 1959; thereafter Under Secretary of State for Political Affairs

Mukarto (also Moekarto), Nodowidigdo, Indonesian Ambassador to the United States

Munro, Sir Leslie, New Zealand Ambassador to the United States

Murphy, Robert D., Deputy Under Secretary of State for Political Affairs until August 1959; Under Secretary of State for Political Affairs August 1959–December 1959

Nash, Walter, New Zealand Prime Minister and Minister of External Affairs

Nasser, Gamal Abdel, President of Egypt until February 1958, thereafter President of the United Arab Republic

Nasution, Major General Abdul Haris, Chief of Staff, Indonesian Army

Natsir, Mohammed, First Deputy Prime Minister of Indonesia September 1950–March 1951; later Chairman of the Masjumi Party Executive Council

Nixon, Richard M., Vice President of the United States

O'Sullivan, James L., Deputy Director, Office of Southwest Pacific Affairs, Bureau of Far Eastern Affairs, Department of State

Parsons, J. Graham, Deputy Assistant Secretary of State for Far Eastern Affairs, Department of State, until June 1959; thereafter Assistant Secretary of State

Prawiranegara, Sjafruddin, Prime Minister of the Revolutionary Government of the Republic of Indonesia

de Quay, Jan E., Prime Minister and Minister of General Affairs of the Netherlands from May 1959

Robertson, Walter S., Assistant Secretary of State for Far Eastern Affairs until June, 1959

Roijen, Jan H., van, Netherlands Ambassador to the United States

Simbolon, former Indonesian territorial commander in North Sumatra

Stabler, Wells, Officer in Charge of Swiss-Benelux Affairs, Office of West European Affairs, Bureau of European and Canadian Affairs, Department of State, September 1958–May 1959

Staf, Cornelis, Minister of Defense of the Netherlands from 1959

Steeves, John M., Deputy Assistant Secretary of State for Far Eastern Affairs, Department of State, from October 1959

Stump, Admiral Felix B., Commander in Chief, Pacific and Commander in Chief, Pacific Fleet to February 1958; thereafter Commander in Chief, Pacific to August 1958

Subandrio (also Soebandrio), Dr., Indonesian Foreign Minister

Sukarno (also Soekarno), Dr. Achmed, President of Indonesia, concurrently Prime Minister from 1959

Sukendro, Colonel, Deputy Chief of Staff for Intelligence, Indonesian Armed Forces

Sumual, Lieutenant Colonel, former territorial commander in East Indonesia

Supeni, Madame, Chairperson, Indonesian Parliament Foreign Relations Committee

Suryadarma, Indonesian Air Marshal

Taylor, General Maxwell D., Chief of Staff, United States Army, until June 1959

Twining, General Nathan F., Chairman of the Joint Chiefs of Staff until September 1960

Underhill, Francis T., Jr., Officer in Charge of Indonesian-Pacific Island Affairs, Office of Southwest Pacific Affairs, Bureau of Far Eastern Affairs, Department of State, until February 1959

Vittrup, General Russell L., Deputy Chief of Staff for Operations, U.S. Army Headquarters in the Pacific

Wallner, Woodruff, Deputy Assistant Secretary of State for International Organization Affairs from August 1959

Wenzel, Robert H., Office of Southwest Pacific Affairs, Bureau of Far Eastern Affairs, Department of State

Wilopo, Indonesian Prime Minister from April 1952–June 1953; leader of the Partai Nasional Indonesia

Yeh, George Kung-Chao, Foreign Minister of the Republic of China until 1958; thereafter Ambassador to the United States

Young, Philip, Ambassador to the Netherlands from March 1957

Yu Ta Wei, Minister of Defense, Republic of China

Indonesia

January–May 1958: U.S. Concern Over the Political Orientation of Indonesia and the Regional Rebellions in Sumatra and Sulawesi

1. **Memorandum From the Assistant Secretary of State for Far Eastern Affairs (Robertson) to Secretary of State Dulles**

Washington, January 2, 1958.

SUBJECT

United States Policy Towards Indonesia

The Special Report

Late in December 1956 regional dissatisfaction with the Central Government erupted into proclamations of defiance of central authority issued by Army-led local "councils" in the outer islands. President Sukarno proposed as a solution to the Cabinet crisis growing out of this development the formation of a new government in which all major parties, including the Communist, would be represented, and the creation of a National Council representing the "functional groups" in society to advise the government. He also advocated an ill-defined political theory of "guided democracy" which appeared to be inspired by the material accomplishments if not the ideology of Yugoslavia, the Soviet Union and Communist China. The new government formed in the spring of 1957, while without open Communist party representation, included three extreme leftists, and the National Council created shortly thereafter had a strong leftist representation. In Regional Council elections on Java during the late spring and early summer of 1957, the Communists scored substantial gains. Because of the indications of progressive growth in Communist strength and concern that anti-Communist forces

---

Source: Department of State, Central Files, 611.56D/1–258. Top Secret. Drafted by John Gordon Mein. Prepared to brief Secretary Dulles for a meeting on Indonesia scheduled for later that day. A handwritten note on the source text indicates that Dulles saw the memorandum.

on Java were unwilling or unable to resist adequately this trend, a special group was appointed by the National Security Council on August 1 to evaluate developments in Indonesia and submit recommendations on what action the United States should take. The Committee's Report, which was submitted to the National Security Council at its meeting on September 23, can be summarized as follows:[1]

The Committee finds that the most promising approach for the United States at this stage of developments in Indonesia lies in exploiting the political resources and economic leverage available in the outer islands and recommends that we utilize and develop these assets. Specifically the Committee's main recommendations are:

1. *In the outer islands.* The U.S. should employ all feasible covert means to strengthen the anti-Communist forces in the outer islands in order through their strength to affect favorably the situation in Java and to provide a rallying point if the Communists should take over Java; and that more forthright means be undertaken if the situation in Java continues to deteriorate.

2. *Java.* The United States should a) seek to promote effective action among the non-Communist elements against the Communists, b) seek to prevent the growth of the military potential of the government forces on Java while at the same time utilizing and supporting the non and anti-Communist forces in the military and para-military forces on Java and in the Central Government, c) induce a psychological awareness of the menace of Communism on Java, d) seek to focus world opinion on the Communist menace on Java.

3. *U.S. Aid Programs.* The abrupt termination of economic aid and information programs in Indonesia is not desirable but they should be handled so as to give no indication that we are reconsidering our policies, and our Technical Assistance Program and our Economic Development Program should be oriented toward the outer islands.

4. *Military Action.* There is a split position on Par. 9 of the paper. Defense representatives took the position that not only should the United States Government proceed with planning for action in case the Communists gain control of Java or having gained control of Java attempt to acquire control over the outer islands, but also that we should at this time decide that we will act under such circumstances if necessary with U.S. armed forces. The Department's position was that we should go no farther at this stage than to plan for such an eventuality in accordance with the provision of Par. 12 of NSC 5518 on Indonesia[2] and that no decision should be reached now on what action we will take at a future date under circumstances not now known. Also that even if such a decision were taken at this time it should not be set forth in the paper which will be distributed throughout the government.

---

[1] The Special Report is printed in *Foreign Relations,* 1955–1957, vol. XXII, pp. 436–440. A memorandum of the NSC discussion on September 23 is *ibid.,* pp. 450–453.

[2] NSC 5518, "U.S. Policy on Indonesia," approved by the President on May 12, 1955, is *ibid.,* pp. 153–157.

5. *Diplomatic Relations.* For the time being our official diplomatic relations with Indonesia should be maintained as near as possible to what they have been in the recent past.

A copy of the NSC Action on the Report is attached at Tab A.[3]

Mr. Allen Dulles, who will also be present at the meeting, will wish to brief you on implementation of the Report in the covert field. A summary of the pending requests from the Indonesian Government and of the status of our overt programs is attached at Tab B.

Ambassador Allison had certain reservations concerning the Report of the Special Committee and was of the opinion that certain possible courses of action which might have been helpful had not been considered. He was of the opinion that Sukarno is not "beyond redemption" and that it was still possible to reduce his reliance on the Communists. He also felt that we should support the Indonesian position on West Irian as a means of winning Sukarno over, at the same time weakening the Communist position in Indonesia. The Ambassador has also felt that we should have supported the efforts of the present Indonesian Government since, in his opinion, the main influences in the Cabinet are non-Communist. He has also felt that we should make an effort to influence President Sukarno through Djuanda, who is a moderate. The Ambassador has also made specific recommendations on the sale of military equipment to Indonesia and the extension of economic aid. A more detailed discussion of the policy recommendations made by Ambassador Allison is attached at Tab C, with the telegrams and despatches containing his recommendations attached at Tab D.[4]

---

[3] No tabs were attached to the source text. Reference is to NSC Action No. 1788, by which the President approved the action taken on the Special Report at the NSC meeting of September 23, 1957; see *ibid.*, footnote 5, p. 452.

[4] Many of the telegrams and despatches containing Ambassador Allison's recommendations are *ibid.*

2.   Memorandum of Conversation

Washington, January 2, 1958, 5 p.m.

INDONESIA

PRESENT

Department
The Secretary
The Under Secretary (part of the meeting)
FE—Mr. Robertson
FE—Mr. Howard Jones
FE—Mr. Gordon Mein
EUR—Mr. John Jones
INR—Mr. Cumming
S/S— Mr. Howe

CIA
Mr. Allen Dulles
Mr. Frank Wisner
Mr. Al Ulmer
[*name not declassified*]

Defense
Secretary Sprague

The Secretary expressed the view that our policy should be as follows, which was generally agreed to be the existing policy:

1. We should not make any deal with Sukarno or the present government.
2. We should let it be known that if a reconstituted government without Communist support or influence came into power, it would get our backing.
3. Meanwhile, we should build up a position of strength in the outer islands and should be ready with assistance we might want to render at a later date on short notice.

In further discussion of point No. 2 above, the Secretary pointed out that we should make known our position "in confidence" and "to friends who might do something about it." He also said that we should be very clear, both with the Dutch and with any others, that we did not mean that in backing a government we would support all of its policies and in particular its West Irian policy.

Source: Department of State, Central Files, 756D.00/1–658. Secret. Drafted on January 6 by Fisher Howe, Director of S/S. This meeting was held in the Secretary of State's office.

In this connection it was accepted that in seeking to make our policy known we would try not to appear to be completely under Dutch influence. We should also avoid the impression we were trying to force Sukarno out for this would tend to strengthen his position in Indonesia.

Discussion

The Under Secretary reviewed the present situation in Indonesia including Japanese shipping, food supplies, seizures of Dutch property and the position of Sukarno, Hatta and others. [*1 line of source text not declassified*]

The Under Secretary indicated that there were differing views of what should be done. Ambassador Allison and his Military Attachés (Djakarta's 1859)[1] and Admiral Stump felt that we should put pressure on the Dutch to hold discussions with the Indonesians; the others felt that we should not take any step in this direction or deal with Sukarno and Djuanda, as Allison also thought we should, until we see whether the situation will stabilize or will shift radically either to the Communists or to the ultra Conservatives.

Mr. Robertson noted that the US-UK working group had had two meetings and generally reflected a similarity of views as between the US and the UK [*2-1/2 lines of source text not declassified*].

Mr. Robertson explained that Ambassador Allison believes support of the Indonesian position on West New Guinea is a requisite but also the only thing required to get Sukarno over to our way of thinking. He believes that we need only to support this government and the Moderates will prevail.

There was agreement that Sukarno was in fact wholly undependable. The Secretary at one point indicated his view that Sukarno was dangerous and untrustworthy and by character susceptible to the Communist way of thinking.

Mr. Robertson reported that the Dutch position now is that they could not possibly talk with the Indonesians since the blackmail conditions had been laid on by the Indonesians. Johnny Jones noted also that the Dutch position on shipment of any arms would be extremely strong because of the possibility that arms would be used against the Dutch in an attempt forcibly to take over West New Guinea.

Gordon Mein noted from his recent trip[2] the following:

1. That no government coming into power in Indonesia could avoid the Dutch-Indonesian problem which now is wider than just West Irian.

---

[1] For text, see *Foreign Relations, 1955–1957*, vol. XXII, pp. 576–578.
[2] Mein was in Indonesia December 14–21, 1957.

2. The Indonesians still suspect Allison principally as a result of the Communist fabricated *"Blitz* telegrams*"* published in Bombay newspapers alleging that Allison had sought arms for elements opposed to the government.[3]

3. The Indonesians complained that they had received no support on any issue from the US.

4. There is urgency in the problem since we may have to deal with the situation before Sukarno returns or on very short notice with any successor government to Djuanda.

---

[3] See *Foreign Relations,* 1955–1957, vol. XXII, footnote 4, p. 507.

---

3.   Memorandum of Conversation

Washington, January 2, 1958.

SUBJECT

> Situation in Indonesia

PARTICIPANTS

> Ambassador J. H. van Roijen, Embassy of the Netherlands
> Mr. D. Ketel, First Secretary, Embassy of the Netherlands
>
> Mr. Walter S. Robertson, Assistant Secretary for Far Eastern Affairs
> Mr. James L. O'Sullivan, Deputy Director, Office of Southwest Pacific Affairs

After an exchange of amenities, Ambassador van Roijen noted that the situation in Indonesia looks bad. He said that 10,000 Dutch nationals left Indonesia in December. In response to a question, Mr. Ketel said that there were approximately 46,000 Dutch nationals in Indonesia as of November, of whom approximately 20,000 are believed to be Dutch ethnically as well as from the point of view of citizenship.

In response to a question, Ambassador van Roijen said that he believed Sukarno suffered a severe nervous shock as a result of the attempted assassination in late November and needs a real rest. An additional consideration in the present Presidential trip[1] is that he

---

Source: Department of State, Central Files, 756D.00/1–258. Confidential. Drafted by O'Sullivan.

[1] President Sukarno was scheduled to embark on January 6 on a 6-week tour of Asia and the Middle East.

planned to visit Latin America about this time and had been prevailed upon by the political parties to postpone that official trip. His present journey now becomes a matter of pleasure as well as a face saving device. The Ambassador thought that during his absence the chances would be better for obtaining a favorable change in the Government. In reply to a further question, when asked by Mr. Robertson whether there was any strong man in Indonesia to replace Sukarno, the Ambassador said that he has confidence in Hatta, who has the backbone to resist what he believes should not be done but who does not have the drive necessary for an active counter-policy. The Ambassador continued that Sukarno wants Hatta to return to the Government as Vice President, a position which Hatta refuses to accept because it does not meet the conditions, such as abolition of the National Council, which Hatta has laid down for re-establishing his collaboration with Sukarno. Mr. Robertson noted that Hatta, in his recent attack upon the Government, criticized only the Government's methods and timing of taking over the Dutch interests and did not oppose the principle involved.

The Ambassador said that the clock could not be turned back in Indonesia and that even if a moderate government came in, it could not be expected to reverse the present anti-Dutch trend. He said that the Dutch are convinced the game is up for them and eventually for the West in Indonesia. The anti-Dutch campaign may have been triggered off by New Guinea but, he said, "Even if we gave them New Guinea on a silver platter, another excuse would have been found."

When asked if he had any hope for Indonesia Ambassador van Roijen stated that it depends upon the moderates. Mr. Robertson said that the Army is now begging us for arms but that we have not responded due to the threats to take New Guinea by force, the unlawful seizure of private property and the uncertainties as to the future orientation of the Government. He also mentioned that large elements of the Army are opposed to the current drift towards the Communists and do not want the Army to become dependent upon the Soviet bloc equipment.

Ambassador van Roijen was emphatic that under present circumstances to give arms to Indonesia would be most unfortunate, for if Sukarno gets arms, it will give the impression that his activities have a seal of approval from the U.S.

Mr. Robertson replied that we had never considered giving arms to Sukarno but asked the question of the Dutch attitude if there were a coup in Indonesia and Sukarno departed.

Ambassador van Roijen replied that any arms sent to Indonesia would be to the credit of Sukarno. He believed Army Chief of Staff Nasution is an opportunist although if there were a coup or an attempted coup by the Communists he might turn against them. He believed that the PKI has penetrated the Army in about the same percentage, both of officers and men, as the PKI has penetrated the population. He noted that Deputy Army Chief of State [*Staff*?] Gatot Subroto, while pro-western, is a Japanese and therefore has a disadvantage in the eyes of the military leaders in the outer-islands. After noting that Hatta seems disinclined to take any long risks, Mr. Robertson asked if the Ambassador believed Indonesia is lost to the free world. The Ambassador replied that Java will go Communist if it continues along the same lines as it is now proceeding. In reply to a further question from Mr. Robertson the Ambassador said that force might have to be used to protect the outer-islands should the Communists take over Java. He believes if Java were to go Communist a free Indonesia would be established in the outer-islands. The Ambassador suggested that Colonel Simbolon was the strongest of the dissidents but that he had no troops.

As there seemed to be some confusion in Ambassador van Roijen's mind, Mr. Robertson made clear that in asking these various questions he was simply trying to ascertain the Dutch views. He said that no one in Washington is arguing for support of Sukarno and that there is no possibility of this Government supporting him although there is a strong feeling in Washington that we should support a moderate element in Indonesia.

In reply to a further question the Ambassador said he knew of no figure who might replace Sukarno. He speculated that Hatta might become Prime Minister but he doubted that Hatta would take any action against Sukarno. Mr. Ketel added that if there were a PKI coup on Java, Sjafruddin might become the center of moderate opposition. The Ambassador then noted that the Sultan of Djogakarta was a very hard headed, ambitious man but his authority was limited to Java. He recalled that the Sultan in the October 1952 episode[2] was in a position to attempt a coup but got "cold feet" at the last moment. Mr. Ketel added that Natsir,[3] Roem[4] and Wilopo[5] represented strong moderate figures. The Ambassador had no explanation as to why the PKI had done so well in the elections in Djogakarta.

---

[2] Reference is to an incident that occurred on October 17, 1952, during which elements within the Indonesian Army sought unsuccessfully to have President Sukarno make certain changes in the Indonesian Government, including the dissolution of Parliament. For related documentation, see *Foreign Relations, 1952–1954*, vol. XII, Part 2, pp. 245 ff.

[3] Mohammed Natsir, Indonesian Prime Minister September 1950–March 1951 and a leader of the Masjumi Party.

[4] Mohammed Roem, Indonesian First Deputy Prime Minister March 1956–March 1957 and a leader of the Masjumi Party.

[5] Wilopo was Indonesian Prime Minister April 1952–June 1953 and a leader of the PNI (Partai Nasional Indonesia).

Mr. Robertson reiterated that we believe there are many moderates in Indonesia opposed to Sukarno and he pointed out that a group might arise in Indonesia to which support might have to be given quickly. The Ambassador reiterated his belief that anything done now will only help Sukarno. Djuanda, he said, is a moderate and non-Communist who is dragged along by Sukarno. The President has had his ups and downs with the people but he still has the ability to sway the masses. Mr. Robertson noted that President Sukarno while in the United States said he had seen little here that was comparable to the problems he faces in Indonesia but that in China he had clearly been affected by Mao Tse-tung's ability to run the masses who suffered the same illiteracy and poverty that Sukarno has seen in Indonesia.

Ambassador van Roijen then said that several governments have offered to mediate between the Dutch and Indonesians and have been given a categoric "No" by The Hague. He said that on New Guinea the Dutch are not going to negotiate although they remain willing to submit the matter to the International Court of Justice. Mr. Robertson said this made a perfect impasse because the Indonesians wanted to discuss New Guinea.

The Ambassador said that Subandrio, the Foreign Minister, is still thinking in terms of Dutch refugees from Indonesia putting pressure on the Dutch Government to negotiate. He said that their information indicated also that Subandrio believes the West will not allow the situation to drag on and that eventually the West will take a move to straighten out the situation as it did with Nasser. The Ambassador emphasized that Subandrio is miscalculating completely and said that the view of his Government is, if Java falls to the Communists, the outer-islands would rally and form a free Indonesia with new leader emerging.

The Ambassador left for informational purposes only an exchange of notes between the Dutch and the Indonesians on recent Indonesian actions (see attachments).[6] He said under normal circumstances the Dutch would have refused to accept the Indonesian note. However, because the Dutch do not wish to give the Indonesians any excuses to break diplomatic relations they have not done this.

Just before the Ambassador left there was some discussion of the Indonesian law which purported to draft foreigners for the use of the State. The Ambassador apparently was not aware of the most recent law, news of which came in a few days ago. He said, however, that to his knowledge which might not be complete no Dutch nationals had been drafted under the previous law of six months ago.

---

[6] These notes, December 10 and 27, are not printed.

4.   Editorial Note

On January 3 Deputy Under Secretary of State for Management Loy Henderson sent a cable to Ambassador John M. Allison which began:

"In response to your message to Robertson through Mein, we would like to recommend to President your appointment as Ambassador to Czechoslovakia. It would be appreciated if you would advise immediately whether or not such appointment would be agreeable to you. This matter rather urgent since Johnson is leaving Czechoslovakia in near future.

"Prague as you know is one of our key posts in Eastern Europe. It would be helpful to have in Czechoslovakia an ambassador with your experience and knowledge of communist objectives and tactics."

Henderson suggested tentatively that Allison begin to make arrangements that would make it possible for him to depart from Indonesia about February 1. (Telegram 1644 to Djakarta, January 3; Department of State, Central Files, 123 Allison, John Moore) See Supplement.

The referenced message from Allison to Robertson through Mein has not been found in Department of State files. Allison summarizes this message, however, in his book, *Ambassador From the Prairie or Allison Wonderland* (Boston, Houghton Mifflin Company, 1973), page 337. According to Allison, the message contained his recommendations for handling the present situation in Indonesia. If Washington was not prepared to go along with those recommendations, he wrote, "I did not believe I should remain in Indonesia."

In telegram 1943 from Djakarta, January 6, for Henderson and Robertson, Allison replied:

"Appreciate your message and have carefully considered offer you make. I assume from first sentence reference telegram that policy to be carried out in Indonesia lacks those elements which I told Mein I considered essential. If this is so, as I told Mein, it would be extremely difficult if not impossible for me to carry out such a policy and the government would undoubtedly be better served if there were another Ambassador here.

"Mrs. Allison and I have seriously thought over whether I should accept Czechoslovak post if offered. While neither of us is happy about it, we agree that as a career officer I should be willing to go where the Department desires." (Department of State, Central Files, 123 Allison, John Moore) See Supplement.

5.   **Editorial Note**

On January 6 at the 350th meeting of the National Security Council, Director of Central Intelligence Allen Dulles discussed Indonesian developments during his briefing on significant world developments affecting U.S. security. According to the memorandum of discussion, drafted on January 7 by S. Everett Gleason, Dulles' briefing was as follows:

"The Director of Central Intelligence stated that the Indonesian Government had apparently decided to turn to the Soviet bloc for the purpose of acquiring arms, although the Government would also shop for arms in Western Europe. Their first effort will be to try to get arms from Yugoslavia, and thereafter from Czechoslovakia or Poland. It also appeared likely that the Djuanda cabinet would try to induce the Indonesian Parliament to ratify the $100 million barter agreement concluded many months ago with the Soviet Union.

"Sukarno left yesterday on his rather lengthy visit to various foreign states. He will be accompanied to certain of these capitals by his Foreign Secretary. A main objective of Sukarno will be to secure support from the governments of the countries he visits for the Indonesian claim to West Irian. Mr. Allen Dulles speculated that Sukarno might be making this extensive trip in order to permit certain changes to be made in the Government of Indonesia without loss of face for Sukarno himself. There were conflicting reports on this point.

"Meanwhile, further measures against the Dutch were being planned by the Indonesians. It now appears that they are going to try to repudiate all their financial obligations to the Dutch. Such a repudiation would have the most serious repercussions. The deteriorating economic situation in Java has led to further defections from the Central Government on the island of Borneo, as had occurred earlier in Sumatra and the Celebes." (Eisenhower Library, Whitman File, NSC Records)

6.   **Telegram From the Embassy in Indonesia to the Department of State**

Djakarta, January 7, 1958, 1 p.m.

1962. Department pass CINCPAC for POLAD for information. At close of general conversation this morning on internal situation Djuanda said he would like to speak to me not as Prime Minister to Ambassador but as friend-to-friend. He then told me that Russians had been recently putting extreme pressure on Indonesians to accept ships and military equipment for use in present emergency. Djuanda says that for this purpose Soviet Ambassador Zhoukov apparently returned to Djakarta earlier than had been anticipated. (In this connection press reports that Zhoukov had "courtesy" interview with Djuanda yesterday morning.) Djuanda said that Russians were offering equipment on understanding that conditions of payment could be settled later after arrival of equipment.

Prime Minister expressed gratitude that arrangement for ships from Japan had been completed prior to Russian offer so that there was no compulsion on that part of Russian proposal. With respect to rest of proposal, Djuanda said he was hopeful it would be possible to stall until return of Sukarno when there might be different situation. He said that it was his intent only to go ahead with already negotiated Soviet loan which he anticipates will come before next Parliamentary session. This loan provides only for some factories, some communication and transportation equipment and for no military equipment other than jeeps.

Previously Djuanda had told me that one of reasons he had been anxious for Sukarno to visit Cairo was so that he could have good talk with Nasser and learn from him some of problems connected with receiving Soviet equipment. Djuanda believes, apparently on basis of reports from Indonesian Embassy Cairo, that Nasser has become somewhat disillusioned with Russians and that his experience will give Sukarno food for thought.

At no time did Djuanda mention question of whether or not America would provide Indonesia with military equipment, and I believe he is honestly concerned at prospect he may be forced into position of taking some such equipment from Soviets. He did say that Indonesian Government was getting in recent weeks increasing evidence that both arms and equipment were being air-dropped in various parts of Eastern Indonesia and that small Dutch Naval vessels had been calling at isolated points in Eastern Indonesia and were apparently giving aid and comfort to local insurgents.

Allison

Source: Department of State, Central Files, 756D.56/1–758. Secret.

7.   Telegram From the Embassy in Indonesia to the Department
of State

Djakarta, January 21, 1958, 3 p.m.

2192. Limit Distribution for Henderson and Robertson. Department's 1881.[1] If information in reference telegram had been received immediately in response to my 1943[2] or before Department had publicly announced my reassignment, news of which reached Djakarta some three or four hours before reference telegram, it might have been possible to save government considerable embarrassment.

Reference telegram shows misunderstanding my position on Indonesian policy. At no time have I recommended immediate military or economic aid to Sukarno. I have recommended negotiation and carefully controlled token deliveries. I do not recall my recommendations for additional economic aid to Sukarno. My last recommendation in this regard, [less than 1 line of source text not declassified] was that if a new and, from our point of view, satisfactory Indonesian government should come into being we should be prepared to grant it military and economic aid. I further recommended that immediate opening of negotiations with present government might forestall purchases by it of military equipment from iron curtain countries, but I said that deliveries could be delayed until we saw results of present political activities in Indonesia. I also stated my belief that any Indonesian government, which came into power, whether or not dominated by Sukarno, would demand return of West Irian and that we would eventually have to face that issue as part of over-all Dutch-Indonesian relationship. However, I have never advocated immediate handing over of West Irian to Sukarno and my last message on that subject[3] pointed out I believed there was possibility this issue of Dutch-Indonesian relations could be handled in

---

Source: Department of State, Central Files, 123 Allison, John Moore. Confidential.

[1] Telegram 1881 to Djakarta, January 20, reads in part as follows:

"First sentence Deptel 1644 referred to your message to Robertson through Mein to effect that Department should start thinking about possibility you might have to be replaced Djakarta since you encountering difficulties seeing leaders and your usefulness becoming limited as result recent campaigns against you, including *Blitz* telegrams, attempts implicate you in recent developments Indonesia, etc. This estimate your position, plus facts as previously reported by you and confirmed by Mein that you were disappointed Department could not concur your recommendation that US support Indonesia claim West New Guinea and extend immediate military and economic aid to Sukarno, and that you did not approve Department's tactics in present situation, were reasons for your assignment to Czechoslovakia." (*Ibid.*) Telegram 1644 is quoted in Document 4.

[2] See Document 4.

[3] Reference is most likely to telegram 1495 from Djakarta, December 9; for text, see *Foreign Relations, 1955–1957,* vol. XXII, pp. 537–539.

first instance through economic talks and that US would not at this time have to give up its neutral position.

I also told Mein that, as I had previously made known to Department, I believed much of Embassy–Department differences might be straightened out if I could be recalled to Washington for consultation, and I expressed hope this could be done after arrival new DCM. It will be recalled that I specifically requested such recall last August but it was not then permitted. I greatly regret that I was given no opportunity to discuss this matter personally with the Department before final action was taken.

With respect to first sentence Department's 1881, I had thought my message regarding New Year's reception at Palace would show that government leaders were no longer avoiding me but on contrary making every effort, short of public denial of *Blitz* articles, to indicate continuing confidence.

Statement that I did not approve Department's tactics in present situation is correct but I remain of opinion that if I had been given opportunity for personal consultation this might have been worked out.

I regret this misunderstanding but in all fairness I believe the record should be put straight.

Allison

---

8.   **Editorial Note**

On January 22 at the 352d meeting of the National Security Council, Allen Dulles briefly discussed Indonesian developments during his intelligence briefing:

"With regard to Indonesia, Mr. Dulles pointed out that the dissidents on the island of Sumatra have decided to postpone for the time being their plan to set up a rival government to the government at Djakarta. On the whole, we think that this was a wise decision." (Memorandum of discussion by Gleason, January 23; Eisenhower Library, Whitman File, NSC Records)

At a State–Joint Chiefs of Staff meeting on January 24, Indonesian developments were again considered. According to a memorandum of discussion, prepared by Richard Finn (Robert Murphy's Special Assistant), the discussion was as follows:

"General Twining said that the Joint Chiefs are greatly concerned about Indonesia and wanted the views of the State Department. Mr. Murphy said that there has been some encouraging news involving Sumatra but that it is too early to predict with assurance what future developments will be.

"Admiral Burke wondered whether there might not be a blow-up in the next few days. Mr. Murphy replied that in his view it is too soon and that any blow-up would be more likely in February rather than in the next three or four days. Mr. Murphy commented, however, that in some respects the trend in Indonesia appears to be favorable from the U.S. point of view."(Memorandum of Substance of Discussion at a State–Joint Chiefs of Staff meeting; Department of State, State–JCS Meetings: Lot 61 D 417)

---

9.   **Letter From the Assistant Secretary of State for Far Eastern Affairs (Robertson) to the Deputy Assistant Secretary of Defense for International Security Affairs (Irwin)**

Washington, January 27, 1958.

DEAR MR. IRWIN: The Secretary has asked me to reply to your letter I–17128/7 of December 26, 1957[1] in which you recommend that action be initiated requesting the President, pursuant to Section 401 (a) of the Mutual Security Act of 1954,[2] as amended, to make the necessary determination so that token military assistance may be provided to Indonesia.

I agree that the U.S. should be prepared to extend quickly to Indonesia military assistance should it be decided to do so, and that we should continue contingency planning for such a course of action. I feel, however, that it would be premature to seek a 401 (a) determination at this time. Such action will, of course, be kept under continuing consideration, and, should we decide to proceed with token aid, could be undertaken if it appeared necessary in the light of the Indonesian response to notification of U.S. preparedness to make arms available and the internal political situation at that time. In any event, the Department of State would wish to be certain that any arms made available by the United States would not be used in support of Indonesian claims to West New Guinea.

Sincerely yours,

Walter S. Robertson[3]

Source: Department of State, Central Files, 756D.5–MSP/12–2657. Top Secret. Drafted by Francis T. Underhill and cleared with Mein, C. Douglas Dillon, Robert Barnes, and J. Wesley Jones.

[1] Printed in *Foreign Relations, 1955–1957*, vol. XXII, pp. 566–567.

[2] For text of the Mutual Security Act of 1954, approved by the President on August 26, 1954, see 68 Stat. 832. The Mutual Security Act of 1955 added section 401 (a); for text of that law, approved by the President on July 8, 1955, see 69 Stat. 286.

[3] Printed from a copy that bears this typed signature.

10.   **Memorandum From the Assistant Secretary of State for Far Eastern Affairs (Robertson) to Acting Secretary of State Herter**

Washington, January 29, 1958.

SUBJECT

Contingency Paper on Indonesia

There is attached a paper on "Possible Contingencies in the Indonesian Situation" prepared at your request by a special working group consisting of representatives of State, Defense and CIA, with Mr. Howard Jones as Chairman.

At the meeting in which it was decided that such a paper should be prepared,[1] the question of referring it to the NSC Planning Board was discussed but no decision was reached. In view of the sensitivity of the subject I believe it would be better not to pass this paper to the NSC Planning Board but to discuss it only with those of its members who must have this information.

Attachment

POSSIBLE CONTINGENCIES IN THE INDONESIAN SITUATION

I. The dissidents repudiate all Central Government control without formal declaration of independence

or

Declare themselves to be the legal Indonesian Government

or

Declare an independent Sumatra State

Assumptions:

1) The dissidents are able to maintain control of the areas presently under their jurisdiction even in the face of Central Government military pressure.

2) There is no outbreak of open hostilities.

U.S. Courses of Action:

a) Pending an assessment of the situation, continue to recognize the Central Government at the same time maintaining such relations

---

Source: Eisenhower Library, Project Clean Up, Indonesia. Top Secret. Drafted by Mein and concurred in by Howard P. Jones, Cumming, and Reams. On February 3 Max V. Krebs, Special Assistant to Under Secretary Herter, transmitted the contingency paper to Cutler at the request of Herter. His note indicates that the paper was not circulated to all members of the NSC Planning Board but that it was available to the Defense and CIA representatives on the Special Working Group.

[1] No record of this meeting was found.

with the regional authorities as generally accorded a de facto regime but without extending them de jure recognition.

b) Urge American-owned interests operating in the areas under the control of the regional authorities to maintain similar relations with the regional authorities.

c) Extend overt economic aid to the regional authorities.

d) Continue present programs of technical and economic assistance.

e) [2-1/2 lines of source text not declassified]

f) Encourage a reasonable settlement of differences between the Central Government and the regional authorities which would lead to the accession to power of a Central Authority prepared to reduce Communist influence in Indonesia.

II. *The present Government or one resembling it remains in power; the outer islands take no further steps to establish separate political identity nor claim to represent the legitimate Government of Indonesia; there are no significant outbreaks of armed violence; Sukarno continues to maintain his power and influence.*

U.S. Courses of Action:

a) Maintain our relations with the Central Government.

b) Continue our technical assistance and economic development programs with special emphasis given to projects in the outer islands.

c) Seek to encourage the growth of anti-Communist strength on Java.

d) Encourage discreetly the political and economic development of the outer islands.

e) Employ all feasible means to strengthen the determination, will and cohesion of the anti-Communist forces in the outer islands.

f) Withhold military assistance from the Central Government.

III. *A new moderate anti-Communist Government, which is prepared to seek a reasonable settlement with the dissident elements and to take action against the Communists, comes to power.*

[U.S. Courses of Action]

a) Continue and be prepared to expand economic assistance to the Government, concentrating as much as possible in the outer islands.

b) Encourage a reasonable settlement of differences between the Central Government and the regional authorities which would lead to the accession to power of a Central Authority prepared to reduce Communist influence in Indonesia.

c) Through strengthening of the government, seek to exploit any tendency Sukarno may have to adjust himself to the situation and/or reduce his influence.

d) Extend token military assistance and be prepared to negotiate for the sale of military equipment to the Indonesian Government.

e) Seek a settlement to Dutch-Indonesian problems, including the West New Guinea issue.

f) Encourage the government to take action against the Indonesian-Communist party.

g) Continue, and as appropriate expand, other programs of assistance and cooperation, e.g. education, leader grants, etc., with the Indonesian Government.

IV. Civil War.

U.S. Courses of Action:

a) Consider extending de facto recognition to the regional authorities.

b) [*1-1/2 lines of source text not declassified*]

c) Pending an assessment of the situation, continue to accord recognition to the Central Government.

d) Consult with the U.K. and ANZUS on military measures which might be necessary.

(*Note:* The extent of U.S. action under this contingency will depend on the assistance, if any, given by the Soviet Bloc.)

V. The Central Government is taken over by the Communists.

U.S. Courses of Action:

a) Encourage the outer islands to declare themselves as the legitimate Indonesian Government and extend to this government de facto or if necessary de jure recognition.

b) In case of de jure recognition seek the support of other governments for the new government.

c) Extend all necessary assistance to enable this government to maintain this position.

d) Encourage anti-Communist elements on Java to rise against the Red regime.

e) Consult with the U.K. and ANZUS on military measures which might be necessary.

VI. The Central Government purchases from the Soviet Bloc arms of a kind and in such quantity as to endanger the position of the anti-Communist forces in Indonesia.

(*Note:* This contingency could either precipitate a breaking away of the outer islands and the outbreak of civil war or could follow such action should the Central Government seek to re-establish its control by force.)

U.S. Courses of Action:

a) Maintain the position of the outer islands to resist military pressure from the Central Government.[2]

---

[2] This contingency plan was discussed at a luncheon meeting of the OCB on February 5. According to informal and preliminary notes on that meeting by Arthur L. Richards, the Operations Coordinator, Murphy responded to Cutler's question regarding action required by the plan "that the Contingency Plan was exactly that; that no action was to be taken by anyone at this time; that action would be taken only if one or more of the contingencies should arise." (Department of State, S/S–NSC Files: Lot 62 D 1, Indonesia)

---

11.   Memorandum by Director of Central Intelligence Dulles

Washington, January 31, 1958.

PROBABLE DEVELOPMENTS IN INDONESIA

1. We believe that the Padang group probably will deliver its ultimatum to the central government on or about 5 February. While the Padang leaders are still reluctant to take the final step of breaking with Java and, possibly, causing a civil war, they appear committed to pursue their objectives of gaining a new government in Djakarta which will act to reduce Communist strength, will permit more autonomy to the outer islands, and will give the latter a greater share of national revenues. Because of their reluctance, they will probably be willing to negotiate with the central government even though the negotiations are prolonged far beyond the five day limit. However, if no progress is made in the negotiations, if the central government should reject their demands out of hand, or if the central government begins to receive large quantities of Bloc arms, the chances are better than even that the Padang group would break with Java and establish a "Provisional Government of Indonesia."

Source: Eisenhower Library, Project Clean Up, Indonesia. Top Secret; Eyes Only. Distributed to the following officials: Eisenhower; John Foster Dulles; Cutler; Robertson; Cumming; Admiral Stump; Major General Robert A. Schow, Assistant Chief of Staff, Intelligence, Department of the Army; Rear Admiral Laurence H. Frost, USN, Assistant Chief of Naval Operations, Naval Intelligence; Brigadier General Richard Collins, USA, Deputy Director for Intelligence, Joint Staff; and Major General Millard Lewis, Assistant Chief of Staff, Intelligence, Department of the Air Force. The source text is Cutler's copy; it was forwarded to him on January 31 by J.S. Earman.

2. The major factors which support this estimate are as follows:

a. The group of provincial army leaders, Hussein, Barlian, and Sumual, plus Simbolon, Djambek, and Lubis,[1] seem fully united on undertaking some action to force a change in the central government. They probably believe they have or can gain the support of most of the military on Borneo and in the Moluccas, and the Darul Islam groups on Java and those which control most of South Celebes.

b. The leaders of the Natsir wing of the Masjumi party and their families have recently moved to Sumatra. We believe this action is important as an indication of the seriousness of Natsir intentions. Thus, the Padang group seems assured of the support of major elements of one of the four principal Indonesian political parties. Natsir will have the active support of the Masjumi on the outer islands and at least the passive support of a large part of the Masjumi on Java. The Padang group also has some support from the small PSI party which has its strength among the intellectuals and in the civil service.

c. The Padang group probably estimates that the position of Djuanda and Sukarno has been weakened by the troubles which have resulted from the anti-Dutch campaign. The dissident leaders also know from Masjumi negotiations with the PNI that some of the PNI leaders are deeply concerned about the growth of Communist influence and are in agreement that there should be a change of government. They probably also estimate that Djuanda, even though committed to no change of government until Sukarno's return, desires to resign.

d. Most important of all, the Padang group probably estimates that it can obtain Western, particularly US support. Moreover, the group, in present circumstances, believes it could successfully resist any military action by the forces loyal to the central government, unless the latter should obtain a massive supply of arms, including planes and warships, from the Bloc.

Probable Immediate Response of the Central Government to the Ultimatum[2]

3. We believe that Sartono, the Acting President, and Djuanda will refuse to capitulate to the ultimatum, but will do so with a "soft" answer

---

[1] Lieutenant Colonel Ahmad Hussein, territorial commander of the Indonesian Army in West Sumatra; Lieutenant Colonel Barlian, territorial commander in South Sumatra; Lieutenant Colonel Sumual, former territorial commander in East Indonesia; Colonel Simbolon, former territorial commander in North Sumatra; and Colonel Zulkifli Lubis, former Deputy Chief of Staff of the Indonesia Army. Djambek has not been further identified.

[2] On January 30 at the 353d meeting of the NSC, CIA Deputy Director Charles P. Cabell discussed the probable Indonesian reaction to an ultimatum from the dissidents during his intelligence briefing:

"Turning to Indonesia, General Cabell said that the Sumatra dissidents would probably present the Djakarta government with an ultimatum in early February, demanding that the government resign within five days or proclaim a new Free Government of Indonesia, which would be an internal reform government stressing regional autonomy and anti-communism. The Djakarta government appeared unlikely to surrender, and would probably insist that all discussion of government reforms must await Sukarno's return. If pressed, however, the Djakarta government might stall for time by proposing a compromise. Meanwhile, the Djakarta government was continuing its negotiations with the Soviet Bloc for arms shipments. For example, 17 MiG planes had recently been obtained from Czechoslovakia." (Memorandum of discussion by Gleason, January 31; Eisenhower Library, Whitman File, NSC Records)

which will probably suggest negotiation. Neither of these leaders wishes to push the situation to the breaking point nor to bring about a civil war. However, their ability to maneuver is restricted because both appear determined to honor their commitment to Sukarno to maintain the status quo until he returns. The central government, at least in the short run, probably will not attempt to put pressure on the outer islands by cutting off the pay of army units and subsidies to provincial governments in the dissident provinces, by strengthening garrisons of Javanese troops on Sumatra and the other outer islands, or by increasing blockade operations to halt barter trade.

4. The Padang group would probably agree to the government's offer to negotiate and would not hold to the five day period given in the ultimatum. It is difficult to say how long the Padang group would be willing to talk and the extent to which their determination to act might drain away.

5. The outcome of such negotiations is unclear. The Padang group's bargaining position would be strengthened by its growing military capabilities and the possibility of outside support, both of which will be evident to the central government. Pressure against the government by anti-Communist elements on Java who sympathize with the Padang group's objectives will also be a factor. On the other hand, the central government would have strong and vociferous support from the PKI and extreme nationalist elements in the non-Communist parties on Java. It would continue to draw on Sukarno's influence and prestige, which, though reduced, would continue to be great, particularly among the masses and certain elements of the armed forces. Its position would be greatly strengthened if either Hatta or the Sultan of Jogjakarta had refused to have anything to do with the Padang group's proposals. The central government is aided also by the disinclination of the PNI leaders to collaborate with the Padang group because of the close association of their chief rival, the Masjumi, with this group and because of the demands of the group for considerable provincial autonomy.

6. The central government's initial purpose in seeking to negotiate would be to stall until Sukarno returns, or at least until it can obtain his views. For Sukarno, three courses of action would be possible: he could agree to the formation a new government; he could seek to prolong the talks while taking steps to weaken or to destroy the Padang group; or he could close out the negotiation and undertake forceful measures to defeat the Padang group. In the event Sukarno should prolong his stay abroad and the Padang group became restive, Djuanda and Nasution might be forced eventually to act on their own initiative and either install a new government or break off the negotiations.

The Appointment of a New Government

7. We believe that the chances are better than even that Sukarno will accede to the appointment of a new government, especially if it can be done in a manner which "saves his face." However, it would probably not meet fully any of the major points contained in the Padang group's ultimatum. It would probably be made up of non-Communist political leaders and might include Hatta, but it would probably not be a government committed to rigorous action against the Communists. At best, it might agree to the removal of a few known Communists from key positions. Such a fuzzy outcome, while not satisfactory, would probably be accepted by the Padang group, at least for a trial period. The provincial leaders would probably attempt to maintain their cohesion during such a trial period in order to negotiate with the new government for their other objectives, and, if necessary, to issue a new and stiffer ultimatum.

Prolongation of Negotiations

8. If the central government adopted this tactic, the Padang group would be in a dilemma. If they broke off the talks, they would bear the onus and probably lose support on Java. Such action might also tend to bring the PNI and the PKI together. On the other hand, if the talks continued the central government would be gaining time in which to seek the defection of various elements among the outer islanders and to build up its own armed strength.

9. The chances are probably somewhat better than even that in this situation the Padang group would hold together and would eventually send another ultimatum. Evidence of an extensive build up of the capabilities of the armed forces on Java would probably speed up such a decision by the Padang group. If the government in reply gave little or no satisfaction, this might become the point at which the outer islands break with Java.

A Break-off of Negotiations by the Central Government

10. If, upon Sukarno's return, the central government should adopt a firm line and break off negotiations, the chances are about even that the Padang group would in reaction set itself up as the "Provisional Government of Indonesia", cut off all revenues to the central government, seek to initiate covert operations on Java to bring down the government, and appeal for international recognition and more arms. In turn, the central government would adopt similar courses of action and would stop the flow of revenues to the rebel areas, would seek to establish a blockade of these areas, and would also appeal for international support and assistance. It would probably denounce the US as the cause of the situation. Although both sides would be reluctant to initiate

serious military action, the chances of a full blown civil war developing would be greatly increased.

A Civil War Situation

11. If a full break should occur between Java and the outer islands, and if hostilities should begin before the Djakarta government had obtained substantial supplies of military equipment, the Padang group would have a better position in the outer islands than would the central government. It could probably count on the loyalty of the people and of the forces directly under its command on Sumatra and northern Celebes. It would probably also have the support of the Atjehnese in northern Sumatra, the Darul Islam forces in South Celebes, the Amboinese and groups in the other Moluccas which support the East Indonesian Republic movement, and some elements on Borneo. We are unable to estimate the outcome of an effort by the Padang group to defeat the central government on Java. It would depend in large measure on the loyalty of Javanese army units to the central government, the capabilities of the Communists, the possible reaction within the army should the Communists seize or be given the role of leadership of the government, and on the military capabilities of the forces loyal to the Padang group. At a minimum, the Padang group could probably launch fairly widespread guerrilla warfare on Java. While it probably would not be able to land significant forces from the outer islands, it could count on the Darul Islam, the Moslem Youth Group (GPII), possibly some units from the Silawangi Division in West Java, and some volunteers from the Masjumi and possibly from the PNI and the NU.

Reactions of Non-Communist Countries

12. The presentation of the Padang group's ultimatum and the negotiations, which we think likely to follow, will probably elicit little response either from the Afro-Asian countries or other non-Communist countries. However, if the Djakarta government publicly charged the US as acting in support of the outer islanders, the Afro-Asian press would almost certainly echo such charges.

13. If the Padang group declared a "Provisional Government of Indonesia", most non-Communist governments would seek to remain neutral and some of the Afro-Asian governments would probably offer their good offices in hopes of averting a civil war. Most of these countries would be concerned that unless the situation was resolved fairly quickly, the Soviet Bloc would intervene to the greatest extent possible on the side of the central government, thus raising the possibility of a civil war of the Spanish variety, which potentially could blow up into a major war. At the same time, the neutral Moslem countries would also have sympathy for the Moslem leaders of the Padang group. Support for the Padang group would probably increase considerably, even

among the Afro-Asian neutrals, if the Communists should attempt to seize control of the government on Java.

14. If civil war actually broke out, most Afro-Asian countries would continue to remain neutral and would not extend recognition to the Padang group. A major factor determining their attitude would be whether or not the Communists had seized power on Java; if this happened, probably Malaya, Thailand, South Vietnam, the Philippines, Nationalist China, South Korea, and possibly Japan would recognize and at least extend diplomatic support to the Padang group. The general trend on the part of most Afro-Asian countries would be to seek to close out the hostilities as quickly as possible.

Reactions of the Sino-Soviet Bloc

15. The Bloc has already made generous offers of assistance to the central government and the presentation of the Padang group's ultimatum would have relatively little immediate effect on Bloc actions. If the Bloc leaders came to estimate that the US was involved in some manner, the Communist press would scream about "US imperialism", and would press its arms and technicians on the central government with increased urgency. It is possible that the Soviet Union would raise this issue in the United Nations. There would be little change in the character of the Bloc campaign against the West and the US if the Padang group broke with Java but the intensity might increase. The Bloc leaders might at this point order the PKI to launch a major effort to seize control of the Indonesian government.

16. If civil war should begin, the Sino-Soviet Bloc would continue to offer diplomatic and material assistance to the Indonesian government. If the Communists had come to power on Java, the Sino-Soviet Bloc might talk in terms of sending volunteers. However, we believe that the Sino-Soviet Bloc would not attempt to intervene with its own forces or major numbers of volunteers, even to save a Communist government. The chances would be much greater that the Soviet Union would raise the issue in the UN.[3]

---

[3] John Foster Dulles briefly referred to this memorandum during a telephone conversation with Allen Dulles on February 4. According to a memorandum of that conversation, prepared in the Secretary of State's office and marked "one-sided," he remarked: "Sec said re your memo about the Archipelago, one point does not seem covered: during the stalling period the present regime is going to get a lot of military stuff. Sec said he would think that would be their tactic; have we anything more in mind?" (*Ibid.*, Dulles Papers, General Telephone Conversations)

12.   Memorandum From the Deputy Assistant Secretary of State
        for Far Eastern Affairs (Jones) to the Deputy Under Secretary
        of State for Political Affairs (Murphy)

Washington, February 6, 1958.

SUBJECT

Tripartite Talks Regarding Indonesia

You will recall that when you were in Paris at the NATO talks in December, you agreed with Mr. Lloyd to the establishment of a small U.S.-U.K. working party on Indonesia which was to discuss U.S.-U.K. cooperation [less than 1 line of source text not declassified] "to consider longer term policy matters" in Indonesia.[1]

At the organizational meeting, which took place in late December, the British insisted that the Australians be included. So far five meetings have been held, at the last four of which there has been representation from the Pentagon (Mr. Sprague's office).[2]

[2 lines of source text not declassified] The meetings revealed that the British objective was to obtain a firm statement regarding United States policy toward Indonesia which they apparently feared was directed at establishing a fragmented Indonesia.

In the course of the first meeting we explained that we envisaged a two-pronged operation in Indonesia: the first designed to attempt to bring about a new government on Java by encouraging the non- and anti-Communist elements there to cooperate with each other in the face of the threat from the PKI; at the same time both to reinforce non- and anti-Communist elements on Java and to assure a fall-back position should Java be lost, [8 lines of source text not declassified].

The rest of the meetings have been devoted to an examination of the considerations involved in supplying the Indonesian Government with rice and arms; what, if anything, could or should be done about West New Guinea; by whom and under what circumstances should the gap left by the Dutch be filled, particularly with regard to shipping; and finally, what would be the best manner in which to proceed to delay delivery of the four warships the Indonesian Navy now has on order in Italy. The consensus of the group, which reflected the views of London and Canberra, was that the risks involved in trying to prevent the imminent delivery of two frigates was not worth the advantages to be gained,

---

Source: Department of State, Central Files, 756D.00/2–658. Top Secret. Drafted by O'Sullivan on February 5.

[1] Dulles was in Paris for the NATO Heads of Government meeting, held December 16–19, 1957; see Foreign Relations, 1955–1957, vol. XXII, pp. 552–553.

[2] No other record of these meetings has been found in Department of State files.

as the frigates will not provide the decisive military advantage to the Central Government. The question of whether to attempt to delay the delivery of the two corvettes (now scheduled for May) is under urgent study.

In addition, agreement has been reached regarding a joint estimate of developments in Indonesia since August 1957. A copy of this is attached. (Tab A)[3] A subcommittee is also working on a joint contingency paper which will contain recommended courses of action regarding the diplomatic and legal attitude to be assumed toward the dissidents.

The Australians have had little to contribute and on instructions from their Government have spent most of their time raising questions and seeking information. [2-1/2 lines of source text not declassified]

Further meetings will be held, but I think it best to keep these on an ad hoc basis to face specific problems as they may arise, a position which at this point would appear to satisfy the British but may not be too palatable to the Australians. Should we try to terminate the working group, however, it is not impossible that the Australian reaction will be to send Mr. Casey to this country or even to call a special ANZUS meeting. Neither of these developments at this juncture would seem to me to be helpful.

---

[3] Not attached to the source text and not found.

---

13.   Editorial Note

On February 6 at the 354th meeting of the National Security Council, Allen Dulles discussed Indonesian developments during his intelligence briefing:

"Turning to the situation in Indonesia, Mr. Dulles said that if there was to be a climax in Indonesia, we were on the point of reaching it; but one has to be very skeptical about the Indonesians and about any climax. As a people, the Indonesians often do a lot of talking, accompanied by very little action; but it seems that the dissidents will join in submitting an ultimatum to the Djakarta government on the 7th of February. In brief, the ultimatum will say 'clean up or clear out'. Meanwhile, an envoy of the dissidents has been in contact with Sukarno in Tokyo. Reports of this meeting seemed to be in character with what we know about Sukarno. He is alleged to have wept; but after the envoy had departed, Sukarno had sent instructions to Djakarta to make no change in policy. Accordingly, his tears may have been of the crocodile variety. The date of Sukarno's return to Indonesia has now been set for February 15.

"Meanwhile, there have been some negotiations between the Central Government and the dissidents on Sumatra. The latter have now in readiness a complete new Cabinet for Indonesia. Mr. Dulles thought it likely that the ultimatum would be presented by the dissidents, and that the government would then suggest further negotiations. Sukarno would then return, after which anything could happen—possibly a blow-up. The great problem is where the Army stands, particularly the forces in Java. These forces seem divided in their loyalty between the dissidents and the Central Government. The military capabilities of the dissidents have recently improved, although they profess to fear greatly an air attack from Java.

"The Sultan of Djogjakarta has arrived in Washington, allegedly to take part in a conference on tourism. This was very queer conduct for the Sultan, but a great many Indonesian fence-sitters are busy getting out of the way until the situation clarifies. Mr. Dulles concluded by predicting the possibility that, whatever happened, the outer islands would split off from Java."(Memorandum of discussion, drafted by Gleason, February 7; Eisenhower Library, Whitman File, NSC Records)

On February 4 and 5, the Sultan of Djogjakarta had a series of meetings with Department of State officials during which he offered his assessment of current Indonesian developments. Memoranda of these conversations are in Department of State, Central File 756D.00.

---

14.   Memorandum of Conversation

Washington, February 7, 1958.

SUBJECT

Dutch-Indonesian Relations

PARTICIPANTS

Ambassador J.H. van Roijen, Ambassador of the Netherlands
Baron S. G. M. van Voorst, Netherlands Embassy
Mr. D. Ketel, Netherlands Embassy
The Secretary
EUR—Mr. Elbrick
L—Mr. Becker

Ambassador van Roijen began the conversation with the statement that Indonesian actions against Dutch interests in Indonesia had created

---

Source: Department of State, Central Files, 656.56D/2–758. Confidential. Drafted by Turner C. Cameron, Officer in Charge of Swiss-Benelux Affairs, Office of Western European Affairs. C. Burke Elbrick briefed Dulles for this conversation in a February 6 memorandum. (*Ibid.*, 656.56D13/2–658)

an economic vacuum in that country. The Dutch Government was very anxious that the vacuum not be filled by Communist bloc countries. The Dutch Government felt that it was its duty to take the initiative with friendly Governments to work out ways by which this could be avoided. The Ambassador said he hoped the present conversation would be followed by others in which there might be a full and frank exchange of views on various aspects of developments in Indonesia. His Government considered that such an exchange of views should concern not only developments in Indonesia but also the policies which the two Governments intended to follow in that area.

The Dutch Government took the position, he said, that should conditions in Indonesia develop in a direction which might justify assistance from Western countries, such assistance should be conditioned on the willingness of the Indonesian Government to reach an agreement with the Dutch Government concerning the confiscation of Dutch interests in Indonesia and Indonesia's failure to meet its financial obligations to the Netherlands. As examples of what his Government had in mind, he cited U.S. policy toward Iran in 1952 and the blocking of Egyptian accounts after the nationalization of the Suez Canal in 1956. He asked for U.S. cooperation with any Dutch efforts to obtain compensation for damages which it had sustained in Indonesia.

The Ambassador then referred to the possibility that private firms might wish to take over certain Dutch interests in Indonesia. In order that these firms should avoid complications resulting from Dutch claims for damages he said that the Dutch considered that the foreign firms should work out with the Dutch firms a mutually agreed basis for any take-over operation. The Ambassador then handed the Secretary an Aide-Mémoire, copy attached, which covered the points he had made. He also gave the Secretary a copy, in translation, of the Dutch note to the Indonesian Government, dated December 30, 1957, protesting Indonesian actions against Dutch interests. (Copy attached).[1]

The Ambassador explained that a similar approach had already been made to the British Foreign Minister who had received it sympathetically. He added that approaches along the same line were being made in Brussels, Paris and Bonn and that his Government also intended to talk to the Japanese Government in this general sense.

The Secretary commented that the Dutch Government was faced with many problems arising out of developments in Indonesia and said that the Department would be prepared to exchange views informally with the Dutch Government on this general subject. He then added that he wished to comment on one point which the Ambassador had made.

---

[1] Neither printed. See Supplement.

He said that U.S. action in blocking Egyptian assets in 1956 had not been undertaken as a form of reprisal. He explained that this action had been designed to protect our shipping companies from double jeopardy.

The Secretary then said that there seems to him to be at least a superficial inconsistency between the Dutch position that non-Communist countries and enterprises from these countries should fill the vacuum in Indonesia and the statement putting everyone on notice that unless acceptable compensation arrangements were worked out with the Dutch there would be interminable legal complications. Van Roijen said that in his opinion the apparent inconsistency could be removed if the problem was considered in terms of the situation which the United States faced in Iran in 1952. Van Roijen added that his Government did not wish to appear unreasonable. The Dutch did not expect to be compensated for the entirety of the losses they had suffered in Indonesia. As another example of the fact that the Dutch were taking a reasonable attitude, he mentioned their position on the furnishing of arms and equipment to Indonesia. He said that the European Allies of the Dutch had been informed that the Dutch Government was not opposed to the shipment of all military equipment to Indonesia but that it did not wish to see military equipment supplied Indonesia which could be used against West New Guinea. The Secretary asked what was the Dutch attitude toward the providing of military equipment which might be used against Sumatra. The Ambassador replied that he believed that his Government would also oppose the shipment of such equipment to Indonesia at the present time, adding, however, that his Government would wish in this connection to avoid giving the appearance of interfering in internal Indonesian affairs.

At this point, Ambassador van Roijen said that he was confident that Hatta, if he should ever become the head of the Indonesia Government, would be in favor of establishing at least the principle of adequate compensation. The Secretary commented that Hatta appeared to him to have lost some of his sound Moslem virtues and suggested that his trip to China might have contributed to his present attitude. Van Roijen indicated that he continued to have confidence in Hatta but said that Hatta's deteriorating physical condition might have resulted in making him a less efficient leader.

Van Roijen then returned to his Government's request for a continuing full and frank discussion of Indonesian problems and developments. The Secretary again acquiesced, commenting that, as he understood it, the Dutch Government had in mind an informal exchange of views. He pointed out the Indonesian actions against Dutch interests were setting an unfortunate precedent and referred to the position which the Afro-Asian Conference in Cairo had taken towards private investment.

Prior to leaving, it was agreed that the Ambassador if he was questioned by the press would say that he had had a discussion of Dutch interests in Indonesia and the effect of Indonesian actions on these interests.[2]

---

[2] The Department transmitted a summary of this memorandum of conversation to the Embassy in the Netherlands in telegram 1449 to The Hague, February 7. (Department of State, Central Files, 856D.19/2–358)

---

15.   Memorandum From the Special Assistant to the Joint Chiefs of Staff for National Security Council Affairs (Triebel) to the President's Special Assistant for National Security Affairs (Cutler)

Washington, February 10, 1958.

SUBJECT

U.S. Policy on Indonesia (NSC 5518)[1]

1.   Enclosure A, which was developed by the Joint Chiefs of Staff in November 1957, is forwarded herewith for Planning Board consideration in connection with the scheduled review of NSC 5518.

2.   Paragraph 5–d of Enclosure A recommends an immediate token military aid program for Indonesia. Subsequent to the development of Enclosure A and the recent unrest in Indonesia, the Joint Chiefs of Staff have stated that in view of the general political instability of Indonesia, recent developments affecting the interests of U.S. Allies, and the uncertainty as to the manner in which military assistance would be utilized, it now appears that political and other considerations may dictate whether or not token aid should be provided to Indonesia, and if so, when it should be delivered.

C.O. Triebel
Rear Admiral, USN

Source: Department of State, S/S–NSC Files: Lot 62 D 1, Indonesia. Top Secret.

[1] NSC 5518, "U.S. Policy on Indonesia," approved by the President on May 12, 1955, is printed in *Foreign Relations*, 1955–1957, vol. XXII, pp. 153–157.

Enclosure A

U.S. POLICY TOWARDS INDONESIA

1. The Joint Chiefs of Staff have been increasingly concerned in recent months by political developments in Indonesia and with the probable effectiveness of U.S. policy and action to forestall or cope with the rising influence of Communism in that country. If this strategic area should be lost to the Communist Bloc, the position of the United States and its allies in the Far East would suffer irreparable and catastrophic damage. U.S. policy and concepts for its implementation must be directed toward avoidance of disaster if possible, in addition to dealing with disaster if and when it occurs.

2. NSC Action 1788[2] approved the Special Report on Indonesia[3] with certain amendments and directed that the Special Report be used in a review of U.S. Policy toward Indonesia. This report, among other things, suggests three approaches toward achieving U.S. objectives in Indonesia:

"a. Employ all feasible covert means to strengthen the determination, will and cohesion of the anti-Communist forces in the outer islands, particularly in Sumatra and Sulawesi, in order through their strength to affect favorably the situation in Java, and to provide a rallying point if the Communists should take over Java.

"b. If the situation on Java continues to deteriorate, then move to more forthright means in pursuit of the course of action outlined in a.

"c. Utilize such leverage as is available and may be built up by the anti-Communist forces in the outer islands to continue our efforts to try to unify and stimulate into action, singly or in unison, non- and anti-Communist elements on Java against the Communists."

The conclusion is reached that the approach in subparagraph c above has the greatest promise of achieving U.S. objectives. As regards Indonesian military forces, the recommendation is made to:

"Seek to prevent the growth of the military potential of the government military forces on Java, as these may ultimately fall under Communist influence and be used to reduce the anti-Communist forces in the outer islands. However, utilize and support the non- and anti-Communist elements in the military and paramilitary forces on Java and in the Central Government."

3. Although U.S. policy as stated above provides, among other things, for strengthening anti-Communist elements in outlying islands

---

[2] For text of NSC Action No. 1788, see *ibid.*, footnote 5, p. 452.

[3] The Special Report, September 3, 1957, is *ibid.*, pp. 436–440. See also the memorandum of NSC discussion of September 23, 1957, *ibid.*, pp. 450–453.

as a means of influencing policies of the Central Government, it is essentially negative. It implies that Java may ultimately fall to Communist control. The Joint Chiefs of Staff are of the opinion that concepts for the implementation of U.S. policy in Indonesia must take cognizance of the following:

a.   Java contains two-thirds of an estimated total Indonesian population of 85 million. Although the island itself possesses only a small proportion of the natural resources of the nation, its people are the more politically sophisticated, the best organized, and have traditionally exercised political and economic leadership. Essentially all Naval and Air Forces are based on Java, as are over 100,000 of the 180,000 Army troops. To lose Java and permit the influence of this concentration of military, economic, and political strength to be exploited by the Communists is virtually to lose Indonesia over the long term.

b.   Nationalism is and will probably continue to be the strongest single force within Indonesia, and it overrides the many divisive elements which exist. Whatever government controls Java it will be able to speak with the voice of nationalism and will almost certainly be able to advance itself as the legitimate government of Indonesia before the world forum. It must be recognized that a Communist controlled nationalist government in Java would receive the immediate and complete overt support of the Communist Bloc, and ultimately the support of the Afro-Asian Bloc within the UN, to a degree which would make it substantially impossible for the West to rectify the situation. On the other hand, if the West were adequately prepared to give timely and effective support to, and if necessary to assist in the creation of, a non-Communist nationalist government on Java in time of crisis, it would have good prospects of being able to achieve long term success.

c.   The principal obstacle facing the West in its attempt to influence Indonesian affairs is the heritage of anti-colonialism and continued Indonesian suspicion of Western motives. The Indonesians are quick to resent any real or fancied attempts to influence their internal affairs and can be expected to react sharply under all such circumstances. For this reason, covert activity must be extremely circumspect and by its nature must be limited in size and scope. It must be augmented by and coordinated with the efforts of other governmental agencies under an accepted concept for the implementation of national policy.

d.   Achievement of U.S. objectives over the long term is unlikely unless a non-Communist nationalist government in some form continues to exist in Java. The United States must be able to immediately exploit favorable developments toward that end. We must plan for timely and adequate support of such a government and, if necessary, assist in its creation when the inevitable crisis in Indonesia comes to pass.

e. In time of crisis in Java, it is probable that Indonesian military forces particularly the Army, will be a decisive factor. Although it is known that the Communist apparatus has infiltrated the Indonesian Air Force and Army to a considerable degree, the latter continues to be the principal stabilizing force within the nation and the element which has the most promising capability of maintaining a national orientation favorable to the West. At this time, Indonesia, although preferring U.S. arms, is actively considering offers from Communist Bloc sources. Provision of a controlled military aid program to forestall direct Communist influence in military affairs is considered necessary as a calculated risk. A token military aid program for Indonesia should be initiated at an early date. No military aid should be provided which would enhance appreciably the mobility of central government forces with respect to the possible employment of Javanese troops in the outlying islands. Further study of the internal Indonesian situation governing the distribution of such arms, and observation of the results of token aid, would be the governing factors in a possible more extensive aid program. Such a military aid program is not regarded as contravening the provisions of paragraph 7. b. of the "Special Report on Indonesia."

4. It is realized that U.S. actions in Indonesia will be subject to close scrutiny by our SEATO allies and other confirmed pro-Western governments in Southeast Asia. Any overt moves on our part should be associated with a program to explain our objectives and convince our allies of the strategic necessity of insuring a pro-Western orientation of the Indonesian Government.

5. The Joint Chiefs of Staff therefore recommend that the above views on the implementation of U.S. policy in Indonesia be brought to the early attention of the National Security Council, specifically to point out:

a. The loss of Indonesia to the Communist Bloc would do irreparable and catastrophic damage to the position of the U.S. and its allies in the Far East.

b. A Communist-controlled nationalist government, once established in Java, would receive the immediate and overt support of the Communist Bloc, and ultimately the support of the Afro-Asian Bloc in the UN, to a degree which would make it substantially impossible for the West to prevent consolidation of Communist control throughout the island chain over the long term.

c. To insure continued non-Communist control of Java in time of crisis, the United States must be adequately prepared to give timely and effective support to, and if necessary assist in the creation of, a non-Communist nationalist government when the inevitable crisis in Java comes to pass.

d. An immediate token military aid program, with particular reference to the Indonesian Army, is necessary to forestall direct Communist Bloc influence in Indonesian military affairs. Such an aid program should not enhance to a significant extent the mobility of forces under the control of the central government with respect to their possible employment in the outlying islands. The distribution and use of U.S. token aid to Indonesia should be carefully observed. Should the program matériel be distributed or used contrary to U.S. interests, the aid should be terminated. Should the program enhance U.S. interests, it might then provide a useful means of measuring a more extensive aid program for Indonesia.

e. Increasing influence of Communist elements on the Central Government of Indonesia must be countered by resolute implementation of a more positive concept for the achievement of U.S. objectives in Indonesia. The scope, nature and quality of the effort now being made to this end by cognizant departments and agencies of the U.S. Government should be re-examined on an urgent basis.[4]

---

[4] In a February 12 memorandum to Triebel Cutler wrote "I am not clear to whom the Joint Chiefs were making this recommendation or why, if they thought the recommendation should be brought to the early attention of the National Security Council, it was not forwarded until some three months after its date and then to the Planning Board instead of to the Secretary of Defense for the Council." (Eisenhower Library, Special Assistant for National Security Affairs Records)

In a February 13 memorandum to Cutler Triebel explained that when he forwarded the JCS report under cover of his memorandum of February 12, a meeting of the Planning Board to discuss Indonesia had been scheduled for February 13. The JCS felt that their views should be considered by the Planning Board in connection with the over-all policy review and Triebel's February 10 memorandum was prepared so that Planning Board members could have the JCS views prior to consideration of policy toward Indonesia. Planning Board consideration of Indonesia policy, however, had been postponed. (Department of State, S/S–NSC Files: Lot 63 D 351, NSC 5518 Series)

16.   **Memorandum From the Deputy Assistant Secretary of State for Far Eastern Affairs (Jones) to Acting Secretary of State Herter**

Washington, February 12, 1958.

SUBJECT

Indonesian Developments

There follows a brief summary of the most recent Indonesian developments, with particular reference to the activities of the regional dissidents.

1) A series of mass meetings by the regional dissidents in Central Sumatra has culminated in the issuance on February 10 of "The Charter of the Struggle to Save the State". Speaking for the dissidents over the Padang Radio, Lt. Col. Hussein reiterated the long-standing grievances of the regionalists against the Central Government and presented the following demands to President Sukarno:

(a) That the Djuanda Cabinet return its mandate within five days.
(b) That former Vice President Hatta and the Sultan of Jogjakarta be appointed to form a "National Business Cabinet", composed of honest and respected leaders and free from "atheistic elements", to remain in office until the next general elections scheduled, in principle, for 1959.
(c) That Sukarno resume his constitutional status and rescind his unconstitutional actions of last year (i.e. eliminate the Djuanda Cabinet, the declaration of the State of War, and the National Council).

2) The "or else" portion of the regionalists' demands is not clear. Hussein stated simply that if their demands were not met, the dissidents would "take action according to our own policy" and would "consider ourselves free from the duty of obedience to Dr. Sukarno as Chief of State." No mention was made of any plan to establish a rival Indonesian government in Sumatra.

3) Following the Padang broadcast, the Djakarta Radio on February 11 announced a Cabinet decision rejection the regionalists' demands and dishonorably discharging four of the rebel colonels (Simbolon, Hussein, Djambek and Lubis) from military service. Prime Minister Djuanda called for firm but patient action by the Government in facing this grave danger to national unity posed by the regionalists' activities. A statement by Chief of Staff Nasution tended to implicate the Central Sumatra regional movement in the assassination attempt on Sukarno last November since the Padang group is presently harboring Lt. Col.

Source: Department of State, Central Files, 656.56D13/2–1258. Confidential. Drafted by Robert H. Wenzel of SPA and sent through Arthur Richards.

Lubis who has been named by Army Headquarters as the ringleader in the plot against the President.

4) President Sukarno is expected to return to Djakarta from Japan this week-end, several days earlier than originally planned. According to press reports from Japan, Sukarno has announced his intention to call a special conference to study the demands of the dissidents.

Comment

Assuming no volte-face on the parts of Sukarno and Nasution, the key to resolving the regional problem appears to lie in the hands of such moderates as Hatta, the Sultan of Jogjakarta and certain Nationalist and Moslem party leaders. If these moderate leaders, particularly Hatta, should assume a more forceful role in bringing to bear what pressures they can on Sukarno to compromise his position, at the same time attempting to hold in check the more irrepressible regional elements, then an equitable and peaceful solution might eventually be found. While civil war does not appear to be imminent, an effort by the dissidents to establish a rival Indonesian government in Sumatra could lead to an attempt by the Central Government to force a solution by arms.

---

17.   **Telegram From the Embassy in Indonesia to the Department of State**

Djakarta, February 12, 1958, noon.

2506. Foreign Minister Dr. Subandrio asked me to call at 9:30 this morning. He opened the conversation by saying that it had been his understanding up to now that the United States was maintaining a position of strict neutrality on the West Irian question and on all issues concerning the internal affairs of Indonesia. Therefore he was disturbed this morning to read UP report quoting critical observations by Secretary Dulles on Indonesia's guided democracy (see Embtel 2503).[1] The Foreign Minister said he had conferred with the Prime Minister, and if the UP report was accurate, the Indonesian Government would regard Mr. Dulles' statement as unwarranted interference in the internal affairs of

---

Source: Department of State, Central Files, 656.56D13/2–1258. Confidential; Niact. Repeated to Singapore.

[1] Telegram 2503, February 12, contained an Embassy translation from the Indonesian-language newspaper *Antara* of John Foster Dulles' remarks regarding Indonesia, which were made during his press conference of February 11. (*Ibid.*, 611.56D/2–1258) For text of these comments, see Department of State *Bulletin*, March 3, 1958, p. 334.

this country. He referred to the last two paragraphs of the UP release and observed that these were inconsistent with the unfavorable remarks about Indonesia's "guided democracy".

The Foreign Minister then said that he also deplored the statement of Mr. Dulles if it proved to be true because he believed it would place Indonesia in the position of being a pawn in the cold war between the East and the West. He said the Russians had some time ago asked him if he would like to have them support publicly the Indonesian position on the West Irian and other issues but that he had requested the Russians not to give such public support. He did this because he said he felt Russian public support would provoke a reaction from the West and make Indonesia a battleground in the cold war.

Foreign Minister then said that he thought it would be in the best interests of the US to refrain from statements such as those allegedly made by Mr. Dulles because he was sure that in any psychological contest in Indonesia the US would be at great disadvantage and that the Communist position would be regarded much more favorably by the general public. This, he said, was because the Indonesian people equated the Dutch attitudes with Western attitudes and were inclined to regard Communist support and sympathy with satisfaction.

Finally the Foreign Minister said that the Indonesian Government thought Mr. Dulles' statement was particularly unfortunate since it came the morning after the ultimatum from Hussein. He said the Indonesian Government had decided to dishonorably discharge from the Army Hussein, Lubis, Djambek and Simbolon for their insubordination. He said the Indonesian Government did not object to legitimate political opposition since this was truly democratic but it would not tolerate military insubordination. He said if the government did not act firmly now it would find itself faced with outrageous demands by many other areas.

In conclusion, the Foreign Minister said he would appreciate my conveying these views to my government. I assured him I would do so.[2]

Cottrell

---

[2] In telegram 2173 to Djakarta, February 12, the Department instructed Cottrell to call upon Subandrio at the earliest opportunity and hand him the text of Dulles' statements regarding Indonesia. (Department of State, Central Files, 611.56D/2–1258) In telegram 2575 from Djakarta, February 15, Cottrell reported that he met with Subandrio that morning and presented him with the text of Dulles' remarks. According to Cottrell, Subandrio remarked in part as follows: "Please convey to your government my statement that I shall be very pleased to receive any private criticisms your people care to make about Communism, 'guide democracy' or any other aspect that displeases your government, but I do not appreciate public statements on these subjects and I am bound to react publicly. I am sure this is not the way to maintain friendly relations. Of course, if your government has something else in mind perhaps such tactics might advance your interests but I would not be able to judge this." (Ibid., 756D.00/2–1558) See Supplement.

18.   Editorial Note

On February 13 at the 355th meeting of the National Security Council, Allen Dulles discussed developments in Indonesia in his intelligence briefing:

"The Director of Central Intelligence pointed out that Colonel Hussein, dissident leader on the island of Sumatra, had broadcast a demand on February 10 that the Djuanda Government resign within five days. The Government had rejected the demand and ordered the discharge of Colonel Husein and the other chief leaders of the dissidents. If, continued Mr. Dulles, the dissidents stick to their earlier demands, they should proceed to set up a rival government. However, they are showing reluctance to take this step, and conversations between them and the Central Government are more likely. Mr. Dulles said that it was extremely hard to predict the outcome of the crisis in Indonesia. Sukarno was expected to return to Java in a few days, and it is thought that he will try to pull his forces together. Hatta, who should have been the leader of the reorganization forces, has been reluctant to act in Sukarno's absence. He is proving unwilling to head the dissident movement or to take over the government. This is the existing situation. We may expect a renewed crisis in another ten days after the Central Government makes its decision."(Memorandum of discussion by Gleason, February 14; Eisenhower Library, Whitman File, NSC Records)

After the NSC meeting Dulles and Herter discussed Indonesia, among other matters, during a telephone conversation. According to a memorandum of that conversation, prepared in the Under Secretary's office, the discussion regarding Indonesia was as follows: "CAH told the Secretary that the President did not attend the NSC meeting this morning, but after the meeting CAH and Allen Dulles spoke with the President to bring him up-to-date on the covert side of the Indonesian matter." (Eisenhower Library, Herter Papers, Telephone Conversations) No record of the conversation among Herter, Allen Dulles, and Eisenhower has been found.

On February 15, dissident leaders in Padang, Sumatra, proclaimed an independent Revolutionary Government of the Republic of Indonesia (PRRI). Sjafruddin Prawiranegara was named Prime Minister.

19.   Telegram From the Department of State to the Embassy in
Indonesia

Washington, February 19, 1958, 9:10 p.m.

2246. Your 2402.[1] You may reply to Subandrio along following
lines:

1) U.S. is gratified by atmosphere of friendship trust and confidence which has become progressively more characteristic of U.S. Indonesian relations during recent years and will seek to maintain this atmosphere. U.S. and Indonesia not only have no basic conflicts, as Subandrio has stated, but share same basic objectives. History U.S.–Indo relations bear testimony U.S. desires for Indonesia what Indonesians desire for themselves, to build strong, prosperous, democratic, unified, and independent state.

2) U.S. recognizes Indonesia's need for arms and military equipment to maintain internal security and has demonstrated since 1950 its willingness to assist in meeting this need. Arms were supplied under the Constabulary Agreement of August 1950[2] and were provided for in the Cochran–Subardjo Agreement[3] which unfortunately did not come to fruition. Since 1950 some 400 Indonesian Officers have been trained in U.S. Service Schools and this program is continuing at increased levels in the current fiscal year. Military equipment for internal security purposes has been and is currently being supplied to the Civil Police under ICA Police Training Program.

3) List of Indonesian military requirements submitted late July 1957[4] represents hundreds of millions of dollars worth of equipment, and price and availability study list this size and complexity takes normally from four to six months. Agreements for sales of military equipment in such quantities are both technically complex and politically sensitive and cannot be concluded rapidly.

Source: Department of State, Central Files, 756D.56/2–458. Secret; Priority; Limit Distribution. Drafted by Francis Underhill, cleared with Murphy, and approved by Walter Robertson.

[1] Telegram 2402, February 4, reported on a discussion between Subandrio and Chargé Cottrell about obtaining U.S. arms for Indonesia. (Ibid.) See Supplement.

[2] For text of this agreement, concluded on August 15, 1950, see 2 UST 1619.

[3] For documentation on this abortive agreement, by which the United States sought to conclude a military assistance agreement with Indonesia under the terms of the Mutual Security Act, see Foreign Relations, 1951, vol. VI, Part 1, pp. 729 ff. and ibid., 1952–1954, vol. XII, Part 2, pp. 245 ff. H. Merle Cochran served as American Ambassador in Indonesia December 1949–February 1953; Achmad Subardjo was the Indonesian Foreign Minister.

[4] The Indonesian list was given to the Embassy on an informal basis on July 23 and transmitted to the Department under despatch 42 from Djakarta, July 25, 1957. (Department of State, Central Files, 756D.56/7–2557)

4) U.S. has been reluctant take emergency action comply with more recent informal urgent requests for arms. This reluctance does not stem from any change in U.S. policy towards Indonesia nor represent a departure from basic U.S. policy of preparedness make available arms to maintain internal security and safeguard Indonesian independence.

5) U.S. has been constrained by uncertainties arising from serious civil and military differences within Indonesia and by fear that at this time supply of arms might jeopardize rather than enhance chances for peaceful resolution current internal difficulties and might encourage younger less responsible elements resort to violence. Further, while recognizing long-standing need for modernizing Indonesian military establishment, immediate action to remedy this situation did not appear essential element in reaching solution current pressing problems.

6) Price and availability study on list Indonesian requirement continues and Indo Govt will be informed when completed. U.S. does not intend to engage in competition with Soviet bloc to supply arms to Indonesia. Choice of sources of arms and military equipment is matter of vital long-range political strategic and military importance which Indonesia will decide in terms its own national self interest. U.S. would hope that this decision would be reached only after careful and sober consideration.

Dulles

---

20.   **Memorandum of Conversation**

Washington, February 20, 1958.

SUBJECT

Netherlands Approach to NATO re Arms for Indonesia

PARTICIPANTS

Baron S. G. M. van Voorst tot Voorst, Netherlands Minister
Mr. D. Ketel, First Secretary, Netherlands Embassy

Mr. Robertson, Assistant Secretary for Far Eastern Affairs
Mr. Mein, Director, Office of Southwest Pacific Affairs

The Minister stated that he was calling under instructions to inform us that his government is instructing its representative on the North At-

---

Source: Department of State, Central Files, 756D.56/2–2058. Secret. Drafted by Mein. Mein briefed Robertson for this meeting in a memorandum dated February 20. (*Ibid.*, 611.56/2–2058)

lantic Council to request all NATO members to agree that no arms shipments will be made to Indonesia and to request the support of the
United States representative when the matter is raised. The Minister referred to previous discussions by the North Atlantic Council of the
Dutch Government's request for bilateral consultations prior to any
shipments being made by any NATO member to Indonesia. He said that
the earlier request had been based on Dutch apprehension that such
arms might be used by Indonesia against West New Guinea, whereas
the present approach was based primarily on the current situation in
Indonesia and the fear that any arms shipped to Indonesia might be
used by the Central Government against the dissidents. He explained
that his government was not seeking an agreed policy but only a statement by each member that it would on its own undertake not to ship
arms to Indonesia. He said that a similar approach is being made to the
British and to other NATO governments.

Mr. Robertson informed the Minister that we had recently authorized our representative to the North Atlantic Council to make a statement concerning the Indonesian request for the purchase of arms from
the U.S., which he summarized, and that such a statement had been
made. Mr. Robertson added that we have been dragging our feet on the
Indonesian request and that we have no intention of supplying the government with any arms which might be used to eliminate the moderate
and anti-Communist elements in Indonesia. Mr. Robertson stated that
the policy of the United States Government is therefore that which the
Netherlands is now proposing, if he understood the Minister correctly,
and that we have no intention of doing otherwise. Mr. Robertson expressed the opinion that a discussion of this subject in NATO might be
inadvisable since should it become known it might jeopardize the
chances of those forces in Indonesia which are trying to change the situation. He said that we are hopeful that a moderate government will be
set up in Indonesia and we must be very careful, as Ambassador van
Roijen had recently agreed with him, that by our actions we not destroy
that which we wish to see come about. [2 *lines of source text not declassified*]

The Minister mentioned two frigates and two corvettes now being
built in Italy for the Indonesians as an illustration of the type of equipment which might be affected by such a policy. Mr. Robertson commented that we had been given to understand that the Dutch
Government had within the last few weeks informed the Italian Government that it had no objections to the delivery of these ships to Indonesia.
The Minister stated that this position had been taken when the order
had first been placed with the Italian Government but it was his impression that recently the Dutch Government had made a new approach to
the Italian Government. He said that if a common line, such as the Neth-

erlands Government was proposing, were adopted it would be easier for Italy, for instance, to say no to the Indonesians.

(Mr. Ketel telephoned Mr. Mein later in the afternoon to inform him that the Dutch Government had made an approach to the Italian Government concerning these ships during the latter part of January. In this telephone conversation he also informed Mr. Mein that the Indonesians have placed a new order with the Italian Government and that the Dutch have informed the Italians that they do not agree with the Italian Government filling the order. The ships ordered by Indonesia are:

- 2 Corvettes Type APE, capacity 600 tons, maximum speed 16 knots
- 2 Minesweepers, Type DINO, capacity 600 tons, maximum speed 14 knots
- 7 Minesweepers, Class 400, capacity 85 tons, maximum speed 18 knots
- 3 Motor torpedo boats, type WASPER, capacity 40 tons, maximum speed 48 knots
- 1 Frigate, type GRENADIER, capacity 1500 tons, maximum speed 28 knots
- 4 Escorters, type SIRIO, capacity 1000 tons, maximum speed 26 miles per hour

All these ships would be equipped with radar.

(Mr. Ketel also informed Mr. Mein that the British Foreign Office had indicated that it would support the Dutch position in the North Atlantic Council. As to the timing, he said that the Netherlands approach would be made at one of the informal sessions of the Council within the near future.)[1]

---

[1] The Department transmitted a summary of this conversation in telegram 1569 to The Hague, February 26. (*Ibid.*, 756D.56/2–2658) On February 27 Jandrey spoke with van Voorst about the question of arms shipments to Indonesia. He stated that he wished to inform the Netherlands Minister that the U.S. position on the request that the Minister made to Robertson was as follows: "1. The United States hopes that the Dutch Government will not raise this question in NATO at this time. 2. The Dutch know the United States and other NATO members are not furnishing military equipment to the Indonesian Government at present. 3. The United States believes that the present situation in Indonesia is of such delicacy that any knowledge of NATO consideration of this matter would have most unfortunate results on both the Indonesian Government and the Sumatran movement, as well as elsewhere in the Far East." (Memorandum of Conversation by Cameron; *ibid.*, 756D.56/2–2758)

At a closed NAC meeting on March 6, Netherlands representative Eelco van Kleffens made another statement on the question of arms shipments to Indonesia. He stated that the Netherlands Government wanted all of its NATO partners to abstain for the time being from delivering any arms and war material to Indonesia. The text of this statement was transmitted to the Department in Polto G–74, March 10. (*Ibid.*, 756D.56/3–758)

21.   **Telegram From the Embassy in Indonesia to the Department of State**

Djakarta, February 21, 1958, 4 p.m.

2689. In accordance Department's instructions, I called on Foreign Minister Dr. Subandrio at 11:30 a.m. on February 21 and expressed substance Department telegram 2246.[1] The Foreign Minister replied that he understood the United States position and accepted it. He said he appreciated United States reciprocation of his remarks concerning the friendship and confidence existing between the two governments and he was certain that his government appreciated all of the help and support which the United States had provided to Indo in the past.

However, he regretted that the United States apparently did not recognize the present problem as being one of internal security in which it could assist.

He said that everyone should understand that young countries normally pass through very troublesome early years and Indo is no exception. He said the United States successfully met a challenge to its authority during our Civil War and he believed that Indo was now in similar situation. He said the central government had never objected to political opposition but even understood and sympathized with the demands of the regions for a larger share of the national wealth. However, the present effort of the dissident government is led by older military commanders who think 90 percent in political terms and only 10 percent in military terms. He said they were selfish, mercenary individuals who are using their military positions for illegitimate ends and they must be crushed by the central government. Otherwise the country will be torn apart by other separatist movements led by unprincipled military men. He said the problem, therefore, should be divided into the military portion on the one hand and the political-economic portion on the other. He said President Sukarno had decided to attack the military problem first and to use every effective means to destroy the rebel military opposition. After that, the President will address himself to the political and economic problems. He said Dr. Hatta had agreed with the President on this analysis of the problem and had declined to enter the government until the military portion had been solved. I then asked how much time he expected this would require. He said they all understood that it will not be easy, and that the military solution may not be forthcoming soon, but however long it takes it must be the first step. I asked him if he anticipated immediate use of military force against the dissidents and he said the timing would of course depend upon military plans.

Source: Department of State, Central Files, 756D.00/2–2158. Secret; Priority.
[1] Document 19.

He then said he would like to have me know that his government did not appreciate the intervention of SEATO in the present situation. I expressed surprise and asked him if he were sure of SEATO intervention and he said, "We have proofs of this." I then asked him what form this intervention took and he said, "Moral help and encouragement at least." He said that agents of the Sumatra colonels had been in touch with SEATO representatives. I again expressed surprise and asked him if he believed that this encouragement came from official SEATO sources or from individual SEATO members. He said, "Oh, I do not mean that there have been any public pronouncements by SEATO as such."

He then switched the conversation and said he regretted the United States decision but his government would now proceed to secure arms in India and elsewhere on an urgent basis. He said this will be done on strictly commercial terms with no strings attached. He concluded by saying he appreciated my call and the Department's frankness in setting forth the United States position on this matter of arms.[2]

Cottrell

---

[2] In telegram 2428 to Djakarta, March 3, the Department informed Cottrell as follows:

"Request you see Subandrio and referring his allegations SEATO intervention Indonesian internal situation, state US as member SEATO cannot remain indifferent such statements from Foreign Minister and request he submit 'proof' he claims have of such intervention. You should also point out to Foreign Minister that blaming SEATO for present difficulties his country, is Communist line being pushed by Peking and Moscow broadcasts, and that we are disturbed by Foreign Minister's apparent willingness lend credence to such obviously unfounded and erroneous allegations." (Department of State, Central Files, 756D.00/2–2158)

---

22.   **Memorandum of Telephone Conversation Between Secretary of State Dulles and Director of Central Intelligence Dulles**

Washington, February 21, 1958, 4:42 p.m.

TELEPHONE CALL TO ALLEN DULLES

They talked about Indonesia. D said he talked with Herter and they will meet at 10 tomorrow.[1] D does not think they will curl up right away

---

Source: Eisenhower Library, Dulles Papers, General Telephone Conversations. No classification marking. Drafted by Phyllis D. Bernau, Dulles' secretary.

[1] No record of this meeting has been found.

but they don't have force to go on indefinitely. If we let them take over it may be you have lost it to Communism. AWD thinks we should be a little readier—the closest thing is 3 days away. We may have the problem of protecting American citizens. [*less than 1 line of source text not declassified*] AWD has talked with Burke. The Sec is in favor of doing something but it is difficult to figure out what or why. A said you can tie the Communists into it a good deal but it is not an actual takeover. They are pushing it more vigorously. The Sec said we have no treaty engagements or Congressional authority to justify action in this area. If you get involved in a civil war he is not sure what kind of a case you have. He is in favor of helping the people. [*1 line of source text not declassified*] AWD mentioned belligerent rights. The Sec said he had brought it up at staff meeting—declaring them de facto belligerent govt. Will it help the insurgents? AWD said the others could blockade the ports. AWD said they are entitled to buy arms. The Sec thinks so—we would be entitled to sell to them but also Djakarta could blockade. AWD said it would help if we can get them in—[*less than 1 line of source text not declassified*]. AWD said there is not too much time to consider all we have to consider. This is the best crowd we could get together. The Sec said he has left it to Herter. AWD said he has called him. The Sec said he can call on his own—he has received the tickers etc. AWD referred to the meeting at 10 and can tell Burke to be readier than 3 days. The Sec said he does not visualize what we will do. AWD mentioned sending something to get citizens out. This is more urgent than what we did before. The presence of something might be of moral value and a deterrent to the others because they would not know what we are going to do.

---

23.   Memorandum From the Under Secretary of State (Herter) to Secretary of State Dulles

Washington, February 21, 1958, 5:10 p.m.

I telephoned Admiral Burke with regard to the reported bombings in Sumatra[1] and said that you and I had discussed it and that on the

---

Source: Eisenhower Library, Herter Papers, Miscellaneous Memoranda. Secret.

[1] Earlier that day, Allen Dulles called the Secretary of State to say that the CIA had just received a bulletin that the Indonesian Air Force had dropped some bombs near Padang in Sumatra. (Memorandum from Phyllis D. Bernau to the Secretary of State, February 21; *ibid.*, Dulles Papers, General Telephone Conversations)

whole we would be more comfortable if there were something nearby.[2] Admiral Burke asked what we would think about having a cruiser or a couple of destroyers around Singapore. He said they would not stay in Singapore but would go in and out of port. Admiral Burke said his people had been divided on this and that those who were opposed felt that the presence of our ships could be misinterpreted publicly by both sides, each claiming we were there in support of its position. However, Admiral Burke and I agreed that if necessary we could say our ships were there because of the American citizens in the area and the need to be in a position to evacuate them if it became necessary. Admiral Burke said he would order a cruiser down there right away since the next few days will be the worst and then will probably settle down to a slow simmer for several months.

C.A.H.

---

[2] Dulles and Herter spoke about this matter over the telephone at 5:06 p.m., February 21. Dulles indicated that he thought it would be a good idea "to ask Burke to start something down in that direction." They agreed that Herter would call Burke to discuss this question further. (Memorandum of telephone conversation, drafted by Bernau; *ibid.*)

---

24.   Memorandum From Robert H. Johnson of the National Security Council Staff to the President's Special Assistant for National Security Affairs (Cutler)

Washington, February 24, 1958.

SUBJECT

Are We Running out of Policy to Deal with the Indonesian Situation?

My only justification for writing still another memo on Indonesia is the rapid development of the situation there—the apparent hardening of positions on both sides over the weekend—along with a continuing concern that we are running out of Presidentially approved policy to

---

Source: Eisenhower Library, Project Clean Up, Indonesia. Top Secret; Special Handling.

deal with the situation. Would it be desirable to have the NSC briefed on Thursday on (a) what we are doing and what we plan to do, and (b) our current estimate of what is likely to happen (including our estimate of the rebels' prospects and the will and determination on both sides)? The NSC should be entitled to an oral progress report.

The ultimate question by which we may be faced in the civil war situation now developing is our response in the event of a rebel request for direct U.S. military intervention. Para 12 of NSC 5518 and para 4 of the Special Report[1] provide for the possibility of such direct U.S. intervention in the event of a threat of *Communist* takeover of Java or the outer islands. They do not indicate what action we should take if such aid is requested but the Communists continue to lie low and do not take over the government of Java.[2] We had, I believe, expected to face a cleaner Communist- anti-Communist split than we now face and had not expected, short of a Communist effort to take over, that the lines of both sides would harden to the extent that they have now apparently done. When Mr. Lay raised in the PB discussion of the Special Report the question of whether the U.S. would intervene in a civil war which did not involve a Communist takeover of Java, Ambassador Cumming, according to my notes, stated that the U.S. should *not* intervene in such a situation.

The question of what we are prepared to do in the event of a request for military intervention is not an academic question [3 *lines of source text not declassified*]. The worst thing that could happen would be for the U.S. to become publicly committed to the rebel side without being willing to follow through with direct military help if it were to be requested. It is possible, I believe, to interpret paras 1-b and 4 of the Special Report to justify overt provision of military assistance to the rebels now on the grounds that there has been a further "deterioration" of the situation on Java (para 1–b), though not of precisely the sort we anticipated; and on the grounds that the political situation is less "fluid" (para 4). However, I believe we are approaching the margins of the situation that the policy was designed to cover and that therefore some sort of NSC review is justified.

Bob

---

[1] For text of NSC 5518, approved by the President on May 12, 1955, see *Foreign Relations, 1955–1957*, vol. XXII, pp. 153–157. The Special Report, September 3, 1957, is printed *ibid.*, pp. 436–440.

[2] Admittedly, para 12 of NSC 5518 is so broad as to be capable of being interpreted to justify almost any possible U.S. action under almost any contingency. [Footnote in the source text.]

25.   Telegram From the Embassy in Indonesia to the Department of State

Djakarta, February 24, 1958, 4 p.m.

2727. Aide of Deputy Premier Idham Chalid told Embassy officer that at February 18 meeting with Djuanda and three Deputy Prime Ministers Sukarno talked at length regarding relations with US. Sukarno said that during visit to Delhi Indian officials assured him *Blitz* story regarding plotting of Ambassador Allison was false. Sukarno expressed high regard for Allison and asserted, "Allison was removed because he attempted to understand Indonesia." In Sukarno's opinion US opposed to him and his concept because he refused permit Indonesia be dragged into imperialist camp. He said he did not know what new American Ambassador's attitude would be, but if US attempted interfere in Indonesia's affairs he would deal with such interference in firm manner.

Source stated Chalid wanted him to pass on to Embassy that Sukarno exceedingly suspicious of US intentions and he (Chalid) hoped Embassy would "relax" and not antagonize President.

Comment: While Sukarno was still abroad pro-government journalist told Embassy officer that Secretary General of National Council Abdulgani had attributed similar views to President. Sukarno reportedly believed at that time US had "written him off" and consequently he was determined to convince State Department that if US intended to have satisfactory relations with Indonesia it would have to get along with him. Abdulgani reportedly said Sukarno considered Secretary Dulles personally responsible for recent lack of sympathy for Indonesia on part of US. Sukarno planned upon his return from abroad to give personal attention to all matters related to US-Indonesian relations and future of all US interests, both official and private, would henceforth depend on his personal decisions.

Cottrell

Source: Department of State, Central Files, 611.56D/2–2458. Secret; Limit Distribution.

26.   Editorial Note

On February 27 at the 356th meeting of the National Security Council, the following exchange took place during Allen Dulles' intelligence briefing:

"Turning to the situation in Indonesia, Mr. Dulles stated that the United States faced very difficult problems in that area. He sketched the latest developments, most of which had been set forth in the newspapers. While there had been raids on Central Sumatra by Djakarta government forces, there had not as yet been an all-out attack on the Sumatra forces. Mr. Dulles said that CIA was inclined to believe that Sukarno was not entirely sure of his army. Mr. Dulles estimated that perhaps half of the army forces deployed on Java would prove loyal to Sukarno. But even so, they were not very enthusiastic about an attack on Sumatra.

"Sukarno was to make a major speech on March 3, on which occasion he will presumably indicate his policy decisions with respect to the dissidents. This is likely to be a strong position against the rebel or patriot forces, either by the application of military force against them or by starving them out.

"Mr. Dulles expressed the opinion that the dissidents had moved rather too fast and made their decision and delivered their ultimatum without carefully counting their military assets. This did not mean, however, that they had lost the fight; indeed, they have a reasonable chance of winning it. The Sumatran soldiers were the best fighters in the Indonesian armed forces.

"Mr. Dulles said that the great problem confronting us is how far we go into the matter. [2 *lines of source text not declassified*] Mr. Dulles predicated that if this dissident movement now went down the drain, he felt fairly certain that Indonesia would go over to the Communists. In this judgment Secretary Dulles expressed agreement. Secretary Dulles also pointed out that in past policy we have gone so far as to state that we could not afford to let this happen. We should therefore, in his opinion, be willing to take some very substantial risks in the situation.

"The President stated his belief that we would have to go in if a Communist take-over really threatened. Secretary Dulles went on to point out that our chances for successful intervention were better today, with the assistance of an indigenous government on Sumatra, than they would be later on, when we might have to intervene without such a cover." (Memorandum of discussion by Gleason, February 28; Eisenhower Library, Whitman File, NSC Records)

27.   Telegram From the Embassy in Indonesia to the Department of State

Djakarta, February 28, 1958, 3 p.m.

2806. At dinner given by Yugoslav Ambassador last night Foreign Minister Subandrio took me aside and said three things worried him and the Cabinet in connection Sumatran situation: SEATO, the Philippines and United States.

Concerning SEATO Subandrio repeated previous allegation that his government has proof of SEATO interference. He said among other proofs he had a photograph of a submarine surfaced off the Atjeh coast. He did not say when this took place. I told him I was not speaking under instruction but I knew that general purpose of SEATO was for defense and SEATO not organized for purpose take action within borders non-member countries. Also SEATO has no military forces. Submarine if sighted would belong specific nation not SEATO. I said I doubted anyone could produce evidence that SEATO as an organization had dealings with Central Sumatra. I said local press is echoing Moscow charges against SEATO but this of course is usual Communist slander. Subandrio then said Russian Ambassador had offered expose SEATO activities publicly but Subandrio told him not to do so as this would merely intensify cold war with Indonesia in middle. I remarked that Russia apparently had not heeded Subandrio's request.

Subandrio then said that from Indonesia's experience during struggle against Dutch, he knew many Filipinos would be willing supply men, arms and planes for a price and he hoped Secretary Dulles would use his influence in Manila to discourage traffic with Sumatrans which might have serious consequences for Indonesian-Philippine relations. I suggested he might care to mention this to Ambassador Jones when he arrives next week.

Concerning United States he said we should not aid Sumatrans "because Soviets have substantial interest here and they will not desert us." I made no reply so he continued talking. Said he had heard report which he did not believe but would like my reaction. Said he was told there were U.S. Marines in Philippines ready at moment's notice to be dropped by aircraft near oil installations Sumatra to protect American property and people. I said I thought part of this report was probably true. He looked very surprised and I added, "because U.S. Marines for over 150 years have prided themselves on readiness go anywhere do

Source: Department of State, Central Files, 756D.00/2–2858. Confidential; Priority. Repeated to Singapore, Bangkok, and Manila.

anything at moment's notice." We both laughed. I then said this might be opportune time tell him if GOI Army landed Bankalis or near Palembang he could expect me in his office immediately to ask that he instruct GOI commanders give safe passage tankers evacuating oil company dependents all nationalities. I said I assumed he would have no difficulty granting such request. He replied, "Of course I would agree. You could count on it". I then said, "Well, in that case no U.S. marines would ever be needed, would they?" We both laughed and ended the conversation.

Cottrell

28.   Editorial Note

At 9 a.m. on March 4 the Secretary General of the Indonesian Foreign Office called Cottrell to inform him that Indonesia had decided to bomb the petroleum storage dumps at Padang and Menado to prevent them from being used by the Sumatran rebels. Secretary General Suwito told Cottrell that Indonesia would warn the oil facilities' personnel of the raid and was prepared to discuss compensation with the owners, STANVAC, and BPM. Cottrell warned of serious consequences should American personnel be hurt and stated that the raid would affect U.S.-Indonesian relations for the worse. Suwito said he was sorry to have to inform Cottrell of the decision, but it was absolutely necessary and would be carried out without loss of life. (Telegram 2847 from Djakarta, March 4; Department of State, Central Files, 756D.00/3–458) See Supplement.

After conferring with Suwito, Cottrell called Jack Berlin, the manager of STANVAC, and discovered that there was only a 15-day supply of kerosene and gasoline at Padang, which Berlin thought could have already been decanted into oil drums and dispersed by the Sumatrans. Cottrell returned to Suwito's office at 11:30 a.m. to ask him to verify the STANVAC estimate, to formally protest the planned destruction of the American facility at Padang, and to ask for an assurance that the raid would not be carried out. Cottrell reiterated again to Suwito the serious consequence of such a bombing raid on U.S.-Indonesian relations. If the STANVAC information were true, Suwito hoped that the Indonesian military would call off the raid, although he remarked that they had unusual authority during the emergency. (Telegram 2852 from Djakarta,

March 4; Department of State, Central Files, 756D.00/3–458) See Supplement.

At the Secretary's staff meeting on March 4, the possible Indonesian bombing of U.S. oil installations was discussed. According to the notes of that meeting, the discussion was as follows:

"Mr. Parsons called attention to a message from Djakarta reporting a conversation between the Foreign Minister and our Chargé during which the Central Government gave notice that it plans to bomb US-owned oil storage tanks at Padang. Our Chargé expressed his concern for the safety of American dependents; and the Indonesian Foreign Minister said that his government would consider the question of compensation for property damage after the bombing. Mr. Becker said he planned to discuss the question with the general counsel of STANVAC. The Secretary said he wished a study to be made to determine whether there is any justification in international law for the US to take steps in advance to protect US citizens and American-owned property in such a situation.

Action: Asked L, in coordination with FE, to consider whether there is any justification in international law for the US to take steps to protect American citizens and American-owned property in Indonesia in the light of the probability that the Central Government plans air raids to destroy certain US-owned oil properties there." (Notes of Secretary's staff meeting; Department of State, Secretary's Staff Meetings: Lot 63 D 75)

Following the staff meeting, the Secretary of State spoke with Allen Dulles on the telephone about developments in Indonesia. According to a memorandum of that conversation, prepared by Phyllis Bernau, the conversation was as follows:

"The Sec referred to the threat to bomb US property and people and said he thinks we should see if that is a case for usefully doing something or not. A said if they try it they might get a bloody nose. The Sec said then you don't think it desirable to send forces in to protect American lives and property. A said no, he is inclined to think it good if they did it—then we have a good basis for yelling and screaming and also get a better reception." (Eisenhower Library, Dulles Papers, General Telephone Conversations)

29.   **Telegram From the Department of State to the Embassy in Indonesia**

Washington, March 6, 1958, 8:15 p.m.

2482. Deptel 2461.[1] Embtel 2886.[2] Concur your view aide-mémoire might be useful although doubt that Suwito or Subandrio could later claim no protest made in view Berlin–Djuanda conversation[3] and additional conversation between Anderson[4] and FonOff officials reported by STANVAC New York.

On balance believe you should orally confirm, if you have not already done so, to Suwito that he should now consider your statements (your 2847 and 2852)[5] to have been made under instruction. At same time you should leave with Suwito aide-mémoire of your conversations re Stanvac Padang oil installation, making following points: (1) Destruction appears unnecessary and unwarranted in light supply situation reported by STANVAC and therefore U.S. feels constrained lodge formal protest (2) Destruction of installations would receive considerable publicity in U.S., would likely evoke critical U.S. public reaction, and would certainly not help promote good Indo-U.S. relations; and (3) If GOI persisted in pursuing plan attack installations, U.S. would hold GOI responsible for damage U.S. property and injury U.S. nationals and would look to GOI for full compensation.

Believe it preferable this be done by Cottrell so as give impression this is follow-up his discussion and indication Department approval his actions rather than new approach by Ambassador.

Dulles

Source: Department of State, Central Files, 756D.00/3–658. Secret; Priority. Drafted by Underhill and Wenzel, cleared with Legal Advisor Becker, and approved by Robertson.

[1] In telegram 2461, March 5, the Department informed Cottrell that it concurred entirely in the representations he made to the Indonesian Government with regard to the proposed bombing of U.S. oil facilities. (Ibid., 756D.00/3–558)

[2] In telegram 2886, March 6, Cottrell informed the Department as follows: "Only other step it occurs to me we might take at this time to exert pressure against intention GOI bomb oil installations at Padang is for me to leave with Foreign Minister an aide-mémoire of my representations to Secretary General Suwito on this subject described Embtel 2852." (Ibid., 756D.00/3–658)

[3] On March 4, Berlin lodged with Djuanda a strong protest against the proposed bombing of STANVAC installations at Padang. Cottrell reported on his conversation to the Department in telegram, 2866 from Djakarta, March 5. (Ibid., 856F.2553/3–558)

[4] Robert Anderson, STANVAC representative in Indonesia.

[5] See Document 28.

30.   Editorial Note

At the Secretary's staff meeting on March 6, developments in Indonesia were discussed as follows:

"Mr. Becker recalled that he had been asked to study whether the
US had rights under international law to intervene in the present Indonesian situation in behalf of US citizens and property interests. He said
he has circulated a memorandum stating that the facts do not justify intervention by the US at this time. He explained that, if an attack on US
citizens were planned, the US could justify intervention despite the provisions of the UN Charter; but that the action now being taken by the
Central Government against insurgents with only incidental danger to
US citizens and property gave no such right to the US under international law.

"Mr. Parsons said there are increasingly believable signs of progress in the Sukarno–Hatta talks and noted that another meeting between
the two is scheduled for today. A face-saving compromise, which
would establish Hatta as Vice Premier or Head of Cabinet, restore the
Sumatran dissidents to their former status and eliminate PKI influence
from the government without repudiating Sukarno's 'guided democracy' appears possible.

"Mr. Robertson added that a CALTEX official told him that both the
Indonesian Government and the insurgents are very friendly to his
company's representatives. He said the dissidents are aware that his
company is continuing to pay royalties to the Central Government but
have shown great understanding for the company's position." (Notes of
the Secretary's staff meeting; Department of State, Secretary's Staff
Meetings: Lot 63 D 75) Becker's six-page memorandum is *ibid.*, Central
Files, 656D.00221/3–158.

Later that day, at the 357th meeting of the National Security Council
Allen Dulles reviewed the Indonesian situation during the course of his
intelligence briefing as follows:

"With respect to the situation in Indonesia, Mr. Dulles pointed out
that Sukarno had postponed setting forth his policy statement with respect to the rebellion, from March 3 to March 8. The intelligence community believed that he had done this in order to have his armed forces in
place for a possible invasion of rebel territory immediately after he
made his pronouncement. Meanwhile, Sukarno has been having conversations with Hatta which do not seem to have come to anything, but
it was possible that Sukarno would propose some kind of compromise
with the dissident forces.

"Meanwhile, likewise, the military build-up on both sides has continued, and this build-up was described in some detail by Mr. Dulles, as
was the possible shape of an attack by the forces of the Central Government against central Sumatra.

"Secretary Dulles interrupted to inquire as to the loyalty of the
troops of the Djakarta government. Mr. Allen Dulles replied that the

Djakarta regime had chosen carefully the troops it would use for the invasion, and that among them would be some very good fighters. On the other hand, he was not sure that either side had much appetite for fighting the other.

"The President observed that if the clash really occurred and the Sumatrans had a few good aircraft, they should be able to throw back the Djakarta invaders.

"Mr. Allen Dulles continued by pointing out that the Djakarta government had informed our attaché of its proposal to bomb the oil installations of the US-UK oil companies in Sumatra. It now appears that they have probably been talked out of this proposal, though Mr. Dulles rather wished they had gone through with it without telling our attaché in advance.

"General Cutler inquired whether, if the Djakarta forces did bomb U.S. oil installations and kill U.S. personnel there, we could move in with U.S. armed forces. Secretary Dulles thought this a possibility, and inquired of Admiral Burke what U.S. forces were available for operations in this area. Admiral Burke described these forces briefly." (Memorandum of discussion by Gleason, March 7; Eisenhower Library, Whitman File, NSC Records)

---

31.   Telegram From the Embassy in Indonesia to the Department of State

Djakarta, March 7, 1958, 7 p.m.

2949. Manila pass COMNAVPHIL and 13AF. Dept pass AFCIN–1A1, ACSI, CNO. CINCPAC also for POLAD. Manila for MLG. Three meetings between Foreign Minister and Cottrell took place today,[1] during which oil situation was discussed, upshot of which was assurance (1) that Padang oil installations would not be destroyed and (2) that Prime Minister Djuanda would advise Saturday[2] morning whether he recommends evacuation of CALTEX dependents from Pakanbaru.

At 9 a.m. meeting Cottrell again sought GOI assurances that American owned oil installations in Padang would not be destroyed by gov-

---

Source: Department of State, Central Files, 856F.2553/3–758. Secret; Niact. Repeated to Canberra, Bangkok, The Hague, Manila, and CINCPAC.

[1] Accounts of these meetings were transmitted in telegrams 2944, 2950, and 2951 from Djakarta, all March 7. (*Ibid.*, 756D.009/3–758, 756D.00/3–758, and 856F. 2553/3–758) See Supplement. See also Document 32.

[2] March 8.

ernment forces, referring to protest made to Secretary General Suwito on March 4 (see Embtel 2852).[3] Foreign Minister replied that he was unable to give such assurances. He said the government has given full consideration to this request and that he and the Prime Minister had supported it. However, he said Foreign Office views on many things do not prevail during this emergency. He said best he could do would be to assure Cottrell that if the installations were destroyed full compensation would be provided.

Cottrell replied that he was very sorry to hear this because the reaction to destruction under the present circumstances would cause repercussions which were exactly those that he was sure the Foreign Ministry would like to avoid. Cottrell reiterated reasons why he believed such an act would be disastrous to relations between two countries.

Cottrell then referred to Pakanbaru situation and asked if Foreign Minister would care to comment on any government decision to take over the CALTEX fields. The Foreign Minister said that the GOI must take over CALTEX fields because they could not permit the rebels to retain control. Cottrell then reviewed the many reasons why such an operation on the part of GOI would be counterproductive. The Foreign Minister agreed to logic of every point raised by Cottrell except one. He said real reason was psychological; that the government must do it to indicate they could impose control wherever they wished in Indonesia. Unable to dissuade the Foreign Minister from this position, Cottrell said this left CALTEX in a completely untenable position since either GOI or rebels had power to cut down or destroy CALTEX installations. Cottrell asked what Foreign Minister thought they could do. Did he suggest CALTEX shut down operations now and evacuate? The Foreign Minister replied yes, since this appeared to be only course open. He said if CALTEX shut down, it would probably provide less reason for either side to destroy any installations.

Cottrell raised point of timing. Could the Foreign Minister say when the GOI attack would be made because no evacuation could be orderly in the midst of battle. The Foreign Minister said this was military secret and he did not know. Cottrell said he would immediately confer with CALTEX and would request an appointment later in the morning with Foreign Minister to discuss evacuation plans if the company decided to undertake them. Report on second and third meetings follows.

Jones[4]

---

[3] See Document 28.

[4] Ambassador Jones arrived in Indonesia March 6 and presented his credentials to President Sukarno March 10.

32.   Editorial Note

In telegram 2950 from Djakarta, Cottrell reported his second discussion with Subandrio at 10:45 a.m. on March 7. The Indonesian Foreign Minister complained about a newspaper report that Department of State Spokesman Lincoln White had commented publicly on the proposed bombing raid. Subandrio considered this a breach of confidence and he described the Indonesian military as "furious" over it. (Department of State, Central Files, 756D.00/3–758)

The relevant portion of White's press briefing was transmitted in telegram 2499 to Djakarta, March 7, and reads:

"Q. There is story out of Indonesia that central government has warned American concern, CALTEX, its installations at one of rebel-held villages will be bombarded or subject to bombing.

"A. We have heard same reports, and Embassy in Djakarta has this matter up with Indonesian Government.

"Q. In what vein? We don't want them to do it?

"A. One, to find out if these reports are accurate; and I would assume (2) to caution them about any such thing." (Ibid., 856F.2553/3–758)

Concerning the third meeting, Cottrell reported in telegram 2951 from Djakarta, March 7, that Subandrio met with him at 1:30 p.m. to tell him some "good news." The Indonesian military had called off the bombing raid against Padang, but Subandrio asked that the United States make no public reference to the decision because of the military's sensitivity to foreign pressure. Cottrell promised to inform the Department of this consideration. Subandrio also promised a decision by the next day on the question an evacuation of the personnel at the CALTEX facility at Pakanbaru prior to an Indonesian attack.When Subandrio complained again about Lincoln White's statement, Cottrell showed him the text and the Indonesian Foreign Minister was much relieved. (Ibid.)

---

33.   Telegram From the Embassy in Indonesia to the Department of State

Djakarta, March 8, 1958, 10 p.m.

2969. Manila pass COMNAVPHIL and 13 AF. Department pass AFCIN–1A1, ACSI, CNO. CINCPAC also for POLAD. Manila for MLG.

Source: Department of State, Central Files, 856F.2553/3–858. Secret; Niact. Transmitted in two sections and repeated to Manila, The Hague, Canberra, Bangkok, Singapore, Kuala Lumpur, and CINCPAC.

Deptel 2501.[1] In view of rapidly moving events here prior receipt of reference telegram I had already requested informal appointment with Djuanda and reference telegram was handed to me during conference with him at his home at which I reviewed points previously made as well as arguments in reference Department telegram and investment and market considerations emphasized by Arnold of CALTEX. Every effort was made to impress Prime Minister with serious repercussions military action this area as well as necessity for prior evacuation dependents in event thereof, but to no avail. Decision had been made as to military action, Djuanda said, and plan outlined in Embtel 2961[2] was only feasible evacuation program under circumstances obtaining.

I was accompanied by Arnold of CALTEX and Cottrell and Foreign Minister Subandrio was also present. Upon arrival Prime Minister greeted me cordially as an old friend and both he and Foreign Minister waved aside questions of protocol under current urgent circumstances. Prime Minister ushered group into living room and then took me aside in small sitting room for private talk. After exchange of appropriate courtesies he inquired as to whether I was familiar with the plan for evacuation and whether this plan was satisfactory to us. I pointed out that primary responsibility for this decision rested with CALTEX but that I had discussed plan thoroughly with Arnold and that we both considered it unsatisfactory in that if there were to be military action in area, dependents should be evacuated not merely held in camp at location which might become involved in hostilities. More satisfactory plan in CALTEX view with which I concurred was orderly evacuation of dependents by tankers down Siak River.

I underlined serious risks involved to dependents and consequently to US-Indonesian relations in leaving dependents in area which might become battleground. Djuanda replied that he too would have much preferred to have moved dependents out of the area but that timing of military action was such that this was impossible. He pointed out further that evacuation via Siak River tanker would (present) opportunity for rebels either to (a) sink tanker and thus obstruct passage on river or (b) follow along behind tankers and meet opposing forces farther downstream.

---

[1] Telegram 2501, March 7, requested Jones to bring a number of additional points to the attention of the Indonesian Government with regard to the planned occupation of Pakanbaru in an effort to dissuade the Indonesian Government from undertaking any military action. (*Ibid.*, 846F.2553/3–758) See Supplement.

[2] Telegram 2961, March 8, reported on a conversation that day between Subandrio and Cottrell during which Subandrio outlined the Indonesian Government's plan for the evacuation of Americans from Pakanbaru. (Department of State, Central Files, 256F.1122/3–858) See Supplement.

I then urged postponement or cancellation of proposed military action in accordance with point (1) reference telegram.[3] I said my government found it very difficult to understand why Pakanbaru had been singled out as target for first military action against rebels.

Prime Minister then launched into long exposition of central government philosophy in which he made points that (1) government's authority must be established on Sumatra; (2) solution must be reached which would preserve Sukarno from appearance of actual defeat yet reestablish authority and influence of Hatta in an anti-Communist government; (3) main reason for action thus was psychological though obviously economic reasons played part; (4) no damage should occur in Pakanbaru oil fields since they would not be military target and would not be occupied; (5) he did not wish CALTEX to close down and was confident that entire matter would be resolved within a week or two.

There was no disposition on anybody's part to put any of dissidents in jail or even punish them, he said, except that dissident colonels would not be permitted to rejoin army.

When I pressed further point as to how much time we had in which to evacuate dependents under his plan or any other which CALTEX was willing to accept, he shook his head and replied, "Not much—you must start at once."

We then adjourned to living room to join others where with permission of Prime Minister I outlined briefly points he had made. Arnold said time element was such it would be impossible to evacuate dependents in tankers using river except to extent tankers were already up river at Prawang. He also emphasized that unless tankers could continue to use river, operations would have to be shut down. Questioned by Prime Minister as to seriousness of a week or two shutdown, Arnold replied that unless there were damage to installations, principal problem was one of markets. With a surplus of crude currently on the market any introduction of uncertainty in Indonesian supply would result in purchasers seeking sources elsewhere and market would have to be rebuilt from scratch. After further discussion, Arnold concluded that in view of Prime Minister's assurances and lacking any alternative, there was nothing to do but accept situation and under protest implement GOI evacuation plan. He informed Prime Minister he would get out instructions immediately to this effect and order his tankers to proceed down river to Pakning.

---

[3] Point 1 of telegram 2501 reads: "Military economic psychological reasons for singling out Pakanbaru for target first military action against rebels remains unclear Washington."

After conference with Djuanda both Arnold of CALTEX and Berlin of STANVAC dispatched instructions to carry out evacuation plan in accordance GOI.

Comment: After careful consideration of all elements that can be assessed here, I believe CALTEX and STANVAC are following best available course of action to ensure protection of both American lives and property. Least satisfactory feature of plan is concentration of dependents in Rumbai camp but if Prime Minister's assurances can be accepted, they should be safe there. Only alternative course of action I can see at moment would be helicopter lift for which preparations might be made in event of further deterioration in situation.[4]

Jones

---

[4] In a March 9 letter Acting Secretary Herter informed Dulles of recent developments with regard to Indonesia. The letter was transmitted in telegram Tedul 5 to Manila where Dulles was for the SEATO Council meeting. (Department of State, Central Files, 256F.1122/3–958)

In telegram 3264 to Manila (sent to Djakarta as telegram 2522), March 9, the Department requested that Jones inform Djuanda that as a precautionary measure it was taking the necessary steps to ensure that U.S. facilities would be available for the immediate evacuation of all Americans from central Sumatra. (*Ibid.*) See Supplement.

---

34.   Telegram From the Embassy in Indonesia to the Department of State

Djakarta, March 10, 1958, 3 p.m.

2998. Manila pass COMNAVPHIL and thirteen AF; COMNAVPHIL pass CINCPAC 92. Department pass AFCIN–1A1. CINCPAC also for POLAD. Manila for MLG. Instead of my first courtesy call on Foreign Minister Subandrio Saturday morning March 8 being confined to usual amenities he utilized occasion to outline his philosophy as to

---

Source: Department of State, Central Files, 756D.00/3–1058. Secret. Transmitted in two sections and repeated to The Hague, Manila, Canberra, Bangkok, Kuala Lumpur, and Singapore.

development of Indonesian Republic, to comment on current situation, and make a strong plea for US understanding and cooperation in critical days ahead. He covered briefly in turn principal elements in current Indonesian situation: Growth of Communism, position of Sukarno, West New Guinea, and rebel government, without however referring to Dutch.

Indonesia must work out her own solution to her own problems without outside interference and his nation would not be cast in image of any other nation, he said. America must also understand that Indonesia's foreign policy of active independence was just that. He referred to Secretary's and Walter Robertson's comments to him on subject of Communism on occasion his visit to Washington[1] and said that he did not need to be warned against Communism. "We recognize that if Communists' strength continues to grow here they will destroy us," he said earnestly. "No Indonesian wants to live under Communism." He blamed selfishness and corruption of many politicians of non-Communist parties for increase in Communist strength, saying in critical period they had been more interested in lining pockets than in developing strong republic thus creating situation ripe for Communist exploitation. Finally, political parties had awakened to situation and he indicated united front was developing on this subject.

With amazing frankness he turned to subject of Sukarno, pointing out that US press was characterizing him more and more as Communist. "Let me be frank," he said. "Whether we like it or not, Sukarno is an element in situation that must be reckoned with. He cannot be gotten rid of. But Indonesia is bigger than Sukarno, Hatta and all the others." He sketched portrait of Sukarno as a sensitive man, a brilliant orator with strong hold on masses, but a man who loved fleshpots. "Let him remain and have his pleasures," he said. "He is no Communist. He is first, last and always Indonesian Nationalist." But he indicated Sukarno's reaction to being called Communist was one of indignation at the name calling and he said this plays into Communist hands. They are shrewd enough to exploit this and other US actions in such way as to drive Sukarno emotionally away from west.

Reading between these lines partly in light of what Djuanda told me subsequently, it seems clear Foreign Minister was spelling out hoped for solution to present impasse in which Sukarno would retain titular title but would be less of power factor.

Turning to West New Guinea for moment, he related this issue primarily to Sukarno's emotional reactions in such way that he seemed to

---

[1] Dulles and Subandrio met in Washington on October 4, 1957; a memorandum of that conversation is printed in *Foreign Relations, 1955–1957*, vol. XXII, pp. 471–475.

be saying something might be done about this except for Sukarno. Or, he might have been simply appealing delicately for further US consideration of Indonesia viewpoint. But I have never noted delicacy in Indonesia approach this subject and inclined to view this was effort give indication that door might be opened by Indonesian Government if Sukarno could be calmed down.

On rebels Foreign Minister was less tenuous and more forthright. He said government had made up its mind its authority must be reestablished on Sumatra and military force would be used to quell rebellion. He spoke in uncomplimentary terms of rebel colonels calling them adventurers who were feathering their own nests financially.

Aside from appropriate remarks regarding my pleasure at returning to his lovely country et cetera, I made only two substantive points in our exchange:

(1) As to Sukarno, I said I too believed he was not a Communist [and?] experts at this game had been using him. Foreign Minister nodded, saying PKI were past masters at playing up to Sukarno and giving him what he wanted.

(2) US had no desire to remake Indonesia in our own image; it was our policy to help in any way we could without interfering in internal affairs of Indonesia, we did believe strongly that it was in interest of Indonesian people, US, and free world—"indeed", I added, "all mankind"—for your important country to remain free and independent (I referred to magic word of Indonesia—"Merdeka") and said it was US objective to help Indonesia retain Merdeka. I believed that this created strong identity of interest between our two countries.

Foreign Minister expressed satisfaction with my response and then observed significantly that it was a pleasure to talk with Americans because one could speak frankly and discuss problems with viewpoint of both sides being taken into consideration. He said he had found in his experience as Ambassador to Soviet Union and subsequent relations here that one could not do that with Soviets. "Soviets know what they want, say what they want and that ends it," he said. One cannot discuss matters or have free exchange of views.

Comment: Subandrio, whom I had not met before, is most intelligent, articulate man. While above may have been skillfully designed purely for American consumption, he spoke with great earnestness and fervor and seemed sincere. His references to Sukarno were most surprising, indicating attitude of mind, even as between Cabinet members of this Sukarno-appointed government, that Sukarno himself represented real problem from their point of view. Recognizing that Asians frequently say what they think one wants to hear, nevertheless these personal allusions to President went much farther than anything I have ever heard from Indonesians in past and may well have significance.[2]

Jones

---

[2] Jones met with Subandrio again on March 12. Their conversation primarily concerned military aspects of the situation in Sumatra. According to telegram 3058 from Djakarta, March 12, the discussion in part was as follows: "Ambassador then said US Government deeply appreciated cooperation to date in form advance information and assurances that effects, lives and property are being and would be protected and asked this be conveyed Prime Minister as well as other points in conversation." (Department of State, Central Files, 756D.00/3–1258.) See Supplement.

---

35.   Memorandum of Conversation

US/Del/MC–2   Manila, March 12, 1958, 8 a.m.

UNITED STATES DELEGATION TO THE
FOURTH COUNCIL MEETING OF SEATO
Manila, Philippines
March 11–13, 1958

PARTICIPANTS

U.S.	*Philippines*
Secretary Dulles	President Garcia
Assistant Secretary Robertson	Acting Secretary Serrano
Ambassador Bohlen	

SUBJECT

Indonesian Situation

During breakfast this morning with President Garcia and Secretary Serrano, at which Assistant Secretary Robertson and Ambassador Bohlen accompanied the Secretary, there was a general discussion on the Indonesian situation.

Source: Department of State, Conference Files: Lot 63 D 123, CF 989. Top Secret. Drafted by Charles Bohlen and approved by Joseph N. Greene. The meeting was held at President Garcia's residence.

President Garcia and Secretary Serrano were very much concerned at the developing situation in Indonesia and were inclined to be extremely pessimistic as to the outcome. They appeared convinced from their information that Sukarno would succeed in crushing the rebellion by military force in a relatively short period of time and that as a result: (1) he would feel a deep debt of gratitude towards the Soviet Union and Communist China for the international support they had given him; and (2) for the same reason would feel very beholden to the Indonesian Communist Party for its support; and (3) that having successfully quelled by force a rebellion he would be disposed to use force against any form of opposition in the future to his personal power and policies. President Garcia on this point said that from his knowledge of Asian psychology he believed that a military victory over the rebels would swing most of the uncommitted masses of Indonesia to the Sukarno bandwagon.

The Secretary and Mr. Robertson, while agreeing that this was a possibility not to be excluded, felt that there were other factors in a confused situation which might work against that result. For example, it was by no means clear that Sukarno would be able to dispose of the rebels so easily, and an extended period of guerrilla warfare might ensue. If this happened there was a distinct possibility that Sukarno would be disposed to find some form of compromise which would in effect limit his personal power and force him to eliminate the Communists from the government. They pointed out that Hatta, who had consistently and stubbornly refused to cooperate with Sukarno unless he cleaned out the Communists from his administration, was a key factor in the situation. The Secretary mentioned in the conversation that it was clear that the rebels did not have much military equipment since they were receiving no help from any government, but were forced to pick up what they could from the commercial market. He also said that he thought that the support of the rebels in the Masjumi Party was strong and that this might be a factor to produce the compromise deal to which they had referred.

It was apparent that President Garcia and Secretary Serrano were both extremely concerned and worried about the possible outcome of the Indonesian developments on the situation in the Philippines and the entire area of Southeast Asia.

36.   Editorial Note

On March 13 at the 358th meeting of the National Security Council, Allen Dulles discussed Indonesian developments during his intelligence briefing. The following exchange took place:

"Turning to Indonesia, Mr. Dulles stated that the Sukarno government had moved with unexpected rapidity in its military operations against the rebels. He thereafter described current military operations. He pointed out that the dissidents had not planned their defense around the Pakanbaru area because of the threat to the civilian operatives in the oil installations, and furthermore, that neither side wished to be deprived of the revenues which flowed from the oil installations.

"Meanwhile, said Mr. Dulles, there had been apparently no progress toward a settlement of the civil strife in Indonesia. Not only was there no agreement between Sukarno and Hatta; he had a recent report that Hatta had been put under house surveillance.

"There was no doubt that the military action of the Djakarta Government had been positive and vigorous. The position of the dissidents, while precarious, was not yet hopeless. The Djakarta Government's control of the air above Sumatra might prove to be crucial. Moreover, the Air Force of the Djakarta Government was the branch of the armed forces most heavily infiltrated by the Communists.

"The Djakarta Government, said Mr. Dulles, had recently issued a statement from the Indonesian Army which indicated awareness of weapons and ammunition drops, although the foreign country which was the source of these weapons had not been specified.

"Mr. Dulles repeated that the situation for the dissidents was critical. If Sukarno succeeded in knocking them out quickly, it would be a feather in Sukarno's cap and in that of the Communists. While Sukarno himself was almost certainly not a Communist, he was becoming more and more a prisoner of the Communist Party.

"The President inquired whether the United States would have a lawful right to intervene with force in Sumatra if the Djakarta forces seized the oil installations. Secretary Herter replied that if these installations were seized by the Djakarta Government with a promise of compensation, there would be no right under international law for U.S. intervention. On the other hand, if the lives of American citizens were threatened, we could lawfully intervene. Mr. Dulles commented that the lives of American citizens do not seem to be in any immediate danger in this area." (Memorandum of discussion by Gleason, March 14; Eisenhower Library, Whitman File, NSC Records)

37.   Letter From the Assistant Secretary of Defense for International Security Affairs (Sprague) to the Deputy Under Secretary of State for Political Affairs (Murphy)

Washington, March 14, 1958.

DEAR MR. MURPHY: Reference is made to your letter of February 4, 1958, requesting the views of the Joint Chiefs of Staff on the strategic importance of the island of New Guinea to the United States.[1]

The Department of Defense concurs in the following conclusions that have been reached by the Joint Chiefs of Staff regarding the strategic importance of New Guinea and Indonesia:

a. New Guinea lies astride the sea-lines of communication between the Indian and Pacific Oceans. Based on experience in World War II, only the north coast of New Guinea is considered militarily useful. For Australia, New Guinea represents a shield against invasion from Asia. Australia has always regarded the control of New Guinea by a friendly nation of paramount importance to Australia's national security.

b. The strategic importance of Indonesia lies in (1) the impact upon the rest of Southeast Asia of eighty million Indonesians who recently won independence from colonial rule; (2) its strategic location astride the sea-lines of communication between the Indian and Pacific Oceans; and (3) its raw materials of rubber, tin, copper, and petroleum. Indonesia is a world-supplier of these materials.

c. In consideration of current U.S. military plans, there are no specific U.S. military requirements in Indonesia or West New Guinea. However, encroachments by the Sino-Soviet Bloc would disrupt the United States policy on Communist containment in the Far East, and would partially isolate Australia. Domination of this area by the Sino-Soviet Bloc would (1) deny to the United States and make available to China and the USSR certain rich national resources; (2) threaten the vital sea lanes through the Indonesian Archipelago; (3) jeopardize U.S. plans for the defense of Southeast Asia, including the Philippines; and (4) greatly weaken the determination of some Southeast Asian states to remain oriented primarily to the West.

d. Accordingly, the Joint Chiefs of Staff concluded that the principal U.S. military interests in New Guinea and the Indonesian Island chain are the denial of these islands and their resources to the Sino-Soviet Bloc. In this connection, and in consonance with current United

---

Source: Department of State, Central Files, 656.56D13/3–1458. Top Secret.
[1] Not printed. (*Ibid.*, 656.56D13/8–2757) See Supplement.

States policy objectives toward Indonesia, the Joint Chiefs of Staff consider that the United States should oppose, by appropriate measures, any attempt by a Communist-oriented Indonesia to seize West New Guinea. In recognition of our ANZUS, SEATO, and NATO commitments, the Joint Chiefs of Staff believe that the United States should continue to consult Australia and the Netherlands regarding West New Guinea.

Sincerely yours,

Mansfield D. Sprague

---

38.   Telegram From Secretary of State Dulles to the Department of State

Taipei, March 14, 1958, 1 p.m.

Dulte 11. During meeting yesterday with Casey and Lloyd[1] I threw out suggestion that if the rebel movement did not immediately collapse and if sustained fighting seemed likely, US might say to Sukarno that since early military solution seemed unlikely US must inquire as to likelihood of a political solution, and that in the absence of this likelihood, US would have to consider according belligerent rights to rebels.

I suggested that this statement if accurately timed might strengthen hands of those seeking political solution.

Lloyd remarked that it would have to be carefully considered whether such a move would have productive or counter productive result. Casey made no comment.[2]

Dulles

Source: Department of State, Central Files, 756D.00/3–1458. Top Secret. Repeated to Djakarta.

[1] The meeting took place in Manila.

[2] On March 19 Secretary of State Dulles spoke with President Eisenhower about a number of matters, including the recent SEATO meetings. A memorandum of that conversation, prepared by Dulles, reads in part: "The President asked whether there was much concern about Indonesia and desire that we should take a stronger course. I said there was such concern, particularly on the part of the Philippines and Australia." (Eisenhower Library, Dulles Papers, Meetings with the President)

39.   Telegram From the Embassy in Indonesia to the Department of State

Djakarta, March 14, 1958, 2 p.m.

3143. Manila pass COMNAVPHIL and 13th AF; COMNAVPHIL pass CINCPAC 129 and CINCPACFLT. Department pass AFCIN–1A1, ACSI, CNO. CINCPAC also for POLAD. Manila for MLG. This is sixth in series of current broad evaluations by country team of changing Indonesian situation.[1] It covers period March 7–14, 1958.

Since GOI commenced military action against Central Sumatra, approximately March 5, Padang regime has been loser both geographically and psychologically. Reassertion Central Government's authority at Pakanbaru has boosted GOI morale. Nevertheless recognized here too early take initial GOI success as indication Hussein's forces will be quickly overrun when invasion moves on Padang.

Apparent that General Nasution (whose fate depends on result) and others are anxious crush rebels in military action, but feeling seems growing in Djakarta that military action has accomplished main purpose—showing rebels, fence-sitters and world that Central Government has power move at will in Central Sumatra—and that time has come for negotiation.

Game Sukarno playing is unclear except obvious he is hedging all bets. While it could be concluded Sukarno has less reason consider compromise with Padang than before capture Pakanbaru face-saving as result re-establishment authority Central Government over part Central Sumatra may actually make compromise easier bring about. Particularly if central military run into tough sledding from now on. This possibility still exists for Hatta's return to top executive position in Central Government. If Nasution successful, Sukarno may consider his position strong enough to make unnecessary any further concession to moderates. He has not closed door to agreement with Hatta, however, and if military venture bogs down he may turn more quickly than is currently forecast to efforts patch together something with Hatta which would be palatable to rebels.

While waiting for smoke to clear, Sukarno is on speaking tour, exhorting army officers and troops and mass meetings to cooperate and contribute their share to settlement of rebellion "by positive measures."

Source: Department of State, Central Files, 756D.00/3–458. Secret; Niact. Repeated to The Hague, Canberra, Bangkok, Kuala Lumpur, Manila, and Singapore.

[1] The Embassy sent its first country team evaluation of the Indonesian situation to the Department in telegram 2348, January 31. (Ibid., 756D.00/1–3158) None of these previous five telegrams is printed; they are all ibid. 756D.00.

Sifting available information, our present impression of Hatta's position re Sukarno and Hatta talks is following:

1. At March 3 meeting Sukarno appeared accept Hatta view that military campaign against Sumatra would be indecisive and Sukarno tentatively agreed to replace Djuanda cabinet with government headed by Sukarno–Hatta and to send A.K. Gani[2] as emissary to Padang to propose status quo ante February 16.
2. Further Sukarno–Hatta meeting arranged for March 6 then postponed until March 7. Sukarno sent Hatta letter March 7, further postponing meeting until he completed consultations other political leaders. By March 7 it clear to Hatta that Central Government planned proceed with military attack on Sumatra.
3. March 10 Hatta sent strongly worded letter Sukarno expressing disappointment their mutual discussions had been fruitless and belief attack on Sumatra would fail. Hatta reportedly now tends view Sukarno's motives in their mutual negotiations as insincere. However, he reportedly is prepared resume these negotiations with aim taking responsibility for government himself if military solution abandoned.

Sukarno is still speaking of rebellion at Padang and Menado being used or manipulated by foreign powers, as yet unidentified. Also presence US naval vessels nearby and US concern for safety of Americans and American property in Central Sumatra have been widely noted. Although GOI considers foreign interests subordinate to military requirements restore "unity of Indonesia" they are fully aware danger disregard safety American personnel. Sukarno exhibited cordiality on reception of Ambassador Jones' credentials and his reaffirmation on that occasion of his friendship for US.

Is possible that reverses in Sumatra or flare-up of troubles elsewhere could lead to less cordial GOI relations with US. Communists and other leftists are eagerly calling attention to US "big-stick" policy toward current Indonesian situation, and there is no assurance if things go wrong for GOI that clamor against US would not take the day.

Jones

---

[2] Former Minister of Trade of the Republic of Indonesia and a leader of the PNI.

40.   Telegram From the Embassy in Indonesia to the Department of State

Djakarta, March 15, 1958, 1 p.m.

3165. Taipei for Robertson. In course of two hour conference Foreign Minister this morning raised subject of arms dropped by planes in Pakanbaru.[1] There were two drops regarding which Indo Government had specific information, he said—one on February 26 and one on March 12. The drop on 26th was still on airfield in unopened cases when central government forces took field, he said.

On March 12 4-engine, unidentified plane dropped 20 cases of arms by parachute including Browning 50 caliber machine guns, Sten guns, Bazookas and 75 millimeter rifles. Some of arms still bore stamp of manufacturer in Plymouth, Michigan (Kekeyhayes).

I pointed out that American arms are available for purchase on international market, particularly older types, and observed that indeed bombing operations of central government against rebels were carried out by Indo Air Force using American planes. Foreign Minister said he did not imply US was involved. He referred to statement of Prime Minister reported in Djakarta press this morning showing that Prime Minister had taken same line.

Fortunately Linc White's comments at March 14 press conference[2] and Defense Department release[3] had just been handed me as I left Chancery for Foreign Office and I showed him these statements remarking that I was sure he would be interested and that I planned to have USIS release them here.

Source: Department of State, Central Files, 756D.00/3–1558. Top Secret; Niact; Limit Distribution. Repeated niact to Taipei.

[1] Jones summarizes this conversation with Subandrio in *Indonesia: The Possible Dream* (New York, Harcourt, Brace, Jovanovich, 1971), pp. 116–117.

[2] During his daily press briefing on March 14, White was asked if he would comment on the Indonesian charge that American arms and ammunition were picked up at Pakanbaru after paratroopers seized rebel airfields. He replied as follows as transmitted in telegram 2623 to Djakarta, March 14:

"No. All we know about this, aside from press reports, is the Embassy has informed us of public announcements from Indonesian official sources that American-made arms were air-dropped to insurgents. Further than that we have no information on subject. Now we do note, however, from the tickers that in connection with these reports Indonesian officials have stated there is no evidence of US complicity in this matter. We have received no protest, and as Indonesian officials themselves pointed out, American arms are pretty generally scattered around world, and there is just no indication of source—who bought these, how they got them, etc." (Department of State, Central Files, 756D.00/3–1458)

[3] Not further identified.

Several times during long conversation, however, he deftly introduced subject of foreign support for Sumatran rebels. At one point, discussing military situation, he said that Sumatran forces were equipped
with three weapons to one man whereas central forces had one weapon
for every 3 men. At another point he said that from beginning Indonesians had been convinced of foreign participation because laying down
of ultimatum followed by proclamation was not Indonesian way of doing things. Indonesians preferred to enter into long discussions and
leave way open for compromise. He added GOI had some evidence
Taipei involved in assistance to rebels.

I made no comment above observations.

Other subjects discussed being reported separately.[4]

Jones

---

[4] The Pakanbaru incident was discussed at a Secretary of State's staff meeting on
March 13. According to the notes of the meeting, the discussion was as follows:

"Mr. Parsons also reported on the fighting in Indonesia and called attention to the
statement by an Indonesian Army spokesman that a foreign aircraft dropped weapons of
foreign manufacture for the rebels at Pakanbaru. In response to Mr. Henderson's questions Mr. Parsons and Amb. Allison expressed the belief that, although the Indonesians
feel some rancor toward the US, they have also experienced a sense of relief, that the US
has not intervened. Mr. Parsons added that he did not consider it likely that Indonesia
would manufacture a charge that the US had 'plotted' the overthrow of the Central Government as the Egyptians and Syrians have done. Ambassador Allison expressed general
agreement with this view." (Department of State, Secretary's Staff Meetings: Lot 63 D 75)

**41.   Telegram From the Embassy in Indonesia to the Department
of State**

Djakarta, March 15, 1958, 8 p.m.

3173. Taipei for Robertson. During interview this morning Foreign
Minister said Secretary's observations to press on subject of de facto recognition rebel regime[1] were discussed at Cabinet meeting last night.

Source: Department of State, Central Files, 756D.00/3–1558. Secret; Priority. Repeated to Taipei.

[1] Reference is to comments that Dulles made during his press conference on March
13 in Manila. In reply to a question Dulles noted that the United States was studying the
possibility of granting belligerent status to the Indonesian rebels. The text of his remarks
was transmitted to the Department in Secto 41 from Manila, March 13. (*Ibid.,*
756D.00/3–1358) See Supplement.

Cabinet was quite distressed by Secretary's remarks, Foreign Minister said, and he undertook to explain them in such a way as to quiet reaction. He had informed Cabinet, he said, that it was apparent Secretary had been asked an unexpected question by press and that his answer had no significance whatever in terms of the US Government having reached a decision to recognize rebel regime on a de facto basis. He sought confirmation that what he had said was satisfactory from standpoint of Embassy because he would not wish to have to retract his remarks.

I confined myself to saying that Secretary's comments were obviously offhand, that it was natural that the US Government would be studying the legal questions involved in a situation of this kind and that he was certainly correct in his assumption that the Secretary had no intention of indicating a decision had been made to grant de facto recognition.

He then inquired as to what I understood de facto recognition to involve. I replied that I, like the Secretary, would prefer to have this spelled out by Department Legal Adviser but in general terms I was confident we both knew that question involved actual control over specifically defined territory by insurgents in any country and such questions as payment of taxes and revenues to insurgents. As example, I pointed out international law precedents held such payment to insurgents renders unreasonable subsequent exaction of payment by titular government. Many other problems, of course, arose in situation of this kind.

Foreign Minister expressed interest in summary of State Department interpretation of international law in this respect and said he would appreciate anything I could give him on generally accepted standards with respect to de facto situation. I promised request such information from Department and would appreciate brief summary by telegram followed by more comprehensive memorandum by pouch.[2]

Jones

---

[2] In telegram 2656 to Djakarta, March 17, the Department informed Jones that it concurred with his interpretation of the background of Dulles' comments and provided the Ambassador with a short statement of the relevant legal points involved in according belligerent status to insurgent forces. (*Ibid.*, 756D.00/3–1558) See Supplement.

42.   Telegram From the Embassy in Indonesia to the Department
of State

Djakarta, March 15, 1958, 9 p.m.

3174. Taipei for Robertson. Embtels 3172[1] and 3173.[2] Foreign Minister two-hour interview this morning continued outline of Indonesian thinking with respect to problems facing country begun in first interview (Embtel 2998).[3] He expressed appreciation for American aid but said most important thing to develop was mutual confidence between us and our two countries and he hoped we should be able to accomplish much in this direction over period of time. He reverted to question of West New Guinea and pleaded for some "leniency" in our position on this question. This was especially important, he said, because of its emotional content within Indonesia and also because Sukarno has fixation on subject and laid greater emphasis on it than almost all other questions. He said Dutch had misjudged Indonesian reaction and had showed little imagination in their approach to this and other problems. Indonesians actually like Dutch people, he said, and even now it was not too late to restore Dutch-Indonesian economic relationship. He said he was not asking me to comment at this time but hoped that in my conversation with Sukarno I might be able to handle this question in such a way as to give Sukarno at least some hope that US might be able to do something in present impasse.

He then turned to subject of communism, referred again to his conversation with Secretary Dulles which apparently made a great impression on him, and reiterated strongly what he had said earlier to effect that he and others in government were alert to communist threat in Indonesia. Leaders of present government as well as political party leaders in Indonesia viewed with trepidation approaching elections toward end of 1959 because of growing communist strength indicated in local elections. There was no doubt, he said, that in Indonesia Communists did not have "balance of power" but they did have what he termed "balance of solidarity". PKI was a vigorous, well financed, shrewdly directed, hard-hitting organization and that so far none of the non-com-

---

Source: Department of State, Central Files, 756D.00/3–1558. Secret; Priority. Repeated to Taipei.

[1] In telegram 3172, March 15, Jones reported on other aspects of his conversation with Foreign Minister Subandrio that morning. The telegram primarily concerned their discussion regarding the military situation in Sumatra and its effect on the American oil companies. (*Ibid.*, 756D.00/3–1558) See Supplement.

[2] Document 41.

[3] Document 34.

munists political parties separately could boast of such effective organization.

Foreign Minister reverted to question of mutual understanding between our two countries which he had very much on his mind. He pleaded for appreciation on US side that Indonesian way might be different from US way but our objectives were same in respect to their desire to establish and maintain free and independent republic in which communism represented no threat. He indicated settlement between Hatta and Sukarno was in making. He emphasized that this would not mean that Hatta and Sukarno saw eye to eye on situation, but in his view this might well prove to be virtue. If successful compromise were reached, there would have to be some face-saving on both sides, he said, touching then on sensitive subject of guided democracy. Since this had never been defined, he indicated that phrase might be preserved but interpretation altered. It would no longer be democracy guided by Sukarno but, recognizing that Indonesian people had much to learn, it would be altered to educational concept in which all Indonesian leadership would participate. This still is fuzzy but what he was obviously trying to say was rose by any other name smells as sweet and to convince me that in their own way Indonesians would tackle problem of communism and come out on top.

As I was about to depart Foreign Minister again said earnestly, "Let us work to achieve a meeting of the minds between us. We should be able to understand each other. America was once a colony too."

Jones

---

43.   Telegram From the Embassy in Indonesia to the Department of State

Djakarta, March 19, 1958, 9 a.m.

3230. At Bogor Palace this morning I had approximately an hour and a half's conversation with President Sukarno during which he complained vigorously regarding lack of understanding in US of him and

Source: Department of State, Central Files, 756D.00/3–1958. Secret. Transmitted in four sections.

his position, particularly with ref to communism. [1] Sukarno had nothing new or startling to say, replaying old records to large extent, but I am reporting conversation fully because of nuances and shifts of emphasis which may have significance.

President seemed his old enthusiastic, jubilant self, albeit he looked older than when he visited US, his face more rugged and lined although not so haggard as in *Time*, cover portrait. [2] He welcomed me with great cordiality, extended both hands and chatted volubly during first few moments while coffee and cake were being served.

After coffee he grew suddenly serious and asked, "Well, how are things?" I parried by answering in a personal vein and turned question back to him.

President referred to his response to my credential presentation, [3] then quoted Frank Graham [4] as saying, "Indo is strategic in place and in time—politically, militarily and economically". US should recognize importance of Indo. Relations between our two countries are not and have not been what they should be, he said. There is a lack of understanding between us that I regret. He cited failure of US to support Indo on West New Guinea and general impression that people in US had that he was Communist and that present govt was Communist-inclined. He referred specifically to Minister of Education Prijono and said he was no Communist, that he received the Stalin Peace Prize because of his educational work in the field of peace; Minister of Vet Affairs Saleh, he said, was a left-wing nationalist but no Communist; Minister Hanifi was only one in Cabinet who could really be called fellow traveler, though not, he felt certain, a member of PKI.

Another factor in this lack of understanding, he said, was Indo request for arms to which there had been no response.

As for himself, he was no Communist. He stood firmly and Indo stood firmly on the Pantjasila. [5] (As defined in preamble of constitution: (1) divine omnipotence, (2) humanity, (3) national consciousness, (4) democracy and (5) social justice.) He said he was referred to as "Creator of

---

[1] The Department transmitted suggestions for this talk with Sukarno in telegram 2635, March 16. (*Ibid.*, Conference Files: Lot 63 D 123, CF 990) See Supplement.

[2] Reference is to the March 10, 1958, issue of *Time* magazine.

[3] Jones presented his credentials to Sukarno on March 11. In response to his speech, Sukarno said that he took back no word of what he said when he was last in the United States in May 1956. (Telegram 3031 from Djakarta, March 11; Department of State, Central Files, 611.56D/3–1158) See Supplement.

[4] Former U.S. representative on the Good Offices Committee of the U.N. Security Council, 1947–1948, which had been formed to help settle the Dutch-Indonesian dispute.

[5] The Pantjasila, or Five Principles, were first set forth by Sukarno in a speech of June 1, 1945, and were endorsed in the Indonesian constitution of 1950 as the basis for the Indonesian state.

Pantjasila", that was an exaggeration—the Pantjasila "had been dug out of the soil of Indo". He, it was true, had been the instrument. He said he recognized there were two political elements in Indo endeavoring to destroy the Pantjasila: (1) Fanatical Moslems and (2) Communists.

There were three basic policies under which Indo was operating: these were (1) Pantjasila, (2) neutralism as we called it or active independence as he called it or policy of non-alignment as Nasser of Egypt called it, (3) restoration of West Irian to Indon Republic. These three policies he could assure us would "never, never change".

Indo was endeavoring to stride across centuries in few years, he said, and then reviewed his trip to US, Soviet Russia and Commie China in 1956.[6] He pointed out that US was so far advanced economically and industrially that Indo had no hope of catching up, that Soviet Russia too was in an advanced state of development industrially, but that Commie China, which had been "a miserable country" only 8 years ago, had made tremendous advance and that he had been greatly impressed by what he had seen there. His conclusions, he emphasized, were also the conclusions of Hatta and Minister of Public Works Noor of the Masjumi Party, who had visited Commie China after his recent visit to US.

"When I say that methods adopted by Commie China in achieving this development may hold lessons for Indo, I do not include their political doctrine," he said. "This I reject." But rejecting of their political philosophy did not mean he could not gain ideas on economic front.

"Americans do not seem to understand this" he complained. "I am called a Communist by American press and even Secretary Dulles said that Indonesia was drifting towards Communism. I am not a Communist. Every word I said in America I still stand by. I tried to point out that Nationalism was the fire that was sweeping Asia and this is true. I am a Nationalist but no Communist".

At this point I interjected and made two points:

(1) that Communist-China was country in which individual freedom had been lost—Merdeka had been destroyed—and where only 1-3/4 percent of people were Communists, led by handful of leaders and this small handful was forcing its will upon the vast majority. I was confident that Indonesians did not want to follow this road.
(2) that I did not think His Excellency was a Communist and neither did most Americans—certainly none of those who knew him did, but I said it is difficult for Americans to understand growth of Communism within your country and to understand why steps are not taken to reduce Communist influence.

---

[6] Sukarno arrived in the United States on May 16, 1956, for a 3-day State visit, following which he made a 14-day tour of the country. Between late-August and mid-October 1956, Sukarno visited the People's Republic of China, the Soviet Union, and several Eastern European countries.

President picked this up immediately and said that US must share responsibility, that our position was major factor in growth of PKI, Indonesian people did not understand America's failure to help Indonesia achieve one of its basic national aspirations—that of regaining West Irian—whereas Soviet Russia and other Communist countries supported Indonesia on this issue right down the line. He then repeated what he has said frequently in the past—if US would change its position on West Irian he could change this situation in a moment, snapping his fingers to emphasize point.

"This is true and yet America stands mute!" he said. "Mute! and why? Why can't America change its position on this one issue?"

I observed I knew he understood our position quite well—that this was a bilateral dispute between two of our friends, Indonesia and The Netherlands, and that this was one issue on which we must assume a position of neutrality. "This I do not understand," he shouted "if you changed your position little Holland would be annoyed—yes, but how do you balance that against the annoyance of Indonesia?"

I admitted that Indonesia was a bigger country of greater resources but I said there was a principle here that one did not desert one's old friends. I pointed out that our position had not won US popularity with the Dutch either. However, President must understand our position clearly—cases of this kind in which it is very difficult for a country to take sides in a bilateral controversy occur not infrequently. I referred to Kashmir and pointed out in this dispute Indonesia had, despite much pressure from both India and Pakistan, refused to take sides.

President quickly changed subject and reverted to Communism within Indonesia. Indonesian people are not Communists, he said. Even most of those who vote PKI are not Communists. They are left-wing nationalists. He cited case of what is called the "Holy City," that section of Surabaya in which is located the Sacred Mosque of Ampel. "These people are 100 percent Moslem," he said. "They pray five times a day. But the Holy City voted 100 percent Communist!" He also cited case of two leaders he knew in PKI who were strict Moslems. I observed that Islam and Communism seemed to me as oil and water and I found it difficult to understand basis on which PKI leaders referred to could rationalize their position. In case of Surabaya Moslem, I could understand because they had no idea as to meaning of Communism. I pointed out that PKI orators in Surabaya carried copies of Koran with them and quoted it in their speeches. This, I emphasized, came under heading of deception rather than conviction.

I observed further that I was prepared to agree with him that most Indonesians that voted PKI were not Communists but Nationalists. This, however, did not reduce danger of Communist takeover since party could equally well exploit vote for PKI whether cast by Commie or non-Commie and I assured him US Government did not believe that Indonesian people would ever willingly go down road to Communism. Instead it was our fear that if Communists' power within country was permitted to grow, ultimately time would come when, even with minority, Communists might stage coup and take over. This was not new to history of Communist expansion.

I then cited Eastern Europe's experience, using Czechoslovakia as prime example. I pointed out that President Benes had felt it necessary in reconstruction of Czechoslovakia after war to have represented in government all elements of political community including Communists. In period from 1945 to 1948, I emphasized, Communists posed as champions of national freedom and independent foreign policy, took great care to operate within framework of Czechoslovak national psychology and appeared to make no moves which were not generally politically acceptable, but when time came Communists believed they were strong enough they moved quickly to take over. I was sure he knew that Jan Masaryk was found dead in Foreign Office, generally believed to have been assassinated by the Communists and that President Benes, broken body and spirit, his influence gone, retired to country. Sukarno nodded soberly at this point and it was clear parallel was not lost upon him.

He then raised question as to why we were so worried about Indonesia's percentage of Communist votes. "You aren't worried about France and Italy yet theirs is higher." I pointed out that at present time Communist vote in France and Italy is decreasing as compared with earlier years.

"We were worried about communism in these countries," I said. "That is what the Marshall Plan was all about: to enable these European countries to rehabilitate themselves after the war, regain lost standards of living and give people hope once more. We think it accomplished its purpose. But in Indonesia, the strength of the Communists is increasing, not decreasing."

President turned to his well-known concept of guided democracy and referred to Secretary Dulles' remarks on this subject, complaining that his idea had been generally misunderstood in US. "This is no Communist conception", he insisted. "This is my idea to correct a trouble from which we suffer—over-democracy". He claimed that there are 47 political parties in Indonesia, each representing special points of view or special interests. "This is nonsense", he said, emphasizing that no country can function with its people divided like this. No government can act. His concept of guided democracy was one which would correct some of these evils, reducing number of political parties. It was designed to correct evils in body politic not destroy democracy.

Only time President showed violent emotional reaction during conversation was when he referred to Secretary Dulles' observation on belligerent status of rebels.[7] "This is way to Hell", he said tensely, and repeated himself. Reaction to such a move would be serious throughout Indonesia but would not be confined to Indonesia, he said.

I took liberty of picking up Secretary's cue in Dulte 11 from Manila,[8] repeated information Djakarta unnumbered March 14, pointing out that early settlement of internal conflict would avoid necessity for facing this issue. Sukarno said nothing but looked thoughtful. I am confident planting of this seed served good purpose.

I then queried as to whether President had anything he wished to say on subject of possible settlement in current conflict, prefacing my question by emphasizing US desire to see cessation civil war and our strong conviction dismemberment of Republic of Indonesia against interest of entire free world. President reacted strongly to this, "yes", he said, "this would be against interest of whole world". He then said, "we will reach a settlement as soon as rebellion is quelled". He pointed out that Central Government was not using great force or violence and did not wish to but that it must reestablish its position and authority on Sumatra. He had tried to settle controversy as soon as he returned from Japan but actions of rebels in proclaiming revolutionary government had made this impossible. He then said head of NU[9] had last week come to him with request for a conference of all political party leaders, including the PKI, he added significantly, and Hatta. He was considering this but had not yet made up his mind.

I took advantage of appearance of President's aide, indicating other visitors were waiting, to say to President that I felt we had great many things to discuss and I hoped this would be one of a series of conversations. President seemed pleased and readily agreed, adding that he had intended to suggest this had I not done so. I assured him that I considered most important aspect of my mission establishment of close understanding between our two countries, that I appreciated very much his frankness and I felt that as between friends this was the way to establish understanding and discuss matters on which even friends might disagree.

President smiled and said he wanted to see me often. Would I prefer to see him next in Bogor or Djakarta? I indicated this was a matter of his convenience. He replied Bogor and he would tell me when. As I walked out, he added, "keep close to me," and repeated it for emphasis.

---

[7] See footnote 2, Document 41.

[8] Document 38.

[9] Probably a reference to Idham Chalid.

Before my departure he introduced me to Indonesian Ambassadors to Pakistan and Yugoslavia who were visiting palace and then took me on inspection tour of palace and to view his collection of paintings. At entrance to palace under porte cochere were parked two bubble helicopters which President now uses to fly back and forth to Djakarta.

Comment: Some of immediate impressions I had of conversation were:

(1) Sukarno appeared eager to present his case fully and frankly, showed great cordiality and seemed to be demonstrating genuine interest in keeping door to US open.
(2) Showed no indication of readiness to compromise current conflict; in this connection avoided subject of his relations with Hatta which is generally conceded to be key to solution.
(3) Showed great concern at possibility US recognition belligerent status for revolutionary regime.

Jones

---

44.   Editorial Note

On March 20 at the 359th meeting of the National Security Council, Allen Dulles opened his intelligence briefing with a discussion of developments in Indonesia:

"The Director of Central Intelligence indicated that he would first go over briefly the strategic developments in Indonesia over the last week. These were hard to evaluate. Our intelligence sources describe the events as something like a chess game. It was in any event a strange kind of war. After Mr. Allen Dulles had dealt with the situation at Medan and at Pakanbaru, Secretary Dulles inquired whether there was any solid evidence that fighting was continuing in the Medan area. Mr. Allen Dulles replied that there had apparently been little contact fighting on the ground, and that such losses as the dissidents had sustained had been occasioned by strafing from the air.

"Mr. Allen Dulles indicated that there had been no change in the situation on the southwest coast, which was still held firmly by the dissidents, with no attempt yet at a landing by Djakarta forces. In South Sumatra, Colonel Barlian, the commander, was still proclaiming his neutrality. Mr. Dulles felt that he might have gone over to the rebels if they could have held Medan after they captured it. Turning to the Celebes, Mr. Dulles indicated that the northern areas were still strongly held by the dissidents under Lt. Col. Sumual.

"The President inquired whether any portion of Borneo had been affected by the civil war. Mr. Dulles replied in the negative, and stated that the Djakarta forces still held Borneo, although they held it somewhat thinly. He then went on to point out that in recent days the dissident leaders had become very belligerent in their public statements, despite their difficult military situation. These statements did not, of course, help in realizing the possibility of a negotiated peace. Nor was there very much evidence of real fighting. Very poor communications facilities made it difficult for the dissidents to mount and sustain a concerted military operation.

"The President inquired about the character of the terrain in the area where the fighting was occurring, and asked Mr. Dulles to provide a brief report on this subject at the next Council meeting. Apropos of the comment that the dissidents lacked the means of effective communication, [2 *lines of source text not declassified*]. Mr. Dulles replied that [*less than 1 line of source text not declassified*] the great need of the dissidents was for aircraft, which they totally lacked. The President found it difficult to grasp what use aircraft would be in jungle fighting. Mr. Dulles pointed out that aircraft could be used against the very few roads in Sumatra. The President replied that he would have imagined that the kind of roads to be found in the fighting area could readily be repaired after they had been bombed.

"Mr. Dulles concluded his comments on Indonesia by indicating that the Soviets have already delivered to Djakarta ten small merchant vessels. Moreover, Djakarta expects from Prague early in April IL–28 light bombers and MiG–15 and –17 fighter aircraft. The crews to man these planes were already being trained in Egypt and Czechoslovakia. Receipt of these aircraft, together with trained crews, could produce a serious change in the military balance in the near future." (Memorandum of discussion by Gleason, March 21; Eisenhower Library, Whitman File, NSC Records)

45.   Telegram From the Embassy in Indonesia to the Department of State

Djakarta, March 21, 1958, 4 p.m.

3300. Embtel 2978.[1] During course hour's talk this morning Prime Minister made following points among others:

1. Government timing military program had been somewhat upset Medan affair but was still proceeding generally according to plan.

2. Prime objective continued to be Padang and GOI would immediately move toward settlement when this objective reached. He said he personally would do utmost to bring pressure on Hatta and Sukarno to get together as he saw no satisfactory alternative to Sukarno–Hatta government if Indonesia was to move forward. He said he himself was willing to resign as soon as Sukarno–Hatta agreement could be reached.

3. He said considerable political maneuvering was going on behind scenes these days to accomplish this objective. Wilopo of PNI was being very active in effort to bring about conference of party leaders with Sukarno and Hatta with view to laying basis for settlement. NU leadership was also working toward same end but Prime Minister indicated thinking somewhat different as to timing of settlement, PNI wishing to bring about settlement soonest, NU interested in some delay, primarily, he hinted, for reasons of political patronage.

4. He reverted to period before rebel ultimatum and proclamation establishment revolutionary government. On February 8, he said, he had sent a message via Roem to Padang leaders pleading with them not to take overt action which would prevent satisfactory compromise from being reached. He had informed them, he said, that within two weeks after return of Sukarno he would resign and pave way for Hatta–Sukarno government. He was confident this could have been done because, he said, it was only with great reluctance that Sukarno had yielded to pressure to take military action. He said he himself was as much responsible as anyone for military action after ultimatum because he said he felt it was necessary to establish for all time in Indonesia that open rebellion was not way to accomplish objectives.

5. I expressed appreciation my government for advance notification and careful planning of GOI to insure adequate protection US persons and property. He said it was a great relief to him that things had

---

Source: Department of State, Central Files, 756D.00/3–2158.Top Secret; Limit Distribution.

[1] In telegram 2978, March 10, Jones reported on a conversation he had that day with Djuanda. During their talk, the Prime Minister stated that an agreement had been reached between Hatta and Sukarno on the formation of a new government with Sukarno as President and Hatta as Vice President. He explained that this agreement would not be announced for 2 weeks in order to give time for the Central Government to exert authority in Sumatra. (*Ibid.*, 756D.00/3–1058) See Supplement.

turned out as they had. He also informed me that unit of General Sukanto's mobile brigade would be assigned to CALTEX area to assure continuance such protection.

6. Since this was first opportunity since receipt Deptel 2545,[2] March 10 to bring up point re SEATO directly with Prime Minister I took occasion to do so, emphasizing I was certain in his mind this was water over dam, but I nevertheless wished to record with him personally my government's assurances SEATO character along lines outlined in reference Department's telegram. Prime Minister expressed appreciation.

7. In moving against Communists within Indonesia, Prime Minister expressed importance build-up of Democratic Trade Union make possible clip SOBSI claws.

Jones

[2] In telegram 2545, March 10, the Department noted that recent private and public statements by Sukarno and Subandrio indicated "underlying area of misunderstanding and misinterpretation of U.S. policy towards Indonesia." It suggested that Jones should stress to Sukarno that the "U.S. had no desire draw Indonesia into SEATO. This policy remains unchanged." Jones was also to remind Sukarno that "History of U.S. relations with Indonesia, as well as with India and Burma, bear ample testimony on sincerity this policy. SEATO has no objective other than mutual defense. It is not and cannot become an instrument of interference in the domestic affairs of any nation." (Department of State, Central Files, 756D.00/2–2858)

---

46.   Telegram From the Embassy in Indonesia to the Department of State

Djakarta, March 21, 1958, 10 p.m.

3312. Dr. Hatta welcomed me warmly when I called at his home at 5 p.m. today.[1] We talked for more than an hour covering most of current issues at least briefly. In summary Hatta appeared optimistic as to possibility of reaching agreement with Sukarno on formation of new government on terms satisfactory to himself but somewhat pessimistic as to bringing about early cessation of conflict in Sumatra. Sukarno had written him recently saying he wanted third meeting in near future, he said. Hatta displayed none of fuzziness of thinking indicated by quotations available here from his *Foreign Affairs* article.[2]

Source: Department of State, Central Files, 756D.00/3–2158. Top Secret; Niact; Limit Distribution. Transmitted in two sections.

[1] Jones summarized this conversation in *Indonesia: The Possible Dream*, pp. 126–127.

[2] Reference is to Hatta's article, "Indonesia Between the Power Blocs," *Foreign Affairs*, XXXVI (April 1958), pp. 480–490.

Hatta said he and Sukarno had fundamental disagreement on how to cope with Communist problem. Sukarno was deeply worried about PKI's growing strength and believed that Communist gains made entirely on basis promises which they not required fulfill. Sukarno therefore thinks Communists should be brought into government and be forced accept responsibility for their promises. Their failure would weaken them by showing them up. Hatta said he entirely disagreed with Sukarno's view and repeatedly pointed out to him that PKI not conventional political party and would use position in government to burrow into army and bureaucracy.

Nevertheless Hatta said he believes Sukarno even willing to yield to him on this critical point and is prepared in principle to give him power and responsibility for forming government. I asked Hatta about current status his personal relationship with Sukarno. Hatta indicated there was no personal acrimony in his relations with Sukarno and spoke of latter in dispassionate and understanding terms.

Issue on which previous Sukarno–Hatta talks have floundered, [*foundered*?] Hatta said, was constitutional framework for next government. Hatta stated that this was no mere legal quibble but reached down to basic power factors in Indonesian politics. Hatta said he unwilling to form government if he must clear important questions with political party leaders in Parliament since parties in their present state development tend to place patronage above other issues. Therefore unless Hatta can bypass parties he thinks he will be unable to take necessary steps to eliminate corruption and lay foundations for orderly development of economy. Hatta said that Sukarno did not seem personally opposed to "presidential" Cabinet envisaged by Hatta as opposed to Parliamentary form, but was representing PNI objections which Hatta said are strong.

While Hatta seemed convinced that restoration of his partnership with Sukarno based on exclusion of Communists from government was possible, he said that military problem much more difficult to solve. Hatta said he does not know how long military struggle will last but fears it will be protracted. He believes that Padang group will put up a great resistance on one hand, and army headquarters is adamant on necessity for re-establishing what it considers primarily problem of military discipline.

Hatta said he thought Djuanda Cabinet should remain in office until he and Sukarno agree on next Cabinet. In this connection Hatta said that in his earlier talks with Sukarno they had not reached point of agreeing on personalities for next government. Although Hatta did not respond to my query as to what parties would be represented, he indicated that certain types of politicians in present Cabinet would be excluded.

On subject of National Council, he had told Sukarno he had no objection to use of term but would not agree to presidential appointment of members. He was willing to have council in form of pre-Senate with, however, purely advisory powers (since no such body provided for in constitution) and with member selected from regions by provincial legislatures. Sukarno, he said, had agreed to this.[3]

He said Indonesia would be faced with many problems when stable government was finally established because printing press had been running so freely. Also there was considerable hoarding of currency in country due to lack of confidence in present situation and lack of goods to buy. Under stable government this money would come out of hiding and create additional inflationary pressures, he believed. He was currently working on a plan to solve this problem, he said.

Second immediate problem would be that of rice. He emphasized that most difficult aspect this problem was distribution rather than supply. Third major problem area was economic development with a view ultimately to raising standard of living. He said he had had many arguments with Sukarno on this subject, having advocated that way to fight Communism was with positive program so that people could see accomplishments rather than negative approach favored by Sukarno in past and described above. He indicated substantial outside assistance would be required.

Hatta emphasized several tragic aspects of current situation:

(1) Division of country with anti-Communist fighting anti-Communist, thus giving greater opportunity to Communists. He pointed out that one of strongest anti-Communists in country was Nasution. He said Communists referred to Dr. Hatta as enemy number one and Nasution as enemy number two.

(2) Wasting of resources in military conflict that were so badly needed in solution serious economic problems of country.

(3) Sacrifice of outstandingly capable leaders such as Sjafruddini, Natsir and others. He said somehow these men must be re-integrated into public life.

(4) Split in Masjumi Party and serious weakening in Masjumi Party on Java resulting from conflict.

Commenting on PKI infiltration army, Hatta said despite clever approach it had not succeeded in reaching more than 10%. PKI method in dealing with army, he said, was not to ask soldiers to join PKI or preach Communism to them or seek support but to do exactly reverse—tell soldiers that PKI was interested in them, that it knew all about their poor pay and bad living conditions and that its program was to remedy these.

---

[3] *[text not declassified]*

I raised question with him as to possibility united front of non-Commie parties. Repeated efforts had been made to accomplish this, he said, but each time clash of personalities had prevented. However, he planned to continue such efforts and was receiving much encouragement from younger Party leaders, particularly in PNI, who believed this essential to save their party and prevent further PKI gains.

Re General Sukanto and mobile brigade I asked him whether he thought its divorce from politics included neutrality in event of Commies resorting to open violence. He replied emphatically in the negative. Mobile brigade could be counted on in event of trouble of this kind, he assured me.

Hatta indicated he would like to see me again soon to discuss economic problems and program in greater detail.

Jones

---

47.   Editorial Note

On March 27 at the 360th meeting of the National Security Council, Allen Dulles opened his intelligence briefing with a discussion of developments in Indonesia:

"As requested by the President at the last Council meeting, the Director of Central Intelligence first presented a brief analysis of the topography of Sumatra. This was actually done by [less than 1 line of source text not declassified] of the Central Intelligence Agency. Thereafter Mr. Allen Dulles gave an account of the recent developments in the civil war in Indonesia. He provided estimates of the relative strength of the dissident forces and the Government forces, the former being well out-numbered. On the other hand, the Government forces are now moving into more difficult and mountainous terrain on the western side of the island. Their progress would be slowed up, and the major danger now facing the dissidents was an amphibious landing on the western coast of Sumatra, with the objective of capturing Padang. Mr. Dulles summarized the situation of the dissidents as not very happy. On the other hand, they have not yet shown signs of giving up. The dissidents were holding their own in the Celebes, and were planning to attack the airfield at Morotai if they could find the planes and the pilots." (Memorandum of discussion by Gleason, March 28; Eisenhower Library, Whitman File, NSC Records)

48.   Telegram From the Embassy in Indonesia to the Department of State

Djakarta, March 27, 1958, 3 p.m.

3403. Manila pass COMNAVPHIL and THIRTEENAF; COMNAV-PHIL pass CINCPAC 173 and CINCPACFLT. Department pass AFCIN 1A1 CNO. CINCPAC also for POLAD. Manila for MLG. This is eighth in series of current broad evaluations by country team of changing Indonesian situation. It covers period March 20–27.

GOI military operations in Sumatra have proceeded successfully during past week. Short-lived coup at Medan week before and uncertainty concerning the future in that area may have slowed down timetable of GOI military clean-up of rebel held areas and drive on Padang will probably be delayed about two weeks. GOI however, has not suffered a military setback and recently has kept propaganda machinery in high gear boasting of success of its armed forces. Again this week Americans and American property in Sumatra have not suffered; as precaution, however, American dependents from Medan area have been temporarily evacuated to Singapore. CALTEX and STANVAC are back in operation and their dependents are moving back to usual places of residence in Central Sumatra.

Hampering the Central Government's satisfaction at its successes in the initial stages of the Sumatra campaign are irritations, and in some cases fear, concerning "foreign intervention". This has been a dominant issue in Djakarta for many days and during past week has taken variety of forms.

PKI and PNI elements, reportedly instigated by persons in authority, have made SEATO their target and singled out US as SEATO member most involved. Student, youth and "farmer" groups have called in person at Embassy and residence to present petitions, and have painted slogans and hung banners on streets in front of US establishments, condemning SEATO. Almost as prominent have been allegations that arms are being supplied rebels from Taiwan, and pro-GRC Chinese are fearful that GOI, or leftists with GOI concurrence, will take out their spite on them next. PKI interest in the campaign to discredit SEATO is evident in the Communist newspapers call to intensify the anti-SEATO action with massive effective actions throughout entire country. Air drop at Pakanbaru of US-manufactured arms has continued to receive heavy publicity.

Source: Department of State, Central Files, 756D.00/3–2758. Secret; Niact. Transmitted in two sections and repeated to The Hague, Canberra, Bangkok, Kuala Lumpur, Singapore, and Manila.

Another aspect of "foreign meddling" which may have far-reaching consequences is Soviet aid. Privately Prime Minister Djuanda has expressed his concern at accepting ten ships from USSR but has assured Ambassador Jones that Russian officers and crews will not remain in Indonesia. According other reports, however, Russian officers and engine crews will stay. Publicly opposition papers (including PSI daily which military authorities have since closed down) have suggested arrival of Soviet vessels constituted intervention which invited retaliation.

Official statements of foreign involvements have verged on the sensational but have kept in bounds by the narrowest of margins. Prime Minister and Foreign Minister, however, have passed up opportunities freely opened to them by newsmen to press the attack on SEATO. Their restraint and caution has been equally noticeable and no doubt reflects their understanding of the actual situation, in their affirmations that GOI is responsible for and capable of safeguarding Americans in zone of operations and that therefore US Seventh Fleet vessels should depart adjacent waters. In this context should be considered also Sukarno's insistence that military moves in Sumatra are only police action. Several Indonesian observers have linked this comment to Secretary Dulles' suggestion that legal aspects of granting belligerency status to rebels required further review by legal experts.

International insurance and liability problems led to decision to return to Dutch owners KPM ships interned in Indonesian harbors since last December. This has not been popular with labor and leftist groups. Indeed, on this issue Communists and Communist labor union have taken their most outspoken exception to GOI action and brought unstuck somewhat GOI-PKI solidarity on some recent problems.

Sporadic banning of specific issues of American publications, recent banning of *Time* magazine until further notice and exclusion from Indonesia of many foreign reporters show growing sensitivity of GOI to reporting abroad which puts Central Government in unfavorable light. Domestic censorship has continued also. Newspapers *Keng Po* (Independent) and *Pedoman* (PSI) have been closed down, reportedly on orders from the top, for not having followed strict government line in reporting Sumatran developments. Simultaneous muzzling of two Communist line papers generally regarded as window-dressing since ban is expected to be temporary only.

Although political mixture remains much the same as before, Hatta has indicated he considers himself still force to be reckoned with, Djuanda is speaking again of Sukarno–Hatta cooperation once rebellion has been militarily suppressed, and NU and others are talking of new non-Communist Cabinet after Padang is subdued. Still to be heard from in significant military or political manner are Padang leaders. Their stock has not been enhanced by their unreliable pronouncements on Padang Bukittinggi radio and military retreats of their troops before GOI advances. Hopes for their eventual success, however, have not been abandoned by their adherents in Djakarta.

Some moderates in Djakarta still claim prospects are good that Sukarno will soon take positive stand against Communists, but definite action in this direction seems to remain as remote as ever.

Jones

49.   Memorandum of Information

Washington, March 28, 1958.

SUBJECT

Sino-Soviet Bloc Assistance to Indonesia

1. Increasing Sino-Soviet economic and military assistance to Indonesia, in conjunction with rapidly deteriorating economic and political conditions in the archipelago, might well lead to Indonesia's early domination by the Bloc.

2. Soviet Bloc economic assistance to Indonesia now totals $129 million. This aid first assumed importance in late 1956 with the initialing of a Soviet $100 million economic development loan by Indonesia. The first purchase under this loan was 10 small merchant ships. A $9 million credit from the European Satellites is being used for the construction of a sugar refinery, an agricultural tool factory and several smaller installations. Communist China recently offered a $20 million credit for the purchase of rice and textiles and development of the Indonesian textile industry.

3. A contract for the purchase of 4,000 jeeps was signed by Indonesia early in 1957; 3,600 have been delivered. A military purchasing mission departed Djakarta in December 1957 for Yugoslavia and the

Source: National Archives and Records Administration, RG 218, JCS Records, 092 Asia (6–25–48). Secret. Prepared by Director of Naval Intelligence Frost. Attached to JCS 1992/650. On April 3, the Chief of Naval Operations, Arleigh Burke, forwarded this memorandum to the Joint Chiefs of Staff for their information.

European Satellites seeking various type weapons and equipment. It had at its disposal $250 million, reportedly stemming from hard currency credit extended by Communist China. Reports of air aid to Indonesia include the sale by Czechoslovakia of 30 MiG–17 jet fighters and the probable provision of technical assistance and pilot training. The delivery of 14 aircraft of unknown type in the "very near future" has also been reported. Naval assistance thus far is limited to the probable ordering of several small ships from Yugoslavia. However, the mission is known to have been interested in a destroyer, submarines, minesweepers and other naval items. Ammunition, small arms and artillery probably have been contracted for but quantities and exact types are not known.

4. The receipt of Bloc aid will serve to heighten differences within Indonesia, strengthening those leaders favoring closer ties with the Bloc while antagonizing moderate elements as well as the dissidents. The arrival of assistance is being handled skillfully, however, and the likelihood of significant anti-Sukarno reactions appears slight. The Soviet short-term objective re Indonesia appears to be to support Sukarno in the hope that he will eventually reassert his authority over the entire archipelago, and that in this process the indigenous Communists will gain a dominant position in the central government. In the event Sukarno cannot reassert his authority over the outlying areas, an alternate Soviet objective probably is to ensure Communist control of Java, and then to extend this control. In any event, the ultimate Soviet objective seems clear: by controlling Indonesia it hopes to gain control of the vital sea lanes between the Indian and Pacific Oceans together with access to the country's rich natural resources and its maritime facilities, thus facilitating the projection of its sea power into East and Southeast Asia.

---

50.   Memorandum From the Under Secretary of State (Herter) to Secretary of State Dulles

Washington, April 1, 1958.

I have studied the attached paper by Walter Robertson[1] very carefully and have some reservations as to its implications. I have no objec-

---

Source: Eisenhower Library, Herter Papers, Miscellaneous Memoranda. Top Secret.

[1] Robertson's memorandum, March 31, has not been found. Robertson discussed Indonesian developments on April 13 at the Secretary's staff meeting, with Deputy Under Secretary of State Loy W. Henderson presiding:

Continued

tion to Jones taking the line with the Sukarno Government which Robertson recommends. [2 lines of source text not declassified] Last night's reports indicated real fighting in which the dissidents seemed to have the advantage both in Central Sumatra and in the Celebes. There is an implication in this paper that we would write-off the dissidents and I am certainly not prepared to do this as yet.

C.A.H.

"In response to Mr. Henderson's questions, Mr. Robertson said communist control of Indonesia's 80 million inhabitants would be a catastrophe and that the likelihood of it has caused concern among other Asians, particularly our Philippine allies. He noted that the rebel movement has not won the support from the people as the leaders had hoped, that the rebel forces offered practically no resistance at Pakanbaru, and that there seems to be among the people of Indonesia no awareness of the communist menace and no will to fight. In answer to another question from Mr. Henderson, Mr. Robertson explained that if the US were to recognize the belligerency of the rebels we would very probably alienate large segments of the Indonesian public whose interests are identical with our own, namely maintenance of the country's national independence."(Notes of a Secretary's Staff Meeting, Department of State, Secretary's Staff Meetings: Lot 63 D 75)

51.   Memorandum of Conversation

Washington, April 4, 1958.

SUBJECT

    Summary Discussion re Indonesia

PARTICIPANTS

    The Secretary
    Walter S. Robertson, Assistant Secretary of State
    Sir Harold Caccia, British Ambassador
    Lord Hood, British Minister

The British Ambassador came in at the request of Foreign Minister Lloyd to discuss the Indonesian situation and to see if their evaluation of developments corresponded with ours. [8 lines of source text not declassified]

The Secretary responded that while there was some conflict in our own intelligence reports, the UK view of the situation corresponded

Source: Department of State, Central Files, 656.56D13/4–458. Top Secret. Drafted by Robertson.

substantially with our own. In fact we were having a meeting on Monday[1] to review and consider all aspects of the problem and determine what action is now indicated. He mentioned we were considering the advisability of an approach to Sukarno to see if it were possible to exact a satisfactory political settlement. We would express our concern at the continuation of the unsettling situation, advise him of our knowledge of the Communist bloc support being given the Indonesian Government, and that we could not be expected to stand by and passively watch Indonesia being taken over by the Communists.

It was agreed that we would consult again with Caccia after our meeting on Monday.[2]

---

[1] April 7.

[2] According to Dulles' Appointment Book, he met with Allen Dulles to discuss Indonesia at 2:35 p.m. on Monday, April 7. At 2:37 p.m. they were joined by Cabell, Ulmer, Irwin, Robertson, Herter, Mein, Reams, and Cumming. At 3:15 p.m. they were joined by Parsons and at 3:25 p.m. by Becker. At 5:40 p.m., Dulles met with British Ambassador Caccia; at 5:41 p.m, they were joined by Robertson. (Eisenhower Library, Dulles Papers, Dulles Appointment Book, 1958–59) No record of these meetings has been found.

---

52.   Telegram From the Embassy in Indonesia to the Department of State

Djakarta, April 6, 1958, 8 p.m.

3565. For Assistant Secretary Robertson from Ambassador Jones. Following observations may be useful in consideration Indo situation.

Main power factories in current situation are Sukarno, Communists, insurgents, and army. Hatta may ultimately prove to be key to settlement with outer islands but as result role he has chosen to play, he can exert very little leverage at present. Men like Djuanda, who represent middle ground and who conceivably might rally enough support from various non-Communist sources to accomplish something, seem unable to employ their strength for decisive political action.

Where Sukarno stands at present not clear. His position unquestionably bolstered by central government military successes in Sumatra.

Source: Department of State, Central Files, 756D.00/4–658. Secret; Niact. Transmitted in two sections.

At same time Sukarno has left door open for compromise settlement and most people who see him regularly claim that he is deeply worried about difficulty rebuilding national unity. Sukarno's tolerance of communism now generally recognized as one of main causes for insurrection and he is under considerable psychological pressure to break with left wingers. As this would represent almost 180 degree turn for Sukarno it probably unreasonable to expect him make change himself. However most Indonesians agree Sukarno capable of turning against Communists if necessary to preserve his own position. While still major power factor, Sukarno may be more passive than active at present stage because he is center of pressures from Communists and anti-Communists.

As for Communists, while events of past few years seem to have moved steadily in their favor, with non-Communists fighting each other and with great expansion of economic relations with Soviet bloc, nevertheless there are straws in the wind indicating that army is on verge of adopting position hostile to Communist interests. Aidit's April 1 report to PKI central committee seems clearly aware of this possibility. Much of the PKI growth in recent years might be swept away if Indonesian political system changed from parliamentary form to military dictatorship which could dispense with elections and deal resolutely with economic development. This is perhaps less likely than increased utilization military within present framework in implementation government decisions. Although PKI probably has succeeded in building small armed force of its own and has infiltrated to small extent regular army, it apparently has nothing like capability for seizing power. Moreover, it is prevented from resorting to violent tactics by fear of offering opportunity which anti-Communist army officers have been vainly seeking for years to suppress PKI by force.

Rebels are losing ground fast militarily. Pakanbaru was serious blow and expectations they would take advantage mountainous terrain resist central forces advances across Sumatra have not been realized. It now appears they may not defend Padang, and from reports of progress made by GOI troops over land toward Bukittinggi, it begins to look as though rebels will not even attempt defend that city (their capital). This leaves guerrilla warfare as their only resort. Hussein might keep up harassment DI style for many years, but prospect of developing alternative government by military and economic pressure on Djakarta seems almost to have faded out. Although main center rebel military strength in Menado area has not yet been tackled, insurgent movement has not proved successful enough to attract open support from other dissident outer island areas and appears to have lost its momentum.

Of four power factors army headquarters seems to have come out ahead. Its successes in Sumatra have raised its prestige and it generally is conceded to be final authority in economic and civil matters. Success of army is something of personal triumph for Nasution who strongest and most consistent advocate of military action against insurgents. Nasution's current measures aimed against PKI, which Embassy has reported, which have been placed in motion at very moment of central government successes in Sumatra, tend to bear out evaluation of Nasution as basically anti-Communist. As Department aware, Nasution is one of very few prominent Indonesians who in earlier years publicly on record in favor alignment with US.

Consideration of above factors leads me to conclusion that army is emerging as most reliable machinery available for anti-Communist action at present and heightened prestige over Sumatran successes may be expected increase its confidence in ability to handle Communist action of any kind, whether violent or subversive. Latter, of course, is great danger here and army has not yet demonstrated its capability this front.[1]

Jones

---

[1] In telegram 3680 from Djakarta, April 12, the Embassy reported further on the role of the Indonesian Army and especially that of Army Chief of Staff Nasution. "Embassy reporting past ten days suggests shift in political position army headquarters may be developing," the telegram reads in part. "Owing extensive intrigue prevalent Djakarta at present it has been unusually difficult pinpoint origin of shift or determine its magnitude. However Nasution appears to be main figure this development. Unless military trend in Sumatra sharply reversed it seems likely Nasution's importance will continue grow." (*Ibid.*, 756D.00/4–1258) See Supplement.

---

53.   Memorandum From the Joint Chiefs of Staff to Secretary of Defense McElroy

Washington, April 8, 1958.

SUBJECT

Indonesia

1. The Joint Chiefs of Staff are seriously concerned over the rising influence that the Russians are achieving throughout Indonesia by their introduction of merchant ships, crews, supplies, and the impending arrival of Russian aircraft. Conversely, the plight of the Revolutionary Government becomes increasingly worse.

Source: National Archives and Records Administration, RG 218, JCS Records, 092 Asia (6–25–48). Top Secret. Attached to JCS 1992/651. Another copy of this memorandum is in Department of State, Central Files, 756D.00/4–858.

2. [*1-1/2 lines of source text not declassified*] Defeat of the dissidents would almost certainly lead to Communist domination of Indonesia. Such a turn of events would cause serious reaction in Malaya and Thailand, probable trouble in Laos and possible trouble in Cambodia. It could result in the disappearance of SEATO as a viable pact, and an extension of Communist influence in the Moslem Middle East. Consequently, if Communist domination of Indonesia is to be prevented, action must be taken, including overt measures as required, to insure either the success of the dissidents or the suppression of the pro-Communist elements of the Sukarno government.

3. The Joint Chiefs of Staff recommend that you support a relaxation of restrictions on United States policy toward Indonesia and accelerated efforts to prevent the fall of this nation to Communism.

---

54.   Telegram From the Embassy in Indonesia to the Department of State

Djakarta, April 8, 1958, 5 p.m.

3585. Foreign Minister asked me to call this morning to continue previous discussions we had on US-Indonesian relations and internal developments Indonesia affecting those relations. Conversation covered a wide variety of topics highlights of which are as follows:

1. Appeal for at least some gesture that might be taken as representing a more forthcoming attitude on US part. PL–480[1] rice and token military aid were two specific examples mentioned. Anything would be better than nothing, Subandrio said, even so small a thing as granting licenses for spare parts for Mustangs and Convairs which they are now getting from Egypt.

2. Government beginning to reach conclusion Communists could not be beaten by ordinary democratic means in elections. Program of gradual elimination of Communists by police and military to be followed by outlawing of Communist Party was not unlikely in comparatively near future, he said.

Source: Department of State, Central Files, 611.56D/4–858. Secret; Priority.

[1] Reference is to P.L. 480, the Agricultural Trade Development and Assistance Act of 1954, approved on July 10, 1954; for text, see 68 Stat. 454.

3. Third meeting of Hatta and Sukarno would be held within a week and he anticipated agreement would be reached at such meeting.

4. Presidential Cabinet rather than Parliamentary Cabinet would probably result from Sukarno–Hatta agreement, he said. He made point almost exactly corresponding to those made by Hatta in Embtel 3312[2] on this subject.

5. Foreign Minister was recommending to Cabinet that West New Guinea issue be allowed cooling-off period and if his recommendation accepted matter would not be brought up at UN this year.

6. Indonesians detected softening of Dutch attitude toward Indonesia, he said. There was no major item but number of small things added up to this conclusion. One example: Restraint with which Dutch had dealt with matter of KPM ships.

7. Commenting on Indonesia's relations with other countries, Foreign Minister said while this would take a great deal of education within Indonesia, he could foresee the time when Indonesia might wish to join with Australia, Philippines and maintain mutual defense pact or pacts. This would take years, he admitted, but felt that this was direction in which Indonesia ultimately must move.

Comment: This is most forthright statement we have received from Foreign Minister to indicate probability definite change in direction but bits and pieces we have been putting together tend to confirm that something of the sort is in offing. Prime Minister had asked me to see him at this [garble] tomorrow evening (April 9) at 5 p.m. for further discussion current situation in Indonesia and I shall withhold further comment until after this meeting. However, it begins to appear that US should be preparing itself to make some positive moves in event what appear to be favorable trends continue.[3]

Jones

---

[2] Document 46

[3] In telegram 2905 to Djakarta, April 8, the Department informed the Embassy: "Trends reported your recent telegrams encouraging but before reaching any positive decision would be helpful have further clarification government's plans and evidence of anti-Communist measures. We await with interest therefore report your conversation with Prime Minister tomorrow and your further comments on current situation." (Department of State, Central Files, 756D.00/4–858) See Supplement.

Jones reported on his conversation with Djuanda in telegram 3629 from Djakarta, April 10. "Subandrio balloon reported Embtel 3585 partly collapsed by Prime Minister Djuanda in frank and forthcoming talk yesterday evening," he stated. "Djuanda made it clear that while government was broadly moving along lines US objectives no precipitate action could be anticipated." After summarizing the Prime Minister's comments, Jones offered the following observation: "There is no apparent explanation for discrepancy between Djuanda–Subandrio statements. Subandrio is regarded as being closer to throne and may be playing up to US on theory that is way wind is blowing. Or he may merely have been leading us on hoping to pry some assistance from us." (Department of State, Central Files, 756D.00/4–1058) See Supplement.

55.   Memorandum of Telephone Conversation Between Secretary
of State Dulles and the Under Secretary of State (Herter)

Washington, April 8, 1958, 12:15 p.m.

TELEPHONE CALL TO GOV. HERTER

The Sec. said he heard that a bad story may break in connection
with Indonesia. Herter said he had talked to Allen Dulles about it, who
was going to look into it right away.[1] Herter thinks it is better to have it
come from Allen than us. If it breaks it will be bad enough. The fellow
who was going to write the story was just intimating. He may not do it. It
came from Sjafruddin. Herter said it was a little naive to put it mildly.
They seemed to have a pretty full story on the drops. The Sec. said we
would have to be thinking what we would do if it breaks. The Sec. said
he was asked at his press conference if we were giving help to the rebels.
The Sec. had said no.[2] Herter said he was afraid we would have to play it
that way. Herter said even if the thing was published, they would not be
able to get the hard facts.[3]

Source: Eisenhower Library, Dulles Papers, General Telephone Conversations. No
classification marking. Drafted by Mildred J. Asbjornson, Dulles' secretary.

[1] Reference is to Dulles' press conference held earlier that day; for text, see Department of State *Bulletin*, April 28, 1958, pp. 684–685.

[2] Herter spoke with Allen Dulles on the telephone that morning at 11:20, saying that
two newspapermen were going to file stories indicating that the United State was aiding
the Indonesian rebels. Herter asked Dulles if he felt he could stop these stories through
David Lawrence and James Knight. Dulles replied he could handle Lawrence and he knew
Knight and would see what he could do. (Memorandum of telephone conversation, April
8; Eisenhower Library, Herter Papers, Telephone Conversations) David Lawrence was
president and editor of *U.S. News and World Report* and a syndicated columnist; James L.
Knight was executive vice-president of Knight Newspapers, Inc.

[3] Allen Dulles and Herter spoke again on the telephone about this matter at 6:05 p.m.
the following day. Dulles said, "he had run down the two stories. The *Chicago Daily News*
story was out this morning and was fairly discreet. He had talked with David Lawrence,
who had had a long story from his man which will probably be published Monday. His
man also is quite discreet. Only descriptive line is that the drops came like manna from
heaven."(Memorandum of telephone conversation, April 9; *ibid*.)

56.   Telegram From the Embassy in Indonesia to the Department of State

Djakarta, April 12, 1958, 3 p.m.

3681. For Assistant Secretary Robertson from Jones. Two approaches have been made by top level officers to Army Attaché[1] within 24 hours on subject of American assistance to rebels by arms dropping. First was by Colonel Jani First Deputy Chief of Staff, who said US assistance to rebels has placed pro-American officers in Indonesian Army in untenable position and unless something is done to support them their influence in picture will seriously deteriorate.

Second approach was by Lt. Colonel Sukardjo, who is Acting Deputy Chief of Staff for Intelligence in absence of Colonel Sukendro, who is now in Sumatra. He said Colonel Sukendro urgently wishes to see Army Attaché on his return—that dropping of American weapons to Nainggolan's[2] troops two weeks ago has produced violent anti-American reaction among officers and troops of Regiment 2 which has been anti-Communist in orientation. Losses following drops have exacerbated reaction.

Colonel Sukardjo then related following incident as illustrative of position in which pro-American officers were being placed as result of arms dropping. Last week after Cabinet meeting at which Colonel Sukendro briefed the Cabinet on current situation Minister Hanafi[3] asked Sukendro in the presence of Sukarno, "What are these good friends of yours, the Americans, in which you have put so much faith, doing to you? Dropping weapons they are helping to kill our brothers. Don't you think you have trusted them too much?"

Sukarno said, "What the Americans are doing is not Sukendro's fault." Sukendro said, "The Americans who brought the weapons to Sumatra are not my friends. My friends are the official Americans and they have had nothing to do with this."

Hanafi said, "Prove it," and walked away.

Jones

Source: Department of State, Central Files, 756D.00/4–1258. Top Secret; [distribution indicator not declassified].

[1] Colonel William R. Cole.

[2] Major W.F. Nainggolan, a dissident Army officer in Sumatra.

[3] A.M. Hanafi, Minister for Mobilization of People's Energy.

57.   Memorandum of Conversation

Washington, April 13, 1958.

SUBJECT

Indonesia

PARTICIPANTS

The Secretary
Mr. Reinhardt
Sir Harold Caccia, British Ambassador
Lord Hood, British Minister

The Secretary told Sir Harold about the meeting Saturday with the Joint Chiefs of Staff, Mr. Allen Dulles and others on Indonesia.[1] He said there had been agreement on some immediate action, but to be performed only if it could be kept covert. He said there had also been agreement on the preparation of measures of a more overt character in line with his view that we should explore more intensively the possibility of getting into a position when we could act more overtly in this situation. Three possibilities presented themselves for study:

1. *Recognition of a state of belligerency.* This action would presumably be dependent on the government's failing for the time being in driving the opposition into the mountains.
2. *The secession from the Indonesian Republic of Sumatra which we would then recognize and perhaps guarantee its independence.* This action would be similar to the events in Panama which led to its recognition by Theodore Roosevelt. Unfortunately, the rebels so far had shown interest only in being the Government of Indonesia but if Sumatra were under anti-Sukarno control it would enjoy economic domination in the whole area. The Secretary observed that the original concept in the United Nations had been that Indonesia should be a loose confederation of the independent states. Perhaps this original idea could be explored.
3. *The possibility that there would be so much damage to the U.S. property that U.S. troops would have to be sent in.* This would of course be a departure from standard practice and would require a procedure designed to accomplish the result under a cover which would be acceptable to the opposition as having adequate justification.

The Secretary said he hoped the British would undertake to study the foregoing possible lines of action. The meeting yesterday had come

---

Source: Department of State, Central Files, 756D.00/4–1358. Top Secret. Drafted by Reinhardt.

[1] According to Dulles' Appointment Book, a meeting regarding Indonesia was held at 4 p.m., Saturday, April 12. The following were listed as participants at the meeting in addition to the Secretary of State: Burke, Irwin, Robertson, and Cumming. The meeting was held at Dulles' house. (Eisenhower Library, Dulles Papers, Dulles Appointment Book 1958–59) No record of this meeting has been found.

to the conclusion that covert action would not be adequate under the circumstances and that no political solution was possible unless we had plans and the determination to go farther. We thought Rob Scott's[2] suggestion of doing something with Nasution was doubtful. We would not exclude the possibility of going to Sukarno and giving him the opportunity to change his line but we must have the determination to act if he proved unwilling. It was conceivable that Sukarno might agree to set up a government with such elements as Hatta and then having gotten rid of the rebels revert to the status quo ante. In any event we did not think there was any possibility of a political solution unless it was backed by the determination to do something.

Sir Harold thought there were two approaches: one was to help the opposition and the other was to try to open up chinks on the government side. This was the rationale that had led to Scott's suggestion.

The Secretary said we believed we should do nothing overt unless it was linked with political action and for the present time, therefore, we had to limit ourselves to covert action. He did not want to give the impression that we had decided on any of the three possibilities he had outlined but we were studying them and he did want to talk with Sir Harold about them in a few days. Sir Harold observed that London was very doubtful that the plan for recognition of belligerent rights would work. It might, however, logically follow after possibility 2 or 3 outlined by the Secretary.

---

[2]Sir Robert H. Scott, U.K. Commissioner General in Southeast Asia.

---

58.   Editorial Note

On April 14, at the 362d meeting of the National Security Council, Allen Dulles discussed developments in Indonesia during his intelligence briefing. The following exchange took place:

"With respect to the situation in Indonesia, Mr. Dulles predicted that the amphibious attack by the Djakarta forces against the dissident stronghold of Padang might start at any time. He gave a summary of the details of the military plans for this amphibious attack.

"There had been no great change in the military situation since last week. The situation of the dissidents was extremely difficult, but if they were prepared to fight to the end, they still had some chance. The absence of all air cover was hard on the morale of the dissident forces. They do have anti-aircraft guns located around the Padang airfield.

"The President said it looked to him as though what the dissidents mostly needed was a submarine or two to deal with the Djakarta

Government's amphibious attack. One considerable disaster to the Djakarta forces might change the whole direction of the struggle. Mr. Dulles replied that an even greater need was for aircraft. [*2 lines of source text not declassified*] (Memorandum of discussion by Gleason, April 15; Eisenhower Library, Whitman File, NSC Records)

---

59.   Memorandum From the Director of the Office of Southeast Asian Affairs (Mein) to the Assistant Secretary of State for Far Eastern Affairs (Robertson)

Washington, April 14, 1958.

SUBJECT

Major General Nasution

During the past year, Major General Abdul Haris Nasution, the Chief of Staff of the Indonesian Army, has emerged as a primary political as well as military force in Indonesia. This rise to power has been due in part to the ineffectiveness of civil leadership, in part to the military problems arising from the regionalist rejection of the central Government authority, and in part to the powers invested in the Chief of Staff under the Indonesian Emergency Legislation. General Nasution represents also Indonesia's most prominent political enigma. By his public activities he has established a reputation for being a staunch anti-Communist and friend of the West. At the same time, he has been a firm supporter of President Sukarno and the present Government. He has insisted on crushing the strongly anti-Communist rebel Government with military force and has shown no current disposition to use his considerable authority to check the growth of Communism on Java. Because of the position he now occupies and the likelihood that he may in coming weeks accede to positions of even greater authority, an investigation of the background, attitudes, and activities of this man appears appropriate.

Curriculum Vitae

General Nasution was born on December 3, 1918 in the Tapanuli area of North Sumatra. Like many senior Indonesian Army officers, he is a Batak, and like his first cousin and bitter enemy, Col. Zulkifli Lubis he is a devout Moslem. Nasution went to Java in 1936 and graduated

---

Source: Department of State, Central Files, 756D.551/4–1458. Secret. Drafted by Underhill.

from the Normal School in Bandung in 1938. He taught school in West Java, and in 1940 entered the Royal Netherlands Academy in Bandung. Following his graduation he was commissioned a 2nd Lieutenant in the Netherlands East Indies Army. During the Japanese occupation, Nasution performed both civil and military services and following the proclamation of Indonesian independence he was appointed Chief of Staff of the West Java command in 1945. He rose rapidly in the military service becoming Chief of Staff of the Army in 1948 and following the final achievement of independence continued in this office until 1952.

General Nasution was from the beginning a strong advocate of a small professional army, and in September of 1952 joined forces with other senior Army officers in opposition to efforts of some political leaders to maintain a large irregular guerrilla element in the Indonesian military establishment. This conflict erupted into the "October 17 Affair" in which Nasution and other senior officers took control of Djakarta, and urged President Sukarno to dissolve the Government, take power into his own hands, and hold immediate national elections. Sukarno refused to take this action and in December 1952, Nasution was relieved as Army Chief of Staff and placed on inactive duty. Nasution, convinced that the Army needed a political voice in the Indonesian Parliament, participated in the formation of a political party called the Association of Defenders of Indonesian Independence (IPKI). In October 1955, Nasution was again appointed Chief of Staff of the Indonesian Army.

Nasution at present appears to avoid personal contact with foreign military and diplomatic representatives. However, during his first tour as Chief of Staff he was on close friendly terms with a number of U.S. military observers, who regarded him as an outstanding professional Army officer keenly interested in the strategic and technical aspects of this profession, strongly anti-Communist, and outspokenly pro-Western. He speaks excellent English and is fluent as well in Dutch and Japanese. His written works indicate further a good reading knowledge of French and German.

Attitudes towards Communism and the West

The first incident in General Nasution's career suggesting his attitude towards Communism occurred in July 1947 when as Commander of the First Division in West Java he broke up a local unit of the Bambu Runtjing, an irregular Communist-controlled paramilitary organization commanded by a political disciple of the Trotskyite Tan Malaka. Following the outbreak of the Communist coup effort at Madiun in 1948, Nasution, as Army Chief of Staff, ordered an all-out offensive against the Communist stronghold and succeeded in crushing the revolt in a bloody and ruthless fashion. In December of 1950, as Chief of Staff of the Army, he drew strong criticism from Masjumi and the Indonesian Parliament for a statement to the press strongly implying that Indonesia should take a firm position on the side of the U.S. and the U.N. in the war in Korea. Following the October 17 affair in 1952, he was strongly attacked by the Communist press for his part in the abortive coup, and following his reappointment to the office of Chief of Staff in 1955, was again attacked by Communist representatives on the floor of the Indonesian Parliament. He is credited with preventing the Communist-dominated veterans organization, Perbepsi, from gaining control of the All-Indonesian Veterans Conference which took place in Bandung in December 1956. In March 1957, following Sukarno's announcement of his "conception", Nasution was reliably reported to be strongly opposed to the participation of the Indonesian Communist party (PKI) in the Cabinet.

During his period of "inactive duty" between 1953 and 1955, Nasution produced two highly regarded monographs on military subjects; the first, *The Essentials of Guerrilla Operations (Pokok Gerilja)*, a study of the political and tactical aspects of guerrilla warfare, and the second, *Notes on Indonesian Military Policies (Tjatatan Sekitar Politik Militer Indonesia)*, a broad review of Indonesia's defense potential and the international forces affecting this potential. From these works a clear idea of his views on Communism and the West can be drawn.

In the latter work, Nasution writes that the Communists place before all else the national interests of the Soviet Union. They hold that if the interests of the Soviets are served, all other interests, including Indonesian national interests, can and must be sacrificed. This conception, he states, cannot be accepted by any Indonesian patriot. In the international sphere, Nasution makes it clear that the only important outside military threat to Indonesian independence is Communist China. (This was written immediately after Dien-Bien-Phu.) In considering Indonesia's foreign policy, Nasution sets as the basic objective of the Indonesian Armed Forces the preservation of a free and independent Indonesia. After cataloging the nation's political, economic and military weaknesses, he finds Indonesia's cherished "active and independent foreign policy" a sterile and negative shibboleth. Nasution as a military man refrains from proposing a specific alternative, but in his appraisal of Indonesia's strategic position his views are made clear.

"To develop military and economic potential [Nasution writes] we must have foreign capital and foreign experts. In attempting to satisfy these needs we must recognize reality. We are in fact in the Western sphere. We can attempt to get assistance from neutral countries, such as India, Switzerland, and Sweden, but these sources of supply are of limited value. An effort to balance our economic relations between the Western and Eastern blocs is equally unrealistic. Our geographical position within the Western sphere clearly makes this impossible. We must recognize and adjust to the fact that the bulk of our needs do come only from the West . . . Indonesia lies inside the Western defense line and among the SEATO nations. It is in Indonesia's interests to maintain good relations with these countries."[1]

Elsewhere in the book Nasution states with equal bluntness that Indonesia must expect Western intervention if a Communist takeover of the Indonesian Government appears imminent.

A cold and realistic judgment of Indonesia's national self-interest is the standard by which Nasution measures Communism and the West. He opposes Communism at home and abroad, not primarily on the grounds of ideological antipathy, religious conviction, or sentimental attachment to the West, but rather because it represents a menace to Indonesian freedom. His advocacy of closer ties with the West rests on equally pragmatic arguments.

Professional Life

Nasution is one of Indonesia's outstanding professional soldiers. He is one of a very few in the Indonesian Army who have had formal officer training under the Dutch and served prior to World War II in a commissioned capacity in the Netherlands East Indies Army. He has a superior record as a field officer in the fighting against the Dutch during the revolution, and his published works on military subjects show a broad knowledge of the technical literature of his profession. He has, since Indonesia achieved its independence, devoted himself with single-minded intensity to the task of creating for his country a modern, well-trained, and effective defense establishment. Training of army officers in U.S. service schools was inaugurated under Nasution, and this program has continued without interruption even during the 1953–55 tenure of a strongly leftist Defense Minister, Iwa Kusumasumantri.

Nasution was one of the principal exponents of a small, professional, and highly trained army, and it was his efforts to reduce the size of the army by retiring non-professional officers and discharging irregular guerrilla units absorbed into the army during the revolution which first brought him into conflict with political leaders and President Sukarno and precipitated the October 17th Affair.

During the two year period of enforced separation from active military duty Nasution continued to work towards his objective. From his own experience in the October 17th Affair, it was apparent to him that the Army would continue to be plagued by irresponsible political meddling in its internal affairs. To meet this problem, Nasution, with the support of officers on both active and inactive duty, established a political party, IPKI, which had as its avowed purpose the representation of army interests in Parliament. IPKI succeeded in electing four delegates

---

[1] Brackets and ellipsis in the source text.

in the general elections of September 1955, but in general was not a political success. Whatever its possible usefulness to the Army, Indonesia had no need for one more political party.

It is clear that Nasution regards as an essential element of a military establishment a rigid code of military discipline. Without a chain of command an army becomes nothing more than a rabble in arms. His preoccupation with discipline can be seen clearly in his actions following his return to the position of Chief of Staff in 1955. The territorial commanders had by 1955 become to all intents and purposes local warlords. They were in many instances local sons who through long service as the military commanders in their home areas had become deeply embroiled in local problems and local aspirations. They obeyed orders from Djakarta when it suited their purposes. This Nasution regarded as potentially dangerous, and he instituted a program of regular transfers and tours of duty. Kawilarang in West Java was sent to Washington as military attaché, Warrouw in Celebes was sent to Peiping in a similar capacity, and Simbolon in North Sumatra was slated for transfer when Hussein in Padang, another native son, announced in December 1956 that he would no longer recognize the authority of Djakarta.

Political Outlook

A dominant factor in Nasution's life, clearly evident in his public actions as well as his published works, is a fierce and uncompromising loyalty to the concept of the free and independent Indonesian state. This loyalty appears further to go beyond both his Sumatran Batak origin and his Moslem faith, and determines his attitudes towards his profession, Communism, and the strong regionalist sentiments of many of his brother officers. He is reported to have the support of the NU and the Masjumi, but is at present not known to be associated with any political party. Throughout his books Nasution stresses again and again the necessity of Indonesian unity. This preoccupation stems not from the mystic emotionalism of Sukarno, but from a sober conviction that Indonesia as a state cannot long exist if it is not strong internally. Writing in 1955 he emphasized that Indonesia had no defense potential whatever until it succeeds in ending the Darul Islam rebellions in West Java, Atjeh, and South Sulawesi. Not only is civil war a source of military weakness, but even worse, a standing invitation to foreign intervention. Both he and General T.B. Simatupang, a fellow Sumatran Batak, point out that Indonesia has in the past fallen under alien control principally because Indonesians have shown a tragic readiness to fight each other. This attitude serves to explain, at least in part, his stand on the regionalist movements and the Padang regime. It is clear that he has no quarrel with their anti-Communist posture, and he may well be in sympathy with their demands for greater regional autonomy. Their resort to open rebellion, however, seriously weakens the nation's overall defense potential and encourages foreign intervention. This he cannot tolerate.

Summary Evaluation

The dominant influences on Nasution appear to be loyalty to Indonesian independence and devotion to his profession. Accepting these as the principal motivating forces, his actions fall into a reasonably consistent pattern, and he emerges as considerably less of an enigma. Like relatively few Indonesians, he thinks in national rather than in local or regional terms—will a certain course of action serve the long-term interests of all of Indonesia, and specifically, will it safeguard Indonesian independence. Like Sukarno, but for completely different reasons, he is convinced that Indonesia must be united to remain free. He is unquestionably opposed to Communism, both at home and abroad, because he regards it as a threat to this freedom. He would oppose with equal fervor foreign intervention from any quarter. Anti-Communism as such, however, is not a dominant motivating factor, and his actions are clearly not determined in the first instance by the service or disservice they do the Communist cause. He believes in discipline, and this to him means obedience to his superiors and from his subordinates. Transcending even this concept, however, is his loyalty to the republic. If after careful consideration he should decide that Sukarno, on balance, has become a divisive rather than unifying force, he would undoubtedly move quickly and decisively to neutralize or eliminate his commander-in-chief. He reaches decisions coldly and logically after sober consideration of all the factors, and once his mind is made up he acts with resolution and firmness. This turn of mind, uncharacteristic of most of his countrymen, has given him a reputation of mental inflexibility. In his self-assurance and dedication to principle he has further tended to ignore the personal and human factors. He has apparently no close friends or confidants, and is admired and respected rather than liked by the colleagues and subordinates. Like most strong personalities, he has also made enemies. His determination to crush the rebels is ascribed in part to the mutual hostility which exists between him and his cousin Zulkifli Lubis, a sentiment which dates at least from the October 17th Affair. He is unquestionably ambitious, but there is in his ambition no discernible strain of self-aggrandizement or megalomania. He is no political theorist, and appears to have no ideological ax to grind. He has no facility for popular leadership, nor the politician's flair for compromise and the "science of the possible". Under ordinary circumstances he would appear to be almost the prototype of an effective army chief of staff. The flow of events in Indonesia, however, may force him into a role which he may not be ideally suited, either by talent or temperament.

60.   Memorandum of Conversation

Washington, April 14, 1958.

SUBJECT

    Indonesia

PARTICIPANTS

    Mr. Howard Beale, Australian Ambassador
    Mr. M.R. Booker, Counselor of Australian Embassy

    The Secretary
    Mr. Farley, Special Assistant for Atomic Energy Affairs
    Mr. Mein, Director, Office of Southwest Pacific Affairs

1. The Ambassador said he wanted to inform the Secretary that the Indonesians have been complaining to the Australian Government that the Australian Broadcasting Company has been sending out too much propaganda in favor of the dissidents in Indonesia. He said that the Australian Government does not intend to stop these broadcasts.

2. The Ambassador said he understood we were considering a possible approach to Sukarno with the suggestion that if the struggle in Indonesia were settled by compromise we would be prepared to extend economic and military aid.

The Secretary said that such an approach is one of the things we have thought about but that no decision has been taken. The difficulty at the moment is that Sukarno has things well in hand and is not in a position where he needs to negotiate. A great deal depends, however, on events during the next few days. If the dissidents can hold out then we might take another look at the situation with a view to determining what if anything we might be able to do.

3. The Ambassador said that according to Australian intelligence the dissidents are disunited and are not likely to make a successful stand. [2-1/2 lines of source text not declassified]

The Secretary said that if the dissidents survive the Central Government's efforts to suppress them [1-1/2 lines of source text not declassified] we might have to consider giving them belligerent status but not unless they do better than they have been doing lately.

The Ambassador said that the Australian Government has some anxiety about according recognition to the dissidents and asked whether an approach to Sukarno might be accompanied by a hint that if

---

Source: Department of State, Central Files, 756D. 00/4–1458. Top Secret. Drafted by Mein.

he does not compromise we would recognize the dissidents. The Secretary said we do not have that possibility in mind at the present time. He agreed with the Ambassador that if the Communists got control of Indonesia it would be a very serious matter, adding that if we could see clearly how to deal with the situation we would be prepared to take some risks if there were any assurance that they might be successful.

---

61.   Memorandum of Telephone Conversation Between Secretary of State Dulles and Director of Central Intelligence Dulles

Washington, April 15, 1958, 2:40 p.m.

TELEPHONE CALL FROM ALLEN DULLES

AWD said Goodpaster called indicating the Boss' deep interest particularly re use of American personnel. AWD told him about the meeting and suggested G might want to be present.[1] The meeting is to discuss that problem. The Sec thought the meeting Sunday covered it.[2] AWD said there is a question or two raised by Stump since then. The Sec said he knows of one—more? AWD does not know. AWD said to G it is getting beyond his charter. Things are under consideration but nothing finally decided on that point and AWD imagines that is what they are going to discuss subject to the Sec's and the Boss' approval. The Sec said he was talking with Herter and Robertson. AWD thought the Sec might want to discuss it—the handling of it etc. Then he said we are reaching the hour of decision and little time will be left to do that so as to have the impact on what is happening. The Sec assumed what Stump raised could be done covert. AWD and the Sec agreed he indicated doubt on that. The Sec said if he raises the question, he (who is stout-hearted) feels there is doubt. AWD said he is on the spot. AWD mentioned some inconsistency. AWD said we can just have the meeting and have it ad referendum to the Sec and the Boss. The Sec said if you decide no, he would

---

Source: Eisenhower Library, Dulles Papers, General Telephone Conversations. No classification marking. Drafted by Bernau.

[1] Reference is to a meeting with the President that was scheduled for later that day; see Document 62.

[2] Possibly a reference to the meeting between Dulles and Caccia on April 13; see Document 57.

not think there need be any referendum. AWD said he would raise points about other types of American personnel—not employed by us. The Sec said if the Pres is going to take it up, he would like to be in on the discussion. The Sec said he thinks the important thing is to try to develop some of the lines he raised Sunday—find a political basis to do it overt rather than get caught covert. The Sec said the only thing now is to study it. If there is a possibility of action along this line, then discuss with the Pres, and if he thinks it worth pursuing then get word to these people we are giving consideration to it and if they survive the first assault then they could look forward to something. If the Executive thinks there is a possibility see if these people are willing to accept it especially with the Sumatran thing which seems to have the greatest degree of possibility.

---

62.   Memorandum of Conversation With President Eisenhower

Washington, April 15, 1958.

PRESENT

    Secretary Dulles
    Under Secretary Herter
    Assistant Secretary Walter S. Robertson
    Mr. Allen W. Dulles

We first discussed the question of whether or not the United States should be tolerant of U.S. nationals acting on a purely private and "soldier-of-fortune" basis (e.g. CAT) in performing services for the patriots in Sumatra. The President indicated that he did not want any U.S. Government personnel or persons detached from the U.S. Government only for the purpose of taking part in any operations partaking of a military character in Indonesia. But he did not think we should extend this principle to private persons operating on their own.

I then discussed the future, pointing out that it did not seem likely that the patriots could gain a victory or in the long run sustain them-

Source: Department of State, Central Files, 756D.00/4–1558. Top Secret. Drafted by Secretary Dulles. Another copy of this memorandum of conversation, initialed by Dulles, is in the Eisenhower Library, Dulles Papers, Meetings with the President.

selves without overt support from outside. On the other hand it seemed as though their willingness to fight needed to be better demonstrated before they would be entitled to overt support. This willingness to fight might, however, in turn be promoted if they knew that if they fought vigorously and well and accepted some casualties, there was some future ahead.

I suggested [*less than 1 line of source text not declassified*] a communication to the leadership of the patriots on a highly confidential basis that our feeling is if they put up a stubborn resistance to the imminent attack by the Central Government threatened on the West Coast off Padang, the United States would be disposed to consider some form of recognition which might permit of overt support from the U.S. or Asian countries which might join in that recognition. On the other hand, if they did not show a real will to fight and dedication to their cause, they could not expect such support.

We discussed various alternatives which recognition might take. One was the recognition of belligerency against the Central Government. Another was recognition of the government of the Sumatran State on the assumption, however, that that state would be part of an Indonesian federation as soon as an appropriate constitution was adopted. A third step was merely to recognize them as the de facto government of the area they controlled. A fourth measure that might be considered was for the United States to land forces for the protection of American life and property on Sumatra, notably at the oil fields.

I recommended against this latter course on the ground that the use of the U.S. military to protect oil interests in that part of the world would receive a very adverse reaction. The President authorized a message, as indicated, leaving for further study the question of what form of recognition should be favored in the event that there was the kind of active fighting by the patriots which would justify giving consideration to such a move given the international practice in these matters and the national interest of the United States which was also a factor, often indeed a controlling factor, in matters of diplomatic "recognition". [*1-1/2 lines of source text not declassified*]

63.   Telegram From the Embassy in Indonesia to the Department of State

Djakarta, April 15, 1958, 7 p.m.

3729. For Assistant Secretary Robertson from Jones. Embtels 3565[1] and 3680.[2] It seems to me time may have arrived to make some positive gesture of support toward Indonesian military if we are to preserve pro-American anti-Communist loyalties among top officer group here.

Two apparently conflicting developments are to be observed here:

(1) Recent gestures toward US by government leaders, top army officers and Sukarno which make it apparent Indonesians opening door to new rapprochement with US;
(2) increasing conviction on part GOI military that US is actually aiding rebels.

Both of these developments have been clearly established in opinion all elements Embassy.

It is self-evident that with regard to second point growing conviction of US support to rebels, whether or not actual proof is available, may cause loss of long and carefully nourished relations with Indonesian Army. It is unanimous view Embassy staff that pro-American officers still hold balance of power in army but this could be upset by development such conviction.

I should like therefore to pursue thought included in my recommendations sent you separately April 6[3] but based upon analysis situation Embassy reference telegrams. As I see it, army is becoming more and more likely determine future course followed by Indonesia. It is gathering more and more power and authority unto itself in both political and economic spheres. If army remains anti-Communist I believe it can be induced to take positive action to prevent Communist takeover by political means or otherwise. In any event, if new anti-Communist government is formed, it must depend upon army for support and implementation its policy. If such government is not formed, then we may find army is sole remaining major asset in preventing Communist takeover Java.

Army does not regard struggle with rebels as battle between Communists and anti-Communists and neither do most influential Indone-

---

Source: Department of State, Central Files, 756D.00/4–1558. Top Secret; Priority; Limit Distribution; No Distribution Outside Department. Transmitted in two sections.

[1] Document 52.

[2] See footnote 1, Document 52.

[3] Not further identified. This telegram was probably not sent through normal Department of State communications channels.

sians here so consider it. See for example Hatta's comments in Embtel 3312.[4] To army issue is simple one of discipline since Nasution and American-trained officers with whom he has surrounded himself are all regarded as strongly anti-Communist.

With or without a political settlement which includes rebel demands we favor, Indonesian Army foreseeable future will remain major power factor which we must continue to influence in our direction. While gesture may not completely counteract (2) above, absence of support is certain to be taken as substantiation their suspicion and evidence complete lack of sympathy.

If we want to save Java it appears impossible to base policy solely on Padang even if Padang can win real military victory. I have always thought of Padang—and I think you agree—as a tactic, as a means of bringing leverage on situation in Java to force new political direction on central government. I think Padang as a tactic has already succeeded to this extent: precipitation of issues has resulted in increased awareness of them here.

I recognize arguments on other side. Briefly summarized, they are: (1) effect on rebel morale of any US gesture toward GOI military; (2) interpretation of move as support for Sukarno and present government; (3) confirming Sukarno in policy playing off US against Communist bloc and obtaining aid from both; (4) removing in Sukarno's mind necessity for reaching agreement with Hatta and reorganization of government.

I shall deal with each of these briefly:

(1) I believe this can be overcome by conditions which might be attached to announcement of forthcoming aid.

(2) Unless rebels achieve clearcut victory, Sukarno will emerge with increased prestige anyway, and must be recognized as potent factor for foreseeable future. Our objective must be to hem him in which will be difficult if not impossible with army against us, since army may be only strong counterweight to Communists.

(3) This is fact of life being practiced by Burma, India and other neutrals. But seems clear army wants help from US not Soviets and there seems possibility of backtrack on bloc equipment if we step in fast.

(4) Believe this decision will in any event be based upon other considerations and not upon US aid or lack of it. However, extension of military aid will put us in better position to bring pressure on Sukarno through army and other channels to obtain reorganization of government.

---

[4] Document 46.

Finally, I think arguments in favor of doing nothing here may be outweighed by possibility irretrievable damage our position in current situation.

If Department concurs with this analysis, Secretary may wish consider making early announcement of US willingness extend military aid to GOI under condition delivery will follow settlement current struggle.

In implementing such course of action following possible steps are suggested:

1. Secretary might say something along following lines in press conference: Reiteration of earlier statement that as matter of general policy US does not supply arms to contending forces within any friendly country which may exacerbate internal conflicts, but at same time US recognizes need of every government to maintain order. Therefore US Government has decided to honor longstanding request of Indonesian Government for military equipment. At same time, consistent with our overall policy, these arms will be delivered after resolution of present military dispute in Indonesia.

2. Almost simultaneously Pentagon announce invitation to General Nasution, his wife, aide and two officers to come to US at his convenience as guest of General Taylor.

3. Indicate through Attaché channels:

(A) That we are looking forward to two officers accepting appointments to the Command and Staff School at Leavenworth.
(B) After visit of General Nasution, we would be happy to receive six or seven officers to spend a month or two looking over the military equipment required.
(C) We would be glad to offer training for officers and noncoms in handling equipment.
(D) Inform Army that parachutes on order will be covered by revocation of suspension export license as soon as military hostilities cease.

4. Agree immediately to switch of cotton for rice in accordance with conditions departure from current thinking in Washington. However, I feel altered situation justifies careful scrutiny possible complementary courses of action.[5]

Jones

---

[5] Telegram 3754 from Djakarta, April 16, from Jones for Robertson, reads as follows: "Australian Ambassador invited me to luncheon today with British Ambassador and we discussed general situation. I took occasion to outline very generally some of thinking contained in Embassy telegram 3729. Both my colleagues agreed time was ripe for some gesture support Indonesian military. British Ambassador said he had thought for some time something of this kind should be done." (Department of State, Central Files, 756D.00/4–1658)

64.   Memorandum of Telephone Conversation Between Secretary of State Dulles and Director of Central Intelligence Dulles

Washington, April 17, 1958, 12:31 p.m.

TELEPHONE CALL TO ALLEN DULLES

The Sec said he is leaving in an hour.[1] [*1-1/2 lines of source text not declassified*] There has been fighting for 24 hours. The one point was corrected. [*6 lines of source text not declassified*] The Sec said it is a diminishing thing. AWD said it took place 2 days later than expected. We don't know how well it has gone. The Sec said it has happened with far greater efficiency, speed and precision than he had expected from what he heard Sunday. A and he discussed this impression—A was not surprised at what happened.

Source: Eisenhower Library, Dulles Papers, General Telephone Conversations. No classification marking. Drafted by Bernau.

[1] Dulles was scheduled to leave for a vacation at Duck Island, April 17–22.

---

65.   Memorandum From Director of Central Intelligence Dulles to President Eisenhower

Washington, April 17, 1958.

SUBJECT

Sukarno

Sukarno, in speaking on 3 April to students in Djakarta, denied accusations that he is a Communist. He explained that these accusations result from a misunderstanding of his own efforts to combat colonialism and capitalism and to find working solutions for Indonesia's numerous economic and political problems, as well as from a misinterpretation of Indonesia's neutral foreign policy.

On 7 April in Demak, Central Java, in commemoration of a Moslem holiday, Sukarno made what might be termed a religio-political speech

---

Source: Eisenhower Library, Staff Secretary Records. Secret; Noforn.

in which he explained himself as peculiarly endowed to screen and blend all trends and ideologies into a philosophy which would be right for Indonesia. He said that although he is a follower of Karl Marx, he is also a religious man and understands "the entire scope between Marxism and religion. . . .[1] I know all trends and understand them."

The contradiction between the two speeches is only an apparent one. Sukarno has repeatedly stated and appears to believe that basically he can be a Marxist, can establish a socialist state, and can use Communist techniques without threatening Indonesia with Communism. Sukarno told the American Ambassador on 19 March[2] that he was no Communist but that he had seen in Communist China such tremendous economic advances that he believed Communist Chinese methods held lessons for Indonesia. Sukarno sees no contradiction in his own attitudes toward Marxism and Islam since he sees the former as promoting the same "social justice" which the latter seeks.

President Sukarno, now aged 57, plays three political roles which are variously emphasized in relation to his audience and surroundings. These are (1) a more or less constitutional president in a more or less parliamentary cabinet system of government; (2) a national revolutionary leader in a newly independent country which is involved in political, economic, and social changes; and (3) an Asian potentate in whom the Indonesians, but particularly the 50,000,000 Javanese—most of them poor, ignorant, superstitious, and starved for excitement and color—see the embodiment of a mystical, divinely endowed, and foreordained king.

Sukarno enjoys the second and third roles far more than the first and is far better qualified to fill them than he is the first. He has all the theatrical techniques of the consummate crowd-pleaser and is in fact a rabble-rouser when he wishes. He has a insatiable desire for public acclaim and wishes to hold all the reins of power and to be the originator of all major decisions. Yet he refuses to accept definite responsibility and is childishly jealous when anyone else appears to share the acclaim usually accorded him or to assume responsibility which might lead to the loss of any of his power. In one important particular, he has virtually no knowledge of economics and no appreciation of the complex economic problems which afflict the nation. He is vain and pleasure loving to a marked degree.

Paralleling these characteristics is an identification with Indonesia and with a dream of Indonesia as a strong, united nation—the home of a prosperous and confident people. In relation to Indonesians, Sukarno

---

[1] Ellipsis in the source text.

[2] See Document 43.

sees himself as father, leader and guide, one who must study, interpret, and blend the best and most appropriate of the modern world with the best of whatever he sees as genuinely Indonesian, to create a truly Indonesian nation. This is a superhuman order for one person, or even one generation, but Sukarno's vanity and ego refuse to let him share the work substantially with anyone of real ability.

In addition, Sukarno has led a life of tension which has repeatedly included revolution, insurrection, imprisonment, exile, conspiracy, and attempted assassination. This undoubtedly tends to emphasize and exaggerate many of his personality traits.

Allen W. Dulles

---

66.   Memorandum of Conversation

Washington, April 18, 1958.

SUBJECT

    Indonesia—Possible Action U.S.

PARTICIPANTS

    Sir Leslie Munro, New Zealand Ambassador
    Mr. G.D.L. White, Counselor, New Zealand Embassy

    Mr. Robertson, Assistant Secretary for Far Eastern Affairs
    Mr. Mein, Director, Office of Southwest Pacific Affairs

Mr. Robertson explained he had asked the Ambassador to come in to correct an impression he had evidently gathered from a conversation with someone concerning possible action by the United States in the Indonesian situation. Mr. Robertson explained that our Ambassador in Wellington had reported that Prime Minister Nash had been informed by Sir Leslie that the U.S. was planning to intervene with force in Indonesia, and that the Prime Minister felt he must make a public statement on this matter.

Source: Department of State, Central Files, 756D.00/4–1858. Confidential. Drafted by Mein.

Mr. Robertson told the Ambassador that the U.S. is not considering going into Indonesia with force. He reviewed briefly the picture on Sumatra, pointing out that the dissidents at the present time controlled very little of the area and were giving up Padang and other areas without a fight. Mr. Robertson said he agreed with Prime Minister Nash that nothing could be more catastrophic than our going in with force.

Mr. Robertson said that the Department would inform our Embassy at Wellington of this, pointing out that Sir Leslie must have been misinformed or must have misunderstood his informant.

The Ambassador asked whether Mr. Robertson's statement meant in effect that the U.S. had written off the rebels. Mr. Robertson replied in the negative, adding that from the information available to us it appears that a stalemate might develop and that as a result of this and the deteriorating economic situation a compromise may be worked out. He indicated we would welcome a compromise since we fear that if the dissidents are wiped out or disappear, Hatta and other moderates may lose any leverage they may have and Sukarno may become difficult to deal with. He pointed out that many people are of the opinion that the army may be the only element capable of checking the Communists. Nothing in the situation, therefore, would justify such action as the Ambassador had been given to understand we were contemplating.

Sir Leslie said that he wanted Mr. Robertson to know that he had not gotten the information from anybody in the State Department, but he also wanted to make it clear that he had not misunderstood his informant. Sir Leslie assured Mr. Robertson he would convey the information given to him to Prime Minister Nash.

---

67.   Letter From the Chief of Naval Operations (Burke) to the Under Secretary of State (Herter)

Washington, April 18, 1958.

DEAR CHRIS: Colonel Berlin, the STANVAC representative in Indonesia, who is on a short visit to the United States, called on me yesterday evening. He has spent some thirty years in that area and is well acquainted with many of the key political and military leaders, both within and outside of the present government.

Source: Department of State, Central Files, 756D.00/4–1858. Secret; Personal.

Colonel Berlin opened the conversation by stating that he had been asked by the anti-communist Chief of Army Intelligence, speaking for Nasution, to convey the following to U.S. Government representatives in Washington:

1.   A request that the U.S. offer to supply arms to the Indonesian Army before the Soviet-promised 16 MiGs and 8 bombers arrive.
2.   A request that the U.S. make available twenty billets for Indonesian Army officers at the Fort Leavenworth School.
3.   An invitation for a group of U.S. military personnel to come to Indonesia for six months or so, in order to make an extensive visit of military establishments, and to satisfy themselves that the Army is not communist. Successive groups were also invited.

Nasution personally confirmed the foregoing to Colonel Berlin.

During our conversation, Colonel Berlin expressed his opinion that Indonesia is rapidly going communist—that certain Cabinet Portfolios, which are the early beach heads of communist penetration, such as the Ministry of Information, Ministry of Labor, Ministry of Trade Unions, are already held by known communists. He regretted that he had no ready solution to offer which was feasible, and which would be sure of stopping the deteriorating situation. He did, however, state that there are elements and individuals within the government who are aware of the danger and who are in a position to show some effectiveness in retrieving the situation. His assessment of certain key figures follows:

Djuanda, the Prime Minister, is anti-communist and believes that once the Central Government can control that part of Sumatra which it believes essential to its economy, it will cease fighting. Then, under the leadership of Hatta (who refuses to rejoin the government until the fighting is ended) the anti-communists will take steps to regain control.

Nasution, Chief of Staff of the Army, is anti-communist, and although loyal to Sukarno, is resentful of the latter's interference in Army affairs. Nasution is politically ambitious and might be receptive to ideas which would further that ambition.

Barlian, Commander of South Sumatra, is strongly anti-communist and, while not declaring himself for the dissidents as hoped for, has refused to take up arms against them.

Sukarno appears to be completely in the pocket of the communists. Although his stature in the eyes of the intelligentsia has definitely diminished, he still has a tremendous popular following and probably could not be successfully challenged by any single individual.

Queried as to what might be done, Colonel Berlin made these observations:

1. A military victory on the part of the dissidents might induce Barlian and, following his lead, other Army leaders in the outlying islands to swing over, actively.
2. The Atjeh tribes (N. Sumatra) might be induced to fight.
3. A gesture of support from the U.S. might encourage the anti-communist officers on Java to take action.
4. Nasution might be approached to employ the Army in exerting pressure to control Sukarno. The question of approach is delicate and the U.S. must be prepared to disavow sponsorship.
5. Acceptance of Nasution's invitation might provide opportunities for the U.S. to exert a favorable influence over the Army.

Colonel Berlin repeatedly emphasized the danger of failing to act promptly to rally those forces in the GOI which may be in a position to do some good. It seems unlikely that the situation will develop in which the United States can take any sort of military action, although this is still a possibility. If the dissidents fail to win over additional supporters and fail to retain control over a considerable portion of Sumatra, the Central Government will be entrenched without serious jeopardy. The only force in the GOI which will prevent that government from becoming communist is in the Army. I agree with you that we should do everything that we can to encourage the anti-communist elements in the GOI to exert all the influence possible to prevent the communist domination of Indonesia.

Ambassador Jones apparently has a firm grasp of the situation and perhaps he could offer some suggestions as to how Nasution could be approached and how to build up the anti-communist forces in the Army and the GOI. If we could act on his suggestions quickly and at the same time not destroy our assets among the dissidents, the United States may be able to assist in preventing Indonesia from becoming communist dominated.

I realize that you have all this knowledge, but I would like to give what support I can to helping the dissidents and the anti-communist elements in Indonesia to save their country.

With warmest personal regards,

Sincerely yours,

Arleigh

68.   Memorandum From the Joint Chiefs of Staff to Secretary of Defense McElroy

Washington, April 18, 1958.

SUBJECT

   Indonesia

1. It is increasingly evident that the defeat and ultimate liquidation of the dissident movement in Indonesia can be prevented only by overt U.S. military assistance to them. In the absence of a timely decision to take such action, the United States must seek other means to achieve our basic objective of preventing the communists from taking over all of Indonesia.

2. There are continuing indications that the Indonesian Army under the Chief of Staff, Nasution, if given some positive gesture of support by this government, might emerge as an anti-communist force in Java. Prior to the current military operations, the Indonesian Army under Nasution was considered to be the strongest anti-communist force in Indonesia. U.S. support of Nasution, or other influential Indonesian Army leaders arranged through appropriate channels, might influence him to take positive action to prevent a communist take-over by political or other means. This does not mean that the dissident forces should be abandoned. It should be clearly understood that the provision of material or financial support to Nasution or the Central Government has the objective of causing removal of communist influence from the Central Government and the cessation of hostilities.

3. The Joint Chiefs of Staff recommend that the matter of an approach to Nasution be re-examined on an urgent basis, taking as a point of departure the recommendations of Ambassador Jones in his message number 3729 of 15 April 1958.[1] However, they do not concur in his proposal that the Secretary of State make a public announcement prior to a covert approach to Nasution, because of the danger of its failure.

4. The Joint Chiefs of Staff recommend that these views be forwarded to the Secretary of State.

For the Joint Chiefs of Staff:
Maxwell D. Taylor
General, United States Army
Chief of Staff

Source: Department of State, Central Files, 756D.00/4–2158. Top Secret. Transmitted to John Foster Dulles on April 21 under cover of a memorandum from John N. Irwin II, whose covering memorandum reads in part: "This Department believes that the Joint Chiefs' suggestion warrants serious consideration but at the same time recognizes that many factors are involved. This Department and the Joint Chiefs will be happy to participate in any way you wish in reviewing this matter further." (*Ibid.*)

[1] Document 63.

69.   Memorandum of Telephone Conversation Between Secretary of State Dulles and Director of Central Intelligence Dulles

Washington, April 23, 1958, 12:49 p.m.

TELEPHONE CALL TO ALLEN DULLES

The Sec and AWD talked about Indonesia. AWD said there is no fight in them. AWD thinks it surprised the leaders. There is a possibility in the North. The Sec mentioned our switching around and backing the govt. AWD said that would probably be a decision for about a week from now. The story re the Chief of Staff being in the papers did not help.[1] AWD is coming over for OCB.

Source: Eisenhower Library, Dulles Papers, General Telephone Conversations. No classification marking. Drafted by Bernau.

[1] Not further identified.

---

70.   Editorial Note

On April 24 at the 363d meeting of the National Security Council, Allen Dulles opened his intelligence briefing with a discussion of developments in Indonesia:

"The Director of Central Intelligence indicated that dissident resistance on Sumatra had practically collapsed in the course of the last week. There seemed to be no willingness to fight on the part of the dissident forces on the island, and the dissident leaders had been unable to provide their soldiers with any idea of why they were fighting. It was a very strange war, because each side was penetrated by the other, and each knew in detail the forthcoming moves of the other. Our people there had had a very frustrating time. While it was impossible to judge what the capabilities of the dissidents for guerrilla operations might prove to be, Mr. Dulles doubted whether very much could be expected on the basis of past performance. Meanwhile, the Central Government was mounting an attack on the dissidents in the Celebes, and Lt. Col. Sumual and his troops seemed to have somewhat more fight in them than had the dissident forces on Sumatra. Nevertheless, Mr. Dulles doubted if they could hold out long. Accordingly, we were pretty close to the end of organized dissident resistance to Djakarta. As for Sukarno's future course of action, this was extremely difficult to estimate.

"The President said it looked to him as though we might well have to mount an operation against Sumatra if Communism appeared about to take over." (Memorandum of discussion by Gleason, April 25; Eisenhower Library, Whitman File, NSC Records)

---

71.   Memorandum of Conversation

Washington, April 24, 1958.

SUBJECT

   Indonesian Problems

PARTICIPANTS

   Dr. Joseph Luns, Foreign Minister of the Netherlands
   Dr. J. H. van Roijen, Ambassador of the Netherlands
   The Secretary
   EUR—Mr. Elbrick
   WE— Mr. Cameron
   Ambassador Philip Young

Following a discussion of the French-North African problem, Ambassador van Roijen commented that this situation was another confirmation of his conclusion that extreme nationalism and communism were the two greatest dangers to the Western Alliance. Foreign Minister Luns said that these two dangers in combination were highlighted in the persons of both Nasser and Sukarno. Ambassador van Roijen said that in his view Sukarno was probably worse than Nasser since Sukarno dealt with the communists not only in the international field but also used their support domestically, whereas Nasser apparently confined his dealings with them to the international sphere. At this point Foreign Minister Luns commented that it appeared that the United States was going to have Sukarno on its hands in Indonesia since the dissident movement had all but completely collapsed. The Secretary said that it

---

Source: Department of State, Central Files, 756D.00/4–2458. Confidential. Drafted by Cameron.

seemed to be the way things were going, adding that the rebels at no time had shown any inclination to fight.

The Foreign Minister then said that as far as the Netherlands was concerned the problem of Indonesia had become one of preventing its take-over by the communists. Dutch citizens were moving out of Indonesia rapidly and the Dutch had gradually accommodated themselves to the fact that their economic holdings and interests were lost. Dutch possessions such as plantations and warehouses had already begun to deteriorate substantially and under Indonesian management or lack thereof they could be expected to deteriorate further. The impact on the Indonesian economy was severe since economic relations with the Netherlands accounted for approximately 50% of the Indonesian national income (these relations amount to only 3% of the Dutch national income). There were, of course, the Foreign Minister said, certain residual problems and he cited in this connection the problems of Indonesian refugees in the Netherlands. The Foreign Minister commented that both he and the Secretary would probably miss the problem of Dutch-Indonesian relations since he had had many occasions to discuss it with the Secretary in the past.

The Secretary then asked the Foreign Minister for his views on West New Guinea. Foreign Minister Luns said that he had intended to mention West New Guinea to the Secretary because he thought that there was a potential development in that area which should be carefully watched. Sukarno after successfully defeating the dissidents might undertake military action against West New Guinea. Foreign Minister Luns said that Sukarno might be impelled into such a venture by the communists or might undertake it to divert attention from internal problems in Indonesia. The Dutch Government had no evidence at the present time that Sukarno intended such a move. Foreign Minister Luns said, however, that he wished to raise it because he thought it was a possibility which we should keep in mind. The Secretary asked about the state of Dutch defenses in the area. The Foreign Minister said that for the time being they had sufficient military forces in West New Guinea to take care of any attack. He mentioned the following components: 2 new destroyers, 1 old destroyer, auxiliary naval craft, 2,000 Royal Dutch Marines, 24 fighter planes (not jets) and 18 amphibious planes. Foreign Minister Luns then said that recent Indonesian purchases of jet planes did give him concern and this would be increased when Indonesian pilots had completed the necessary flight training. The Secretary suggested that this might not be too far away since Indonesian pilots were currently being trained in Egypt and Czechoslovakia. He added, however, that jet planes did not seem to him the type of equipment which could be used either against the dissident movement in the outer islands or against West New Guinea. He assumed that Sukarno wanted these planes since they had come to be considered the modern dictator's symbol of power.

The Secretary asked whether there was any unrest within West New Guinea. Foreign Minister Luns replied that there was none and that the natives cooperated fully with the local administration. He said that they were able to deal easily with very minor attempts at infiltration of one or two agitators at a time. Luns explained that the natives either apprehended and reported these agitators to the local administration or they ate the agitators. He said there was only one variation to this latter practice and that existed among the more Christianized natives who would only eat fishermen on Fridays.

The Secretary reverted to the serious internal problems which exist in Indonesia and said that the United States might decide that it was in its interest to provide Indonesia with a small amount of assistance. He explained that this would give the United States an opportunity to retain some influence on the Indonesian situation by giving the Indonesians the impression that they could play both sides. Foreign Minister Luns commented that if the United States did decide to give Indonesia some aid he hoped that the Indonesians would be reminded of their international obligations. Ambassador van Roijen asked what kind of things we had in mind furnishing the Indonesians. The Secretary replied that we were thinking about releasing some rice to them. This request, he explained, had been on our books for some time and in view of the local serious food situation it might be desirable to go ahead and supply Indonesia with a small amount of rice. In response to a question, the Secretary said that we did not have the intention of furnishing military assistance to Indonesia.[1]

---

[1] In telegram 3101, April 25, the Department authorized the Embassy to negotiate a new P.L. 480 agreement with Indonesia, which would provide Indonesia with approximately $5.5 million of rice. (*Ibid.*, 411.56D41/4–358) A previous P.L. 480 agreement with Indonesia was effected by an exchange of notes in Djakarta on March 2 and 5, 1956; for text see 7 UST 361.

72.   **Editorial Note**

On April 24 President Eisenhower sent a letter to British Prime Minister Harold Macmillan that dealt with Indonesia, among other matters:

"The rebellion in Sumatra seems to have flattened out so that the problem there, while certainly as grave as ever, does not have the same time factor that seemed at one time to be the case.

"If you want Caccia to have some talks with Foster about this before you come over, I would see no objection. However, I think that four-power military planning at this stage carries more risks than advantages at least in advance of political decisions. Incidentally, Foster has the impression, derived from the SEATO Meeting, that Prime Minister Nash of New Zealand is much less disposed than was his predecessor to vigorous action that could have military implications." (Eisenhower Library, Whitman File, International File) The full text of the letter is printed in volume XVI, pages 39–40.

73.   **Editorial Note**

On April 29 a meeting regarding Indonesia was held in Secretary of State Dulles' office. The following officials attended the meeting, which began at 12:01 p.m.: the Secretary, Robertson, Murphy, Wisner, Burke, Irwin, Parsons, Mein, and Cumming. At 12:04 p.m. they were joined by Allen Dulles. The meeting lasted approximately 1-1/2 hours after which the Secretary met alone with Allen Dulles. (Eisenhower Library, Dulles Papers, Dulles' Appointment Book, 1958–59) According to a memorandum for the record by Burke, April 30, the group decided to respond favorably to the request by Indonesian anti-Communist elements in the army for substantial military aid, as long as it was not used against the dissidents and as soon as a political settlement with the dissidents was reached. The sense of the discussion was to deal initially with trusted Army leaders, rather than Sukarno, on a preliminary basis. (Naval Historical Center, Burke Papers, Originator File)

The following day, the Secretary met again with Robertson, Cumming, Mein, and Allen Dulles to discuss Indonesia. The meeting, which began at 5:31 p.m., lasted approximately 25 minutes, after which Secretary Dulles met alone with Herter and Allen Dulles. (Eisenhower Library, Dulles Papers, Dulles Appointment Book, 1958–59) No record of the April 30 meeting has been found.

74.   Telegram From the Embassy in Indonesia to the Department of State

Djakarta, April 30, 1958, 2 p.m.

3965. Foreign Minister summoned me this morning at 9 a.m. to request US mediation with Government of Republic of China on supply of arms to rebels and informed me that Djuanda would make strong speech today charging foreign intervention and make a plea for US assistance in preventing further deliveries to rebels.

Documents which had been captured proved that rebels in Sumatra had received 10,000 small arms in addition to bazookas, artillery and planes and their sources of information in Menado had reported 3,000 items small arms supplied recently. Possession by Menado of three bombers and two Mustangs plus cost of air raids which they had verified at $75,000 per raid, had made it evident to Indonesian Government that rebels were not equipping themselves from own sources of revenue but were receiving actual assistance in form of military equipment from foreign government sources. He was not accusing the US of being involved, he said, and neither would Prime Minister in speech, but GOI had established fact that planes were from Taiwan and they were being piloted by Americans and Chinese, and Prime Minister would say so.

He made strong plea for US taking some action in response to his request if for no other reason than to prevent serious reaction against Chinese Kuomintang community in Indonesia. There was basic undercurrent of hatred against Chinese in Indonesia anyway, he said, and continued evidence of Taiwan participation in active aid to rebels might well be spark setting off explosion.

Everyone knew US Government had great influence with GRC whereas Indonesian Government, not recognizing GRC, was not in position to make direct formal protest. He hoped US Government would undertake this on behalf GOI.

I made no comment on Foreign Minister's request except to say that I would transmit it to Department. Foreign Minister did not at any point charge GRC with official participation in aid to rebels but indicated that use of facilities was not possible without at least knowledge or blessing of government.

Comment: I think at this stage it would be most helpful to us here if Linc White could mention Foreign Minister's request and indicate US Government would discuss matter with GRC in accordance therewith, without of course admitting implication GRC complicity. It would also

---

Source: Department of State, Central Files, 756D.00/4–3058. Secret; Niact.

be helpful if this could be coupled with repetition of previous statements to effect that US regards conflict as Indonesian affair and that it is against US policy to intervene in internal struggle.

In my view this would tend discourage growing conviction here that US Government is directly involved, continuing identification of US with rebel cause certain to provide Communists with unparalleled opportunity exploit their position here. In this connection see Embassy telegram 3966[1] immediately following.

Jones

---

[1] Document 75.

---

75.   **Telegram From the Embassy in Indonesia to the Department of State**

Djakarta, April 30, 1958, 5 p.m.

3966. Embtel 3965.[1] Prior to making démarche reported reference telegram Foreign Minister discussed for nearly an hour current political situation in Indonesia and thinking of leaders within government, particularly himself and Djuanda, and leaders of PNI. Basic theme of this presentation was realization that growth of communism within Indonesia must be halted by democratic means or otherwise and that this was point on which all responsible elements in official and political area agreed.

Foreign Minister opened discussion by saying that he recognized that US had great confidence in Dr. Hatta and that we considered Hatta's participation in a reorganized government as signal that government would be anti-Communist in orientation and one with which we could actively cooperate. He inquired as to whether this was not generally accurate. I replied by saying that it was of course true that Americans had confidence in Dr. Hatta, that we considered him an able administrator and that there was general feeling America that he represented policies which were in interest of Indonesia. Foreign Minister pressed this further by inquiring whether Dr. Hatta's known anti-Communist attitude was perhaps not major element in this reaction. I replied that this was correct.

He then launched into exposition of efforts to get President Sukarno and Dr. Hatta to work together. He said quite frankly that in

---

Source: Department of State, Central Files, 756D.00/4–3058. Secret; Niact. Transmitted in two sections.
[1] Document 74.

very real sense both Sukarno and Hatta constituted difficult problem for Indonesians because of great difficulty in past as well as present of getting them to work together. Sukarno was imaginative, creative, magnetic, with capacity to appeal to the masses but with no patience with details of administration or implementation of general policy. One could not discuss economic or financial questions with Sukarno, for example. Sukarno was always the political leader, flexible, adjustable within the overall framework of his emotional rationalism. Hatta was rigid, inflexible, competent administrator, impatient with political conceptions, hard working and interested in doing something instead of talking or dreaming. He implied desirability of getting these two men to work together in view of their complementary characteristics was only equalled by difficulty of bringing this about. He hoped, however, that it would be possible to get Hatta back into government and Sukarno and Hatta would have another talk after Sumatran business was finished.

However, he said, US would be making great mistake if our policy was based on assumption that Hatta was key to anti-Communist attitude in Indonesia. He said Dr. Djuanda, himself, Nasution and, a bit late perhaps, PNI leadership here equally anti-Communist. Present government recognized that coming year was most critical in Indonesia's history and that during this year growth of communism in Indonesia must be halted. Last thing that Indonesians wanted was for their country to go Communist. He himself had serious question whether PKI increase could be stopped by democratic means. He agreed with US analysis to this extent—if PKI won even so much as 30 or 35 percent of votes at next election which he thought was probable unless something were done to counteract it, Indonesia would go Communist.

At same time PKI and Leftist elements were doing utmost to capitalize on rebel opposition and in effect turn this into Communist-anti-Communist battle. Prime Minister Djuanda had three times told Sukarno that as long as he was Prime Minister he would not permit PKI to capitalize on current conflict in such a way as to turn GOI course more to left. Indonesian Government wanted and needed to feel closer to US in this current period, he said. Elements within political parties and government who were friendly to America needed some gesture from US to enable them to counter accusation that US had deserted legitimate Government of Indonesia and was backing rebels.[2] US seemed very far away, he said.

---

[2] On April 30 President Eisenhower was asked during a press conference for his reaction to Djuanda's charge that Americans were flying rebel planes. He replied that U.S. policy was "one of careful neutrality and proper deportment," and added that every rebellion has its "soldiers of fortune." For text of Eisenhower's remarks, see *Public Papers of the Presidents of the United States: Dwight D. Eisenhower, 1958*, pp. 357–358.

I commented that I was very glad to hear that official and political leaders of Indonesia had become convinced that positive action had to be taken to prevent further Communist growth and to weaken influence. I raised two questions in this connection:

(1) Did President Sukarno agree with what Foreign Minister was now saying, and
(2) What steps were planned to be taken against PKI.

Foreign Minister replied frankly that he did not think Sukarno had as yet come around to this way of thinking, but they were working on him and after settlement current conflict army could be brought into picture more directly. He could not answer second question specifically, but result of PNI conference at Semarang winding up tomorrow would be significant. Both Masjumi and PSI had failed to curb growth of communism. Now was country's last chance and PNI would have to adopt vigorous program. Even so, he reiterated he was not convinced that PKI could be disposed of in democratic manner. If not, army which was still strongly anti-Communist must be used. If tactics within democratic framework were to be successful silver tongue of Sukarno would be needed. PKI activity was carried on by professional, trained organizers working full time at job and moving from place to place. Non-Communist political parties were rank amateurs in spare time who could not meet competition of professionals. GOI had no proof as to how hard working, effective PKI was financed but they assume it was financed through Soviet and Communist Chinese governments. In response to my query he admitted they had to make similar assumption that PKI was therefore not responsible to Indonesian interest but to interests of outside power. History had demonstrated that if a country went Communist there was no going back. Democracy ceased functioning at point where Communist Party took over government.

This led to conclusion that if effective opposition to PKI within democratic framework was to be developed, some means must be found to influence masses now becoming more and more subservient to PKI organization. Only weapon they could see was voice of Sukarno to whom masses had always responded. If Sukarno could be won over to active campaign against communism, he thought still possible reduce influence PKI without use of force. Without Sukarno army remained only answer.

In this connection and leading into démarche reported reference telegram he pleaded for gesture of support from America—rice, granting of licenses for spare parts to Dakotas, arms to army, anything which would enable friends of America within official family to continue to exercise influence. He then turned to question of arms supply to rebels and interview was concluded with request reported reference telegram.

Comment: This was frankest talk I have ever had from Foreign Minister. He appeared earnest—almost desperate—in his appeal for US understanding, actually becoming emotional at one or two points on subject of determination of GOI leaders fight communism within country.

At same time it must be remembered Subandrio is articulate, skillful advocate, master at creating impression he desires to make. Nevertheless, I think this represents démarche of great significance on part GOI to which we must react soonest.

Jones

---

76.   Editorial Note

On May 1 at the 364th meeting of the National Security Council, Allen Dulles discussed Indonesian developments during his intelligence briefing:

"Turning to the situation in Indonesia, Mr. Dulles pointed out that dissident forces based on Menado had staged an amphibious operation and seized Morotai, situated in Helmahera Island and one of the best airfields in Indonesia. From the base at Menado the dissidents have staged a successful series of air strikes—almost too effective in certain instances, since they had resulted in the sinking of a British and of a Panamanian freighter. These raids were still run on a shoestring basis with a few P–51s and B–26s.

"Meanwhile, on Sumatra dissident resistance has now been reduced to guerrilla operations. The dissident leaders have stayed behind in the Sumatran hills.

"The Indonesian Army has given some indications, through various channels, that it would like to acquire U.S. weapons and then turn against the Communists. While such reports must be treated with reserve, there is still some hope that the regular Indonesian Army might turn against the Communists. The President commented that it would be a great success if the dissidents could seize Macassar." (Memorandum of discussion by Gleason, May 2; Eisenhower Library, Whitman Library, NSC Records)

77.   Telegram From the Embassy in Indonesia to the Department
      of State

Djakarta, May 2, 1958, 2 p.m.

4004. Manila pass priority COMNAVPHIL and 13th AF; COM-
NAVPHIL pass CINCPAC 241 and CINCPACFLT. Department pass
AFCIN–1A1 ACSI, CNO. CINCPAC also for POLAD. Manila for MLG.
Embtel 3974.[1] Djuanda's statement concerning aid provided by American and Taiwanese adventurers to rebels is climax of and puts official
stamp of approval on propaganda build-up which was started in Indonesia weeks ago against foreign intervention as result of GOI conviction
rebels have had active assistance foreign powers. Fact that Prime Minister himself made statement and his reference to government's possession of "sufficient proof" of foreign assistance to rebels take whole
matter out of realm of speculation or Communist-inspired propaganda
and put Free China and particularly US on the spot. Embassy considers
implications for future relations between US and Indonesia (and US policy toward Indonesia) are as serious as suggested by Djuanda himself, in
point 7 of his statement.[2]

British and Australian Ambassadors told me yesterday they considered statement most temperate in light situation here and had concluded it was carefully drafted so as not to be too inflammatory and
avoid direct accusation any foreign government as such of intervening.
In Embassy view, however, statement is merely slightly veiled and will
be taken by most Indonesians as conviction on part GOI that US is in fact
involved. This gives rise to important question of what next GOI step
will be.

Source: Department of State, Central Files, 756.D.00/5–258. Secret; Priority. Transmitted in two sections and repeated to The Hague, Manila, Canberra, Bangkok, Kuala
Lumpur, and Singapore.

[1] Telegram 3974, April 30, transmitted the text of a press release that was issued by
Prime Minister Djuanda that afternoon. In this statement Djuanda stated that the Indonesian Government had collected sufficient proof about foreign assistance in the bombings
of various regions in the eastern part of Indonesia. "The conclusion could be drawn," the
statement read in part, "that the pilots being employed by the rebels are foreigners and the
reports which we have received from Menado indicate that these pilots are Americans and
Taiwanese. Apart from that, it should also be inferred that the gasoline used has been illegally imported from abroad." (Ibid., 756D.00/4–3058) See Supplement.

[2] Point 7 of Djuanda's statement as reported in telegram 3974 from Djakarta, reads as
follows: "As a consequence of the actions taken by these United States and Taiwan adventurers there has emerged a strong feeling of indignation amongst the Armed Forces and
the people of Indonesia against the United States and Taiwan and if this is permitted to
develop it will only have a disastrous effect in the relationships between Indonesia and the
United States."

Created by centuries of antagonism against Dutch and, spilling over to all Western "colonialists and imperialists", latent xenophobia is perhaps even nearer surface here than most Asian countries. Recent West Irian and anti-SEATO campaigns are examples of anti-foreign sentiments which can be aroused without provocation. Chinese minority hated by Indonesians as cat's paw of Dutch and exploiters of people are special case and represent specific target against which Indonesia feeling in past frequently manifested by outright massacre. Indonesians also have common penchant for placing blame on others for many of their own troubles. Djuanda's charges, therefore, can be expected find emotionally conditioned and receptive audience here. Foreign appeal, principally to Asian-African nations, to condemn US and GRC intervention can hardly fail to evoke response from many sides and especially Communist countries and fellow neutrals.

According to Djuanda's statement, GOI, using all means and strength available to it, is confident she will shortly destroy all rebel remnants in eastern part of Indonesia. Embassy's Military Attachés believe that establishment of military command under Colonel Rukmito in Central Sulawesi is indication that GOI plans further military action in Central and North Sulawesi as soon as possible after completion action in Sumatra. Attachés also believe recent bombings either by rebels or on rebels' behalf have served to stiffen GOI resolve to settle issue by force. Djuanda's statement lays groundwork for increased public support of such action by making possible transformation of civil war, or internal police action, into fight against foreigners and foreign supporters of rebel cause. If Djuanda's lead is followed, original issues may well come out of focus entirely and rebel goal of reformed, non-Communist, "constitutional" government may be lost sight of completely as struggle becomes identified as part of cold war and thus an international affair. If this happens, however, issues unfortunately will not be Communist/anti-Communist to Indonesians, but Indonesians versus foreign interventionists and public opinion here will be easily marshalled against US.

Whatever chances may previously have been for settlement by negotiation or compromise, they would appear to have considerably dimmed as result Djuanda's charges of foreign intervention. If GOI continues this tack, possibility of overt Soviet assistance, even Soviet "volunteers" should not be ignored although GOI would unquestionably withhold approval until last extremity. In one portion Djuanda makes this clear when he warns that aid provided to rebels by American and Taiwan adventurers might invite "other quarters" to interfere and thus make Indonesia battleground for interests of foreign powers. Whether this materializes may depend to considerable degree, in Embassy's view, on response which US makes to Djuanda's appeal that American citizens be prevented from providing aid to rebels and on whether GOI has cause for believing "American adventurers" are continuing to assist rebels. Simultaneous diplomatic démarche by Indonesian Foreign Minister reported Embtel 3965[3] provides us opportunity to respond without in effect "putting on shoe which fits".

Regardless of longer-range implications, Djuanda's official pronouncement appears to be shrewdly conceived effort to put Indonesia's Civil War in new framework of Indonesians versus foreigners as well as accomplish basic purpose of quieting activity rebel behalf. By-product may well be to render ineffective whatever pressures rebels may have built up for changes in central government by associating them with universally-feared "foreign intervention."

Jones

---

[3] Document 74.

---

78.   **Telegram From the Embassy in Indonesia to the Department of State**

Djakarta, May 3, 1958, 8 p.m.

4028. Foreign Minister summoned me this morning to discuss rebel bombings and evidence American adventurers and Taiwan involvement operations. He made strong plea for US Government to do anything it could vis-à-vis Government of Republic of China, or otherwise, to stop bombings.

Some within Indonesian Government believed, he said, that these bombings were prelude to war. Both Admiral Subijakto[1] and Air Marshal Suryadarma had advised Prime Minister and President that they convinced American naval and air forces are planning attack Indonesia. He said neither President, Prime Minister, Nasution nor himself believed this but cited it as example of intense emotionalism within Indonesian Government this whole subject. He further said killings of innocent people by bombings has resulted in such strong reaction

---

Source: Department of State, Central Files, 756D.00/5–358. Secret; Niact; Limit Distribution. Transmitted in two sections.
[1] Commander of the Indonesian Navy.

within Indonesia against rebels that (a) rebel movement has become object violent popular reaction in Ambon and other places and (b) difficulty of GOI settling conflict at this time immeasurably increased.

He said both he and Djuanda had deprecated talk within Indonesian Government of breaking off diplomatic relations with US. In this connection he said Indonesian Government found itself on horns of most serious dilemma: In America lay its main hope of aid in opposition communism yet Indonesians were convinced that America was actively helping rebels. He said forces within government had wanted to include direct charge to this effect in Djuanda's statement but that Djuanda was unwilling to accept this because he felt it would play into hands of Communists and alienate America at critical stage.

He reported interesting conversation between himself, Sukarno and Djuanda yesterday in which Djuanda had told the President that what Communists have been in past they will be in future and that present cooperative attitude was mere matter of tactics. Djuanda had said flatly "Indonesian Communists are run by international Communists and cannot be trusted." Result of long conference was that President had agreed that PKI could "exist but must grow no stronger." He said President had finally become convinced that four leg concept guided democracy[2] was unsound because PKI represented alien, not indigenous element and that guided democracy meant indigenous democracy and had no element of communism within it. I urged Subandrio to attempt induce Sukarno to make this clear in public statement.

In connection with strong appeal for US help in matter of bombings, and other gestures of US support for Indonesia, Foreign Minister returned to question of arms. Army is the key to effective anti-Communist action in Indonesia, he said, "Don't antagonize the army." He indicated anti-American sentiment in army was growing as result of conviction strong US support for rebels and urged America to do something soon which would reverse this trend.

In connection with discussion bombings he said "Please help us not to accelerate conflict but to bring it to close" and at this point he said evidence of foreign assistance was so great that if conflict was not settled soon Indonesian Government planned bring matter before UN.

He then went into discussion of evidence foreign assistance to rebels. He first showed me an intercepted cable to Colonel Djambek in Bukittinggi from R. S. Hirsch, American Sales Company, 684 McAllister Street, San Francisco, which read: "can offer up to 50,000 each 7.35mm

---

[2] On several occasions Sukarno had referred to the four major Indonesian political parties—the PNI, PKI, NU, and Masjumi—as constituting the "four-legged horse" of guided democracy.

semi-automatic rifles and up to 15 million rounds ammunition for same for prompt shipment. Particulars promptly upon request".

He also said they had uncovered documents linking Chiang Kai Min, chairman of National Security Bureau in Taiwan, with supply of planes. These documents revealed, he said, referring to intelligence report, that Chiang had turned over C–47s to rebels and that planes were piloted by American pilots and Chinese co-pilots. Chiang had taken this action on instructions of US Navy in Singapore, he alleged documents revealed. He also said they had proof that General Li Chung Sie was with rebels as military adviser. This man sometimes has been known by name of Lie Chi-chun and Indonesian intelligence circles refer to him commonly as C.C. Li. He is a long-time GRC intelligence operator with serial number of 2621–1504–6108, he said and formerly was active in Indonesia as Kuomintang intelligence agent.

He further said that financial information obtained showed that total barter deals consummated by rebels amounted to from 8 to 10 million Straits dollars. He said complaints already received by GOI from merchants in Singapore to effect 3 million Straits dollars for rice, armored cars and road equipment have not been paid and are long overdue. He said Chinese merchants Singapore had made large commissions out of actions and indicated considerable bad faith involved. This was reason for assassination of Wan Tan Nea in Menado by rebels recently. Wan Tan was formerly Indonesian Army lieutenant stationed in Bandung.

Connection with above "evidence" I pointed out telegram from American in San Francisco, of whom I had never heard, constituted no evidence whatever of American official or unofficial involvement—that on face of it this was merely businessman trying to make sale and that reference to arms available did not even mean these arms were available within US since international arms purveyors have stocks in many countries.

Foreign Minister quickly cut in and denied any implication of American Government involvement in what he or Djuanda had said but that he felt evidence was sufficient to prove that rebels were receiving outside assistance and that he felt if US Government desired to do so it could be helpful in situation. I pointed out that Secretary Dulles had opened door by saying he would welcome any suggestions from Foreign Minister on this subject. Foreign Minister repeated request Embassy telegram 3965, saying he felt approach to GRC would be productive but that what he was asking was any help which we could give by way of discouraging continued bombings.

He then returned to subject of Communism and Sukarno in obvious effort to convince us that US and GOI objectives were identical on this point although ideas and method might differ. What President has been talking about, he said, is indigenous democracy and they recognize that PKI is least indigenous party. PKI's strategy has been most skillful; leaders have told Sukarno that they would do anything he wanted— they did not insist on being in Cabinet, they were satisfied merely to be his errand boys. Sukarno found this difficult to oppose but was appreciative of danger. Sukarno had said "I have slept with Musa in one bed but I will kill him if he tries to impose Communism on Indonesia". Sukarno keeps referring to Madiun[3] in this connection.

President yesterday also queried: "Why do Americans think I am Communist or pro-Communist? If I were, Indonesia would long ago have been Communist. Communists want power. I do not seek power. How many times have I been urged to become a dictator or to run the government as an active President? I have always refused. I do not want this. I want Indonesia to have democracy which will work".

Foreign Ministry cited this, he said, to show that Sukarno was not [beyond?] redemption in this matter and could, he was convinced, be won over to side anti-Communists. In support his claim that Sukarno beginning lean in right direction in spite anger at foreign intervention, Foreign Ministry cited reference in Sukarno's Bandung speech to remarks he made at my credentials ceremony.[4] This deliberate effort to keep door open, he said.

Subandrio reiterated point reported Embtel 3966[5] that Sukarno's silver tongue was needed if Communist growth were to be checked within democratic framework but that ultimate hope of checking communism was Army. He concluded his presentation on this note, simply adding that on Wednesday he would have to appear before Parliament to discuss this whole subject of rebel bombings and relations with US and he sincerely hoped US could take some step or make some gesture which would be helpful to him in this difficult task.

Before leaving I referred to matter of Robertson testimony before Senate Foreign Relations Committee[6] and read him correct version. I said although incorrect version has not as yet been published here, I did not want him to be taken off guard because I felt it was important to our mutual relations that sensitive subject of this kind be handled carefully.

---

[3] Reference is to an unsuccessful rebellion by the Indonesian Communist Party that broke out in Madiun, Java, on September 18, 1948; related documentation is in *Foreign Relations*, 1948, vol. VI, pp. 353 ff.

[4] Reference is to the speech that Sukarno delivered at Bandung on May 2. Telegram 4055 from Djakarta, May 5, briefly summarized the speech. (Department of State, Central Files, 756D.00/5–558.) For information on Sukarno's response to Jones' credentials speech, see footnote 3, Document 43.

[5] Document 75.

[6] Robertson testified before the Senate Foreign Relations Committee on U.S.-Indonesian relations on May 2; circular telegram 1034, May 2, summarized his remarks. (Department of State, Central Files, 756D.00/5–258) See Supplement.

He expressed appreciation for information and said he did not believe this would create problem. He said first part of Robertson's comments on subject of anti-colonialism would be welcome in Indonesia and implied it would balance later reference to West Irian.

Comment: 1. Foreign Minister was obviously anxious to accomplish two things: (A) Provide me with an understanding of feeling of desperation bombings had created in GOI; (B) demonstrate that in spite of everything, GOI felt it must have support of US if growth communism to be halted. Although trying to impress me with seriousness Indonesian reaction to "foreign bombing" and making fairly strong remarks, his manner was most cordial and as I left, he said, appealingly, "you think we can straighten out these things, don't you?" I replied in affirmative but not to be misunderstood as acceding to his specific request, spelled out desire of my government to help Indonesia, but emphasizing difficulty of so doing in current situation.

2. At luncheon in honor Indian Ambassador, immediately following Subandrio interview, British Ambassador drew me aside to obtain brief rundown of conversation. He then commented that in his view it was absolutely essential for two things to be done at once: (A) Bombings must somehow be brought to stop or situation will get out of hand; (B) Indonesian military must be provided with at least part of what it asks—both from US and British sources. He doesn't see how we can lose by taking such action.

3. Subandrio interview covered two-hour period so I have not attempted to give play-by-play account and in interest of space have omitted most of my comments and rejoinders designed in each case to spur Subandrio on in his anti-Communist thinking and at same time leave impression US genuinely interested helping Indonesia.

4. Anything Department could provide by next Wednesday[7] that would enable Subandrio to report to Parliament sympathetic attitude on part US would be useful at this point, for example, statement by Secretary that US proceeding to explore situation on basis of information supplied by Foreign Ministry.[8]

Jones

---

[7] May 7.

[8] The Department transmitted pertinent excerpts from this telegram to the Embassy in Taipei in telegram 700, May 5. (Department of State, Central Files, 756D.00/5–358)

79.   Memorandum of Conversation

Copenhagen, May 4, 1958, 5:15 p.m.

UNITED STATES DELEGATION TO THE 21ST MINISTERIAL
MEETING OF THE NORTH ATLANTIC COUNCIL
Copenhagen, Denmark, May 5–7, 1958

PARTICIPANTS

United States	*United Kingdom*
The Secretary	Foreign Secretary Lloyd
Ambassador Burgess	Ambassador Frank Roberts
Mr. Elbrick	Sir Roderick Barclay
Mr. Reinhardt	Sir Anthony Rumbold
Mr. Porter	Mr. Denis Laskey

SUBJECT

Indonesia

The Secretary said that the Sumatran affair had pretty well folded up. It had been a lamentable performance [1 *line of source text not declassified*].

In the Northern Celebes, however, there was more activity and a rickety amphibious operation had just succeeded. [*less than 1 line of source text not declassified*]

At the present we were trying to talk with friendly elements in Djakarta to see whether there was any leverage and any prospects of a political solution. The Secretary said he was very skeptical. Although Sukarno was, of course, highly undependable, we were trying to see what was possible in this regard. The leaders in Sumatra were all right, but their troops had refused to fight.

Mr. Lloyd raised the question of open intervention. The Secretary observed that he did not see any possibility of this character which would not have the most disastrous consequences for us throughout the Far East. He said we might have proceeded to recognition of belligerent rights if the rebels had really fought. He concluded by saying that although the situation was very thin, it was not altogether hopeless.[1]

Source: Department of State, Conference Files: Lot 63 D 123, CF 1006. Top Secret. Drafted by Reinhardt. Dulles and Lloyd were in Copenhagen for a meeting of the NATO Council of Ministers.

[1] [*text not declassified*]

80.   Telegram From the Embassy in Indonesia to the Department
      of State

Djakarta, May 6, 1958, 1 a.m.

4063. Deptel 3184.[1] Prime Minister received me at his home tonight,
his manner more grave and serious then I have seen before.[2] Foreign
Minister Subandrio was only other person present. Prime Minister
seemed to fear that relations between US and Indonesia were at cross
roads and that next few days might determine outcome.

He started out by saying that he had originally hoped that capture
of Padang and Bukittinggi would make it possible to bring about political settlement in conflict with rebels. Foreign bombings however had
introduced new element which had so aroused Indonesians that government was determined to push on with military campaign. He knew
that there was internal conflict in Minnehasa and until bombings took
place government had simply planned to blockade Menado and let matter settle itself over period of time. Now this was no longer possible. He
had made every effort to draft his statement of April 30 in such a way
that no specific accusations were made against us but he implied he
knew we were involved and could not understand our motives. It now
looked to GOI as if purpose of US was to split Indonesia in two in order
to insure that one part of Indonesia at least would remain non-Communist. This would be tragic for everybody, he said. It would be playing
into hands of Communists who had been delighted by predicament in
which bombings had placed both GOI and US. PKI was making capital
of this, he said, endeavoring to induce President and cabinet to take
steps from which there would be no return and President himself was so
furious that it was with greatest difficulty Djuanda had been able to persuade him not to make speech openly attacking US. His references to
splitting Indonesia in Bandung speech[3] were mild compared to his
original thinking.

I broke in at this point to assure Prime Minister that US had no such
objectives, that US objectives with regard to Indonesia were what I had

---

Source: Department of State, Central Files, 756D.00/5-658. Top Secret; Niact; Limited Distribution. Transmitted in two sections.

[1] In telegram 3184, May 3, the Department informed Jones that he could tell Subandrio: "Our Ambassador in Taipei has been instructed to inform GRC of substance his
charges that aircraft involved recent air raids came from Taiwan and were piloted by citizens GRC and his request that U.S. mediate with GRC in behalf Government Indonesia to
prevent future assistance to Indonesian rebels." (Ibid., 756D.00/5-358)

[2] Jones summarized this conversation with Djuanda in Indonesia: The Possible Dream,
pp. 133–134.

[3] See footnote 4, Document 78.

repeatedly told him they were—a united Indonesia able to stand on its own feet and maintain its own freedom and independence. US did not desire fragmentation of Indonesia which we felt would not be in interest of Indonesia, US or free world. We were of course most concerned about growth of communism in Java and fact that no steps apparently were being taken to do anything about it. Prime Minister said he, Dr. Subandrio and others realized that something must be done about it and he was glad to be able to tell me that the PNI in its meeting in Semarang had decided to take positive steps. He said he would be conferring with Deputy Prime Minister Hardi and others in next few days to work out specific positive program. He also said he hoped that Hatta could be induced to join government but that whether Hatta did so or not, we could be sure steps would be taken to curb growth of communism. At least this would be case unless US involvement in current struggle provided PKI opportunity turn Indonesian leadership against America.

Prime Minister said he had just received advice from his Indonesian Embassy in Manila to effect that new preparations were being carried out at Clark Field for additional plane and MTB assistance to rebels.

Foreign Minister interjected at this point observation that Serrano had said he was planning protest to Ambassador Bohlen against use of Clark Field to mount program of assistance to rebels. He did not know whether this had yet been done.

I expressed shocked surprise that Clark Field would have been directly involved in operation of this kind and asked whether he had specific evidence. Prime Minister replied that he had reports of observers from Indonesian Embassy Manila. I indicated this was hard for me to believe but I would transmit allegations to my Government.

Prime Minister continued by making strong appeal for action by US Government to halt bombings and further aid to rebels. He hoped Secretary could say something to indicate US intention to do what it could. This he said would help immeasurably to clear air and enable those within government who were endeavoring pour oil on troubled waters to continue this course. Further bombings would provide Communists with such leverage that it would be impossible for non-Communists and friends of America to hold line.

At this point I pulled out of my pocket paraphrase of Deptel 3184 which I had received shortly before leaving chancery and said I had some news for them which was responsive to Foreign Minister's earlier appeal this subject. After I had finished reading substance of reftel Prime Minister nodding appreciatively said that more threatening area at moment seemed to be build-up at Clark Field in Manila and he hoped that something could be done about this.

Prime Minister repeated very earnestly that he felt future of US-Indonesian relationships depended on US responsiveness to his appeal. He indicated America's friendship was so important to Indonesia that he was willing to overlook American past participation but he pleaded for hands-off in future and let Indonesians settle their own internal conflicts.

Prime Minister concluded his comments by saying that he recognized this was very unusual procedure for him to make appeal of this character to Ambassador but that he felt he could do so on basis our personal friendship and that this was perhaps only way in which matter could be resolved.[4]

Jones

---

[4] In telegram 4079 from Djakarta, May 6, the Embassy reported: "On basis several conversations at Parliament reception last night, Canadian Chargé today told Embassy officer he concluded widespread consensus members of Parliament is that air activity on rebels' side would not be possible without at least tacit US approval. He believed this attitude indicative that US-Indonesian relations gravely jeopardized particularly since GOI had made no effort, as he thought it should, to draw distinction between official US policy and whatever action individual American adventurers might be involved in." (Department of State, Central Files, 756D.00/5-658)

---

81.   Telegram From the Department of State to the Embassy in Indonesia

Washington, May 6, 1958, 1:57 p.m.

3207. Embtels 4028[1] and 4063.[2] Following points should be made to Djuanda and Subandrio:

1. We appreciate frankness their discussion with you and would welcome any additional comments or suggestions they may care make. We agree that best method for eliminating any misunderstandings which may exist or arise is through such talks.

2. Reassure them that US objectives are an economically viable, politically stable, united, free and independent Indonesia, and not a split or a communist dominated or influenced Indonesia.

Source: Department of State, Central Files, 756D.00/5–658. Top Secret; Niact; Limit Distribution. Drafted by Mein, cleared with Cumming and Robertson, and approved by Herter. Jones summarized this telegram in *Indonesia: The Possible Dream*, pp. 134–135.

[1] Document 78.

[2] Document 80.

3. Pass to them statement made by Foreign Minister Yeh (Taipei No. 909 repeated Djakarta as 12)[3] in reply to approach by our Ambassador (Deptel to Taipei No. 694, repeated Djakarta as 3185)[4] made in reply to Subandrio's request (Embtel 3965).[5]

4. US has no control over bombings by rebels or adventurers whom rebels may have hired. As regrettable therefore as these bombings are there is nothing we can do to stop them.

5. As to "evidence" of US involvement cited by Subandrio you should inform them that:

(a) if C–47s were indeed turned over to the rebels in Singapore as alleged US has no knowledge of and US Navy issued no instructions for such transaction in Singapore or anywhere else. If Indonesians have "documents" you can assure them they are false.

b) in addition to points already made by you re Hirsch cable that

(1) American Sales Company is not registered with Department of State as arms dealer;
(2) Company has made no application for export licenses for any types of arms;
(3) 7.35 mm semi-automatic rifles not manufactured in United States nor used by United States armed forces.

6. Assure them Clark Field not being used as base for assistance to rebels, and therefore no build-up taking place there as alleged by Djuanda.

7. Inform them US is prepared to sell Indonesia 35,000 tons of rice (Deptel 3101).[6] Expect instructions for conclusion this agreement along lines Embtel 3999[7] will be sent you today but there is no reason why our willingness proceed with this deal should not be made known and capitalized upon as a gesture on our part in line point made by Subandrio in earlier talk with you (Embtel 3966).[8]

---

[3] Telegram 909, May 5, reported that during a conversation with Foreign Minister Yeh that afternoon Ambassador Drumright was informed that the Republic of China had given no clearance to any of its Air Force planes to go to Indonesia and that it had not cleared ammunition shipments to any place abroad. Yeh said the United States could inform Subandrio of these facts. (Department of State, Central Files, 756D.00/5–558) See Supplement.

[4] Telegram 694, May 4, asked the Embassy in Taipei to inquire about Indonesian charges of GRC pilots and arms shipments aiding Indonesian dissidents. (Department of State, Central Files, 756D.00/5–458)

[5] Document 74.

[6] Dated April 25. (Department of State, Central Files, 411.56D41/4–358)

[7] Dated May 2. (Ibid., 411.56D.41/5–258)

[8] Document 75.

8. We are seriously concerned over Aidit message to you (Embtel 4018)[9] because a) it demonstrates ability representative of political party, and especially communist, address threat to representative of friendly foreign government, and b) of implications contained in threat. You should protest strongly and ask what action Government intends take.

9. Make point in paragraph numbered One of Deptel 2635.[10]

10. You may wish also point out to them invitations extended Indonesian Armed Forces to send observers to Oceanlink[11] and weapons demonstration sponsored by CINCPAC[12] as indication our desire establish close working relations with those Forces.

11. We welcome Djuanda's assurances that steps will be taken to curb growth of communism. You may wish point out that would make your mission and decision by U.S. Government much easier if such steps were actually taken on the basis of which further discussions could then take place.

FYI. We are considering your recommendation for issuance statement. Will advise separately. End FYI.

Herter

---

[9] Telegram 4018, May 3, transmitted the text of a letter from PKI Chairman D.N. Aidit to Jones concerning U.S. assistance to rebels in Indonesia. After citing proof of help by "American adventurers to the rebels" Aidit continues: "As your government probably knows, so far our party has not been propagating that action be taken against USA economic interests in Indonesia, but if aid, both open and covert of weapons from your country to rebels is not immediately stopped then we will deem it necessary to consider starting of campaign on actions against USA economic interests in Indonesia." (Department of State, Central Files, 756D.00/5–658)

[10] Telegram 2435 to Djakarta, March 15, suggested specific points for Jones to make in his meeting with Sukarno. The first paragraph suggests that if Sukarno requests additional aid, Jones should point out that difficulties of U.S. public and Congressional opinion preclude additional aid until a non-Communist government comes to power and is able to take action against the Communists and reach solutions to Indonesia's internal problems. (*Ibid.*, Conference Files: Lot 63 D 123, CF 990) See Supplement.

[11] A SEATO naval exercise was held May 1–14.

[12] The Department of Defense was planning to conduct a weapons demonstration and symposium for delegations for 18 Pacific powers in mid-May under the auspices of CINCPAC.

82.   Memorandum of Conversation

Copenhagen, May 7, 1958, 11:30 a.m.

UNITED STATES DELEGATION TO THE 21st MINISTERIAL
MEETING OF THE NORTH ATLANTIC COUNCIL
Copenhagen, Denmark, May 5–7, 1958

PARTICIPANTS

United States   Netherlands

The Secretary   Foreign Minister Luns

SUBJECT

Indonesian Designs on West New Guinea

Foreign Minister Luns thanked the Secretary for his exposition on
Indonesia during the restricted NATO Council meeting, [1] but urged that
the US make more emphatic to the Indonesian government that there
would be no tolerance of an armed attack on West New Guinea. The
Foreign Minister said that he was convinced that if the Indonesian government knew this in advance, there would not be any such attack.

The Secretary replied that he was not entirely sure that an attack
would in the long run be bad because if it took place it would expose the
disregard by the Indonesian government of the provisions of the UN
Charter. Also the Secretary thought that the permissible reaction to such
an attack would be such as to give a bloody nose to the Indonesian government.

Foreign Minister Luns said he thought the Dutch could do that, that
they were good fighters and the Indonesians were not, as shown by the
fact that a handful of the Dutch had been able for many years to exercise
complete control and authority over the many millions of Indonesians.

Source: Department of State, Secretary's Memoranda of Conversation: Lot 64 D 199.
Secret. Drafted by Dulles. The meeting took place at Christiansborg Palace.

[1] In Secto 49 from Copenhagen, May 7, Dulles reported on the restricted NATO
Council meeting of May 7. The following summarized his statement on Indonesia: "In
meantime, Secretary reported on situation in Indonesia, citing increasing tendency of
Sukarno to follow more dictatorial methods with support of Soviet bloc. He reviewed action in Sumatra and the Celebes and political situation in Djakarta. He indicated that these
events as well as those in Middle East show Soviet has new techniques in supplying military and economic aid to back dictatorial leaders. It was a form of indirect aggression
which is very difficult to deal with under established international law." (Ibid., Central
Files, 396.1–CO/5–758)

83.   Telegram From the Commander in Chief, Pacific (Stump) to the Chief of Naval Operations (Burke)

Honolulu, May 7, 1958, 5 p.m.

080332Z. Sent CNO. State for Robertson only. Exclusive for Adm Burke from Stump. Deliver during working hours. We have just reviewed Djakarta's 4028[1] passed as CNO 061757Z and Djakarta's 4063[2] passed as CNO 062245Z together with your exclusive to me 061759Z.[3]

Riley, Steeves and I are of the opinion that Djuanda's presentation of views to Jones reported in Djakarta's 4063 reveal that the situation is grave indeed and that there is an imminent possibility of a break of relations between Indonesia and US. If this should transpire, the fat is really in the fire and we will have forced beyond the point of no return anti-Communist elements which may still exist within the framework of the Djakarta government.

If Washington is convinced, as some in State seem to be, that there is possibility that no real will resist communism exists the army or in any other effective area in Djakarta then, of course, we have no alternative but to turn a deaf ear to such pleading as Djuanda presents. If, however, there is any basis to the recent reports that there are strong elements who are still anti-Communist in Djakarta, we are of the opinion that greater risks may be required in order not to turn our backs irrevocably on any possible non-Communist cooperation from Djakarta. We may be asking too much of Djuanda, Nasution and non-Communists of like mind to take the steps which you have outlined in your 061759Z before we indicate any willingness to cooperate.

[1 paragraph (11 lines of source text) not declassified]

It seems to us that Jones should be allowed to make a forthright proposition to Djuanda and Nasution with possibly knowledge of our offer coming to the ears of men like Soekanto, Hatta, and possibly Subandrio, that we are prepared to mediate between the GOI and the dissidents, to offer aid promptly, both military and economic, to non-Communist forces if they will give us any encouragement that they are willing to take a stand.

Even if we should launch such a program, we can still play a cat and mouse game if their anti-Communist protestations turn out to be deceitful; [2-1/2 lines of source text not declassified].

Source: Department of State, Central Files, 756D.00/5–858. Top Secret. Repeated to the Department of State, which is the source text.

[1] Document 78.

[2] Document 80.

[3] Not found.

84.   Telegram From the Embassy in Indonesia to the Department of State

Djakarta, May 7, 1958, 11 p.m.

4112. Deptels 3207[1] and 3213.[2] Immediately on receipt of reference telegrams I sought appointment with Foreign Minister and he received me at his home at 5:30. When he learned subject to be discussed, he telephoned Prime Minister who asked us to come to his home at once. There I carefully presented all points reference telegrams.[3]

Both Foreign Minister and Prime Minister expressed appreciation for prompt response, informing me that question of military planning as well as action against PKI would be discussed at special executive cabinet meeting with Nasution present at 9 a.m. tomorrow. Under head of interesting coincidence, prior receipt reference telegrams today, army headquarters telephoned to make appointment for me to see General Nasution at 8 a.m. tomorrow—hour before his meeting with Prime Minister.

Foreign Minister said my news could not have been better timed—that pressures were building up and tomorrow's meeting might have been critical. PKI was engaged in feverish activity designed to push GOI into irrevocable anti-American position. This information would enable Djuanda and himself to put shoe on other foot. Both Djuanda and Subandrio were obviously greatly relieved by indication adjustment US position.

Prime Minister, while expressing gratification at reassurance and offer of help from US, said that Indonesian Government would not be willing to consider offer which carried conditions with it affecting internal operations of country; that Indonesia, in other words, would not bargain away its independence of action. Indonesia Government would

---

Source: Department of State, Central Files, 756D.00/5–758. Top Secret; Niact; Limit Distribution. Transmitted in two sections.

[1] Document 81.

[2] Telegram 3213, May 6, referred to a "supplementary message" from Jones that had been sent "through other channels" and to a message that the U.S. military attachés in Indonesia were authorized to pass on to certain Indonesian Army leaders. Neither of these messages has been found. The telegram authorized Jones to meet with either Djuanda, Nasution, or Subandrio and explore with them the approach laid down for the attachés. It also instructed him to emphasize point 11 of telegram 3207, "pointing out to Djuanda that in order take definite measures assist Government we need concrete demonstration Indo Govt intention deal effectively with Communists." (Department of State, Central Files, 756D.00/5–658)

[3] Jones summarized his conversation with Subandrio in Indonesia: The Possible Dream, pp. 136–137.

follow course it believed sound for country; if that course enabled US to help, so much the better. He believed that this would prove to be case.

I said I understood this thoroughly and that I was not putting forward proposition with conditions but simply informing them what we would like to do and were prepared to do. At same time I was indicating ways in which they could be helpful to us in creating situation that would enable us to do what we would like to do by satisfying US public opinion.

Prime Minister acknowledged distinction with smile and then proceeded to say that he was planning two moves in near future: (1) reshuffle of government and (2) more positive actions to curb PKI. He said he could tell me confidentially that he as well as army was very much concerned about current activities of PKI. With large part of effective military forces now outside Java, as Minister of National Defense, he was seriously concerned as to capability of forces left on Java to maintain security if Communists stepped up activity as reports indicated they were planning to do. He was not only thinking of coup but of disruption of economy through strikes, boycotts, et cetera. Parenthetically, he said that he had instructed military to crack down on any action taken by Communists against foreign interests. Prior receiving reference telegrams I had made representations to both Foreign Minister and Prime Minister on subject Aidit message to me. (On this point he could assure me specifically that PKI would not be permitted to take any action against American property or personnel). Subject of how to handle Communists and capability of military on Java would be discussed with General Nasution at tomorrow's meeting.

On subject reshuffle cabinet, Prime Minister said he still hoped to get Hatta into cabinet but could not be sure. There were two reasons for this uncertainty:

(1) Hatta's own rigidity and (2) fear of some army leaders that he would favor Sumatrans to such extent that control of army might actually pass to rebels. Sultan of Jogjakarta, however, was certain to be included in cabinet either as Minister of National Defense or Minister of Economic Affairs. New cabinet would be anti-Communist in orientation and its objectives would coincide with US objectives. Sukarno agreed with general concept, he said, but task would not be easy with many conflicting groups and interests and he counselled patience. He might not succeed but he would do his best.

In commenting on arms offer, he carefully avoided direct reference to settlement current conflict (probably because of sensitivity to conditions expressed or implied) but touched on point obliquely by saying that he could assure me that no arms from US would be used against dissidents.

Prime Minister also expressed deep appreciation for decision on rice which was urgently needed, as well as for message from Foreign Minister Yeh of GRC,[4] and other information from US Government. Although US could not assure him that bombings would stop, he appreciated assurance that Clark Field was not being and would not be used as base for aid to rebels.

I informed Prime Minister of appointment with Nasution tomorrow morning and he concurred in suggestion I should supply him with highlights of reference telegrams. He thought this would be mutually helpful. I also mentioned both SEATO and modern weapons invitations. Although it was impossible for GOI to send military representatives to SEATO exercises for reasons previously reported, Prime Minister's initial reaction to possible second invitation from Admiral Stump[5] was favorable again depending on timing and availability of personnel. He suggested I discuss it with Nasution tomorrow.

Will advise results Nasution interview soonest.

Jones

---

[4] See footnote 3, Document 81.
[5] To attend the "modern weapons" demonstration.

---

85.   Editorial Note

On May 8 at the 365th meeting of the National Security Council, Allen Dulles opened his intelligence briefing with an analysis of Indonesian developments:

"The Director of Central Intelligence indicated that the dissident forces on Sumatra had been reduced to guerrilla activity. While the dissident leaders, both military and political, had not been captured, the prospects for effective guerrilla warfare were not very good. In the northern Celebes, on the other hand, the dissidents had been having quite a few successes since they had taken the air base at Morotai. Their bombing attacks have stirred great anger and apprehension in Java. Charges have been made that U.S. and Chinese Nationalist personnel have taken part in these air raids. On the other hand, the government seems to have no definite intelligence or information to back up this charge. Incidentally, it had been reported that four Soviet instructors had been killed in one of these dissident bombing attacks.

"Mr. Dulles pointed out that a few feelers had been extended at lower Army levels in Djakarta. The Army was the most anti-Communist branch of the armed services, as the Air Force was the most Communist-penetrated. Certain Army officers had been in touch with our Military Attaché. While there had been no real progress as yet in these conversations, Mr. Dulles was not without some hope that they would ultimately amount to something. In any event, our Ambassador was pursuing the matter diligently. Meanwhile, there are increasing reports of the arrival of Soviet military matériel—MIGs, some transport planes, and a few light bombers. These aircraft have not yet seen action, and probably wouldn't for some days, until training was completed. Mr. Dulles thought that Secretary Herter might wish to make a comment at this point.

"Secretary Herter replied that it was hard to assess the true situation in Djakarta. However, it seemed that Sukarno was as determined as ever to run the show as he wished, i.e., with the support of the Communists.

"The President observed that if the Indonesian Army could really work effectively, it could completely neutralize the Communist-inclined Air Force by simply seizing the airfields." (Memorandum of discussion by Gleason, May 9; Eisenhower Library, Whitman File, NSC Records)

---

86.   Telegram From the Embassy in Indonesia to the Department of State

Djakarta, May 8, 1958, 8 p.m.

4116. Deptels 3207[1] and 3213.[2] Made call on General Nasution this morning accompanied by Col. Cole, Army Attaché.[3] General treated my call as important occasion. Honor guard had been turned out and he later informed me this was first time he had ever received a call from an Ambassador. With him at conference were General Subroto, Col. Ibnu, Lt. Col. Sukendro, and interpreter for Subroto among others. General Nasution's English turned out to be quite fluent.

General Nasution struck me as a highly intelligent, determined man of character with definite philosophy and most attractive personal-

---

Source: Department of State, Central Files, 756D.00/5–1858. Secret; Niact. Transmitted in two sections.

[1] Document 81.

[2] See footnote 2, Document 84.

[3] Jones summarized his talk with Nasution in *Indonesia: The Possible Dream*, pp. 137–139.

ity, latter feature I had not anticipated. After we had established rapport he opened up and talked freely, at one point nearly 15 minutes without pause.

General received me standing, flanked by his staff officers and we spoke for some minutes together before coffee was served and we sat down. In connection usual exchange of courtesies. I observed that I had heard a great deal about him since coming to Indonesia and that it had all been good. I expressed regret that it was impossible for him to attend my dinner for Admiral Frost[4] tonight but that I understood completely, knowing how busy he must be. However, I hoped that when he saw Admiral Frost tomorrow morning he would not treat the Admiral's call as a courtesy call but would discuss Indonesian situation frankly with him and anything else he had on his mind. I said this would be mutually beneficial.

General Nasution responded that he would do so. He said, "There have been serious misunderstandings between United States and Indonesia." I agreed, commenting that I hoped these were in process of being cleared up.

Expressing regret but also understanding that he had been unable to send observers to SEATO exercise, I then led into invitation from Admiral Stump to attend or send representatives to modern weapons demonstration and handed him draft of Admiral Stump's letter.[5] Nasution replied that he would have liked to have sent observers to SEATO exercise but that in present situation it was impossible as he needed every competent officer. He said he sincerely welcomed Admiral Stump's invitation, indicated that if timing were different he would have accepted with pleasure but that he was afraid he would have to make same response as to SEATO. However, he appreciated invitation and would write Admiral Stump.

I then referred to long standing arms request which Indonesian military had with US Government and outlined substance of reference telegrams in less detail but otherwise as presented to Foreign Minister and Prime Minister last night (Embtel 4112).[6] General appeared gratified by news that US was now prepared to be responsive to arms request but made no specific comment. I emphasized my government wished to demonstrate its confidence in leadership Indonesian Army by this

---

[4] Admiral Laurence H. Frost, Chief of U.S. Naval Intelligence, arrived in Indonesia on May 8 as part of a larger trip to the Far East for the purpose of inspecting U.S. naval intelligence operations. (Ibid., p. 147)

[5] Not further identified.

[6] Document 84.

move. Statement evoked gratified nods from staff officers present and this was point at which Nasution himself began to unbend.

He said he wanted me to know his thinking on position of Indonesian Army within democratic government structure. (General had previously been described to me as officer who talks over heads of associates. This characteristic was clearly evident as General pursued theme of place of Indonesian military in hierarchy.) He was disciple of late General Sudirman, founder of Indonesian Army and Chief of Staff during revolution, he said, in his strong conviction that Indonesian Army must be protector of democratic Indonesian state based upon constitution and Pantjasila. Constitution was important but Pantjasila with its five principles was basis of philosophy establishing republic.

He wanted me to understand this because this was reason Army would never permit Communists to take over government. PKI did not agree with two points of Pantjasila and Army considered all five points fundamental to Indonesian philosophy of revolution. Army had fought for individual freedom as well as independence of country and was determined to preserve this.   .

For same reasons, he was equally and unalterably opposed to Moslem state which would violate principles Pantjasila. This was old-fashioned concept. It might have been all right 500 years ago in period absolute monarchies but not today. He knew Natsir intimately. They had worked together during revolution but he had never been able to subscribe to Natsir's philosophy.

He was likewise opposed to military junta concept, he said. Indeed, differences between himself and former members of his staff, such as Colonel Lubis, revolved around this central point. There was no difference in their attitude toward communism and he said this represented basis misunderstanding on America's part of issues involved in current conflict. Colonel Lubis wanted to use army as road to political power; other dissidents were merely interested in "commercial aspects of Warlordism". This was great evil in Indonesian Army as it had been in Chinese Army in old days, and he was determined to crush this and develop strong, vigorous, cohesive army responsive to commander-in-chief with function of preservation Indonesian democracy. He implied China might never have gone Communist had this been true.

Position of Indonesian military was different and would continue to be different from that of military in any other country in world that he knew of, he said. He has repeatedly been urged to take over power and establish military dictatorship. "I will not do this," he said. "This is what happens in Latin America. It must not happen in Indonesia. If I seize power today someone else will seize power tomorrow and throw me out. This does not make for stable democracy, which is our objective".

Neither, however, would Indonesian military ever accept traditional position of military in European democracies and under all circumstances take orders from civilian politicians. Indonesian military would continue active in policy. They had fought and won revolution and considered they had right to be heard in councils of nation. They did not want to take over power—their objective, he repeated, was to protect and preserve fruits of revolution. "It is our job to preserve freedom in Indonesia," he said, "and to prevent its curtailment from whatever source. This is what Pantjasila means to us."

To carry out this concept, Army would insist on strong emergency powers being provided in constitution. They must be able to move in and take over legally when threat to democratic state loomed on horizon. What he seemed to be saying was that Indonesian Army would in effect be policeman to constitution and guardian of Indonesian liberties and that he was determined to weld it into effective instrument for this purpose.

Comment: I was much impressed with General Nasution and believe conversation was most useful from standpoint both sides. Better assessment of results, however, can be made after discussions within Cabinet are known and Indonesians follow up this approach.

Department's prompt action relation above matter deeply appreciated. It apparently was close thing. British Ambassador informed me today he was waiting for Subandrio yesterday at 1 p.m. and that Foreign Minister was delayed considerable length of time in Cabinet meeting. His aide informed Ambassador, "there is terrible argument going on in there", and when Foreign Minister finally emerged he confirmed this and indicated in meeting great pressure had been brought to attack US openly as aggressor. Events of last night and this morning already appear to have brought great change in atmosphere.

Jones

87.   Telegram From the Embassy in Indonesia to Secretary of
       State Dulles, at Copenhagen

Djakarta, May 9, 1958, 2 p.m.

2. For the Secretary. I earnestly hope that you can disavow or at
least soften by public statement UP story Copenhagen front page all
Djakarta papers today to effect that you warned yesterday that an Indonesian attack on West New Guinea would have "most serious consequences" for Southeast Asia and whole Western world. Full text story
follows:

Begin verbatim text:
"United States Secretary of State, John Foster Dulles, warned yesterday that an Indonesian attack on Western New Guinea (Irian) would
have most serious consequences for Southeast Asia and the whole Western world, a high conference source disclosed last night.

"Dulles, the source said, brought up Indonesia during a secret session of the NATO Council yesterday morning. He was said to have
pointed to the Communist danger and intimated that Washington was
"deeply disturbed" over developments in that area.

"He was quoted as saying he felt bound to bring this to the Council's attention.

"Netherlands Foreign Minister Joseph Luns, the source disclosed,
then gave the Council a full report on developments in Indonesia according to the latest information reaching the Dutch Government."

End verbatim text.

I had no sooner finished dictating above when I was summoned by
Foreign Minister, who stressed seriousness of this statement coming at
this time. He said as soon as it had been published he received telephone
calls from both President and Prime Minister who were inclined to react
at once with strong statement attacking United States. Foreign Minister
pointed out this was third-hand information and urged that they wait
until he had opportunity to consult American Ambassador. He also told
them he could not believe that United States would deliberately exacerbate United States-Indonesian relations after having just made strong
gesture in behalf friendship in Ambassador's approach to Prime Minister on subject Indonesian arms request and rice for Indonesia.

I informed Foreign Minister that I believed he was correct in his assumptions and that I doubted Secretary had made any such statement in

Source: Department of State, Central Files, 656.56D.13/5–958. Confidential; Niact.
Repeated to the Department of State as telegram 4134, which is the source text.

context in which it was published. Indeed, as soon as I had read story, I had dictated telegram seeking accurate information and would advise him as soon as I had a response.

Foreign Minister pointed out that they were doing best to play down issue of West New Guinea. I believe this to be accurate, particularly at this time when strenuous efforts being made to heal wounds.

In this highly emotional situation here in which Indonesian Government on verge of charging United States as aggressors reference to West Irian is most inflammatory. As you aware, West Irian is most sensitive subject on which all Indonesians are united. Juxtaposition remarks of Luns also unhelpful except that Foreign Minister concluded from this that Dutch obviously had violated confidence secret meeting.

It would be most helpful to us here if you could say something to effect source badly distorted your remarks and then make statement designed calm Indonesians.[1]

Jones

---

[1] In Tosec 75 to Paris, May 9, Herter and Robertson informed Secretary Dulles that it would be helpful if he could make a statement or direct Jones to make a statement that could be released in Djakarta regarding the UP story on West New Guinea. (*Ibid.*) See Supplement. In telegram 8 from Paris to Djakarta, May 9, (repeated to Washington as Secto 64), Dulles authorized Jones to tell Subandrio or Djuanda that the UP story "is obviously fabrication since I made no remarks of any kind regarding a possible Indo attack on New Guinea." (Department of State, Central Files, 656.56D13/5–958) In telegram 5157 from Djakarta, May 10, Jones expressed appreciation for the Secretary's prompt response and indicated he informed the Foreign Minister who indicated the information would be "most helpful." (*Ibid.*, 656.56D13/5–1058) See Supplement.

88.   Memorandum From the Joint Chiefs of Staff to Secretary of Defense McElroy

Washington, May 9, 1958.

SUBJECT

Indonesia

1. The Joint Chiefs of Staff, in a memorandum dated 18 April 1958,[1] recommended to the Secretary of Defense that the United States explore the possibilities of making some positive gesture toward the Indonesian Military Services to halt the trend toward a Communist takeover in Indonesia.

2. It is understood that such an approach has been authorized.

3. Recent reports from various sources indicate that the political climate in Indonesia may be evolving into a situation where it would be timely to take steps to expand the approach to the military Services into more public action of greater scope.

4. The most urgent problem facing Indonesia, besides the immediate problem of the rebellion of the dissident groups, is the deterioration of the economy of the country. Indonesian economy has steadily declined since the Japanese occupation. The recent expulsion of the Dutch has aggravated further an already bad situation. It seems obvious that, if Indonesia is to survive as an independent nation, she must be assisted by the free nations of the world to a position of economic stability. If she is assisted by Soviet Bloc countries, Indonesia will inevitably swing into the Sino-Soviet orbit.

5. Therefore, the following courses of action for the immediate future are proposed:

a. The United States make an official public policy statement concerning Indonesia, in order to establish a world understanding of the U.S. position and serve as a basis for further action. It is envisaged that this statement would express:

(1) United States support of the independence of all free nations, and desire to help preserve the sovereignty of Indonesia in particular.

(2) United States concern over a pattern of events in Indonesia, which has in the past in other countries led to the loss of the sovereign independence of the nation concerned, and its reduction to that of a virtual colony of an imperialistic power.

Source: Department of State, Central Files, 756D.00/5–1458. Top Secret. McElroy forwarded this memorandum to Dulles on May 14 under cover of a letter that reads: "The enclosed copy of a memorandum dated 9 May 1958 sets forth the views of the Joint Chiefs of Staff on the current Indonesian situation. Although I understand that certain steps are already being taken along these lines, I believe their comments and recommendations merit serious consideration."

[1] Document 68.

(3) The conviction that the current internal strife in Indonesia both facilitates and obscures the rise of foreign agents and their followers to power through exploitation of Indonesian political and economic troubles.

(4) An offer of U.S. good offices in working out a peaceful solution to Indonesian internal problems.

(5) An offer of U.S. assistance in working out ways and means of establishing a strong, prosperous, and independent Indonesian economy.

b. The current deteriorating economic situation in Indonesia is one is which all Indonesians, especially the Rebel leaders, recognize the need for help. The United States should offer a moderate "impact program" of economic aid. This program should provide immediate, visible contributions to the capital plant of the Indonesian economy; for example, land, sea, and air transportation equipment. The scope and promptness of this program should be at least comparable to the recent Russian deliveries of ships. Deliveries, especially initial deliveries, should be made promptly.

c. The United States should, on the assumption that the approach to the Indonesian Military will prove successful, take steps to insure immediate delivery, upon agreement, of an initial increment of a military aid program. A token grant military aid program, the bulk of which is army equipment has been assembled and ready for some months. Negotiation or financing should not be allowed to interfere with prompt execution.

6. The above courses of action would neither negate previous actions taken nor necessarily preclude their continuation for the time being. Properly timed, they should serve to establish a logical overt cold war beachhead for future U.S. operations in Indonesia:

a. The public statement will establish in world opinions the moral basis of U.S. concern. It will also serve notice to all concerned in Indonesia of the new lines of U.S. action.

b. The impact economic program will provide an initial boost toward Indonesian economic recovery, as well as a favorable basis for further U.S. interest and activity in the economic field. It should be followed up by longer-term programs designed to put the potentially prosperous Indonesian economy on its feet.

c. The token military aid program will establish a small initial requirement for spare parts and training; this will provide an opportunity for some degree of continuing U.S. influence over the Indonesian Armed Forces. Consideration should be given to subsequent additional programs, possibly including the establishment of a U.S. Military Mission.

7. It is recommended that the above views of the Joint Chiefs of Staff be submitted to the National Security Council for consideration.

For the Joint Chiefs of Staff
N.F. Twining
Chairman
Joint Chiefs of Staff

89.   Telegram From the Embassy in Indonesia to the Department of State

Djakarta, May 10, 1958, 4 p.m.

4154. Department pass to CNO, ACSI, DWI and AFCIN. Rear Admiral Frost sends. Following my call and talk with General Nasution 9 May, which followed same lines as his earlier talk with Ambassador Jones (Embtel 4116),[1] Nasution sent Lt. Colonel Sukendro to me to discuss some items Nasution did not have time to cover during my visit.

First Nasution wanted to tell me he planned to bring about changes in Cabinet to replace leftist-oriented members. Second, Nasution was deeply concerned about economic situation result recent bombings of shipping by rebels. Third, that rebel bombings had completely upset his timing for taking action against Communists because he could not, and would not, make any such move until rebel problem was solved. Effects of bombings had greatly disturbed him and had forced him to consider economic factor which he could not now control because of dependence of Indonesia upon outside shipping and other trade relationships. At same time, he wished me to know Communists were becoming more active in exploiting economic situation. He did not give details, his only comment being that I would understand how Communists would go about using this new tool which had been put in their hands.

During this 2-hour discussion, Sukendro again questioned sincerity of US motives. I did not emphasize Communism or anti-Communism but developed what we in US consider to be aspiration of new republic. These items included an independent Indonesia, in no way controlled by international Communism or any other influence, the vital requirement for maintaining the principles of the constitution of the Republic; economic control of country by Indonesians and finally necessity for tying together many divisive forces through their maritime communications; their navy and their political representation from all regional areas.

Sukendro stated General wished to ask me to convey message frankly to CNO and many other government level officials with whom he knows I have contact. "What can US do, what support can I expect from US?" he asked. It was apparent that General Nasution has serious doubts about US because of alleged support of rebels. Colonel Sukendro said General Nasution cannot understand why US would support such persons as Warouw who in 1948 during Communist uprising at Madiun

---

Source: Department of State, Central Files, 756D.00/5–1058. Top Secret; Niact; Limit Distribution.

[1] Document 86.

was on "red side". My only response was again to ask him to explain to me and to representatives here specific facts relating to those individuals on rebel side who were pursuing their own self-interests as opposed to those of country, or who sought to be "war lords" in various areas. This took some time as Sukendro was talking to me for first time without an interpreter. I told him I would again review background of all rebel leaders which has been fully reported by Embassy.

In summary, General desired to advise me that we were rapidly coming to "climax" in US-Indonesian relations and in current situation here and that he could not, and would not, hazard his chances of success without knowing how he was to control PKI activities and solve developing economic crisis. Everything hinged on whether or not US would support him. To accomplish his objectives, bring about political changes in Cabinet and move against PKI, he must know unequivocally and soon what US Government intends to do.

Comments: While there are many factors in this complex situation, I believe Nasution is only person who has strength to change trend of Soviet influence. As indication his cooperativeness, he made immediate arrangements (through Sukarno and FonOff) for Subijakto to receive me this morning after latter had declined all invitations both for himself and for navy and having stated he was too busy to see me.

Atmosphere my call on Subijakto was barely cordial and about only item he discussed was to play old record of Indonesia's requirement for control of West Irian before anything else can be done. He thought Admiral Stump's invitation to the Baguio Conference for 18 May was interesting but it came at time when he was too busy. There is no doubt that loss of their Corvette cuts him very deeply and he would seek to attribute this loss to alleged participation of US in rebel cause.

I must acknowledge that my visit here would have been a complete failure without assistance of General Nasution who has, I believe, gone further in disclosing his real position than at any time in past. I can see no other internal element in Indonesia through which we may promote best interests of Indonesia than Indonesian Army. Ambassador Jones comments follow and I am deeply grateful to him and to his staff for their determined and ever helpful assistance while in Djakarta.

Ambassador's comments: I am deeply appreciative of Admiral Frost visit which has been more helpful. It was not only a real personal pleasure to have him here. Admiral Frost himself has made real contribution in terms of personal relations and developing confidence of General Nasution and other important military figures that US genuinely exploring ways and means of helping Indonesian situation. His visit also has tended to allay suspicion US Navy directly involved in aid to rebels. He has accomplished much in short visit.

As clear from above message, Admiral Frost has independently reached conclusion already reached by me that General Nasution and army represent majority in unlocking door to solution Indonesian problem. Interesting observation made by Admiral Frost on way to airport was strong impression of complete lack indication any Indonesians desire to get rid of President Sukarno. Control of him within democratic framework, not elimination, has been attitude throughout conversations. Admiral Frost departed with feeling Sukarno was still symbol of independence and should be regarded by US as fact of life in this situation.

Also on way to airport, Admiral Frost pithily remarked he was convinced "Nasution is reason we are still in ball game." Admiral's final observation was that as Yankee visitor in Djakarta, he felt a little like a Russian must feel visiting Washington.

In our discussions prior departure, we both shared great sense of urgency in moving off dead center and giving Nasution some positive tangible evidence of our willingness to back him.

During visit, Indonesian Army also indicated preparedness send mission to Washington or anywhere else to discuss implementation of my approach to Djuanda and Nasution and set forth frankly position of army in current difficult situation. Acceptance of this suggestion might be way of moving ahead promptly on arms for army without immediate commitment or necessity for shipment until resolution conflict. However, should this suggestion be adopted, we must recognize we have crossed Rubicon because such mission could not return empty-handed. To avoid PKI exploitation, fact of mission should be held confidential, Nasution stressed.

In conversation with Admiral via Lt. Colonel Sukendro, Nasution also emphasized vital importance keeping his plans secret. Admiral was not only first foreigner but first one out of family with whom we had shared his program. Even cabinet had not been taken completely into his confidence.

If any of this got back to Indonesians via US channels, this could be fatal to mutual objectives.

Jones

90.   Telegram CX–158 From the Army Attaché in Indonesia (Cole) to the Department of the Army

Djarkarta, May 12, 1958, 1:20 p.m.

[Source: Department of State, Central Files, 756D.00/5–1258. Secret; Niact. 4 pages of source text not declassified.]

91.   Telegram From the Embassy in Indonesia to the Department of State

Djakarta, May 12, 1958, 5 p.m.

4175. Department pass AFCIN–1A1, ACSI, CNO, CINCPAC for POLAD. For Robertson from Jones. Reference: ARMA CX 158.[1] Situation has now developed to point where I believe we must move decisively and immediately to prevent fragmentation of Indonesia, jeopardy to US policy through fight with Indonesia in UN, possible break of relations, and Java alignment with Soviet bloc.

Following is my understanding of our objective, basic elements of present situation as of today, and recommended course of action:

The objective: An independent, politically stable, economically sound unified, anti-Communist Indonesia.

Present situation:

1.   A military stalemate now exists in sense that the GOI cannot subdue the rebels if latter continue to enjoy foreign support. Conversely, rebels cannot achieve a military victory over the GOI unless rebels receive massive foreign support.

2.   If fight increases in tempo, more Soviet bloc aid, "technicians" and finally "volunteers" will be accepted by GOI and rebels will call for more "volunteers" and aid from the West. Each side will damage other with no progress towards US objective.

3.   Under above circumstances:

Source: Department of State, Central Files, 756D.00/5–1258. Top Secret; Niact; Limit Distribution.

[1] Document 90.

(A) Soviet bloc will become established solidly as ally of GOI and US will be regarded as enemy by majority of Indonesians.

(B) In UN GOI will brand US as an aggressor and debate with evidence supplied by GOI (see ARMA reftel) will have most serious repercussions on US foreign policy and seriously damage our position in Asia.

(C) GOI Cabinet has already debated breaking relations with US and probably will do so if military fight is intensified with continuing foreign support to rebels.

4. I believe above deterioration US position can be avoided if we act promptly. I think elements exist in present situation which can be exploited to resolve current impasse and turn tide in new direction.

5. These elements are:

(A) GOI–rebel conflict is not a fight between Communists and anti-Communists. Both GOI Army and rebels are anti-Communist.

(B) Bulk of GOI Army are sympathetic to rebel political objectives although opposed to rebel military defections.

(C) Rebel movement in its inception has primary goal of forcing political changes, not destroying military strength of GOI.

(D) Both GOI Army and rebels share US desire for a unified, democratic, independent non-Communist oriented Indonesia.

6. Successful negotiation between GOI Army and rebels on initiative of either side is now apparently impossible after failure Andi Jusuf compromise attempt (ARMA reftel). It is evident compromise becomes more difficult as lines become more sharply drawn and personal bitterness increases.

7. Since military situation is at an impasse, and since neither side can prevail without outside help, US presumably now holds balance of power to settle issue in our favor if our power is applied before Soviets induce GOI abandon West and side with Communists.

8. This balance power can be applied by exerting immediate pressure and inducements on both GOI and rebels in following recommended steps to be taken:

(A) Inform Colonel Kawilarang and General Nasution immediately through attaché channel that US believes fighting should cease and that this is in best interest Indo and US. Tell them first steps are to stop rebel bombings, and GOI build up against Celebes.

(B) Offer unofficial US mediation to both commanders and then ascertain their respective minimum terms for settlement of military and political differences.

(C) Compare Nasution and Kawilarang terms and decide what we consider equitable basis agreement, rejecting unreasonable demands from either side.

(D) Inform Kawilarang US will exercise its full influence to eliminate rebels support unless he agrees to adjusted terms.

(E) Inform Nasution if he will agree to adjusted terms US will furnish him immediately military, economic and political support, provided he follows through his proposed plan to: (1) settle military differences with rebels and unify army; (2) bring about cabinet changes eliminating leftists; (3) exercise controls over Communists.

9. I believe exercise of our power and influence along above lines has fair chance to succeed. In any event, I believe that it is worth real try and that our efforts would be understood by both sides and might stave off imminent danger of fast GOI slide into Soviet bloc orbit.

10. I continue to urge strongly that Secretary make some public statement along lines earlier recommended to demonstrate US sincerity in last week's démarche. Suspicion that US does not mean what it says here is apparent on all sides. "US Ambassador tells us one thing but we hear no echo of his words in Washington" is way one Indo put it. They cannot understand this silence. British and Australian Ambassadors concur in my view voice from Washington needs to be heard unless value last week's détente be lost. If above recommendations are adopted, it is important approach Nasution in atmosphere in which he is convinced we are honestly attempting to help him and not merely playing rebel game.

11. If Department agrees above courses of action are worth undertaking, they must be pursued quickly. We have bought a little time but not much. It is essential to get off dead center. I hope I may be authorized immediately to approach General Nasution through attachés and someone must approach Kawilarang in Manila. I suggest attachés make initial approach to Nasution through deputy or assistant and that if reaction favorable, I follow up with Djuanda and Nasution. Advise soonest. Admiral Frost and attachés [less than 1 line of source text not declassified] concur.

Jones

92.   Telegram From the Department of State to the Embassy in Indonesia

Washington, May 13, 1958, 10:10 p.m.

3300. Your 4175.[1] From your recent messages it appears that General Nasution and Prime Minister Djuanda feel that until there has been cessation to the activities of the dissidents it will not be possible for them to bring about the contemplated changes in the Cabinet or to take action against the Communists and that in fact a military stalemate exists. This being the case it would appear that the best course of action would be for cessation of military activities in order to permit the anti-Communist elements in Djakarta to take the contemplated steps in attainment their objectives which in essence are the same as those of the dissidents.

In addition to presenting the verbal statement (Deptel 3301)[2] you should also explore with General Nasution (or Djuanda, in your discretion) the possibility of a cease-fire during which Nasution would be in a position to take such action as he contemplates. As we see it events could follow in approximately this order:

1. If General Nasution agrees to a cease fire the Secretary at a press conference could make a statement along the lines suggested by Foreign Minister Subandrio to the effect that the U.S. Government hopes that a settlement of the rebellion will be brought about soon and peace and stability restored to the area and suggesting at the same time that both parties agree to a cease-fire.

2. It is hoped General Nasution and Sumual would then reply openly to the Secretary's suggestion accepting a cease-fire and also undertaking that during the cease-fire period there would be no build-up by either side. We have no assurance that Sumual would accept a cease-fire, but believe it worth a try.

3. During the cease-fire period Nasution would take such action as he contemplates to bring about a change in the Cabinet and against the Communists.

4. General Nasution should be told that if effective action is taken against the Communists he can be assured of receiving U.S. military and economic support. You should reiterate that a token shipment of military equipment totaling approximately $7 million could be made on

---

Source: Department of State, Central Files, 756D.00/5–1258. Top Secret; Niact; Limit Distribution. Drafted by Mein, cleared with Parsons and Robertson, and approved by Dulles. Repeated to CINCPAC.

[1] Document 91.

[2] Document 93.

short order and that in addition we would be prepared to assist in other fields such as shipping, civil aviation, training in Service Schools.

5. Once action had been taken against the Communists we would hope that the two parties to the present struggle would seek an amicable settlement of their differences. We assume this would be possible since it would appear to us that the objectives of the dissidents and of Nasution and the Army and other anti-Communists on Java is the same, that is, to stop the Communists in Indonesia.

FYI: The Secretary will probably not have a press conference before Tuesday [3] next week. We hope it would be possible to conduct the necessary discussions in Djakarta in time for a statement to be made by him at that time assuming of course Nasution accepts the suggestion. In view of the seriousness of the situation however we believe that we should move as expeditiously as possible.

Dulles

---

[3] May 20.

---

93.   **Telegram From the Department of State to the Embassy in Indonesia**

Washington, May 13, 1958, 10:11 p.m.

3301. From previous messages reporting your conversations with Djuanda, Subandrio and Nasution, not clear what specific action government or Nasution intends take against Communists or whether what they say is more than talk. It would appear that they wish some definite action by us without at the same time taking concrete measure to check the rising tide of Communist influence. We are also not clear what you mean by "Nasution plan" in these messages.

You are, however, authorized to speak along following lines, preferably to Sukarno himself, after previously informing in your discretion

---

Source: Department of State, Central Files, 756D.00/5–1358. Top Secret; Niact; Limit Distribution. Drafted by Mein and Dulles, initialed for Robertson by Parsons, and approved by Dulles. Repeated to CINCPAC for POLAD.

Djunda, Subandrio and Nasution of your purpose. Outline of verbal statement follows:

U.S. policy toward Indonesia proceeds from the premise that it should be a vigorous independent member of the society of free nations. This policy led us to give support to the desire of the Indonesians for independence. Our policy in this respect has never wavered and under it we have given moral, political and economic support to the Government of Indonesia.

We have, however, become deeply concerned at the growing influence and ambitions of the Communist Party in Indonesia. We are convinced that here as elsewhere the Communist Party is an instrument of International Communism, and that it takes its direction from Moscow. The recent statement by Mr. Nehru that the Communist Party in India is guided from without applies equally to the Communist Party in Indonesia. The influence of that party, coupled with the large degree of Indonesian military dependence, both in terms of equipment and technicians on the Soviet bloc, cannot but cause deep concern to all who had such high hopes for Indonesia as a truly independent nation. It has been demonstrated time and again, most recently by Soviet action in Hungary, and by its present policy toward Yugoslavia, that it is intolerant of genuine independence if it is able, directly or indirectly, to impose its will.

This situation is inevitably of deep concern to peoples of the free world who are in close proximity to Indonesia. This vast archipelago, projecting from the Indian Ocean to the Western Pacific, is geographically close to many free countries, the peoples of which cannot but have deep concern lest there be a militant Communist regime in their very midst.

The Government of Indonesia complains that a few people from the surrounding areas are as individuals helping elements within Indonesia who are in rebellion against the Communist trend to which we allude. No one could realistically expect that Indonesia should be moved into the Sino-Soviet orbit with the total good will and acquiescence of all the neighboring peoples who would be greatly endangered thereby. There is no rule of international law to stop this.

The United States Government itself has exercised the greatest circumspection in this matter. It is not possible for us to control the activities of all Americans, some of whom are "soldiers of fortune" and interested in freedom, and there is no international obligation on our part to do so. If there are any, the number must be insignificant and the rumors of large participation by Americans are wholly without basis in fact. We have to this date ignored repeated pleas by the rebels that we recognize their belligerent status.

We suggest that the Indonesian Government must realistically recognize it as a fact that there cannot but be at least a minimum of reaction on the part of all those, Indonesians and neighbors of Indonesia, who see in rising Communist influence the prospect of alien domination, so long as the Central Government seems to be moving in a Communist direction.

If the Government takes definite measures for the elimination of the Communist threat which would in itself greatly enhance the prospects for a peaceful settlement of the present struggle, we would use full extent of our influence everywhere including our influence with neighboring states to try to compose the situation which now threatens to disrupt the normal life of the Indonesian Republic. Furthermore, under those conditions, the United States would be prepared to extend substantial economic aid, and such military aid as would seem appropriate to maintain internal order as against any Communist subversive threat.

The United States seeks for itself nothing whatsoever from Indonesia other than that it should be a genuinely independent nation. We are deeply distressed that events jeopardize that independence and impair the economic prospects of Indonesia, whose people deserve an improving rather than a deteriorating social and economic prospect. We would eagerly welcome knowledge of any concrete measures with which the United States might cooperate, if this be the wish of the Government of Indonesia.

Instructions for talk with Nasution follow separate cable.[1]

Dulles

---

[1] Apparent reference to Document 92. In a telephone conversation with British Foreign Minister Selwyn Lloyd at 12:50 p.m. on May 13, Dulles spoke of "a rather important message we are thinking of sending to Indonesia," referring evidently to Document 92 and telegram 3301. A memorandum of that telephone conversation, prepared by Bernau, reads in part as follows: "The time has probably come to put maximum pressure on for a political settlement. The Sec does not think it will work but no harm in trying. L said he thinks he knows what it is and will agree." (Eisenhower Library, Dulles Papers, General Telephone Conversations)

94.   Memorandum From the Chief of Naval Operations (Burke) to Secretary of State Dulles

Washington, May 13, 1958.

SUBJECT

Indonesia

1. This morning General Twining and I talked over the views I expressed in yesterday's conference in regard to Indonesia.[1]

2. We both feel, and I believe the remainder of the Joint Chiefs of Staff would concur, that the Indonesian situation as of this date presents as favorable an opportunity for the U.S. to influence the turn of affairs as we are likely to get.

3. In summary, my views are:

a. The maximum the rebels can attain by themselves is an independent Celebes government, but, since they have no civilian leadership, even this appears unlikely.

b. [1-1/2 lines of source text not declassified]

c. The recent successes of the rebels in the Celebes have caused elements in the GOI to consider compromise negotiations.

d. The solution to attaining U.S. objectives and keeping the Communists from gaining control of Indonesia is to influence elements of the GOI to establish a communist-free government, control the PKI, and minimize the influence of the Soviets in Indonesia.

e. The Indonesian Army, under Nasution and other leaders, appears to be the only anti-communist element in the GOI which is possibly strong enough to persuade Sukarno to establish a communist-free government.

f. Nasution has stated that his success in bringing about political changes in the Cabinet, moving against the PKI, and solving the developing economic crisis depends on whether or not the U.S. will support him.

g. The U.S. has been reluctant to promise support to Nasution because of his possible lack of ability to deliver and also because of the possibility of trickery.

Source: Department of State, Central Files, 656.56D13/5–1358. Top Secret.

[1] Possibly a reference to a meeting that was held in Dulles' office on May 12 at 4:19 p.m. According to Dulles' Appointment Book, the Secretary, Robertson, Mein, Arneson, Herter, Reams, Allen Dulles, Cabell, Ulmer, and Irwin met to discuss Indonesia. (Eisenhower Library, Dulles Papers, Dulles Appointment Book, 1958–59) No record of the meeting has been found.

h. It is my opinion that although an approach to Nasution might very well fail, he represents the only means available to the U.S. for influencing the GOI. Therefore, I believe that it would be profitable for Ambassador Jones to approach Nasution with a statement that the U.S. could not be expected to support the Indonesian government unless it were assured that the GOI would discontinue its trend towards communism. Specifically, the U.S. would expect Nasution to bring about:

(1) Negotiated settlement with the rebels.
(2) Cabinet changes eliminating all leftists.
(3) Exercise of control over the PKI.

i. Perhaps Nasution could be persuaded to move before actually receiving other than a general promise that the U.S. would support an anti-communist government.

j. Should Nasution insist upon specific support before he moves, it is my opinion that the Ambassador could promise such support including specific funds and specific military aid as listed in the Token Military Aid Program for Indonesia.

k. If an approach is made to Sukarno, I believe that, because of his wavering and susceptibility to communist control, he should be made fully aware that the U.S. will support the GOI on the basis that Nasution and the Army are able to control the communist elements.

Very respectfully,

Arleigh Burke

95.   Memorandum of Conversation

Washington, May 13, 1958.

SUBJECT

West New Guinea: "Denial of U.P. Report from Copenhagen"

PARTICIPANTS

Dr. J.H. van Roijen, Ambassador of the Netherlands
Mr. David Ketel, First Secretary, Embassy of the Netherlands
The Secretary
FE—Mr. Robertson
EUR—Mr. Jandrey
WE—Mr. Cameron

Ambassador van Roijen opened the conversation by expressing his appreciation for the opportunity of seeing the Secretary so soon after his return from the NATO Meeting in Copenhagen. The Ambassador explained that Foreign Minister Luns had asked him to express urgently to the Secretary the Dutch Government's concern at the effect in Indonesia of the denial of the UP story from Copenhagen which had reported the Secretary to have said at the NATO Meeting that an Indonesian attack on West New Guinea would have most serious consequences for Southeast Asia and the Western Alliance. The Dutch Government feared that the Indonesian Government and military would interpret this denial to mean that the United States would be indifferent to such an attack. The Secretary replied that when he had considered the problem of denying the UP story he had had very much in mind the possibility that the Indonesians might place such an interpretation on the denial. He had, therefore, instructed the Department that the story be denied in such a fashion that the Indonesians could not draw this inference. He was satisfied that this had been done. He did not believe that the Indonesians were under any illusions about our position. They were aware of the fact that the United States opposed the use of force for the resolution of differences. In this respect he believed that the situation was being handled as the Dutch would want. Whatever the Indonesians may say publicly, they know that the United States would not be indifferent to the use of force against West New Guinea.

The Secretary recalled that the possibility of an Indonesian attack on New Guinea had been mentioned in the corridors at Copenhagen in a brief exchange between him and Foreign Minister Luns.[1] The Secretary

---

Source: Department of State, Central Files, 656C.56D/5–1358. Confidential. Drafted by Cameron.

[1] See Document 82.

said that he had jokingly remarked that it might perhaps be a good thing if Indonesia should try to attack West New Guinea. Foreign Minister Luns replied perhaps so, adding in the same vein that the Dutch had proved themselves good soldiers in the past and the Indonesians were still far from successful in demonstrating this capacity.

Ambassador van Roijen said that the Dutch Government, of course, understood that the United States was opposed to the use of force against West New Guinea. Foreign Minister Luns, however, was going before the First Chamber of the Dutch Parliament today to defend the Foreign Office Budget and he expected questions based on the denial of the UP story. He added that there had been considerable public reaction in The Hague and speculation about the possibility that the Indonesians might conclude from the denial that the United States would be indifferent to an attack on West New Guinea.

The Dutch Ambassador and Mr. Ketel left the Secretary's office for several minutes while the following statement which the Secretary drafted was discussed:

"The Netherlands Ambassador called upon the Secretary of State to inquire whether the denial by the United States of the Secretary's alleged statement at the NATO Council Meeting at Copenhagen with reference to West New Guinea meant that the United States would, in fact, be indifferent to an armed attack against West New Guinea. The Secretary said that the United States had no reason to anticipate any such attack. The Secretary went on to affirm that the United States, as its conduct had shown, was dedicated to the principle of the United Nations Charter that situations which might lead to a breach of the peace should be settled by peaceful means and in conformity with the principles of justice and international law."

The Ambassador and Mr. Ketel rejoined the Secretary and he gave them copies of this statement. After studying it the Ambassador said that in all frankness he must point out that he did not believe that the statement would entirely meet Foreign Minister Luns' needs since it did not contain a specific warning to Indonesia against the use of force. The Secretary replied that that was quite true but that the inference could be drawn that we would not be indifferent to the use of force against New Guinea. The Ambassador again said that the absence of a specific warning would make Foreign Minister Luns' task in answering questions in Parliament more difficult. The Secretary replied that the Dutch were in effect asking for us to change our policy and issue a public warning to Indonesia. He recognized Foreign Minister Luns' problem but he said that he would not agree to issue such a warning to Indonesia when we have no reason to anticipate an attack on West New Guinea. It was not good international practice to issue such a warning when there was no evidence to justify it. In addition, the Secretary said that Indonesian Government and military leaders know our position on this question.

They were informed of it, Mr. Robertson remarked, when we refused to sell them arms last November. The Secretary said that we are trying to maintain a position in the area so that elements in Indonesia opposed to communism can take control and unite the people of Indonesia. It would be in our opinion an act of folly to inject at this time the issue of Western New Guinea into the delicate Indonesian situation. If this was done, the Communist versus non-Communist character of the present struggle would be destroyed and the conflicting forces in Indonesia united in an anti-colonial campaign. The danger of increased Communist control would thereby become much greater. If the Communists did gain control the threat would not only be against West New Guinea but against Singapore, Philippines and Australia.

Ambassador van Roijen again returned to the likelihood of questions in Parliament and said that Foreign Minister Luns would be asked whether the United States was in fact indifferent to an attack on West New Guinea. In reply to these questions the Ambassador asked whether the Foreign Minister could say that he was convinced that the United States was opposed to such an attack. The Secretary said that he could not agree to the Foreign Minister's making such a statement.

The Ambassador said that he would transmit the Secretary's statement to the Foreign Minister. He asked what the Secretary had in mind about releasing the statement. The Secretary replied that he thought it might be released immediately after this conversation by the Department's spokesman. It was agreed that in replying to press questions Ambassador van Roijen would say that he had discussed the denial of the UP story with the Secretary and that the Department was releasing a statement. The Ambassador then said that Foreign Minister Luns had requested him to inform the Secretary that neither the Foreign Minister nor Dutch sources had leaked the story. The Secretary commented that because of the great Dutch interest in this problem we had thought it might have been Dutch sources, or press speculation on something which some Dutch source had said. The leak had indeed created a very awkward situation and he appreciated receiving the Foreign Minister's assurances.[2]

---

[2] In telegram 4165 from Djakarta, May 12, Jones reported that, according to UP representatives, Foreign Minister Luns was the source of the UP story, and suggested that Robertson might wish to pass the information to Dulles. (Department of State, Central Files, 656.56D13/5–1258)

96.   Memorandum of Conversation

Washington, May 15, 1958.

SUBJECT

Indonesia

PARTICIPANTS

Sir Harold Caccia, British Ambassador
The Viscount Hood, Minister, British Embassy

The Secretary
Mr. Robertson, Assistant Secretary for Far Eastern Affairs
Mr. Mein, Director, Office of Southwest Pacific Affairs

The Secretary said that in light of developments in Indonesia and the situation facing the dissidents it appeared that this might be the psychological moment when we might be able to get the most by seeking a political solution in Djakarta. General Nasution has made several approaches which would seem to indicate that he feels he might be able to swing the government into taking action against the communist threat. He has indicated, however, that to do so he must first liquidate the rebels. It is necessary, therefore, to find a way to have the two things, cessation of hostilities and anti-communist action, move concurrently, especially since Sukarno may not be a party to these approaches and there is no indication whether he will associate himself with such a solution. It would appear, therefore, that this is the best time to move.

The Secretary said that we are instructing our Ambassador to see Sukarno and to make a statement along the following lines: The Indonesian Government alleges that assistance is being given to the rebels; that he cannot move his country to the communist camp without expecting reaction from the free world and that some of the free peoples are bound to help the rebels; that the only way to avoid that is to stop the trend to communism; that if he takes action to stop this trend we are willing to discuss the allegations with the Philippines, ChiNats, etc; also that if the trend shows any real significance we would then be prepared to give economic and military assistance but only if we were convinced by the actions of the government that such would happen.

The Secretary said that we would also inform Nasution, Djuanda and Subandrio of this approach to President Sukarno with the thought that they might reinforce our position.

Mr. Robertson stated that we were also proposing to the government a cease-fire to give Nasution time to carry out such action as he

Source: Department of State, Central Files, 756D.00/5–1558. Top Secret. Drafted by Mein.

might contemplate against the Communists. Nasution is extremely anxious for some indication of sympathy from the United States.

The Secretary said that it is important that there be no build-up during a cease-fire period if one is accepted, and that such must be a condition to such a proposal. He said the Indonesians must also realize that what is happening in the area is the inevitable counterpart of what they are doing. They cannot expect to turn over their country to communism without something being done about it by the free world.[1]

---

[1] [text not declassified]

---

97. Telegram From the Embassy in Indonesia to the Department of State

Djakarta, May 15, 1958, 1 p.m.

4230. For Assistant Secretary Robertson from Ambassador Jones. Deptels 3300 and 3301.[1] Démarche contained in reference telegrams was seed sown on stony ground, but I believe clarification of GOI attitude brought about thereby can be considered productive. Djuanda made clear (1) GOI was unified in rejection any consideration of negotiation with rebels; (2) principal leaders GOI aware dangers of Communist growth and have moved from talk stage to action stage; (3) reorganization of Cabinet now imminent.

Immediately upon receipt of reference telegrams, I requested appointment with Prime Minister Djuanda and was received at his home at 6:15 p.m. Foreign Minister has been ill for several days so was not present. I instructed ARMA to seek appointment with Nasution so that information would reach him simultaneously.

I presented verbal statement outlined in Deptel 3301 almost verbatim and informed Djuanda that I was planning to see Sukarno to speak to him along same lines. I then explored with Djuanda possibility of a cease-fire along lines contained Deptel 3300.

Source: Department of State, Central Files, 756D.00/5–1558. Top Secret; Niact; Limit Distribution.

[1] Documents 92 and 93.

Before I could complete what I had to say, almost at first mention of words "cease-fire," Prime Minister interrupted and inquired what I meant by "cease-fire". When I explained, he shook his head incredulously and said, "but this would mean negotiating with the rebels. This we could never accept".

I pointed out that both he and General Nasution had emphasized their problem of two-front fight and difficulty of taking positive action against Communists within Java until cessation of military action. This would seem to lead to logical conclusion that less dangerous enemy should be eliminated by peaceful settlement which would permit concentration effort on enemy representing more serious threat to independence of nation. We were not suggesting terms of settlement—that was GOI business. We were simply offering use of US as voice to propose cease-fire.

I referred to Foreign Minister Subandrio's suggestion that Secretary make statement on settlement of rebellion and that if GOI were willing to agree to a cease-fire Secretary would be willing to take initiative in publicly suggesting that both parties agree to cease-fire.

Djuanda rejected this flatly, commenting that there was one thing upon which he, President Sukarno, Suwirjo, head of PNI, and Army were in complete agreement—that was that there would be no negotiations with Indonesian Army officers who had sought foreign assistance in fighting other Indonesians. They were adamant on this point, he said. If GOI negotiated with rebels at this stage, it would be regarded as sign of weakness and blood of Indonesians shed in Sumatra would have been shed in vain, that is, authority of government and Army Headquarters would not have been reestablished. If they had been willing to negotiate they would have negotiated earlier. They certainly would not negotiate now with Colonel Sumual and Colonel Warouw.

We had long discussion of various aspects proposal but he was immovable. Basis of his position was cease-fire must lead to negotiations, GOI would not negotiate. I argued that GOI had insisted rebels in Menado had no popular support. If premise correct and cease-fire obtained, then GOI could simply await inevitable collapse of Sumual–Warouw. Djuanda said if GOI accepted cease-fire and rebels did not, GOI would appear weak. I countered with argument instead sign weakness, moral position of GOI would be greatly strengthened thereby.

I pointed out further that GOI might be risking Indonesian independence in order to carry out policy of crushing rebels. Prime Minister replied hotly, "Not if foreign interventionists stop supporting rebels. We can handle rebels if they do not receive additional foreign assistance. If rebels continue to receive additional foreign assistance then we too shall require additional foreign assistance". If US would not help, they would be forced to go elsewhere.

I again pointed out effect this would almost inevitably have on independence of Indonesia and he said he recognized this only too well.

If US would not help even to extent of discouraging foreign assistance and GOI were faced with necessity of seeking additional aid from Soviet bloc, combination of external pressures from bloc plus internal Communist pressures might conceivably result in loss of independence and Communist Indonesia. He recognized fate of himself and others who were opposed to Communism under those circumstances but, he said, we have taken position from which we cannot withdraw.

This would be great tragedy, he said, particularly since GOI was beginning finally to take positive steps against Communists and adopt course in line with US thinking and was not because of pressures, he emphasized, but because it was right course to take and Indonesian leaders had finally awakened to fact. He summarized recent moves against PKI previously reported (May Day prohibitions, cancellation demonstrations against US, protection US economic interests after Aidit threat, etc.)[2] and said government was continuing to move in this direction as rapidly as possible. Within last three days, for example, he had succeeded in obtaining agreement of President, PNI leadership, and army to reorganization of cabinet which would dissolve ministries headed by Hanafi and Tobing.[3] Sultan of Djogjakarta had finally agreed to enter cabinet but it still remained to be determined which portfolio to take, probably that of Economic Affairs. With this reorganization as first move he hoped that he could induce Hatta to join government at a later stage. He indicated Hatta, while opposing rebellion, would not join Cabinet until military action had ceased because of Hatta's strong views that it never should have been thwarted and that affair could have been settled by negotiation.

Above program should be carried out within matter of days, he hoped. Agreement of NU was only element needed to enable him to

[2] In telegram 4440 from Djakarta, May 28, the Embassy summarized these anti-Communist actions in part as follows:

"1. Prohibition of 'foreign intervention' demonstrations against U.S. Embassy in March 1958 in face of strong leftist propaganda linking U.S. to Sumatran arms drops.

"2. Prohibition of leftist rallies on 1 May and huge anti-intervention mass meeting on 16 May which would have been focused primarily against the U.S. on charge of intervention in Sumatra and North Sulawesi.

"3. Following threat by CP Sec Aidit against U.S. commercial enterprises in telegram to Ambassador, Gen. Nasution announced that army would not tolerate any interference with foreign-owned oil interests and Prime Minister pledged protection to all U.S. interests." (Department of State, Central Files, 611.56D/5–2858)

[3] Ferdinand Lumban Tobing, Minister of Inter-Regional Affairs.

move ahead immediately. Deputy Prime Minister Chalid, head of NU, agreed with program and would attempt to obtain NU concurrence at meeting of NU leaders Thursday and Friday.

Djuanda pleaded for US understanding of his government's position and said if US sincere in desire to help and if we really meant what we said in my earlier statement (last two paragraphs Deptel 3301), there was one thing which his government needed more than anything else at present time—assurance US would do everything in its power to discourage further support to rebels from Philippines and Taiwan. He referred specifically to oil and gas supply from Philippines and Borneo by ship and air to Menado.

He knew, of course, he said, that US had power to influence events in Pacific area from which rebel support derived. Severance of rebel supply lines through US discouragement further aid to rebels he knew was within US capability if we were sincere and really wanted to end conflict. If, as he believed, withdrawal of further foreign support enabled GOI military forces end conflict, outcome, he felt strongly would be in mutual interest US and GOI. Should rebels reach point of being willing surrender, they would, in accordance Indonesian tradition, be treated generously. He thought Sumual, wealthy man now as result personal profit barter transactions during dissidence, would probably go abroad in any event.

While I was talking with Prime Minister, Col Cole (ARMA), was endeavoring to reach General Nasution, but General had previous commitments and Cole was received by Lt. Col. Sukendro at 8 PM. Col. Cole therefore did not cover reftels fully but did outline general idea on which reftels based, touching in exploratory way cease-fire suggestion.[4]

Colonel Sukendro, whom ARMA considers closest staff officer to Nasution in terms personal relations, expressed same view as Djuanda, that anything less than victory over rebels was out of question and that while Army was equally determined to crush rebels and Communists, General Nasution considered rebels must be liquidated to achieve his objectives and he would never consider negotiation with them. Army, however, had already begun to move against Communists within present capability and would do much more when rebel affair wound up. Sukendro expressed same view as Djuanda above that if intervention is stopped, GOI forces capable of rapid elimination of Menado rebels. With US assistance Army there would be in position to bring about changes in Cabinet apparently Sukendro not privy to or not privileged

---

[4] See Document 98.

to reveal what Djuanda told me re prospects imminent Cabinet reorganization and intensified action against PKI.

My comments in telegram immediately following.[5]

Jones

[5] See Document 99.

---

98.   **Telegram From the Army Attaché in Indonesia (Cole) to the Department of the Army**

Djakarta, May 15, 1958.

CX 161. Reference: Embtel 4230.[1] After discussing, in general terms, context of Deptels 3300 and 3301[2] with Lt. Colonel Sukendro, authorized spokesman for General Nasution, ARMA is convinced that GOI will not accept any terms involving direct or indirect negotiations with current rebel regime. This is predicated on fact that GOI is now confronted with 4 major problems which must be settled in order listed. First, GOI and army strongly believe that US could use influence to eliminate or reduce outside air and other logistical support to rebels as previously reported. This intervention by so-called "soldiers of fortune" has upset timetable for GOI plans to solve rebel problem, reorganize cabinet favorable to US, and initiation of actions to control PKI influence. Also, Sukendro states that intervention has created adverse public opinion against GOI owing to failure to properly explain matter or take positive action to stop this practice. Second, Sukendro states that GOI policy envisions crushing Menado rebels, probably before taking effective steps toward solving latter two problems. Sukendro strongly indicated that GOI was capable of quick defeat of [garble] foreign support to rebels. Otherwise, he believes this problem will be time consuming and may force GOI to accept active Soviet bloc assistance. Third, Sukendro

---

Source: Department of State, Central Files, 756D.00/5–1558. Secret; Niact. Sent to the Department of the Army for the Army Chief of Staff for Intelligence and the Air Force Chief for Intelligence and repeated to the Department of State, which is the source text.

[1] Document 97.

[2] Documents 92 and 93.

emphasized that GOI plans to bring about changes in cabinet had progressed to point which would permit early completion of move. This, according to source, must be timed so as to take place concurrently or after Menado rebels are defeated, to eliminate possibility of unfavorable reaction from Indonesian public, rebels and PKI. Source realizes that PKI will react but believes GOI forces capable of handling situation. Sukendro mentioned that Sultan of Djogjakarta was definitely included in new cabinet. Fourth, Sukendro stated that army realized PKI threat and indicated that after solving first two problems and receipt of US assistance would be in position to initiate further actions to control such activities. *Comment:* In solving these problems, ARMA feels that if foreign assistance is eliminated, GOI could defeat Menado rebels quickly without outside assistance. Sukendro stated that assistance would be needed to ensure successful implementation of last two problems. Signed Cole.

---

99.   Telegram From the Embassy in Indonesia to the Department of State

Djakarta, May 15, 1958, 6 p.m.

4234. Embtel 4230.[1] *Comment:* In light strong position taken by Djuanda which I am certain reflects President's views, unless Department instructs otherwise, I shall not seek immediate interview with Sukarno to present points embodied Deptel 3301.[2] He and Madame Sukarno are lunching with us on May 22 and this may provide opportunity for brief serious conversation. If not I shall ask him for appointment for another talk at which time I can cover these points among others. I also hope that in next press conference, Secretary will feel able take opportunity to say something reassuring to GOI. I have strong impression events here moving in direction favorable US interests and repeat that in my view time has come to give GOI more encouragement. I commented earlier that rebel action had been successful in precipitating issues. I think we can now go farther and say that this precipitation has resulted

---

Source: Department of State, Central Files, 756D.00/5–1558. Secret; Niact. Transmitted in two sections.

[1] Document 97.

[2] Document 93.

in decisions along lines favored by US. In my view we are at turn of tide in events which if seized can lead to gradual realization US objectives.

My discussion with Djuanda (Embtel 4230), Col. Cole's talk with Lt. Col. Sukendro (ARMA CX 161),[3] and information I have reported from various other sources convince me that Sukarno, Djuanda, Subandrio and Nasution are united in conviction GOI can work with US only on following basis:

1. US to exercise its influence to bring about cessation of foreign support to rebels, especially air support.
2. GOI to reorganize Cabinet.
3. GOI to proceed to win military victory over rebels in Menado area.
4. GOI to move against Commies with US military aid supporting GOI forces.
5. GOI economic rehabilitation and development with US support.

You will understand extraordinary difficulty of obtaining clear-cut delineation of above items which stems from Indonesian sensitivity on subject strings to aid and consequent impossibility of setting forth US position to GOI in terms of quid pro quo. However, above appears to be essence of Indonesian attitude.

Points 2, 4, and 5 are in consonance with US objectives, but points 1 and 3 we recognize pose very difficult problems.

If as appears to be case, GOI is determined not to try again to open negotiations with rebels, and now insists on achieving military victory even at cost of accepting greater Commie support, then I believe we face new situation estimate of which might be somewhat as follows:

1. Rebel objectives at inception of revolt were set forth in proclamation reported Embtel 2489,[4] February 11. In summary they encompassed following principal objectives:

(A) Restoration of Government based on constitution.
(B) Elimination of corruption.
(C) New cabinet formed by Hatta and Sultan to operate pending new constitution.
(D) More equitable distribution of revenues contributed by the regions.

2. GOI was not prepared at that time to accept these changes so rebels set up revolutionary Government and GOI launched military action. Now, however, issues have been precipitated by intervening events and GOI appears to be preparing to move in parallel line toward objectives originally set forth by rebels.

---

[3] Document 98.
[4] Not printed. (Department of State, Central Files, 756D.00/2–1158)

3. Time may be ripe, therefore, for reassessment of current rebel objectives. If rebel goals limited to achievement original political objectives, these appear to be in process realization. If, on other hand, rebels now look forward to military victory with foreign support and either complete takeover of GOI Government or fragmentation their country, these objectives would appear neither feasible nor in best US interests because they appear from here almost certain to involve swing of Java into Communist orbit.

4. If above reasoning sound, it would appear time has arrived to put brakes on rebel military effort. Since rebel movement has apparently exerted leverage sufficient to bring about GOI decision, it has served constructive purpose but I believe this is as far as it can go without pushing GOI to breaking point and alignment with Soviet bloc.

In view above considerations and uncompromising rejection US démarche on subject cease-fire by Djuanda which was, however, softened by news GOI seriously moving toward reorganization cabinet. I recommend consideration of following steps:

1. Statement by Secretary at next press conference deploring bombings, expressing hope conflict will soon be concluded and peace and stability restored to area and assuring GOI that US will do what it can to discourage foreign adventurers.

2. Take any steps available to us to slow down further material support for rebels.

3. Arrange if possible approach to rebels to:

(A) Ascertain present objectives, pointing out probably early fulfillment of their primary political objectives.

(B) Convey view of US that point has been reached at which further military action will play into hands of Communists.

(C) Urge rebels to move toward peaceful settlement of dispute.

I am convinced it is in US interest to get this conflict settled soonest. It has served its purpose and continuance of fighting will, in my view, not serve US interests. It is clear that GOI will not serve US interests.[sic] It is clear that GOI will not make first overt move and covert move on their part was flatly rejected (ARMA CX–158, May 12).[5] It would seem, therefore, that next step should be to induce rebels to make covert overtures toward settlement.

Jones

---

[5] Document 90.

100.   Telegram From the Embassy in Indonesia to the Department of State

Djakarta, May 16, 1958, 7 p.m.

4254. Department pass AFCIN–1A1, ACSI, CNO. Department pass CINCPAC. CINCPAC also for POLAD. For Assistant Secretary Robertson from Jones. In addition to seeking solution to basic problems considered in Embtel 4234,[1] I believe we can make substantial progress if we do certain things now within present framework.

I believe we can progressively accelerate number and effectiveness of GOI anti-Commie moves by adopting a policy of encouraging each anti-Commie move they make. Example: Forceful anti-Commie step was taken by army at our request to cancel large "anti-interventionist rally" scheduled today. Rally was cancelled yesterday despite fact that almost all political parties had agreed to participate and after notices were sent to employers ordering them to allow employees to leave their jobs to attend. Cancellation was not easy for army and demonstrated their power versus politicians.

I think we should follow up by letting GOI know that we not only appreciate army action but desire to show our approval in concrete form. (A) We should provide political support by statement by Secretary recommended my telegram 4234; (B) military support could include Department Defense invitation Indo military mission proceed US soonest accordance Embtel 4154;[2] (C) economic support could be Sumatra highway construction project, diesel electric project outlined in ICATO 1092[3] of May 2, and the Jap yen loan (TOICA 1198).[4] These three are mainly outer island projects which have no military significance and can be delayed later in case we cared to drag our feet. Meantime, approval along above lines would give me a valuable psychological weapon.

By above "carrot" technique we can focus attention, particularly of army, on what we are most interested in—anti-Commie action. If they are rewarded after they make an effective move, it will not smack of "quid pro quo" or "test rings" which are psychologically distasteful to Indos, but will illustrate to them what is the key that unlocks American policy.

Source: Department of State, Central Files, 756D.00/5–1658. Top Secret; Niact; Limit Distribution.

[1] Document 99.

[2] Document 89.

[3] Not printed. (Washington National Records Center, ICA Files: FRC 59 A 2458)

[4] Not printed. (*Ibid.*)

I fully understand our policy to date of denying any kind of support to GOI in order to build up pressure for change of government. At same time I think it is now necessary for us to unbend a little as suggested in this telegram. I do not recommend opening dam wide because this would relieve pressure we still need, but opening crack on above basis will definitely help at this particular moment.

Jones

---

101.   Telegram From the Embassy in Indonesia to the Department of State

Djakarta, May 17, 1958, 7 p.m.

4266. CINCPAC also for POLAD. For Assistant Secretary Robertson from Ambassador Jones. Foreign Minister summoned me this morning to inform me that battalion of Chinese troops had landed in Sulawesi to fight with rebels. I said I found this hard to believe and inquired how they got there. Foreign Minister said he believed they had arrived by corvette but had no further details. He took very serious view of this, pointing out difficulty of resisting pressure for foreign volunteers on behalf GOI under circumstances this kind.

He indicated that this and other evidence of continued build-up rebel forces combined with my démarche to Prime Minister May 15 (Embtel 4230)[1] had convinced Indonesian Government that there had been considerable retrogression in US position since my original exploration of arms subject of May 7 (Embtel 4112).[2] I denied that this was case, I pointed out PL 480 rice had been authorized, arms shipment under active exploration, and finally, that démarche referred to was exploration in attempt to help them solve problem. Foreign Minister asked me for summary of what I had told Djuanda. I reviewed conversation fully. When I had finished, he said he appreciated motives, but that cease-fire would imply recognition rebel regime or at least willingness to negotiate and this they would never consider.

Source: Department of State, Central Files, 756D.00/5–1758. Secret; Niact; Limit Distribution. Transmitted in two sections and also sent to CINCPAC.

[1] Document 97.

[2] Document 84.

Djuanda was terribly discouraged and was talking of resigning, he said. If Prime Minister took this step, reorganization of government would move in opposite direction than that desired by US. Djuanda felt that he was just reaching point of success in obtaining reorganization of government (NU had yesterday agreed to program reported Embtel 4230, paragraph 12) but that combination foregoing events plus bombing of Ambon market place last Sunday had given him feeling US not interested in helping. Bomber hit market place at most crowded time when people were shopping and on their way to church (Ambon being Christian) and more than 100 civilians had been killed. Ambonese were now violently bitter against both US and Menadonese.

Meanwhile, he pointed out, PKI was hammering away on slogan—"It is war, war against foreign country." Almost every day that went by brought new evidence which they could exploit.

Foreign Minister pleaded for some positive gesture from US soonest. At moment moral support more than material support was required. Doubt of US intentions was growing on all sides. Djuanda government could not last much longer under present circumstances, he said. Its policy of discussions with us in attempt to obtain US assistance in discouraging foreign interference on side of rebels was certain to be branded as failure in near future. Should this happen, open attack on US would follow almost inevitably and acceptance of volunteers from Soviet bloc. Conviction was also growing in Djakarta, he said, that US Government was determined to cause Djuanda cabinet to fall. He knew reorganization of cabinet represented US desire, but he and Djuanda had hoped that US pressure was not directed at Djuanda as Prime Minister. He also thought that if it were, US was making grave mistake.

I assured him that this was certainly not the case. As he aware I had great confidence in Djuanda and was convinced he was man of integrity and sincerity of purpose, that he was known in US and that I could categorically deny that US policy was directed at liquidation Djuanda leadership.

If we wanted to help instead of hurt, then, Foreign Minister said, and assist Prime Minister in his desire to reorganize cabinet most helpful thing we could do would be for Secretary to make statement clearly indicating that US was willing to let Indonesian Government handle rebellion as internal affair. Public statement was urgently needed to reassure GOI that US was doing what it could to discourage foreign aid to rebels and was willing to let GOI fight it out and defeat rebels if such were outcome.

Comment: It is self-evident from above pressure is mounting here. Exact moment to ease up on our side is delicate decision but as I have indicated in Embtels 4234 and 4254,[3] I believe that moment has arrived. Unless some positive evidence of US good will is forthcoming soon, I think we may anticipate explosion in near future which almost certain to be deleterious to US interests and objectives.

I think, for example, resignation of Djuanda would be contrary to US interest. It is difficult to know how seriously to take this possibility. Djuanda has threatened to resign before but had been holding on, anticipating possibility of ultimately getting Hatta, for whom he is willing to step aside, into cabinet. But there is apparently no chance of getting Hatta into cabinet before fight with rebels is over, on basis his own position.

Djuanda then becomes hope of (A) obtaining early reorganization of cabinet to get rid of world [?] elements, Hanafi and weak sister (Tobing) adding Sultan of Djogjakarta as member and (B) ultimate take-over of cabinet by Hatta. I am convinced if Djuanda resigned with lack of US support as contributing factor, alternative will be most unsatisfactory whereas if we can take some action that will be interpreted as favorable to him, I believe we have good chance of progressing toward what we want: action against PKI.

Let me reemphasize that there are no views that I know of in this community—American, British, Australian or anti-Communist Indonesian—in disagreement with idea that it is time for America to make strong positive gesture of support for GOI. My own view is that this can best come in public expression by Secretary, but it should be accompanied by real effort to discourage additional support for rebels and particularly bombing which has roused antagonism of even those elements sympathetic rebel objectives.[4]

Jones

---

[3] Documents 99 and 100.

[4] In telegram 3339 to Djakarta, May 17, the Department informed the Embassy that it could not confirm that Chinese troops landed in Sulawesi nor was there any indication that such a movement was underway. (Department of State, Central Files, 756D.00/5–1758)

In telegram 4292 from Djakarta, May 19, Jones informed Robertson that he concurred that the Indonesian Government was apparently adamant against any open negotiations with the rebels, but noted that it had made covert approaches in the past. Consequently, Jones recommended that if General Kawilarang could be induced to contact General Gatot Subroto in Tokyo where both would be attending the Asian Games, "this would enable exploration possible settlement." (*Ibid.*, 756D.00/5–1958)

102. Telegram From the Department of State to the Embassy in Indonesia

Washington, May 17, 1958, 2:03 p.m.

3335. Pass CINCPAC for POLAD. Embtels 4230,[1] 4235,[2] 4254.[3] You should inform Djuanda that we will explore with Philippine and GRC governments Indonesian Government's allegations that their nationals are assisting and their territory is being used in support of rebels which those governments have repeatedly denied. You should point out however that as in case US, Philippine and GRC Governments may have difficulty in controlling actions their nationals abroad. You should also reiterate that the situation in Indonesia is inevitably of deep concern to peoples of free world who are in close proximity to Indonesia and that no one could realistically expect that Indonesia should be moved into Sino-Soviet orbit with the total good will and acquiescence of all the neighboring peoples who would be greatly endangered thereby. Indonesian Government should therefore realistically recognize it as a fact that there cannot but be at least a minimum of reaction on the part of all those, Indonesians and neighbors of Indonesia, who see in rising Communist influence the prospect of alien domination, and that the best way to avoid assistance by few people in surrounding areas who may be assisting rebels is for Indonesian Government to eliminate reasons for their action by taking steps against internal Communist threat. (Deptel 3301)[4]

With specific reference to several points raised in your messages:

1. You should make points in Deptel 3301 to Sukarno at early opportune moment unless you perceive objection.
2. Statement by Secretary at press conference still under consideration. Whether Secretary makes statement may well depend on developments next few days.
3. Regarding approach to rebels with suggestion they seek settlement conflict there would appear be no reason why an approach by them would be likely to succeed in view of adamant position taken by government that it will not negotiate with rebels. If you have reason believe government's attitude would be different we will be glad reconsider.

Source: Department of State, Central Files, 756D.00/5–1858. Top Secret; Niact; Limit Distribution. Drafted by Mein, cleared in draft with Herter, and approved by Robertson.

[1] Document 97.

[2] Telegram 4235, May 12, is about an unrelated matter; the reference is an apparent mistake.

[3] Document 100.

[4] Document 93.

4. You should express to Djuanda and Army appreciation for action taken in canceling "anti-intervention rally" scheduled for yesterday.

5. We will explore question of military mission (Embtel 4154)[5] in light developments in Indonesia.

6. In line suggestion your tel 4254 that we show our approval for recent action taken by Army and Government we are:

> a) granting license requests which have been pending for several months;
> b) proceeding with action on Sumatra highway construction and diesel electrical projects, and;
> c) issuing instructions to you for implementation Japanese yen loan.

7. We are not making any announcement regarding these steps. Issuance licenses will of course become immediately known to Indonesians but we leave to you how and when Djuanda, Subandrio and Nasution should be informed of yen loan. Until you receive further instructions from us which we will attempt get out soon as possible you should not discuss with Indonesians highway and diesel projects. Indonesians may not be aware however that these projects have been held up for other than technical reasons. You may wish also reiterate items paragraph 4 of Deptel 3300.[6]

Dulles

---

[5] Document 89.

[6] Document 92. In telegram 4298 from Djakarta, May 19, Jones reported that he conveyed the contents of telegram 3335 to Subandrio at the Foreign Minister's home that evening. The telegram read in part as follows: "I covered contents reftel thoroughly insofar as appropriate, emphasizing responsiveness my Government to earlier specific requests was act of faith based upon our confidence in intentions of GOI to move in direction we considered sound. Foreign Minister responded with expression of appreciation, stressing that most important things in what I had told him was that it represented expression of confidence in GOI and belief in sincerity and determination of its leadership." (Department of State, Central Files, 756D.00/5–1958) See Supplement.

103.   Memorandum of Conversation

Washington, May 18, 1958, 5:30 p.m.

PARTICIPANTS

Allen W. Dulles   The Secretary
General Cabell
[name not declassified]

We discussed the situation in Indonesia and report of an air battle that had occurred with a loss of one rebel plane with two crewmen[1] and the probable destruction of three or four government planes.[2] There was apparently a large government build-up and considerable pressure to get authority to strike it again.

I expressed the view that we should use our influence to prevent this, as I could not see in the long run any possibility of this being a winning course and either the political move must succeed or we would have to consider backing more overtly the anti-Communist elements in the neighborhood. [2-1/2 lines of source text not declassified]

Source: Department of State, Secretary's Memoranda of Conversation: Lot 64 D 199. Secret. This meeting took place at Secretary Dulles' residence.

[1] American flier Allen Pope was one of the two crewmen shot down and captured by Indonesian Government troops on May 18. He was shot down while flying a bombing mission for the rebels over Ambon.

[2] On May 19 Secretary of State Dulles discussed the capture of Allen Pope in separate telephone conversations with Cabell, Robertson, and Allen Dulles. (Memoranda of telephone conversations, prepared in the Secretary of State's office; Eisenhower Library, Dulles Papers, General Telephone Conversations)

104.   Memorandum From the Chief of Naval Operations (Burke) to the Assistant Secretary of State for Far Eastern Affairs (Robertson)

Washington, May 20, 1958.

SUBJECT

Indonesia

1. Following is a quotation of a message received from Admiral Stump this date.

"There follows report of my first conversations with Indonesian Delegation and some random impressions: Immediately after arriving Lenqe Baguio, Subroto and Sukendro made it known they wanted to have private interview to which I agreed and saw them for 2 hours Sunday afternoon with their interpreter Sunario who speaks excellent English.[1] I am keeping memoranda of conversations for later dispatch and will only pass highlights now.

1. It seems quite obvious that Sukendro is the spokesman and gives impression of sincerity and friendliness.

2. Subroto nodded assent to all that was said but took very little part in the interview.

3. Sunario although allegedly interpreter is bright mop [and?] glib and does not hesitate to throw in his own opinions and ideas.

4. There is no doubt that they have come to this demonstration to talk and have already indicated to some of my staff that they want to discuss matters further.

5. On the situation in Indonesia Sukendro says that they want to draw closer to the United States, and take steps to rid government of commies and isolate Sukarno from leftist advisers. They stress this will take time and imply that we must have patience in bringing this about for to be precipitous would invite failure. Their plan involves using Sukarno but controlling him.

6. They emphasize that everything depends upon an early cessation of rebel activities.

7. They indicate that a few of dissident leaders could be forgiven but feel very bitter toward Lubis. They refer to Sjafrudden as patriot.

Comment: Their presentation thus far could equally be explained as genuine attempt at reproachment with us or as clever device to affect

---

Source: Department of State, Central Files, 798.00/5–2058. Secret.

[1] These Indonesian military officials were in the Philippines for the U.S. weapons demonstration.

dissident operations. I and my staff will try to assess this more accurately as time goes on. Sukendro has asked for special arrangement to go to Manila today which may mean he wants to send out some messages through his embassy. I would appreciate being kept informed of anything from Djakarta or Washington that would assist my discussions with these men this week. Signed Adm Stump."

2. I think this meeting between Adm Stump and representatives of Indonesia attending the Weapons Demonstration will provide Adm Stump with an excellent opportunity to judge the future trend in Indonesian affairs. I also think it important that we give Adm Stump every bit of counsel possible in order that he can make the most of the opportunity to talk with these people and to elicit from them information which will help us plan our future actions vis-à-vis Indonesia.

3. I concur with the views expressed by Adm Stump above. I would appreciate your reactions. We stand ready to assist in any manner possible.

Arleigh

105.   Telegram From the Embassy in Indonesia to the Department of State

Djakarta, May 20, 1958, 5 p.m.

4301. For Assistant Secretary Robertson from Ambassador Jones. Deptel 3343.[1] I am more and more convinced most important single step US can take in present situation is public statement sympathetic to GOI by Secretary (or President). I cannot emphasize too strongly importance of official statement being made in Washington. Everybody here is

---

Source: Department of State, Central Files, 756D.00/5–2058. Top Secret; Niact; Limit Distribution.

[1] Telegram 3343, May 18, informed Jones that the Department regretted the bombings at Amboina just as Jones was exploring the situation further and was pursuing the matter as expressed in telegram 3335 (Document 102). Jones was also informed that at the Secretary's upcoming press conference he is considering making "statement along lines suggested by Subandrio Embtel 4266 [Document 101]." (Department of State, Central Files, 756D.00/5–1858)

hanging on hope of favorable statement from Secretary and Djuanda said so explicitly at reception this morning (Embtel 4300).[2] Forthright statement now on part US can be, I believe, turning point in US-Indonesian relations and serve concomitantly to weaken Indonesian ties with Soviet bloc. In terms of maximum usefulness here, it seems clear from Indonesian reactions during conversations in past few days that strong point to be made in statement is US support for GOI and US willingness to intercede in effort to put a stop to bombings and foreign aid to rebels. At minimum statement should include following:

1. Strong expression of concern over continuing bloodshed combined with expression of hope and confidence conflict will soon be concluded and peace and stability restored to area.
2. US view GOI rebellion is internal affair and reassurance to GOI that US is doing what it can to discourage foreign adventurers and aid to rebels.
3. Unequivocal [indication?] of US good will toward and active support for GOI in efforts to maintain independence and national integrity.

At this stage I trust no conditions will be stated or implied since Indonesian sensitivity is so great on this point, even implication of conditions would largely destroy value of statement.[3]

Jones

---

[2] Telegram 4300, May 20, reported that President Sukarno delivered a speech that day for National Reawakening Day that was "more favorable to US than any previously delivered since rebellion." (Ibid., 756D.00/5–2058) See Supplement.

[3] During his May 20 press conference Dulles stated that the United States believes "that the situation can be and should be dealt with as an Indonesian matter by the Indonesians without intrusion from without, and we hope that there will be quickly restored peace and stability in the Indonesian Republic." For text of his remarks, see Department of State Bulletin, June 9, 1958, pp. 945–946.

According to telegram 4323 from Djakarta, May 22, Foreign Minister Subandrio told the press on May 21, after meeting with Prime Minister Djuanda, that Dulles' statement "can be seen as step forward if his words are to be taken as affirmation of U.S. Government's attitude reflecting its full confidence in Indonesian Government's ability to deal with present situation in interests of and for good of Indonesian people themselves. Indonesian Government certainly hopes for an observance of Dulles' statement so that there will be no more misgivings on part of Indonesian people as to U.S. Government's attitude toward rebels." (Department of State, Central Files, 756D.00/5–2258)

---

106.   Editorial Note

On May 22 the United States and Indonesia concluded an agreement by which the United States agreed to provide Indonesia with 35,000 tons of surplus rice, worth approximately $5.5 million, under Public Law 480. The agreement was effected by an exchange of notes in

Djakarta May 22 between Ambassador Jones and Foreign Minister Subandrio. For text of the agreement, see 9 UST 1083. The Embassy reported on the signing ceremony in telegram 4339 from Djakarta, May 22. (Department of State, Central Files, 611.56D/5–2258) See Supplement.

Following the ceremony at the Foreign Office concluding the rice agreement, President Sukarno, Foreign Minister Subandrio and other Indonesians lunched with Ambassador Jones at his residence. Jones reported that Sukarno was "in warm, expansive mood, joking throughout luncheon." Responding to Jones' toast, Sukarno said that "he wanted to speak from the heart" about his friendship with Americans and his desire for closer U.S.-Indonesian relations. (Telegram 4341 from Djakarta, May 22; Department of State, Central Files, 611.56D/5–2258) See Supplement. Jones discussed his luncheon engagement with Sukarno in *Indonesia: The Possible Dream*, page 150.

---

107. Memorandum of Conversation

Washington, May 22, 1958.

SUBJECT

Indonesian Situation

PARTICIPANTS

Mr. Howard Beale, Australian Ambassador
Mr. M. R. Booker, Counselor, Australian Embassy

The Secretary
Mr. Mein, Director, Office of Southwest Pacific Affairs

The Ambassador stated [*1-1/2 lines of source text not declassified*] that he would like to discuss the current situation. The Secretary said that our basic philosophy had been to encourage the dissidents to a point where they might serve as leverage on the government to reverse the trend toward communism. He said that as a result of this policy many accusations have been made against the United States and many untrue allegations of U.S. involvement have been made by the Indonesian Gov-

---

Source: Department of State, Central Files, 756D.00/5–2258. Top Secret; Limited Distribution. Drafted by Mein.

ernment. It seemed to us now that the operations had been carried to a point where they could no longer be effective without more overt action on our part. Also, there have recently been feelers from Djakarta implying that if we would dissociate ourselves from the dissidents it might be possible for the anti-Communist elements to shift the orientation of the government away from communism. It is doubtful that such an approach will succeed and more likely that they are playing a come-on game to put a stop to any support to the rebels. It is not a question of intentional misleading on their part but rather that the people in Djakarta do not have the power to do what they would like to do.

The Secretary continued that we were faced with a situation where the dissidents had failed and the undesirability of taking overt action was so great that we did not want to proceed further along those lines at this time. For that reason it was decided to give the political approach a chance. Accordingly, we have within the last few days taken the necessary steps to withdraw any support to the group in the Celebes.

The Secretary said that Ambassador Jones had recommended that he make a press statement, adding that he had made one yesterday. He commented also that other things must be tried for a reasonable period, possibly two or three months, to determine the intentions of the group in Djakarta. In the meantime, however, we are going to keep certain assets on the shelf to be used in case the political approach is not successful.

[1 paragraph (5 lines of source text) not declassified]

The Ambassador asked whether any conditions would be imposed on the sale of military equipment to Indonesia, [1 line of source text not declassified]. The Secretary stated that no proposal has as yet been submitted to him on the sale of military equipment so he did not know what position we might take. The Secretary informed the Ambassador that we had decided to issue some licenses for spare parts but there had been no decisions as yet on military equipment.

The Secretary commented that the Dutch were greatly concerned about this problem also but that he did not think there was any appreciable danger at this time of overt Indonesian action against West New Guinea. The Indonesian Government is in a very difficult economic situation and it is hard to imagine Indonesians precipitating a war on account of West Guinea, which would simply provide a basis for counteraction. The Secretary said that if military equipment is sold to Indonesia there will be definite undertakings required of the Indonesian Government.

[1 paragraph (6 lines of source text) not declassified]

The Ambassador [1-1/2 lines of source text not declassified] wondered if the success of the Indonesian military forces in mounting and carrying out the campaign in Sumatra might not change the picture. The Secretary commented that the operations had been far more effective than he had been led to believe the Indonesians were capable of, but there had been no resistance. In case of an attack on West New Guinea there would of course be resistance and he thought that without Soviet Bloc assistance Indonesia would not be capable of mounting any such operation.

The Ambassador asked whether any conditions would be attached to any token shipment of arms to Indonesia, [*1-1/2 lines of source text not declassified*]. The Secretary said that we had not as yet undertaken to make a token shipment of arms and therefore no conditions had been set forth to the Indonesian Government. The Secretary emphasized that we were moving gradually.

[*1 paragraph (4 lines of source text) not declassified*]

The Ambassador returned again to the point of public relations and inquired whether any thought had been given to how any change in policy toward Indonesia might be presented to the [*less than 1 line of source text not declassified*] public. The Secretary said that if we do anything publicly we will have to be careful how it is expressed so that any statement will not offend the Indonesians and at the same time will satisfy our public that what we are doing is based on an expectation that the Government of Indonesia wishes to maintain friendly relations with us. We are not entering into any formal agreement with the Indonesian government but merely taking gradual steps hoping thereby to encourage them to take definite action to reverse the trend toward communism.

108.   Telegram From the Embassy in the Republic of China to the Department of State

Taipei, May 22, 1958, 8 p.m.

984. Eyes only Secretary and Robertson. President Chiang summoned me late this afternoon. Foreign Minister Yeh was present.

Chiang referred to Indonesian situation saying position of revolutionaries is deteriorating and will become hopeless within one week unless substantial help is received meantime.

He spoke of flow of Communist assistance to Djakarta government including Russian-made planes flown through Red China and Rangoon and of dire consequences to free world if Indonesia is allowed to come under Communist control. Taiwan and Philippines would then be exposed from south and route to Australia interdicted. Position and prestige of US would be gravely affected and whole world situation altered in favor of Communists. Communist control of Indonesia would hold us up to ridicule of Communist world and facilitate their goal of world conquest.

Chiang said if Chinese Reds attempt to use Taiwan Strait area to move troops or supplies to Indonesia he will immediately order his forces to attack them. In any case he is considering issuance of public announcement to this effect. He is prepared, he said, to intervene militarily if Chinese Reds intervene.

Chiang said he has received urgent request from Indonesian revolutionaries to send men and equipment to assist in recovery of Morotai. Bringing out map, he expatiated at length on importance of Morotai to control balance of struggle. He is proposing to send one regiment of marines and a squadron of aircraft to assistance of revolutionaries who otherwise will be defeated and men and equipment already supplied lost. Chiang hoped US would provide help and in any case not impede him in his plans. He asked me to communicate foregoing to Secretary Dulles and I said I would of course do it.

I said to President I was not very conversant with developments in Indonesia and could not speak with authority. I recalled what you had said to him about difficulties of giving help when you saw him on March 14.[1] I said I gathered help of some kind had been provided, but fact was revolutionaries had failed to fight effectively and they therefore faced utter defeat. It would be most risky for outsiders to fight their battles for

---

Source: Department of State, Central Files, 793.00/5–2258. Top Secret; Niact.

[1] A memorandum of the Dulles–Chiang conversation of March 14 is printed in vol. XIX, pp. 8–12.

them and I urged President to reconsider carefully his proposal to send proposed fighting forces. I read to him extract from your Tuesday press conference on subject of Indonesia[2] and said I inferred from your remarks that US would not intervene. I also said his proposed intervention would provide Reds with pretext they seek to intervene openly on side of Djakarta and surely he would not want to provide them with that opportunity. I also referred to news reports of dissident approaches to Djakarta for final compromise settlement and asked if it would not be risky for him to proceed with his proposed intervention if these reports proved to be true. President replied that Sukarno would not compromise with insurgents. He also scouted possibility that agreement could be reached among Djakarta adherents whereby Reds could be eliminated. In his view only solution is sufficient aid to revolutionaries in men and equipment to defeat Djakarta. In agreeing to pass his remarks on to you I intimated it to be my opinion that his proposed course of action would be received with astonishment and dismay in Washington.

Chiang spoke earnestly and with emotion at times. He appeared to be in dead earnest but I doubt whether he will move to implement his proposals before receiving your reactions. I would suggest that these be transmitted soonest for communication to him. Of course any information of an encouraging nature about Indonesian developments would be highly useful for diverting him from the risky course he is contemplating so seriously.

For your information, Foreign Minister Yeh is out of sympathy with Chiang's proposed course of action and told me after interview that he had spent an hour this morning attempting to dissuade President from intervening.[3]

Drumright

---

[2] See footnote 3, Document 105.

[3] Telegram 749 to Taipei, May 22, for Ambassador Everett F. Drumright, reads: "You should inform President Chiang that

"1. In view of collapse of dissidents on Sumatra due to their unwillingness to fight and small leverage of Celebes group we are seeking develop anti-communist assets in government in Djakarta in effort to curb Sukarno and drift toward communism;

"2. We urge him suspend any moves he is contemplating until we can determine whether government will move. If our hopes of action by the government are not realized we will want to discuss this matter with him at a later date." (Department of State, Central Files, 793.00/5–2258)

In telegram 986 from Taipei, May 23, Drumright reported that he saw Chiang that afternoon and conveyed to him substance of telegram 749. "He asked me to thank you for your reply," the Ambassador noted, "and to tell you he will hold up contemplated action until he hears from you as to further developments." (*Ibid.*, 793.00/5–2358) See Supplement.

109.   Memorandum of Conversation

Washington, May 23, 1958.

SUBJECT

Indonesian Situation

PARTICIPANTS

Mr. Mukarto, Indonesian Ambassador

The Secretary
Mr. Mein, Director, Office of Southwest Pacific Affairs

The Ambassador said he had requested an opportunity to see the Secretary 1) to express the gratitude of his government for the Secretary's recent press statement, which had been very well received in Indonesia; 2) to express the appreciation of his government for the agreement to sell rice under PL–480 agreement, which was very timely especially in view of the famine in Central Java; 3) to discuss in general terms the situation in Indonesia.

The Ambassador stated that Indonesia faces some very serious problems among which are the growth of communism, inflation and communications. During the last year the communists have made considerable progress not because of the acceptance by the Indonesians of their ideology but primarily because of their change in tactics. One of the new tactics they have been using is in their approach to Sukarno, which they have handled very well. Although Sukarno is not a communist and in 1948 suppressed the communists at Madiun, they have nevertheless been approaching him. It is not a question of Sukarno working with the PKI as much as it is of the PKI using Sukarno. As an example of their method in dealing with him the Ambassador cited their support for the Pantjasila, the President's concept of "Democracy of leadership" ("guided democracy", which the Ambassador said is a mis-translation), and of the West New Guinea issue, which they know is dear to Sukarno's heart. The effect of communist support of the West New Guinea issue has been to make the Indonesian case more difficult. Nevertheless the communists have used that issue. The latest example of their tactics is their position on the rebellion, which they are also using to appeal to the people.

The Ambassador said that about 10 days ago he had cabled Sukarno pointing out in frank terms the danger of his playing with the communists, and the U.S. thinking on Sukarno, and emphasizing that if

Source: Department of State, Central Files, 756D.00/5–2358. Confidential. Drafted by Mein.

Sukarno does not change his attitude he is taking great risks not only domestically but in Indonesia's relations with the U.S. The Ambassador said he pointed out to Sukarno also that it is necessary for Indonesia to maintain close friendship with the U.S.

The Ambassador said that the way to deal with Sukarno is not to ridicule him, as the press is inclined to do, but rather to flatter him. The Ambassador added that he had told Sukarno that the American people still love him but are worried about the way he is going. He said this had made an impression on Sukarno. Immediately after receipt of the Ambassador's message Sukarno had called in Wilopo who had gotten the impression that Sukarno is changing his attitude. The Ambassador commented that Sukarno's attendance at a luncheon yesterday at the American Embassy in Djakarta was in itself significant and also a further indication of the change in his attitude. The Ambassador believes that the most important thing we can do in Indonesia at the present time is to approach Sukarno and seek to influence him. He emphasized again the need to flatter him adding that in his opinion Sukarno is changing his mood and his thinking.

The Ambassador said that as a result of the rebellion Nasution is emerging as a new power and that he may well be the balance of power in the present situation. The Ambassador said that Nasution is an anticommunist. He suggested that we should approach Nasution as well as Sukarno in an effort to bring about closer relations between the two men. There are also changes in the attitude of the political parties. The PNI, which formerly worked with the PKI, is now definitely anticommunist. As a result of the shift in political power among the parties the picture now is the PKI on one side, the PNI, Masjumi and NU on the other, and Sukarno in the center. The best way for the U.S. to proceed, therefore, would be to approach Sukarno and Nasution to strengthen this new force represented by the three parties.

The Ambassador said that they would like to see the PKI take some action which would precipitate a showdown but the communists would not do that. That is another reason why they have changed their tactics in handling the situation.

The Ambassador said that Foreign Minister Subandrio has suggested to Ambassador Jones a token shipment of arms of approximately $7 million, which would assist Nasution and also help create a new atmosphere by strengthening the Army. He is afraid that if nothing is done to strengthen the Army there is danger of the communists taking over as a result of the 1959 elections. The inflation in Indonesia is also playing into the hands of the communists.

The Ambassador commented that in his opinion there was need for more technical assistance, which has been very helpful to Indonesia, with emphasis placed on small projects, small industries, rather than for any large-scale economic assistance. In his opinion this would also tend to stop inflation.

The Ambassador said that the long-term economic prospects are good although the situation is bad now, and that they will improve as soon as barter trade is stopped and the foreign exchange situation is improved.

Summarizing, he said that there is good prospect of improvement in the political situation, but the help of the U.S. is needed; the economic situation is bad now but long-term prospects are good, there is need for immediate action and for that reason they were especially grateful for the Secretary's statement and the sale of rice. The Ambassador said also that they were very glad to have Ambassador Jones in Djakarta and expressed appreciation for the role he was playing.

The Secretary thanked the Ambassador for his comments on the situation in Indonesia. He said we have a good opinion of Sukarno who is an able politician and we don't quarrel with his concept of "guided democracy". In a situation like that in Indonesia where the people have had to take over without any training, there is need for greater centralization of authority. As long as this leads toward genuine independence we do not object to it but if it leads toward communism we are against it. We have been concerned that because of the similarity of what we understood to be the concept of "guided democracy" and what the Russians referred to as the "dictatorship of the proletariat" there was a danger that people might be misled and Indonesia might become more dependent on the communists.

The Secretary said that Indonesia in our opinion cannot be a happy, prosperous country without ties with the West. It is surrounded by the free world, its markets are primarily in the West, and if Indonesia goes down the communist path it would be impossible to prevent economic dislocation within the area.

110. Memorandum of Conversation

Washington, May 23, 1958.

SUBJECT

Indonesian Situation

PARTICIPANTS

Mr. Moekarto, Indonesian Ambassador

The Secretary
Mr. Mein, Director, Office of Southwest Pacific Affairs

In a discussion of the Indonesian situation the Secretary said he wished to assure the Ambassador that we are seeking to prevent acts from neighboring countries designed in some form to help those who seem to be trying to stop the drift of Indonesia toward communism. He said that we cannot go on exerting this pressure, and he is not sure we will wish to do so, unless something is done by the Indonesian Government to stop the drift. The Secretary said he hoped, therefore, that the government would take such action as is possible to curb the trend.

Source: Department of State, Central Files, 756D.00/5–2358. Top Secret; Limited Distribution. Drafted by Mein.

111.   Telegram From the Department of State to the Embassy in Indonesia

Washington, May 23, 1958, 10:20 p.m.

3409. Embtels 4340,[1] 4368.[2] In considering what reply you should make to Subandrio concerning his desire to meet with Secretary or your suggestion that Djuanda as Minister of Defense be invited come Washington would be helpful to know whether Cabinet changes contemplated near future and whether these two men will retain present portfolios. It would seem that if any talks were to take place it would be far more profitable have them with new ministers rather than those in present cabinet.

FYI. Not only would it be most difficult arrange visit at this time for Indonesian Ministers but pending further evolution Djakarta moves to work with us and curb communists we would consider such visit premature. We will discuss feasibility Nasution visit with General Taylor and advise you later. End FYI.

Secretary's statement, issuance of licenses,[3] also of rice, appear to have lessened tension somewhat. Before we can go much further, however, we must have some indication of effective action by Indonesian Government against communist threat. If there were cabinet change and if new cabinet composition satisfactory this would be considered step in right direction. There is danger however that improvement in U.S.-Indonesian relations in last few days might serve to bring about relaxation in Djakarta thereby postponing action for reorganization of cabinet or against communists. This would only play into hands of communists. You should therefore urge that there be no let-up and that such

---

Source: Department of State, Central Files, 756D.00/5–2358. Secret; Limit Distribution. Drafted by Mein and approved by Parsons. Repeated to CINCPAC for POLAD.

[1] In telegram 4340, May 22, Jones informed Robertson that, prior to the PL 480 signing ceremony, Subandrio had raised the possibility of visiting the United States for discussions with the Secretary of State. He also suggested that it would be useful if Djuanda could visit the United States sometime later in the year. Jones urged favorable consideration of both of those suggestions. (Ibid., 611.56D/5–2258) See Supplement.

[2] In telegram 4368, May 23, for Robertson, Jones stated that he had some second thoughts on the subject of a visit by Subandrio to the United States "because I would prefer to see Djuanda and/or Nasution be intermediary between US and Indonesia in developing situation." Accordingly, he recommended that the Department consider authorizing him to invite Djuanda to the United States at an early date, accompanied by Subandrio, and to renew the invitation to Nasution to visit the United States, previously extended by General Taylor. (Department of State, Central Files, 756D.00/5–2358) See Supplement.

[3] On May 22 the Department of State issued export licenses for the shipment of certain materials to Indonesia.

action as contemplated be taken as soon as possible if we are expected to take any further action here at this time.

Dulles

---

112. Telegram From the Department of State to the Embassy in Indonesia

Washington, May 26, 1958, 8:30 p.m.

3446. From Robertson for Jones. Following basic philosophy which guides us presently in our policy toward Indonesia is for your background guidance and discreet use at times and with persons of your choice. FYI. Following was dictated by the Secretary. End FYI.

We have regard and admiration for the abilities of President Sukarno. President Eisenhower well remembers his visit here, and Secretary Dulles recalls not only that but his visit to Djakarta. The Congress and the American people obtained, and retain, a very favorable impression of President Sukarno.

There is, however, a distinct impression which is not exclusive to the United States, that the Communists are taking advantage of the fact that President Sukarno feels a need for greater authority at the top in the situation that confronts him. The Communists are seeking to impose upon Indonesia a Communist-type "dictatorship of the proletariat" which will end up by taking the Indonesian Republic into the Communist camp and making Sukarno in effect a prisoner.

As pointed out, this is not a United States judgment, it is the judgment of many Indonesians of high responsibility. It is also shared by the free world nations which are Western Pacific neighbors of Indonesia and which want to be its friends.

It is utterly unrealistic for anyone to believe that Indonesia can in tranquillity wend its way into the Communist camp. Once it became

Source: Department of State, Central Files, 756D.00/5–2658. Top Secret. Drafted by Mein and approved by Robertson. Jones refers to this telegram and quotes from it in *Indonesia: The Possible Dream*, p. 139. The telegram was based on a May 23 memorandum with a virtually identical text from Dulles to Robertson. A copy of that memorandum is in the Eisenhower Library, Herter Papers, Chronological File.

clear that that was the course, the now dying embers of revolution would burst out in flames and it would not be possible for the United States, even should it so desire, to restrain the impulses of governments and individuals who are dedicated to freedom and some of whom would feel they were imperiled by the course Indonesia was taking.

Furthermore, the economy of Indonesia is so fragile and is so dependent upon the free world and the West, that it would be impossible for long to maintain a viable government and prosperous society if the economic pattern were to be readjusted to dependence upon the Sino-Soviet bloc.

The United States is exerting itself strongly to permit of an orderly and peaceful evolution of Indonesian policy in a direction which will avoid, and preclude, the danger of the Republic being captured by the International Communist movement. The situation cannot, however, for long stand still. We are hoping to see, concretely, the start of a new trend and some action responsive to our own.

Dulles

---

113.   Telegram From the Embassy in the Republic of China to the Department of State

Taipei, May 26, 1958, 2 a.m.

992. Eyes only Secretary and Robertson. Admiral Doyle[1] came to see me to say when he landed at airfield late this afternoon on return from seeing Admiral Stump he was requested to see Defense Minister Yu Ta Wei at once. He accordingly called at Yu's residence where he was given to understand President is about to despatch forces to Indonesia to assist insurgents. Doyle states he argued against such action and asked for two days grace. Doyle then sent urgent message to Admirals Stump and Burke urging a US commitment to Chiang that Indonesia will not be permitted to fall in hands of Communists.[2] Tonight, after din-

---

Source: Department of State, Central Files, 793.00/5–2558. Top Secret; Niact.

[1] Vice Admiral Austin K. Doyle, USN, Commander, Taiwan Defense Command/MAAG.

[2] Not found.

ner given by President for Secretary Douglas,[3] which number of Americans including myself attended, Doyle was asked to remain for talk with President. According to Doyle, President informed him he is on point of sending forces to assistance of Indonesian insurgents. Doyle said he urged President not to send forces, asking that US be given chance to work out settlement through Djakarta friendly elements. President replied there was no possibility of satisfactory settlement in this way. Doyle accordingly repeated request he had made to Yu for two days' grace and President gave it.

I had informed Doyle prior to his departure to see Stump of President's approach to me and of your reply,[4] so that he could discuss problem with Stump. I informed Doyle tonight of President's assurance not to take action pending further word from US Government of results of its actions in Indonesian situation and told Doyle I relied on President to live up to his word. I then suggested to Doyle that he send a followup message of his conversation with President.

At President's dinner tonight there was no suggestion in President's talk with Douglas that he planned to take military action although he stressed importance of not permitting Indonesia to fall to Communists and he asked Douglas to convey his views to President Eisenhower. Neither was there any reference of military action to me on part of Defense Minister Yu, Foreign Minister Yeh or Chief of General Staff Wang. President appeared relaxed and in good humor. Therefore Doyle's report came as a surprise to me, although I knew Chinese to be anxious and preoccupied with Indonesian development.

After Doyle left my residence I got in touch with Foreign Minister Yeh. He said he was uninformed of any intent on part of President to resort to immediate military action, adding he believed President would live up to assurance not to move pending word from US. Besides President could not move without consulting United States pursuant to mutual defense agreement.[5] Yeh said he was uninformed of President's and Yu's talks with Doyle. But he did know from talks he had yesterday with Yu and Deputy Chief of Staff Pak Yu that President yesterday morning had instructed Defense Minister Yu to make plans for deployment of GRC forces to Indonesia and that Defense Minister Yu had in turn asked Deputy Chief of Staff Yu to draw up such plans. Latter had come to Foreign Minister last night asking for information as basis for drawing up plans. Yeh said he was unable to provide much helpful information and

---

[3] James H. Douglas, Secretary of the Air Force, was in Taipei for a brief visit.

[4] Reference is to telegram 749 to Taipei; see footnote 3, Document 108.

[5] Reference is to the mutual defense treaty between the United States and the Republic of China signed in Washington on December 2, 1954; for text, see 6 UST 433.

he expressed view preparation of plans would be prolonged and difficult job. He also said he thought implementation of plans might be beyond China's capacity and had so intimated to planner Yu. Yeh and I agreed to meet tomorrow morning to discuss situation further. I propose to urge him to see President and remind latter of his pledge and of provisions of defense treaty. If Yeh thinks it desirable I shall probably see President again.

Meanwhile, if Department has any favorable information on Indonesian developments or even expectations of such developments I would urge that they be passed on to President without delay. While I find it hard to believe that he will actually despatch forces as he threatens to do, he is plainly deeply troubled, is apprehensive that US will not move effectively to stop Communist takeover of Indonesia and may just possibly take desperate action. Doyle and I agree that his subordinates would deprecate such actions, but none dare stand up and oppose him.[6]

Drumright

---

[6] Drumright met with Yeh again on May 27. The Foreign Minister explained to him that both he and Yu believed that armed intervention on behalf of the Indonesian rebels would be a most hazardous undertaking and they were in the process of making this known "gently" to Chiang. (Telegram 1002 from Taipei, May 27; Department of State, Central Files, 793.00/5–2758) See Supplement.

---

114.   Telegram From the Commander in Chief, Pacific (Stump) to the Chief of Naval Operations (Burke)

Honolulu, May 26, 1958, 9:22 p.m.

S–39. 270722Z. Exclusive for Admiral Burke, Assistant Secretary Robertson. Information Ambassador Jones, Vice Admiral Riley, Rear Admiral Cruise. From Stump. Deliver during working hours. Following

---

Source: Department of State, Central Files, 756D.00/5–2758. Top Secret; Priority. Also sent to the Department of State, which is the source text, and repeated to Djakarta, CINCPAC ADMIN, and CINCPACREPHIL.

receipt of Robertson's message, passed as CNO 240825Z,[1] I fortunately was able to have a further lengthy discussion with Indonesian group consisting of BGen Subroto, Col Sukendro and their excellent translator Maj Sunario. I conveyed to them the points which were authorized for me to make to the group and in order to give them assurance that this was being coordinated in Djakarta as well, I pointed out that this was essentially what Amb Jones would be passing on under instructions in Djakarta.

From this conversation and previous interviews with this group, my best estimate is that they have been impressed with our willingness to assist them in this new approach, that they are honestly determined to carry out their part of the responsibility. This was illustrated by the fact that they requested that their return schedule be altered so that they might reach Djakarta more expeditiously in order to help guide delicate reorientation of attitudes there to one of cooperation.

Delicately tried to suggest certain things which they could do to create a better impression on their anti-Communist Asian neighbors and most of all on US officials and public opinion. Of course the first point that we have always emphasized is that in some manner they must take steps to prove that they are making genuine effort to exclude PKI and Communists from government influence. I further pointed out that if it is humanly possible they must see to it that a muzzle is placed on Sukarno to avoid upsetting the applecart during this delicate period. Thirdly while we did not name names or appear to have too much vested interest in the dissidents, we did point out that insofar as possible their willingness to demonstrate generosity (using the illustration of Magsaysay's[2] extremely successful technique in exhibiting magnanimity in reconverting many of the Huks) would be most effective in influencing international opinion with respect to their sincerity. They seemed to accept all of this philosophy with very good grace, and I believe our association with them here will contribute a great deal to the overall effort being made to getting our relationships back on the track with the right forces in Indonesia.

---

[1] Reference is to the telegram from Robertson to Stump, May 23, repeated to Djakarta as telegram 3403. In this telegram Robertson summarized recent U.S. actions with regard to Indonesia and suggested that it would be useful if Stump could: "1) Review with Indonesians what we have done in last few days as indicative of our attitude toward Indonesian Government; 2) express hope early cessation hostilities; 3) emphasize strongly need for some effective action in Djakarta in curbing the communist threat; and 4) reiterate our willingness to help if action taken urging them to use their influence in seeing that some action is taken. You may wish in this connection to point out that Congressional and public opinion in this country would not tolerate sale of military equipment unless there is some change and that it is in their interest to take action at earliest possible time." (*Ibid.*, 756D.00/5–2358) See Supplement.

[2] Ramon Magsaysay, President of the Philippines from 1954 to 1957.

The group is now departing Tokyo 2200 local 28 May in company with Gen Arellano,[3] will spend one day in Manila at Sangley and return via Singapore thereafter. Incidentally, I believe Gen Arellano's personal influence on them has been good and trip to Manila in his personal company is fortuitous.

They have not desired any publicity regarding their attendance weapons demonstration and intend to say in Djakarta that they have "been to Tokyo to see Asian games." So far believe no mention in press of their presence weapons demonstration.

---

[3] Lieutenant General Alfonso Arellano, Chief of Staff of the Philippine Armed Forces.

---

115. Memorandum of Conversation

Washington, May 27, 1958.

SUBJECT

Dutch Protest Lack of Consultation Concerning Indonesian Developments

PARTICIPANTS

Dr. J. H. van Roijen, Ambassador of the Netherlands
Baron van Voorst, Minister, Netherlands Embassy
Mr. D. Ketel, First Secretary, Netherlands Embassy
The Secretary
FE—Mr. Robertson
EUR—Mr. Jandrey
WE—Mr. Cameron

Ambassador van Roijen came in to see the Secretary at his own request. On instruction of his Government, the Ambassador strongly protested the lack of prior consultation with the Dutch Government and with NATO concerning recent United States approval of export licenses for the purchase of small arms and aircraft spare parts by Indonesia, reports of which had appeared in the press on May 22. The Ambassador characterized these transactions as "arms deliveries to Indonesia". He recapitulated a series of conversations which he and the Dutch Foreign Minister had had with the Secretary and other officials of the Depart-

---

Source: Department of State, Central Files, 756D.56/5–2758. Secret; Limit Distribution. Drafted by Cameron on May 28.

ment during the course of which he asserted the Dutch had received assurances that such deliveries would not be made to Indonesia and that
the Dutch Government would be informed of any change in United
States policy towards Indonesia, particularly in the fields of military and
economic assistance. The Ambassador stated that without consultation
or even an informal exchange of views the United States Government
had acceded to Indonesian requests for military and economic (the substitution of rice for cotton under the 1956 P.L. 480 Agreement) assistance. He emphasized that the Dutch Government was sorely
disappointed by these developments; its confidence in "promises given
by the American Government had been severely shocked" and consequently it will be compelled to draw its own conclusions. He said further that there was no assurance whatsoever that the Indonesian armed
forces would not receive additional United States support. In view of
this situation and in view of Soviet bloc military assistance to Indonesia
the Netherlands Government would have to consider seriously "adapt-
ing the defense forces of Netherlands New Guinea to this new threat".
Such a move on the part of the Dutch Government, he continued, would
necessarily have effects on Dutch contribution to the defense of Western
Europe. The Dutch Government considered it necessary, therefore, to
inform the other members of NATO of these developments so that they
could take fully into account the changed situation. The Ambassador
handed the Secretary a note covering these statements, the text of which
is attached. [1]

The Secretary replied that if he had understood the Ambassador
correctly it would appear that the Ambassador was saying that the
Dutch Government no longer had any confidence in the United States
Government because of what the Dutch read in the newspapers. He said
that this was an extreme and unjustified conclusion for the Dutch Government to reach. Why, he asked, had not the Dutch Government inquired about the facts? The Ambassador referred to a talk which Baron
van Voorst had had with Mr. J. Graham Parsons (FE) on May 22, and
asserted that Mr. Parsons had not been responsive to Baron van Voorst's
request for information on this subject. [2] The Dutch Government, therefore, had been impelled to give great weight to the press reports. Mr.
Robertson commented that he had complete confidence in Mr. Parsons
and that he was certain that Mr. Parsons had been correct and helpful in
his conversation with Baron van Voorst. Mr. Robertson added that in his
experience it was unusual to raise questions of this nature during the
course of a talk which had been arranged as a courtesy call.

---

[1] Not printed.

[2] A memorandum of this conversation is in Department of State, Central Files,
756D.56/5–2258.

The Secretary referred to his conversation with Foreign Minister Luns on April 24[3] and recalled that he had told the Foreign Minister at that time that the United States was considering supplying the Indonesians with a few things (some rice had been specifically mentioned) in an attempt to maintain some influence in Indonesia by giving the Indonesian leaders the idea that they could play both sides. The Secretary said that he did not consider that the approval of export licenses for a very limited list of items constituted arms deliveries to Indonesia. He explained that the only arms covered by these licenses were 250 Colt revolvers for the Indonesian Navy, four sporting rifles and three 22-caliber pistols. The value of these items was $14,582. The total sum involved amounted to approximately $1.2 million. Of the items covered by the licenses 95% were aircraft spare parts. All involved commercial purchases from private American companies. It had not occurred to the Department that the Dutch would consider these transactions as arms deliveries to Indonesia. The Secretary said he could now see that we had been wrong in not informing the Dutch Government and he regretted that we had not done so.

Ambassador van Roijen said that the Dutch Government not only felt very strongly about the lack of consultation but that it was completely in the dark concerning the reasons for United States assistance to Indonesia at this time. The Secretary explained again as he had done on May 13 in his conversation with the Ambassador[4] that the United States was attempting to create a situation in Djakarta which would permit the United States to continue to exercise some influence in the swiftly moving and very delicate Indonesian developments. We hoped to use this influence to encourage the Indonesian civil and military leaders to institute government reorganization and other steps favorable to the Free World. We were pursuing these objectives in the interest of the Free World. He noted with regret that we seemed to receive only sniping and a complete lack of understanding from the Dutch.

The Secretary then commented that he also placed a high value on consultation but he did not consider that consultation was a substitute for confidence. He believed that in this case the ally which had the primary responsibility in a very difficult situation was due a modicum of confidence and a certain degree of flexibility of action. Over-emphasis on consultation could result in a web so entangling that the consequences would be only more consultation and no action.

The Ambassador then asked why the Dutch Government had not been informed concerning the moves which the United States had de-

---

[3] See Document 71.
[4] See Document 95.

cided to take in Djakarta. The Secretary replied that the emotional involvement of the Dutch in the Indonesian situation was so great that he had judged it unwise to keep them as closely informed as he would have liked. He emphasized this point by saying that he was taking a calculated risk in talking as frankly to the Ambassador as he was doing today. He stressed the confidential nature of his remarks and said that any public disclosure would have disastrous consequences. The Secretary again described the insignificant character of the actions which the United States had decided to try in Indonesia. These, he said, were in effect tactical moves designed to let the Indonesian leaders think that they had an alternative to Soviet assistance. Should these actions have the results which we all desired of encouraging the anti-Communist elements in Indonesia and reversing the leftward movement there, which he personally thought very doubtful, the United States would be disposed to consider further steps designed to strengthen this trend. The exact nature of these steps could not be anticipated. However, our actions would be geared to concrete moves which the Indonesian Government might take to reverse the current Communist orientation. The Ambassador asked whether he should take the Secretary's statement to imply that if this reversal takes place the United States would be prepared to consider furnishing additional military assistance to Indonesia. The Secretary replied that he questioned the Ambassador's use of the word "additional" and repeated that we did not consider the export licenses in question as constituting deliveries of military assistance to Indonesia. He said, however, as he had done to the Ambassador on May 13, that if we were satisfied with steps being taken to reverse the anti-Communist trend the possibility should not be excluded that we would be prepared to consider the desirability of furnishing arms and military assistance to Indonesia under certain circumstances.

In response to a statement of the Ambassador about the concern of the Dutch Government for the security of West New Guinea, the Secretary said that he would like to repeat that the Dutch Government need have no concern now or in the future about the United States attitude towards an Indonesian military attack on West New Guinea. He said that the Dutch Government knew officially that the United States would be greatly concerned about such an attack. He added that we had recently received a new declaration from Foreign Minister Subandrio that Indonesia had no intention of using force against West New Guinea. He said this declaration had been responsive to a statement by Ambassador Jones in Djakarta that good relations between the United States and Indonesia would have to exclude the use of force against West New Guinea. The Secretary said he remained strongly opposed to a public statement to this effect which in his considered judgment would make impossible the achievement of the desired orientation of the Indonesian

Government. Unless we are successful in bringing about such an orientation Free World Nations will not be able to influence developments there.

Ambassador van Roijen introduced at this point the Dutch Government's strong feeling that aid to Indonesia should be contingent upon a satisfactory settlement of Dutch-Indonesian problems. He said that the observance of international obligations which such a settlement would imply was in the interest of the entire Free World. The Secretary said that the United States also placed great weight on the sanctity of international obligations, but that in this case, as in the case of Iran which the Ambassador had raised, it was necessary first to have a government amenable to Western influence and willing to carry out its obligations. Without such a government it was clearly impossible to expect observance of international obligations and commitments. The Secretary then said that the United States and the Netherlands should face squarely the fact that in our relations with Indonesia we placed emphasis on different things. The United States placed primary emphasis on preventing a Communist take-over of Indonesia, whereas the Dutch appeared to place primary interest on their economic and business interests in that area. The United States would not like to be identified with the idea that commercial interests are primary.

The Secretary said he wished again to confirm to the Ambassador that we had no intention at the present of furnishing arms or military equipment to Indonesia. He said he was prepared to consider how we might make consultation between our two governments on Indonesian matters more effective. In conclusion he suggested that Ambassador van Roijen and Mr. Robertson agree on the line the Ambassador might take with the press concerning this conversation.

116. Memorandum of Conversation

Washington, May 27, 1958.

SUBJECT

Dutch Protest Lack of Consultation Concerning Indonesian Developments

PARTICIPANTS

Dr. J. H. van Roijen, Ambassador of the Netherlands
Baron van Voorst, Minister, Netherlands Embassy
Mr. D. Ketel, First Secretary, Netherlands Embassy
The Secretary
FE—Mr. Robertson
EUR—Mr. Jandrey
WE—Mr. Cameron

In explaining the background of current United States efforts to en-courage and influence Indonesian military and civil leaders to take steps to reverse the Communist orientation of Indonesia, the Secretary said that we had first tried to encourage the rebel movements in Sumatra and then in the Celebes. He commented that our efforts would make an epic story. Unfortunately, these rebel movements had apparently spent themselves. Arms supplied to the rebels had fallen into the hands of In-donesian Government forces, lives had been lost and the Indonesian Government, in fact, now holds an American. [*1-1/2 lines of source text not declassified*]

When the movement in the Celebes appeared to be following a pat-tern similar to that of the Sumatran rebellion it was decided that the mo-ment had come when we should try to influence Indonesian military and civil leaders. We consulted with Australia and the United Kingdom and it was agreed that we should try this line. Our three Ambassadors in Djakarta believe that there is a chance of success. Others, with whom the Secretary associated himself, think that success is very unlikely. Never-theless, all concurred that this line should be tried. We have, therefore, decided to make some small gestures towards the Indonesian Govern-ment. We shall delay anything substantial until that government takes advantage of the opportunity to perform on its side. For example, if there should be a cabinet reshuffle within the next few weeks, we might have some basis for judging whether steps have been taken to reverse the present communist orientation.

In the meantime, we shall try to keep other assets in being, with the idea of possibly reviving them if the efforts in Djakarta fail. In other

---

Source: Department of State, Central Files, 756D.00/5–2758. Top Secret; Limit Distri-bution. Drafted by Cameron.

words, we shall try to keep those embers warm so that they can be fanned into flames if necessary.

If all these things do not work, it may be necessary to consider taking more overt action, possibly involving the assistance of the Philippines and Taiwan. In view of the extreme gravity of such a course of action, it was decided first to try to influence Djakarta.

The Secretary expressed in the strongest terms the top secret character of this information. Mr. Robertson reinforced the Secretary's statements by explaining how closely this information was being held in this Government. Both the Secretary and Mr. Robertson stressed that any disclosure of what the Secretary had told the Ambassador would be disastrous not only for the United States but for the Free World in Asia. Ambassador van Roijen said he understood what was involved and said his government would guard the information with the greatest care.[1]

---

[1] The Department summarized this conversation in telegram 2101 to The Hague, May 31. (*Ibid.*, 756D.00/5–3158)

June–December 1958: Establishment of a Token Military Assistance Program for the Indonesian Armed Forces and U.S. Encouragement of the Anti-Communist Elements Within the Indonesian Government

117. Telegram From the Embassy in Indonesia to the Department of State

Djakarta, June 3, 1958, 6 p.m.

4544. For Assistant Secretary Robertson from Ambassador Jones. To ascertain Gen. Nasution's views re possible US visit ARMA made discreet inquiry through staff officer who reported Nasution said he was prepared leave for US any time but only if it were possible during such visit to sign agreement obtain military equipment.

Nasution also said he would be glad see me later this week if I cared to call assuming I had something of substance to discuss with him.

I think now might be an opportune time to follow up my previous conversation (Embtel 4116)[1] ascertain Nasution's current thinking and make sure he understands real basis of US support to GOI as outlined urtel 3403[2] to Admiral Stump and also limitations urtel 3409.[3]

I believe timing is right for this kind of talk with Nasution because (A) PNI are coming out publicly with anti-PKI stand (see Embtel 4431)[4] and will step up political opposition to Commies; (B) imminent Cabinet change expected weaken Commies; (C) Sukarno's recent mild speeches and attitudes are reportedly viewed with alarm by PKI; (D) improved US-Indo relations are obstructive to Commie objectives and; (E) end of rebel armed resistance when army takes Menado means troops will return to Java to strengthen anti-Commie forces.

All above developments may cause Commie reaction which army must be prepared to meet and continue to control if GOI pursues harder line against Commies.

Source: Department of State, Central Files, 756D.00/6–3358. Top Secret; Niact.

[1] Document 86.

[2] See footnote 1, Document 114.

[3] Document 111.

[4] In telegram 4431, May 28, the Embassy reported that the PNI Central Board issued a statement in Djakarta on May 27, "which, although not naming PKI, amounts to attack on Communist Party." (Department of State, Central Files, 756D.00/5–2858) See Supplement.

In this interview it may be useful to lead Nasution into discussion of Commie reaction and his estimate of army requirements to maintain internal order against this threat. We can then consider supply of these requirements under the above rationale to coinside with Cabinet changes and resolution military campaign in Sulawesi.

In addition to exploration of above subject with Nasution it would be very helpful if I were able to be immediately responsive to request of Foreign Minister (Embtel 4503)[5] that we supply non-combat engineering bridging equipment to army on priority basis for restoration of land communications in Sumatra. This material is similar to items which appear on master list of arms and equipment long pending and orginally called for equipping twelve combat engineering companies. If Department can authorize me to say that we will deliver this kind of material as quickly as possible after Nasution specifies what he needs, I am sure it would go long way with Indonesian army, which has not yet received any material among export licenses recently approved for other branches of Government and armed forces. It would also help offset effect Pope case and have the distinct advantage of showing Nasution that we are not merely talking about support but are actually prepared to provide it.

Department views would be appreciated before Friday.[6]

Jones

---

[5] Dated May 31. (Department of State, Central Files, 256D.1122–Pope, Allen Lawrence/5–3158)

[6] The Department replied in telegram 3613 to Djakarta, June 5, which reads in part as follows: "Believe further conversations with Nasution along lines suggested by you would be helpful especially in assessing his thinking and plans. Although no specific gesture toward Army has yet been taken by us all steps which have been taken contribute to army's apparent objective strengthening hands of anti-communist and pro-U.S. elements." (*Ibid.*, 756D.00/6–358) See Supplement.

---

118. Telegram From the Embassy in Indonesia to the Department of State

Djakarta, June 6, 1958, 8 p.m.

4615. Department pass ACSI, CNO, AFSI. CINCPAC for POLAD. On 5 June ARMA met with Lt. Colonel Sukendro, Chief Army Intelli-

---

Source: Department of State, Central Files, 756D.00/6–658. Top Secret; Niact. Transmitted in two sections and also sent to CINCPAC.

gence, to discuss his recent visit to US weapons demonstration. Sukendro stated demonstration was most impressive and well-planned. He was grateful for excellent treatment and deeply appreciated courtesy and kindness extended by Admiral Stump and Staff.

Sukendro stated that on 27 May in Tokyo, Admiral Stump had indicated US Government had issued licenses for small arms for Indonesian police, aircraft spare parts, communication facilities and shipping. Sukendro then asked if Embassy had received any information re delivery dates. ARMA stated that except for "shipping" State Department had approved considerable number of export licenses. ARMA further explained that approval of licenses completed US Government action with respect to these commercial transactions and that arrangement for payment and delivery should be settled by GOI representatives and US private business companies.

Sukendro then said Admiral Stump had indicated US prepared furnish additional aid provided effective measures were taken by GOI against Communists. ARMA said he would discuss matter with Ambassador. Sukendro agreed and said he would appreciate clarification June 6 since he was required brief President Sukarno.

On 6 June after conference with Ambassador Jones, Cole and Shuman called on Sukendro who opened conversation by saying Admiral Stump had clearly stated the US position and Sukendro inquired if Embassy had received corresponding information. Cole and Shuman replied US support would be responsive to Nasution's plan to end hostilities, bring about Cabinet changes, and take action against PKI. Attachés also pointed out that action in good faith had been already made by both sides. On our side US influence had been exerted to halt intervention and export licenses had been approved for a number of items. A list of these items was given to Sukendro.

Sukendro then said the inner group (Sukarno, Nasution, Djuanda and Subandrio) would appreciate US detailed planning on token shipment $7 million arms, shipping assistance, civil aviation, service schooling so that US could rapidly deliver upon completion groups next step. They envision this step to be the end of fighting, reshuffling Cabinet to exclude Leftists, and identifiable action to control PKI. Sukendro indicated government reorganization would be in two phases reshuffle Cabinet now and basic changes in government later. He said action against PKI would be continuous rather than a short term affair.

Sukendro said the group feels that they would qualify for $7 million token arms after first step outlined above and it must come fast to support them in their continued moves against the PKI.

Nasution has established a commission of officers to study the needs and determine specific terms to be included in the $7 million arms and in the service schooling. Sukendro said in general terms he could tell us what they initially needed in this category was equipment to support six mobile battalions composed of two amphibious KKO Commando Corps, and four paratroops. He said these mobile units would be needed to move rapidly to counter Communist reaction as the GOI applied pressure. He said the technical assistance should be both formal instruction and technical maintenance to support the initial arming with these weapons and the amount of this technical assistance would depend upon the type and amount of the weapons.

General Nasution desires to go to the US to work out details of future relations and negotiate further assistance after the above US and Indonesian moves have been made and the government is under control. Sukendro warned not to discuss these plans with any one other than identifiable group listed above.

Sukendro further stated following: Major Marsudi of town command would be transferred. Sukendro would inform attachés as soon as decision made on handling Pope case. Menado would be finished soon. Nasution would try arrange interview with Ambassador Jones on June 9. When arms forthcoming air delivery was not only acceptable but welcomed.

Comment by attachés Cole and Shuman: We believe the Indonesian group understands situation and is working in good faith according to plan and that this plan has an excellent chance to succeed if we properly support. To expedite subsequent action list of items in $7 million arms package is requested including conditions and terms of purchase.[1]

Jones

---

[1] In telegram CN 5721 to CNO, June 9, Stump commented that he felt the United States must move rapidly to fulfill its commitments to the Indonesian army for assistance. He also raised the possibility of sending a technical military mission to Indonesia, a forerunner of a military advisory group, and suggested that the United States offer to train a selected group of intelligence officers at the rank of captain and major in the United States. (Ibid., 756D.00/6–958) See Supplement.

In telegram 282141Z to CNO, June 28, Stump submitted a detailed outline plan for the implementation of the token aid program for Indonesia for consideration by the JCS. (Department of State, G/PM Files: Lot 64 D 341)

119.   Telegram From the Department of State to the Embassy in Indonesia

Washington, June 16, 1958, 6:32 p.m.

3758. In farewell call on Robertson June 9 Mukarto made following points:[1]

1. PNI Central Committee in recent Semarang meeting decided adopt anti-Communist resolution and call for Cabinet change with recommendation that Mukarto or Wilopo be appointed formateur. Sukarno indicated preference for Mukarto and he was returning Djakarta for this purpose.

2. Mukarto would establish following as preconditions for forming or heading a government:

    a. PKI must be placed in opposition.
    b. PNI, Masjumi, and NU must work together.
    c. Armed Forces must support his government.
    d. Sukarno must make clear to people that he is prepared fight Communists.

3. Hatta would probably not be included in government but would act as Cabinet adviser attending meetings but without any specific responsibility.

4. U.S. assistance in constructing barracks for Armed Forces would be important step in strengthening pro-U.S. orientation Indonesian Army. Such construction might be financed by approximately Rupiahs 50 million of PL–480 funds and perhaps $5 million in foreign exchange.

5. He would like be assured that any government he headed would receive U.S. moral and financial support.

Robertson replied that U.S. objective is a strong independent Indonesia, but prerequisite to any large-scale assistance to Indonesia is concrete demonstration that Indonesians prepared take action prevent drift toward Communism. Mukarto asked if formation of government of type he had described would receive U.S. support. Robertson replied establishment such a government would facilitate extension U.S. assistance.

Source: Department of State, Central Files, 756D.00/6–1658. Drafted by Underhill on June 13 and approved by Robertson.

[1] A 5-page memorandum of this conversation was drafted by Mein on June 9. (*Ibid.*, 756D.00/6–958) See Supplement.

Mukarto said he would be in touch with you following his arrival in Djakarta June 20. Memo of conversation pouched. Request foregoing be closely held.

Dulles

---

120. Editorial Note

On June 10 Secretary Dulles spoke with John M. Raymond, the Assistant Legal Adviser, about the Allen Pope case. A memorandum of their telephone conversation, prepared by Bernau reads as follows:

"Re the Pope case—all the Sec can say is he is an American citizen— he may have violated laws of Indonesia but we expect him to receive treatment at least as lenient as that given to others in the same category. R said we expect him to be treated fairly—we will watch what is going on and protect him in that respect. R said as far as we know he has violated no law of the US. They agreed he is not guilty of treason. R mentioned his being tried by a military court. Jones has sent various laws under which he could be tried but don't know which it will be." (Eisenhower Library, Dulles Papers, General Telephone Conversations)

121.   Memorandum of Conversation

Washington, June 11, 1958.

SUBJECT

Defense of Southeast Asia

PARTICIPANTS

U.S.	U.K.
The Secretary	The Prime Minister [1]
Mr. Allen Dulles	Sir Harold Caccia
Mr. Reinhardt	Sir Norman Brook
Mr. Elbrick	Sir Patrick Dean
Mr. Green	Lord Hood
Mr. Dale	Mr. Carter
	Mr. Morris
	Mr. Bishop

The Prime Minister repeated his recommendation that we should give guidance to the military planners to the effect that they should deal primarily with general matters in defense planning for Southeast Asia, such as command arrangements, force contributions, and timing, so that all concerned could have a general idea of what they could rely on in case of emergency. He did not suggest that we engage in detailed planning but rather a general stocktaking of our military and other resources and seeing how we could move rapidly if and as required. He suggested that Ambassador Caccia and Admiral Denny [2] start conversations with our people soon. Sir Norman Brook [3] said that there are two questions which must be decided: first, what exactly are the limits within which military staff planning might take place and second, which staffs "should do the job".

The Secretary reported that we shall need to make some very important decisions relating to Indonesia in the near future. He explained that we had [2-1/2 lines of source text not declassified] concentrated on trying to bring about a reorientation of the Indonesian Cabinet away from Communist influence. We had hoped to persuade Sukarno to face up to the Communist issue.

Source: Department of State, Conference Files: Lot 63 D 123, CF 1020. Top Secret; Limited Distribution. Drafted by William N. Dale, Officer in Charge of United Kingdom and Ireland Affairs.

[1] Prime Minister Macmillan was in the United States for a 5-day unofficial visit, June 7–11.

[2] Admiral Sir Michael M. Denny, U.K. representative on the NATO Standing Group.

[3] Secretary of the Cabinet.

The Secretary said that he personally had never thought that this would work and now Sukarno appears to be reneging. He relies heavily on Communist support and the regime is in danger of passing under Communist control. [2 lines of source text not declassified] We shall have to determine, probably within the next ten days, whether or not our political effort with the present government can succeed[4] and, if not, whether to support the rebels.

Mr. Allen Dulles pointed out that guerrilla activity in Sumatra and Sulawesi is continuing and that fighting is still underway on the outer Islands in the Celebes area.

The Secretary reported that the Filipinos, South Koreans, and Nationalist Chinese want very much to help the Indonesian rebels. [1-1/2 lines of source text not declassified] he wanted the Prime Minister to know what the decisions are that face us and that we realize we cannot say where these decisions may lead.[5]

---

[4] In another conversation on June 11 between Macmillan and Secretary of State Dulles the subject of Indonesia came up briefly. According to a memorandum of that conversation, drafted by William N. Dale and John Foster Dulles, Allen Dulles made the following points:

"Mr. Allen Dulles raised the question of how to deal with situations in which a country has been penetrated by Communists and there exists the danger of a Communist takeover. He distinguished between two types, one, in which there is para-military activity (in which case covert military preparations can be made), and a second type in which there is the creeping spread of Communism through the electoral process. [3 lines of source text not declassified]" (Department of State, Conference Files: Lot 63 D 123, CF 1020)

[5] Later that day Eisenhower met with Macmillan with Dulles present. A memorandum of this conversation by Dulles included the following comments: "We spoke of the situation in Indonesia, of which I had spoken to the Prime Minister during our morning session, and the fact that it might be necessary to consider our present political effort a failure and to choose between more overt measure against the government or acquiescence in Communist domination." (Ibid.)

---

122. Telegram From the Embassy in Indonesia to the Department of State

Djakarta, June 17, 1958, 11 a.m.

4752. CINCPAC for POLAD. Department for Assistant Secretary Robertson from Ambassador Jones. Foreign Minister telephoned this

---

Source: Department of State, Central Files, 756D.00/6–1758. Secret; Limit Distribution. Also sent to CINCPAC.

morning and asked me to call at his home at 8:15 to inform me that rebel B–26 had strafed Gorontalo Sunday morning at 9 o"clock.

Since all useable airfields in Menado and vicinity are now under GOI control, including Morotai, only airport from which plane could have come, Foreign Minister said, was Sanga Sanga in Philippines. Foreign Minister said Indonesian air force wanted to follow plane and destroy it but Foreign Minister and Prime Minister prevented, not wishing to become involved in international incident in last stage of military effort. Foreign Minister said obvious reason for strafing instead of bombing was that plane could not travel distance from Sanga Sanga to Gorontalo and return with bomb load.

Foreign Minister requested that US Government make further representations to Government of Philippines along lines of previous efforts to discourage further aid to rebels. He said GOI knew that Colonel Warouw middle of May had visited both Taiwan and Korea in effort to obtain additional B–26's and B–17's. GOI had assumed this mission was unsuccessful in view of developments since then but Sunday strafing has caused considerable concern. At this stage it would seem in interest of all concerned to end conflict as soon as possible at least to keep conflict within framework of Indonesian internal problem. Foreign Minister said he had already instructed his Ambassador in Manila to approach Philippine Government in effort to discourage further use of Sanga Sanga by rebels.

Menado military campaign was progressing most favorably, he reported. Government troops were approaching Menado from three sides and were now within 40 kilometers of city.[1]

Jones

---

[1] In telegram 170258Z from Djakarta, June 17, Naval Attaché Perry Shuman reported that Sunario informed both Shuman and Cole, on instructions from Nasution, that a rebel B–26 bomber had attacked Gorontalo on June 15. "Sunario said that Nasution understands that flight was probably without our knowledge and beyond our control," the message noted, "but desires any reassurances you may desire to make because he is being pressured by strong faction of senior Javanese colonels." (*Ibid.*, 756D.00/6–1758) See Supplement.

In telegram 3799 to Djakarta, June 19, the Department informed the Embassy as follows: "You may assure Subandrio US deplores the B–26 attack on Gorontalo and what appears to be evidence military assistance to rebels originating outside of Indonesia." (Department of State, Central Files, 756D.00/6–1758)

123.   Memorandum From the Director of the Bureau of
       Intelligence and Research (Cumming) to Secretary of State
       Dulles

Washington, June 20, 1958.

SUBJECT

Intelligence Note: *Intelligence Analysis of Prospects for Effective Anti-Communist
Action in Indonesia*

Recent reports from Embassy Djakarta indicate that a number of Indonesian leaders are considering plans to halt the progress of the Indonesian Communist Party (PKI). Among these leaders are the Chief of Staff of the Indonesian Army, Major General Nasution, Prime Minister Djuanda, Foreign Minister Subandrio; national and regional leaders of the Indonesian Nationalist Party (PNI) and the two major Muslim parties.

Proposed courses of action include a reshuffle of the present cabinet, a moratorium on political activity, a postponement of general elections for another five years, and a major economic development program to raise living standards and lessen the attraction of PKI promises. However, none of these leaders has prepared a well-defined anti-Communist program. The extent to which they represent the Army, the cabinet, and major non-Communist political parties is not clear. While General Nasution probably speaks for his immediate circle in Army headquarters, recent reports indicate that a number of senior Army officers oppose his action in seeking American support against the Communists. Proposals for a cabinet reshuffle have not advanced beyond a nebulous stage. Various other suggested actions against the Communists apparently have not been cleared by the cabinet or by President Sukarno. It cannot yet be taken for granted that the major non-Communist political parties are able or willing to commit their membership to an effective anti-Communist program.

In considering what action might be taken by the Indonesian government with the support of some of the elements mentioned above, the following considerations are relevant:

1) Indonesia will probably not abandon the "independent and active" foreign policy characteristic of its external relations since independence.
2) No really major changes in overall domestic policy are in prospect, for virtually all political groups are in general agreement on the main lines of present political, economic, and social policy.

Source: Department of State, Central Files, 756D.001/6–2058. Secret.

3) The personality and outlook of President Sukarno is a basically limiting factor on the formulation and execution of any anti-Communist program. While Sukarno's understanding of democracy sometimes varies with the US interpretation, he appears attached to most of the forms and some of the substance of democracy. An anti-Communist program which would appear to be clearly anti-democratic in outlawing a political party would most likely encounter his heavy opposition.

4) The Army, cabinet, and political party leaders who have recently spoken of the need to halt the progress of the PKI generally regard Sukarno with respect and even reverence because of the historic role he played in the achievement of Indonesian independence. Sukarno is still the dominant figure in the central government, and it is doubtful that Army, cabinet, or party leaders would be able or even willing to carry out an anti-Communist program without Sukarno's support or at least acquiescence.

5) The Indonesian Communists have made most of their progress by legal means. With every prospect of further expanding its electoral base in 1959, the PKI is likely to continue to emphasize legal means.

Embassy Djakarta has reported that non-Communist elements in the central government have already taken action against the PKI: prohibiting PKI action against US-owned property, limiting PKI exploitation of the celebration of May Day, prohibiting a mass rally against "foreign intervention" in the Indonesian rebellion, and statements by the PNI identifying the PKI as the servant of a foreign power. However, close analysis indicates these actions are of little substance in themselves. The prohibitions of PKI action against US property and of the mass rally may have been intended to prevent further deterioration in relations with the US. The regulations on the celebration of May Day were merely a repetition of similar regulations issued in 1957. The PNI statements were similar to statements issued by the PNI in 1951, 1954, and 1957. In any case, the power position of the PKI has not been disturbed by these actions.

No rumored central government action against the PKI holds out much hope of successfully blocking the Communists. While a cabinet reshuffle may take place their replacements will probably not impart a clearly anti-Communist flavor to the cabinet. Postponement of the 1959 general elections will be increasingly difficult, as preparations are already well-advanced, and this would be a clearly anti-democratic act which both Sukarno and the political leaders would probably find distasteful. A major economic development program to raise living standards would be a long-term project which Indonesia could hardly carry out with its limited resources. Domestic policies followed by the central government have effectively discouraged most private foreign investment, and Western government loans have been inhibited by the prospect of further Communist advances.

None of the foregoing courses of action, singly, would solve the Communist problem, and the prospects of the government's taking all of them together are remote. A possible solution was recently suggested to Ambassador Jones by a group of Moslem political leaders: the Communists could only be halted through satisfactory solution of the status of Western New Guinea and low living standards. They urged that the US contribute to a solution of these problems. From all indications successful resolution of the Western New Guinea question might be a sufficient price for Sukarno's cooperation in a campaign against the Communists. Improvement of the very low standard of living in Indonesia would in the long run tell significantly against the Communists, much of whose electoral support probably represents a protest vote against poverty.

A similar memorandum has been addressed to The Under Secretary.

---

124.   Telegram From the Embassy in Indonesia to the Department of State

Djakarta, June 24, 1958, 4 p.m.

4868. CINCPAC for POLAD. Foreign Minister informed me this morning that President would announce "strengthening of Cabinet" program some time today. He summarized actions to be taken as follows:

1.   Sultan of Djogjakarta would replace Sunardjo as Minister of Trade.
2.   Ministries of Hanafi and Tobing would be abolished but both would remain in Cabinet as Ministers without Portfolio.
3.   NU would obtain two additional Cabinet positions.

I pointed out that these changes in Cabinet were hardly sufficient to convince objective outsider that Indonesian Government was in fact taking steps to solve problem of Communism within Indonesia and said frankly that I was disappointed in result. Elimination of Hanafi had become a kind of symbol of genuineness of Indonesian determination to move against Commies. As long as he was in Cabinet American public would hardly consider Cabinet to be effectively anti-Communist.

Source: Department of State, Central Files, 756D.00/6–2458. Secret; Priority; Limit Distribution. Transmitted in two sections. Also sent to CINCPAC.

Foreign Minister explained that pressures had been very great but that army was still determined to get rid of Hanafi and he thought this would come as a second step in two or three months. However, strength of PKI was so great that with troops still in Sumatra and Sulawesi Sukarno had decided open challenge to Communists at this time was too dangerous. He pointed out that Hanafi would have no power in this Cabinet which actually had been and would continue to be run by an inner steering group and since he had no govt Department to supervise his claws had been rather effectively clipped. He also emphasized that new Cabinet actually represented move in right direction even though not as satisfactory from our standpoint as he had originally hoped and indeed been led to believe by Sukarno's assurances of several weeks ago.

I recalled statements I had made to him and Prime Minister in connection with US readiness provide military and economic support in accordance paragraph 4 Deptel 3300[1] and emphasized that this did not give us much to go on. We had hoped that Cabinet reshuffle would be more meaningful and that, as he knew, we were prepared to send token shipment of arms just as soon as rebellion over if effective action is taken against the Communists. I cautioned reaction of Washington to new Cabinet might well be so negative as to render such token shipment difficult if not impossible at this time.

Foreign Minister said he understood this but that number of unfortunate events had occurred which tended influence Sukarno not to move too far at this time. There was first most unfortunate Hensley story which had aroused President and made him suspicious. There were other recent events with which we both familiar (presumably he was referring to Pope case and repercussions therefrom). Much though he regretted pace could not be faster, what was done was in accordance with realities of Indonesian politics and he urged that I not be discouraged since, while result might take longer to achieve, outcome would ultimately be the same.

Comment: I felt it wise to be negative in my reaction to Subandrio's news in order maintain our pressure and stress necessity for continued anti-Communist action. Actually I do not feel as pessimistic as indicated in above summary. The fact that any action at all has been taken at this time should be encouraging to us, especially in light of adverse factors,

---

[1] Document 92.

e.g. Pope case, Hensley article,[2] continuing discovery by Army mopping-up units in Sumatra of new US-made equipment stored in rebel caches. While meaning and importance of Hanafi retention remains to be seen, elimination of his ministry could be distinctly helpful development since its principal function was as leftist propaganda machine. Nasution remains determined as ever in anti-Communist stand and in resolution eliminate Hanafi from Cabinet. While this might be taken as evidence Nasution cannot stand up against Sukarno, it must be appreciated at present time Nasution's hands tried as result of forces being otherwise occupied. On whole although shuffle not as good as hoped it may be great deal better than we had reason expect in present situation. If Sultan actually joins Cabinet, his presence may prove to be of real significance as time goes on in providing solid cornerstone for future improvements.

Since dictating above, I have been informed that Cabinet announcement will be postponed until tomorrow.[3]

Jones

---

[2] Reference is to an article by Stewart Hensley, a Washington-based reporter for United Press International, which was carried by the Indonesian News Agency Antara on June 11, stating that diplomatic authorities recently said that relations between the United States and Indonesia continued to improve and predicted that the next few weeks would bring even greater harmony. The text of Antara's summary of Hensley's story was transmitted to the Department in telegram 4691 from Djakarta, June 12. (Department of State, Central Files, 611.56D/6–1258)

[3] The Indonesian Cabinet reshuffle was announced on June 25 and Jones commented on the changes in telegram 4928 of June 27. "From US viewpoint," the telegram read in part, "reshuffle is somewhat disappointing but in light of factors Embassy has reported over period of time probably best that could be expected at this moment." (Ibid., 756D.00/6–2758) See Supplement.

125.   Telegram From the Embassy in Indonesia to the Department
of State

Djakarta, June 26, 1958, 2 p.m.

4904. Embtel 4883.[1] At dinner Embassy residence last night Ambassador Moekarto informed Director USOM Baird and me in effect that ball was now in US court and future US-Indonesian relations would depend on how we played it. He admitted Cabinet change did not go as far as he would have liked—he had argued for complete elimination Hanafi—but it was step in right direction and considering political, economic and military situation, he believed, as he had indicated to me earlier in day and reported reftel, this was best that could be done. He repeated that situation was much more complex than had been apparent to him from Washington. He was amazed at variety, scope and intensity of Communist activity and at campaign they are conducting to discredit him. He was also dismayed at attitude of Prime Minister and Foreign Minister—they have stated to him frankly that the policy towards US has failed despite fact that they have followed his advice step by step.

Asked if GOI had actually followed his advice, he replied, "Yes, in every detail." Source close to President had also told him that President shared these views as to failure of policy and also of Moekarto effectively to represent his country in US. He has attempted to explain realities of political attitudes of US towards Indonesia and necessity of Indonesia to make more definite moves against Communists. He was surprised to find that not only officials of government but PNI leaders as well are firmly convinced that they have made such moves, yet US has not recognized them and has not reciprocated. That, he says, has created an apparent stalemate which must be broken if free momentum of improvement of relationships between the two countries is to be sustained.

He was surprised to find that Djuanda, who has always been considered an American stooge by Indonesians, he said, is so negative towards US in his present thinking. Apparently Djuanda feels he is being

---

Source: Department of State, Central Files, 611.56D/6–2658. Secret; Priority. Also sent to CINCPAC for POLAD.

[1] In telegram 4883, June 25, Jones reported on a conversation he had that morning with Moekarto, during which Moekarto informed him that the reason for the Indonesian Government's postponement of the announcement of changes in the cabinet was the Sultan of Djogjakarta's decision that he would not join the cabinet under present conditions. (*Ibid.*, 756D.13/6–2558) See Supplement.

228 Foreign Relations, 1958–1960, Volume XVII

forsaken by US and is not receiving support, understanding or appreciation of significance of anti-Communist moves that have taken place.

Moekarto said that Indonesian military within coming year are going to equip themselves with modern arms and they want them from US. However, they will not wait any longer and will turn to Russia if US fails to act. Moekarto expressed great distress at this possibility and indicated his awareness of Soviet penetration and increasing influence Indonesia under these circumstances.

Moekarto said he had failed to understand US position as he felt that not only American press but Congress was much more understanding and sympathetic towards Indonesia than State Department. He felt informed public opinion in US would support bolder moves in extending assistance to Indonesia in her current struggle against economic disruption and Communist infiltration.

He brought up subject of construction military barracks from counterpart funds and said he had discussed this at some length with Assistant Secretary Robertson. He felt this gesture would be much appreciated by military and had impression that action of this kind would strengthen his position against criticism now being directed against him. He is preparing list of Export-Import Bank applications currently stalled for submission to Ambassador.[2]

Jones

---

[2] In a subsequent conversation with Baird on June 27, Moekarto clarified his remarks concerning Djuanda, indicating that he had not meant to imply that the Prime Minister was becoming anti-American. (Telegram 4940 from Djakarta, June 28; Department of State, Central Files, 611.56D/6–2858) See Supplement.

---

126. Editorial Note

On June 26 at the 370th meeting of the National Security Council, Allen Dulles discussed Indonesian developments during his intelligence briefing. The following exchange took place:

"In Indonesia, the fight for Menado still goes on. In that area the rebels were putting up a very good show, though they are likely soon to lose the town. We are in close touch with their activity, and after the fall of Menado guerrilla fighting is likely to continue in the Celebes as it is still continuing in Sumatra. The rebels have warned that unless we provide them with assistance they will undertake reprisals against U.S. oil installations on Sumatra, as they have already been attacking British and Dutch installations. They argue that to deprive the Central Government of oil revenues may be the only way to bring the Djakarta Government to its knees.

The President commented that it was queer that the Indonesian rebels put up such a poor showing [*less than 1 line of source text not declassified*]. Now that the organized fighting is over, they begin to show greater forcefulness. Was it their object to induce the United States to intervene? Mr. Allen Dulles thought that [*1-1/2 lines of source text not declassified*] the recent shift in the composition of the Djakarta Cabinet was so minor in character as not to constitute a significant change. The Sultan of Djogjakarta had been asked to join the new Cabinet, but declined to do so. Secretary Dulles asked Mr. Allen Dulles whether he was certain that the Sultan had been requested to join the Cabinet. Mr. Allen Dulles said he was quite sure that this had been the case. Meanwhile, we have alerted the American oil companies against the threat of guerrilla attacks by the rebels against their installations." (Memorandum of discussion by Gleason, June 27; Eisenhower Library, Whitman File, NSC Records)

On June 23 President Eisenhower wrote a 9-page personal letter to Paul Hoffman, former head of the Economic Cooperation Administration, in which he discussed "the things that seem constantly on my mind." The letter included the following comments on Indonesia:

"There is very little to be said about Indonesia that you do not already know, except to observe that it remains a worry to the Administration. With Sukarno's ambitions and his leftish leanings, with his readiness to take Communist support, and his seeming preference for the radicals rather than the more conservative sectors of Moslem people, the situation could well become serious in that area of the world. At the moment we can do little more than remain alert." (Eisenhower Library, Whitman File, Eisenhower Diaries)

127. Memorandum of the Substance of Discussion at a Department of State–Joint Chiefs of Staff Meeting

Washington, June 27, 1958, 10 a.m.

PRESENT

Defense

General Twining, USAF
General Taylor, USA
Admiral Burke, USN
General White, USAF
General Pate, USMC
Lt. General Picher, USAF
Maj. General Wheeler, USA
Vice Admiral Libby, USN
Maj. General Cary, USAF
Brig. General Mangrum, USMC
Brig. General Wentworth, USAF
Captain Carde, USN
Rear Admiral Triebel, USN
Maj. General Barnes, USA
Colonel Moses, USA
Colonel Phillips, USA

JSSC

Maj. General Timberman, USA
Rear Admiral Dudley, USN

ISA

Mr. Sprague
Lt. General Fox
Lt. General Byers

State

Mr. Robert Murphy
Mr. Frederick Reinhardt
Mr. Gerard Smith
Mr. Walter Robertson
Amb. Joseph S. Farland
Mr. Stewart Rockwell
Mr. Allen Stewart
Mr. Roswell McClelland
Mr. Richard Finn

CIA

Mr. Robert Amory

NSC

Mr. Gleason

1.   *Indonesia.*

General Taylor said that we are moving pretty fast in Indonesia but maybe not fast enough. The situation in Indonesia has improved somewhat with a Cabinet change. It is important to give General Nasution material support right away. It might be desirable to get Presidential approval for the $7 million package in assistance and we would then be in a position to move rapidly if the situation required it.

Mr. Robertson described the background leading up to the recent Cabinet changes, noting that the changes were disappointing, that the Indonesians had indicated that the changes would be more drastic and

---

Source: Department of State, State–JCS Meetings: Lot 61 D 417. Secret. No drafting information indicated on the source text. The meeting was held at the Pentagon. A note on the source text reads: "State Draft. Not cleared with the Department of Defense."

that Hanafi, the extreme leftist, remains in the Cabinet. A telegram has gone out authorizing additional assistance;[1] the Army Attaché is to advise General Nasution directly and the Indonesian Government is not to know. Sukarno remains the dominant personality and it is a calculated risk to attempt to strengthen Nasution's position.

Admiral Burke said that Nasution is now the only hope we have in Indonesia. His position is being weakened by certain Javanese officers. It is important we try to strengthen his position. The program for training ten Indonesian officers in intelligence matters should be got under way.

General Taylor stressed the importance of getting authority to expend funds for various items of military assistance to Indonesia. General Byers[2] noted that funds are not currently available and special Presidential authorization will be necessary; the intelligence training program will cost only a very small amount.

It was agreed that steps should be taken to obtain Presidential authorization so as to be prepared to move when political conditions warrant.

Admiral Burke noted that the UK is evidently planning to sell some airplanes to Indonesia. Mr. Robertson said we had not been consulted and that this would be raised with the UK. Mr. Murphy noted that the French may also be planning to sell planes to Indonesia.

[Here follows discussion of other subjects.]

---

[1] Reference is presumably to telegram 3858 to Djakarta, June 25, which approved additional assistance for the Indonesian Army, including the furnishing of radio sets, the issuing of export licenses for transmitting sets, gasoline generators, and dry radio batteries, and the provision of training for Indonesian Army intelligence officers. (*Ibid.*, Central Files, 756D.00/6–1958) See Supplement.

[2] Lieutenant General Clovis E. Byers, USA, Military Adviser to the Assistant Secretary of Defense for International Security Affairs.

128.   Telegram From the Department of State to the Embassy in Indonesia

Washington, June 27, 1958, 9:48 p.m.

3901. For the Ambassador from the Secretary. Indonesian leaders have repeatedly told you that they would not be able to conduct military campaign and take action against Communist threat simultaneously but that upon conclusion military campaign definite action against Communists would be taken. We assume therefore that since Army has announced Menado has fallen and since military campaign now concluded something will be done going beyond the insignificant Cabinet reshuffle announced June 25.

Governments of neighboring countries have been repeatedly expressing to us their concern at growing influence and ambitions Communist Party and increasing activities Sino-Soviet bloc in Indonesia. They feel this endangers them. We believe we should let Sukarno know of this concern on part neighboring countries and seek determine from him nature his plans now that military campaign over and obtain from him assurances on which we might rely in defining our attitude.

You should therefore seek appointment with Sukarno soon as possible and speak along following lines.

Some governments in Far East have recently approached US Government and expressed grave concern at growing strength and influence of Communist Party in Indonesia and at increased activities Sino-Soviet bloc in area. They fear that with successful conclusion of military campaign against rebels the Communist threat might increase thereby jeopardizing their own security and independence and ultimately that of the entire area. This concern on their part appears to us to be genuine and justifiable unless the government of Indonesia is prepared in fact to arrest the growth of influence of PKI which seeks bring Indonesia's political and military structures more and more under the domination of International Communism which will then in turn seek to subvert neighboring countries.

We would like to be able to indicate to these governments that we have confidence that the Indonesian authorities will take the necessary internal measures to check the growth of Communist power and thus to prevent Indonesia from being moved into the Communist camp and effectively losing its independence.

It must be clear to all who study international affairs that PKI is an instrument of Sino-Soviet imperialism and that it takes its direction

---

Source: Department of State, Central Files, 756D.00/6–2758. Top Secret; Limit Distribution. Drafted by Mein, O'Sullivan, and Dulles and approved by Robertson and Dulles.

from leaders of Sino-Soviet bloc and their Communist parties. Recent statements by Nehru that Communist Party in India is guided from without applies equally to PKI and every other Communist Party that follows the International Communist line. It has been demonstrated time and again, most recently by Soviet action in Hungary and by its present policy toward Yugoslavia, that International Communism is intolerant of genuine independence. The President should realistically recognize it as a fact that there cannot but be some reaction on the part of those, Indonesians and neighbors of Indonesia, who see in rising Communist influence prospect of alien domination. They are not, in fact, going to be placidly acquiescent in that.

The President should know that US policy proceeds from the premise that Indonesia should be a vigorous independent member of society of free nations. We assume that this is also the President's desire. Our policy led us to give support to the desire of Indonesia for independence in the postwar period. Our policy in this respect has never wavered and under it we have given moral, political and economic support to government of Indonesia so long as we could feel confident that such support was helping Indonesia to be independent. In further implementation of this policy US Government would be prepared, if the government of Indonesia takes definite measures toward eliminating Communist threat, to extend additional substantial economic aid and such military aid as would seem appropriate to maintain internal order as against any Communist subversive threat.

The US seeks for itself nothing whatsoever from Indonesia other than that it should be genuinely independent nation. We are sure this is also the desire of the other countries in the area. We would therefore welcome knowledge of concrete measures which the Indonesian Government contemplates taking and also an indication of what the US might do to assist Indonesia in maintaining its freedom and independence. This would put us in a position to enable us to reassure Indonesia's neighbors who bring to us their concern which we also share.

We are not seeking to align Indonesia with SEATO as occasionally charged. We fully respect the decision of any government to avoid international alignments, even though we ourselves believe that collective security is the best security. History of US relations with Indonesia, as well as with India, Burma and Afghanistan bear ample testimony on sincerity this policy.

SEATO itself has no objective other than mutual defense. It is not and cannot become an instrument of interference in the domestic affairs of any nation.

FYI. You should let Nasution and Djuanda know of this approach to the President to strengthen their hands in their discussions with him for definite action against Communist threat. Also, to strengthen further Nasution's and Army's position we are taking steps listed Deptel 3858.[1]

Dulles

---

[1] See footnote 1, Document 127.

---

129. Telegram From the Department of State to the Embassy in Indonesia

Washington, June 28, 1958, 4:12 p.m.

3911. For Ambassador from the Secretary. Supplementing Deptel 3901[1] you may also wish to point out to the President that while the Government has dealt with the overt and organized aspects of the rebellion it cannot, without moving away from Communism, deal with the economic or underground aspects of the problem.

The rebels have not been exterminated to any appreciable extent. They have been driven underground where they remain as embers which could flare up to keep the economy and the solvency of the nation in a precarious state. The economic prospect is indeed bleak unless the GOI can assure good long-term relations with the free world nations which regard Communism as their enemy. The Soviet bloc has ample surplus military equipment. But it cannot provide the markets which Indonesia requires for its natural products nor can it provide the agricultural products which the West, notably the United States, possesses in surplus, but which are in very short supply in the Soviet Union and China. The Communist leaders in Indonesia, probably taking orders from outside, may, like International Communists everywhere, be indifferent to human misery if it gives them opportunity, and they may feel that it is to their political advantage to invite economic and fiscal chaos on the theory that where such chaos exists they can increase their political power. But surely this is not in the interest of the people or Government of Indonesia.

Dulles

Source: Department of State, Central Files, 756D.00/6–2858. Top Secret; Priority; Limit Distribution. Drafted and approved by Dulles.

[1] Document 128.

130. Telegram From the Embassy in Indonesia to the Department of State

Djakarta, June 28, 1958, 4 p.m.

4945. Deptel 3858.[1] ARMA saw General Nasution this morning immediately following his return from 3 day inspection trip Palembang.[2] General was obviously pleased and asked that Col Cole meet Col Ibnu on June 30 to work out details and determine specific requirements bridge equipment. I am seeing Foreign Minister tonight and will pass on similar information.

Nasution also told ARMA meeting would be held next week by Prime Minister with three chiefs of staff to discuss long list of requirements submitted to us year ago and consider how to renew request. General emphasized vital importance getting something started in arms support area.

As for economic sabotage by rebel action Sumatra, General said he fully aware danger and had issued orders to military commanders to establish armed guards for estates. He said Col Ibnu had responsibility for preventing damage oil fields. He also pointed out significantly that Army has now a Colonel as Cabinet minister who will be able to look after economic matters.

Comment: It is clear from what Nasution said that he believes he will shortly have qualified for military assistance on basis my original approach authorized by Deptel 3300.[3] With conclusion Menado campaign, reshuffle of cabinet and assurances as to army plans gradually to curb communism in Indonesia, General made it obvious he now looks to us for support.

Jones

Source: Department of State, Central Files, 756D.00/6–2858. Secret; Niact.

[1] See footnote 1, Document 127.

[2] Cole reported on his meeting with Nasution in telegram CX 216, June 28. He stated that he passed on the information contained in telegram 3858 to Nasution and the General "seemed quite pleased." (Department of State, Central Files, 756D.00/6–2858) See Supplement.

[3] Document 92.

131. Memorandum of Conversation

Paris, July 5, 1958.

SUBJECT

The Secretary's Talks with the French Minister of Foreign Affairs, Paris,
July 5—Indonesia

PARTICIPANTS

French Foreign Minister Maurice Couve de Murville
French Ambassador, Hervé Alphand
M. Louis Joxe, Secretary General of the French Foreign Office
M. Jean Laloy
M. Pierre Sebilleau
M. Jacques Baraduc
M. Jean Daridan

The Secretary
Ambassador Amory Houghton
Mr. Cecil Lyon
Mr. C. Burke Elbrick
Mr. Andrew Berding
Mr. Philip Farley
Mr. Randolph Kidder
Mr. John Tuthill
Mr. Matthew Looram

With regard to Indonesia, the Secretary noted that there had been a
spontaneous revolt, particularly in Sumatra and the Celebes, against
Sukarno's trend toward Communism. [1 *line of source text not declassified*]
In view of the arms they had received, the rebels in Sumatra could have
made a serious stand, but unfortunately they did not do so. They had
since withdrawn to the jungle, but had not as yet given up. In the
Celebes the rebels had shown more will to fight and this was partly due
to outside air support. In Sumatra the Indonesian Government had had
complete control of the air, which had had a demoralizing effect.

Some six weeks ago, the Secretary said, we had concluded that the
rebels were going to collapse unless they received overt assistance. We
accordingly decided to see if, before the embers of the rebellion became
completely cold, we could not get the Indonesian Government to move
away from the Communist camp. We were then told that Sukarno
would revamp the cabinet. This was in fact done, but the new cabinet
had reflected no basic change in orientation. As a result, we had given
our Ambassador instructions to tell Sukarno that unless he took positive

---

Source: Department of State, Central Files, 756D.00/7–558. Top Secret. Drafted by
Looram of WE. Dulles was in Paris for talks with French leaders July 3–5.

steps away from Communism, it would not be possible to prevent the neighboring countries from rendering assistance to the rebels. In the Philippines, Taiwan and Korea, there was great concern over developments in Indonesia and accordingly a desire to help the rebels. The situation might therefore come to a head very soon: either Sukarno would come around or increased rebel activity would be permitted. It must be recognized, the Secretary stated, that Sukarno was extremely adroit and was getting considerable matériel of a military nature from the Soviet Union and Communist China.

In response to the French Foreign Minister's request for the Secretary's over-all estimate of Sukarno, the Secretary said that Sukarno was like Nasser in many respects. He undoubtedly wished to be independent. However, he thought that he could accept Communist aid and still remain independent. In fact he was becoming more and more dependent on the Soviets. Of course, it must be noted, the Secretary stated, that there was a very large and effective Communist party in Indonesia. The economic conditions of the country were deplorable and the Communists thrived on this situation. If elections were held today, the Secretary said, the Communist party would undoubtedly receive more votes than they had obtained the last time.

---

132.   Telegram From the Embassy in Indonesia to the Department of State

Djakarta, July 7, 1958, 1 p.m.

83. CINCPAC also for POLAD. In absence of Foreign Minister who is on 4-day leave, Secretary General Suwito summoned me at 9 o'clock this morning to inform me that 4-engine bomber at 12:55 local time July 6 had flown over Donggala in north central Sulawesi (west coast) from west to east and dropped oil drums on roofs of houses in small village of Wani. Latter is located between Taiwaeli and Laeba (map coordinates 0039 south 11949 east). Amount of damage still under investigation.

When I pressed him for details he said he had none but would supply them as soon as obtained. I expressed amazement because I could

---

Source: Department of State, Central Files, 756D.00/7–758. Secret; Niact; Limit Distribution. Transmitted in two sections and repeated to Taipei, Manila, and CINCPAC.

not conceive what could be purpose of such raid. Suwito said GOI did not know, but in strictest confidence he would tell me that Major Samba was hiding in village of Donggala or vicinity and that GOI speculation was that drums were to supply oil and gas for rescue plane.

What distressed Indonesian Government was that this represented continuance of outside interference. Prime Minister, he said, was very much upset this morning because there was no place in Indonesia not under control of GOI forces from which 4-engine plane could operate. This meant plane was either based in Taiwan or Philippines but GOI believed it to be Taiwan. Whether purpose of raid was to cause damage or to rescue rebel leader made no difference to GOI, he said—both cases constituted continuance of foreign intervention.

Coming at this time, he said, event was particularly unfortunate. GOI would do everything possible to prevent incident reaching newspapers but this was not easy with this incident added to B–26 actions of June 15 and 27. He did not imply that US Government had anything to do with this but requested that we do everything possible to suppress further actions of this character. Should story get out, he emphasized, nothing could prevent Communists from exploiting situation in such a way as to cause serious deterioration in US-Indonesian relations and destroy much of what had been accomplished in last two months.

He described plane as probably B–29, whereupon I pointed out there were no B–29's in this part of world and that I would appreciate further details of aircraft description if possible. Since drop took place at noon one could assume good visibility this time of year. My own guess was that if in fact this was 4-engine aircraft it was probably DC–4.

Suwito said that what distressed Prime Minister was that this kind of thing should still continue after rebel forces had been defeated. Since big plane of this kind could easily be identified and must be serviced at sizable airport, GOI recognized that effort of this character could not take place without cognizance of government of whatever territory involved. In interest of improving US-Indonesian relations he pleaded that US exert all possible pressure on governments in area to prevent further occurrences, mentioning again particularly GRC on Taiwan and Philippine Government.

Comment: In view Taipei despatch 739[1] of June 4 there seems no doubt that plane came from Taiwan. At this stage of improving relations here continuance of this kind of thing makes no sense. Possibility of Communist takeover of Indonesia can be greatly enhanced if mutual effort to improve relations can be nipped in bud. Following on heels of Pope case I can think of nothing more likely to accomplish this than publicity on these incidents which will inevitably follow their continuance. It is impossible to convince Indonesians that US does not have sufficient influence in Pacific to stop this kind of thing if we wish to and if this continues they will believe it to be case of right and left hand regardless of how strong our assurances to them may be. They know GRC could not exist without US support and consequently will continue to believe US lending tacit support to this kind of thing unless incidents cease.

Taipei despatch 739 indicates GRC see advantages continue limited support Indonesian rebels. I regard continued rebel resistance as providing absolutely no leverage whatsoever in moving Indonesians towards anti-Communist position. On contrary such action only exacerbates situation and ties down GOI army preventing its return to Java where it has and we believe will continue exert pressures against Communists. Therefore I recommend Department authorize Ambassador Drumright outline our views to Foreign Minister Yeh and seek withdrawal GRC support to rebels.[2]

Jones

---

[1] In despatch 739 Ambassador Drumright reported a conversation he had on June 4 with Foreign Minister Yeh during which the Foreign Minister summarized a conversation he had in Taipei with Indonesian insurgent leader Colonel Warouw 4 or 5 days earlier. Warouw had appealed for military assistance from the Republic of China and Yeh told Drumright "that the Chinese are continuing to assist the Indonesian dissidents. He said that an unspecified quantity of small arms made in Chinese arsenals had recently been dispatched to the dissidents." (*Ibid.,* 756D.00/6–458) See Supplement.

[2] In telegram 20 to Taipei, July 8, the Department asked Drumright to discuss with Foreign Minister Yeh the points raised in telegram 83 from Djakarta, "urging him for reasons discussed by Jones to discourage any further raids against Indonesian forces if they are in fact being staged by ChiNats." (Department of State, Central Files, 756D.00/7–758) See Supplement.

In telegram 118 from Djakarta, July 9, Jones reported that during a call on Djuanda that morning he informed the Prime Minister that the United States deplored the air raid by a four-engine plane reported in telegram 83. The Ambassador said the United States also deplored what appeared to be evidence of military assistance to the rebels originating outside of Indonesia. "He expressed appreciation," Jones noted, "and seemed convinced that I meant what I said and was not merely going through motions." (Department of State, Central Files, 756D.00/7–958) See Supplement.

133. Telegram From the Embassy in Indonesia to the Department of State

Djakarta, July 9, 1958, 5 p.m.

130. CINCPAC for POLAD. Department pass CNO, ACSI, AFCIN. Admiral Riley[1] reported following his conversation today with General Nasution that General had told him he was working out detailed plan under Djuanda's instructions for control of Communism within Indonesia. Essence of this plan was that reliable anti-Communist officers would be appointed as links in nationwide system of supervision in various military territories. This would apply down through village level as well as to specific functional areas such as trade unions, business, shipping, veterans organizations and the like. These officers would report through special channels to regional commanders, to General Nasution, to Djuanda. Plan had not yet been submitted to Djuanda for approval.

Nasution also said plan called for this control to be exercised directly by Djuanda acting as Minister of Defense without involving cabinet which would not be informed of program.

General also referred to foreign intervention as one of most difficult obstacles he had to face in posing armed forces in anti-Communist direction. Admiral Riley responded that US had exerted all possible influence to quell outside assistance to rebels.

Re damage to Sumatran estates, Nasution said he was doing everything possible assure protection but this would be difficult because of shortage of troops.

Admiral Riley said he was much impressed with General Nasution and believed he was officer on whom we could count.

Comment: What General Nasution appears to have envisaged is an organization to control Communist activity but invisible to general public. He has been under considerable criticism for his regulations controlling political activity in outer areas and is sensitive to this.

He does not want army to appear to be undermining democratic institutions in Indonesia but does wish to create military organization to combat Communism.

Details of this plan are not yet available, although we have heard it referred to frequently in past. Since plan has not yet been submitted to

---

Source: Department of State, Central Files, 756D.00/7–958. Secret; Priority. Also sent to CINCPAC and repeated to Canberra, Manila, and Taipei.

[1] Vice Admiral Herbert Riley, CINCPAC Chief of Staff, was in Indonesia on a brief visit.

Djuanda, presumption is that it is still in tentative form. Embassy will report further information as soon as available.[2]

Jones

---

[2] During his visit to Indonesia, Admiral Riley also met with Foreign Minister Subandrio. In telegram 120 from Djakarta, July 9, the Embassy reported that Subandrio emphasized that such visits were of great importance in bringing about understanding between the armed forces of the United States and Indonesia, and he was only sorry that the visit had to be so short. (Department of State, Central Files, 756D.00/7–958) See Supplement.

Riley reported on his trip to Indonesia in telegram 100600Z from ALUSNA Melbourne to CINCPAC, July 10. He noted in part that there was complete agreement among all the U.S. military attachés in Indonesia "about attainment of US objectives in Indonesia hinging on strengthening army so that it can control communism, prevent further destruction of economy, and influence political changes we are seeking. Priority of US objectives should provide for assistance to Army as first objective to facilitate attainment other objectives." (National Archives and Records Administration, RG 218, JCS Records, CCS 092 Asia (8–22–46)) See Supplement.

---

134.   Telegram From the Embassy in Indonesia to the Department of State

Djakarta, July 15, 1958, 6 p.m.

220. Department pass CINCPAC. CINCPAC also for POLAD. Foreign Minister asked me to call this afternoon to discuss two matters primarily: (1) Continued bombings of North Sulawesi and (2) Iraq situation.

Re bombings he said three places in North Sulawesi—Wori, Kema, and Pitung—had been bombed last night by B–26. He has been requested to report to Cabinet meeting tonight on this matter and particularly US attitude regarding it. Cabinet would discuss preparation of appeal to UN against foreign aggression, he said. He deplored this because of its effect on US-Indonesian relations at a time when these relations were improving but he said reaction of President, Prime Minister and majority of Cabinet was so strong that he was afraid unless bomb-

---

Source: Department of State, Central Files, 756D.00/7–1558. Secret; Niact; Limit Distribution. Transmitted in two sections and repeated to Taipei and Manila.

ings stopped decision would be taken. He did not imply US involvement; he did recognize that part of evidence would be submission Pope diary and other exhibits which would have unfortunate effect here. Among other evidence which he had not mentioned before were labels from crates containing arms showing shipment from Taiwan via Clark Field. He added that President, Prime Minister, Deputy Prime Minister, Chief of Staff and himself were meeting tomorrow to consider this whole question.

I repeated what I had said on earlier occasions, that US Government deplored continuing air raids and what appeared to be evidence military assistance to rebels originating outside Indonesia. I also told him that in response to earlier request (Embtel 83)[1] further representations had been made. He reiterated what he had said earlier, that GOI military controlled all airports within Indonesia from which B–26 could operate. Therefore plane must be serviced on foreign territory. I said we would appreciate any information as to probable location of airport of origin. As he was aware, US Government was doing its best to discourage outside assistance from whatever source.

He reverted to earlier request that Secretary Dulles make some statement (Embtel 4946).[2] I pointed out that my response constituted in effect a statement by Secretary since he had authorized me to provide the Foreign Minister with such assurances on his behalf. Subandrio said that important thing about statement on part of Secretary was effect on Indonesian people generally as well as upon President Sukarno in particular. If Dulles made public statement it would be taken as gospel here. Witness tremendous effect May 20 statement had upon situation.

I responded along lines of Deptel 3935[3] and emphasized that it would appear somewhat gratuitous with world-wide attention focused on Middle East for Secretary to make a statement regarding Indonesian rebellion which everywhere in America was considered as having been concluded. Foreign Minister continued to plead, leading me to conclusion that Sukarno himself had suggested this. I said that I would of course report what he had said but in light of considerations I had mentioned I could not be too optimistic. Foreign Minister indicated global point of view and recognized it appeared as small matter but he earnestly considered it could be helpful to US-Indonesian relations here.

Re Iraq said Cabinet would raise question with him tonight as to recognition of rebel regime and he inquired as to US attitude. I told him I had no information as to Iraqi situation except what I had heard on radio

---

[1] Document 132.

[2] Dated June 29. (Department of State, Central Files, 756D.00/6–2858)

[3] Dated June 30. (*Ibid.*) See Supplement.

and that this obviously came from rebel source. I counseled "wait and see" attitude. He indicated this was line he would take but requested that I obtain as soon as possible for his information analysis of situation as US saw it and an indication of our position. He would appreciate my calling him at any time in office or at home in view of urgency of matter and seriousness of crisis. He had already been informed that US naval vessels were in Arabian Sea. I promised that I would advise him soonest. I again raised question of when I might see President and informed him of conversation Embtel 186.[4] He had no information but would advise me.

There has been mutual cooling off between President and PKI in recent weeks, Subandrio said. This presents US with real opportunity. "We cannot save Indonesia from Communism without President," he said. "And we must have help from US." I countered with observation this was Indonesian not US problem—that we wanted to help but it was up to them. Foreign Minister agreed. "But you must lead us—you must push us," he said. President has idea US and perhaps Russia too is adopting "wait and see" attitude toward Indonesia. This is no good. They were not expecting dramatic help but they did need to be shown US was not inactive.

This connection continuation of rebel bombings was serious psychological problem to Indonesians. Even Nasution did not understand it. He was saying on subject of communism, "give me the tools and I will do the job." And he wanted US arms. But he was baffled by bombings which kept resistance going, delayed possibility his using troops for anti-Communist purpose and generally upset schedule he and Prime Minister had in mind.

"Let us not reach an impasse," Subandrio pleaded. I replied we were just as anxious as he to avoid an impasse. But we had to work this out together. US had to have some indication of GOI intentions. One of purposes of my talk with Sukarno would be to find out what he is thinking about—where do we go from here?

Comment: Indonesian charges before UN of foreign intervention would be most unfortunate at this time in view Middle East tensions. It is possible Foreign Minister was bluffing or tossing out thinly veiled threat, but this is not my judgement. We appear to be gradually sliding backward as result of continued bombings to something resembling situation immediately prior May 2.

---

[4] In telegram 186, July 14, Jones reported that during an outing for the Diplomatic Corps the previous day he told Sukarno that he was "very anxious to have a talk with him." Jones and Sukarno agreed to meet at Bogor Palace rather than in Djakarta indicating that they could talk longer there without interruption. (Department of State, Central Files, 756D.11/7–1458)

As to request for Secretary to make some statement on continuation of bombings, I recognize validity of considerations raised in Deptel 3935. However in view of recent publicity here on B–29 and B–26 raids, perhaps Department could plant question in Secretary's press conference which would bring out brief comment that would help us here. I make this suggestion with considerable hesitation because I am reluctant to add to Secretary's burdens at time when his full attention needs to be concentrated elsewhere. But this might be of considerable importance in preventing deterioration relations with GOI leaders particularly Indonesian military so important to realization US objectives.[5]

Jones

---

[5] Telegram 163 to Djakarta, July 19, explained that an unsolicited public statement by the Secretary on bombing raids appearing in the U.S. press would be certain to raise other questions that might be more harmful than the original statement would be helpful. Jones should inform Subandrio of the above and let him know that the United States was again approaching governments of neighboring countries regarding continued bombing missions. (*Ibid.*, 756D.00/7–1558) See Supplement.

In telegram 320 from Djakarta, July 23, Jones reported that he called on Foreign Minister Subandrio that afternoon and apprised him of the Department's reaction to his suggestion that Dulles make a statement about the recent bombings. (Department of State, Central Files, 756D.00/7–2358) See Supplement.

---

135. Telegram From the Commander in Chief, Pacific (Stump) to the Chief of Naval Operations (Burke)

Honolulu, July 16, 1958, 12:06 p.m.

162206Z. Personal for Adm Burke from Stump. Despite transcendency of MidEast situation, I urge favorable response to AmEmb Djakarta niact tel 220[1] to Dept State, in form of (ALFA) statement by Sec State (bravo) stronger representations to Presidents Chiang and Garcia.

My thought is that if we permit Indonesian situation to retrogress while attention is focused on MidEast, we will be providing the Com-

---

Source: Department of State, Djakarta Embassy Files: Lot 63 F 50, 350.21 Communism. Secret; Priority. Repeated to Djakarta.

[1] Document 134.

munist bloc exactly what it needs for diversionary action through which another bonfire may be started which could lead toward a possible catastrophic loss to the free world. Without use of ChiNat and/or Philippine bases continuation of rebel bombings would not be possible. It would be impossible for me if I were an Indonesian and it is impossible for me as CINCPAC to believe that the US is impotent enough to be unable to stop these raids, which are encouraging to the rebels and which involve retention of GOI troops outside of Java where they are needed to guard against PKI uprisings, which are feared by those in the GOI whom we hope are anxious to move in the direction we want them to go.[2]

---

[2] A marginal notation on the source text, apparently by Jones, reads: "Good for Stump!"

---

136. Telegram From the Embassy in Indonesia to the Department of State

Djakarta, July 21, 1958, 6 p.m.

301. CINCPAC also for POLAD. Deptels 3901,[1] 3911[2] and 163 (paragraph 2).[3] President was in most serious mood when I saw him at Bogor this morning. He greeted me cordially but even before serving coffee, he said, shaking his head, "Trouble, trouble, trouble." Then before I had chance to comment, he said urgently, "Tell me about Middle East. What will happen there?"

[Here follows brief discussion of the Lebanon crisis.]

President then said the psychological situation between Indonesia and US was not good and was beginning again to deteriorate. He said improvement that had occurred few weeks ago had been pretty well wiped out by continuation of bombings by B–26s. I commented along

---

Source: Department of State, Central Files, 756D.00/7–2158. Secret; Niact; Limit Distribution. Also sent to CINCPAC. Transmitted in three sections.

[1] Document 128.

[2] Document 129.

[3] See footnote 5, Document 134. Paragraph 2 informed the Embassy that the Department intended to approach "neighboring countries" with regard to the continued bombing missions in Indonesia.

lines of Deptel 163 and then made point that, unlike Soviet Russia with satellites, we could not give orders to independent countries in Far East and consequently had no control over situation. Repeated representations had been made to these countries. If bombings were continued it was undoubtedly reflection of grave concern of neighboring governments at growing strength and influence of Communist Party in Indonesia. I pointed out such concern was only natural. I was certain Sukarno would feel the same way if he believed Malaya was about to go Communist and then I developed points in Deptel 3901, emphasizing character of PKI as foreign controlled party within Indonesia, referring to Nehru's statements and breaking off presentation prior to presenting statement of what US was prepared to do. At this point I said we recognized that new situation had developed as result of military victory over rebels and Cabinet reshuffle and my government would be most interested to know what President had in mind by way of next steps to solve problems from which country was suffering and establish political and economic stability. This, I emphasized, was what my government as well as governments of neighboring countries wished to see in Indonesia.

At this point President interjected, "I can assure you that I will never permit a Communist coup d'état in this country." I said I recognized that this was true—that he had so demonstrated at Madiun. What Indonesia's neighbors feared was not this so much as growing political strength of PKI which would enable it to seize power as result of exploiting ordinary processes of democracy. "How, in other words, are you planning to curb growing influence of PKI within your country", I asked.

"This is a complex question," President replied slowly. "It involves economic, political and military considerations. I can assure you that Indonesia will never follow the route of Czechoslovakia".

I pressed him to be specific. I said that US Government would be prepared to extend additional substantial economic aid and such military aid as would seem appropriate to enable Indonesia to maintain elimination of Communist threat.

In commenting President led off with discussion of cabinet reshuffle. "I abolished Petra, Hanafi's ministry, because I had been informed that this was Communist dominated. I will tell you why I was unwilling to throw him out of Cabinet. When I was in exile in Benkoelen in South Sumatra, Hanafi was a young boy. He comes from Benkoelen. I became acquainted with him there and taught him revolutionary way which Indonesia must follow. He became an ardent follower of mine and later when he organized our revolutionary army I appointed him Lt. Col. He has been close to me through years. He is even indirectly related to me. His brother, a newspaperman in Medan, named Hadi, is married to my foster daughter. Hanafi is no PKI member. He is Leftist revolutionary. He is loyal to me but he understands feeling of the masses. He is popular with labor union members throughout Indonesia.

Sukarno then turned to PNI Party. "I will tell you exactly what I have been telling PNI leaders," he said. "This is a struggle to win masses, I say to them, why do you not do as PKI does? Why do you not organize masses? You must become more Left and fight PKI on its own ground. PNI is my own child," he said, but PNI has not been as effective as PKI.

I pointed out that PKI had advantage of being well-financed, well-trained under professional organizers, uninhibited in what they could promise, etc.

"That is what my PNI people tell me," President rejoined, "but that is no excuse. I had no money to start revolution. It takes work and determination and small contributions from many people".

"Then your answer to Communist threat is basically political one, I suggested. "Pantjasila front led by PNI".

"That is correct," President replied.

"But" I objected, "this will take time. Time is running out. What plans have you to deal with interim contingencies?"

President pointed to himself and said, "I and the military. I can control 99% of military. We will do what needs to be done".

I reminded him that there were already indications of Communist arrogance in certain parts of Java. He nodded, pointed to military control of demonstration, etc., and reiterated firmly that this kind of thing would be prevented.

In economic field, overlapping military and educational field, President said he was establishing national planning board to prepare blueprint for Indonesian development. This was board for which special planning committee headed by Djuanda was now working out structure and function. Board would be composed of technicians and experts, he emphasized, not politicians. It would be broadly representative of functional groups and of regions throughout Indonesia. This board would go to work intensively after establishment and prepare blueprint by next year.

Meanwhile he hoped America would give evidence of its support for Indonesia, "I want America and Indonesia to come closer and closer together. Above all" he said, "I hope America will not be negative but will be positive, that you will not do things and take positions which play into hands of PKI here and strengthen their hold on the people". He reverted to B–26s and then referred to West Irian. "This is an obsession with me," he admitted. "But if America would support Indonesia on West Irian I could (and he snapped his fingers) change Indonesia's attitude towards America overnight. I have said this many times but it is still true. It is hard for our people to understand why Russia can support without equivocation our claim to Irian and why US—claiming to be our friend—remains silent. If America could only say that they consider our claim a just claim, this would make all the difference" he went on in this vein for several minutes playing old record.

When he had finished I did not argue case but simply said, "Mr. President, I think that whole subject of West Irian needs cooling off period". I then pointed out that fear on part of her neighbors of Indonesia's going Communist was, entirely aside from Dutch position, element in Irian problem. If neighbors no longer had fear of Communist Indonesia and believed Indonesia to be politically and economically stable, some neighbors might feel differently about Indonesia possessing Irian. I emphasized this was personal observation.

I then made additional points in Deptel 3901 and economic points in Deptel 3911.

When President indicated he must leave for luncheon in Djakarta, I suggested desirability of continuing conversation in near future and of keeping in close touch now that some progress had been made in improvement of US-Indo relations. President readily agreed but with reservations such meetings should not be too visible. He suggested my stopping at Bogor en route to Puntjak occasionally on weekends when visit would have appearance of informal social call and would be unobserved by any but his own staff.

Comment: Throughout conversation Sukarno was intensely serious. There were none of the histrionics for which he is famous, no turning on either of his magnetic charm or his flushing indignation. He spoke gravely and quietly but impressively.

I had impression that he was convinced of sincerity of US policy with regard to preservation Indonesian independence and non-interference with Indonesian foreign policy. My frank remarks about Indonesian misunderstanding of SEATO were well received.

Further comments follow.

President's parting words were, "Let us have no war, no war. This would be bad for everybody."

Jones

137. Telegram From the Embassy in Indonesia to the Department of State

Djakarta, July 24, 1958, 2 p.m.

324. CINCPAC for POLAD. Embtel 301.[1] After consideration content and general tenor President's remarks made in course my July 21 meeting with him at Bogor, I have following additional comments:

1. Believe Sukarno, as strong advocate Afro-Asian bloc concept, genuinely disturbed at what he and others in government, confusing struggle to realize popular aspirations with unprincipled, externally supported power grabs, have felt is western suppression legitimate nationalist manifestations in Middle East. Have impression my presentation of limited US objectives and motives fairly convincing to him; in any case his desires study US position, and evidence on which based, is heartening.

2. President for first time personally confirmed many reports that he cognizant PKI danger and that new posture of PNI has his endorsement and encouragement. I also consider significant his admission that army main instrument to curb PKI (thus implicitly acknowledging army strength and often-reported anti-communist firmness of army leadership), pending political control through Pantjasila front device. If, I hope, more frequent meetings with President materialize, opportunity can be sought discuss with him desirability that anti-communist political front, if it expected cope successfully with regional and economic problems, include non-Javanese Party representation.

3. President deeply concerned by continuation B–26 raids and while it my impression he wishes accept at face value US position, he still perplexed by and possibly skeptical my assertion that US powerless to stop them. He may have had raids in mind when he cautioned against US action that could be exploited by PKI. Lack of publicity concerning raids (most recently reported incidents not yet publicly released) and restrained handling Pope case and other "evidence" foreign support rebel cause is of course regarded by GOI as favorable to US and anti-Communist position in that PKI deprived of highly exploitable and anti-US material.

4. Atmosphere this meeting with President most gratifying since my arrival. He gave impression of man conscious his burden and endeavoring find best solution by candid consultation with minimum

Source: Department of State, Central Files, 756D.00/7–2458. Secret; Priority; Limit Distribution. Also sent to CINCPAC. Transmitted in two sections.
[1] Document 136.

pretense or playing for effect. I left with impression that President desires friendly relations with US; is at long last becoming disturbed by Communist threat to Indonesia; is now prepared to encourage moves against PKI although I see no early prospect of his taking public stand against Communists. Also implicit although never explicit in conversation was assumption future of Indonesia security and area security dependent US. I propose take early opportunity test his declaration that more frequent meetings in relative privacy Bogor Palace would be welcome.

5. Sukarno's recognition of army role in curbing Communists and admission of necessity for inter-related military and political action against PKI ties in with information we have received from Nasution and other government leaders. It presents US with opportunity to provide tools for accomplishment of objective I believe is becoming mutual. There was definite indication in Sukarno conversation President beginning to be aware that US and GOI interests coincide in this respect. Although President was not as specific as might be desired in outlining anti-Communist program, what he said makes clear to me that he is supporting Djuanda and Nasution in their efforts.

It is always possible, of course, that Sukarno was saying what he thought we wanted to hear, but this was not my impression. Sukarno has always cut off head of any individual or any group that threatened his supremacy. It seemed clear he has reached point where he considers PKI to be in this category and I believe we can count on his following same course with PKI as he has in case of all other challengers.

On this basis, it seems to me new posture of Sukarno and repeatedly demonstrated anti-Communist attitude of army provides us with sufficient justification for taking next step in inducing further anti-Communist action in Indonesia. As I see it, we must take whatever calculated risk may be involved in betting on army if we are to be successful in advancing our objectives in Indonesia. Army has consistently given not only oral assurances but also specific examples of determination prevent Communist take-over (Embtel 4440 May 28)[2] and discourage Communist exploitation, most recent and impressive instance of which was sharp warning to PKI not to turn July 21 mass meeting into anti-western demonstration (Embtel 299).[3]

There is no question in anybody's mind here but that army is determined to obtain arms it requires. Pro-US army leaders want equipment to come from US but if we will not supply it others will. Thus US deci-

---

[2] Telegram 4440 listed some of the recent anti-Communist steps taken by the Indonesian Government and Army. (Department of State, Central Files, 611.56D/5–2858)

[3] Dated July 21. (Ibid., 756D.00/7–2158)

sion will not determine whether Indonesian army gets equipment or not but simply whether source of supply is US or Soviet bloc.

After consideration President's words to me, taking into account earlier expressions Djuanda and Subandrio, army assurances and performance over extended period of time, and recent information concerning Nasution plan to control PKI activity (ARMA CX–237)[4] (Embtel 130),[5] I believe next move is ours. Army leaders who have been defending US are under heavy pressure provide tangible evidence US support. I am convinced it is time for positive US action in support of army. I therefore recommend Department give urgent consideration to supplying Indonesian Army soonest with at least token shipment arms (Deptel 3300)[6] and engineering equipment (Embtel 203[7] and ARMA CX–232[8]). This action on our part may not produce all results we hope for, but failure to act would, I believe, be needless forfeiting best opportunity yet seen to induce anti-Communist action in order preserve independence this strategic country.

6. I have discussed above in substance with Australian Ambassador McIntyre who departs on home leave tomorrow.

While he cannot speak for his government, he personally strongly endorses recommendation, believing now is time to act.[9]

Jones

---

[4] Not found.

[5] Document 133.

[6] Document 92.

[7] Telegram 203, July 14, called the Department's attention to telegram CX 232 concerning General Djatikusumo's request for U.S. assistance to the Indonesian Corps of Engineers in order to enable them to work on public construction projects in remote areas. "This kind of project," the cable read in part, "combined with army appointment selected officers in territories to supervise anti-Communist activities is grass roots kind of opposition to PKI that may be well worth US support." (Department of State, Central Files, 756D.5/7–1458)

[8] Not found.

[9] Telegram 200 to Djakarta, July 26, for the Ambassador from Robertson, reads:

"As you know your recommendations Embtel 324 require major decision on our policy towards Indonesia. In view Secretary's pre-occupation with Middle East situation and his departure yesterday for Europe, we will not be able meet with him until July 31. Hope after that meeting be able advise you what our position will be and what steps we might be prepared take. In meantime would welcome any additional comments or recommendations you may care make." (Department of State, Central Files, 756D.00/7–2458)

138.   Memorandum From the Assistant Secretary for Far Eastern Affairs (Robertson) to Secretary of State Dulles

Washington, July 30, 1958.

SUBJECT

Indonesia—U.S. Policy

A meeting is to be held in your office on Thursday, July 31, with representatives of Defense, JCS and CIA also present, to review our policy toward Indonesia and determine what our next move should be. The following comments and recommendations are submitted as a basis for the discussions at that time:

1. Tension between the United States and Indonesia has abated significantly since the decision on May 20 to encourage the anticommunist and pro-U.S. elements in the Army and Government.

2. During this period the Government of Indonesia has given evidence, both in word and in action, of a desire to improve relations with the U.S. and of its determination to take action against the communists. (Tab C)

3. The momentum has, however, slackened. Considerable impatience is developing due to the alleged lack of U.S. responsiveness. At the present moment we appear to be in a period of drift.

4. During this period it has again been demonstrated that (a) Sukarno is the key to the situation, (b) Sukarno believes the pendulum has swung too far to the PKI, and (c) the communists are the most serious threat to his position.

5. Also, during this period the anti-communist orientation of the Army has become more evident, and the PNI has moved as a party into active opposition to the communists.

6. There has been nothing to demonstrate that the dissident movement can exert any leverage on Djakarta. On the contrary, their continued activities result in greater economic and fiscal chaos, which serves the purposes of the communists, who take advantage of such conditions to increase their political power. The Government has been able to learn in great detail the source and scope of outside assistance to the rebels, on the basis of which it has made its charge of "foreign intervention". Any encouragement to the dissidents from outside Indonesia would, in view of developments in the Middle East, be considered as "indirect aggression" and could lead only to further deterioration of the U.S. position.

Source: Department of State, Central Files, 611.56D/7–3058. Secret. Drafted by Parsons and Mein.

Conclusion:

In light of the foregoing circumstances Ambassador Jones is convinced the time has come for the United States to strengthen the hand of the Indonesian Army. Admiral Stump has recommended we initiate shipment at once of a phased delivery of the $7 million arms package which has been held in readiness. He has also recommended that an officer be sent to Indonesia to coordinate this program with the Indonesians. Additional courses of action for which we recommend approval and progressive implementation are at Tab A. If the U.S. does not embark on a positive policy, our potential for influencing the situation will decline.

A more extended analysis of the Indonesian situation appears at Tab B.[1]

Recommendation:

That you approve the courses of action at Tab A.[2]

Tab A[3]

POSSIBLE ACTIONS U.S. CAN TAKE[4]

1. Military.

a) Furnish token military aid—particularly to the Army—totaling about $7 million. CINCPAC strongly recommends this be done. CINCPAC also recommends that a senior officer be sent to Indonesia to coordinate such a program with the Indonesian Army.

---

[1] See the Supplement for Tab B, entitled "Factors Affecting U.S. Policy," and Tab C, "Attitudes Towards the U.S. and the West and Anti-Communist Actions and Statements."

[2] In a July 31 memorandum to Dulles, Herter stated that he had read the material provided by FE and INR and was "struck by the wide divergence in the interpretion of some of the factual material." In view of this divergence Herter suggested that the Intelligence Community be asked to prepare a paper on the situation that Dulles should have prior to making the decisions recommended by FE. Herter also recommended that the July 31 meeting be postponed until after Dulles' return from Brazil and the estimate by the Intelligence Community is received. (Eisenhower Library, Herter Papers, Miscellaneous Memoranda) Cumming's intelligence summary, July 30, is attached to a memorandum from Cumming to Irwin, August 1. (Washington National Records Center, RG 330, OASD/ISA Files: FRC 64 A 2170, 092 Indonesia) See Supplement.

On July 31 Robertson telephoned Dulles and mentioned that Herter wanted to put off the scheduled meeting on Indonesia until the following week. (Eisenhower Library, Dulles Papers, General Telephone Conversations) See Supplement.

[3] Secret.

[4] Dulles approved these courses of action at the August 1 scheduled meeting; see Document 139. At the end of the first sentence Dulles added a phrase so that it read: "a) Furnish token military aid—particularly to the Army—totaling about $7 million on phased basis and on military level so far as practicable."

b) Provide additional slots for Indonesian officers in U.S. military schools.

c) Agree to the use of counterpart funds for the construction of barracks for the Indonesian Army.

2. *Aviation.* Authorize the Embassy to resume negotiations with the Indonesian Government on a Civil Aviation Agreement. The Indonesians have recently indicated a desire to do so. This would also permit American carriers to discuss with Garuda possible assistance in the personnel and maintenance fields.

3. *Shipping.*

a) Explore ways in which the U.S. might be able to assist Indonesia in meeting the inter-insular shipping problem.

b) Furnish instructors, books and other training aids to the Indonesian Merchant Marine Academy in Djakarta.

c) Offer training to Indonesians in the State merchant marine academies in the U.S.

4. *Licenses.* Issue on a continuing basis licenses covering equipment, small arms and ammunition similar in type and quantity to those previously authorized.

5. *EXIM Bank.*

a) Withdraw our objections on political grounds to an Ex-Im Bank loan ($12 million) for three Commercial Lockheed Electra Turbo-prop Jets for Garuda, to be delivered in 1960.

b) Support an Indonesian application for financing the design and construction of a Urea Fertilizer Plant in South Sumatra ($36 million).

c) Consider with Ex-Im Bank the possible financing of power plants to be built by Westinghouse (which otherwise are expected to be financed and built by the Czechs).

6. *Impact Projects.*

a) Assistance to the IBU Sukarno Children's TB Hospital, Djakarta, for the purchase of equipment ($1.65 million).

b) Consider the possibility of using IMG (Information Media Guarantee Agreement) counterpart funds for the construction of schools in Indonesia.

139. Memorandum of Conversation

Washington, August 1, 1958.

SUBJECT

Indonesia

PARTICIPANTS

The Secretary	Defense
The Undersecretary	
	Mr. Irwin
FE	Admiral Stroh
	Captain Robbins
Mr. Robertson	
Mr. Parsons	
Mr. Mein	CIA
INR	Mr. Allen Dulles
	Mr. Frank Wisner
Ambassador Cumming	Mr. Alfred Ulmer
Mr. Bartlett Wells	Mr. FitzGerald

Before considering the memorandum submitted by Mr. Robertson on July 30[1] recommending several courses of action which might be taken by the United States, the Secretary was given a short briefing on current developments in Indonesia. Ambassador Cumming reviewed especially recent activities by the dissidents.

Mr. Irwin stated that the Department of Defense felt that the U.S. should attempt to build up Nasution's strength as an anti-communist step in Java since he has displayed good-will toward us and his prestige in the government has increased. Mr. Irwin pointed out that Nasution has said that he agrees with the objectives of the rebels although not with the methods used by them in attaining those objectives. He would therefore also seem to be the logical person through whom a reconciliation of the various factions in Indonesia might be attempted.

After a short discussion of the situation in Indonesia the Secretary 1) said there appeared to be general agreement that we should go ahead with the actions listed in Tab A of Mr. Robertson's memorandum of July 30 (copy attached). Mr. Robertson pointed out that Admiral Stump had recommended phased delivery of the military package. Mr. Herter said that it was important also that the actions taken be developed in such a way as to permit Nasution to get the maximum benefit from them. In the light of this discussion the Secretary added at the end of the first sen-

---

Source: Department of State, Central Files, 756D.00/8–158. Secret. Drafted by Mein. Robertson initialed the memorandum, indicating his approval.

[1] Document 138.

tence of Paragraph 1(a) of the Courses of Action "on phased basis and on military level so far as practicable". He approved the courses of action with that change. 2) said there should be a minimum of publicity and that our actions should be played down as much as possible. 3) asked Mr. Allen Dulles to prepare a study of the present status and strength of the dissidents.

Admiral Stroh stated that Admiral Burke, who had planned to be present at the meeting, favored pointing our actions as much as possible toward Nasution in line with the opinion expressed by the Department of Defense. Mr. Robertson stated that he agreed with this but that it should not be overlooked that this is primarily a government-to-government problem and that it is impossible to keep the government completely out of the picture.

Mr. Allen Dulles suggested that some effort might be made to bring the dissidents and the anti-communist forces in Java together.

Mr. Irwin said that CINCPAC and Defense recommend that in addition to the package of $7 million military equipment bridges also be made available to Indonesia and that the original package be augmented. He said that Defense would need three things: 1) a 451 determination[2] to proceed with the $7 million package; 2) a 451 determination for approximately $2-1/2 million for bridges; 3) the Secretary's approval for an increase in the amount of military equipment to be made available to Indonesia. He said that a letter concerning this increase was on its way from the Department of Defense to Mr. Robertson.[3]

The Secretary said that he had no information on the bridges and hesitated to make a decision on the basis of an oral request. Mr. Robertson said that this would be submitted to him in writing in due course.

Mr. Robertson raised the matter of consultations with other governments, recommending that we inform the UK and Australian Governments here immediately and that Ambassador Bohlen be authorized to keep the Philippine Government informed of developments. As to informing the Dutch Government, he recommended that they be told as the actions were implemented. The Secretary agreed.

---

[2] Reference is to the Mutual Security Act of 1958, approved on June 30, 1958, which provided the President with a special "contingency fund." For text, see 72 Stat. 261.

[3] Reference is to a letter of July 31 from Irwin to Robertson. That letter, along with a letter of July 23 from Sprague to Dillon, gave Department of Defense concurrence in Ambassador Jones' recommendation that the United States initiate a program of token and limited military assistance to the Indonesian Armed Forces and suggested specific military equipment that could be offered to the Indonesians for that purpose. The letters are in Washington National Records Center, RG 330, OASD/ISA Records: FRC 64 A 2170, 092 Indonesia.

140. Telegram From the Embassy in Indonesia to the Department of State

Djakarta, August 5, 1958, 5 p.m.

467. Department pass AFCIN–1A1, CNO, ACSI. CINCPAC also for POLAD. ARMA and ASTARMA informed Lt. General Nasution at 1300 today of items paragraph 1 Deptel 255.[1] Colonel Jani and Major Jusuf were present. After explaining US decision furnish arms support on phased basis, additional schooling spaces and agreement to use counterpart funds for barracks construction, General Nasution appeared delighted and said, "I am very happy to hear this good news". With reference to US military representative coming to Djakarta, Nasution said, "the sooner the better". He also indicated that speed was of essence in obtaining equipment and said he preferred air delivery. Replying to ARMA query as to Nasution's opinion on publicity this matter, he stated, "no publicity at this time". He explained he wanted to make biggest impact possible with US aid and enthusiastically welcomed suggestion it be flown in. He had earlier indicated when equipment starts to arrive, he plans meet first plane personally. He then explained he was acting as a policeman trying to offset hostile pressures (such as PKI and DI). Nasution stated there are certain groups who would like to turn Indo-nationalism into anti-westernism, and also "group of Indonesians that would like to sabotage US arms support". If equipment started arriving soon he would be in position to prevent such adverse action. That would be the time for publicity. ARMA commented on possibility of leaks and Nasution said he recognized this was always possible.

Turning to Irian problem, Nasution stated Army has no plans for military action against West Irian and that Prime Minister Djuanda has so informed Parliament. He said "the useful thing about Irian is the uniting force it provides, which is something we need at this time". Nasution said sooner or later Indonesia will get Irian back through the UN or other political means.

In view of the above I recommend:

1. That no publicity be given this matter until further notice.

Source: Department of State, Central Files, 756D.5–MSP/8–558. Top Secret; Niact. Also sent to CINCPAC.

[1] Telegram 255, August 4, authorized Jones to have Cole see Nasution and inform him that the United States was (a) prepared to supply Indonesia with military equipment (without mentioning the kind of equipment or the total amount of the aid); (b) providing additional slots for Indonesian officers in U.S. military schools; and (c) providing for the use of counterpart funds for the construction of an Indonesian Army barracks. (Ibid., 756D.5–MSP/8–458) See Supplement.

   2. That CINCPAC representative (CINCPAC 020328Z)[2] come to
Djakarta immediately.
   3. That equipment be despatched by air soon as possible upon signal from the CINCPAC representative after talks with General Nasution.[3]

Jones

---

  [2] Not found.

  [3] In telegram 470 from Djakarta, August 6, Jones reported that he met with Djuanda
that morning, who was "most gratified" to learn about the U.S. military aid package.
"Prime Minister commented that he had been confident in his own mind that US and Indonesia would cross this bridge to improve relations sooner or later," Jones noted in part,
"but he had not thought this development would come so soon." (Department of State,
Central Files, 756D.5–MSP/8–658) See Supplement.

---

141. Special National Intelligence Estimate

SNIE 65–58   Washington, August 12, 1958.

THE OUTLOOK IN INDONESIA

The Problem

   To assess the current situation in Indonesia, and to estimate the
probable main lines of development.

Conclusions

   1. Events in Indonesia during the last year have greatly strengthened the position of the Indonesian Communists (the PKI). If the national elections scheduled for 1959 are held, the PKI will probably
emerge as the largest party in Indonesia and be in a strong position to
demand cabinet representation. (Paras. 22–23, 25)

   Source: Department of State, INR–NIE Files. Secret. According to a note on the cover
sheet the CIA and the intelligence organizations of the Departments of State, the Army, the
Navy, the Air Force, and the Joint Staff participated in the preparation of this estimate. All
members of the IAC concurred with the estimate on August 12, except the representatives
of the AEC and the FBI, who abstained on the grounds that the subject was outside their
jurisdiction.

2. We believe that the PKI will continue its present policy of seeking to attain power by legal means. The PKI will probably not attempt to seize power by force during the coming year, even if large numbers of army units are still committed in the outer islands. (Para. 24)

3. The continuing guerrilla actions of the rebels constitute a considerable military and financial burden on the government. The rebels can continue such actions for a prolonged period and, with outside arms support, could seize and temporarily hold sizable areas. Even in these circumstances, however, the rebels could probably neither develop widespread political support nor create sufficient military pressure to cause the government to seek a negotiated settlement. (Paras. 12–14)

4. The leaders of the armed forces gained self-confidence and prestige in their operations against the rebels. In the face of the increasing power of the Communists, army leaders have considered measures to move against the PKI, including a proposal that the elections be postponed. However, we do not believe that they will take any decisive action unless they have at least the tacit approval of Sukarno. (Paras. 15–16, 19–21)

5. Sukarno is also concerned by the growing power of the PKI. However, he is reluctant to use force or to abandon his position of being above party struggles. We believe that he will at first seek to consolidate and strengthen non-Communist parties so that a balance between them and the PKI may be achieved. If he becomes convinced that the Communists seriously threaten his position, he will probably yield to army pressures to postpone the elections. However, we believe that the chances are no better than even that he could be convinced that his position would be threatened. (Paras. 26–27)

6. Economic conditions, which have been deteriorating for years, have worsened since the seizure of Dutch economic interests and the outbreak of civil war. Most productive facilities and foreign trade transactions are now in inexperienced hands. Due to the shortage of raw materials the industrial sector of the economy faces partial paralysis, although the peasant economy, in which some 80 percent of the population is included, has been comparatively little affected. (Para. 28)

7. Continuing and substantial US aid would increase the ability and determination of non-Communist leaders to resist the growing power of the PKI. However, the best that could be hoped for would be that non-Communist forces would be so strengthened that the PKI could not come to power, although it would still remain a major force in Indonesian politics. (Para. 34)

[Here follows a 6-page Discussion section; see Supplement.]

142.   Editorial Note

On August 10 Major General R.L. Vittrup, USA, arrived in Djakarta for discussions at the service level with Indonesians on the terms of U.S. military assistance. Vittrup headed a technical military mission and operated under the guidance of Ambassador Jones. The Departments of State and Defense provided him guidelines for his discussions with the Indonesians. (Telegram 280 to Djakarta, August 7; Department of State, Central Files, 756.5 MSP/8–758) See Supplement. Vittrup met with Prime Minister Djuanda and with General Nasution on August 11. After these meetings, Ambassador Jones reported that the "political impact" of token military aid would be much greater if air deliveries of equipment already authorized by the Department of State could reach Indonesia before August 17, its independence day. The Department of State agreed and authorized Vittrup to conclude an agreement. (Telegrams 539, 540, and 541 from Djakarta and telegram 307 to Djakarta, all August 11; Department of State, Central Files, 765D.5 MSP/8–1158) See Supplement for all.

On August 13 the United States and Indonesia concluded an agreement by which the United States agreed to provide Indonesia with approximately $7 million in military assistance. The agreement was effected by an exchange of notes in Djakarta between Ambassador Jones and Foreign Minister Subandrio. For text, see 9 UST 1149. In telegram 570 from Djakarta, August 13, Jones reported on the exchange of notes, explaining that the Indonesians accepted the text contained as proposed by the United States without change. "Prior to meeting Foreign Minister," Jones noted, "I had long conference with Prime Minister Djuanda during which I clarified all points in accordance instructions and stated US regards assurances to mean also that equipment, materials and services will not be used to obtain control of West New Guinea by military forces." (Department of State, Central Files, 756D.5–MSP/8–1358) See Supplement.

In telegram 247 to The Hague, August 13, the Department instructed Ambassador Young to inform Foreign Minister Luns at the earliest opportunity of the U.S. decision to sell a limited amount of military equipment to Indonesia. It emphasized that the Indonesians desired no publicity until a scheduled public announcement on August 20. (Department of State, Central Files, 756D.56/8–1358) See Supplement. In accordance with the Department's instructions, Young met with Luns on August 14. In telegram 259 from The Hague, August 14, he reported on the meeting in part as follows:

"I believe Luns was pleased with assurances contained in text of agreement and with added confidential assurance that equipment, material and services would not be used to obtain control Netherlands New Guinea by military force. I pointed out to Luns that perhaps flat statement by Ambassador Jones to Djuanda to this effect was better than including this assurance in written agreement, inasmuch as Dutch point of view has always been Indonesians did not live up to provisions of any agreements made in past. Luns agreed that this interpretation put it in positive light, which would be helpful to him." (Department of State, Central Files, 756D. 56/8–1458) See Supplement.

143.   Telegram From the Embassy in Indonesia to the Department of State

Djakarta, August 14, 1958, 5 p.m.

589. Department pass AFCIN–1A1, ACSI, CNO. CINCPAC also for POLAD. Embtel 570.[1] Supplementing reference telegram, following comments made by Prime Minister and Foreign Minister in connection with exchange of notes re military aid will be of interest. Djuanda said he had seen President that morning and had given him news. President's reaction was one of disbelief followed by an expression of great gratification. President then raised question as to what had caused this sudden change of policy toward Indonesia on US part. Prime Minister said he had also been wondering. He wasn't asking me but he thought the President would probably raise query when I saw him. I said I had no hesitation whatever in answering the question—that it was due to increasing confidence on part US Government that GOI was beginning seriously to face up to handling problem of communism within Indonesia and that this conviction had developed as result of actions taken by GOI to control PKI excesses, Djuanda's own statements as to GOI intentions, clear evidence of PNI late awareness Communist danger in Indonesia and finally Sukarno's own statements indicating his support for anti-Communist moves. Djuanda was obviously gratified by this statement. He referred to his statement in earlier talk to effect that he had not anticipated such early change in US attitude (Embtel 518).[2] He had been

---

Source: Department of State, Central Files, 756D.5–MSP/8–1458. Top Secret; Priority. Also sent to CINCPAC and repeated to The Hague.

[1] See Document 142.

[2] Dated August 8. (Department of State, Central Files, 756D.5–MSP/8–858) See Supplement.

confident that US would ultimately come to decision it had now reached but he had not expected it so soon.

He referred to arrogant behavior of PKI in East Java and Central Java and said that more and more Indonesian leaders were becoming alert to problem presented by PKI.

As I rose to leave in order to join the Foreign Minister at his home to exchange notes, Djuanda again said how deeply gratified he was at this turn of events. He recalled how close US and Indonesia had come to parting of ways at the time he made his statement on foreign intervention (Embtel 3974)[3] and said he hoped that this was beginning of long period of improving relations. I added I too hoped it was beginning of new era.

I then went to residence of Foreign Minister accompanied by General Vittrup. Following exchange of notes, Foreign Minister commented that as this represented major political decision on part of US, he wanted me to appreciate that acceptance of military aid also represented a major political step toward America on Indonesians' part. He recalled fall of Sukiman cabinet in 1952[4] and said that he would have to be prepared for considerable questioning in Parliament and barrage of criticism. He was pleased by what had happened but wanted US to appreciate significance of move from Indonesian side.

Jones

---

[3] See footnote 1, Document 77.

[4] The Sukiman cabinet fell on February 23, 1952, largely on the issue of accepting aid from the United States under the Mutual Defense Assistance Program; for documentation, see *Foreign Relations*, 1952–1954, vol. XII, Part 2, pp. 245 ff.

---

144.   Telegram From the Embassy in Indonesia to the Department of State

Djakarta, August 14, 1958, 10 p.m.

586. Embtel 570.[1] President's first words in receiving me at Merdeka Palace at noon today were, "I am very grateful. I am tremendously pleased."

Source: Department of State, Central Files, 756D.5–MSP/8–1458. Secret; Priority.

[1] See Document 142.

I said I assumed he had heard the news of our decision regarding military aid from others but that I wanted to inform him officially myself. I said news had arrived when he was in Bali otherwise I would have asked to see him immediately.

He said yes, he had heard the news from others—in fact Prime Minister, General Nasution, Admiral Subyakto and Marshal Suryadarma all had come to see him and all were very gratified by US Government decision. He said he assumed package included aid for Navy and Air Force as well as Army since all three were essential for Indonesian security. I confirmed that Navy was included and then explained that Air Force had not been included because we did not know what equipment they had received from other sources and consequently could not assess their requirements. I said General Vittrup had seen Marshal Suryadarma and had discussed his current needs with him. President nodded and said he had instructed Marshal Suryadarma to make available to us information as to his priority requirements. I threw in caution saying I hoped something could be done for Air Force but I was not in position to make commitment at this point.

Bearing in mind Prime Minister's comments last night,[2] I observed President should consider that this decision of my government was directly responsive to our last conversation in which President outlined determination prevent Communist take-over (Embtel 301)[3] and represented tangible evidence of US conviction that GOI was taking steps to solve its problems. I then pointed out that decision was made at highest level US Government upon recommendation Secretary Dulles. President was obviously pleased to know that both Secretary and President had been involved in decision. The President then suggested General Vittrup be invited to attend August 17 ceremonies.

In summarizing program briefly, I informed him of anticipated arrival first two aircraft on August 15 or 16 bearing signal and ordnance equipment.

Jones

---

[2] See Document 143.
[3] Document 136.

145.   Telegram From the Department of State to the Embassy in the Netherlands

Washington, August 19, 1958, 12:43 a.m.

286. As you have seen from Deptel 345 to Djakarta,[1] rptd The Hague 269 and Djakarta's 628 to Department, rptd The Hague 18, original package of military equipment contained four helicopters and one 173-ft. sub-chaser. In addition package included six LCVPs (36 feet long). 90% total package consisted equipment for Indonesian Army, but these three items were included as marginal items for use with Air Force and Navy when needed in order to avoid putting Nasution too much on spot with his Air Force and Naval colleagues and to avoid creating impression he is US chosen instrument. US Mil Rep and Ambassador consider that program is already building up considerable suspicion and intrigue against Nasution by Navy and Air Force. In order alleviate Navy pressure Department has decided permit delivery of six LCVPs. These vessels already on way from Philippines and scheduled arrive Surabaja August 21. Preparation for their reception already made. We learned only this morning of arrival date which is much sooner than we expected.

Delivery of sub-chaser and helicopters will be postponed for several months. FYI. CINCPAC being instructed not to effect delivery of sub-chaser to Indonesia prior 1 Dec. End FYI. However, it will probably be necessary to deliver these items at some point as required to reduce inter-service rivalry and pressure on Nasution.

You should see Luns as soon as possible to inform him of these three items. You may say that you had just been told about them and use above material as you think desirable. In deciding to go ahead with six LCVPs Department has not overlooked Dutch protest of last winter when there was question of furnishing similar craft to Indonesian police under ICA assistance programs. Navy assures us these vessels will not increase Indonesian offensive capabilities.

Source: Department of State, Central Files, 756D.56/8–1958. Secret; Niact. Drafted by Cameron and approved by Elbrick. Repeated to Djakarta and CINCPAC.

[1] Telegram 345, August 16, requested Ambassador Jones' explanation of what has been done to four helicopters that were originally included for Air Force in list of military equipment for Indonesian armed forces. "While info provided Dutch correctly referred to program 'primarily' for Army," the telegram read in part, "they have no knowledge four helicopters and the 173 foot subchaser included in package. We greatly fear progress made in gaining Dutch acceptance our policy and current program would be jeopardized if these two parts package either a) delivered or b) made public now." (Ibid., 756D.5–MSP/8–1458) See Supplement.

We know that Dutch will be greatly concerned by Sukarno August 17 speech.[2] Preliminary reports of what he said are indeed disturbing and we shall examine text when received most carefully within context present tactics toward Indonesia. It should be remembered, however, that present tactic is not directed toward Sukarno but towards elements in armed services (principally in Army) and in Government who have showed some evidence that they would be prepared to take steps to reverse pro-Communist orientation Indonesian Government. We have hoped and we still expect that these elements will serve eventually to bring some helpful influence to bear on Sukarno himself.

In view outstanding performance in persuading Luns accept 90% of package deal we leave your judgment tactics presentation these items to him, fully cognizant that this will be much more difficult. If in your judgment strength of Luns' reaction requires some public statement on West New Guinea you are authorized to inform him that Department agreeable his using statement along following lines: "Prior to signature of agreement Department of State obtained from Indonesian authorities satisfactory assurances that items of military equipment and material purchased by the Indonesians from US would not be used against West New Guinea." Such a statement may cause us serious difficulties in Indonesia. We would hope that Luns would use it publicly only if he considers that there is real necessity.

We shall, of course, inform the NAC of these three items when we make statement at next regular session.[3]

Herter

---

[2] See Document 146.

[3] Ambassador Young met with Foreign Minister Luns on August 19 to inform him of the three additional items in the U.S. military equipment agreement with Indonesia. (Telegram 292 from The Hague, August 19; Department of State, Central Files, 756D.56/8–1958) See Supplement. Upon instructions from Luns, Netherlands Chargé Baron van Voorst called on Elbrick on August 22 to express his government's "serious dissatisfaction" with the U.S. decision to supply Indonesia with military equipment that could be used against West New Guinea. A memorandum of this conversation, drafted by Cameron, is in Department of State, Central Files, 756D.58/8–2258.

146. Telegram From the Department of State to the Embassy in Indonesia

Washington, August 19, 1958, 12:44 a.m.

357. Department has been shocked and disappointed note initial report Sukarno's speech set forth Embtel 624.[1] Sukarno's identification of West with obstruction aspirations Asian nationalist powers and his at least implied alignment with "progressive" countries of bloc are not only un-neutral but represent perversion of facts. Communist Bloc imperialism is seeking stifle independence of countries world over while U.S. as leader of West seeking prevent it. Sukarno's speech has seriously undermined potential this Government's continuance policy on which we recently embarked. Recognize later reports may place speech in better perspective but unless this is clearly the case Sukarno will have to understand that he cannot at one and same time gratefully accept U.S. assistance and denigrate and castigate everything for which U.S. stands.

We had been led to believe that prompt delivery on 15th of first token shipment would demonstrate desire U.S. work with Indonesian Government and might influence tone of Sukarno's speech. Sukarno himself registered his gratification this action our part. In absence unmistakable indications attitude reflected in preliminary reports this speech not Sukarno's and Indonesian Government's true attitude, U.S. may have reconsider its position. Provision equipment predicated on belief in sincerity Indonesia desire follow independent neutral course. If highest authority in Indonesia instead should effectively align himself with enemies of U.S. and free world, basis of our support is destroyed.

If Sukarno's speech not essentially different from report contained reftel request you express our disappointment Djuanda and Nasution along foregoing lines. In your discretion you may point out that Sukarno's statement at West Irian front ceremony re necessity to build up power to obtain West Irian may have created such tremendous problems with Dutch that we may have to authorize Luns to make public Indonesia's assurances re West New Guinea. (See separate telegram for instructions to Hague.)[2] You should subsequently and in light their comments seek appointment with President and try to make him understand neither U.S. nor any other country can be expected continue prof-

---

Source: Department of State, Central Files, 756D.00/8–1758. Secret; Niact. Drafted by Parsons and approved by Robertson. Repeated to The Hague and CINCPAC.

[1] Telegram 624, August 17, transmitted to the Department the official English text of Sukarno's scheduled independence day speech, which was to be delivered that day. (Ibid.) See Supplement.

[2] Document 145.

fering friendship when referred to publicly in terms which suggest U.S. and West are real enemy.[3]

Herter

_____

[3] In telegram 625 from Djakarta, August 18, Jones reported that Sukarno adhered strictly to the previously distributed text of his independence day address. Jones noted that the United States could not "draw any comfort" from Sukarno's speech, but observed that neither could the Communists. (Department of State, Central Files, 756D.11/8–1858) See Supplement.

_____

147. Telegram From the Embassy in Indonesia to the Department of State

Djakarta, August 20, 1958, 2 a.m.

661. For Assistant Secretary Robertson from Ambassador. Deptel 357.[1] I share Department's disappointment that military aid agreement failed to effect material change in Soekarno's well-known public attitudes.

Of even more moment, however, is that according to Department's 357 US policy now seems predicated on lines which I had not heretofore understood. I refer specifically to statement that "if highest authority in Indonesia instead should effectively align himself with enemies of US and free world, basis of our support is destroyed".

I am sure Department will agree that President is no more aligned with enemies of free world and US than he was before the speech. Yet we reached a decision to give aid to Indonesian Armed Forces in belief that they would thereby be enabled to take effective action against internal Communist subversion which may otherwise capture control of Indonesia by Parliamentary or other means.

To conclude now that, because of one piece of July 4 oratory received by the Indonesian people as one more playing of a broken record, [we] must change our policy of assisting anti-Communist and potentially anti-Soekarno elements, would be in [my] view extreme folly.

_____

Source: Department of State, Central Files, 756D.5–MSP/8–2058. Secret; Niact. Repeated to The Hague and CINCPAC.

[1] Document 146.

Of course I will see Djuanda and President and report disappointment which my government feels that he should have attacked everything we stand for. As explained Embtel 660,[2] it would be difficult to raise point regarding "assurances" since I do not understand GOI has given assurances beyond those in exchange of notes. Meanwhile I feel that our thinking here and that of the Department should be brought closer together than appears to be case from reference telegram.

As I see it, our military aid has been predicated on the proposition of first things first. The immediate threat is not Soekarno's leftish bent, third force ambitions or flirtations with both sides at once, but the PKI which may even now be strong enough to capture Indonesia with or without the President. There is today only one effective force in opposition—the Indonesian Army. We have understood it to be our purpose first of all to strengthen that force and to rally all anti-Communist elements around it. If this succeeds, the external relationships of Indonesia will most certainly move in the direction of our international objectives. If this fails we will have lost Indonesia. In view of these stakes, we can hardly be diverted by Soekarno demagoguery, although I realize that his utterances justifiably create resentment in the US and the free world.

In considering the case of Soekarno it is necessary to remember that we are dealing with a man who is convinced that the US gave active help to the rebellion against his government. He also believes this support was directed against himself. Further, he undoubtedly suspects that the military aid program is intended as support for Nasution against himself, an argument constantly dinned into his ears by the PKI.

At no point have I understood that the objective of our aid was to win over Soekarno, although I had been led to hope that his remarks on Independence Day would be softened, and apparently were softened, by the aid agreement. Although we have not written off entirely the idea that Soekarno might be changed by arraying sufficient internal anti-Communist power against him, if this occurs it will be a welcome by-product by [of] our immediate objective—to prevent a Communist take-over of Indonesia.

I would appreciate Department's comments.

Jones

---

[2] Telegram 660, August 20, reported Jones' conversation with Djuanda on August 17 about the U.S. position on the use of American military equipment and services in an effort to gain control of West New Guinea. (Department of State, Central Files, 756D.5–MSP/8–2058) See Supplement.

148.   Telegram From the Department of State to the Embassy in Indonesia

Washington, August 20, 1958, 7:24 p.m.

373. Ambassador from Robertson. Your 661.[1] From your experience in Department I am sure you will recall that policy we are now following in Indonesia is subject to divided counsel and you can well imagine that serious doubts exist as to its wisdom. Many sectors of U.S. public opinion do not make distinction between support for Nasution, Army and other non-Communists and support for Sukarno. These sectors of opinion also sympathize readily with dissidents who are patently anti-Communist and therefore less readily understands how it is that our present policy is anti-Communist. There is confusion as to why we seem not to support anti-Communist dissidents but rather President, who castigates us and who permitted Indonesia to slide into present precarious situation (remember *New York Times* editorial, August 6).

It is not only public, however, which is skeptical. I have been on notice for some days to meet with Senators Knowland[2] and Bridges to explain and justify why we are backing this horse.[3] Moreover, you know about debates not only within Executive branch but within Department which have occupied us right down to present. There has been no unanimity of conviction on our present policy at any time.

Given this situation, Sukarno undermines our policy every time he confirms and fortifies views of those who hold he is playing both sides and making suckers of us. If it is true that what we and our press say about Sukarno and Indonesia can cause reactions there and threaten basis for our cooperation, reverse is also true. If Sukarno wants to destroy our current policy one of the best means surely is for him to make more speeches along August 17 line. Basis of policy is fragile although we hope with time its wisdom as only possible course which would strengthen anti-commie centers of power, principally army, will become evident. I of course agree Sukarno is no more aligned with our enemies after than he was before speech; point is he unfortunately appears no less aligned than before.

Source: Department of State, Central Files, 756D.00/8–2058. Secret; Limit Distribution. Drafted by Parsons and approved by Robertson. Also sent to CINCPAC exclusive for POLAD.

[1] Document 147.

[2] William F. Knowland (R.–California), member of the Senate Foreign Relations Committee.

[3] On August 20, Senator Styles Bridges (R.–New Hampshire), member of the Senate Foreign Relations Committee, made a statement in the Senate criticizing the U.S. Government's decision to sell arms to Indonesia as "shocking." The Department transmitted a summary of his remarks to the Embassy in telegram 380 to Djakarta, August 21. (Department of State, Central Files, 756D.5–MSP/8–2158) See Supplement.

Similarly it is dangerous for continuance of our current policy for Vittrup to raise hopes of broader and more extensive cooperation with and aid to Indonesian armed forces than we now have authority for or any prospects of getting, particularly if Sukarno continues to beat his unhelpful drums. It is natural for him to be zealous but he must be kept within limits of authority granted.

We are sending you other messages on this and also question of assurances received about use our token packet of arms. I would like to conclude this one by saying I do not think there is any difference between you and me in our understanding of what our policy is predicated on and I appreciate your continued skillful handling of a very difficult situation. I also welcomed your strong caution against changing our policy merely because of another Sukarno broadside but to be defended successfully it must give signs of paying off in reasonable time.[4]

Herter

---

[4] In telegram 687 from Djakarta, August 22, Jones informed Robertson in part as follows: "Deeply appreciate your comment reference telegram. I understand situation fully. At same time your reassurance most helpful." (Department of State, Central Files, 756D.5–MSP/8–2258)

Jones met with Djuanda on August 22 and expressed to him the U.S. Government's disappointment with Sukarno's speech of August 17. (Telegram 688 from Djakarta, August 22; *ibid.*, 756D.11/8–2258) See Supplement. On August 23 the Ambassador met with Subandrio "and conveyed Department's reaction to Sukarno's August 17 speech emphasizing especially our deep concern with respect to his attacks on the West, and making same point as in previous conversation with Djuanda (Embtel 688)." (Telegram 708 from Djakarta, August 23; Department of State, Central Files, 756D.11/8–2358) See Supplement.

---

149. Telegram From the Embassy in Indonesia to the Department of State

Djakarta, August 26, 1958, 6 p.m.

743. CINCPAC also for POLAD. Deptels 357[1] and 390.[2] Interview with Sukarno lasted 1 hour plus lunch. I expressed fully Department's

---

Source: Department of State, Central Files, 611.56D/8–2658. Secret; Niact. Repeated to The Hague, Manila, CINCPAC, and Singapore.

[1] Document 146.

[2] Telegram 390, August 20, requested Jones' clarification of the assurances that he had received from Indonesian officials at the time of the military sales agreement. The

Continued

reaction Independence Day speech. Sukarno response was he had been misunderstood. He intended no attack on America, although added that he thought America made mistakes, such as going into Lebanon. After discussion pros and cons this issue Sukarno reiterated that he had no intent attack America. Said that in speech in Bandung September 1 he would try "to say something nice about America". Reverting again to US mistakes cited Marines in Singapore but I believe accepted my statement that their presence there nothing do with Indonesia. Conversation concluded on this note: "You should have no doubt as to how I feel about America. I am sending my son Guntur, whom I love dearly, to America to be educated. Arrangements have already been made through our Embassy in Washington." Later at luncheon he expressed desire to take ride in C–124 making arms delivery.

Full telegraphic report follows.[3]

Jones

Department indicated that it would appreciate Jones' recommendations on how to proceed to obtain assurances from Indonesia that the material, equipment, and services that it received from the United States would not be used to obtain control of West New Guinea, if such an assurance had not already been obtained. (Department of State, Central Files, 756D.5–MSP/8–2058) See Supplement.

[3] Telegram 744 from Djakarta, August 27. (Department of State, Central Files, 756D.00/8–2758) See Supplement. On August 29, Sukarno took a hour and 20 minute trip with Jones on a U.S. Globemaster aircraft. In telegram 796 from Djakarta, August 29, the Ambassador reported that the flight was a "complete success from standpoint improvement US-Indo relations." (Department of State, Central Files, 756D.5–MSP/8–2958) See Supplement.

---

150. Telegram From the Embassy in Australia to the Department of State

Canberra, August 27, 1958, 9 p.m.

68. My telegram 52.[1] Prime Minister Menzies requested me call this morning. In presence Defense Minister Sir Philip McBride he spoke at

---

Source: Department of State, Central Files, 656.56D13/8–2758. Secret; Priority; Limited Distribution.

[1] In telegram 52, August 15, Sebald reported on a conversation with Casey regarding the West New Guinea problem. Casey said that his cabinet had discussed the issue three

Continued

length re Australian reactions toward United States policy of supplying arms to Indonesia. He stated latest available information indicates United States has now supplied landing craft and also proposes supply anti-submarine vessels.

Menzies said with considerable earnestness one problem which could defeat his government in coming election would be wave of Australian resentment against growing strength Indonesia because of United States arms policy and possibility Indonesia might in consequence take aggressive action against West New Guinea. This would pose government with dilemma whereby on one hand if open support were given to Dutch, government would be charged in United Nations and elsewhere with support colonialism, whereas if nothing were done and West New Guinea fell to Indonesia, government would be pilloried for jeopardizing Australian security.

Menzies thought in length [long?] term interest Australian security it most essential some deterrent be formulated against Indonesian ambitions. He thought United States only country which can provide such deterrent and hoped something could be worked out whereby United States would make it crystal-clear to Indonesians that if any arms furnished by United States were used for aggression against New Guinea United States would take appropriate action. He thought present Indonesian assurance this context meaningless as Indonesia could claim West New Guinea entirely domestic problem and not within contemplation its assurance or United Nations Charter.

Menzies drew parallel with Taiwan situation and pointed out United States had made it clear that any attack on Taiwan would be countered by United States. Likewise it could be said Australia's security demanded it be made clear that attack on West New Guinea would be attack on Australia. He said considerable portion of cabinet inclined adopt this as official policy toward New Guinea but he prefers not do so at this time.

In comment upon Taiwan situation Menzies parenthetically said considerable body of Australian opinion including some great newspapers feel strongly Australia should recognize Red China. He felt New Zealand would do so within one or two years and thus raise Australian pressures but even then if still in power he would refuse. He would not

---

times in the past week to reach agreement on a position for discussions Casey will have in The Hague, London, and presumably Washington. Casey felt that immediate objective "should be work out some deterrent to Indonesians using force against West New Guinea. He feels first shot fired by Indonesians would cause chain reaction ultimate results of which cannot be foreseen. Casey also told Sebald that Australian public opinion has "been built up to point where West New Guinea has become symbol of Australian security and use of force by Indonesians would cause violent reaction here." (*Ibid.*, 656.56D13/8–1558)

wish have Communists successfully drive wedge between United States and Australia. This policy has been firmly adopted by government notwithstanding continuing accusations by opposition that government's foreign policy is too subservient to United States.

Menzies said Casey would explain these matters to Secretary.[2] He thought Australian public has apparently accepted small arms aid but United States action in making available potentially offensive-type equipment such as landing craft will not be understood and could have serious repercussions. He also mentioned Australia's efforts to dissuade British from furnishing Indonesia aircraft and other equipment.

I told Prime Minister that insofar as I aware there is no indication whatsoever Indonesia plans or intends attack West New Guinea by force and while I was not informed re landing craft, any arms or equipment made available by United States were in fact for internal use only. Although I had not seen precise wording of undertaking given by Indonesian Government, it seemed clear that point re possible use these arms for aggressive purposes was very much in mind my government. It seemed to me his concern could be divided into short-term problem of domestic considerations and long-term problem of Australia's security. Re latter particularly I felt certain nothing would be done to undermine or weaken security of Australia with which we were so closely allied. I said this problem is one which is heavily charged with emotion and as he knew, Dutch particularly often greatly exaggerated situation. Question of supply arms was delicate one of preventing Commies from moving into vacuum which would otherwise be created, and yet not supplying too much until situation further clarified and stabilized. Menzies said he understood this and our need work with Nasution but as previously indicated our policy giving rise difficult problems Australia.

As Menzies had to leave for party caucus being held adjoining room I said would pass his views to Secretary who would be most interested in receiving them.

Comment: We have additional indication cabinet greatly exercised over Indonesian situation and reports United States apparently unduly strengthening Indonesia military. I gained impression pressure being put on Menzies by Cabinet (Embtel 67)[3] and that this interview was de-

---

[2] External Affairs Minister Casey was scheduled to visit the United States in early September, prior to the ANZUS Council meeting, which was to be held in Washington on October 1. See Document 153.

[3] Telegram 67, August 27, provided a summary of the Australian attitude regarding West New Guinea. (Department of State, Central Files, 656.56D13/8–2758) See Supplement.

signed partly assuage colleagues who could not help have knowledge I was closeted with Menzies and McBride.

[1 paragraph (3 lines of source text) not declassified]

It would be useful if Department could send me its comments and any views which I might pass along to Menzies who will be in Canberra most of next week.[4]

Sebald

---

[4] In telegram 2233 to London, August 28, the Department transmitted a message for Australian External Affairs Minister Casey, explaining the U.S. position regarding military sales toward Indonesia and the West New Guinea dispute and suggesting that he convey this information to Luns during their upcoming talks in the Netherlands August 29–30. (Department of State, Central Files, 756D.56/8–2858) In telegram 64 to Canberra, August 29, the Department instructed Ambassador Sebald to make the same presentation to Prime Minister Menzies. (*Ibid.*, 756D.56/8–2958) Young reported on his conversation with Casey in telegram 382 from The Hague, August 29; Sebald reported on his conversation with Menzies in telegram 78 from Canberra, September 3. (*Ibid.*, 756D.56/8–2958 and 756D.56/9–358)

---

151.   **Letter From the Ambassador to Indonesia (Jones) to the Assistant Secretary of State for Far Eastern Affairs (Robertson)**

Djakarta, September 2, 1958.

DEAR WALTER: I have been here just six months and have several times started to write you, only to have events in this fast moving situation overtake what I had wanted to say. I am also keenly aware of the tremendous burden of reading in FE and have not wished to add unnecessarily to it.

First, I do want to express my deep appreciation for the wonderful support you have been giving us here. This goes for all of FE and the Secretary, of course, but no one knows better than I who has led the fight and no one appreciates more than I the difficulties involved in some of the problems and situations we have had to pass to you for solution.

I am confident that we are embarked on the right course. Since the announcement and actual delivery of military aid here, the very atmos-

---

Source: Department of State, Central Files, 611.56D/9–258. Secret.

phere in Djakarta has noticeably changed. When my car passes by, people wave and smile and several times this past week, teenagers on their bicycles have waved and cried, "Hi, Mr. Jones." This has even happened to Mary Lou when she has been alone without a flag on the car. And several Indonesians have commented that all Indonesia heaved a great sigh of relief when the bridge was crossed which seemed to them to prove that America was with them instead of against them.

The President's taking a ride in the Globemaster had a significance out of all proportion to the event itself. It helped to avoid any impression that we were backing Nasution against Sukarno and removed the impression in some circles that the President was less enthusiastic about American military aid than Djuanda and the Army. Finally, it tended to line up the President with the US in Indonesian eyes and was considered here as more a political gesture than anything else.

In saying the above, I don't mean to imply that I am in any sense betting on the President. He continues to be "all things to all men". But he is not merely *a* power factor here today; he is the dominant power factor and part of the problem we face here is to keep him genuinely neutralized while anti-Communist forces within the country are built up to do the job that must be done here. I know that the Secretary does not want Sukarno to get the credit for US assistance and I think he is absolutely right.

So far, Sukarno has not only not gotten the credit, he has made no effort to take the credit. This, frankly, is what worried me more about his August 17 speech than anything else. His failure at least to give US aid a nod in the speech was to me an indication that he doubted we meant business or that he interpreted it as an anti-Sukarno move. This, too, was one of the reasons that putting on the airplane ride for the President assumed, from our side, an exceptional importance. I am glad we were able to do it. Had we not done so after his request, the negative implications would have been just as strong against us as the positive implications have been since we carried it off successfully. All this may have seemed "Much ado about nothing" in Washington, but it represented a US triumph locally.

I believe that we have turned the corner and that if we are able to maintain the momentum we now have, our chances of achieving our objectives are reasonably good. Again, let me emphasize that I think we certainly should not at this point be led into putting our faith in or our chips on Sukarno. Gestures in his direction are important—they help to keep him on course with those Indonesians whose objectives are the same as ours. That is why I think it imperative for us to break loose the TB hospital equipment. The amount of money involved is small compared with the good it will do in terms of keeping Sukarno in line. Don't let anyone in Washington consider that at this stage I or anyone in the

Embassy has any illusions on the subject of wooing Sukarno. Let's do what we can to keep him from being completely taken in by forces actively moving against us. This requires, as I see it, a skillful combination of power factors moving Indonesia in the direction we wish to see it go and to which Sukarno will bend if they are sufficiently strong, and enough gestures toward the President at least to encourage him to support this internal struggle against the PKI.

There is another reason for a gesture or two in Sukarno's direction: to keep him from moving against Nasution. His natural suspicions are being fanned by the PKI. He can cause us no end of trouble if he reaches the conclusion which I am convinced he is testing in his mind that we are building up the Army in a move against him as well as against the PKI. The same reasoning applies, of course, to at least limited aid for the Indonesian Air Force. But I need not elaborate on that. You have had our cables.

I should like to revert to a suggestion I made sometime ago—the possibility of Djuanda's visiting the US. I think that if we move forward as we hope here that visits by both Djuanda and Nasution would be most useful. I am not advocating this at present. First, we have to come closer together with the Indonesians. Also we have the President to worry about. It could hurt both men if the President thought we were beginning to play up to them rather than himself. Our tactics in connection with any such invitations will have to be thought through very carefully. But we should bear the above in mind in planning FE area official visits to Washington next year.[1]

[Here follow brief personal remarks.]

Howard

---

[1] Robertson responded on September 26. His letter to Jones reads in part as follows:

"I share completely your view of Sukarno. We know, and I suspect most politically aware Indonesians also realize, that he has been in the past few years a divisive and disruptive influence. He is nonetheless a primary political force and a political fact of life that we are going to have to live with. We should be under no illusions that we can make him over into a genuinely constructive influence and a champion of the Free World. We must at the same time do what we can to neutralize and contain his disruptive capacities, and deny to the Communists his continued hold over the masses." (*Ibid.*)

152. Telegram From the Embassy in Indonesia to the Department of State

Djakarta, September 8, 1958, 10 a.m.

882. CINCPAC also for POLAD. I fully support recommendations which General Vittrup is making to CINCPAC for types and quantity of additional material for Indo armed forces under military aid agreement. (ALUSNA Djakarta to CINCPAC 060445Z).[1]

It is of the utmost importance that we maintain the momentum of the program if we are to sustain and expand Nasution's confidence in US and improving atmosphere between Indo Government and US.

Nasution and other Indo leaders having been in their view responsive to US moves, any indication on our part that we are going to dole out military assistance in such a way as to obtain concrete pay-off for each new parcel would nip in the bud the developing Indo belief that they can in fact count on US for continued and meaningful support. Only when that confidence has come to full flower will top Indo leaders feel safe in burning their bridges behind them by outright repudiation of PKI support.

As matter of fact Nasution already has burned some of his bridges and would be extremely vulnerable should it turn out that his confidence in US had been misplaced. PKI strength would be greatly increased, probably to the point where Sukarno would be forced to go all the way with them in order to maintain his position.

I feel sure Sukarno, Djuanda, Nasution feel that their response to aid agreement so far has been all that could be expected in light of their uncertainty as to how far we were willing to go.

Likely we will have to rely to some extent on intangibles for evidence that arms aid is paying off, such as President's public identification with program through publicizing Globemaster flight, Foreign Minister's American Association speech[2] and private assurances from President and government of desire to establish closer relations and resist domination by Communists.

Nevertheless, there has been definite progress of a more measurable sort, such as limitations on propaganda activities and demonstra-

---

Source: Department of State, Central Files, 756D.5–MSP/9–958. Secret; Priority. Repeated to The Hague, Canberra, and CINCPAC.

[1] Not found.

[2] Reference is to Subandrio's speech before the American Association luncheon in Djakarta, during which he spoke of a "fresh wind" that was infusing Indonesian-American relations. The Embassy summarized the speech in telegram 853 from Djakarta, September 4. (Department of State, Central Files, 611.56D/9–458) See Supplement.

tions by PKI, assumption of control by army over veterans organization, the apparent though as yet unannounced decision to postpone elections as means of averting Communist takeover, and goverment's position on foreign investment.

Lifting of the ban on *Time* Magazine, indefinite delay of Pope trial, prohibition of strikes and lockouts of oil company workers, assumption by army of control of national front, all are positive developments in our favor. We can expect more such actions if the momentum of our arms aid program is not lost.

Of course I am constantly aware of the political problems with our Dutch and Australian allies which are inherent in our present policy in Indonesia. It is necessary to keep equally in the forefront that we do not nor does anyone, have capability of preventing Indonesia from building up her military forces to whatever size Indonesians feel appropriate. The only question is whether this is to be done with our aid, and with those restraints that we may be able to impose in our role as grantor, or with the aid of the Soviet bloc which encourages Indonesia to defy both the Netherlands and Australia on the West Irian question.

This applies with equal force to question of offensive and defensive weapons. Of course it is not possible to draw a meaningful line between offensive and defensive equipment in military field and in my opinion we should not attempt to do so. (The Hague 417 to Department September 4.)[3] However, should we deny adequate equipment to Indonesian Army, Navy or Air Force, which has internal security and self defense responsibilities to 85,000,000 scattered through a chain of more than 3,000 islands, we will have accomplished nothing for our allies, we will have irreparably damaged our own interests, and we will have opened door wide for a permanent Soviet foothold in this part of the world.

I hope the Department will press forward as swiftly as possible in implementing General Vittrup's well-considered program.

Jones

---

[3] In telegram 417, September 5, Young reported on a conversation with Luns in which the Netherlands Foreign Minister complained strongly about a proposed U.S. statement to the NAC on U.S. military assistance to Indonesia. Luns stated that it was a watering down of previous statements, would start a chain reaction of commercial arms sales to Indonesia by other NAC members, and did not make a distinction between offensive and defensive weapons. (Department of State, Central Files, 765D.56/9–458) The Netherlands Chargé, Baron van Voorst, also protested the proposed statement to U.S. officials in Washington. (Memorandum of conversation, September 5; *ibid.*, 765D.56/9–558) See Supplement.

153. Memorandum of Conversation

Washington, September 9, 1958.

SUBJECT

Indonesia

PARTICIPANTS

The Hon. R.G. Casey, Australian Minister for External Affairs
The Hon. Howard Beale, Australian Ambassador
Mr. J. Plimsoll, Assistant Secretary, Dept. of External Affairs
Mr. Malcolm Booker, Counselor, Australian Embassy

The Secretary
Mr. Robertson, Assistant Secretary for Far Eastern Affairs
Mr. Mein, Director, Office of Southwest Pacific Affairs

Minister Casey said that the Australians were exercised over the threats to West New Guinea. He said they do not believe that the Indonesians are likely to use force to get West New Guinea within the next six to twelve months but that there was genuine anxiety in Australia as to what might happen beyond that period. The Dutch have asked the Australian Government for assurances of support in case of an Indonesian attack against West New Guinea. The Australians have given them no such assurances although they have discussed with the Dutch all aspects of the problem. When the Dutch raise the issue, Mr. Casey said, the Australians pass it off by pointing out the danger of leaks and suggest other deterrents to the use of force. The United States is in the best position to exercise the most effective deterrent by placing conditions on any economic or military aid it might extend to Indonesia. The Minister asked whether it would be possible for the U.S. to inform the Indonesians that it plans within the next 18 months to give additional aid to Indonesia but only on condition that they will not use force against West New Guinea. Such conditions could be stated privately, but it would be preferable if they could be made public.

Minister Casey said he had spent two days in Ottawa in talks with Prime Minister Diefenbaker. He had asked the Prime Minister if while in New Delhi in the course of his forthcoming visit to several countries in the area he would talk to Prime Minister Nehru in an effort to get Nehru to exercise some moderating influence on Sukarno. Prime Minister Diefenbaker agreed to do that. Minister Casey thought this would be helpful since Canada has good relations with India and Diefenbaker apparently hit it off well with Nehru at the Prime Ministers' Conference.

Source: Department of State, Central Files, 756D.00/9–958. Secret. Drafted by Mein.

Short of that, Minister Casey said there did not appear to be any deterrent to the use of force by Indonesia to obtain possession of West New Guinea. Sukarno is a fanatic and may not under any conditions be deterred. The Australian position is that they have supported the Dutch in the UN and that since they have been influential in preventing any Indonesian resolution from getting a two-thirds majority they feel an obligation to the Dutch and would find it difficult not to support the Dutch in this case. The Australian Government is aware, however, that should it give support to the Dutch in case of an Indonesian attack against West New Guinea the firing of the first Australian shot would cancel out all Australian influence not only in Indonesia but in all of Asia. The Asian countries,whether they agree with the merits of the Indonesian claim or not, would certainly support Indonesia in such a case. The Minister thought this would be true even of the Philippines. He said that on the basis of private conversations they had reason to believe Serrano agrees with the Australia-Dutch position but in public he must take a different stand.

The Secretary commented that the issue here is the same as that of the offshore islands in that Indonesia claims that West New Guinea is part of Indonesia and therefore wishes to liberate it. The Secretary said that he did not think there is any fear of Indonesia taking West New Guinea by force unless Indonesia falls under communist control. They make speeches and so on for public consumption but we do not believe their intentions are to use force. We feel that if they get a moderate amount of arms from us we may be in a position to influence them. Out of the revolutionary situation which developed there during the early part of the year there seems to have emerged an apparent willingness on the part of the armed forces to work with us and to take steps against the communist threat. The situation there has worked out not too badly.

Minister Casey said there was no question in the Australian mind concerning the sale by the United States of arms for internal security. The Secretary commented that any attack against West New Guinea would, of course, be disastrous and that we would throw our force against such an attack. He said we do not have Congressional authorization to do so but some way could be found if such developed. Minister Casey wondered if there were any sanctions which we could apply to prevent such development. The Secretary commented that there were many things we could do, such as economic sanctions. If Congress were in session we could of course get authorization if necessary for the use of force. Ambassador Beale commented that the important thing, however, is that on these issues we must take the position that force cannot be used to reach settlement. A world opinion supporting this position must be created.

Ambassador Beale referred to the assurances obtained by the U.S. from the Indonesians in connection with the sale of military equipment and pointed out that we had not gotten a specific reply from the Indonesians on this point. Mr. Robertson said that the legal people in the Department feel that the assurances given us do cover the use of the arms for an attack against West New Guinea. Ambassador Jones also feels that he has obtained the necessary assurances. The Secretary commented that it might help if further discussions on this issue take place to have more explicit assurances.

The Secretary said he wished to comment on Minister Casey's referring to Sukarno as a fanatic. In his opinion Sukarno is not a fanatic in the same sense as Syngman Rhee, Chiang Kai-shek and Nasser, but rather a schemer, and a smooth and adroit politician.

Mr. Casey in departing reiterated that although the Dutch were most anxious to have a formal commitment from the Australian Government to come to their assistance in case of an armed attack against West New Guinea he wanted us to know that he had not given them such assurances. The Secretary commented that he would not have objected had the Australians given the Dutch such assurances.[1]

---

[1] Following the meeting with Dulles Foreign Minister Casey met with Assistant Secretary Robertson. A memorandum of that conversation, drafted by Mein, is *ibid.*

---

154. Memorandum of Conversation

New York, September 17, 1958, 11 a.m.

Mr. Luns said his Government realized that the problems of West New Guinea and of Indonesia were perhaps not of first importance to the United States in the face of our many other worldwide problems and responsibilities. Nevertheless, they were very important to the Dutch.

He wanted to say first that the Netherlands would support our China policy in the exclusion of China from the UN. Also they would support our position as regards Taiwan and the offshore islands.

Source: Eisenhower Library, Dulles Papers, General Memoranda of Conversation. Confidential. Drafted by Dulles. The meeting was held at the Waldorf Astoria. Dulles and Luns were in New York for the 13th regular session of the U.N. General Assembly, which opened September 16.

The Dutch felt that they had had a "raw deal" in the postwar period, particularly from the US. Some members of the Dutch Government constantly urged him to appeal to the UN Commission to reestablish the conditions that had been foreseen, but he knew that this, while legalistically sound, was practically impossible. The past could not be erased.

The Dutch recognize that this US Administration had no responsibility for what they regarded as the sins of the preceding. He did feel, however, that we had been lacking in that we had not sufficiently opposed the scandalous behavior of Indonesia in stealing Dutch property and repudiating even commercial debts. They were "gangsters". We had taken a strong line with Iran when it seized the Abadan refinery. We had taken a strong line with Egypt when it seized the Suez Canal Company. But we had been indifferent in Indonesia. The Dutch were inclined to feel that our arms policy was unsound. It would not stop them from getting arms from the Soviet bloc. In some ways, the danger to West New Guinea was greatest if Indonesia was not Communist. There would then be less restraint because the Soviet Union would exercise a measure of restraint, and there would be less free world opposition.

I said that these matters could all be discussed in Washington.[1] I did want to disabuse him of the idea that we did not consider the Indonesia-West New Guinea situation as important. We gave it high priority indeed. It was part of the whole problem of the West Pacific position and keeping the far shore of the Pacific in friendly hands. This was not only important to the free world but to the security of the United States.

I said there might be differences of opinion between us as to how to carry out our objectives, but the objectives were the same. Implementing these was difficult and there were differences of opinion within our own government. Therefore it was not surprising that there might be differences of opinion with the Dutch Government, but our basic propositions were united.

I said (with Ambassador Young being present) that I expected to state our China position in general terms which would equally apply to an attempt by Indonesia to seize West New Guinea by force.

JFD

---

[1] Dulles met with Luns on September 30 in Washington and discussed West New Guinea and Indonesia. (Memorandum of conversation, September 30; Department of State, Central Files, 611.56D/9–3058) See Supplement.

155. Editorial Note

On September 22 Prime Minister Djuanda announced that the Indonesian elections, scheduled for 1959, would be postponed for 1 year. At the Secretary's staff meeting the following day this matter was briefly discussed:

"Mr. J.G. Parsons called attention to an announcement by the Indonesian Prime Minister that the 1959 elections would be postponed. In reply to the Secretary's inquiry, Mr. Parsons said this development was a good one from our point of view." (Notes of the Secretary's staff meeting, September 23; Department of State, Secretary's Staff Meetings: Lot 63 D 75)

On September 25, at the 380th meeting of the National Security Council, Acting Director of Central Intelligence Charles Cabell mentioned the election postponement during his intelligence briefing:

"In Indonesia Prime Minister Djuanda informed Parliament last Monday that the national elections scheduled for 1959 would be postponed for one year. This move was the result of Army pressure designed to check the growth of Communist influence in Indonesia and must have had Sukarno's advance approval. The Indonesian Communist reaction has so far been moderate although the Indonesian Communists will certainly go after Chief-of-Staff Nasution and his followers." (Memorandum of discussion by Gleason, September 25; Eisenhower Library, Whitman File, NSC Records)

---

156. Minutes of ANZUS Council Meeting

ANZ MC–1   Washington, October 1, 1958, 10:05 a.m.–5:55 p.m.

[Here follow a list of participants (24), discussion of other subjects, and statements by Foreign Minister Casey and Prime Minister Nash.]

Begin Top Secret

Secretary Dulles: We see the problem of West New Guinea within the context of the larger problem of Indonesia. The big stake in the area

---

Source: Department of State, Conference Files: Lot 63 D 123, CF 1128. Top Secret; Limit Distribution. Attached to a November 3 covering note by Dudley Miller of the Reports and Operations Staff. The meeting was held at the Department of State. For documentation on the ANZUS Council meeting, see vol. XVI, pp. 45–58. The full text of the minutes is included in the Microfiche Supplement for volume XVI, Part 1.

284 Foreign Relations, 1958–1960, Volume XVII

is Indonesia itself rather than the problem of West New Guinea. We say if West New Guinea and all of Indonesia goes under Communist control, the situation will be very bad. [*11 lines of source text not declassified*]

Begin Secret

I think we have achieved a measure of success in that respect, although it would be premature to say that it had been a complete success. I think it has created a situation where at the present time the government of Indonesia—and I agree that in that government by far the most potent force is Sukarno—sees now the danger of allowing the Communist influence to grow and alienating the West and perhaps leading to a revival of subversive activities, and they have switched to a more truly neutralist policy in the sense of trying to have a policy which would not seriously antagonize either the Communist world or the Western world and particularly the United States.

That has been brought about in part by [*1 line of source text not declassified*] encouragement to Nasution, in particular, the army people who are disposed to be anti-Communist.

There have been a number of developments which indicated that there was growing resistance in Indonesia to Communism and to the possible Communist take-over. Perhaps one of the most significant episodes in that respect has been the postponement of the elections, which will give more time to organize the anti-Communist parties. At the moment the organization of the Communist party has been so effective that probably if there were early elections it would be preponderant in the returns.

The policy that we embarked upon here may require us to continue and possibly to extend somewhat our military assistance. That I must say is not in the form I think you used the word of "gifts" at one point. There are no gifts involved in the military field. They are all sales.

Mr. Robertson: On this $7,000,000 deal, it is a sale, but it is a sale on which there is a low value. It is a sale at a reduced price.

Secretary Dulles: Whether that is a gift, below value, is a debatable question. I am sure the Defense Department would like to get a higher price for it, but it is a question of how you value this more or less obsolete, secondary equipment. That is a debatable point.

I had a long talk yesterday with Mr. Luns,[1] who I would say takes, according to my estimation, a more reasonable view of this situation than some of his associates, and I do not think that he is strongly opposed to our policy although we did not give any indication as to what the development of that policy might involve in the way of further

---

[1] September 30. (Memoranda of conversation by Stabler; Department of State, Central Files, 611.56D/9–3059) See Supplement.

equipment. Indeed, we have come to no conclusion about that ourselves. There are various recommendations made to us from Djakarta which are in process of being evaluated at the present time, and they have not come up to me yet with any recommendation, so I am in ignorance as to what the plans may be, although I do know that they contemplate some assistance to both the Air Force and the Navy and that they involve a category of goods which could be used for either aggressive or defensive purposes.

It is not easy to draw a line, as you are well aware, between so-called offensive and defensive weapons. Almost any weapon can be used offensively. Obviously if you give them pistols and sidearms, they are less effective than if you give them other types of arms.

Now from the standpoint of the armament business, I would say first of all that we think that the Indonesians are extremely foolish in devoting as much of their resources as they are to armament. They are in a desperate economic position and I think it is folly for them to be spending as much of their diminishing resources as they are upon armament. They are mortgaging themselves to the Soviet bloc to a very considerable extent already. We make such arguments to many countries of the world, and always my experience is that those arguments fall upon deaf ears. I have never talked with anybody anywhere in the world that I know of, including in the United States, who spends less money on armament because of economic necessities and the need for a balanced budget and considerations of that kind. And I think the situation is one where the demands of the military people will to a considerable extent be met, and the problem is, will they be met from the United States or from the Soviet Union or from whatever sources which will be available to them.

Of course, as I said, there are other markets in Europe to which they would turn, just as they were able to buy a considerable amount from the United Kingdom and other countries of Europe which will have potential markets open to them.

We are in a sort of curious situation in these matters, because whenever a country turns to the Soviet Union for military aid we throw up our hands in horror and consider that to be a very serious political defeat, and then when they turn to us for military aid and assistance, we do not put the same interpretation upon their actions. Of course, in fact, the nation which supplies military equipment does get a certain control over the country that receives it, because of the dependence upon replacements and spare parts and the like. And it is far better, we think, that Indonesia should be dependent upon us in that respect than dependent upon the Soviet Union or the Soviet bloc.

Now we have given quite a lot of consideration to a request made by Mr. Luns to see what if anything we could do further to discourage the Indonesians from the possible use of force against West New Guinea, and to indicate a measure of support to West New Guinea if it should be attacked.

The principle involved is, as we see it, the same principle as is involved in China today, where a country claims that it is entitled to do it and that to establish that claim would be in effect a civil war and therefore they are justified in doing it. They can make that case against West New Guinea, or, as they call it, West Irian, and that would doubtless receive some support in some quarters. But we would ourselves reject that thesis just as we rejected it in Korea and just as we rejected it in China. And we do not believe that force ought to be used for these purposes and that it is a pretense to say that it is a purely internal affair when in fact we know that it does involve external international factors.

I told Mr. Luns that we would explore the possibilities of putting him in a position to make some statement of our views on this subject when he got back. It is a delicate thing to do because we do not want by anything we say to imply that we reject the sincerity of the number of statements which the Indonesian Government has made disavowing any intention to use force. I admit some of their statements are equivocal, and on the other hand some of their statements are unequivocal, and we don't want in a sense to release them from these unequivocal statements by indicating that we don't believe them or rely upon them. So I don't know yet whether we will find the formula that we will consider would enable Mr. Luns to carry out his purposes without doing such harm to our Indonesian relations that would make it undesirable, but we are studying that very actively at the present time.

I think there is no doubt in the world but what if there were such an attack, that the Government of the United States would be disposed to be as helpful as it could to the Dutch in resisting such an attack. We are not in the same position as regards that area as we are as regards the SEATO area or the area around China and Korea, which is covered by treaties, or by Congressional Resolutions or by both, and where the will of Congress has been manifested to the degree that the President has authority without further reference to the Congress to use military force.

However, we certainly could and I think would give logistical assistance under those circumstances, and would strongly oppose in the United Nations, and otherwise, the action. We would think it was a highly improper breach of the principles of the Charter and that the law-abiding countries ought to unite to oppose and resist it with moral and material strength. We do not think that any change ought to occur there by the use of force, and I hope that perhaps we would find a way to make that clear which would not be offensive or dangerously offensive to the Indonesians. But our basic position is that we do not think that any change should be effected by force, and if it were attempted by force that we would strongly oppose that in our political actions. We would be disposed logistically to assist the defenders. Whether or not it would be necessary or desirable to get Congressional action to permit actual military activity is a matter that could not be answered at this time, and perhaps it would depend upon the circumstances of the time.

If our relations with Indonesia develop as we expect, or at least as we hope, and there does develop a considerable dependence upon the United States, we would think it highly unlikely that they would in fact attempt to take West New Guinea by force. And, as I say, that is perhaps the best hope in the situation. It is not easy to get the Dutch to place confidence in that line of policy, and I can well understand and sympathize with the problems which Mr. Luns has in Parliament with his public opinion, which is convinced that there is (an Indonesian intention) to take it (West New Guinea) by force, and they see us as supplying the sinews of war to Indonesia to be used against the Dutch. I can understand that problem, and I would like as well as we could to alleviate it. We are confident that the policy we are following is the wisest policy from the standpoint of both trying to prevent Indonesia falling into the grasp of the Communists and also from the standpoint of preventing armed attack against West New Guinea.

Minister Casey: If there were an attack in due course in spite of everything, I imagine that would be bowled into the Security Council at once, wouldn't it?

Secretary Dulles: I would suppose so.

Minister Casey: I would hope by you.

Secretary Dulles: If it happens when I am here, I will not be reluctant. I can't commit my successor.

Minister Casey: I want to commit you. That is all. (Laughter)

Secretary Dulles: Of course you can get a veto there quite surely.

(Off-record discussion.)

Mr. Robertson: What is the size of your program there?

Minister Casey: Indonesia—I just can't remember offhand, but we have got now in Australia, I would guess, three or four hundred students and we are getting more all the time. We have got more students from Indonesia than any other Asian country.

Secretary Dulles: I would think I can just say this. I would very much doubt the wisdom of putting anything in the communiqué.

Minister Casey: Oh, not mentioning this directly, no; but broadening out what is said about the use of force any place at any time.

Secretary Dulles: Well, that might be.

Minister Casey: Broadening out this question.

One other point, Mr. Secretary: There was being considered generally at one time, I think, whether or not you came to a decision about it, that you should be the sole supplier of arms as far as the NATO countries are concerned.[2] Has that gone by the board completely or is that a possibility still?

Secretary Dulles: I don't think it is a very good possibility, although I do think this, I think there should be, if it can be practically arranged, an exchange of information between friendly countries, members of NATO, so that we each know what the other is doing and do not run the risk of an excessive action in that respect through each being ignorant of what the others may be doing. We tried to have arrangements of that sort in regard to Israel at one time. It tended to break down in practice. But I would think it highly useful if we could have some kind of informal understanding at least among the NATO members and perhaps some others that in this traffic-in-arms business we should try to keep each other informed so that the aggregate amounts are not too excessive.

Minister Casey: Do you think you would be in a position to get at least a statement from them in specific terms against the use of force, not tacking it onto any tranche of arms that you were providing them with?

Secretary Dulles: We have, of course gotten a lot of these, and I don't attach a great deal of importance to those things. Whenever they get anything from us, they have to get it under the terms of the conventional agreements that state they must not use the arms for any aggressive purposes. And we have obtained statements from them that they would not use it against West New Guinea and the like. I don't attach a great deal of value to those statements. Even among the more reliable countries, France for example, we have had agreements which would preclude use of arms in Algeria; but to stop them once they get these arms and their political policy calls for them—they go ahead and use them. They are not dependable.

I think the most dependable thing is, in fact, the dependence of the country upon us, so that it will not commit any action which would seriously disrupt that relationship. Certainly any act of force against West New Guinea would seriously disrupt our relationship there, and they know that very well. If they only got help from one side, the Communist side, they then wouldn't mind at all whether they disrupt it. They would not have any relations to disrupt. It would not be a factor.

Allen, do you want to comment on this Indonesian situation? I know you have given it a great deal of thought.

[2] See Document 20.

Mr. Allen Dulles: I have here certain figures on the aid that we discussed this morning. The economic aid granted is about $200 million from the Soviet bloc. This is the Sino-Soviet bloc.

Ambassador Beale: Are you speaking of arms aid now?

Mr. Allen Dulles: No; this is just economic aid. I will come to the other in just a moment. The amount obligated so far is about $118 million. Now, a good deal of that has not reached Indonesia. For example, there is a block here of $40 million from Poland for shipping. A good deal of this is shipping, and it has not reached Indonesia and will not reach it for some time. It is much more difficult to give amounts as to the arms aid, but it probably is in excess of $100 million. A great deal of that is from, supposedly, Czechoslovakia. It may be furnished by Russia. About $63 million of it is in aircraft, including about 35 MIG–17's, 20-to-30 IL–28's, 20 IL–14 transports, 20 MIG–15 jet trainers, and some helicopters. Of this, however, only a relatively small part appears to have been delivered as of a few weeks ago. About six of the jet fighters, six to eight of the jet bombers, 15 of the jet trainers have been delivered. Now, there have been agreements with Poland, also, with regard to four destroyers and two submarines. It is quite extensive; it may be almost massive.

Minister Casey: You, too, have come around to "massive." (Laughter)

Mr. Allen Dulles: On the side of technicians, we estimate that they have about 270 bloc technicians on the economic side and about 130 technicians on the military side, or a total of about 400.

[1 paragraph (8-1/2 lines of source text) not declassified]

(Discussion off the record.)

Mr. Allen Dulles: We do not estimate that they are at the moment planning military operations.

Minister Casey: But you will get some advance, possibly considerably advance knowledge of their plans?

Mr. Allen Dulles: I would think we would. We ought to. I would hope so. We ought to get some advance warning.

Secretary Dulles: Have you anything from the standpoint of the question that Mr. Nash put: Is it worthwhile for the Dutch to hold on here? What is the answer to that question?

Minister Casey: What is that?

Secretary Dulles: Is it worthwhile for the Dutch to hold onto it? Are they getting anything out of it?

Minister Casey: No. They are putting an equivalent of seven or eight million pounds into it each year. They haven't any chance of getting any dividends out of it.

Mr. Robertson: They told me the other day it was close to $20 million U.S. dollars. I hadn't known it was as high as that.

Minister Casey: Close. Their oil is not impressive there and I believe it is declining, so it is likely to be a sink for money.

Secretary Dulles: I think it seems to me that the danger we need to face there is perhaps more the danger that the Dutch would pull out than the danger that the Indonesians will take it by force. Of the two dangers, I reckon that danger as greater, because, as I understand it, a lot of their business people realize that this issue is poisoning their relations and (depriving them of the) opportunity to get their property back or at least to get some compensation for their (lost) business in Indonesia and at least to start up business again. There is quite a lot of pressure from the business people to say, "Why in the world don't we give this wretched business away and start fresh and build our relationship with Indonesia." And from a purely business point of view, that makes a lot of sense, and the Dutch have a great reputation for being pretty hard-headed about these things rather than sentimental. And I would imagine that while at the moment they are quite emotional about this one issue, that one must anticipate that their attitude will change and that they may be disposed to just let this thing go, realizing that there is more in it for them if they can reestablish their good relations with Indonesia and get some of their property back and get business going again rather than to hold onto this wretched affair (West New Guinea) which is going to cost them more money if they are going to have to get ready to defend it against possible armed attack.

And of course you know I have talked about giving logistical support and perhaps even more support—that is only possible if the fellow primarily involved is himself willing to fight for it. A foreign country can't come in and fight for the territory of another country which isn't willing to do anything about it itself. So aid that we could give, or maybe that you could give, even though you are not directly involved, would be largely dependent upon their making an effort and their willingness to fight. If they are not willing, we would be out.

Minister Casey: At the moment they are not only willing but determined to resist any aggression—at the moment.

Secretary Dulles: I think they are at the moment.

[Here follows the remainder of the discussion on Indonesia and other subjects.]

157.   Memorandum of Conference With President Eisenhower

Washington, October 2, 1958, noon.

OTHERS PRESENT
Netherlands Foreign Minister Luns
Ambassador Young
General Goodpaster

The President recalled that he had last met Foreign Minister Luns in Paris at the NATO meeting and had enjoyed the opportunity to talk with him.[1] Although the meeting was intended to be quite informal and non-substantive, the discussion immediately turned to Dutch New Guinea when the President asked Mr. Luns for his views. Mr. Luns stressed the difficulty that the government in the Netherlands is experiencing in terms of public opinion because of their effort to maintain a moderate attitude toward the United States on this matter. He said he and the government fully understood the United States position—of avoiding actions which would drive the Indonesians into the arms of the Soviets. Certain types of arms the United States is supplying the Indonesians, however, cause a great deal of concern. Ambassador Young confirmed that Mr. Luns and the government had been extremely understanding in this matter. Mr. Luns said that the Indonesians of course have no claim on Dutch New Guinea, since the natives are non-Indonesian, and strongly desire to stay free of the Indonesians. The land is very lightly settled, however, and the possibility exists of the Indonesians making small landings at various places. He felt that a "deterrent" in the form of a joint Dutch-Australian statement would be very important and hoped that the United States would support that.

The President commented with regard to the limited amounts of arms being furnished the Indonesians, that many of these require ammunition and spare parts in order to be effectively utilized, and that this gives us a degree of control over their misuse; also, any recipient must undertake not to use the arms for aggressive purposes.

The President recalled that we have recently been stressing very strongly in the Far East the principle of "no territorial expansion by force of arms." He asked whether this would not have application in Indonesia.

Source: Eisenhower Library, Whitman File, Eisenhower Diaries. Secret. Drafted by Goodpaster on October 7. A note on the source text indicates the conversation was "off the record."

[1] Reference is most likely to the NATO Heads of Government meeting, held in Paris December 16–19, 1957. No record has been found of a conversation between Eisenhower and Luns.

The President and Mr. Luns next discussed Dutch New Guinea in more detail, as to population, area, economic development, etc. The President asked what value Dutch New Guinea had to the Dutch. Mr. Luns said that it does not have much real value, but that the Dutch feel they have an obligation to administer and protect it. He added that other UN members should honor this feeling.

The President said he would talk in more detail to the Secretary of State regarding this matter.[2]

The President concluded by asking Mr. Luns to remember him to his many friends in Holland, mentioning particularly Prime Minister Staf, Prince Bernhard and Queen Juliana.

AJG
Brigadier General, USA

---

[2] Luns and Dulles had already discussed the issue in Washington on September 30. (Memorandum of conversation, September 30; Department of State, Central Files, 611.56D/9–3058) See Supplement.

---

158.   Letter From the Assistant Secretary of Defense for International Security Affairs (Irwin) to the Under Secretary of State for Economic Affairs (Dillon)

Washington, October 7, 1958.

DEAR MR. DILLON: The decision taken on 1 August 1958 to implement the token military aid programs for Indonesia was based, among other things, upon an estimate that: (1) The Indonesian Army is the only non-Communist force in Indonesia with the capability of obstructing the progress of the Indonesian Communist Party (PKI) toward domination of the country, and (2) given some encouragement in the form of

---

Source: Department of State, Central Files, 611.56D/10–1558. Secret. A draft of this letter was prepared by Rear Admiral W.S. Post, Jr., USN, Regional Director, Far East Region, ISA, and forwarded to Irwin for his approval on September 24. (Washington National Records Center, RG 330, OASD/ISA Records: FRC 62 A 1698, 091.3 Indonesia) The letter was based on a September 22 memorandum from the Joint Chiefs of Staff to the Secretary of Defense. (National Archives and Records Administration, RG 218, JCS Records, 092 Asia (6–25–48)) See Supplement.

U.S. aid, Indonesian Army Chief of Staff Nasution will carry out his plans for the control of Communism. Therefore, the bulk of the equipment programmed is intended for the Indonesian Army, but will be paralleled by some assistance to the other Services.

The first shipments under this token program commenced arriving in Djakarta on 15 August. There is evidence through official channels that the reaction in Indonesian political and military circles was very favorable. An initial momentum has thus been gained, and it is important that this momentum be maintained.

It is recognized that there are risks and uncertainties ahead in pursuing our current policy. Indeed, by its magnitude the comparison to the massive economic and military aid Indonesia has already received from Bloc countries, the token military aid program could hardly be expected to produce more than that which has already been accomplished—plus an opportunity for personal association between U.S. and Indonesian military personnel. However, it is the view of the Department of Defense that the token military aid program, by creating a momentum in Indonesia favorable to the United States, is accomplishing the purpose for which it was designed. What is important now is to maintain this momentum with further actions designed to convince General Nasution and the anti-Communist Indonesian politicians that the United States can be depended upon for continued support in return for further moves on their part to curb the Indonesian Communist Party (PKI).

The Department of Defense recognizes the sensitivity of the Netherlands to military assistance to Indonesia, and the staunch support of the United States by the Dutch both in NATO and the United Nations. Yet continued delay in our Indonesia program because of Dutch objections may readily result in the deterioration of our position in Indonesia and the ascendancy of the Communist Bloc.

Under other circumstances the Department of Defense would recommend the establishment of a MAAG organization in Indonesia. However, in view of the difficulties discussed above concerning the impact of this program on our relations with the Netherlands, as well as the desire of the Indonesian Government to keep the program on an informal basis, the continuation of military assistance to Indonesia should be at the present time by means other than a formal program. Such arrangements should not preclude the eventual establishment of a MAAG.

It is suggested that appropriate arrangements be made for conducting a continuing program of military assistance for Indonesia informally, although on an unclassified basis. Delivery of U.S. equipment

could then continue to be supervised by qualified U.S. military personnel, but their operations should be conducted with minimum publicity.

In light of the above considerations, the Department of Defense recommends:

a) Prompt completion of the initial token military aid program in
its entirety.

b) Approval of the augmented program forwarded to the State Department by the Department of Defense in memoranda dated 23 and 31
July 1958,[1] to include necessary funding and authority to implement the
programs as soon as possible.

c) Early determination of a permanent Military Assistance Program
on a continuing basis for Indonesia with minimum detriment to our relations with the Netherlands.

Sincerely yours,

John N. Irwin, II[2]

---

[1] See footnote 3, Document 139.
[2] Printed from a copy that bears this typed signature.

---

159.   Memorandum of Conversation

Washington, October 8, 1958.

SUBJECT

Statement for the Netherlands Foreign Minister

PARTICIPANTS

Dr. J.H. van Roijen, Netherlands Ambassador
Mr. David Ketel, Counselor, Embassy of the Netherlands
The Secretary
Ambassador Young
FE—Mr. Robertson
EUR—Mr. Jandrey
WE—Mr. Stabler

The Secretary handed to Ambassador van Roijen the attached letter
and statement for transmittal to Foreign Minister Luns in New York.[1]

Source: Department of State, Central Files, 611.56/10–858. Confidential. Drafted by
Stabler on October 14.

[1] Neither printed. In the letter, dated October 7, Dulles informed van Roijen that, in
response to a request by Luns for a statement of the U.S. position on the possible use of
force by Indonesia against West New Guinea, he was enclosing a draft statement. The letter and the draft statement are *ibid.*, 756D.00/10–758. See Supplement.

The Secretary said he thought that the statement met the points in which he understood Mr. Luns was interested. We had really tried to be helpful.

After reading the statement, Dr. van Roijen said that the first thought which occurred to him was what would the United States do if Indonesia did in fact use force against New Guinea. The Secretary replied that he could not give an advance commitment on what we would do if force were used without prior consultation with Congress and Congressional authorization. However, he could say that if force were used, the Dutch could undoubtedly count on our following the same pattern in dealing with that situation as we have followed in comparable cases elsewhere. However, since it was not possible at this time to get Congressional authorization, he could not make a formal statement to that effect. He recalled that the United States had acted vigorously to prevent territorial shifts by force. He said that our action in Lebanon, although it was primarily directed against indirect aggression, was an example of what he meant. He had told the Israelis, who had also sought advance commitments in the event force should be used against them, that they could take comfort from our actions in Lebanon. The Secretary said that in cases where we have taken military action we have had advance Congressional preparation and sanction. He did not doubt that we would help the Netherlands to the limit of our legal authority, but he could not put that in the statement. He believed that the statement, as now drafted, provided a good indication to the Netherlands and to Indonesia what our attitude would be with respect to the use of force.

Ambassador van Roijen agreed that the statement clearly set forth our interest and concern with respect to the West New Guinea situation but he said that it was as if we were merely saying that we were against sin. He had doubts whether the statement would serve to quiet the fears which exist in the Netherlands, particularly in the Labor Party, that the Netherlands stands alone with respect to West New Guinea. Dr. van Roijen recalled to the Secretary the background of the resolution on West New Guinea recently introduced into the Netherlands Parliament by the Labor Party[2] and said that although the resolution had been defeated, the Labor Party had fully supported it. The Secretary said that he thought that the statement carried the clear implication that the Dutch do not stand alone with regard to West New Guinea. He stated that many people in Europe do not seem to realize that the Executive in this country is much less free than in other countries to make promises or

---

[2] Reference is to the so-called Burger motion, introduced in the Dutch Second Chamber on September 30 by representative J.A.W. Burger. The motion called for consultations with a number of friendly powers concerning the feasibility of a UN trusteeship for West New Guinea.

take action in the absence of Congressional authorization or sanction. He said that at the time of the Suez situation the US could not have acted militarily because there was no Congressional approval. He recalled that there had been considerable controversy over the legal authority of the Truman administration to act with respect to Korea. He said that although nobody disagreed with the action itself, there were those who felt that no action should have been taken until Congress had been consulted and had approved. He said that President Eisenhower might be termed "conservative" in relation to this point since he was most reluctant to give promises which might strain the Presidential authority. The Secretary stressed that we have always made our opposition to the use of force recognized by more than mere words of condemnation. We have always acted on the principle that force should not be used to settle disputes and he recalled the strong diplomatic stand we took at the time of Suez against our two oldest allies. The Secretary said that it would be unthinkable that we would not do something if force were used against West New Guinea, but he emphasized again that he could not make a formal statement to this effect without Presidential approval, and he did not think the President would give his approval without Congressional sanction.

Dr. van Roijen said that he thought that Mr. Luns would have to explain the background set forth by the Secretary to the Foreign Affairs Commission of the Netherlands Parliament in private sessions. He did not think that the statement by itself without the private explanation would suffice. He said that the real problem was that there were those in the Netherlands who felt that West New Guinea should be given up. He thought that a serious situation would be created if pressures in the Netherlands to give up West New Guinea should increase. The Secretary agreed that if the Dutch should give up West New Guinea, a serious problem would be created, especially if Sukarno should go to the Communists. He said that Australia would be particularly concerned in view of the importance of New Guinea to Australian security.

160. Memorandum From the Assistant Secretary of State for Far Eastern Affairs (Robertson) to Secretary of State Dulles

Washington, October 15, 1958.

SUBJECT

Indonesia: Future U.S. Actions

Discussion:

On August 1 you authorized several steps to be taken, including token military aid, to strengthen the hand of the Indonesian Army and as an indication of our support of the anti-Communist elements in Indonesia (Tab A).[1] The bulk of the equipment provided for in the token arms program will have been delivered by December 1. Because of Dutch objections, however, delivery dates for three L–20 liaison planes for the Army and three helicopters for the Air Force included in the package have not been determined.

These actions have produced in Indonesia a very favorable reaction, and with the postponement of elections and the likelihood of relative political stability for a minimum of two years, our Ambassador has recommended we proceed with programs of economic and military assistance designed to strengthen anti-Communist elements and re-enforce Indonesian ties with the West (Djakarta telegram 1113, Tab B).[2]

The Netherlands Government fears that Indonesia will attempt to take West New Guinea by force and is strongly opposed to Indonesian acquisition of arms and military equipment from any Western source. Failing a complete embargo, the Dutch request that the U.S. supply no "offensive" arms and ask its NATO partners to refrain from selling arms to Indonesia. The Australian Government, both for internal political reasons and because of Dutch pressure, has expressed concern over U.S. supply of "offensive weapons," but is in basic agreement with present U.S. policy. The British Government, although not prepared to sell heavy military equipment to Indonesia "at this time", has informed the Indonesians it will sell them some radar equipment. The Germans have also recently informed the Indonesians that they are going ahead with the delivery of some speedboats for the Navy.

Source: Department of State, Central Files, 611.56D/10–1558. Secret. Drafted by Underhill and cleared by Barnes, Mann, Murphy, and Parsons.

[1] Tab A summarized the actions authorized on August 1. See Supplement.

[2] Telegram 1113, September 29, analyzed the current state of U.S.-Indonesian relations and made certain specific recommendations for augmented U.S. military and economic aid. (Department of State, Central Files, 756D.00/9–2958) See Supplement.

The recent trend in developments in Indonesia has been in general favorable (Tab C).[3] The postponement of elections is a concrete, major step in the right direction, and despite greatly intensified Soviet Bloc efforts to press economic aid on Indonesia, the government and the military establishment clearly prefer closer ties with the U.S. I feel that we should proceed immediately to press our advantage both in the military and civil sectors. There are recognized risks and we can not be certain to succeed, but to turn our back on Indonesia would bring almost certain failure.

The Department of Defense has recommended that further actions be taken in the military field to maintain the favorable momentum created by the token aid program (letter dated October 7, 1958 from Mr. Irwin to Mr. Dillon, Tab D).[4] Admiral Burke, in a personal letter to me, has expressed his feeling of urgency that we proceed with further assistance (Tab E).[5]

Whatever the validity of Dutch and Australian fears, the security of West New Guinea from Indonesian attack can certainly not be obtained by denying to Indonesia western sources of economic and military assistance and permitting unobstructed Soviet Bloc infiltration from without and Communist subversion from within, to say nothing of an unlimited supply of Soviet Bloc arms and ammunition.

Recommendation:[6]

That you approve:

1. The following military program:

    a. Prompt completion of the August 1 token military assistance program in its entirety, that is, the delivery of three L–20 liaison planes for the Army and three helicopters for the Air Force.
    b. An augmented program of military assistance, as recommended by Mr. Irwin in his letter of July 31 (Tab F),[7] to be financed under Title I of the Mutual Security Act of 1954, as amended, subject to a Presidential determination under Section 451 of that Act.
    c. A continuing limited program of military assistance to Indonesia contingent upon future internal developments, and subject to the criteria and guidelines outlined by W/MSC in its memorandum of October 18, 1958 (Tab G).[8]

---

[3] Tab C summarized the recent pro-Western and anti-Communist actions taken by the Indonesian Government. See Supplement.

[4] Document 158.

[5] Dated October 8. (Department of State, Central Files, 741.5622/10–858) See Supplement.

[6] Dulles initialed his approval of all five items.

[7] See footnote 3, Document 139.

[8] Not found.

2. Removal of restrictions on the issuance of export licenses for:

a. All types of civil aircraft.
b. Subject to the approval of the regional bureau, the following equipment and supplies for military and civil use: surplus, propellor-driven military aircraft; small arms and ammunition; and surplus landing craft for police and civil use, since it is inconsistent and self-defeating that we supply arms for local currency under a military sales program and refuse to permit Indonesia to buy for dollars equipment commercially available in the U.S.

3. A program of increased economic assistance utilizing the several available types of economic aid. Among the projects currently under consideration are:

a. A loan of $2.7 million from the DLF for railroad rehabilitation in South Sumatra.
b. Negotiation of a new PL–480 agreement to provide rice and other surplus agricultural commodities.

4. Informing the Ex-Im Bank that for political reasons we wish them to proceed with consideration of projects in Indonesia meeting their criteria. Projects under consideration include:

a. Urea fertilizer plant ($30 million).
b. Thermal power project, Surabaya ($9.4 million).
c. Dredges for land development and reclamation in Borneo and Sumatra ($6.9 million).
d. Lockheed Electras for Garuda ($12 million).

5. That we inform the Netherlands and Australian Governments that we intend to proceed with programs of assistance to Indonesia in the military and economic sectors, that we intend to proceed with their views and concerns very much in mind, that we will inform them of the nature of these programs as they are decided upon, and that we will take all appropriate occasions to impress on Indonesia that we would be strongly opposed to the use of military force in an attempt to resolve the West New Guinea dispute.[9]

---

[9] In an October 30 memorandum to Dulles, Elbrick offered EUR's appraisal of Robertson's October 15 memorandum. Regarding recommendation 2(b) he explained that EUR believed that the Dutch would object to the commercial sale of surplus propeller-driven military aircraft and surplus landing craft for police and civil use and suggested that Dutch reaction could be better handled if the sales remained on a government-to-government basis. (Department of State, Central Files, 756D.5–MSP/10–3058) See Supplement. On November 5 Dulles approved the augmented aid program recommended by Robertson, taking into account EUR's position; see Document 161.

161. Editorial Note

General Maxwell D. Taylor, U.S. Army Chief of Staff, visited Indonesia November 2–4 as part of a larger Asian trip. During his stay in Indonesia Taylor met with President Sukarno, Prime Minister Djuanda, and Foreign Minister Subandrio. In telegram 1504 from Djakarta Jones reported that Taylor's trip illustrated pointedly the new state of U.S.-Indonesian relations and noted that the Indonesian press had commented favorably upon his visit. (Department of State, Central Files, 611.56D/11 258) See Supplement. The Embassy reported further on Taylor's trip in telegram 1520 from Djakarta, November 4, and telegram 1528 from Djakarta, November 3. (Department of State, Central Files, 756D.00/11–458 and 756D.5–MSP/11–358) See Supplement for both.

On November 5 Secretary of State Dulles approved the augmented aid program for Indonesia, recommended by Assistant Secretary Robertson in his memorandum of October 15. According to an excerpt from the Staff Record of November 6, drafted by Dudley W. Miller of S/S, the Secretary

"*Approved* a course of future US actions with regard to Indonesia involving a military assistance program, removal of restrictions on the issuance of export licenses for certain items and a program of increased economic assistance using the several types of assistance available; *agreed* that we should inform the Dutch and Australians of our assistance programs, assuring them that we shall bear in mind their views, that we will inform them of the nature of these programs as decided upon, and that we will impress on Indonesia our opposition to the use of military force to resolve the West New Guinea dispute." (Department of State, SPA Files: Lot 63 D 106, Indonesia 1958)

The Department of State summarized Dulles' decision in telegram 873 to Djakarta, Document 163.

Mein informed British and Australian representatives of the augmented aid program in separate conversations on November 12. (Memoranda of conversation by Mein; Department of State, Central Files, 756D.5–MSP/11–1258)

162. **Telegram From the Department of State to the Embassy in Indonesia**

Washington, November 8, 1958, 5 p.m.

878. CINCPAC for POLAD. FYI only. Following summary main points Subandrio meeting with Secretary Nov 5 based on uncleared memo of conversation.[1]

Subandrio cited US desire find way check communism and Indo adopted policy of Pantjasila and stated wished explore margin for agreement between two countries based on these policies and eliminate past mutual suspicions. Subandrio assured Secretary Indo does not want communism. In past GOI unable openly oppose communist bloc or adopt anti-communist policy because such policy would have led to anarchy. Now however possible for GOI take stronger stand. Subandrio remarked Sukarno no longer popular with communists who regard President as principal competitor for loyalty of masses. Sukarno as well as military having greater voice in daily operations of government. Fon-Min stated Indo must find solution to many of its problems while Sukarno still alive and serving as unifying force. Government must also find ways for administering country without retreating from elections.

Secretary emphasized US dedicated to principles, not alliances or friendships, and cited US position on Suez. Re newly independent former colonies such as Indonesia Secretary said our concern not merely that independence be obtained but that once obtained it be preserved. One of policies of international communism is to promote concept of independence to point of breaking relations of colonial people with West, then after independence move in and consolidate strength. Danger in Far East, Secretary noted, is growing mood of expansion in Communist China and desire dominate area.

Secretary stated until recently we felt GOI not aware communist dangers and therefore might lose independence and remarked that some of revolutionary elements more aware these dangers than central

---

Source: Department of State, Central Files, 756D.000/11–858. Secret; Limit Distribution. Drafted by Wenzel, cleared by Mein, Parsons, and Stabler of EUR/WE, and approved by Robertson. Repeated to The Hague and CINCPAC. In telegram 1493 from Djakarta, October 31, Jones outlined the points which Subandrio hoped to make with Dulles during this meeting. (*Ibid.*, 611.56D/10–3158) See Supplement. On November 4 Robertson forwarded a briefing paper for the Secretary for this meeting with Subandrio. (*Ibid.*, 756D.13/11–458) See Supplement.

[1] The meeting took place at 11 a.m. in Dulles' office. Subandrio was in Washington en route to a meeting of the Consultative Committee of the Colombo Plan November 10–13. An 8-page memorandum of conversation of this meeting, drafted by Mein and approved by Robertson, November 5, is in Department of State, Central Files, 033.56D11/11–558. See Supplement.

government. Secretary said we did nothing to help them but we did nothing to stop others from rendering assistance. We now believe, Secretary said, GOI more aware of dangers and this tends create better relationship between us. As long as Indo alert to dangers and is taking steps counter them, Indo will have nothing but sympathy and support from US and no basis to fear us. Indo will never be under pressure join SEATO but we do wish see Indo remain independent. If it seems Indo slipping into communist hands then we would see what steps necessary help Indonesia preserve independence. Secretary summarized US views as 1) we have no ambition run Indo, force Indo adopt our policies or align itself with us; 2) our one concern is that action be taken by GOI to maintain independence; 3) as long as Indo does that, there will be no basic differences between us.

Secretary acknowledged situation complicated somewhat by West New Guinea issue but stated our attitude toward Indonesia would not be altered or swayed by our friendship with the Netherlands. Secretary reiterated we abide by principles, however unpopular they might be. We assume therefore that Indo will also adhere to its principles and not resort to use force for settlement its territorial claims. Re use of force, Subandrio replied Indo realized such action not only against Dutch or even Australia but against US and he could assure Secretary Indo will never take action against US. Subandrio added that while his government would not be so foolish as to use force, GOI wanted US to be more constructive in helping find solution. Secretary replied he thought there might be opportunity do something in future but that at present feelings on both sides too emotional.

Secretary said also we do not like GOI policy of wholesale confiscation, that it is bad policy to treat property in such a way that it frightens everybody away. Secretary emphasized he raising this issue not because he was talking as agent of Dutch but rather because of its general importance re Indo relations with West. Secretary remarked that when Nasser nationalized Suez he was careful to say there would be fair compensation. In reply Subandrio recalled fruitless negotiations with Dutch on West New Guinea issue since 1950 indicating Indo-Dutch relations had played into hands of communists and implying this forced current GOI measures against Dutch. Stated proposed legislation did not provide for confiscation but for nationalization. Subandrio added GOI had no intention of cutting off economic relations completely with Dutch and declared recent developments Indo-Dutch relations a tragedy. However Indo did not wish isolate itself from West. Now that PKI agitations controllable Subandrio said if US could do something to bring the two countries together this would be helpful.

Re Communist China Subandrio remarked in Indo there was great respect for its material progress, albeit at expense human lives, but also great fear. FonMin added there was not one person in Indo afraid of attack on Indo by US but growing awareness of danger of ChiComs. Subandrio declared one of great problems faced by Indo is resident Chinese and defended GOI actions against them. He tended fail differentiate between KMT and ChiCom elements and cited protest of ChiCom Ambassador as well as discussions with Ambassador Jones.

FonMin stated he anxious promote good relations with Australia and noted he planned visit there at Casey's invitation after national elections. End FYI only.

Dulles

---

163.   **Telegram From the Department of State to the Embassy in Indonesia**

Washington, November 7, 1958, 8:59 p.m.

873. FYI only. Secretary November 5 approved following US actions re Indonesia:

1) Military Programs

a) Prompt completion entire August 1 military assistance program, i.e. delivery 3 L–20 aircraft for army and 3 helicopters for air force.
b) $7.8 million augmentation program as follows: for army $2.4 million for 12 bridges; for navy $2.9 million for one LST, two minesweepers and equipment for one marine rifle company and one 60 mm mortar section; for air force $2.5 million for pilot training and command and general staff school training. To be financed under MSP subject to Presidential determination.
c) Continuing limited program of military assistance contingent upon future internal developments.

2) Removal of restrictions on issuance export licenses for all types civil aircraft, surplus propeller-driven military aircraft, small arms and ammunition, surplus landing craft for police and civil use. In general our program for the sale of military equipment to Indonesia will be on a

Source: Department of State, Central Files, 756D.5–MSP/11–758. Secret; Limit Distribution; Priority. Drafted by Wenzel, cleared in draft with Jandrey, and approved by Parsons. Also sent to Canberra, The Hague, and CINCPAC.

government to government basis. We cannot, however, make a commitment to permit no commercial sales, although such sales will remain subject to export licensing procedures and thus to control by the government.

3) Program of increased economic assistance utilizing several available types economic aid. Among projects currently under consideration are a) $2.7 million DLF loan for railway rehabilitation South Sumatra and b) negotiation new PL–480 agreement for rice and other commodities.

4) Informing Ex-Im Bank that for political reasons we wish them to proceed with consideration of projects in Indonesia meeting their criteria. Projects under consideration include a) fertilizer plant ($30 million); b) thermal power project Surabaya ($9.4 million); c) dredges for land development Borneo and Sumatra ($6.9 million); d) Lockheed Electras for Garuda ($12 million).

Indonesians, Dutch and Australians not yet informed above decision and we presently working out arrangements for notification.

No action should be taken by any addressee pending further instructions. End FYI.

Dulles

---

164.   Telegram From the Department of State to the Embassy in Indonesia

Washington, November 19, 1958, 11:32 a.m.

943. Follow summary major points Robertson–Subandrio conversation Nov 18.[1]

1) Robertson informed Minister we have approved program additional military assistance which will include items not only for Army but

---

Source: Department of State, Central Files, 756D.5–MSP/11–1958. Secret; Priority. Drafted by Wenzel and approved by Robertson. Repeated to The Hague, Canberra, and CINCPAC for POLAD.

[1] Subandrio stopped in Washington on November 18 on his return from the Colombo Plan meeting in Seattle. A 5-page memorandum of Robertson's conversation with Subandrio, drafted by Mein, is *ibid.*, 756D.00/11–1858. See Supplement.

also for Navy and Air Force. Stated until we obtain Presidential determination under Section 451 MSA which we requesting, we cannot make commitment to GOI nor discuss details and added we hope instruct Ambassador Jones shortly advise GOI of this program.

2) Robertson also advised Subandrio we approve in principle GOI request for additional PL–480 program but matter must be considered by Inter-departmental Committee. Stated we do not know magnitude of program but possible it may not be for as much as GOI has requested because among other reasons insufficient quantity surplus rice available at present time. Advised details of program will be discussed with GOI after final approval by interested agencies.

3) Re other economic assistance, Robertson told Minister we have instructed Ambassador Jones explore with GOI possible use DLF funds for financing GOI purchase KPM ships. Re Ex-Im Bank Robertson stated all applications under active consideration and we hope be able act on them soon. Noted contract with STANVAC for natural gas not yet signed by GOI and such contract necessary before application re fertilizer plant can be approved.

4) Robertson impressed upon Subandrio that there should be no publicity concerning these programs either here or in Djakarta until everything had been settled. He reiterated we would instruct Ambassador Jones give GOI all details as soon as we in position discuss them. Minister stated he was "pleasantly surprised" over these prospects though he understood no commitments made. He stated satisfactory atmosphere created and this would make his task easier not only in Indonesia but in his discussions with other governments as he attempts implement Indo foreign policy and he "really grateful" for this prospect.

5) When queried on *Blitz* story re possible GOI nationalization American oil companies in Indonesia,[2] Subandrio replied he had not made any such statement, had seen no newspapermen in India and would see that denial was issued.

6) Robertson stated there was considerable concern here over implications Sukarno's Ambon speech that if Indonesia does not get West Irian it will not make any settlement for nationalized Dutch properties.[3] Minister replied it important consider need meet psychological atmosphere in Indonesia, implying some of such statements made primarily

---

[2] The Indian newspaper *Blitz* quoted Subandrio as saying while in India, en route to the United States, that "the Indonesian Government was seriously contemplating the plan of nationalization of foreign-owned oil companies which are taking a huge bite of the foreign exchange earnings of the country." (Briefing memorandum from Mein to Robertson, November 17; Department of State, Central Files, 756D.13/11–1758) See Supplement.

[3] Jones reported on this speech in telegram 1614 from Djakarta, November 13. (Department of State, Central Files, 756D.11/11–1358)

for domestic consumption. Subandrio continued it unfortunate use GOI attitude toward Dutch as indicative GOI attitude toward private capital, stated that Indonesia has always paid its foreign obligations and asked that we be understanding of problem, adding he confident satisfactory solution would be worked out as soon as dust settles, perhaps within next 6 months.

7) Remainder of conversation devoted to discussion SEATO, neutralism, Soviet Union, Communist China and Communism. Subandrio remarked that in Indonesia they realized now more than ever before danger of communist subversion. Minister added Indonesians wish settle problems themselves and not be accused of blindly following U.S. but that with necessary tools from U.S. he confident GOI could meet the problem. Text memo conversation being pouched.

Herter

165.   Telegram From the Embassy in Indonesia to the Department of State

Djakarta, November 20, 1958, 2 p.m.

1695. CINCPAC for POLAD. President Sukarno made strong appeal last night to ICA Director Baird to help convey true picture of Indonesia to American Government on his return to Washington. President asked Baird to call on eve of his departure for Washington consultation, first time Baird had talked with President on other than primarily social occasions.

Sukarno expressed hope that improvement Indo-US relations could continue. Baird remarked that he felt relations had improved during last six months, and President replied, "Oh, tremendously. But we want this to continue. We always have the feeling you are holding back and not giving us your full confidence. We are peculiar people. If you give us your full confidence, you will be surprised how we will respond."

Source: Department of State, Central Files, 611.56D/11–2058. Confidential. Repeated to The Hague, Canberra, Tokyo, Singapore, and CINCPAC.

President went on to say he had told Secretary two years ago "not to lose this game".

"These fellows up north are pretty rough," Sukarno added. "We don't know how many friends we have in the world. We don't know whether you are really for us; we have the feeling that your aid comes to us reluctantly.

"We have more basic things in common with America than any other country. Please don't lose this game."

President then turned to specifics, noting that press reports had said Subandrio informed in Washington EXIM Bank unwilling make loans for Lockheed Electras, thermal power plant in Surabaya, dredges.

"This is vital. We have to have these things. I don't understand. Why are you so reluctant to help us. We like Americans and we trust America, but we have got to survive. Try to explain this in Washington and get these loans through. We were embarrassed by this."

President's attitude throughout conversation was friendly, sincere, humble. At one point said he was angry about *Herald Tribune* editorial which had accused him of staging trip to Moluccas to divert attention from serious economic situation.

"I don't know why we're so misunderstood," President said. "We don't seem to have projected ourselves as we really are.

"I have received many, many letters from your young people in the States who are more understanding of Indonesia's needs and aspirations than your government."

The President then undertook to analyze the cause for US Government misunderstanding.

"The center of world power and influence has shifted since World War II to Asia from Europe. You are still guided by a European mentality in your attitude and relations with Asia generally, but in particular towards the Republic of Indonesia.

"Why is it that most of the visitors who come here have a completely false picture of Indonesia in their minds? But after even two days in Djakarta, the worst city in the world, they understand us better and see that they have been wrong. Please do not lose this game because of such false attitudes."

At another point in conversation President asked whether "Dutch propaganda" might be responsible for distorted picture of Indonesia in outside world.

Jones

166.   Telegram From the Embassy in Indonesia to the Department of State

Djakarta, November 20, 1958, 3 p.m.

1697. CINCPAC for POLAD. I saw Sukarno at 10 o'clock this morning, he having postponed appointment tentatively scheduled for eighteenth because he was not feeling well. President had three-hour examination by doctors yesterday and he has been ordered to take complete rest. He therefore will leave for 10 days in Bali end of this week returning December 4.

President opened conversation by asking me whether I had recovered from rigors of trip to East Indonesia. I laughed and said I had after two or three good nights sleep. I complimented him on his amazing energy and stamina and said he certainly had not acted like a man who needed medical attention. He admitted stimulation of trip helped not hurt him. He had planned trip to Kalimantan on twenty-seventh of this month to dedicate new airport but he had reluctantly cancelled this on insistence of his doctors. He asked my impressions of trip. I replied that aside from obvious beauty of Moluccas and attractiveness of gay, music-loving people I had received two distinct impressions:

(1) That people of Moluccas were genuine Indonesians and that they thought of themselves as Indos first and Moluccans second. This was significant since when I had been in Indonesia before I had heard much of separatist movement in Moluccas and anti-Javanese sentiment there. I said I presumed considerable anti-Javanese sentiment still exists (at this point President nodded agreement) but that it was evident from people with whom I had talked entirely aside from staged demonstrations that Moluccan people had become in spirit a part of a united Indonesia.

(2) That President himself served as a symbol of this unity and that regardless of anti-Javanese feelings in eastern Indonesia these sentiments did not apply to President for whom obvious genuine affection had been manifested on all sides. I said that some observers in the party inclined at first to be skeptical were convinced by genuiness of his reception. President was right in what he had said on trip, I commented, and quoted his own words back to him "It is easy to arrange a meeting but one cannot prearrange a smile."

President while apparently gratified at my comments seemed to be waiting for me to say something else which I intentionally avoided say-

Source: Department of State, Central Files, 756D.00/11–2058. Secret; Priority. Transmitted in two sections and repeated to The Hague, Paris, Canberra, and CINCPAC.

ing, that is comment on West New Guinea aspect of trip. President, however, did not raise point but instead turned to subject of another trip he had planned as soon as various official visits such as that of President Tito, et cetera were out of way. This would be trip to northern Sulawesi, he said, and indicated he would include me in invitation.

President then referred to his conversation with Mister Baird last night (Embtel 1695),[1] reviewed what he had told him and then inquired whether I had seen press reports re no credit for Lockheed Electras, Surabaya Power and Kalimantan Dredges. If so what did I think about them.

I replied that I had seen press reports, that I had queried Washington as to their significance which I said I failed to understand in view of good news which I had come to impart. I then informed President in accordance with authorization Deptel 925[2] that the US was prepared to consider a program of increased economic assistance to Indonesia on project basis, using the various US lending agencies—DLF, EXIM Bank and PL 480. US Government, I said, was presently in process of reviewing all pending GOI applications and GOI would be informed as [soon as] we are prepared to proceed. President expressed gratification at this news and re-emphasized his concern re Lockheed Electras. It would be very embarrassing if after all this time this request were turned down. Need for these planes was very great but much more important at this point was question of pride. I responded that I had had no official word which would lead me to believe that this request had been rejected and I counseled patience, pointing out that newspaper reports are often misleading.

I then informed President US Government had also approved program of additional military assistance, including items for army, navy and air force. In order not to raise his hopes too high felt it desirable to mention some of specifications contained in Deptel 191,[3] emphasizing however that this constituted advance notice and did not represent final decision. I pointed out as Sukarno aware presidential determination was required for this assistance and in this connection I stressed impor-

---

[1] Document 165.

[2] Telegram 925, November 17, reads: "You are authorized inform Sukarno and Djuanda along lines final para your 1664 emphasizing our desire that there be no publicity. (Department of State, Central Files, 756D.5–MSP/11–1758) In telegram 1664 from Djakarta, November 17, Jones requested that the Department authorize him to tell Sukarno and Djuanda of the general nature of the planned assistance programs. (*Ibid.*)

[3] Reference is most likely to telegram 911 to Djakarta, November 14, which authorized the Embassy on a service-to-service basis to inform Nasution as well as the Indonesian Navy and Air Chiefs of the proposed augmentation in the U.S. military assistance program, including mention of potential specific items. (*Ibid.*, 756D.5–MSP/11–1458) See Supplement.

tance of no publicity at this time, pointing out obvious embarrassment to President Eisenhower in event news broke before he had had opportunity to act. I also noted current meeting of NATO parliamentary group in Paris and observed that I was sure he would agree that it would not be in the interest of either of our governments for this to become an issue [at] that meeting.

President readily assented. He went on to say that he hoped the US Government would not be like the British—that we would not feel it necessary to seek Dutch approval in advance for anything we did for Indonesia. I assured him that as he by now must be aware US policy toward Indonesia stood on its own feet. President then expressed gratification at this news. He also obviously appreciated my coming to him first (although for Department's information this was result of chance not of planning since I had asked for appointments with PriMin and Sukarno simultaneously). Sukarno then said "please keep this aid coming—gradually but quickly." He then repeated this phrase "gradually but quickly." "It is important for it to come quickly."[4]

Jones

---

[4] In telegram 1704 from Djakarta, November 20, Jones reported that he passed on to Djuanda the same information that he had given Sukarno regarding the additional U.S. military and economic assistance programs. The Prime Minister was "very appreciative" and "said he was gratified at this indication of improving US-Indo relations." (*Ibid.*, 756D.5–MSP/11–2058) See Supplement.

---

167. Telegram From the Embassy in Indonesia to the Department of State

Djakarta, December 4, 1958, 9 a.m.

1819. Department pass DEPTAR for ACSI. CINCPAC also for POLAD. Department telegram 873.[1] We believe moment has arrived when we must discuss with Indonesian armed forces more fully and frankly than has heretofore been possible our long range intentions re military assistance. If we do not do so, we may find ourselves providing

---

Source: Department of State, Central Files, 756D.5–MSP/12–458. Secret; Priority. Transmitted in two sections and repeated to The Hague and CINCPAC.

[1] Document 163.

considerable assistance piecemeal without accomplishing our political objectives. This would be as unsatisfactory to Indonesians as to ourselves.

I believe we should tell chiefs of armed services that so long as there is no reversal in present favorable political trend in Indonesia US intends furnish such quantities and types of arms for all three services as it is able, consistent with other assistance commitments, requirements of our own military services, and limitation that only self-defense and internal security requirements are to be met.

So far as Indonesian Army now knows we have translated offer of additional military assistance into commitment provide 12 Bailey bridges. While army is glad to have Bailey bridges, it will have difficulty absorbing that quantity all at once. However, it could immediately use large number additional rifles. Army's immediate needs change from time to time, and long gap between first request and actual delivery may produce other such incongruities if we approach problem on item by item basis.

Recently General Nasution and his deputies have informed MIL-TAG army headquarters now giving low priority to proposed equipment in augmentation program. They emphasize immediate need for small arms, transportation and communications.

Natural resolution for such difficulty would be for Indonesian Army to plan its requirements year or so ahead so US could make determinations well in advance as to items it is willing or able to provide. This not now possible since army has no assurances US will be providing it with any form of assistance year, or even month, from now. In any event it could make no plans without knowing what US had available and might be willing to supply. So far US aid has been what the US has decided is best for Indonesia have. Indonesian armed services do not believe they can make adequate long range plans on that basis, especially since they have no clear idea of what US thinks they should have in future. It is inevitable that unless they can see a little farther into future re our intentions, the services, particularly air force, will be tempted to deal increasingly with Soviet bloc as a more satisfactory alternative.

We realize our present program is to proceed only as rapidly as we receive signs that Indonesians are responding as we desire. While I believe this has been valid approach, it can become self-defeating because it prevents adequate planning and produces a situation in which improvement of relations can only proceed by fits and starts.

There is much evidence that General Nasution taking on greatly increased share responsibility for management Indonesian affairs, and it not beyond realm of possibility this trend will continue to point where his influence will be decisive on all questions. Therefore it is vital to our interest that we reinforce, especially at this time, his confidence in US willingness to see him through.

We need a definite plan as to approximate value and categories of weapons US prepared supply Indonesia annually for period of years, subject to favorable political developments. This plan should realistically take into account needs of services and fact that items we cannot supply may be obtained elsewhere.

While it may take some time to develop such a plan, there are certain steps we can take now to make it clear that we are prepared to go farther in future.

Specifically I recommend:

1. That we inform armed services they should regard items cited paragraph 1 reference telegram as token of our willingness to assist and not our idea of meeting their most pressing requirements.

2. That we inform Indonesians we prepared discuss long-range program, subject to availability of funds, which will strike balance between their requirements and our capabilities, military and political.

3. That we substitute small arms, particularly M–1 Garands to equip and standardize complete infantry units, for Bailey bridges as item for immediate delivery to army.

4. That we provide additional supplies and services requested by Marshal Suryadarma (MILTAG to CINCPAC 022330Z)[2] in connection with helicopters.

Above comments relate primarily to paragraph 1 reference telegram and in particular to emphasis in discussing with Indonesians content subparagraph (C) reference telegram regarding future military aid.

In addition it would help greatly if I could inform Indonesians of removal restriction on issuance export licenses for aircraft pursuant paragraph 2 reference telegram.[3]

Jones

---

[2] Not found.

[3] Telegram 1095 to Djakarta, December 12, a joint State–Defense message, responded to Jones' request for a long-range military aid program. (Department of State, Central Files, 756D.5622/12–1258) See Supplement.

168.   Telegram From Secretary of State Dulles to the Department of State

Paris, December 18, 1958, 2 p.m.

Secto 26. Foreign Minister Luns saw Secretary for half hour before December 18 NATO meeting.[1] Luns stated he had complained to Lloyd re British action in selling Fairey-Gannets to Indonesia after previous Dutch understanding British would break contract.[2] Secretary repeated bases for US arms sales to Indonesia which was a typically new country in which army was main effective source of power and barrier to Communism. Secretary added that Dutch intelligence estimates with regard to likelihood attack against West New Guinea were apparently different from ours and accordingly believed we should discuss these estimates together. He also stated his recent Washington talk with Subandrio had been extremely frank.

Luns repeated Dutch information re projected March attack against West New Guinea. [4 lines of source text not declassified] He also concurred in Secretary's suggestion for comparing intelligence estimate. [3 lines of source text not declassified]

Dulles

Source: Department of State, Central Files, 756D.56/12–1858. Confidential; Priority. Repeated to The Hague and Djakarta.

[1] Dulles and Luns were in Paris for a Ministerial Meeting of the North Atlantic Council, December 16–18. On December 17 Luns raised the subject of Indonesia [text not declassified] objecting in particular to Western nations supplying arms to Indonesia. In reply Dulles stated that the modest U.S. arms supplies to Indonesia would not appreciably increase Indonesia's ability to move against New Guinea. He added that the United States thought that it had some influence over the Indonesian Government and was attempting to direct that government away from pro-Communist channels and into more desirable directions. Dulles also noted that the United States had exerted its influence in the most categorical way against the Indonesian use of force against New Guinea. (Telegram 1158 to Djakarta, December 22; ibid., 756D.00/12–2258)

[2] On December 8 the British Embassy informed the Department of State that the British Government had decided to proceed with the sale of Fairey-Gannet aircraft to Indonesia. (Telegram 1071 to Djakarta, December 10; ibid., 756D.5622/12–1058)

On December 16 in Paris, Dulles spoke with Selwyn Lloyd about Indonesia and reported on this conversation in Secto 24 from Paris, December 17, as follows:

"Lloyd then raised Dutch disturbance over announced British intention deliver planes to Indonesians, which he said he had justified on basis that United States had told United Kingdom they would deliver comparable aircraft if British did not. I reviewed with him encouraging developments in Indonesia situation and told him that I had warned Indonesian Foreign Minister that any use of force by his country against New Guinea would find us 'against' them; Lloyd said that he had told Dutch that in such event British would be 'with' Dutch." (Ibid., 756D. 5622/12–1758)

169.   Telegram From the Embassy in Indonesia to the Department of State

Djakarta, December 24, 1958, 10 a.m.

2026. CINCPAC also for POLAD. Department pass Department Army for ASCI. I believe Jani–Benson discussion contained Army Attaché CX 362[1] of utmost importance. It is obvious pressures increasing on Nasution and that his position susceptible of dangerous weakening if US does not come forward soon with positive assistance in line with Indonesian army request to equip 20 Infantry Battalions on austere basis. (reference ALUSNA Dakarta 090735Z)[2]

Unless army thus strengthened, it is possible Suryadarma, in view of air force competent performance against rebels, may be strengthened vis-à-vis Nasution. One indication of a possible trend is report from Medan of razzias carried out by air force personnel, including searches of army officers houses.

Jani's and Gatot Subroto's statements to Benson were extraordinarily frank and blunt for Indonesians indicating they are reaching point of desperation. Approach almost certainly made at request of General Nasution.

Nasution's ability to preserve prestige of army and to maintain his position as dominant Chief of Staff rests on his ability obtain equipment. His need is urgent. If he does not have assurance from US within a short time on our willingness to equip 20 battalions he will have no choice but to deal with Communist sources which have demonstrated their willingness and ability to deliver on short notice.

We now have specific request in which Indonesians have taken into consideration problem they realize we have with Dutch and consequently did not ask for heavy equipment or equipment designed for amphibious type operation but only basic light arms for infantry battalions.

I recommend that both priorities one and two, reference ALUSNA Djakarta 232345Z[3] for equipping 20 infantry battalions be furnished on urgent basis.

Source: Department of State, Central Files, 756D.56/12–2458. Secret; Priority.

[1] Not found.

[2] In this telegram, December 9, Lieutenant Colonel Henry A. McCartney, the Naval Attaché in Indonesia, reported that in a meeting that day with Colonel Jani he learned that the first priority for aid as desired by the Indonesian Army was for small arms and related equipment for their infantry battalions. Accordingly, he recommended, and the Ambassador concurred, that the L–20s not be delivered. (Washington National Records Center, RG 319, Headquarters, Department of the Army Communication Center Files)

[3] Not found.

If the policy we have embarked on is to succeed, we need affirmative answer soonest.[4]

Jones

---

[4] In telegram 2063 from Djakarta, December 30, Jones reported on a conversation that he had with Sukendro the previous night, in which Sukendro stated that the situation in Indonesia was becoming desperate. Jones concluded that a decision on military aid and economic assistance to Indonesia be taken soon. (Department of State, Central Files, 756D.5–MSP/12–3058) See Supplement.

January–July 1959: NSC Consideration of U.S. Policy on Indonesia; Augmentation of U.S. Military Assistance to Indonesia; Concern of the Netherlands Over U.S. Military Aid; U.S. Policy Toward the West Irian-West New Guinea Dispute; and Establishment of Sukarno's "Guided Democracy" Government

170. Memorandum From the Assistant Secretary of State for Far Eastern Affairs (Robertson) to Secretary of State Dulles

Washington, January 9, 1959.

SUBJECT

Additional Military Assistance to the Indonesian Army

Discussion:

On November 5, 1958 you approved a series of future U.S. actions with respect to Indonesia [1] including an augmented program of military assistance totaling $7.8 million to be allocated to the three Indonesian Armed Services as follows: Army—$2.4 million (bridges): Navy—$2.9 million (small vessels and hardware for Marine Corps); Air Force—$2.5 million (pilot training) (Tab A). [2] While the Army is our primary target, it was and is considered important to give some assistance to the Navy and Air Force to prevent inter-service jealousies from working against the Army leadership. A request for a Presidential Determination under Section 451(a) of the Mutual Security Act of 1954, as amended, approving the use of $7.8 million for furnishing military assistance on a grant basis to Indonesia is presently in its final stages of preparation before being sent to the White House.

In preliminary discussions of this possible assistance, however, the Indonesian Army has responded without enthusiasm to our proposed

---

Source: Department of State, Central Files, 756D.5–MSP/1–959. Secret. Drafted by Wenzel on January 8 and cleared by Parsons and Merchant. This memorandum was sent through and initialed by Dillon and Herter.

[1] See Document 163.

[2] No tabs were found attached. According to a note on the source text, however, Tab A was Document 160.

furnishing of bridges and has asked instead that the U.S. consider supplying items of the highest priority—i.e. basic light arms and support equipment for 20 infantry battalions. The equipment requested (small arms, transportation and communications equipment—ALUSNA Djakarta telegram 232345Z[3] December, Tab B) has been "sanitized" by the Indonesians to take into consideration the problem we have with the Netherlands and Australians over the supply of heavy equipment or equipment designed for amphibious operation. Ambassador Jones recommends that we agree to furnish this equipment for 20 infantry battalions on an urgent basis (Embassy telegrams 2026[4] and 2063,[5] Tab C). Assistant Secretary of Defense Irwin has informed us that the Defense Department and the JCS strongly endorse the proposal and has stated that funds are available. The substitution of this first priority Army equipment in place of the bridges would require additional financing of $7.2 million. The total amount of the pending request for Presidential Determination would thus be raised from $7.8 million to $15.0 million.

I believe that it is essential to the success of our policy in Indonesia that we respond favorably and quickly to the Indonesian Army's request that we furnish this basic equipment for 20 infantry battalions. The Army with a strength of about 200,000 men is a potent political force. It is the only force in Indonesia which stands a reasonable chance of being able to stem Communist advances and has made a start in this direction. Compared to the Navy and the Air Force, the Army to date has contracted for only relatively small quantities of military equipment from the Soviet bloc. Our failure to respond favorably to the Army's request will weaken the position of the Army Chief of Staff Nasution and other pro-West officers and almost certainly force the Army to turn increasingly to the bloc as a source of military supply. A favorable answer to Nasution would, on the other hand, enable us at least for the next few months to retain and perhaps increase our influence within the Army and our ability to encourage internal Indonesian developments along a desirable course.

Recommendation:

That you approve an increase of $7.2 million in the pending request for Presidential Determination for Indonesia, raising the total to be requested from $7.8 million to $15.0 million to be allocated as follows: Army—$9.6 million; Navy—$2.9 million; Air Force—$2.5 million; the

---

[3] See footnote 3, Document 169.
[4] Document 169.
[5] See footnote 4, Document 169.

equipment to be furnished to the Army to be as described in Tab B and the equipment to be furnished to the Navy and Air Force to be as originally described in Tab A, and that the Dutch, British and Australians be informed accordingly.[6]

---

[6] On January 20, Dulles approved this recommendation. In telegram 1327 to Djakarta, January 22, the Department informed the Embassy of Dulles' decision, noting that the subject should not be discussed with the Indonesian Government pending further instruction. It explained that a request for a Presidential Determination was being modified to reflect these changes in the augmented military sales program. (Department of State, Central Files, 756D.56/1–2259) See Supplement.

---

171.   Memorandum of Conversation

Washington, January 14, 1959.

SUBJECT

U.S. Military Assistance to Indonesia

PARTICIPANTS

Dr. J.H. van Roijen, Ambassador of the Netherlands
Mr. David Ketel, Counselor, Embassy of the Netherlands
EUR—Mr. Merchant
SPA—Mr. Mein
WE—Mr. Stabler

1.   NAC Statement

The Netherlands Ambassador, Dr. van Roijen, said he has been instructed to speak to the Department further about the question of U.S. arms deliveries to Indonesia.[1] He said that Foreign Minister Luns hoped and expected, on the basis of his talks with the Secretary in Paris,[2] that when we made our statement on arms deliveries to Indonesia in NAC, we would recognize and stress the responsibility which these deliveries imposed on us in connection with the possible use of these arms by Indonesia against West New Guinea. [*11 lines of source text not declassified*]

Source: Department of State, Central Files, 756D.56/1–1459. Secret. Drafted by Stabler.

[1] In a memorandum of January 13, McBride briefed Merchant for this meeting with van Roijen. (*Ibid.*, 756D.56/1–1349) See Supplement.

[2] See Document 168.

[*1 paragraph (15-1/2 lines of source text) not declassified*]

2. *Exchange of Military Information*

Dr. van Roijen said that his Government was most anxious to get on with the exchange of military information regarding Indonesia's intentions and subsequently to proceed to the next stage of secret military talks with United States and others on what should be done if Indonesia should attack West New Guinea. The Dutch Government felt that even though there was a difference between us on the evaluation regarding Indonesian intentions, the possibility still remained that aggression might occur. This aggression could be in a variety of forms. He said that although his Government had mentioned, on the basis of intelligence reports, March as a possible date for Indonesian action against West New Guinea, his Government was not tying itself to this date. His Government believed that we should proceed without delay along the above lines, since this was the minimum which could be done so that the necessary precautions might be taken against Indonesian action.

Dr. van Roijen said that another important point was the building up of a public deterrent against Indonesian action. The Dutch believed that the statement which the Secretary gave to Mr. Luns in October had been useful in this respect, although it had not gone far enough. The Ambassador said that his Government was also anxious to obtain an open commitment of support from the United States. At the present time Dutch public opinion was becoming restive, since it believed that the Netherlands was isolated in its policy with respect to Netherlands New Guinea. The Netherlands held on to New Guinea in the interests of the West. However, it was increasingly difficult without public recognition of this fact, by the United States and others, for the Netherlands to follow this policy. In this connection he referred to the possibility that the Labor Party might be in opposition after the forthcoming elections and that this might complicate the present policy with respect to West New Guinea.

Mr. Merchant said that although the paper on the Indonesian situation which the Ambassador had handed him on December 22 was under study, we could not finalize our comments until we had received the more detailed analysis which Mr. Luns had told Ambassador Young was now being prepared in The Hague. As soon as we received the new paper, we would complete our comments. Dr. van Roijen said that he was unaware that an additional paper was under preparation in The Hague.

Mr. Merchant said that although we and the Dutch are in agreement on general objectives in connection with Indonesia, we have from time to time disagreed with regard to tactics. He reviewed the nature of our military assistance program to Indonesia and said that we place great reliance on our effort to influence the Indonesian Government. He recalled the strong statement which the Secretary had made to Subandrio that the United States would be opposed to the use of force by Indonesia against West New Guinea.[3] There were, of course, great difficulties for us in connection with military planning for an area which was not covered by a treaty commitment. Any action on our part with respect to such areas would be limited to self-defense or to an action pursuant to a Security Council resolution. Dr. van Roijen said he realized the difficulties involved for us in this situation. The main thing was to build up a public deterrent so that Indonesia will realize the grave consequences which would ensue if it should undertake aggression. Even though we might not be able to proceed as the Dutch desire, his Government believed that it was only fair that we should be warned regarding the possibility of an attack against West New Guinea.[4]

---

[3] See Document 162.

[4] The Department summarized this conversation in telegram 1068 to The Hague, January 14. (Department of State, Central Files, 756D.56/1–759) Ambassador Young met with Foreign Minister Luns on January 19 and discussed the West New Guinea problem. In telegram 1157 from The Hague, January 20, Young reported that the Netherlands Government is "making strong effort obtain as far-reaching commitments as possible, both public and private, from US, UK, and Australia to buttress their position in New Guinea based on assumption they must remain in best interests of west. Dutch Government sincerely appreciates US policy and assurances US has given them. However, they will undoubtedly seek statement from US in due course that US wishes Dutch to hold on to New Guinea and will continue to press us for some public demonstration of support." (*Ibid.*, 656.56D13/1– 2059) See Supplement.

---

172.   Telegram From the Embassy in Indonesia to the Department of State

Djakarta, January 17, 1959, 6 p.m.

2245. Shortly after I sent Embtel 2221[1] Dr. Tamzil of President's Cabinet informed me Mrs. Jones was invited to accompany me and he understood we would be expected to stay for lunch at Bogor Palace.

Source: Department of State, Central Files, 756D.5622/1–1759. Secret; Niact.

[1] Telegram 2221, January 16, reported that Jones had just received a call from the palace setting up an appointment with Sukarno for the following morning. (Department of State, Central Files, 123 Jones, Howard P.)

Upon arrival we were greeted by President and Madame Hartini who were accompanied by several other guests, including the Paku Alam and the head of the Indonesia Red Cross.

After usual exchange of courtesies, reason for President's invitation became evident. He drew me aside and said urgently "What about the Electras? Can you assure me that we will get them?" I had seen Sub-andrio's car pass mine leaving Palace as I arrived so I believe Sukarno had been fully briefed on conversation reported Embtel 2229.[2]

Sukarno said that he had three reasons why it was most important for Indonesia to have the Electras. He said the reasons were political, economic and personal. I told the President that I regretted I could not assure him that he would receive the Electras but promised that I would report our conversation in full to Washington. I emphasized that the DC–7 was an excellent aircraft and pointed out that the Export-Import Bank has the duty of determining the soundness of any project for which it loaned money, as is the case with any bank. Sukarno asked if the US did not manufacture aircraft to sell them and stated that Indonesia's credit was good. He said, "we do not want second hand aircraft, we want new aircraft", these Electras we have been talking about for so long. He said that he realized DC–7's were good but Electras were matter of prestige. He implied not only Indonesia's prestige but his personal prestige.

I explained the developments in Washington including Moekarto's exposition of Indonesian Government position.[3] Sukarno said that Ambassador Moekarto had misunderstood his instructions, that the letter cancelling the Lockheed contract should never have been written and the priorities never passed to us as was done. Sukarno appeared highly displeased with Moekarto's performance in this matter. At end of our conversation on other matters, President reverted to Lockheeds and again during lunch he pressed very hard on this subject.

Comment: In view strong personal appeal by President in this case, I believe, contrary to opinion I expressed in Embtel 2229, that US interests require reconsideration this matter. In view of Sukarno's exceptional strong feelings, I believe Department must discount position set forth by Moekarto.

---

[2] Telegram 2229, January 16, reported on a conversation between Subandrio and Jones regarding the Lockheed Electras loan. (*Ibid.*, 956.72/1–1659) See Supplement.

[3] Reference is to a January 8 meeting between Ambassador Mukarto and Assistant Secretary Robertson on the Export-Import Bank's decision to turn down Indonesia's request for a loan to help finance the purchase of three Lockheed Electra aircraft. (Memorandum of conversation, January 8; Department of State, Central Files, 856D.10/1–859) See Supplement.

It was clear in this morning's conversation that President cannot understand our reluctance to sell Electras to Indonesia and that in his eyes his own personal prestige as well as prestige his country involved. This is most sensitive nerve. If our policy is to be successful, Sukarno as well as other leaders here must be convinced that Indonesia will receive support they need from US. In very real sense, Electras have become test case.

In my comment yesterday I thought Subandrio was saying "We want Electras but can live with adverse decision". Sukarno does not subscribe to this view.

Jones

173. Telegram from the Embassy in Indonesia to the Department of State

Djakarta, January 21, 1959, 11 a.m.

2274. Department pass Department Army for ACSI. CINCPAC also for POLAD. Pertinent portions of ARMA telegram to DEPTAR (CX–21)[1] reflects widespread conviction Indonesian Government, armed forces that GRC continuing attempts supply rebels by sea, air.

This conviction most deep-seated in air force, may be responsible for difficulties encountered in establishing US rapport with AURI.

Unfortunate fact is that hand in hand with this conviction goes equally intense belief that US is doing less than best to prevent GRC activity this direction. This flows from obvious dependence GRC on US for military supplies, economic aid, and diplomatic support.

GOI reasons that US could prevent use of its aid goods this fashion by withholding them if necessary or at any rate could apply sufficient political pressure to cut off rebel supplies it so willed.

Source: Department of State, Central Files, 756D.00/1–2159. Secret; Noforn. Repeated to Taipei and CINCPAC

[1] Not found.

Further, there is no prospect of alleviating plight of KMT Chinese here if this aid continues.

So long as suspicion remains alive that US is doing less than utmost to prevent supplies reaching rebels, our influence in total Indonesian picture toward stimulating anti-Communist efforts, shift away from Soviet bloc, will be less than maximum potential. There exists no suspicion that PKI or Soviet bloc are supporting or permitting support of rebellion. On contrary they most ardent, ostensibly unqualified supporters central government.

If GRC is in fact aiding rebels they undermining US policy this area not only to our detriment but their own as well.[2]

Jones

---

[2] In telegram 1394 to Djakarta, February 3, the Department informed the Embassy that Robertson made a strong presentation to Ambassador Yeh on January 29 of the case for current U.S. policy toward Indonesia and the importance of GRC's refraining from any activity that might undermine U.S. influence with the Indonesian Government. (Department of State, Central Files, 756D.00/2–359) See Supplement.

---

174. Telegram From the Embassy in Indonesia to the Department of State

Djakarta, January 23, 1959, 3 p.m.

2308. CINCPAC for POLAD. Paris for USRO. The Hague 1157 to Department.[1] As I read reference telegram Dutch have decided to force issue of US neutrality on New Guinea by insisting on answer to question as to whether US in fact believes continued Dutch presence that area essential to free world interests.

Source: Department of State, Central Files, 656.56D13/1–2359. Secret; Priority. Transmitted in two sections. Also sent to CINCPAC and repeated to The Hague, London, Paris, and Canberra.

[1] See footnote 4, Document 171.

Whether or not Dutch do force issue this manner I believe time has come to answer this question in clear negative. If we do so, we must of course have alternative which would better serve free world interests than continuation of status quo and at same time be compatible with Dutch, Australian, Indonesian national interests.

In suggesting that time has come for Dutch to lay down admittedly heavy burden West New Guinea, I do not imply that immediate acquisition of sovereignty by Indonesia need be involved. On contrary, there could be continuation free world control until such time as there no longer any danger Indonesia passing under Communist domination.

This control could take many forms, such as a UN trusteeship with or without interested parties as trustees; a consortium outside UN or even unilateral US custodianship.

Important factor to obtain Indonesian cooperation, and thus remove issue as political hand hold for Soviet Union, would be an immediate end Dutch sovereignty and assurance that in long run there would be very good possibility Indonesia obtaining sovereignty by peaceful means. Meanwhile whoever assumed responsibility for area should be required prepare population for self-determination in as brief period as possible—for example five years—with provision for appropriate extension should this prove be too short period for such preparation.

For their part Dutch would be relieved of burdensome responsibility and most likely would be able obtain substantial compensation from Indonesia for nationalized Dutch assets—this would be question of bargaining. Australians would be protected against extension communism nearer their boundaries, and a source friction with future power in this part of world would have been removed in timely fashion.

My approach to whole problem is based on conviction that ultimately Dutch will be forced relinquish West New Guinea in any event and that it is in their interest as well as ours do so while some advantage may be gained thereby.

Colonialism is finished and the longer we continue support small western enclaves in Asia the longer we delay winning Asians to our cause, the more we intensify danger of major explosion over minor issue.

Even if it be argued that transfer West Irian to Indonesia is to substitute Asian for western colonialism, fact is that it is combination of white west over colored east that Asians are fighting, rather than imperialism or colonialism per se.

That Dutch withdrawal from the area is inevitable appears clear on other grounds than fact colonialism is dead. These grounds are eloquently stated in reference telegram—business and labor opposition, mounting expense, fear of attack, lack of international support, et cetera.

While US has given and must honor assurances that [it] would stand with Holland in event Indonesian aggression against New Guinea, it certainly in our interest that such situation not arise. Presumably degree popular support among American public for military defense New Guinea could hardly be classed as enthusiastic.

In terms strategic importance New Guinea could not be classed with other places in which free world has dug in, such as Berlin, Okinawa or Taiwan. So far as defense ANZAM concerned, there are several parts of Indonesian archipelago which would present more of a threat to that area should they fall into unfriendly hands than would New Guinea.

Of course there are many practical problems in attempting work out such solution as I have outlined. We should evaluate such difficulties in the light of what it might be worth to US and free world to remove for all time principal anti-west issue in Indonesian politics, to draw teeth of extreme nationalists and Communists alike, to free Indonesia from political dependence on USSR, to facilitate rapprochement between ANZUS and Indonesia.

Certainly it cannot be said that such a solution as I have suggested would damage Netherlands. On contrary our NATO ally would be strengthened.

Thus I think our approach to Dutch at this time should be that while we appreciate sacrifice they have so loyally made in defense of free world, we cannot in all conscience ask them to continue longer, that we prepared instead help them work out solution that will relieve them of their burden and at same time obtain recompense from Indonesia for their nationalized properties.

If there is to be a settlement this problem, there no other nation except US which has capability of taking successful initiative.

Jones

175.   Memorandum of Discussion at the 395th Meeting of the National Security Council

Washington, January 29, 1959.

[Here follow a list of participants and agenda item 1.]

2.   *Significant World Developments Affecting U.S. Security*

[Here follows discussion of an unrelated subject.]

In Indonesia, Mr. [Allen] Dulles stated that President Sukarno had been holding talks with Indonesian political leaders with respect to the re-organization and expansion of the Indonesian Parliament in keeping with Sukarno's concept of "guided democracy". According to Sukarno's present plans, one-half of the members of the Parliament would be appointed by the government and one-half would be elected. Mr. Dulles thought that such a proposal might not be bad inasmuch as he certainly could not look forward, he confessed, to full and free elections in Indonesia with so many disorganized parties on the political scene. Moreover, the Indonesian Communist Party strongly opposed the government's plan for appointing one-half of the members of the new Parliament.

There were also reports from Indonesia that Sukarno was not at all well and was suffering perhaps from a kidney ailment. Mr. Dulles thought that Sukarno might wish to come to Walter Reed Hospital for surgery. In this connection he noted that Prime Minister Sarit of Thailand would presently be operated on again in Bangkok by physicians from Walter Reed. Sarit was a very sick man indeed.

Mr. Dulles then pointed out that the Indonesian Army was continuing to play a very strong political role in Indonesia. Meanwhile, extensive guerilla warfare went on in Sumatra and North Celebes. There were approximately 10,000 armed rebels in Sumatra and 5,000 in North Celebes. In view of these facts it seemed curious to Mr. Dulles that the Indonesian rebels had not done better when they had a chance to fight in an organized way against the forces sent from Java. We ourselves were not giving any aid to the rebels although they seem to be getting some assistance from Nationalist China.

The President inquired whether, if Sukarno were to succeed with his plans for "guided democracy" and excluded the Communists from a significant voice in the Parliament of Indonesia, these moves would tend to end the rebellion in the outer islands? Mr. Dulles replied that he

Source: Eisenhower Library, Whitman File, NSC Records. Top Secret. Prepared by Gleason.

doubted that this would occur unless Sukarno could bring himself to deal directly with the rebels. So far he has refused to do this despite urgings by us and by the British. Meanwhile, the rebel leaders, who included some of the most able men in Indonesia, were still up in the hills. They were probably now ready to negotiate but Sukarno won't hear of it.

Mr. Dulles concluded by pointing out that significant Soviet Bloc military aid to Indonesia was continuing. Likewise, the economic situation in Indonesia was worsening and inflation was increasing.

[Here follows the remainder of this agenda item.]

3. *U.S. Policy Toward Indonesia* (NSC 5518;[1] NSC 5901;[2] Memo for All Holders of NSC 5901, January 21, 1959;[3] NSC Action No. 1788;[4] Memo for NSC from Executive Secretary, subject, "Special Report on Indonesia:, dated September 25, 1957;[5] SNIE 65–58;[6] Memo for NSC from Executive Secretary, same subject, dated January 26, 1959[7])

Mr. Gray briefed the Council on the contents of the proposed new policy statement on Indonesia. (A copy of Mr. Gray's briefing note is filed in the Minutes of the Meeting and another is attached to this Memorandum).[8] When in the course of his briefing, Mr. Gray referred to the problem of West New Guinea and to the fact that the new policy recommended continuation of the U.S. neutral stand on the West New Guinea issue, he called on Secretary Dulles for comment.

Secretary Dulles observed that of course the trouble in West New Guinea between The Netherlands and Indonesia was highly complicated and involved both Dutch domestic policy and the foreign policies of several NATO nations. The present government of The Netherlands has hitherto taken a very strong line with respect to holding on to West New Guinea. Since West New Guinea, continued Secretary Dulles, had

---

[1] NSC 5518, "U.S. Policy on Indonesia," approved by the President on May 12, 1955, is printed in *Foreign Relations*, 1955–1957, vol. XXII, pp. 153–157.

[2] Document 177.

[3] This covering memorandum from Lay transmitted draft copies of NSC 5901. (Department of State, S/S–NSC Files: Lot 63 D 351, NSC 5901—Memoranda)

[4] For text, see *Foreign Relations*, 1955–1957, vol. XXII, footnote 5, p. 452.

[5] For text, see *ibid.*, pp. 436–440.

[6] Document 141.

[7] This memorandum transmitted the views of the Joint Chiefs of Staff on the draft statement of policy on Indonesia. In it the JCS concurred in the adoption of the policy and noted that the draft policy was not "an appreciable change over the policy expressed in NSC 5518." They also noted that "the United States must act now on its programs for Indonesia, and with a degree of urgency not clearly expressed in the policy guidance section of the draft policy statement." (Department of State, S/S–NSC Files: Lot 62 D 1, Indonesia)

[8] See Supplement.

no ascertainable value at the present time, it seemed to him that the Dutch Government was paying a very high price for maintaining prestige. The really useful Dutch investment had been in Indonesia and this was now wiped out, at least temporarily. Moreover, there was a considerable element in The Netherlands, notably among Dutch businessmen, who felt that the policy of the present government of The Netherlands on the West New Guinea issue was silly.

Reiterating that West New Guinea, so far as was known, was pretty nearly valueless, Secretary Dulles did not discount the possibility of a change in the policy of The Netherlands toward West New Guinea. While this might be hopeful, it should be remembered that Australia was even more violently opposed than The Netherlands to turning over West New Guinea to the Indonesians. For our part, we have made quite clear to the Indonesians that if they should attempt to seize West New Guinea by force, the U.S. would be strongly opposed in principle. We have also told the Dutch that in the event that West New Guinea were attacked by the Indonesians, we would at least give them moral and perhaps logistical support although we would not support them with our own military forces. Secretary Dulles added a statement of doubt that the Indonesians would actually move against West New Guinea with armed forces.

In conclusion Secretary Dulles stated that the government of The Netherlands was in a very delicate and difficult position with respect to this dispute and as Mr. Gray had pointed out in his briefing, the Dutch have lately been putting heavier pressure on the U.K. than on the U.S. to obtain support for their point of view with regard to West New Guinea. Nevertheless, the British stand approximately where we stand on the West New Guinea issue and while they may provide the Dutch with moral and logistical support, they are not likely to take military action to support the Dutch, if the Indonesians attacked West New Guinea.

Secretary Quarles said he wished to point out that from the point of view of Defense, he strongly supported the State position of neutrality on the West New Guinea dispute. Mr. Quarles commented that in the course of his recent talks at The Hague, he had observed that the Dutch were taking the possibility of an Indonesian attack on West New Guinea very seriously and were diverting military forces to the defense of West New Guinea even though such resources were needed to discharge Holland's NATO responsibilities. Secretary Quarles added that the Dutch were much annoyed at the military assistance which we were currently providing to Indonesia. In response to these expressions of irritation, Secretary Quarles had pointed out our big objective of trying to prevent a Communist take-over in Indonesia.

With respect to this last point, Secretary Dulles said that the Dutch Foreign Minister Luns had said he would rather have Indonesia go Communist because then one could more clearly move against it.

Mr. Allen Dulles pointed out that while we knew very little about the West New Guinea area, we would presently have on hand a report of what has been going on in the area in recent months.

The President complained that he simply could not understand why any nation except Australia should be very concerned about West New Guinea. Australia was obviously concerned because of geographical proximity.

At this point Mr. Gray continued with his briefing of NSC 5901 and pointed out after he had dealt with the Financial Appendix, that the Joint Chiefs of Staff had expressed some concern about the apparent lack of urgency in carrying out our military assistance program for Indonesia. He called on Admiral Burke who was Acting Chairman of the Joint Chiefs of Staff to comment on this matter.

Admiral Burke explained that the concern of the Joint Chiefs of Staff resulted from the fact that in the past eight or nine months the U.S. has slowly been pulling Indonesia out of the clutches of the Communists, chiefly through the instrumentality of the Army Chief of Staff, General Nasution. The Chiefs were only concerned that this process continue and that we keep the ball rolling and not destroy Nasution or weaken him by not keeping up to schedule with our military assistance.

At this point Secretary Dulles undertook a general defense of the U.S. policy with respect to supporting the rebellion in the outer islands while it seemed to have some chance of success and withdrawing our support at a later time. By and large, [*less than 1 line of source text not declassified*], Secretary Dulles believed that we had played the game pretty well and our policy may now work out successfully. He said he certainly did not dissent from Admiral Burke's views as to the need for an effective military assistance program in order to win the confidence of the non-Communist elements in Indonesia. The delays which had occurred in the delivery of our military assistance to the Indonesians were the result of the need in which we found ourselves to keep the Dutch in line. To do this was often a difficult task but we must at least try to keep the Dutch tolerant of what we are doing to assist Indonesia. Ultimately, thought Secretary Dulles, the Dutch will understand and acquiesce in our program for assisting Indonesia.

The President did not seem wholly convinced by Secretary Dulles' arguments in defense of prior U.S. policy except as he said that we were on a better horse now than we had been during the organized rebellion in the outer islands.

On this point Mr. Allen Dulles commented that a forceful reduction now of rebel guerilla activity in the outer islands would provide Sukarno with a measure of freedom of action which might not be wholly to our advantage. On the other hand, the rebels certainly had not shown the competence necessary to take over Indonesia for themselves. Accordingly, we were placed in a very delicate and difficult situation. Mr. Dulles expressed the hope that the new policy statement would not prevent the U.S. from providing small arms to the rebels later if this appeared to be a desirable action. The President paraphrased Mr. Allen Dulles's comment by stating that he was advocating that we play with both sides.

Mr. George Allen pointed to the fact that on Page 21 of the Financial Appendix to NSC 5901, the program of the U.S.I.A. (information services) was listed under Assistance Programs. He explained that he was somewhat astonished to find the U.S.I.A. program described as "an Assistance" Program. Mr. Gray pointed out that the Financial Appendix did not describe the U.S.I.A. program as such as an Assistance Program. The program was merely listed in a table which covered the estimated costs of carrying out our policies toward Indonesia. Mr. Gray then said he judged that the National Security Council recommended approval of the policy in NSC 5901. The President said this seemed to be the case and while this seemed to be a policy of walking a tightrope, he could see no other solution to the West New Guinea dispute. Mr. Gray pointed out that Secretary Dulles should in effect be permitted to walk the tightrope as best he could. The President, however, suggested that the Dutch were such very good friends of ours and such good allies that we should try to win them over to our point of view. Commenting on the warm personal relationships he had enjoyed with Dutch friends, he was sure that we could find some way to influence them. He commented that perhaps Australia was a harder nut to crack than The Netherlands.

The National Security Council:

a. Discussed the draft statement of policy on the subject contained in NSC 5901, in the light of the views of the Joint Chiefs of Staff thereon, transmitted by the reference memorandum of January 26, 1959.
b. Adopted the statement of policy in NSC 5901.

> *Note:* NSC 5901, as adopted by the action in b above, approved by the President for implementation by all appropriate Executive departments and agencies of the U.S. Government, and referred to the Operations Coordinating Board as the coordinating agency designated by the President.

[Here follows agenda item 4.]

S. Everett Gleason

176.   Telegram From the Embassy in the Netherlands to the Department of State

The Hague, January 29, 1959, 8 p.m.

1231. Paris for USRO. Department pass CINCPAC for POLAD. Re Embassy telegram 1196,[1] repeated London 47, Paris 141, Djakarta 156, Canberra 79.

1.   Saw Foreign Minister Luns for 35 minutes this morning, and he gave me brief report on his talks January 26 and 27 in London.

2.   Luns opened conversation by again stressing importance of building up deterrent which Indonesians would recognize and have constantly in mind if they were tempted to engage in any adventure against West New Guinea. Luns and Foreign Minister Lloyd discussed what UK-Australia-US position would be in event of such Indonesian adventure. Luns advanced Menzies argument (paragraph 6 Embassy telegram 1157,[2] repeated London 41, Paris 133, Djakarta 149, Canberra 74) that in event of Indonesian action, US and UK would necessarily stop assistance to Indonesia thus frustrating policy of West and forcing Indonesia into arms of Soviet bloc. Luns stated that Lloyd was impressed with this argument as it emphasized need for real deterrent to prevent Indonesia from starting anything that it would be difficult to stop. Luns evidently got assurances from Lloyd that in event of Indonesian military action against West New Guinea, UK would stop any assistance to Indonesia.

3.   In connection this question of deterrent, Luns again emphasized and asked me to raise with Department question of having US ship call at West New Guinea port. Luns stated Dutch would not give such call any publicity or capitalize on it or in any way treat it as slap at Indonesia. He regards it solely as demonstration of US friendliness to Dutch for

---

Source: Department of State, Central Files, 656.56D13/1–2959. Secret. Transmitted in two sections and repeated to London, Paris, Djakarta, and Canberra.

[1] In telegram 1196, January 24, Young reported a conversation he had with Luns that morning during which he informed the Netherlands Foreign Minister that the United States had been in touch with the British regarding West New Guinea and that the British were fully aware of the U.S. position with respect to the possible use of force by Indonesia against West New Guinea. Luns was most appreciative and very pleased with the Department's prompt response to his worries, the Ambassador noted, and delighted to have these facts before his upcoming meeting with Selwyn Lloyd. (*Ibid.*, 656.56D13/1–2059)

[2] See footnote 4, Document 171.

benefit to local population to indicate that Dutch are not alone in world. He visualizes one or two-day call with general visiting, at least by Dutch officers and men, with no hoopla. He added Dutch had refrained from saying anything to US when US Naval units visited Surabaya something over year ago. This idea is preying on Luns' mind and I believe may result in formal request. Would be helpful if I could indicate to Luns Department's preliminary reaction. While such visit would obviously be helpful here, we cannot attempt assess repercussions in SEA.

4. Also in connection deterrent question, Luns once again made same statement he has made number of times in past, namely, that both Secretary and Ambassador Jones should from time-to-time repeat to Indonesians US position re any Indonesian action against West New Guinea; it needs constant repetition if it is to serve as general deterrent.

5. Luns evidently did not receive any written statement from British or any copy of statement which British propose to give Indonesians. However, he received substance statements British gave Department, (Department telegram 1106,[3] repeated London 6688, Paris Topol 2420, Djakarta 1326, Canberra 222) and apparently something more for Luns believes UK has gone further than US in two respects in supporting Dutch:

First, UK recognizes validity of Dutch legal claim to West New Guinea, and said so in communiqué issued end Luns' visit (Embassy despatch 656, January 29).[4] In this connection Luns again asked why US does not recognize validity of Dutch claim and feels very strongly that US should review that situation and if it does recognize legal validity, then US should say so.

Secondly, Lloyd told Luns specifically that he would advise Indos, if asked about UK assurances to Dutch, that UK would support Dutch in every way and that Lloyd was prepared to add that this "may well mean military assistance." Luns stated further that Lloyd said of course he would provide Dutch with "logistical support" as US has said it would provide such support.

6. Luns raised question with Lloyd re possible military planning talks as next step in program of sensible preparedness against possible contingencies in New Guinea area. [3 lines of source text not declassified] British emphasized again to Luns that of course whole situation de-

---

[3] In telegram 1106, January 22, the Department transmitted the texts of separate draft statements that the United Kingdom was considering communicating to Indonesia and the Netherlands respectively regarding West New Guinea. (Department of State, Central Files, 656.56D13/1–2259) See Supplement.

[4] Not printed. (Department of State, Central Files, 033.5641/1–2959)

pended on US attitude and position. Luns asked me if Seventh Fleet was familiar with potential Indo threat against West New Guinea, and I told him I was quite sure appropriate military officials in Pacific area were familiar with general situation.

7. On subject of continuing British arms sales to Indo, Luns stated that in his opinion present conservative government was so scared of criticism by Labor Party and of unemployment issue that it could not forbid commercial contracts between British arms manufacturers and Indos. UK, however, would not seek any orders from Indo and regarded arms shipments to Indo as purely commercial operation. Nonetheless Luns said Lloyd made it very clear to him, and promised also to make it clear to Labor Party leaders, that in permitting such arms sales UK assumed very definite responsibility and obligation re their use. Luns went on to make one of most extreme statements he has made to date re Dutch position on this matter. He told Lloyd if Dutch were to find themselves alone on New Guinea issue and could not count on any real assistance, then "there would be one less partner in NATO". While this is obviously a "Lunsism", it reflects Dutch Government's feeling that it should receive same support from its allies that it gives them in NATO.

8. Re foregoing aspects his London talks, Luns commented with tinge of injured feelings and slight suspicion, that he had not detected any indication that US-UK consultations prior his London visit had been conducted at very high level.

9. Re Fairey-Gannet planes, Luns said balance of twelve would not be delivered to Indos until 1960. Luns added that both he and British had heard that Indos were prepared to spend up to 50 million pounds for armament but both hoped this was wrong.

10. I asked Luns how he now viewed possible NAC discussion of this whole situation. He said Lloyd would go along with Dutch suggestion that only those countries should supply arms to Indo which could "guarantee their use". I attempted to get more accurate interpretation or definition of this phrase but Luns would go no further in describing what he had in mind, if he knew himself. He did state that he expected British to draft statement for presentation to NAC which would be presented at same time as US statement. I told Luns I assumed US statement was being revised order bring it up-to-date and that Luns would be consulted on draft prior to its submission.

11. It seems to me two things are important in this connection: First, close coordination with UK on its statement; and, secondly, opportunity for Luns to review proposed US statement and to comment before its final submission. I believe that if this is done chances of blow-up in NAC can be minimized, furthermore, it would provide good opportunity

here for discussion, in advance of meeting, of position Dutch plan to take.[5]

Young

---

[5] In telegram 1228 from The Hague, January 29, Young reported that [*text not declassified*] Luns indicated "that he felt British agreed that Indonesian attack would be forthcoming against West New Guinea, but with no speculation re timing." (*Ibid.*, 656.56D13/1–2959) See Supplement. The British Foreign Office official responsible for Indonesia confirmed this, as reported in telegram 3959 from London, January 30, which reads in part as follows:

"Embassy officer discussed further, January 29, with Indonesia desk officer Foreign Office, discussions ending January 27 between Netherlands Foreign Minister Luns and HMG. Desk officer confirmed that British estimate on likelihood some kind of Indonesian attempt invade West New Guinea agrees with Dutch to extent this might happen and might in turn lead to incidents which would bring UN into picture and result in some kind of gains for Indonesians, though British would not go so far as Dutch do in predicting imminent danger of Indonesian attack." (Department of State, Central Files, 656.56D13/1–3059)

---

177. National Security Council Report

NSC 5901   Washington, February 3, 1959.

STATEMENT OF U.S. POLICY ON INDONESIA

General Considerations

1. The chief danger confronting U.S. policy with respect to Indonesia is that a combination of domestic instability, Sino-Soviet Bloc economic and military aid, and growing local Communist strength may lead to a Communist takeover or to a policy increasingly friendly toward the Sino-Soviet Bloc on the part of whatever regime is in power. The size and importance of Indonesia, together with its strategic posi-

---

Source: Department of State, S/S–NSC Files: Lot 63 D 351, NSC 5901 Series. Secret. Transmitted to the NSC on February 3, under cover of a memorandum by Lay which noted that the President had approved NSC 5901 that day and that it superseded NSC 5518 and the "recommendations" of the "Special Report on Indonesia."

tion in relation to Australia and Free Asia, and the probable serious consequences of its loss to Communist control, dictate a vigorous U.S. effort to prevent these contingencies.

2. Basically, any non-Communist Indonesian regime likely to come to power will desire to follow a "neutralist" policy, seeking aid on its own terms from both the West and the Bloc and balancing each off against the other. It is unlikely that any foreseeable non-Communist regime will depart from this basic policy, even though there is growing concern among Indonesians, including the Army, over growing Communist strength and the extent of aid accepted from the Bloc. Many Indonesian leaders remain suspicious of Western motives. These leaders, preoccupied with colonialism, have found in the Western European attitude towards Cyprus, Algeria, and Arab nationalism, as well as towards the West New Guinea issue, strong grounds for such suspicion of Western motives. Formal political commitments to the West would constitute in their minds unacceptable abridgement of their international freedom of action; and regional military security pacts are opposed on the grounds that they sharpen rather than reduce international tension.

3. Indonesia has certain advantages and points of strength. It shares no common boundary with a Communist state. Although the Indonesians have an extremely low per capita income, a salubrious climate and fertile soil make the crushing poverty and starvation characteristic of some Asian nations unknown in Indonesia. A predominantly subsistence economy cushions most Indonesians from adverse commercial and financial developments. While there is severe overpopulation on Java and much "shared poverty," absentee landlordism and glaring inequalities in land distribution are almost unknown. The Dutch implanted in Indonesia a strong respect for legal processes and the rule of law. Western concepts of individual freedom and democratic government introduced by the Dutch found a parallel in the democratic structure of the Indonesian village and the Indonesian tradition of compromise and collective decision-making.

4. On the other hand, Indonesia was ill-prepared to face the problems and assume the responsibilities of independence. The educational policy of the colonial regime prevented the development of an indigenous civil service and a corps of trained professional men. Dutch economic policy militated against the growth of an Indonesian entrepreneurial class. Dutch policy of regarding all political activity as subversive prevented the acquisition of a healthy political experience and a knowledge and understanding of political techniques, and left in their stead a tradition of negativism and irresponsible obstructionism. Finally, Dutch administrative policies tended to preserve and accentuate regional and ethnic differences.

5.   The Indonesian Communist Party (PKI)[1] is relatively well-organized, well-financed, and well-led. It is unique among Indonesian political parties in its discipline, unity of purpose, and command of the techniques of political action. It also dominates the Indonesian labor movement through its labor federation, SOBSI, and its electoral strength is particularly concentrated in central and east Java. The PKI, which has capitalized on internecine quarrels, venality, and incompetence in the non-Communist parties, demonstrated in 1957 and 1958 local elections its steadily increasing popular support. If the election scheduled originally for 1959 had been held, the PKI would probably have emerged as the largest party in Indonesia and would have been in a strong position to demand cabinet representation. However this election has now been postponed for at least one year. The party has established itself in a strong psychological position by refraining from overt extra-legal activities, strongly supporting the governments recently in power, and more recently backing vigorously President Sukarno and endorsing the government's military action against the rebels. At the same time, it is free of any responsibility for government failures and inadequacies since it has not been formally represented in any cabinet. Open measures of repression against the PKI would be difficult to justify on internal political grounds, and would expose any government undertaking them to charges of truckling to Western pressure. At present the PKI probably lacks the resources to seize power by overt force, and postponement of the elections may delay a bid for power via the polls. However, there is a serious and continuing danger that Indonesia may fall to Communism through government inadequacy, Communist subversion, legal political means, or, as a last resort, by violence.

6.   PKI efforts have been complemented in the external field by the Sino-Soviet Bloc, which since September 1956 offered Indonesia about $350,000,000 in military and economic credits, under which arms and military equipment were provided when Western sources were denied; vigorously espoused Indonesia's claim to West New Guinea; and gave diplomatic support during the difficult days of the recent rebellion.

7.   During recent months some non-Communist leaders and political parties have demonstrated a greater realization of the Communist danger facing their country, and appear more willing than before to cooperate among themselves and with the Army to give Indonesia a more effective government and check the growth of Communist strength and influence. The non-Communist political parties are at present overshadowed by the Army, the President, and the PKI as major power factors in

---

[1] There are no completely reliable figures on PKI membership, but it probably numbers at least 500,000 and may be substantially higher. PKI claims that it is Indonesia's largest party are probably correct. [Footnote in the source text.]

Indonesia. While they won approximately 75 percent of the total vote in the 1957 election, they are faction-ridden and sharply divided among themselves. They represent nonetheless a significant element of Indonesian society seeking to steer a course between military dictatorship on the one hand and Communist dictatorship on the other. As such, they are presently exercising some stabilizing influence, and to the extent that they are able to reconcile and subordinate their inter-party differences, they could, with the backing of the Army, turn the tide against the Communist party in the political field.

8.   The non-Communist posture of the Indonesian Government is now maintained in delicate balance between President Sukarno, General Nasution of the Army, and Prime Minister Djuanda. President Sukarno is Indonesia's paramount political figure. He occupies this position not only because of his personal magnetism and hold on the masses, but because he represents to the Indonesian people the symbol of their revolution and the mystic incarnation of their state. Sukarno exercises a strong general influence on government policies but, unlike other prominent national leaders in Asia, does not direct the course of government operations. He has proclaimed Indonesia's need for a "guided democracy," as yet not clearly defined, but has no desire to assume responsibility for the difficult decisions which accompany the open exercise of power. At the same time no cabinet or public official can remain in office and function effectively in the face of Sukarno's active dislike or disapproval. Unlike other national leaders in Asia, Sukarno is neither the titular nor actual head of a political party machine. The ruling elite appear increasingly aware that Sukarno, whatever his great service to Indonesian independence, cannot provide the constructive leadership required. He appears concerned by the growing power of the PKI but is reluctant to use force or to abandon his position of being above party struggles. He will probably seek to manipulate non-Communist elements to counter-balance PKI strength. Sukarno the symbol is still indispensable; he is a living national monument, a political fact of life which must be lived with.

9.   The Indonesian Army is the largest element of the Indonesian armed forces. The Army and the predominantly non-Communist orientation of its officer corps, represent the principal obstacles to the continued growth of Communist strength in Indonesia. This situation derives to a considerable degree from the favorable impressions made on Indonesian officers trained in U.S. service schools, who now hold responsible positions. These officers have accepted U.S. organization, equipment, and training methods and, upon return to their homeland, have exerted a strong influence in orienting the Army toward the West and toward the United States in particular.

10. Under the leadership of the anti-Communist General Nasution, the Army has assumed an increasingly powerful position in the political arena including a growing policy-making role. The Army is likely to continue to exercise considerable authority in civil affairs barring an open break between Sukarno and Nasution. The Army's increased power has resulted from two factors: the considerable authority it is permitted under the present "state of war," and the prestige accruing from its success in suppressing the regional revolt. The Army's objective is to steer a middle-of-the-road course. Navy and Air Force leaders have had little apparent influence on the policies of the Government of Indonesia. However, their national positions are expected to improve as a result of large amounts of matériel received from the Soviet Bloc, and they may take an increasing interest in the political scene.

11. The Army, which is equipped with individual and light automatic weapons of varied origins and types, including Dutch, British, U.S. and Japanese, has reached the point where it must make major procurements of weapons and equipment. Late in 1957, because the U.S. and other Western countries were unwilling to sell arms to Indonesia, approaches were made to the Soviet Bloc, and an Indonesian military mission is believed to have purchased about $25,000,000 worth of Army hardware in Poland, Yugoslavia, and Czechoslavakia in 1958. In the next two years the Indonesian Navy is scheduled to obtain a significant number of ships from the Soviet Bloc, probably on credit. In early 1958 the Indonesian Air Force contracted to purchase from the Soviets about 115 aircraft, including MIG fighters, jet bombers, transports and trainers. Additional purchases from the Soviet Bloc can be expected.

12. In view of the key importance of the military as a stabilizing force in Indonesia, and in view of extensive Bloc military aid, the question of the quantity and form of U.S. military aid is a major policy issue. Although initially reluctant to accept U.S. terms for military aid, Indonesia is now actively seeking such aid. Because Indonesia previously rendered inoperative a bilateral agreement, it is now legally possible to provide grant assistance only under a Presidential Determination that waives the necessity for the U.S. to obtain certain assurances otherwise required by the Mutual Security Act of 1954, as amended, and usually included in military assistance agreements. In the summer of 1958 such a Presidential Determination was made and a token military aid program of about $7 million was approved. A request is now being processed to seek a further Presidential Determination for an augmentation program in the amount of $14.9 million which would bring the total FY 1959 program to about $22 million.

13. U.S. policy has for a number of years called for the provision of both technical assistance and economic aid to Indonesia, although for the past 18 months our policy has provided that these programs should

be oriented toward the outer islands. The U.S. technical assistance program in Indonesia has concentrated on the important problem of developing technical, professional, and managerial skills, with major emphasis on education. However, prior to about 1955, the Indonesians were reluctant to conclude bilateral agreements which would have facilitated U.S. extension of economic aid. Since 1955 the Indonesian Government has become more receptive to U.S. economic assistance and, because of the serious economic situation, is now actively seeking such assistance.

14. The Indonesian Government fiscal and financial situation is now at about the lowest state since independence. During the past year, additional heavy burdens were imposed on the already unstable economy by a series of developments: the armed uprisings, the expansion of barter trade diverting resources from the central government, the anti-Dutch campaign, and the international business recession. The Indonesian masses living on a subsistence economy remain relatively unaffected by this situation, but the absence of economic development and the inability of the Indonesian Government to provide needed public services such as schools, hospitals, roads, and inter-island communications have contributed to regional dissatisfaction and political unrest, and have been exploited by the Communist Party, particularly on the over-crowded Island of Java, to win popular support. Direct government action to suppress the Communist Party would not bring lasting results unless non-Communist forces in Indonesia at the same time demonstrate to the masses some progress in solving Indonesia's social and economic problems.

15. The shortage of trained professional men, administrators, and technicians is an underlying obstacle to progress in the solution of Indonesia's manifold political, economic, and social problems. The Indonesian Government is making strenuous efforts to remedy this deficiency, and this is one field in which U.S. assistance can pay great long-range dividends.

16. In the recent rebellion, the regionalist leaders and their rebel forces in the outer islands were no match for the government forces in regular military operations. However, the rebels are proving to be effective guerrilla fighters and are seriously harassing the government forces and hampering the reestablishment of civil authority in North and Central Sumatra and North Celebes. Although the rebels lack the military capability and the political following to reestablish their control of major populated areas, they have some local support and can continue guerrilla warfare for a prolonged period, creating serious economic and political problems for the central government. Since Sumatra and Borneo produce a major portion of Indonesian export earnings, they are of great significance to the Indonesian economy. The central government is at-

tempting to satisfy the desires of the outer islands for a larger measure of fiscal and administrative autonomy, and is giving priority to economic development projects off the Islands of Java. Regional distrust of the central government, however, is likely to continue.

17. The unresolved dispute between Indonesia and the Netherlands over West New Guinea has become in Indonesia a major vulnerability not only to the United States and its European allies, but also to moderate elements in Indonesia favoring a rapprochement with the Netherlands and closer ties with the West. It has poisoned Dutch-Indonesian relations, and undermined Indonesia's otherwise excellent relations with Australia. The dispute does not appear at present susceptible of early solution. Both sides have taken irreconcilable positions on the basic question of sovereignty, emotions are high both in Indonesia and the Netherlands, and the Australians are, if anything, more determined than the Dutch that West New Guinea should not come under Indonesian control.

18. The U.S. cannot expect to reap the full benefits of aid to Indonesia while at the same time appearing to oppose Indonesian aspirations on the one international issue which has aroused great nationalist emotion in Indonesia and is a personal idée fixe with Sukarno. Not to support Indonesia on this issue is to leave this key gambit to the USSR. On the other hand, a shift in U.S. policy would create grave complications with the Netherlands and Australia, with unforeseeable results. Moreover, acquisition of West New Guinea might whet Indonesia's appetite for other areas such as Timor, Papua, and British Borneo, whatever assurances Indonesia might give to the contrary. Even U.S. support of Indonesia on the West New Guinea issue probably would not deflect Indonesia from pursuing a basically neutralist course.

19. On balance there are compelling arguments for continuing, under present circumstances, a U.S. policy of neutrality in the West New Guinea dispute. This policy has been followed because of the seriously adverse consequences which would ensue if the United States supported either the Dutch or the Indonesian position. The former would drastically reduce if not eliminate United States influence in Indonesia, deal a serious blow to pro-United States elements and be exploited by the Soviet Bloc and the PKI as proof of United States hostility to the aspirations of the peoples of Asia and Africa. To support Indonesia on the other hand would have an equally serious damaging effect both on our bilateral relations with the Netherlands and Australia and in our working relationships with the former in NATO and the latter in ANZUS. The intensity of public feeling and the firmness of government positions in the three countries directly involved further counsel against any United States effort at this time to urge on the principals a compromise solution such as some form of UN trusteeship, though the latter might

provide a basis for eventual compromise. Such a proposal would probably be acceptable to the Netherlands only if the Netherlands and/or Australia were named the administering power or powers. It would produce in Indonesia scarcely less condemnation than outright espousal of the Dutch cause.

20. U.S. ability to influence Indonesian policy and government actions is limited by Indonesian:

a. Resistance to guidance and direction from any foreign source.

b. Reluctance to undertake ties and associations which would appear to bind Indonesia politically and militarily to the West.

c. Continuing suspicion that the United States may be motivated more by a desire to combat Communism in Indonesia than to assist in the establishment of a strong Indonesian state.

d. Preoccupation with colonialism, both as it relates to its own New Guinea issue and to other current issues between Western European nations and dependent or newly independent states in Asia and Africa and the position which the United States has taken on these issues.

e. Resentment over alleged U.S. moral and material assistance to the rebels.

f. Irritation, frustration, and doubt of U.S. intentions occasioned by the length of time required by the United States in the provision of military and economic assistance.

21. U.S. ability to influence Indonesian policy and actions is strengthened by the following factors:

a. The predominantly Western cultural orientation of the Indonesian governing elite and the moral and intellectual commitment of this elite to the principles of democratic, representative government.

b. A strong desire for economic assistance, military supplies and equipment, and higher education and professional training from the United States and the West.

c. The fact that approximately 95 percent of Indonesia's trade is with the Free World.

d. The teaching of English as the first foreign language in Indonesian schools.

e. Western orientation of the Army, which results in part from training accorded Indonesian officers in U.S. service schools.

Objectives

Short-range

22. Prevention of Communist control of Indonesia, or vital parts thereof, by overt armed attack, subversion, economic domination, or other means.

Long-range

23. The establishment of a politically stable, economically viable nation, friendly to the West, with the will and ability to resist Communism

from within and without, and the denial of its human and natural resources and strategic positions to the Sino-Soviet Bloc.

Major Policy Guidance

24. Employ all feasible means, including, in accordance with constitutional processes, the use of U.S. armed force if necessary and appropriate, to prevent Indonesia or vital parts thereof from falling under Communist control by overt armed attack, subversion, economic domination, or other means; concerting action with other nations as appropriate.

25. While seeking an ultimate pro-Western orientation, accept Indonesia's neutralist policy, as necessary, even though the present regime maintains diplomatic, trade and cultural relations with the Sino-Soviet Bloc and is receiving Bloc military equipment and economic assistance, but endeavor to insure that these relations are reasonably balanced by relations with the Free World.

26. Seek by official and personal relations, as well as through the general character of U.S. relations with Indonesia, to encourage Sukarno to regard the United States as a friend of Indonesia, to direct his influence into constructive channels, and to restrict and contain the harmful aspects of his influence on Indonesian political and economic development.

27. Encourage reconciliation between the rebels and the central government, and cooperation among non-Communist political and military leaders, as well as between political parties, in order to stimulate the development of a more effective non-Communist political force.

28. Maintain and strengthen existing U.S. ties with the Indonesian police and military establishments; and increase their capability to maintain internal security and combat Communist activity in Indonesia by providing appropriate arms, equipment, and training, on a limited but continuing basis. To maximum extent practicable, U.S. training of personnel of the Indonesian armed forces should be expanded and efforts made to curtail Sino-Soviet Bloc training programs.

29. Demonstrate interest in and concern for economic development in Indonesia while avoiding actions which might be interpreted as an attempt to control or take responsibility for Indonesian economic development. To this end:

a. Encourage Indonesia to take steps such as the following to further its economic development:

(1) Improve its basic economic and fiscal policies, including the budgeting of government expenditures and a tax structure and administration which will increase government revenues.
(2) Control inflation and gradually eliminate inflationary pressures.
(3) Create a favorable climate for private investment.

(4) Reduce corruption.

(5) Expand technical, administrative, and entrepreneurial skills among Indonesian nationals.

(6) Foster diversification of the economy without neglecting staple exports.

(7) Maintain and increase close friendly commercial relations with the U.S. and other Free World nations.

b. Support loans to Indonesia by international organizations where consistent with relevant U.S. loan policies.

c. Encourage other Free World nations to continue measures designed to contribute to Indonesia's economic development.

d. Be prepared to provide appropriate economic and technical assistance to Indonesia.

e. Be prepared to provide U.S. loans for economic development which are consistent with relevant U.S. loan policies.

30. Encourage Indonesia to improve administration by modernizing laws and administrative procedures.

31. Seek to broaden Indonesian understanding of the U.S. and the Free World and to convince Indonesia that closer cooperation with the Free World is desirable, by:

a. Assisting Indonesians to travel and study in the U.S. and other Free World countries.

b. Continuing programs for increased training of Indonesians.

c. Making full use of U.S. private organizations to assist educational, cultural, medical, and scientific activities in Indonesia.

d. Identifying the U.S. with willingness to assist peoples struggling with problems of independence, and emphasizing the U.S. tradition of anti-colonialism.

32. Encourage the development of closer relations between Indonesia and other nations of Free Asia, particularly Australia, Japan, the Philippines and the Federation of Malaya, and seek opportunities for improvement in relations between Indonesia and the Netherlands.

33. Give priority treatment to requests for assistance in programs and projects which offer opportunities to isolate the PKI, drive it into positions of open opposition to the Indonesian Government, thereby creating grounds for repressive measures politically justifiable in terms of Indonesian national self-interest.

34. Encourage government officials to oppose Communist activities, to understand the relations of these activities to international Communism, to realize the danger of Communist China, and to foster such understanding and opposition throughout the Indonesian populace.

35. Encourage the development of non- and anti-Communist labor, peasant, business and similar organizations.

344 Foreign Relations, 1958–1960, Volume XVII

36. While for the present maintaining neutrality in the West New Guinea dispute in our relations with other governments, explore within the U.S. Government solutions to this problem compatible with over-all U.S. objectives, for possible discussion with other interested governments.[2]

---

[2] A 10-page financial appendix, January 9, was approved as part of NSC 5901. See Supplement.

---

178. Telegram From Secretary of State Dulles to the Department of State

London, February 5, 1959, 1 a.m.

Secto 8. Paris for USRO. In talks with Secretary afternoon February 4, Selwyn Lloyd raised two problems with respect to Indonesia: (A) danger Indonesian attack on West New Guinea creating situation in which West would have to line up with Dutch thereby pushing Indonesians toward Communists (which he said concerns both Luns and Menzies), and (B) pressure on Her Majesty's Government because of unemployment to fill Indonesian orders for arms (which he said might include 10 million pounds worth of small naval ships), and necessity finding some formula which would permit supply of arms but at same time involving moral obligation to see they would not be used against West New Guinea. Lloyd proposed (1) US-UK intelligence discussion on assessment danger Indonesian attack on New Guinea and implications; (2) NATO discussion arms supply problem.

Secretary suggested possibility Netherlands Government is in domestic political predicament over costly and unprofitable retention West New Guinea. Dutch want us to share burden. We wish avoid actions which might spoil improved situation in Indonesia. We agree Indonesian small scale infiltration and guerrilla operations in West New Guinea possible, but military equipment supplied by us no real factor in

---

Source: Department of State, Central Files, 656.56D13/2–559. Secret. Repeated to The Hague, Canberra, Djakarta, and Paris. Dulles was in London as part of a 6-day trip to the United Kingdom, France, and the Federal Republic of Germany, February 3–8.

such operation. Secretary said he was leery of undertaking vague "moral" obligations. US has been explicit in talking to Indonesians. He had told Subandrio that if Indonesians used force US would be against them.

Secretary agreed to joint intelligence study in Washington of Indonesian intentions limited to Britain and United States to prevent leaks. Secretary said he had discussed arms supply to Indonesians at December NATO meeting expounding same position he had earlier put to Subandrio. Secretary was noncommittal on Lloyd's suggestion of further NATO discussion.

Dulles

---

179. Telegram From the Embassy in the Netherlands to the Department of State

The Hague, February 6, 1959, midnight.

1287. Paris for USRO. Department pass CINCPAC for POLAD. Re Department telegram 1182,[1] repeated London 7091, Djakarta 1402, Canberra 252, Paris Topol 2575.

1. Met with Foreign Minister Luns this afternoon at 5 o'clock for 50 minutes to carry out instructions contained reference telegram. I had prepared in advance summary list of program as outlined paragraph 2 reference telegram, which also showed changes in program as given Luns in November. I left copy of this list with Luns so he would have items and figures correctly stated.

2. Luns quickly noted and commented on increase in amounts over November program. Needless to say, these increases did not arouse great enthusiasm and merely served to emphasize his depressed

---

Source: Department of State, Central Files, 756D.56/2–659. Secret. Priority. Repeated to London, Paris, Djakarta, and Canberra.

[1] Telegram 1182, February 4, informed Young that Eisenhower signed a Presidential Determination the previous day approving the augmented military assistance program in Indonesia. It instructed the Ambassador to see Luns as soon as possible and inform him of the new program and how it had been altered from the program outlined to him in November. (Ibid., 756D.56/2–459) See Supplement.

state of mind when he realized this program was still continuing. There is no need to report Luns detailed comments and reaction as all of these have been reported before and Department is fully familiar with them. He did specifically request me, however, to express to Secretary his great and profound disappointment that US saw fit:

(1) To continue this program at all;
(2) To increase the size of it;
(3) To push it right at this point when everyone seemed to be agreeing that there was potential military threat against Netherlands New Guinea; and
(4) That Dutch are still not given any opportunity to make suggestion or to comment on this program before it is given to Indonesians.

Luns expanded to some degree on this last point, indicating that although Department might not wish to consider any Dutch comments or suggestions, perhaps some day Department might find a Dutch suggestion that might be reasonable and helpful. Luns still feels strongly that US is not playing fair if it does not give Dutch opportunity to comment on this type of program before it is finally decided upon, even though Luns recognizes full well that his comments may have no effect whatsoever. I pointed out to Luns he would have had information on this current program day earlier if I had not been in London, but Luns said this would have made no difference as advance notice period of four days to Dutch was hardly adequate or even respectable if US had any real or sincere intention of getting Dutch reaction ahead of time.

3. I again pointed out that augmentation program was pursuant to August 13 sales agreement and use of equipment governed by provisions of that understanding. I further emphasized criteria set forth in Department telegram 782[2] (repeated Djakarta 893, Paris 1727, Canberra 141) order keep present program in proper perspective. I added that Department was still keeping in mind Dutch views re this program and once again went over US assurances to Dutch, including statements made by Secretary to Subandrio in Washington. I emphasized again that we felt we had gone long way in reassuring Dutch and that, of course, we would not stand idly by if Indonesia should endeavor to attack West New Guinea. I also pointed out to Luns that of course we would keep Dutch informed concerning any items of military significance which would go to Indonesia under export license from the US. I believe that going over this background with Luns had salutary and stabilizing effect on his thinking and it was wise to recall these various statements

---

[2] Telegram 782, November 12, 1958, instructed Young to inform Luns about the recently approved U.S. arms sale program to Indonesia. (Department of State, Central Files, 756D.5–MSP/11–1258)

and assurances to his attention, considering lapse of time since November.

4. I also emphasized to Luns fact we did not plan to issue press release either in Washington or Djakarta and hoped that public knowledge of it would not become available at least until after Subandrio's Australian visit.[3] Luns has assured me that nothing would be leaked from The Hague, or any statement made concerning it. Once again I thanked Luns for his appreciation and understanding and his efforts to handle this program on restrained basis, both within government and with Dutch press and public opinion.

5. Would appreciate advance notice of content and timing any public announcement which may ultimately be planned by US or Indonesians.[4]

Young

---

[3] Foreign Minister Subandrio was scheduled to make a 6-day visit to Australia February 10–15.

[4] On February 6 Deputy Assistant Secretary Foy Kohler briefed Ambassador van Roijen on the recently approved modifications in the U.S. military assistance program for Indonesia. (Memorandum of conversation, February 6; Department of State, Central Files, 756D.56/2–659)

---

180. Special National Intelligence Estimate

SNIE 65–59   Washington, February 10, 1959.

LIKELIHOOD OF INDONESIAN ARMED ACTION AGAINST NEW GUINEA

The Problem

To estimate the likelihood of Indonesia taking armed action against West New Guinea.

Source: Department of State, INR–NIE Files. Secret. According to a note on the cover sheet, the CIA and the intelligence organizations of the Departments of State, Army, Navy, Air Force, and the Joint Staff participated in the preparation of this estimate. All members of the IAC concurred with the estimate on February 10, except the representatives of the AEC and the FBI, who abstained on the grounds that the subject was outside their jurisdiction.

Conclusions

1. Indonesia has the capability to capture one or more of the lesser Dutch settlements in West New Guinea and would have a good chance of launching a small-scale (up to 1,000 men) invasion force without prior detection. Although Indonesia might be able to muster 7,000–8,000 men for an assault on the major Dutch stronghold at Biak, its waterlift capability probably does not exceed 3,500 troops and its airlift capability about 600 paratroopers. Moreover, it could provide little effective fighter cover for such an operation. Indonesian ability to coordinate operations of a scale necessary to seize and hold Biak is very doubtful and preparations for such an operation could probably be detected. (Paras. 7–9)

2. We believe that Indonesia will probably not undertake large-scale armed action within the next six months, primarily because of internal security problems and concern that such an attack would provoke adverse international reaction. Also, Indonesian leaders may believe that present pressures may force the Dutch to yield. (Paras. 10–14)

3. The Indonesian objective in a small-scale action to seize one or more of the smaller settlements in West New Guinea would probably be to provoke Dutch countermeasures which would attract international attention and UN consideration. However, unless the Indonesians could point to strong evidence of military provocation by the Dutch, they would face accusations that they had resorted to armed force and the possibility of UN action favorable to Indonesia would be reduced. Although the arguments against large-scale military action do not apply with the same force against small-scale operations, we have no convincing evidence that Indonesia intends to undertake small-scale action and, on balance, the odds seem to be against it for the near future. (Paras. 15–16)

4. Indonesian military capabilities and the temptation to resort to armed force against West New Guinea will increase over the next two years. However, we believe that Indonesian armed action on any significant scale is and will remain much less likely than Indonesian use or provocation of some incident with the Dutch so as to bring the issue before the UN under favorable circumstances. (Paras. 17–18)

[Here follows the 4-page Discussion section; see Supplement.]

181. Editorial Note

From February 10 to 15 Indonesian Foreign Minister Subandrio visited Australia to discuss with Australian officials the status of West New Guinea. The Embassy in Canberra summarized the results of Subandrio's Australian trip in despatch 338 from Canberra, March 15. It reads in part as follows:

"Dr. Subandrio, Indonesian Foreign Minister, made an official visit to Australia February 10 to 15 for the purpose of holding high-level discussions with the Commonwealth Government toward the principal end of re-assuring Australia that Indonesia does not pose a threat to this country's security.

"To accomplish this objective, it was necessary for Dr. Subandrio to place Indonesia's claims to West New Guinea in a new, and if possible, more favorable context. The visit, therefore, was concerned essentially with the problem of West New Guinea, however much both parties may have endeavored to give the impression that this was not the paramount issue in the discussions.

"Dr. Subandrio's frank and friendly exchanges with Prime Minister Menzies, External Affairs Minister Casey and other Australian officials provided an opportunity for each side to explain its position and policies. The result was the discovery of a broad area of understanding. No definite agreement was reached on the difficult problem of West New Guinea, but in a Joint Communiqué issued on February 14, Indonesia categorically ruled out the use of force as a means to settle this problem and Australia adopted a more flexible policy by agreeing not to impose objections if Indonesia were able to acquire this territory through peaceful negotiations with the Netherlands.

"Dr. Subandrio and the Australian leaders were able to place the West New Guinea problem in the broader context of Australian-Indonesian relations, in consequence of which the air has been cleared of considerable suspicion and distrust, a basis laid for more friendly relations, and the way pointed to a peaceful solution of the West New Guinea problem.

"The understanding incorporated in the Joint Communiqué brings Australia's relations with Indonesia more into line with United States objectives and should serve to reduce Australian concern over United States economic and military assistance to Indonesia. The understanding should also serve to make Indonesia more aware that it does not of necessity have to seek its friends only among the Communist Bloc." (Department of State, Central Files, 033.56D43/3–559)

182.   Telegram From the Embassy in Indonesia to the Department of State

Djakarta, February 19, 1959, 1 p.m.

2580. CINCPAC pass Dillon Anderson. CINCPAC also for POLAD. Dillon Anderson and I called on President Sukarno at 1100 February 17.[1] President was in excellent spirits and expansive mood, showed no sign of illness and asked Anderson to convey personal message to President Eisenhower.

He sent first his warm personal regards and all good wishes; as always, he spoke of President Eisenhower with genuine affection and admiration. He then asked Anderson to inform President Eisenhower that Sukarno was most grateful for recent news of military assistance, particularly small arms and equipment for 20 battalions and that although this represented only a third of Indonesian requirements he was most appreciative.

He also asked Anderson to emphasize that much as economic and military aid from US meant to Indonesia, political support meant even more. In this comment he was obviously alluding to West New Guinea issue, although no specific mention of it was made in this context. Earlier in conversation, however, Sukarno, referring to American leaders who were his idols, mentioned Thomas Jefferson, Abraham Lincoln and Sam Houston.

In skillful parallel West New Guinea, neatly tailored for Texan Anderson, Sukarno smilingly noted that Houston had won independence of Texas from Mexico "by bullets." West New Guinea independence from Dutch would be won by peaceful means, Sukarno said, with, he hoped, the help of the US. Neither Anderson nor I made any comment at this point, none being called for in view Sukarno's familiarity US policy this subject.

Remainder of conversation was devoted to banter in President's usual manner.

President was out of city Sunday and Monday but interrupted his already overcrowded schedule to see Dillon Anderson Tuesday morn-

---

Source: Department of State, Central Files, 756D.00/2–1958. Secret. Also sent to CINCPAC.

[1] Between February 15 and 17 the Anderson subcommittee of the Draper Committee visited Indonesia. On November 24, 1958, President Eisenhower had appointed a special committee under the chairmanship of William H. Draper, former Under Secretary of the Army, to undertake a "completely independent, objective, and non-partisan analysis" of the military assistance aspects of the U.S. Mutual Security Program. (Letter from Eisenhower to Draper, November 24, 1958; Department of State *Bulletin*, December 15, 1958, p. 954) The Anderson subcommittee of the Draper Committee was headed by Dillon Anderson and General J. Lawton Collins.

ing at my request when he found Anderson had to leave Djakarta that afternoon. This was unusual procedure for Sukarno who seldom arranges appointments on short notice and [can?] only be taken as illustrative his change of attitude.

Jones

---

183.   **Telegram From the Commander-in-Chief, Pacific (Felt) to the Joint Chiefs of Staff**

Honolulu, February 24, 1959, 5:11 p.m.

250311Z. Ref AmEmbassy The Hague telegram to State 1381.[1] Am disturbed by repercussions which would result should State act favorably upon recommendation made in referenced msg. Limited U.S. military aid to Indonesia has been based on premise that it does not generate Indonesian military threat to Dutch position in New Guinea. It has been made clear to Indonesia that any military aid from us has the condition attached to it that it will be used for internal security purposes and not as means to settle militarily Indonesia-Dutch disputes over New Guinea. That Indonesia understands and accepts this position has been affirmed most recently by Foreign Minister Subandrio in Australia. For United States to assume that Dutch position New Guinea is thereby threatened and compensatory military aid be furnished Dutch to defend New Guinea would not only imply gross irresponsibility on our part by furnishing both antagonists with weapons to settle dispute militarily but would leave us open to Commie charge of providing military means to sow dissent.

If our military aid policy vis-à-vis Indonesia is designed to retrieve our position in Indonesia the whole purpose might be very largely neutralized by furnishing weapons to the Dutch for a non-existent need.

Source: Department of State, WE Files: Lot 63 D 106, Indonesia 1959. Secret. Repeated by the Department of State to The Hague and Djakarta as telegrams 1312 and 1590, respectively, on March 3. (*Ibid.*, Central Files, 756D.5–MSP/2–2159)

[1] In telegram 1381, February 21, Young reported that Dutch Defense Minister Staf asked to buy four naval items for use in connection with West New Guinea defense. (*Ibid.*) See Supplement.

Strongly recommend that this position be presented to State asking their non-concurrence with the Dutch request and Ambassador Young's recommendation.[2]

---

[2] Jones commented on this telegram in telegram 2736, March 5. (Department of State, Central Files, 756D.56/3–559) See Supplement.

---

184.   Memorandum From the Assistant Secretary of State for Far Eastern Affairs (Robertson) to Acting Secretary of State Herter

Washington, February 27, 1959.

SUBJECT

Indonesian Guided Democracy—1959

In a speech February 20 President Sukarno officially announced a unanimous Cabinet decision on the implementation of "Guided Democracy" within the framework of a return to the Constitution of 1945.[1] The decision supported by the President, the National Council and the military is as follows:

1. Prior to his trip abroad scheduled for April, Sukarno, on behalf of the Government, will go before the Constituent Assembly and recommend that the Assembly adopt the Indonesian Constitution of 1945 as the country's permanent Constitution. If the Assembly accepts the recommendation (as is expected), the President, Cabinet Ministers and Constituent Assembly members will sign a "Bandung Charter" prior to Independence Day, August 17, declaring the Constitution of 1945 as Indonesia's Constitution.

2. Before his trip in April, Sukarno and the Cabinet will ask Parliament for action on two bills: (a) one bill calling for the simplification of the political party system; (b) the second calling for amending the general election law of 1953 to permit the inclusion of functional groups in Parliament. These bills will be submitted to the existing Parliament

---

Source: Department of State, Central Files, 756D.13/2–2759. Confidential. Drafted by Wenzel and cleared in draft with Parsons. A copy of this memorandum was sent to Murphy.

[1] For the English text of the constitution of 1945, see Daniel S. Lev, *The Transition to Guided Democracy: Indonesian Politics, 1957–1959* (Ithaca, N.Y.: Cornell University Modern Indonesia Project, 1966), pp. 290–298.

which shall continue in office until general elections are held and a new Parliament, including functional group representatives, is formed.

3. With the confirmation of the Constitution of 1945, the Djuanda Cabinet will return its mandate to the President, who shall appoint new Cabinet ministers. (Some sources report that Djuanda would continue in his position of Prime Minister or in a comparable role after the return of his mandate.)

4. With the formation of the new Parliament, bills will be submitted concerning (a) the forming of a Supreme Consultative Council, which will also include representatives of functional groups; (b) the forming of a People's Consultative Council, which will consist of members of Parliament, regional representatives and representatives of functional groups.

5. Election of a President and Vice President will be held according to the Constitution of 1945—i.e., by a majority vote of the People's Consultative Council.

Comment:

The 1945 Constitution, which entered into effect immediately after Indonesia's declaration of independence and continued until 1949, provides for a strong, executive form of government, with considerable resemblance to the American system, as opposed to the parliamentary system under the present constitution. Under the 1945 document, power to amend the constitution and to determine the broad lines of national policy is vested in the People's Consultative council. This council, in turn, is composed of members of the People's Representative Council—i.e., the Parliament, and representatives of regional and other groups. The Parliament exercises joint legislative power with the President. A Supreme Consultative Council to advise the President is also provided for. The manner in which members of these three Councils are to be chosen is to be provided by law. The 1945 Constitution also provides for an independent judiciary and appropriate ministries.

The effect of this decision by the Indonesian Government, if carried out along the lines stated, would appear to be to reduce the powers currently exercised by the political parties and the Parliament, while strengthening the hand of the President and his advisors (including the Army). All four major political parties have indicated general approval of the Cabinet decision, although the Communists (PKI) have approved the return to the 1945 Constitution on the condition that "it exclusively serve to realize President Sukarno's conception (1957 version) of embodying Communists in the Government." In this connection, Prime Minister Djuanda informed Ambassador Jones unequivocally February 25 that President Sukarno had definitely abandoned that part of his earlier concept which would call for inclusion of Communists in the Cabinet.[2] In the next few months, the parties, especially the PKI, may be expected to put up a last-ditch fight to retain some of their prerogatives, particularly in connection with the coming legislation on the simplification of the party system and the amendment of the general election law.

It is premature to say whether the implementation of the Cabinet's decision will mean a substantial reduction of the power of the Communist Party, although the tendency would appear to be in this direction. Within the framework of the 1945 Constitution, the power of the PKI could be eclipsed along with that of the other major parties so that any change in the relative PKI parliamentary strength, following the next general elections, might not have as much significance as under the present governmental structure. With the exception of 35 functional representatives of the Armed Services to be appointed to Parliament by the President, the method of selecting the functional representatives of the new Parliament has not yet been made entirely clear. If the Army, directly or through a controlled "National Front" apparatus, can play a major role in the selection of parliamentary functional candidates, the relative parliamentary strength of the PKI could suffer a loss at the expense of Army-approved candidates. The Army, in its advisory role to the President, would also be likely to frustrate any PKI attempts to place Party members in key positions in the Executive.

---

[2] Jones summarized this conversation in telegram 2641 from Djakarta, February 25. (Department of State, Central Files, 856D.2553/2–2559) See Supplement.

---

185.   Telegram From the Embassy in Indonesia to the Department of State

Djakarta, February 28, 1959, noon.

2687. CINCPAC also POLAD. Department telegram 1564.[1] Djuanda as on previous occasion simply smiled understandingly but

---

Source: Department of State, Central Files, 756D56/2–2859. Secret. Also sent to CINCPAC.

[1] Telegram 1564, February 26, reads as follows: "Dept would appreciate information Djuanda's reaction your reiteration US understanding that military equipment provided under August 13 agreement to be used accordance UN charter meaning not to be used obtain control West New Guinea by force." (Ibid., 756D.56/2–2559)

Continued

made no comment. In my view no comment could be expected as he made no comment on my similar statement last August. Embassy telegram 660, August 20[2] sets forth my interpretation of our position vis-à-vis GOI on assurances beyond those contained in exchange of notes. Immediately following my statement this subject to Djuanda last August he proceeded with exchange of notes without protest, and I am convinced there is mutual understanding on point. Repeated public and private statements by GOI that it has no intention use force against West New Guinea, latest of which are Subandrio's private and public assurances in Australia, reinforce this view. See immediately following telegram summarizing Ambassador McIntyre's impressions Subandrio visit.[3]

Jones

In telegram 1209 to The Hague, February 10, the Department had informed the Embassy that Netherlands officials had inquired whether, in informing Indonesians of the augmented arms program, the United States had again stressed its opposition to the use of force by Indonesians against West New Guinea. (*Ibid.*, 756D.56/2–1059) See Supplement. In telegram 1494 to Djakarta, February 16, the Department requested that Jones reiterate the U.S. view that the conditions of the U.S. arms sale program required that the equipment not be used to obtain control of West New Guinea. (Department of State, Central Files, 756D.56/2–1659) See Supplement.

[2] See footnote 2, Document 147.

[3] Not found.

---

186.   Memorandum From the Assistant Secretary of State for Far Eastern Affairs (Robertson) to the Under Secretary of State for Economic Affairs (Dillon)

Washington, March 5, 1959.

SUBJECT

Ex-Im Bank Financing of the Sale of Three Lockheed Electra Aircraft to Indonesia

Discussion:

On March 15, 1957 the Indonesian Government signed a contract with Lockheed for the furnishing of three Lockheed Electra commercial aircraft, spare parts, tools, test equipment, etc., at a total cost of about $12 million to be delivered to Garuda International Airlines in late 1960.

Source: Department of State, Central Files, 756D.5622/3–559. Confidential. Drafted by Wenzel and cleared with SPA and FE.

According to the terms of the contract, Indonesia would deposit about $1.9 million (of which at least $1.2 million has already been paid) and Lockheed would finance a like amount. On April 25, 1957 Lockheed applied for exporter type credit financing by the Export-Import Bank of the balance of approximately $8.2 million. On June 27, 1957 the National Advisory Council (NAC Document #88)[1] notified the Bank that the NAC offered no objection to consideration by the Bank of $15 million financing for the Electras, as well as for three Convair 440s. (Financing of the latter was subsequently approved by the Bank.) During the regional rebellion in the latter part of 1957 and the early months of 1958, the Department adopted the policy that no additional assistance for the Indonesian Government would be considered. The Bank followed this policy as regards pending Indonesian loan applications, and in response to queries received from the Indonesian Government, the Bank indicated that consideration of the Electra loan was being held up for "technical reasons"—i.e. the lack of an agreement to provide technical services to Garuda. On August 1, 1958 the Secretary approved a broad range of future U.S. actions vis-à-vis Indonesia, including the withdrawing of our objections on political grounds to an Ex-Im Bank loan for the Electras. The Bank was notified of this decision. Another series of U.S. actions regarding Indonesia, approved by the Secretary on November 5, 1958, included informing the Ex-Im Bank that for political reasons we wished the Bank to proceed with consideration of projects in Indonesia meeting their criteria, noting the Electra loan application as one of several under consideration. Again the Bank was informed of this decision. Meanwhile, on October 21, 1958, Garuda signed a technical assistance contract with Lockheed thus removing one of the Bank's major objections to the granting of the loan. On December 30, 1958, however, the Bank informed the Indonesian Government that the Electra loan application had been turned down.

The Bank's decision was made primarily on economic grounds. Mr. Waugh pointed out on December 31, 1958 (Tab A)[2] that from the point of view of banking and economics, it was not a good loan, that the Bank had unpaid commitments of over $86 million in Indonesia and pending applications for new loans totaling over $70 million. It should be noted, however, that Indonesia has an unblemished record in servicing these outstanding commitments to the Bank. Some confusion also arose over the priority which the Indonesians attached to the Electra loan in relation to possible loans for other pending projects and this may have con-

---

[1] Not printed. (*Ibid.*, NAC Files: Lot 60 D 137, Documents)

[2] No tabs are attached to the source text. Reference is to a meeting held on December 31 between Waugh and Francis Jarvis and Mary Olmsted of SPA. (Memorandum of conversation, December 31; *ibid.*, Central Files, 756D.5622/3–559) See Supplement.

tributed to the Bank's negative decision. In August and again in November 1958 the Indonesian Ambassador in Washington indicated to the Bank that two or more of the other pending projects were of higher priority than the Electras which was apparently contrary to the position of the Indonesian Government that the Electra loan be pressed as foremost in importance. This matter was clarified around the end of the year with the Electras definitely accorded No. 1 priority by the Indonesians. However, the Bank apparently still felt that the financing of some of the other pending projects—e.g. dredges, fertilizer plant, etc.—would in the long run be more beneficial to the Indonesian economy. A second major reason for the Bank's turndown was a recommendation received by the Air Coordinating Committee that the Bank finance the sale of used piston planes which are about to be replaced by jets. The Bank has indicated its willingness to Indonesia to consider the financing of reconditioned DC–6s and 7s up to $3 million.

The Indonesian Government has expressed great disappointment at the Bank's decision and has asked that it be urgently reconsidered. While the contract with Lockheed has expired, negotiations are currently proceeding between the Indonesian Government and Lockheed in Djakarta whereby a new contract will be signed or the old one extended to keep this transaction open for another 30–90 days. The Indonesian Parliament has not yet been informed of the Bank's turndown which is not yet public knowledge. President Sukarno, himself, has taken a strong personal interest in the loan for the Electras. Regarding DC–6s and 7s, he has told our Ambassador that Indonesia does not want second-hand aircraft. The Bank's turndown, if definitive, will be bound to have an undesirable effect on U.S.-Indonesian relations, but particularly on our relations with Sukarno. This comes at a critical juncture when there is increasing evidence of the President's casting off of Communist Party (PKI) support and an expected reformulation of the Government's structure which could lead to a further eclipse of the PKI. A denial of this loan would likely hand the PKI a strong propaganda weapon by which the U.S. would be attacked for lack of good faith in prolonging negotiations for almost two years, in tying up a substantial amc·unt of scarce foreign exchange thus preventing Indonesia from acquiring such aircraft elsewhere and then turning its back at the last moment. The PKI has already made the Electra loan an issue in Parliament several months ago and the Party would not lose another opportunity to embarrass the Government and press for purchase of these aircraft from the bloc. The prestige of the Government is at stake since it has repeatedly encouraged Parliament to believe the Electra loan would ultimately be received.

I know you are very much aware of the massive assistance drive which the bloc has been carrying out in Indonesia over the past year.

Credits in the economic and military fields offered by the bloc and accepted by Indonesia now stand at about $375 million ($200 million economic and $175 million military), *most of these concentrated in the period since January 1, 1958.* These credits already exceed total U.S. economic and military assistance of $308 million ($282 million economic and $26 million military) in the form of grants, loans and surplus agricultural commodities extended to Indonesia *over the past nine years.* We do not wish nor can we expect to compete dollar for dollar with bloc aid to the non-aligned countries. At the same time we will have to meet this major Sino-Soviet challenge with all the resources at our disposal if we are to retain our influence in these key areas, selecting our projects carefully so as to achieve the maximum possible impact. The Electra loan is, I believe, such a project.

It should be noted here that the Indonesian Government as well as our Ambassador in Djakarta do not share the Bank's views as to the economic soundness of this loan. While the Indonesian arguments in this regard are not completely convincing, I support the Ambassador's recommendation that if there is doubt as to the loan's economic soundness, this doubt be resolved in Indonesia's favor on political grounds. Failure to do so could mean a reversal in the hard-won gains we have made in Indonesia since last May.

Recommendation:

That you call Mr. Waugh and urge, that on the basis of overriding political factors, the Bank approve the Electra loan.[3]

---

[3] A handwritten note on the source text indicates that Dillon talked with Waugh on March 19 and the Export-Import Bank subsequently approved the Electra loan.

---

187. Telegram From the Embassy in Indonesia to the Department of State

Djakarta, March 13, 1959, 10 a.m.

2829. CINCPAC also for POLAD. During 45-minute conversation with Senator H. Alexander Smith,[1] Sukarno made unusually strong

---

Source: Department of State, Central Files, 611.56D/3–1359. Secret. Repeated to Saigon, The Hague, Seoul, and CINCPAC.

[1] H. Alexander Smith (R.–New Jersey), a member of the Senate Foreign Relations Committee, was in Indonesia as part of a larger trip to Asia; documentation on his trip is *ibid.,* 033.1100–SM.

pitch for US to change its position of neutrality on West New Guinea, emphasizing this major question which separates two countries psychologically.

Reaction came in response to Senator Smith's question as to how US could best help Indonesia. President expressed great gratitude for military and economic assistance but repeated statement frequently made in the past that moral and political support even more important to Indonesia than material support. He again said, "Don't let Communists win this game," pointing out that international Communists supported Indonesia strongly on this most sensitive question. He referred to speeches of Ho Chi Minh during visit to Indonesia,[2] pointing out in every speech on whatever occasion Ho had stressed support of Indonesia's claim to West New Guinea. Sukarno put everything he had into appeal. "Change your position on this issue and I will stand up and tell Indonesian people that US is their real friend," Sukarno said.

Senator Smith responded that he was here on goodwill mission and would take back President Sukarno's message but that he was not authorized or prepared to enter into discussion of policy questions.

When Senator Smith referred to Syngman Rhee in commenting on his itinerary, Sukarno said, "Why should Syngman Rhee attack us? Why should he attack me?", indicating two nations had no reason to quarrel with each other. Senator Smith said he would be glad to pass this message on to President Rhee when he saw him.

I asked Sukarno whether he was satisfied with shape taken by his conception of guided democracy as finally worked out involving return to 1945 constitution. President replied with an emphatic affirmative. I observed that this came very close to the American strong President form of government. Sukarno nodded, indicating there were some differences. "Also," he said, "I intend to appoint a Prime Minister", indicating he did not desire to be bothered with details of government administration.

In connection with forthcoming trip President said details were in hands of Doctor Tamzil but he would probably depart Djakarta April 23 and was tentatively planning to stop either in San Francisco or Los Angeles for a few days.[3] "Which would you recommend?," he asked. I indicated I could not be in position of deciding between two such attractive cities and suggested he ought to stop in both. Nothing was said about

---

[2] Ho Chi Minh, President of the Democratic Republic of Vietnam, was in Indonesia in early March for a brief visit.

[3] Sukarno was scheduled to undertake a 2-month tour of Asia, Europe, and Latin America between April 23 and June 27. In despatch 824 from Djakarta, April 28, the Embassy transmitted a copy of Sukarno's itinerary, which included a stop in Los Angeles June 1–3 and a stop in Honolulu June 4–5. (Department of State, Central Files, 756D.11/4–2859)

physical examination and Sukarno, despite rigorous schedule of enter-
tainment for Ho Chi Minh, looked fit, indeed better than when I last saw
him on February 17.

Jones

---

188. Editorial Note

On March 19 British Prime Minister Macmillan and Foreign Minister Lloyd arrived in the United States for a series of consultations with
U.S. officials on matters of mutual concern. During one of these meetings, held at Camp David on March 22, Indonesia was discussed:

"The President asked Mr. Allen Dulles for a report on the situation
in Indonesia. Mr. Dulles said that Sukarno has moved somewhat away
from dependence upon the Soviets. He is moving back toward the old
constitution. Their economic situation is bad, and they have been unable
to put down the rebels in Sumatra and the Celebes. He commented that
the rebels include many of the finest men in the leadership ranks in Indonesia. Exports of rubber and tin remain disturbed by the continuing
rebellion. He thought there was advantage in trying to bring both sides
together, and suggested that the British might be in better position than
we are to attempt to do so. Mr. Lloyd said he understood the United
States is providing some arms to the Indonesians. The UK is doing the
same, he said. This creates a most difficult situation with the Dutch who
recognize but are not persuaded by our argument that if we do not provide these arms the Indonesians will turn to the Soviets. Sir Frederick
Hoyer Millar commented on one new factor in the situation—the Australians said, about two months ago, that they would accept any solution
relating to New Guinea that was agreed upon by the Dutch and the Indonesians." (Memorandum of conversation by Goodpaster, March 28;
Eisenhower Library, Whitman File, Eisenhower Diaries)

Millar was the Permanent Under Secretary in the British Foreign
Office. [text not declassified]

189. **Memorandum From the Assistant Secretary of State for Far Eastern Affairs (Robertson) to Acting Secretary of State Herter**

Washington, March 26, 1959.

SUBJECT

Export Licensing of Lockheed C–130B Military Transport Aircraft for Indonesia

Discussion:

The Indonesian Air Force has ordered ten C–130B's from Lockheed Aircraft Corporation, which has applied to the Department for the necessary export license. The Indonesians have asked us for a decision on the export license by April 2, 1959, in part to insure that delivery of the planes can begin October 1960 as presently scheduled.

I believe the license should be issued for the following principal reasons:

1. Issuance of the license would be consistent with our present policy towards Indonesia. The Secretary's decision of November 5, 1958, (Tab A)[1] approved issuance of export licenses for surplus, propeller-driven, military aircraft. The C–130B's are new, not surplus, but licensing them for export would appear to be in the spirit of the Secretary's decision. The C–130B is a propeller-driven (prop-jet), unarmed airplane designed for the transport of military cargo and personnel.

2. The transaction is a purely commercial one between Lockheed and the Indonesian Air Force. No U.S. Government financing has been requested. The total estimated cost of the ten airplanes is $31 million.

3. Even if the license is promptly issued, delivery of the C–130B's cannot begin until October 1960. Delivery of the ten planes is not scheduled to be completed until October 1961.

4. The C–130B would seem to be particularly well-suited to the needs of a dispersed country such as Indonesia in maintaining internal security. It is designed to provide a high degree of mobility for troops and equipment, and is said to possess unusual ability to land on and take off from rough fields. This plane seems a sensible choice by the Indonesians for their requirements, and is a plane in which they have expressed particular interest.

Source: Department of State, Central Files, 756D.5622/3–2659. Secret. Drafted by Moore on March 25. Mein and Parsons concurred in this memorandum, but EUR did not. In a memorandum of March 27 to the Acting Secretary, Merchant outlined EUR's position, recommending that action on the licenses be suspended pending a study of Indonesia's needs and a projection of what future U.S. assistance to Indonesia might be. (*Ibid.*, WE Files: Lot 63 D 106, Indonesia 1959) See Supplement.

[1] See Document 161.

Should you authorize issuance of the export license for the C–130B's for Indonesia, we would plan to inform the Dutch and Australian Governments of our intention to issue the license, in conformity with our standing practice as established by the Secretary in November 1958.

Recommendation:

That you authorize issuance of the export license covering ten C–130B's for Indonesia.[2]

---

[2] On April 7 EUR withdrew its dissent and Acting Secretary Murphy approved Robertson's recommendation, initialing his approval on this memorandum. According to a handwritten note on the source text, Herter saw Robertson's memorandum and registered no dissent.

---

190.   Letter From the Assistant Secretary of Defense for International Security Affairs (Irwin) to the Assistant Secretary of State for Far Eastern Affairs (Robertson)

Washington, March 28, 1959.

DEAR MR. ROBERTSON: The Department of Defense is concerned that the momentum of improved relations with Indonesia resulting from the token aid program and, more recently, the augmentation to that program, be maintained. Needed action was taken to expedite the interim program and it is our opinion that additional action is now needed to achieve realization of United States objectives in Indonesia.

As Defense is convinced that insofar as practicable further piecemeal actions should be avoided, this office, in conjunction with other elements of Defense, has been discussing initiation of an integrated long-range military assistance program of limited size. During a recent discussion of this matter with Admiral Felt, it was proposed that Mr. Robert Knight and Admiral O'Donnell of this office, who are soon to be

---

Source: Department of State, Central Files, 756D.5–MSP/3–2859. Secret.

in Djakarta, might at that time, in the company of the Ambassador, talk to the Indonesians about the type of limited MAP which the Indonesians would like to have developed on a long-term basis. It would, of course, be emphasized that the United States participants at this meeting could not commit the United States but were simply demonstrating friendly interest in the Indonesian armed forces and engaging in exploratory talks.

The Department of Defense recommends that guidelines governing the development of the proposed Indonesian program reflect that the program:

(1) is politically motivated in recognition of the need that Indonesia be a friend of the United States, rather than in recognition of Indonesia's current military significance to the maintenance of free world security; and

(2) should be kept to the minimum cost commensurate with its purposes.

The guidelines should establish that the purposes are:

(1) the maintenance and strengthening of existing U.S. ties with Indonesian military establishments;

(2) the increase of Indonesian capability to maintain internal security and to combat Communist activity by providing the appropriate arms, equipment and training on a continuing basis; and

(3) the expansion to the maximum extent practicable of the United States training of personnel of the Indonesian armed forces, and the curtailment to the extent possible of Sino-Soviet training programs.

It is presently contemplated that any such program would be carried out substantially on the basis upon which this year's program was formulated.

We would greatly appreciate your comments with regard to the foregoing.

Sincerely yours,

John N. Irwin II

191.   Memorandum of Conversation

Washington, April 1, 1959.

SUBJECT

Indonesia

PARTICIPANTS

Dr. Joseph Luns, Foreign Minister of the Netherlands
Dr. J. H. van Roijen, Ambassador of the Netherlands
FE—Mr. Robertson
SPA—Mr. Mein
WE—Mr. Stabler

Dr. Luns opened the discussion by expressing his regret over the news which he had just heard regarding Mr. Robertson's resignation.[1] He then said that in the talk which he had just concluded with Mr. Dillon[2] he had indicated that the political deterrent against an attack by Indonesia on West New Guinea had worked so far. The Indonesian intention to mount such an attack had been shelved for the time being. Dr. Luns said he thought that it would be most useful for the United States and the United Kingdom to keep up the policy of public and private deterrents against the use of force by Indonesia.

Mr. Robertson recalled that the Secretary had spoken most forcefully to Indonesian Foreign Minister Subandrio last November on the question of force. In Mr. Robertson's opinion Indonesia realized that the state of the world was such that attempts to settle issues between nations through the use of force would not be tolerated. The Secretary had told Dr. Subandrio that if Indonesia used force against West New Guinea, the United States would be against Indonesia. Dr. Subandrio had replied that he knew this and he also knew that if Indonesia should attempt to use force, the opinion of the entire world would be against it. The dispute between Indonesia and the Dutch was not the only dispute in this world, said Mr. Robertson, and the world would not tolerate the use of force to settle these disputes.

Dr. Luns said that while this might be true, there was irresponsible elements in Indonesia which might not be sensitive to world opinion.

Source: Department of State, Central Files, 756D.00/4–159. Secret. Drafted by Stabler.

[1] Robertson was planning to resign for health reasons; see *The New York Times*, April 2, 1959, p. 8.

[2] As reported in a memorandum of conversation, April 1. (Department of State, Central Files, 656C.56D/4–159) See Supplement.

Mr. Robertson replied that in our opinion the responsible elements which were the important ones in Indonesia fully realized that the use of force would not be tolerated.

Dr. Luns said that the Netherlands had no doubt that Indonesia had a plan to use force against West New Guinea and that the plans called for an attack some time in March. The fact that the Indonesians had called it off had caused much disappointment among Indonesian agents in West New Guinea. Dr. Luns then said that his Government was most worried about the intention of Swedish shipyards to build two destroyers of the "Halland" class for Indonesia. These destroyers would be as powerful as any ships the Dutch have in the West New Guinea area. Mr. Robertson said that Indonesia's actions in building up its defensive capacities was because Indonesia held that its most dangerous enemy today was Red China. Dr. Luns pointed out that the Indonesians had taken action against the Chinese Nationalists in Indonesia and not the Red Chinese. Mr. Robertson replied that our reports were that Indonesia had taken action against the Chinese population as a whole because the Indonesians were concerned about the activities of the Chinese population in Indonesia. In our opinion, Mr. Robertson said, Indonesia was more acutely aware of the menace of international Communism than ever before. It was increasingly concerned about becoming overly entangled with the Communists and in this connection Indonesia recently turned down a Soviet loan. With regard to the question of arms, if the Indonesians could not get arms from the United States, they would get them from the Soviets. The Soviet bloc was ready and willing to provide such arms as Indonesia desired. However, the Indonesians did not wish to depend solely on the Soviets for their supply.

Dr. Luns said that he agreed that if the Indonesians had to depend on a foreign source of supply, it would be better for United States to be this source. However, he could not agree that Indonesia's request for arms from Sweden was desirable since the Swedes were only interested in the commercial aspect and had no means whereby they could exercise any responsibility with respect to the use of these arms. The Swedish destroyers were a very heavy type with strong armament. Dr. Luns requested that we look into this question in Stockholm. Dr. Luns added that he would almost prefer the Indonesians to obtain Soviet destroyers because at least there was a chance that at some future time the Indonesians might not be able to get the necessary spare parts.

Dr. Luns summed up by saying that there were two points involved in Indonesia's attitude toward West New Guinea. The first was the political deterrent and this had worked so far. The second point was that if the political deterrent failed, there would be a vaccum because no plans had been devised in anticipation of that situation. If the political deterrent failed, it would mean the failure of the entire Western policy, since

Indonesia would be supported by the Soviet bloc in its actions against West New Guinea.

Mr. Robertson said that the disagreement between the Dutch and ourselves was on how to ensure a non-Communist Indonesia, not on the objective which we and the Dutch shared. The United States believed that there has been steady progress in achieving the objective. Dr. Luns said that in a sense the rabid anti-Dutch feeling in Indonesia has helped United States policy because the Indonesians derived a certain amount of satisfaction from their belief that we were working with Indonesia against the Dutch. Mr. Robertson replied that we took no sides in this matter and that our only aim was to keep Indonesia out of the Communist sphere.

Dr. Luns pointed out that since 1945 almost 288,000 Dutchmen had returned to Holland from Indonesia. Of this number about one-half were Eurasian. The last 50,000, who came last year from Indonesia, arrived in a nearly destitute condition. The influx had placed a heavy burden on the Netherlands whose population had increased during the last six years from about 10,500,000 to about 11,600,000.

Mr. Robertson inquired what in Dr. Luns' view would be the best solution to the West New Guinea question. Dr. Luns replied that he thought the Papuans on the whole, both in Australia and Netherlands areas, should form a single unit. In response to Mr. Robertson's question, Dr. Luns said this would be achieved through self-determination and through the guidance of those now governing and administering the areas. Dr. Luns said that the Papuans detested the Indonesians. They recalled their treatment at the hands of Indonesian officials whom the Japanese had put in charge in the area during the War.[3]

---

[3] Later that day Luns met with Acting Secretary Herter to discuss Indonesian nationalization of Netherlands properties and the need for NATO solidarity. (Memorandum of conversation by Cameron; Department of State, Conference Files: Lot 64 D 560, CF 1235)

192. Letter From the Assistant Secretary of State for Far Eastern Affairs (Robertson) to the Assistant Secretary of Defense for International Security Affairs (Irwin)

Washington, April 10, 1959.

DEAR JACK: Thank you for your letter of March 28, 1959, commenting on the future of the United States military assistance program in Indonesia.[1] The Department of course shares the gratification expressed by the Department of Defense at recent improvements in United States-Indonesian relations, stemming in substantial part from the military assistance program.

We also agree that hard and continuing thought should be given to the future of the program. However, we believe it preferable that Mr. Knight and Admiral O'Donnell neither raise the question of a long-range program with the Indonesians nor respond specifically to Indonesian overtures along these lines which may be made. Should the Indonesians bring up the matter with Mr. Knight and Admiral O'Donnell, as well they may, some discussion cannot be avoided. In our view, while Mr. Knight and Admiral O'Donnell might indicate United States recognition of Indonesian needs, they should carefully avoid any impression of any commitment to provide additional aid or of encouraging expectations of a continuing program.

We hold this view because the present United States policy towards Indonesia remains one of proceeding step-by-step as we assess the strength and determination of non- and anti-Communist elements in Indonesia to move that country in the direction we would like to see her take, for her sake as well as our own. This policy derives from the impossibility of foreseeing now the likely course of (1) internal Indonesian politics and (2) Indonesian foreign policies. Under the circumstances it seems premature to discuss a long-range military assistance program with the Indonesians. To do so might well give them an exaggerated idea of the extent to which the United States is presently willing and able to go to meet their desires for military assistance.

Although we do not favor discussion of a long-range program with the Indonesians at this time, we do believe it would be most helpful for Mr. Knight and Admiral O'Donnell to discuss the matter fully with Ambassador Jones and the MILTAG officers in Djakarta. We believe it is essential constantly to review and evaluate developments in Indonesia to

Source: Department of State, Central Files, 756D.5–MSP/3–2859. Secret. Drafted by Moore on April 6. The following Department of State offices concurred in this letter: SPA, WE, FE, W/MSC, and G.

[1] Document 190.

guide us in the development of our policy towards Indonesia. For example, we shall wish to observe carefully how the projected Indonesian governmental reorganization measures are applied. If these measures are carried out in such a way that a more stable government and a more decisive curbing of Communist influence seem likely to result, it might then be timely to consider the possibility of considering further military assistance programs.

It may be desirable meanwhile to examine the feasibility of engaging in a long-range military assistance program should such a program be determined to be in our best interest. Consideration of a long-range program would have to take into account, for instance, in addition to the guidelines you suggest, the difficulty of planning on a long-range basis when Mutual Security funds are appropriated year-by-year in unpredictable amounts. Any long-range program for Indonesia would have also to be coordinated with the many other demands on MSA funds, a potentially serious problem since these demands invariably exceed the funds available.

Sincerely yours,

Walter S. Robertson[2]

------

[2] Printed from a copy that bears this typed signature.

------

193. Telegram From the Department of State to the Embassy in the Netherlands

Washington, April 10, 1959, 8:32 p.m.

1537. Deptel 1531 to The Hague.[1] Dept (Merchant and Robertson) informed Netherlands Ambassador van Roijen April 10 that after careful examination all factors decision had been reached within past few days and after Luns' departure from Washington to issue export licenses for commercial purchase by Indonesia of 10 C–130B unarmed

------

Source: Department of State, Central Files, 756D.5622/4–1059. Secret; Priority. Drafted by Stabler, cleared by Merchant (draft) and Robertson, and approved by McBride. Repeated to Djakarta, London, Paris, and CINCPAC for POLAD.

[1] Telegram 1531, April 10, informed the Embassy that the Department approved the issuance of export licenses for ten C–130B aircraft for Indonesia and that it planned to explain this decision to the Netherlands Ambassador on April 10. (Ibid.)

cargo-transport aircraft. Delivery would commence October 1, 1960 and be completed by autumn, 1961. Merchant pointed out that US Government not involved in transaction except through granting of export licenses.

Van Roijen said important thing for Dutch was fact Indonesians were getting these aircraft and not degree US Government involvement. Aircraft could be used to drop parachutists and thus in an aggressive sense were in same category as destroyers being built for Indonesia by Sweden (Deptel 1473).[2] Van Roijen said his Government would be "very disappointed and disturbed" by this action. It would cause chain reaction other allied and friendly countries which would no longer see need to use restraint in furnishing arms to Indonesians.

Merchant said we were not surprised by Dutch reaction and it was in view of their probable reaction that we desired inform them soonest of our decision. Merchant made point that in Indonesian archipelago almost any sort of military equipment, even in internal security categories, could be used for aggressive purposes. He also pointed out that Indonesian Air Force has set aside necessary money (about $31 million) needed for this cash transaction and that if US withheld approval of export licenses, Indonesian Air Force would buy comparable type from Soviet Bloc.

Robertson reviewed background of our military assistance to Indonesia and said US had been gratified by progress achieved through our phased assistance of limited nature. Decision to grant export licenses was in line with decisions taken last November and about which Dutch had been fully informed. Robertson stressed that Indonesians did not wish to be dependent on Soviet Bloc and that if we refused licenses for these planes we would impair and reverse satisfactory trend of Indonesia toward Free World. He recalled what Secretary had said to Subandrio last November about our opposition to use of force against West New Guinea and that entire world would condemn it. In reply to van Roijen's statement that Netherlands did not trust Indonesian word and that unstable situation in Indonesia might well get out of hand and result in attack on West New Guinea Robertson said that in final analysis US maintained control over delivery of these aircraft which could be withheld if situation deteriorated. This would not be the case if Indonesia received aircraft from Soviet Bloc.

Van Roijen said that risks involved in furnishing aircraft great and that by 1960 Indonesia would already be receiving these aircraft. It

---

[2] Telegram 1473, March 31, reported that van Roijen had called at the Department the previous day to express concern over Sweden's decision to build two destroyers for Indonesia. (*Ibid.*, 756D.5621/3–3159) See Supplement.

made important difference to Dutch public opinion that such large and aggressive planes were being furnished Indonesia by allies of Netherlands, not by its enemies. He said this transaction would "severely affect relations between us."

Merchant expressed hope that in presenting matter to parliament and public opinion Dutch Government would stress following points:

a. Its confidence in what we have told Indonesia regarding our attitude on use of force;
b. Commitments which US has received from Indonesia that military equipment furnished would not be used for aggressive purposes; and
c. Fact that Indonesia is dependent on West for its future supply of spare parts.

Last point would be added deterrent to Indonesian use of force which would not be case if equipment came from Soviet Bloc. Merchant said we do not believe this decision has created additional risks in connection West New Guinea; we believed it was proper step to take in light of Indonesian Air Force determination obtain these planes.

Van Roijen concluded that while he would make these points to his Government he wished to emphasize again with all strength at his command adverse effect this transaction would have on public opinion. With reference assertion these planes licensed in line with November program he said that we had created "false impression," since in November we had told Dutch program was small. This was not the case. We had also told them that nothing but surplus aircraft would be licensed for Indonesians. This also not true. Robertson said could not understand how Dutch gained such impression. Van Roijen ended conversation by saying he "surprised US ready risk good will it enjoys in Netherlands" through transaction of this sort.

Herter

194.   Telegram From the Embassy in the Philippines to the Department of State

Baguio, April 13, 1959, 8 p.m.

2. From Dillon.[1] Following summary talks Djakarta:

1) Nasution discussed role of army in present Indonesian scene in general terms along lines familiar Department. Only new elements were that, although constituent assembly can fill office vice president, not expected office be filled for two or three years and that army expected have increased representation new government to be formed July with Chief of Staff position possibly raised above cabinet rank. Nasution stressed need for political stability and solving country's economic problems as important to security and attainment of military objectives. He said that Darul Islam more difficult problem for army than PRRI.[2]

2) In meeting with Subandrio and five of his cabinet colleagues, Fon Minister referred improvement US-Indonesian relations, reviewed political and economic problems of newly independent countries especially as being faced by Indonesia and renewed plea for US understanding. He said government giving highest priority to security and that government wishes settle rebellion, for it not only source of friction, but also threat to very existence of state. Finance Minister said government in need of loans and is now negotiating with several US banks for short-term line of credit for importing raw materials and hoped reach agreement possibly by end April.

I took occasion to raise with him as I had earlier with Nasution, security problem on rubber estates. Also mentioned question of internal price oil production and Stanvac needs for additional concessions.

3) Meetings with Djuanda and Sukarno being reported separately.[3]

Bohlen

Source: Department of State, Central Files, 756D.00/4–1359. Secret. Also sent to Djakarta.

[1] Dillon arrived in Baguio on April 13 for the annual meeting of the Far Eastern Chiefs of Mission. Prior to this meeting Dillon made a 2-day visit to Indonesia, April 12–13, and before that he was in Wellington as the U.S. representative to the fifth SEATO Council of Ministers Meeting, April 8–10. During his stay in Indonesia Dillon met with President Sukarno, Prime Minister Djuanda, Army Chief of Staff Nasution, and Foreign Minister Subandrio; see Document 195. Briefing papers prepared for Dillon's visit to Indonesia are in Department of State, Conference Files: Lot 64 D 560, CF 1263.

[2] Telegram 3111 from Djakarta, April 13, reported more fully on Dillon's meeting with Nasution. (*Ibid.*) See Supplement.

[3] See Documents 195 and 196.

195. Telegram From the Embassy in the Philippines to the Department of State

Baguio, April 14, 1959, 10 a.m.

5. From Dillon. Djuanda asked Jones to arrange opportunity for private talk with me which we had after dinner at Embassy. Djuanda gave long exposé of reasons for return to 1945 constitution as apparently Indonesians are very sensitive that we may think they are abandoning democracy in making this shift. After I had reassured him on this point he asked if I had any questions. I told him my primary interest was economic development and I understood one of the main Indonesian problems was the expense of combatting the rebellion. I asked him how long he expected this to continue. Djuanda replied the most pessimistic estimates were that it would take 3 more years to complete the suppression of the rebellion, but he said he hoped and expected that there would be a political solution earlier. He alluded to the government's recent success in negotiating a political solution with Atjehnese and indicated he hoped for something similar in other rebel held territory. He then quickly said the time was not yet ripe for such negotiations and that if it proved necessary to carry matters to ultimate military conclusion then 3 years would be required.

Djuanda then launched into what apparently was main reason he had wished to talk with me. This was his conviction that the many bureaucratic details in implementing US aid projects were largely destroying their psychological usefulness. He emphasized that he was not thinking of any increase in dollar volume of aid but that both the negotiation of projects and implementation once they were negotiated left much to be desired. He pointed out this was particularly so in view of invidious comparison with Soviet aid practices and stated that the majority of Soviet aid programs were being promptly and rapidly implemented. He then asked my view regarding Soviet aid.

I told him US had no objection to the acceptance of Soviet aid as such because a cement plant for instance would serve development purposes equally well no matter who had constructed it. I said we were concerned lest countries unwittingly get into position where they were dependent on Soviet aid. Soviets had shown in the case of Yugoslavia that they were fully prepared to terminate their aid programs at moment's notice for political reasons. Djuanda said he was glad to hear my views and assured me Indonesian Govt was well aware of danger of their dependence on Soviet aid. He then repeated plea that some action be taken to expedite our procedures. I told him we were well aware of

Source: Department of State, Central Files, 756D.00/4–1459. Confidential. Repeated to Djakarta.

problem which was not confined to Indonesia and that we were in process of taking steps to improve situation. I promised to look into particular cases of excessive delays in Indonesian projects on my return. I had impression Djuanda was sincere and felt our implementation procedures were working against best interests of US-Indonesian relations. This impression strengthened when I checked ICA record of implementation which is not good.

I then took opportunity to speak to Djuanda about DLF application for purchase of KPM ships from Dutch which described in separate telegram.[1]

Bohlen

---

[1] Reference is to telegram 4 from Baguio, April 14, in which Dillon reported on his discussion of the prospective DLF loan to finance the purchase of ships from the Netherlands with Ambassador Jones and his staff. (*Ibid.*, 756D.5–MSP/4–1459) See Supplement.

---

196. Telegram From the Embassy in the Philippines to the Department of State

Baguio, April 15, 1959, noon.

14. From Dillon. Deptel 11.[1] After advising with Jones it was decided to mention C–130 only in response to Indonesian question. Sukarno raised matter in most informal way after our interview was concluded and while he was escorting me to my car. We had been talk-

---

Source: Department of State, Central Files, 756D.5622/4–1559. Confidential; Priority. Repeated to Djakarta, The Hague, and Canberra.

[1] Telegram 11, April 14, inquired about the substance of Dillon's remarks to Sukarno regarding the sale of C–130 aircraft. (*Ibid.*, 756D.5622/4–1459) Dillon had met with Sukarno on April 12 and the Embassy reported on this meeting in telegram 3103, April 13. During the meeting Sukarno's principal interest "was desire President Eisenhower visit Indonesia. He made long, ardent plea this respect and promised President would receive finest reception Indonesians capable of producing." Sukarno also commented on the improvement in U.S.-Indonesian relations and "expressed hope and belief" that improvement would continue. Dillon briefly mentioned C–130 aircraft desired by the Indonesian Air Force." (*Ibid.*, 611.56D/4–1359)

ing about economic development in outer islands which in Indonesian view involves transfers of population from Java. Sukarno said if we really wished help in this process C–130's would be most helpful. Since there was no possibility discuss matter in any detail I replied that he had no cause for concern and that I expected good news for him shortly. He was obviously very pleased. Jones intends arrange for formal notification to Indonesians on his return Djakarta at which time our understanding re use of aircraft will be stressed. During conversations with Djuanda and Subandrio I mentioned US gratification at Casey–Subandrio agreement using this as vehicle for re-emphasizing US views re necessity for peaceful settlement West Irian issue.

In Australia Menzies raised matter and indicated some surprise that we were making such aircraft available and wondered how Indonesians could obtain funds to purchase such expensive aircraft. However, when I informed him that we had decided issue license for ten planes he made no protest and seemed to accept matter with equanimity. As result my talk with Menzies I feel we should take great pains to inform Australians in advance and at same time as Netherlands regarding military deliveries to Indonesia.[2]

Bohlen

---

[2] On April 22 Jones informed Subandrio that the United States was prepared to issue licenses for the C–130 aircraft that had been requested by President Sukarno and Air Marshal Suryadarma but "only for internal security and legitimate self-defense purposes." (Telegram 3233 from Djakarta, April 23; ibid., 756D.5–MSP/4–2359) See Supplement.

---

197. Telegram From the Embassy in Indonesia to the Department of State

Djakarta, April 20, 1959, 6 p.m.

3193. Department pass DEPTAR for ACSI. CINCPAC also for POLAD. Deputy Assistant Secretary Defense Knight, Admiral O'Donnell saw ACS Nasution, Foreign Minister Subandrio, Defense Secretary General Hidajat during one-day here April 18.[1]

Nasution described plans return to 1945 Constitution, said army did not intend permit political parties create diversion by holding long talks. Expressed opinion parties would accept but pointed out all had

---

Source: Department of State, 756D.00/4–2059. Confidential. Also sent to CINCPAC.

[1] Knight and O'Donnell accompanied Dillon to the SEATO Council meeting and the Far Eastern Chiefs of Mission meeting at Baguio. Separate memoranda of their conversations with Nasution, Subandrio, and Hidajat were transmitted to the Department under cover of despatch 871, May 14. (Ibid., 756D.00/5–1459) See Supplement.

voiced some objection. Re PKI mentioned rank and file had refrained from participation government-sponsored rallies to support 1945 Constitution.

Under new government Cabinet would be reorganized along lines of general staff with several deputy prime ministers responsible for specific area of interest.

In response to Ambassador's questions, Nasution said he did not believe PKI would be represented in new Cabinet but would seek retention of sympathizers, mentioning Prijono, Hanafi this connection. Described Prijono as Murba member, Hanafi under Communist influence, but these two unable cooperate. President Sukarno "biggest politician of them all" understands this and plays off Communists against Murba and vice versa.

Communists working hard gain control new national front but would not be successful. Army influence in new front would be sufficient prevent PKI penetration.

PKI working to split Sukarno from Nasution, Nasution from commanders, non-Communist political parties from each other. Communists now causing slow-downs on estates and railroads. Communists doing best infiltrate army. Asked whether anything would happen during forthcoming absence of President, Nasution said certain elements may try cause serious situation to develop but army is alert and ready to react against such effort.

Subandrio took line US could be more effective by having positive program rather than placing too much emphasis on anti-Communism. He and his government anti-Communist, Indonesian democracy based on Pantjasila. Communists had cleverly avoided open opposition to these principles, had identified own objectives with these principles.

Foreign Minister said Sukarno would succeed in plan to bring back 1945 Constitution. Principal non-Communist parties more or less in agreement to this end. PKI realized this contrary to their interests but had not come out publicly against it.

Hidajat told visitors it would be necessary to wait and see how 1945 Constitution was implemented before determining whether it would mean improvement. Gave impression his wife, Deputy Chairman of Consembly, not too enthusiastic for change but probably would support.

Said Indonesians happy with military aid program but he felt navy and air force have been neglected. Navy does not want aircraft carriers or guided missiles; want small patrol craft. Admiral Subijakto had reported to him would take two or three years to train people for equipment they have recently purchased.

Jones

198. Memorandum From the Assistant Secretary of State for Far Eastern Affairs (Robertson) to Acting Secretary of State Dillon

Washington, May 7, 1959.

SUBJECT

Political Developments in Indonesia

In view of significant political developments impending in Indonesia, the present situation in that country is discussed in a paper at Tab A, which may be summarized as follows: On April 22, President Sukarno formally proposed, in his own name and that of the Indonesian Government, that Indonesia return to its 1945 Constitution in order to (1) rekindle the revolutionary fervor and unity of that year when independence was proclaimed and (2) stabilize Indonesian Government and politics through "guided democracy". The 1945 Constitution (Tab B) envisages a strong executive in contrast to the present parliamentary system which has proved unstable over the past ten years.

The next few weeks are likely to be marked by political tension in Indonesia as the President's proposal is debated in the Constituent Assembly by representatives of the political parties. Inasmuch as "guided democracy" is designed in part to reduce the importance and power of the parties in the Indonesian political system, the parties are reluctant to accept the scheme. On the other hand, they are also reluctant to oppose Sukarno with his great popular prestige. They must consider as well the extreme but real possibility that the Army might impose a less welcome form of "guided democracy" should the parties fail to accept the President's proposal voluntarily.

Our Embassy reports that the Constituent Assembly probably will accept the 1945 Constitution but that some of the parties may seek to amend it and thus cause an impasse in the Assembly. The Army is reported to be prepared to force approval of the President's proposal if necessary, in the interest of ending the chaotic political situation that has fostered the growth of Communist Party (PKI) strength during the past few years.

The U.S. Departments of State and Defense are exploring possible means of accelerating delivery of arms to Indonesia under our military assistance program, in response to requests from highly-placed Indonesian Army officers that we speed up deliveries and thereby strengthen the Army's position both psychologically and materially in the present delicate situation.

Source: Department of State, Central Files, 756D.00/5–759. Secret. Drafted by Moore on May 5 and cleared with O'Sullivan and Palmer. Both tabs are in the Supplement.

199.   Memorandum From the Assistant Secretary of State for Far Eastern Affairs (Robertson) to Acting Secretary of State Dillon

Washington, May 15, 1959.

SUBJECT

Indonesia: Developments Affecting Foreign Oil Companies

1.   The Draft Petroleum Law

After a long period of delay the Indonesian cabinet recently presented to Parliament a draft petroleum law which includes features considered to be inimical to the operations of the three major foreign oil companies in Indonesia: CALTEX Pacific Oil Company, Standard-Vacuum Oil Company, and Royal Dutch/Shell. Some of the basic features, such as primary dependence on governmental and mixed companies for the development of oil resources, stem from philosophies now prevailing in Indonesia, and objection to those aspects of the legislation will undoubtedly be unavailing. There has, however, been some feeling among the oil companies that certain features of the bill should be the subject of protest. These features are:

(1) The duration of concessions, which will be shorter (30 years plus extension) for private companies than for mixed companies (40 years plus extension).
(2) The non-deductibility of royalties from taxable income.
(3) The requirement that 20 percent of refining, storage and transportation capacity be made available for government use at request.
(4) The transitional provision for current concessions which requires current holders to conform to the new law within two years with the possibility of a year's extension. This feature, incorporated in Article 41, is regarded as a violation of the principle of sanctity of contracts. STANVAC in particular is disturbed by this provision.
(5) The requirement that foreign companies must incorporate under the laws of Indonesia rather than simply register to do business in Indonesia and the requirement that the majority of the Board of Directors of the oil companies be Indonesians.

Approaches to the Indonesian Government

The question of official representation, either by the United States alone or jointly with the United Kingdom and France has been raised. Contrary to the comment attributed to Mr. Wilkinson in London's 5868

Source: Department of State, Central Files, 856D.2553/6–1559. Confidential. Drafted by Olmsted on May 14 and cleared with SPA, SPA/E, FE, and FSD.

(Tab A)[1] both CALTEX and STANVAC have indicated to the Embassy that they strongly oppose the idea of a joint governmental approach on the grounds that it would arouse Indonesian antagonism and do more harm than good (Tab B). Ambassador Jones has likewise indicated his opposition to the idea of a joint approach. He has recommended that he approach the Prime Minister and Acting Foreign Minister by himself but not on a formal basis. He also suggested the possibility that the British Ambassador might do likewise.

Both STANVAC and Shell were requested by the GOI to submit their views on the proposed legislation and both did so (Tab C). CALTEX was not asked to submit its views but after some consideration of the subject decided to do so without being requested. CALTEX believes that strong protests against the legislation would tend to force the present Parliament to take action now, whereas in the absence of pressure, Parliamentary action might be deferred until after the adoption of the 1945 Constitution.

In view of the sensitivities of the Indonesians regarding any indication of foreign intervention, and in view of the possibility that the passage of the petroleum bill may be considerably delayed by internal political factors, we believe that any United States approach regarding the petroleum legislation should be made informally by the Embassy in Djakarta and not in conjunction with the approach of any other Government.

2.   *Cancellation of Existing Mining Rights*

The bill providing for the cancellation of inactive mining rights, which was passed by Parliament on February 4, provides an escape clause by which the Minister of Industries is given the discretion to make exceptions to the law. Although the oil companies view this law as being detrimental to their best interests, it is believed that formal official representation against the law would be counterproductive because of Indonesian sensitivities. We feel that the best approach would be for the oil companies to seek exceptions as needed, but if official representation is found to be appropriate, it should be handled informally.

Tab D provides an indication of the importance of the oil companies to the Indonesian economy.

---

[1] Telegram 5868, May 7, reported that the Embassy in London was recently informed by a representative of the Foreign Office that the Foreign Office was still considering whether the United Kingdom should proceed alone with representations to the Indonesian Government about the draft petroleum bill. The representative also stated that Wilkinson of Shell Oil had seen Dillon and explained Shell's attitude toward the pending law and the fact that both STANVAC and CALTEX also favored joint protests. (*Ibid.*, 856D.2553/5–758) See Supplement. No tabs were attached to the source text.

200. Letter From the Permanent Representative to the North Atlantic Council (Burgess) to the Assistant Secretary of State for Far Eastern Affairs (Robertson)

Paris, May 18, 1959.

DEAR WALTER: I have been giving further thought to the problem of supplying arms to Indonesia which we discussed in Washington in April,[1] and believe it might be helpful to put some of my ideas on paper.

We have two responsibilities here in this matter. One is to execute U.S. policy as effectively and persuasively as possible. The other is to reflect to the Department our own best thinking as a contribution to continuing policy formation. For both these duties I found the talks with you very helpful. This letter is addressed to the second purpose.

We and our NATO Allies recognize the importance of trying to keep Indonesia out of the Communist camp, though there are differing opinions as to the value of arms deliveries for this purpose. I welcome evidence on this score which we can give our colleagues. I do not underestimate this. Arms are often the surest road to the hearts of generals.

It is also essential in our long range policy that we consider the effects of this program on NATO.

From our conversations here, we believe that what the Dutch, and others, are worrying about are three things:

First, that, following the lead of the U.S., other countries will find it impossible to resist commercial pressures to sell arms to Indonesia (a fear that is now being shown to be well founded) and that the cumulative total of military equipment from all sources, both East and West, will give such a degree of strength to Indonesia as to tempt them, at some propitious moment to undertake some kind of military exploit against West New Guinea either openly or under the guise of protecting the Indonesians there.

Second, they are concerned that public pressures at home, in light of this growing Indonesian military strength, may lead to a demand for reinforcing the defense of West New Guinea at the expense of the Dutch contribution to the NATO defense effort in arms, money, and men.

Third, they are concerned at the psychological effect on the whole NATO Alliance, which is the cornerstone of Dutch foreign policy and defense policy, lest public reaction against sales to Indonesia by NATO Allies should be transformed into a real breach with Western Allies.

These three problems, we must agree, are real political problems to which our policy affords no clean answer. We have not given a binding

---

Source: Department of State, Central Files, 756D.56/5–1859. Secret.

[1] No record of this discussion was found in Department of State files.

security commitment to intervene in the event of Indonesian attack on West New Guinea. It is therefore difficult to count on the extent to which the Dutch will be able to satisfy criticism at home by referring to the statements we have made to Sukarno that we would be in opposition to any such move.

Whether or not the Dutch could adequately reinforce their forces in West New Guinea to hold it against an Indonesian assault, or provide adequate protection to their nationals there, the emotional and political pressures on the Dutch Government to make a show in this direction are great. And if substantial reinforcements are sent, as the Dutch have said, it is doubtful that the Netherlands Parliament would vote additional funds to replace the forces that the Netherlands would withdraw from NATO to serve that end. The NATO defense effort would, in political fact, have to foot the bill because Dutch public opinion will hold its NATO Allies in large part responsible for having created this problem.

This is where we have serious problems. The Dutch have been one of the stoutest of our Allies, providing on an outstanding scale the great part of their NATO military requirements. In the political area, the Dutch have taken a sound, practical, tough line against all of the traps the Communists attempt to set in order to destroy NATO. It would have a serious effect on the Alliance should a change of policy result in a diminution of the Dutch defense effort or a change in Dutch attitude towards NATO unity and toughness. We would indeed be losing a leader in the cause we serve, and I fear that there might be other waverers that would use the Dutch example to reduce their defense effort or to vary their policy. I think we can reduce the dangers in this situation in several ways:

1. We should lend an attentive ear to the Dutch request to purchase further military equipment at "surplus" prices.
2. We should limit further sales to Indonesia especially of arms of an offensive character.
3. I think very frankly we can be more forthcoming in dealing with the Dutch than we have been in the past. Granted that they are hypersensitive and granted that they have their own goals in mind, I think we can be a little more considerate in dealing with them in the future. We have now made our position clear, and although it makes them squirm they know what it is. I would urge that in the future we make every effort to advise them *in advance* of the issuance of license for export and *in advance* of the conclusion of sales agreements. I know that the Indonesians are also sensitive, and that if they thought Dutch agreement was involved in our actions, the goal of the program would be jeopardized. But the Dutch can be trusted to keep a confidence for the maybe forty-eight hours involved in advance notification. This would simply be following the accepted procedure for NATO consultation, which is followed in all areas.

I am sending a copy of this letter to Foy Kohler, in Livie Merchant's absence.

Sincerely,

Randy

---

201.   Telegram From the Embassy in Indonesia to the Department of State

Djakarta, May 21, 1959, 2 p.m.

3502. CINCPAC also for POLAD. For Robertson from Ambassador. As you are aware [*less than 1 line of source text not declassified*] Soviets laid on plush reception for Sukarno during his Russian visit[1] but nevertheless distinct coolness apparent between President and Khrushchev. This seems to me present US with opportunity to exploit by means of some warm personal gesture from US when Sukarno arrives Los Angeles.

Of course an informal invitation from President Eisenhower to spend a day at Camp David or Gettysburg would be the best possible means of accomplishing the objective of placing US-Indonesian relations on a close personal basis, which is the only basis which has much impact on Sukarno. At the same time it would play to his vanity, another essential in influencing him. Such tokens have more effect on Sukarno than more material fruits of friendship.

I recognize that time may be too short to arrange anything of this sort and might present precedent problems, but I can suggest two useful alternatives which would be for Vice President Nixon to visit California coincident with Sukarno's stay, with an informal meeting to be arranged as a consequence. Sukarno is a staunch admirer of the Vice President and any courtesy from him would have considerable effect.

Another possibility which I urge to be done in any event would be for President Eisenhower to send a wire to Sukarno at the time of his arrival in Los Angeles, welcoming him to the country and expressing a wish for a pleasant stay there and in Honolulu.

Source: Department of State, Central Files, 756D.11/5–2159. Confidential; Priority. Also sent to CINCPAC.

[1] Sukarno was in the Soviet Union May 7–12 as part of his world tour.

No doubt Sukarno's personal stock in Washington is at even a lower ebb than usual due to erratic performance during his trip. Nevertheless he continues to be the center of political gravity in Indonesia and we must hold his friendship if we are to achieve our objectives here, even if sometimes his visit be repugnant to us.

If, as seems possible, Sukarno arrives on American soil in a frame of mind antagonistic to the Soviet Union, the right human touch could do a great deal to nail down the improvement in US-Indonesian relations that already has taken place.[2]

Jones

---

[2] Telegram 2221 to Djakarta, May 29, explained that Nixon would be unable to visit California at the time of the Sukarno visit, but that Eisenhower had asked Secretary of Agriculture Ezra T. Benson to greet the Sukarno party upon the Indonesian President's arrival in Los Angeles, and Benson had agreed. It also noted that Benson would deliver a personal letter of welcome from Eisenhower to Sukarno and outlined Sukarno's schedule for his 3-day visit to Los Angeles. (Department of State, Central Files, 756D.11/5–2159) See Supplement. The Department transmitted the next of Eisenhower's May 30 letter to Sukarno to the Embassy in telegram 2242 to Djakarta, June 3. (Department of State, Central Files, 756D.11/6–359) See Supplement.

---

202.   Despatch From the Embassy in Indonesia to the Department of State

No. 904   Djakarta, May 26, 1959.

SUBJECT

   The West New Guinea Dispute and United States Interests

Members of the Embassy Political Section have held a series of discussions over the past several months to consider the West New Guinea dispute in its various aspects and, in particular, to seek an answer to the following question:

Are the interests of the United States best served by our present policy toward the West New Guinea dispute, or would these interests best be served by a change of policy?

Source: Department of State, Central Files, 656.56D13/5–2659. Secret. Drafted by Edward C. Ingraham, Second Secretary of the Embassy.

The Political Counselor and the other officers of the Section have jointly come to the following conclusions as a result of these discussions and of independent study of the question raised therein:

1. Present American policy toward the West New Guinea dispute—that of recognizing the existence of the dispute while neither taking sides nor making positive efforts to effect a solution—has in all probability best served the interests of the United States in the past.
2. In the light of the changing situation in Indonesia, the other countries of Southeast Asia, and the Netherlands, this policy is less likely to serve the interests of the United States in the future, and may well operate to the increasing detriment of those interests.
3. The United States should now abandon its present policy toward the West New Guinea problem in favor of a policy of actively seeking a solution to the dispute.
4. To have a prospect of success, any solution must contain provision for eventual relinquishment of Dutch control over West New Guinea and the eventual attainment of at least partial control over the territory by the Indonesian government.

The remainder of this despatch consists of a brief survey of the background of the West New Guinea dispute and a discussion of the various factors which led to the foregoing conclusions. In a despatch immediately following, the Embassy presents a specific proposal for settlement of the West New Guinea dispute.[1]

[Here follows the remainder of the despatch; see Supplement.]

_____

[1] Document 203.

_____

203.   Despatch From the Embassy in Indonesia to the Department of State

No. 905   Djakarta, May 26, 1959.

REF

Embassy Despatch No. 904 of May 26, 1959

SUBJECT

A Proposal for Settlement of the West New Guinea Dispute

_____

Source: Department of State, Central Files, 656.56D13/5–2659. Secret. Drafted by Ingraham. Jones transmitted despatches 904 (Document 202) and 905 in despatch 925, June 1, which reported his concurrence with the conclusions and recommendations reported therein. He concluded: "Our position of neutrality has served its purpose. It is time we developed a formula to remove this major irritant to Indonesian relations with the West." (Department of State, Central Files, 656.56D13/6–1550)

In Despatch No. 904 the Embassy submitted a recommendation that the United States abandon its present policy toward the dispute between Indonesia and the Netherlands over West New Guinea in favor of a policy of actively seeking a solution to the dispute.

In this despatch the Embassy submits a specific proposal for settlement of the West New Guinea dispute, including both a formula for settlement and a suggested method to be followed in obtaining approval of the formula by the two disputants. In summary, the two-part formula envisages (1) a special United Nations trusteeship over the territory for a limited number of years, at the end of which time sovereignty would be turned over to Indonesia, and (2) a bilateral agreement between Indonesia and the Netherlands providing for the payment by Indonesia of adequate compensation for seized Dutch assets and the removal of discriminatory restrictions against Dutch nationals. Steps to effect the settlement would be inaugurated by a General Assembly resolution calling on the two sides to negotiate the dispute, thereby giving the United States an opening to convince both sides to accept the proposed formula.

Part I—The Formula for Settlement

A satisfactory settlement of the West New Guinea dispute is possible only if each disputant receives what it considers to be substantial compensation from the other in return for concessions offered. The elements for mutual compensation can be found in (1) the Indonesian demand for sovereignty over West New Guinea, and (2) the Dutch demands for adequate compensation for Dutch assets seized by Indonesia and for the elimination of Indonesian discrimination against Dutch business, cultural entities, language, etc. A two-part settlement, accordingly, is required, one part covering sovereignty over West New Guinea and the other compensation for Dutch assets. The mutual lack of trust felt by both participants to the dispute makes it necessary that both parts of the settlement come into effect simultaneously, that each part be brought to completion at about the same time, and that execution of the two parts be linked. This can be accomplished through (1) a special United Nations trusteeship which would assume sovereignty over West New Guinea for five years, at the end of which period sovereignty would be transferred to Indonesia if certain conditions were met, and (2) a bilateral agreement between Indonesia and the Netherlands, by which the former agrees to the payment in installments of adequate compensation for seized Dutch assets, and further agrees to the progressive removal of discriminatory restrictions on Dutch enterprises in Indonesia.

A. *The United Nations Trusteeship*

A three-nation trusteeship, to include the Netherlands, Indonesia and a third power, would be established by the General Assembly and given the following terms of reference: To administer the trust territory of West New Guinea for a period of five years and to take measures during this period to effect the orderly transfer of sovereignty over the territory to Indonesia, the Dutch administering power to utilize this period to effect the withdrawal of its prior administrative apparatus, and the Indonesian administering power to utilize this period in making necessary preparations for the assumption of sovereignty. Transfer of sovereignty would be postponed if, at the end of five years, (a) the trustees were unanimously agreed that preparations were not complete, or (b) the United Nations made a finding that such transfer would, under then existing conditions, be a threat to world peace.

The trusteeship would operate under the following general and specific conditions:

1. The administering powers will take over the administration of West New Guinea from the Netherlands government one year after passage of the resolution establishing the trusteeship. (*Comment:* The one-year interval is necessary to allow the Netherlands time to amend its constitution to permit a transfer of sovereignty and to give both countries an opportunity to conclude a bilateral compensation agreement.)

2. Administration of the territory will be placed in the hands of a commission consisting of two members appointed by each of the three administering powers plus one ethnic Papuan member representing the West New Guinea populace, the latter selected by majority vote of the other members of the commission. Decisions of the commission will be by majority vote.

3. The commission will appoint subordinate civil officials to operate the various administrative, security and welfare bureaus of the territorial government. At the outset these subordinate officials will be the Dutch incumbents. In making subsequent appointments the commission will draw up and will follow a schedule by which Dutch officials are progressively replaced by Indonesian nationals and ethnic Papuans over a period of four years. At the end of a four-year period, subordinate administrative personnel will be entirely Indonesian/Papuan. All subordinate officials appointed by the commission must have the approval of at least one of the two Indonesian members.

4. The commission will establish training schools, provide for on-the-job training, and make available other necessary facilities for training Indonesian nationals and ethnic Papuans in the various branches of civil administration, security, welfare and health services, etc.

5. At the end of five years the Dutch and Indonesian members of the commission will report to the commission the satisfactory conclusion of measures undertaken by prior agreement of the two powers to adjust the status of Dutch nationals and of Dutch business and cultural enterprises in West New Guinea and in Indonesia. Upon the receipt of such a report, the commission will surrender its responsibility for administration of the territory to the Indonesian government except in case of postponement as noted above.

6. If such a report by the Indonesian and Dutch members is not forthcoming at the end of five years, the commission will continue to administer the territory until such time as the Indonesian and Dutch members report agreement over the future status of the territory.

7. All expenses incurred by the commission will be borne by the Dutch and Indonesian governments, each paying an equal portion thereof.

The identity of the third nation of the trusteeship would be subject to certain limiting criteria: It should not be one of the former colonies or strong anti-colonialists among the Afro-Asian states, any of whom would be considered by the Dutch as unduly favorable to Indonesian interests; to meet similar Indonesian sensitivities, it should not be either a Western European nation or Australia; it should not be Japan because of its wartime association with West New Guinea; and, in our interests, it obviously must not be a Soviet bloc country.

The United States itself is an obvious candidate for the third trust power. This may, however, be inadvisable. The third trust power will, in effect, be the actual governing power in West New Guinea during the trust period, and will be in the position—particularly during the earlier years—of deciding between opposing Dutch and Indonesian views. Its decisions may at times create strong reactions in the Netherlands and, especially Indonesia. As the United States is already labeled as the chief external enemy by Indonesian leftists, it appears unwise to place us in a position whereby we will provide a standing target for communist propaganda and agitation for five years, particularly as the PKI would use our inevitable "adverse" decisions on the commission to drum up support among other nationalist groups for its anti-American campaign. A further consideration is that United States participation in the trusteeship would bring forth the most strenuous efforts by the Soviet bloc to frustrate its establishment and defeat its objectives. Soviet opposition to the trusteeship can be expected in any event, but its intensity would be increased by direct American participation therein.

The most suitable third power in the trusteeship, accordingly, is one relatively remote from the dispute and one belonging neither to Afro-Asia, Western Europe or the Soviet bloc. Among countries meeting these specifications, the most appropriate may be: Turkey, Mexico, Canada.

B. *The Compensation Agreement*

At the time the General Assembly passes a resolution establishing the trusteeship, Indonesia and the Netherlands would initiate bilateral negotiations leading to treaty or other form of agreement covering (1) the payment of compensation for Dutch enterprises seized by Indonesia, (2) the elimination of discriminatory restrictions on Dutch commercial and cultural activities in Indonesia, (3) the status of Dutch interests in West New Guinea at the conclusion of the trusteeship period, and (4) the re-establishment of normal trade and consular relations between the two countries.

Points two, three and four could be handled in a relatively simple manner by clauses extending to Dutch enterprises and Dutch nationals in all fields the same rights now enjoyed by the enterprises and nationals of other countries in Indonesia, and by an Indonesian commitment to revoke progressively all conflicting laws and regulations over a stated period of time.

The major point, that of compensation payments, presents more of a problem. The key to an ultimate solution would be mutual agreement on arbitration in all cases resulting in a deadlock. The exact formula by which a figure for compensation is reached in the case of individual enterprises might best be left up to the negotiators. Agreement on certain guide-lines, however, would be obtained from both sides as a part of the over-all West New Guinea settlement. They would include the following:

1. Acceptance of present market value as the criterion in fixing compensation.
2. Delegation of the task of setting actual compensation figures for individual enterprises to a binational commission of financial and economic experts, whose decisions would be final.
3. Establishment of a simple and specific procedure for submission to arbitration of those individual cases in which the binational commission is unable to reach agreement, the arbitrator or arbitrators to be designated in advance. (*Comment:* A special arbitration board with, perhaps, a Malayan as the chief figure might be the best arbitration procedure, but this would be decided by the principals.)
4. Once a specific compensation figure is set for each individual enterprise, a schedule of installment payments would be drawn up in such a manner that the final payment coincides with the termination of the trusteeship over West New Guinea.

Part II—The Method for Obtaining Settlement

In attempting to bring about a settlement of the West New Guinea dispute, the United States faces a particular problem in that the current intransigence of both participants all but precludes a direct approach to either. Should the United States approach either side directly with the foregoing proposal, we lay ourselves open to the charge that we are promoting the surrender of what that side considers its just and inalienable right. To avoid this danger the Embassy suggests the following course, admittedly tortuous but with greater prospects of success:

1.   A resolution would be submitted to the General Assembly calling upon both the Netherlands and Indonesia to undertake further negotiations toward settlement of the West New Guinea dispute and related issues, its text carefully drafted to show complete impartiality toward both sides. It would not be introduced or sponsored by the United States but by a group of non-European states. Among likely candidates are the Philippines, Malaya, Japan, Mexico, Argentina, and Brazil—the last particularly useful because its sponsorship would indicate wider support for the resolution than was received by the 1957 resolution.

2.   While the resolution is pending in the General Assembly, the United States would approach the Dutch government. Pointing out that the resolution appears to have a good chance of passage and that we will find it difficult to recommend that friendly non-European members abstain, we would take the opportunity to suggest that the time had come for a re-examination of the entire West New Guinea issue as it affects our mutual interests in Indonesia and NATO. We would then put forth the most persuasive arguments for a final settlement of the dispute in accordance with the formula described in Part I, ultimately presenting the Dutch with the formula itself for study. We would assure the Dutch that, should the formula be acceptable to them, we would make a major effort to induce the Indonesians to accept it, to the extent of applying quiet pressure if necessary.

3.   Should the Dutch reply that their internal political balance or the temper of their populace precludes the voluntary surrender of sovereignty over West New Guinea, we would then propose the following: that the Dutch vote against the pending General Assembly resolution and attempt through other public means to defeat it; if the resolution passes despite their efforts, that they then announce their reluctant decision, as loyal members of the United Nations, to accede to the demand for negotiations notwithstanding their opposition to it. The formula could then be represented as the best obtainable under the circumstances.

4.   While the formula is being discussed with the Dutch, the United States would also approach the Indonesian government. Pointing out that passage of the pending General Assembly resolution would be assured by our open or tacit support, we would affirm our interest in finding a solution to the West New Guinea dispute and our conviction that both sides must accept a compromise. We would then put forth a sug-

gestion for settlement in accordance with the formula, making the point that any other course on which they may embark to obtain West New Guinea would in all likelihood take them at least the five years envisaged in the formula. We would assure the Indonesians that, should the formula be acceptable to them, we would make a major effort to induce the Dutch to accept it, to the extent of applying quiet pressure if necessary.

5. (a) Should both the Dutch and the Indonesians signify general agreement with the terms of the proposed formula, the West New Guinea resolution would come before the General Assembly and be passed with United States support.

(b) Should the formula be definitely rejected by either side or by both, the United States would abstain on the resolution, making no effort either to aid or to block passage. This eventuality would mark the defeat, for the time being, of our attempt to achieve settlement of the dispute, but the proposal would be in the hands of both governments for later second thoughts.

6. Should the settlement pass the stage described in 5 (a), we would suggest a conference of Dutch and Indonesian officials at the Prime Minister or Foreign Minister level at a neutral site—preferably Washington—where they would agree formally to the proposal, petition the General Assembly to undertake action on the trusteeship agreement, and set the time and place for the beginning of negotiations toward drawing up the compensation agreement. The United States would assist informally at this conference but would have no official role.

Conclusion

As stated in Despatch No. 904, the Embassy believes the foregoing proposal for settlement of the West New Guinea dispute to be feasible and to avoid certain of the pitfalls which otherwise will threaten United States efforts to solve the issue. Should this particular proposal be found impractical by the Department, however, the Embassy strongly recommends that steps be taken as soon as possible to draft an alternative proposal.

For the Ambassador:
John W. Henderson
Counselor of Embassy
for Political Affairs

204.   Editorial Note

On May 29 the United States and Indonesia concluded an agreement under Title I of Public Law 480 by which the United States agreed to provide Indonesia with approximately $40.3 million of wheat, cotton, rice, and nonfat dry powdered milk. The agreement, which was signed in Djakarta by Ambassador Jones and Acting Foreign Minister Hardi, entered into force that same day; for text, see 10 UST 1079. Documentation on the negotiations leading up to the agreement is in Department of State, Central File 411.56D41.

205.   Memorandum of Conversation

Washington, June 5, 1959.

SUBJECT

Current Political Developments in Indonesia

PARTICIPANTS

Mr. Robertson, Assistant Secretary for Far Eastern Affairs
Mr. Parsons, Deputy Assistant Secretary for Far Eastern Affairs
Mr. Mein, Director, Office of Southwest Pacific Affairs

Dr. Subandrio, Indonesian Foreign Minister[1]
Ambassador Mukarto of Indonesia

The Minister said he welcomed the opportunity to see Mr. Robertson for a general exchange of information and to reassure himself that as a result of the Secretary's resignation and death[2] and of Mr. Robertson's departure from the Department, there would be no change

---

Source: Department of State, Central Files, 756D.00/6–559. Official Use Only. Drafted by Mein.

[1] During his 2-day visit to Washington, Subandrio, who had been traveling with Sukarno on the President's worldwide tour, also met with Acting Secretary of State Dillon. They discussed current political developments in Indonesia, the security of U.S. rubber estates in Sumatra, Indonesian purchase of KPM ships, and Export-Import Bank and DLF loans to Indonesia. Separate memoranda of these conversations, drafted by Mein, are *ibid.*, 756.00/6–559, 856D.2395/6–559, 756D.5621/6–559, and 856D.10/6–559, respectively. See Supplement for all.

[2] Dulles died on May 24.

in our policy toward Indonesia. He said that he and his Government regretted Mr. Robertson's departure but welcomed the appointment of Mr. Parsons.[3] The Minister said further that upon the receipt of the news of the Secretary's death, President Sukarno had said that although in many things he disagreed with the former Secretary, he would be greatly missed, especially since it was always known where the Secretary stood and he could be relied upon. Mr. Robertson assured the Minister there would be no change in our policy as a result of the changes.

Mr. Robertson said that we were glad that President Sukarno had come back to visit the United States and he hoped that the visit to Los Angeles had gone well. The Minister expressed his appreciation for the way the Los Angeles visit had been handled. He said that President Sukarno now has a grasp of the problems of Indonesia [*the United States*?] and of details which he previously did not have and that this is bound to have a more definite impact on the policy of the Government of Indonesia. The visit to the various countries had therefore been very useful for the President.

Mr. Robertson asked the Minister to comment, if he would, on the recent developments in Indonesia. The Minister said that when President Sukarno left Indonesia in late April on his present tour, the assumption had been that the Assembly would adopt the 1945 Constitution. The political parties had agreed to the return to the 1945 Constitution last February. The only exceptions expected then were the PSI and the Masjumi. The PKI also had some doubts as to the desirability of returning to the 1945 Constitution although for its own purposes it was giving the Constitution its support in the Assembly. At a Cabinet meeting on February 19, the NU had agreed to support the adoption of the Constitution and it was expected until the last moment that they would do so. The position taken by the NU in the Assembly therefore had come as a surprise to both Djuanda and Nasution. The change in the NU position was due primarily to the absence of Chalid from the country immediately prior to the voting. The Minister said that it is debatable whether a two-thirds majority is necessary in such a case or whether a simple majority can approve the return to the 1945 Constitution. The Assembly will now go into recess with the vote not being considered final and will await the return of President Sukarno. Instructions were sent to Djakarta to keep the situation calm and to limit political activities. In the meantime the present Government will stay in power. President Sukarno is confident that he can solve the problem even if a compromise is necessary on the Djakarta Charter.

---

[3] Parsons was appointed to succeed Robertson as Assistant Secretary of State for Far Eastern Affairs on June 5. Robertson resigned on June 30 and Parsons became Assistant Secretary the following day.

The Minister said that President Sukarno is determined to return to the 1945 Constitution and to direct the Government himself. The President is more than ever convinced he wants to get definite results for the people and feels that the country has been experimenting too much already. The President and the Indonesians are proud that to date they have kept the country from disintegration. Mr. Robertson commented that the Indonesians do indeed have a great deal to be proud of and have achieved a great deal in the short period since their independence.

The trip to Latin America and to the United States has been inspiring and helpful. The Minister said he feels that as a result, President Sukarno should visit the United States each year in order to see the situation in this country as it really is. The President has an image of the United States which is different from the actual situation. Indonesia has developed to such a point, the Minister said, that no ideological or military dictatorship would be possible. Only a Sukarno dictatorship would be possible, but the President has repeatedly refused to assume such powers in the past.

Mr. Robertson again referred to the progress made in Indonesia. He commented that he can easily understand the impatience of Asians for improving their standard of living, adding that he is always impressed by what has been accomplished in Asia in just a few years.

Mr. Robertson said that we have been very pleased at our improving relations and that we are especially happy to have Ambassador Jones, who understands and likes Indonesians, in Djakarta. The Ambassador and the United States Government, he said, both wish to improve U.S.-Indonesian relations. The Minister said that President Sukarno is very fond of Ambassador Jones, not only as the representative of the United States but as a personal friend.

---

206. **Letter From the Assistant Secretary of State for Far Eastern Affairs (Robertson) to the Permanent Representative to the North Atlantic Council (Burgess)**

Washington, June 12, 1959.

DEAR RANDY: I appreciate the thoughts which you have set forth in your letter of May 18, 1959 on our Indonesian arms program and its effect on our relations with the Netherlands and on the NATO Alliance.[1]

Source: Department of State, Central Files, 756D.56/5–1859. Secret. Drafted by Wenzel on June 2 and cleared by Mein and Parsons.

[1] Document 200.

We have, as you know, thoroughly reviewed a number of these points during our discussions here in April, and I shall not comment again on all of them in detail at this time. As for responding to your points concerning the Dutch contribution to NATO and the psychological effects on the Alliance, I shall defer to EUR. I would, however, like to offer a few selected views, some of which I have voiced before but which bear repeating.

Concerning the current Dutch concern over increased Western arms sales to Indonesia, recent reports from Paris and other European posts indeed indicate a pick-up in such sales. I do not, however, regard this as an unfavorable development as far as our policy toward Indonesia and the achievement of free world objectives in that country are concerned. While these sales are perhaps substantially the result of commercial pressures, they may also in part reflect a growing confidence in Indonesia's future on the part of these suppliers. I believe this is particularly true in the case of the United Kingdom. The participation of Western countries as suppliers to Indonesia in effect tends to broaden the base of free world influence there, which is much to be desired from our point of view. [*2-1/2 lines of source text not declassified*]

At no time during the discussions here over the past several months did we envisage that other free world countries would not furnish some arms to Indonesia. You will recall, I am sure, that the "sole supplier" concept (the United States alone or in concert with one or more other countries) of arms deliveries to Indonesia was firmly rejected by the Department. I might add that some of these countries which have recently announced their intention of furnishing arms to Indonesia are historical suppliers of Indonesia's military requirements over the past several years.

I do not believe that the present flurry of Western arms sales to Indonesia can be considered unrestrained [*2 lines of source text not declassified*]. Furthermore, the weak Indonesian foreign exchange position is, I believe, a built-in restraint against promiscuous purchasing from Western sources.

But more important—and I cannot make this point more forcefully—a denial of Western sources of military equipment for Indonesia will lead to Indonesia's turning completely to the bloc for these requirements. Since the beginning of 1958, Indonesia has purchased about $250 million of foreign arms, about three-quarters of which are coming from the bloc. Given this current imbalance and the possibility of continued Indonesian purchases from the bloc, I do not believe that we can reasonably say that continued moderate Western arms shipments will do much to tip the scales in favor of an Indonesian military action against West New Guinea. Military shipments by the United States and other free world countries to Indonesia have afforded the free world a foothold in Indonesia through which we have been able to exercise a considerable deterrent to any Indonesian aggressive action against West New Guinea. The removal of this free world foothold would weaken the deterrent and could easily open the way for a Communist-inspired drive against that island.

As for your suggestions on ways to reduce the dangers in this situation, I would offer the following views:

1) FE has posed no objection to Dutch purchases of United States military equipment at "surplus" prices provided in any such transaction it is not stated that such equipment is for use in West New Guinea. I do, however, continue to have serious reservations about the desirability (and the real necessity) of a large influx of United States arms into West New Guinea and the real possibility that this could undermine our accomplishments to date in Indonesia and create further tensions between the Indonesians and the Dutch which could readily lead to the precise incident which the Dutch fear.

2) As you know, our present military program to Indonesia is on a "limited and continuing" basis contingent on future developments in Indonesia. However, in the event of some markedly favorable change in Indonesia in the coming months (or even years), I would not rule out the possibility that we might wish to consider a substantial increase in the present limited level of our assistance. As for what are and are not "offensive" weapons, I am sure you are aware of the difficulty in trying to arrive at an acceptable definition of this term. There comes to mind the recent Danish decision to furnish 5,000 machine guns to Indonesia to which the Dutch offered no objection. In the view of some "military experts" machine guns might be considered considerably more "offensive"—as regards possible use in West New Guinea—than, for example, a World War II subchaser which the Dutch apparently consider in the "offensive" category.

3) Finally, I would not agree with you that we have not been adequately forthcoming in dealing with the Dutch. We have informed them in advance of our government-to-government sales and of the more significant export licenses issued. This is, of course, primarily Livie Merchant's concern, but I cannot help but feel that in our sometimes precipitous and "bits and pieces" notifications to the Dutch, we have perhaps inadvertently tended to play up our arms deliveries to Indonesia out of all proportion to their significance, which has only led to increasing Dutch concern. Advance notification to the Dutch on the issuance of all export licenses would, I am afraid, only worsen this situation. For your information, over the past year we issued approximately 140 export licenses for shipments of Munitions List items to Indonesia—everything from a few dollars worth of aircraft parts to the ten C–130B's. We have, in fact, issued hundreds of such licenses for Indonesia since

1950. Advance notification to the Dutch, in addition to the problem of overemphasis cited above, would be a highly impractical operation. I also have my doubts whether such detailed involvement of another country in the United States Government's licensing operation would be desirable or appropriate.

I have tried to address myself frankly to the above problems and offer you my honest views on them. I am convinced that our present policy toward Indonesia is the correct one and the one most likely to lead to a realization of our objectives there. Progress over the past year has been heartening and there is a good prospect of additional gains although we cannot expect miracles overnight. Progress in countries such as Indonesia is better measured over a period of years or even decades rather than weeks or months. At the same time I wish to assure you that we in FE are most cognizant of the difficulties in NATO over this question of arms deliveries to Indonesia and I hope that we will continue to have the benefit of your helpful counsel in this matter.

I am sending copies of this letter to Foy Kohler.

Sincerely yours,

Walter S. Robertson[2]

------

[2] Printed from a copy that bears this typed signature.

------

207. **Memorandum From the Director of the Office of Southwest Pacific Affairs (Mein) to the Assistant Secretary of State for Far Eastern Affairs (Robertson)**

Washington, June 17, 1959.

SUBJECT

Attached Paper on Indonesian Foreign Policy Reappraisal

The attached memorandum was prepared by Frank Underhill at my request at the time he left the Indonesian Desk. Due to illness, however, he was not able to complete it until recently. I think you will find it of considerable interest in view of his long experience in Indonesia and on the desk.

Source: Department of State, SPA Files: Lot 62 D 409, General. Confidential. Also sent to Parsons and Marshall Green. All recipients initialed the memorandum indicating they had read the attached paper. Green wrote: "Well worth reading. Right to the point." Parsons wrote: "This is a fine paper—let's keep it handy. 7/12/59"

Attachment[1]

INDONESIAN FOREIGN POLICY REAPPRAISAL

Despite chronic internal political crises, continuing Cabinet changes, and eight Foreign Ministers in as many years, Indonesian foreign policy has been remarkably constant. Since independence, the Indonesian people and their governments have accepted as the foundation of their foreign policy a principle and a cause—non-involvement in either major power bloc and pursuit of Indonesia's claim to West New Guinea. Further there can be no doubt that Indonesia will in the future continue to press its irredentist claim and continue to pay lip service to an "active and independent" foreign policy. There is increasing evidence, however, that Indonesian leaders are beginning to question the adequacy of a policy dominated completely by the essentially negative concept of non-involvement and the obsessive quarrel with the Dutch over West Irian, and to weigh the relevance of this policy to the problems which their country must face in the Far East in the coming decades. The insistent question which has prompted this reappraisal seems clearly to be, "What and who is to stand between us and a militant and expansionist China?"

Without attempting to make a comprehensive list, the more obvious indications in recent months of this reappraisal have been:

1. Indonesia's relatively mild official position on the Taiwan crisis.

2. Statements of the Indonesian Foreign Minister to our Ambassador expressing concern over Communist China as an eventual threat to Indonesia. While to some degree self-serving, these statements echo others made by former Foreign Ministers, especially Sunario to Ambassador Cumming.

3. Subandrio's trip to Australia.

4. Actions against the Chinese. While Indonesian Government repressive measures have been directed against Chinese associated with the KMT, our Embassy has pointed out that these actions have been part of a general movement against *all* Chinese. The Indonesian military, and to a lesser degree the civil leaders, have long shown concern over the potential fifth column danger of Indonesia's relatively small, but strategically placed, Chinese minority.

The reasons for this gradual focusing of attention on Communist China as an Indonesian security problem are equally evident. A steady stream of Indonesians have returned from China impressed by the militant dynamism of the CPR. A series of events over the past three or four

---

[1] Drafted by Underhill on June 11.

years: Dien Bien Phu, the Singapore riots, the Sino-Burmese border dispute, have had presumably a gradual cumulative effect. (This appraisal was written prior to the Tibet incident which undoubtedly has intensified considerably Indonesian doubts about the peaceful intentions of Communist China.) Perhaps most important of all is the probable influence of Indonesian military thinking. General Simatupang as far back as 1954 pointed out in his book "Pioneer in War, Pioneer in Peace" that Burma's security problem today will be Indonesia's tomorrow. Nasution in 1955 wrote that in terms of national self-defense Indonesia's cherished active and independent foreign policy was an unrealistic and potentially dangerous shibboleth, and implied clearly that China was the only significant external threat to Indonesia's national security. Indonesian military leaders have expressed privately these sentiments to American officials in even more explicit terms from 1951 to the present, and while again a desire to please American ears may have played some part, the statements were made with evident sincerity.

The Indonesian military is today exercising considerable influence in the political and economic sectors, and it seems logical to anticipate that Indonesia's foreign policy will also show, sooner or later, the influence of strongly held military views in this field.

Projecting this trend into the future, what is the probable direction of Indonesian foreign policy during the coming months and years?

We should anticipate, first, Indonesian efforts to strengthen its position with the major Pacific powers. The coming years should witness especially the development of much closer ties between Indonesia and Japan. Both countries have much to gain from such an association, economically as well as politically. World War II animosities and residual fears of repeated Japanese expansion to the south may delay this trend, but Japan and Indonesia are natural trading partners, and as the two major countries on China's eastern and southern periphery, they have a strong political interest in creating a counterforce to a strong China.

Similar factors should also bring about closer Australian-Indonesian relations. Despite the irritant of the New Guinea question, Australia has made a major effort through the Colombo Plan to assist in the establishment of a stable democratic Indonesia. These close Southeast Asian neighbors are faced by the same underlying military and strategic problem, and with the maturation of Indonesia's foreign policy outlook, even the New Guinea problem may come finally into proper prospective. Australia's security depends more, in the last analysis, on good relations with a democratic Indonesia than on Western control of West New Guinea. Indonesia, for its part, cannot afford an unfriendly southern neighbor.

For the present and foreseeable future, however, the only answer to Indonesia's question "What stands between us and China" is of course the United States. Indonesia has many reasons for maintaining good relations with the United States, but none more important than this one. An Indonesian diplomat once observed privately that he had read that it was initially the British fleet in the 19th Century that had made the Monroe Doctrine possible, and that it was the American fleet today that permitted Indonesia to have an "independent" foreign policy. We should therefore see increasing evidence of Indonesian desires to strengthen its relations with the United States.

The question arises of the influence of this trend on Indonesia's attitude towards SEATO. Paradoxically, the existence of SEATO may well have impeded the development of such a trend since SEATO has in Indonesian eyes a predominantly Western character, and, because of the membership of France and Great Britain, certain colonialist overtones. It appears logical to expect, therefore, continued Indonesian criticism of SEATO while Indonesia at the same time is working towards the same objective of a deterrent to Communist China.

It is clearly in the U.S. interest to follow closely any further signs of this foreign policy reappraisal, and to encourage discreetly such a trend. It is important, however, that we do not attempt to force Indonesia against its will into the broader aspects of the Asian anti-Communist movement. Any rapprochement between Indonesia and the Republic of China is highly unlikely, and close relations between Indonesia and the Republic of Korea are equally improbable. As noted above, Indonesia will continue to remain aloof from SEATO. We should also not expect Indonesia to take a forthright stand against international communism. The appeal of the active and independent foreign policy will remain strong, and Indonesia's policy reorientation, in its first phase at least, will be directed more against China as such rather than against communism.

If the foregoing analysis is valid, and this trend should develop, it would mark a welcomed maturing of Indonesia's international outlook and contribute materially to the attainment of free world objectives in the Far East.

U.S.-Indonesian Relations

Indonesian Attitudes towards the U.S.

Through the years since independence there has been generally convincing evidence that Indonesian policy towards the U.S. has been founded on a substantial basis of admiration, trust, respect, and considerable popular good will. The Indonesians know that the U.S. has no design on their territory and no desire to dominate Indonesia politically. They admire not only our material progress, but also our cultural life and educational system, and even some of our most vocal critics among them aspire to an American education for their children. They may differ strongly on certain aspects of our foreign policy, but they generally give us credit for honest motives.

Despite this significant area of understanding and sympathy, however, there are certain elements in the Indonesian image of the United States which hamper the growth of closer relations, and make it difficult for them to look wholeheartedly towards us for leadership. Indonesians find little if anything worth preserving in their pre-independence past. It represents to them domination, exploitation, and individual humiliation, and they continue even after independence in strong emotional rebellion against it. Further, the economic condition of the masses of the Indonesian people today does nothing to recommend the old economic order. The Indonesian, next to national independence, cherishes most the idea of industrial progress and economic development, and he is prepared to sacrifice much to achieve these goals. The United States, however, has come to be regarded as the principal defender of the status quo, insufficiently aware of and not entirely in sympathy with Indonesia's desire to break away from the past as sharply and as quickly as possible. They see us as a nation clinging to a moribund economic order and unwilling to take a clear and unequivocal stand on colonialism, and while grateful for our past, present, and future economic aid, they tend to see it motivated more by a desire to defend and preserve the old political and economic order than to help usher in the new. Repudiation of the past and a bright dream for the future account for much of the appeal of communism in Indonesia, but even those Indonesians who reject the Communists' claim that they are the wave of the future have not been able to find in our actions and statements any alternative which to them provides sufficiently bold and dynamic ideas and programs with which to attack the economic and social problems facing them. (This theme emerges frequently in Foreign Minister Subandrio's American Association speech early this year.)

There are certain aspects of U.S. life which adversely affect U.S.-Indonesian relations and which are not susceptible to rapid or easy change. Our race problem is perhaps the most notable in this category. The above noted image of the United States as a static, anti-progressive force, however, has been allowed to develop despite the facts in the case, and can be remedied not by more money for Indonesia, but by an effort to place our present aid to Indonesia and other underdeveloped countries in a different framework and context. It is difficult to define precisely the nature of this new context, but it should have the same elements of idealism, humanitarianism, boldness, and dynamism which existed in the original Marshall Plan, in Point Four, and—in the domestic sphere—in the New Deal. The irony of the situation is that we are and have been for some time embarked on such a program in Indonesia, but have not been able to present it in the philosophical and ideological framework which would bring the maximum return.

U.S. Policy towards Indonesia

Since 1952 U.S. policy towards Indonesia has been strongly influenced by our increasing concern over the growth in strength of the Indonesian Communist Party. Prior to 1955 non-Communist Indonesians, apprised of this concern, were prone to pooh-pooh the danger and brush our warnings aside as American anti-Communist emotionalism. However national elections in that year and Javanese provincial elections in 1957 proved to them all too clearly that our fears were well grounded. Despite this clear evidence of a progressively greater Communist threat, there appeared to be, however, no person or organization prepared to take forthright counter action, and we began to cast about with an increasing sense of urgency for some individual or movement that would assume this task. When those we had identified as anti-Communist—Hatta, the Sultan of Djokjakarta, Police Commissioner Sukanto—also refused to act, our feeling of desperation increased, and when the young colonels in December of 1956 repudiated the central government's authority we transferred to them our sympathy and hopes as the saviors of Indonesia.

In the cold light of hindsight there were several basic errors in our appraisal of the situation. We underestimated the strength of anti-Communist forces on Java that remained loyal to the central government, especially the army, and we overestimated both the military and political capabilities of the colonels to succeed in their challenge of central authority. If in February 1958, at the time of the PRRI ultimatum to the central government, an estimate had been required of the situation in Indonesia in February 1959 based on the premise of a quick and complete military defeat of the rebels, we could have predicted little less than an Indonesia hostile to the West and under more or less complete Communist domination. Instead we have a situation which while grave in many aspects is far better than anything we would have any right to expect if the best intelligence estimates of 1957 had been entirely valid. Finally, we overestimated the strength of anti-communism as a primary motivating and unifying factor among the various groups in armed opposition to the central government. The DI on Java and Celebes and the Atjehnese in North Sumatra were and are unquestionably anti-Communist. However, regional interests, personal rivalries, and religious differences proved to have greater strength than anti-Communist sentiment, and neither military support nor other diversionary activities were forthcoming during the PRRI's weeks of dire need. It is noteworthy that the Sulawesi wing of the PRRI did not begin its air attacks until after the fall of Padang, and that representatives of the Sulawesi leaders were in Washington early in 1958 expressing distrust of the Sumatran leaders and seeking to establish direct ties with the United States before the Sumatrans were able to do so.

From these developments certain general conclusions can be drawn:

1. Anti-communism is not in Indonesia, even among those strongly and sincerely professing such views, a primary and overriding motivating force. Rarely if ever are contemplated actions measured in the first instance in terms of the service or disservice they will do to the Communist cause, internally or externally. Nationalism, expressed either as loyalty to the nation or a region, religious ties, political party affiliations, and personal and family hostilities and friendships all clearly play a more important role.

2. We have been perhaps too inclined to view Indonesian public personalities as either heroes or villains, and to endow automatically those of known anti-Communist views with intelligence, maturity, political sagacity, and the other personal and political virtues. When these figures have disappointed us for one reason or another we tend to consign them to oblivion and look about for new champions. Our policy towards Indonesia has thus acquired on occasions a widely fluctuating character, appearing to swing from one extreme to another.

3. U.S. efforts to persuade Indonesia to check communism will be more successful if we give less emphasis on the direct frontal attack and attempt to turn the force of the stronger motivating forces cited above against the PKI. Nationalism is perhaps the strongest of these forces, and Communist strength in Indonesia will suffer most when Indonesians come to believe that communism is *anti-Indonesia*. There is evidence that this sentiment may already be developing and it is clearly in our interest to encourage its growth. We have been perhaps too much inclined to regard nationalism as a force working against Free World interests, and to ignore its potential as a weapon against Soviet-bloc interests.

208. Telegram From the Embassy in Indonesia to the Department of State

Djakarta, June 18, 1959, 5 p.m.

3776. DEPTAR for ACSI. CINCPAC also for POLAD. Deptel 1961.[1] Impasse produced in Constituent Assembly over GOI proposal return 1945 constitution differs only in sharpness of focus from fundamental impasse which has ripped Indonesian political life since independence. It boils down to fact that Moslem parties cannot govern Indonesia alone. No other parties or combination thereof can govern without support or at least acquiescence of Moslem parties.

Sukarno has regularly utilized this fact to help retain power in own hands, thus Indonesia traditionally has been able maintain effective government only through intervention Sukarno. Accordingly his absence now has brought Indonesian political leadership to almost complete road block, and there is no prospect stabilizing political situation until he returns.[2] Most serious consequence is lack of effective government to deal with deteriorating economic situation.

Whether or not this stalemate deliberately produced by army conniving with NU (and there is some evidence to suggest this) fact is that when confronted with opportunity to take strong measures in President's absence, Nasution has failed to move either through reluctance disrupt democratic process or fear of internal army divisions, probably latter. It is all the more certain that any moves that Nasution may ultimately make will be in the name of Sukarno, not against him. Conversely Sukarno unlikely able establish political stability functioning government without, at this stage, full support of the army.

While in past Indonesia has been able to afford political upheavals which have temporarily paralyzed central government, as is the case now, there is serious question whether current [upheaval?] may not result in permanent far-reaching damage to nation unless strong corrective action taken immediately upon Sukarno's return. This danger

---

Source: Department of State, Central Files, 756D.00/6–1859. Secret. Transmitted in two sections and also sent to the Department of the Army and CINCPAC.

[1] Telegram 1961, April 24, noted that the Department was following closely internal political developments in Indonesia as reported by the Embassy and the Army Attaché. "As and if situation begins to crystallize so that Embassy in position make more conclusive evaluation," the telegram reads in part, "Dept would require on priority basis any recommendations Embassy might make as to optimum US courses of action in this situation. Important that such recommendations be submitted in time to permit complete and careful review by all concerned here prior to formulating any decision on possible US action." (Ibid., 756D.00/4–2259)

[2] Sukarno was scheduled to return to Indonesia from his worldwide tour on June 28.

becoming acute now because of the rapidly deteriorating economic situation which may easily become extremely serious unless appropriate remedies applied soon. Yet there is no reason to believe that Sukarno will be any more impressed by this danger now than heretofore; and it would be unrealistic to assume that whatever measures he decides to take in the political field will be taken swiftly and decisively.

Although present economic crisis has not yet affected vast majority Indonesians who subsistence farmers on largely non-monetary economy, it is beginning ominous pinch in cities among laborers, white collar workers, armed forces, from which PKI hopes draw support its ultimate revolutionary goals. (Embtel 3775)[3]

Because of worsening economic picture fact Nasution apparently unable or unwilling act without Sukarno may mean it will be too late for him to take any kind of strong action with the President by the time Sukarno ready to proceed. This true not only because economic difficulties enhance prospects, but because of renewed importance party will have as supporter of President's program where until Consembly crisis PKI was gradually being boxed in by being forced to choose between two unpalatable alternatives; support of 1945 constitution which could curtail its powers or open break with Sukarno which in end it feared more. It now may have opportunity to wiggle off hook, perhaps recover some of position previously lost.

Sukarno certainly will need political strength of PKI for whatever program he determines upon. Colonel Sukendro has informed Embassy he believes he has assurance of enough votes from Moslem parties to vote dissolution of Consembly, after which President would decree 1945 constitution in effect. Even if Sukendro's expectation justified program remains based on support also of PKI, which has taken lead in demanding such course of action.

It has not been PKI but Moslem parties which have frustrated President's plans, and his foremost objective upon return will undoubtedly be overcome Moslem opposition in some way, for which must have aid of PKI as well as PNI. Former will have a price, domestically and internationally, a price which Sukarno probably will not consider unduly high.

In these circumstances it would be wishful thinking to anticipate drastic action against Communists by army or GOI in near future unless PKI provides army with sufficient excuse by jumping traces in some

---

[3] Telegram 3775, June 18, reported on the deterioration of the Indonesian economy and emphasized the extent to which this trend was accentuated by the political crisis. (Department of State, Central Files, 756D.00/6–1859)

way. Sukendro's comments this regard (ARMA to DEPTAR CX–74)[4] encouraging but no certainty he speaking for Nasution. Sukendro privately has long favored provoking clash with PKI.

Assuming that Sukarno still fears PKI threat his own position (I have no reason to doubt that he does) easiest apparent way out would be effect compromise between PNI, Moslem parties, which would bring about legal return 1945 constitution. Common antipathy toward communism then would enable Moslem parties, PNI, army, President work together against PKI. Unfortunately this easier said than done. Fact is religious controversy in part only convenient battleground for other less open but no less fundamental issues, such as support of, or opposition to Sukarno, regionalism versus centralism, Java versus outer islands, et cetera. Consequently, problem of lining up anti-Communist parties against PKI difficult one, and this doubtless primary reason PKI tactic supporting Sukarno and governmental issues.

In determining most effective courses action US must recognize Sukarno essential element political picture for foreseeable future; thus his acquiescence, preferably active support, needed for achievement any objective. If objective is reduction Communist power in Indonesia through GOI repressive action, means must first be found reduce Sukarno dependence on Communists internally, externally. Alternative might be to back strong rival leadership so as to neutralize importance Sukarno, but recent events strongly suggest this is out of question for present. It seems to me the army has shown its present inability to fulfill such a role, and there apparently is no available understudy of suitable talents.

Seemingly then we have only limited freedom of action in dealing with situation. We must be prepared to continue a policy of patient strengthening of anti-Communist elements in ways that may be open to us with a view to surrounding Sukarno with right sort of pressures; we must continue to attempt to convince President and associated leaders Indonesia can count on US friendship and support and that we are not attempting to dictate internal or external policies.

This is what we have been doing for nearly a year with some success. Fact that we may have to expect temporary setback resulting from present situation, with relative position of PKI enhanced, should not tempt us to embark on new, unorthodox methods for mere sake of change. Our cue now is to remain alert for developments capable of exploitation while recognizing that in so complex a situation, trends may not uninterruptedly flow in our favor.

---

[4] Not found.

In the long run we have good ground for optimism because of the political leadership, including Sukarno himself. The underlying antagonism of not only the Moslem but nationalist parties toward communism and all its works, the determination of army leadership to prevent a Communist take-over and our own capability to encourage and strengthen these elements are dependable assets.

Summing up, I am convinced that, considering all factors, our present policy of gradually increasing economic, military assistance, coupled with continuing efforts to build Indonesian confidence in West, exploit Indonesian fear of Communist expansionism, is all we should undertake for the time being. At same time we should not be deterred from doing that much by temporary deterioration of political, economic situation which likely occur next few months.

Jones

---

209. Memorandum From the Assistant Secretary of State for Far Eastern Affairs (Robertson) to Acting Secretary of State Dillon

Washington, June 19, 1959.

SUBJECT

Political Situation in Indonesia

On April 22, 1959, President Sukarno proposed that Indonesia return to its 1945 Constitution in order to (1) rekindle the revolutionary fervor and unity of that year and (2) stabilize Indonesian government and politics. After more than a month's debate, the proposal failed on three successive ballots (May 31, June 1, June 2) to win the necessary two-thirds majority in the Constituent Assembly. The Islamic parties voted solidly against the proposal because the 1945 Constitution lacks explicit provisions recognizing Islam as the pre-eminent religious faith of Indonesia.

Source: Department of State, S/S–OCB Files: Lot 62 D 430, Indonesia. Confidential. Drafted by Moore on June 17 and cleared with Mein. A copy of this memorandum was sent to Murphy.

Following the defeat of Sukarno's proposal, the Army Chief of Staff, General Nasution, acting in his capacity as War Administrator under the existing State of Emergency, on June 2 banned all political activity in Indonesia as tending to exacerbate tensions prejudicial to law and order. He took this action on instructions from Sukarno, then in Los Angeles on his world tour. While banning political activity, the Army denied having any intention of taking over the reins of government. Nevertheless, it is evident that the Army is prepared to intervene actively in the political sphere in order to prevent further deterioration of the political situation.

It is generally expected that there will be no further important developments in the Indonesian political situation until Sukarno returns to the country June 28. We have been told by Foreign Minister Subandrio that Sukarno is confident he can resolve the differences with the Moslem parties which led to defeat of his proposal in the Constituent Assembly and find a mutually agreeable way to return to the 1945 Constitution.

Our Embassy at Djakarta estimates that, while imposition of the 1945 Constitution by Presidential decree remains a possibility, it is more likely the President will work out a compromise formula involving concessions of some sort to the Moslem position. The Embassy looks for the present government thereupon to resign and be replaced by a government in which the principal roles will be played by Sukarno himself, the Army, the PNI (Nationalist Party) and perhaps the NU (a major Islamic party).

210.   Editorial Note

On June 28 Ambassador Young sent an airgram to the Department of State evaluating the current state of U.S.-Dutch relations. He suggested that with the establishment of the J.E. deQuay Cabinet, which had been formed on May 19, the time had come "when we should take [a] fresh, overall look at our relations with the Dutch." (Airgram G–193 from The Hague, June 28; Department of State, Central Files, 611.56/6–2859) See Supplement.

211.   Memorandum From the Assistant Secretary of State for Far Eastern Affairs (Parsons) to the Deputy Under Secretary of State for Political Affairs (Murphy)

Washington, July 1, 1959.

SUBJECT

U.S. Attitude towards Present Political Crisis in Indonesia

Summary

I understand that Mr. Karl Harr[1] will ask you at the July 1 OCB luncheon how U.S. policy towards Indonesia may be affected by the outcome of the current political crisis in Indonesia. It is not possible to state categorically how the U.S. would react to each of the many possible solutions of this crisis. In general, however, none of the probable solutions is likely to require any change in our present policy towards Indonesia.

Discussion

Indonesia's political crisis stems from refusal of the Islamic political parties to support President Sukarno's April 22 proposal to the Constituent Assembly that Indonesia reinstate its 1945 Constitution (see background at Tab A).[2] Our Embassy reports that the Indonesian Government is considering four alternative means of reinstating the 1945 Constitution:

1. Resubmission of the proposal to the Constituent Assembly with necessary concessions to the Islamic parties to secure their support.
2. Submission of the proposal to Parliament, where the Government has a majority and presumably can assure a favorable vote (it is not clear that this procedure would be legal since the Constituent Assembly is the body charged with drawing up a constitution).
3. Imposition of the 1945 Constitution by Presidential decree (this procedure, too, may be of questionable legality).
4. A national referendum.

The Embassy's guess is that Sukarno will proclaim the 1945 Constitution by Presidential decree, probably incorporating in the preamble some reference to Islam which would at least partially meet the Moslem parties' demand for preferential status for Islam. Sukarno might ask Parliamentary endorsement of his decree to meet the letter of legality.

There is no apparent reason for the U.S. to view with alarm the return to the 1945 Constitution in Indonesia. In fact, there is some hope

---

Source: Department of State, S/S–OCB Files: Lot 62 D 430, Indonesia. Secret. Drafted by Moore on June 30 and cleared with Mein.

[1] Acting Chairman of the OCB.

[2] See Document 198.

that this change might bring increased political stability and more effective measures to check the deterioration of the economy, developments the U.S. would welcome.

Ideally the U.S. would like to see the return to the 1945 Constitution accomplished by legal and democratic means. None of the means thought likely to be employed is fundamentally undemocratic, and the Indonesians will probably make every effort to meet at least the letter of the law. In any case, the hoped-for gain in political stability might well counterbalance the disadvantage of any departure from wholly legal procedure as far as overall U.S. interests are concerned.

It is the practical steps which might be taken after the reinstatement of the 1945 Constitution, rather than the act of reinstatement itself, which could ultimately lead the U.S. to consider modification of its policy towards Indonesia. However, the actions we expect the Indonesian Government to take are generally those which would further our objectives. It is anticipated that the new government under the 1945 Constitution, would be heavily weighted with representatives of anti-Communist elements, notably the Army.

Inasmuch as it is the Moslem parties which have opposed Sukarno's proposal to return to the 1945 Constitution, Sukarno will continue to depend in part on Communist Party (PKI) support in his move to reinstate the 1945 Constitution. This is not expected to result in PKI participation in the Government, but it could result in the PKI continuing to enjoy its substantial popular influence and relative freedom to pursue its ends.

Even if the PKI remains in this advantageous position, however, the U.S. would gain nothing by a change in existing policy. Our Embassy strongly recommends that, whatever the outcome of the present crisis (short of marked Communist gains or general civil disorder, of course) the U.S. should simply maintain its present policy of strengthening non- and anti-Communist elements (1) in a material sense through judicious economic and military assistance, and (2) in a psychological sense by showing the U.S. to be a dependable friend of Indonesia. The Ambassador recommends further that we should continue to exploit Indonesian fears of international Communist expansionism.

I concur in these recommendations.[3]

---

[3] The question of U.S. arms supplies to Indonesia was discussed briefly at the OCB luncheon meeting of July 1. During the discussion, both Gates and Murphy offered the view that the supply of arms to Indonesia should continue. (Memorandum from Jeremiah J. O'Connor, Operations Coordinator, to Parsons, July 1; Department of State, S/S–OCB Files: Lot 61 D 385, Indonesia) See Supplement.

212. Memorandum From the Director of the Office of Southwest Pacific Affairs (Mein) to the Assistant Secretary of State for Far Eastern Affairs (Parsons)

Washington, July 8, 1959.

SUBJECT

Indonesia's Return to the 1945 Constitution

His proposal that Indonesia return to the 1945 Constitution having been defeated in the Constituent Assembly by the Moslem parties, on July 5 Sukarno proclaimed by Presidential decree (1) reinstatement of the 1945 Constitution, (2) abandonment of the Provisional Constitution of 1950 and (3) dissolution of the Constituent Assembly. Thereupon the government of Prime Minister Djuanda resigned but was kept on by Sukarno in a caretaker capacity.[1]

The 1945 Constitution is a less complete and detailed document than the 1950 Constitution, but Sukarno (with Army endorsement) recommended returning to it as a means of increasing the stability of the government. Under the 1945 Constitution, the formal power of the executive will be increased, in part through the medium of a Presidential cabinet replacing the unstable parliamentary cabinets that Indonesia has suffered for ten years.

Because it provides for a stronger executive, the 1945 Constitution has been loosely described by the press as a device employed by Sukarno to acquire "dictatorial" powers. This description is misleading on several counts:

1. The proposal to return to the 1945 Constitution is not Sukarno's private brainchild but has had the consistent backing of the Army and the cabinet since the plan was hatched earlier this year in the hope of ending chronic political instability.
2. The 1945 Constitution places numerous checks on the President's power, as may be seen from the underlined portions of the Constitution (Tab A).[2] Sovereignty rests with the people, the Presidency is an elective office, laws may only be enacted with the concurrence of a Council of Representatives (parliament), etc.
3. No powers the President could legally assume under the 1945 Constitution would equal in scope those possessed since March 1957 by the War Administrator (General Nasution, Army Chief of Staff) under

---

Source: Department of State, Central Files, 756D.03/7–859. Secret. Drafted by Moore.

[1] The Embassy summarized these developments in despatch 10 from Djakarta, July 7. (Ibid., 756D.03/7–759) See Supplement.

[2] Not printed. See Document 198.

the State of Danger Law. Nasution's authority under this law to act to maintain order and internal security is virtually unlimited.

There is no apparent reason for the U.S. to view with alarm the reinstatement of the 1945 Constitution. In fact, if this change produces a more stable, non-Communist government and results in firmer measures to check the deterioration of the economy, U.S. objectives in Indonesia will be served. As a matter of internal political reorganization in Indonesia, the change of constitutions as such need have no effect on U.S. policy towards Indonesia.

It is true, of course, that political developments in Indonesia attendant on implementation of the 1945 Constitution could necessitate a reexamination of U.S.-Indonesian relations. The Communist Party (PKI) has supported Sukarno consistently in the matter of the 1945 Constitution so he remains to some extent dependent on PKI support, particularly if the Moslem parties remain uncooperative. However, we do not expect Communists to be included in the new cabinet, and we do expect the anti-Communist Army leadership to be substantially represented therein. And we have been led to believe that the Army and certain civilian elements of the government intend to use the increased executive power provided by the 1945 Constitution to curb the influence of the PKI.

---

213.   Memorandum of Conversation

US/MC/117   Geneva, July 12, 1959, 5:15 p.m.

UNITED STATES DELEGATION TO THE
MEETING OF FOREIGN MINISTERS
PALAIS DES NATIONS, GENEVA, 1959

PARTICIPANTS

The Secretary
Foreign Minister Luns of the Netherlands
Mr. Merchant
Mr. Lewis

SUBJECT

General Discussion

Source: Department of State, Secretary's Memoranda of Conversation: Lot 64 D 199. Secret. Drafted by Geoffrey W. Lewis, First Secretary of Embassy in Paris, and approved by Herter July 14. The meeting was held at the Villa Greta. The Foreign Ministers were meeting on the future of Germany July 13–August 5.

[Here follows discussion of other subjects.]

4)   Indonesia

Mr. Luns said that Mr. Menzies of Australia had assured the Dutch of strong support in New Guinea, but he noted that the Australians can go no further in the military field than permitted by the United States. Mr. Luns then went on to say that he was worried about Indonesia's intentions in New Guinea and the Dutch were preparing a statement [*less than 1 line of source text not declassified*] concerning the amount of arms which the Indonesians had acquired from Western sources. So far, the political deterrent exercised by the United States had worked, but Mr. Luns was concerned that if the Indonesians did attack there were no arrangements for the Dutch to obtain any military help from their Western allies. He urged that the United States strongly continue to exert a political deterrent. The Secretary recalled a recent Indonesian statement that they had no intention of attacking New Guinea.

Mr. Luns then turned to the question of obtaining U.S. surplus weapons for the Dutch forces. He asked the Secretary's support in obtaining the items on the revised list which the Dutch had submitted in response to U.S. suggestions to replace the earlier list.[1] Mr. Luns said the Dutch particularly wanted a tanker. He hoped that the price of the arms sold would be merely token. He would hate to have a situation develop wherein the Netherlands would have to divert funds from their NATO effort for the defense of New Guinea. He noted in this connection that there were some 18,000 Dutchmen there whom it was his duty to protect. He thought that if the Indonesians thought the West considered the island vital to defend, they would be deterred from attacking. He then remarked that there were still 2,800 Dutch left in Indonesia, but he wouldn't be surprised if they would soon be forced to leave. The Indonesians keep saying that they would pay compensation for the properties they had taken from Dutch interests, but they did nothing. The Secretary remarked that during the consideration of our aid program, an amendment had been introduced and adopted in committee that there would be no aid supplied to countries who had confiscated private property.[2] This amendment was in fact aimed at Cuba, but might well apply in the case of Indonesia. The Secretary then asked Mr. Luns for his evaluation of the new Indonesian cabinet. Mr. Luns replied that

---

[1] The revised Dutch list was summarized in circular CG–78 to The Hague, August 11. (*Ibid.*, Central Files, 756D.56/8–1159) See Supplement. Additional documentation is in Department of State, WE Files: Lot 63 D 221, Shopping List.

[2] Reference is to the Mutual Security Act of 1959, which was approved by the President on July 24 with the amendment on confiscation; for text, see 73 Stat. 246. In a memorandum to Mein of July 24, Moore summarized this matter. (Department of State, Central Files, SPA Files: Lot 62 D 409, Netherlands)

he preferred it to a Communist Government, but he had little confidence in Sukarno or Subandrio. He then gave a long dissertation, with examples, on how unreliable he had found the Indonesian leaders to be and how far the Dutch had gone in their attempts to get on with them. He said that the trouble was that the Dutch were to Sukarno what the Jews had been to Hitler and that therefore the whole problem was tremendously discouraging.

---

214.   Telegram From Secretary of State Herter to the Department of State

Geneva, July 15, 1959, 11 p.m.

Secto 319. Selwyn Lloyd raised with me today question of West New Guinea and state of our understanding with the Dutch in event Indonesians attacked.[1] He said that he and Secretary Dulles had agreed on giving warning in identical terms to Indonesians against attack and also mentioned that Mr. Dulles had said in such event US would give Dutch logistical support, it being impossible to go beyond this in absence Congressional approval. We discussed the matter briefly and noted that each of us was under continuing pressure from the Dutch to move in direction of joint military planning with them (and presumably Australians as well) which I indicated we were not enthusiastic over. Matter was left that I would report this conversation to the Department which I thought would be in better position having full earlier records available than I to continue dialogue with Caccia.[2]

Herter

Source: Department of State, Central Files, 656.56D13/7–1559. Secret; Limit Distribution. Repeated to London, The Hague, and Djakarta.

[1] Secto 330 from Geneva, July 16, reads: "Request summary discussions with Dutch re U.S. position in event Indonesian attack on West Guinea." (*Ibid.*, 656C.56D/7–1659) In Tosec 336 to Geneva, July 18, the Department provided the summary and explained that U.S. conversations with the Netherlands regarding the U.S. position in event of an Indonesian attack on West New Guinea had focused on political deterrents and secret military planning. (*Ibid.*) See Supplement.

[2] In telegram 111 from Djakarta, July 18, Jones commented that he "fully expressed our attitude toward any possible Indonesian attack on West New Guinea." Subandrio repeatedly assured Jones that Indonesia would not attack and that it was well aware of the attitude of the United States, the United Kingdom, and others to such a move. Given these assurances and the unlikelihood of an imminent attack, Jones stated such a warning "would not only serve no useful purpose but would have a pernicious effect on US-Indonesian relations." (Department of State, Central Files, 656.5613/7–1859) See Supplement.

215.   Memorandum From the Assistant Secretary of State for Far Eastern Affairs (Parsons) to Acting Secretary of State Dillon

Washington, July 16, 1959.

SUBJECT

New Government in Indonesia

A new government took office in Indonesia on July 10 under the Premiership of President Sukarno who thus becomes head of government as well as head of state. The new Cabinet retains the principal figures from the previous government, including Djuanda, formerly Premier but now First Minister under Sukarno, and Subandrio, who stays on as Foreign Minister. Army Chief of Staff Nasution assumes a place in the Cabinet for the first time as Minister of Security and Defense. Sukarno describes the new Cabinet as a "working" Cabinet which will deal with the country's basic problems in a non-partisan spirit. Cabinet appointees have been required to divest themselves of responsibility to political parties to which they may belong.

From the standpoint of United States interests and objectives in Indonesia, the new Cabinet represents an improvement over its predecessor, even though Sukarno and Subandrio have made it clear that Indonesia's neutralist foreign policy will continue. No known extreme leftists occupy positions in the "nucleus", or inner, cabinet, in which the anti-Communist leadership of the Army is strongly represented. The inner Cabinet can be characterized as technically competent, and, on the basis of its membership, more conservative in political orientation than the previous Cabinet.

Designation of the new ministers follows a revised ministerial set-up. The complete Cabinet, consisting of 38 ministers occupying 43 posts (see Tab A for Cabinet list and Tab B for biographic data on inner Cabinet members)[1] is composed of (1) an inner Cabinet of nine full ministers, (2) deputy ministers who serve under the inner Cabinet ministers, and (3) a group of ex-officio ministers who are heads of certain government agencies other than ministries. This organizational structure centers control in the more conservative inner Cabinet, thus providing the means to restrain the few fellow travelers (and one possible Communist) included among the deputy ministers. At the same time, Army officers have been placed in some key deputy minister posts dealing with labor, communications and economic matters.

Source: Department of State, Central Files, 756D.11/7–1659. Secret. Drafted by Moore on July 14 and cleared with Mein and Marshall Green. A copy of this memorandum was sent to Murphy.

[1] See Supplement for both tabs.

The new government has, in theory, a freer hand to tackle some of the country's basic problems—such as the continuing rebellion and the spiraling inflation—than any previous government. It takes office under the 1945 Constitution, which was reinstated July 5 by Presidential decree to replace the Provisional Constitution of 1950. The 1945 Constitution provides for a Presidential Cabinet with an assured life of five years, in contrast to the previous Parliamentary Cabinets which proved weak and unstable. Only time will tell whether the new government can and will capitalize on its relative insulation from political haggling and give the country effective leadership. The outcome of the experiment will depend in large degree on the performance of Sukarno, who, as the avowed head of a "working" Cabinet, must show unaccustomed willingness to shoulder administrative responsibility if the new government is to have a good chance of success.[2]

---

[2] The Embassy in Djakarta assessed the new Indonesian Cabinet in telegrams 50, July 9 (Department of State, Central Files, 756D.00/7–959); 58, July 10 (*ibid.*, 756D.00/7–1050); and 73, July 14 (*ibid.*, 756D.00/7–1459).

---

216.   Telegram From the Embassy in Indonesia to the Department of State

Djakarta, July 27, 1959, 2 p.m.

174. Also for POLAD. Out of welter of confusion and conflicting interests accompanying revision of structure Indonesian Government and appointment of new Cabinet, two things emerge clearly. First is that Sukarno feels he has achieved or is on way to achieving balance of power factors which he considers essential to maintain his position. The second is that there is at last awareness that something must be done about deteriorating financial and economic situation and an apparent determination to do the necessary even if adoption of politically unpopular measures is required.

With regard to first, this is of course way in which Sukarno has always operated. Balancing one man off against another, one group

---

Source: Department of State, Central Files, 756D.00/7–2759. Confidential. Also sent to CINCPAC. Transmitted in two sections and repeated to The Hague, Canberra, Manila, Tokyo, Bangkok, London, and Singapore.

against another, has been the key to his political strategy. As Department aware, this was what gave PKI its opportunity to stage a comeback when Sukarno some years ago saw black cloud of Masjumi looming on political horizon as direct threat to his own position. This is also reason Hatta and Sjahrir are on sidelines, reason Natsir and Sjafruddin are in Sumatra. For balancing one political force against another neutralizes both and leads not to decision and action but to indecision and inaction, with consequent failure to face up to and attack problems facing country.

Today Sukarno has succeeded in establishing somewhat precarious balance between Army and PKI, and he has aligned himself with army because at least for time being PKI poses greatest threat to his pre-eminence. Sukarno recognizes, of course, that ultimately this balance may be upset, that he is dealing with an ambitious man in Nasution but so far he does not fear him because presumably he still has power to destroy him and he needs him. Nasution has demonstrated capacity to temper ambition with restraint.

Reason previous Cabinet, so-called Karya Cabinet, was able to stay in office as long as it did, its more than two years of service breaking all records for Indonesia, was because it was able to preserve this balance. The government rested on a tripod of three men—Sukarno, Nasution, and Djuanda. This triumvirate has been continued in new Cabinet. For time being at least, each man is dependent upon the other. Djuanda does not count in the power struggle of course. He is simply a dedicated man trying to do a job for his country but therein lies his greatest strength because Sukarno knows he is no rival for power and is willing to trust him—to an extent he probably trusts no other man—to run government. Nasution likewise appears to have same feeling about Djuanda.

Visitors to Indonesia continue to ask me this question—what has brought about change in Sukarno? The situation has changed so that it is no longer to Sukarno's interest to play game the way he played it before. If Sukarno sees threat coming from another direction, he will change his course again.

This raises question as to how long Sukarno–Nasution alliance can continue. Answer, in my view, is a simple one—just so long as Nasution controls army but still lacks power to unseat President. The moment Nasution acquires such power Sukarno will move against him unless Nasution moves first. This is an uneasy alliance between two strong men—each strong in a different way. Sukarno, the superb politician, the beloved of the masses, versus Nasution, the tough soldier, the brilliant commander. If they can continue to work together, much can be accomplished for the good of the country. Claws of PKI can be clipped, an open field can be given Djuanda to tackle financial-economic problems of nation, some measure of political and economic stability may conceivably result. If not, then solution a la Burma, Pakistan is not out of question, as, unfortunately, neither is also a lapse into chaos with resultant emergence of PKI as dominant force although this latter possibility, while ever present, is in my view much less likely than two years or year ago.

To prevent military solution at least until he himself wants one, and to assist in preserving balance within military, Sukarno is clearly playing off Suryadarma against Nasution; also loyalty of some strong subordinate commanders to Sukarno, e.g. Colonel Sarbini,[1] provides further check on Nasution. We have not seen last of antagonism between Nasution–Suryadarma although if I were betting I would put my money on Nasution.

The difficulty with military solution to Indonesian problem is that while this may be temporarily effective in advancing US objectives through curbing Communists there is no more assurance that a military regime will be able find its way through maze of economic and financial difficulties than its civilian predecessors could. And there is no present indication that military are likely to be any less tempted by fatal lure of corrupt practice than have civilians. And should military fail, what then?

Indonesian attitudes today in economic field provide remarkable parallel to political attitudes year and half ago. At that time Indonesian leadership was just beginning to be acutely aware of fact that Communism within country represented a real threat to continued freedom and independence of Indonesian people. Today same leadership has become aware of new danger—inflation—and they are beginning to see that economic instability can not only threaten a better life for their people but that it also presents a situation ready-made for Communist exploitation.

I have been anticipating a direct bid from Indonesian Government for more assistance to tide them over this crisis. If and when it comes, I think we should be responsive, always provided they are willing help themselves to extent they are able, even though this means taking some of the hard decisions I have been talking about.[2]

Jones

---

[1] Military Commander in East Java.

[2] On July 29 John Gordon Mein briefed the OCB on developments in Indonesia. His analysis closely followed that presented by Jones in this telegram. He emphasized that the U.S. position in Indonesia had improved over the past year, but added that this development should not induce complacency. (Memorandum from Jeremiah J. O'Connor to Parsons, July 29; Department of State, Central Files, 611.56D/7–2959) See Supplement.

August 1959–August 1960: President Sukarno's Invitation to President Eisenhower To Visit Indonesia; Khrushchev's Visit to Indonesia; and Heightened Indonesian-Netherlands Tension Over the West Irian-West New Guinea Dispute Occasioned by the Cruise of the *Karel Doorman*

217. Editorial Note

In telegram 276 from Djakarta, August 11, Ambassador Jones reported that he had received recent feelers from Indonesian officials that suggested to him that Indonesia was on the point of requesting an expanded program of U.S. military assistance. Jones asked for an "early indication of U.S. thinking" on this possibility. He added that the signature of a military assistance agreement was a distinct possibility because of the following factors:

"1. Presidential Cabinet not responsible to Parliament removes one of major political obstacles to signature such agreement.
"2. Country is in real economic and financial trouble. Leaders, particularly Djuanda and Nasution, are deeply concerned and determined to take effective steps to deal with situation.
"3. There is growing realization that solution economic problems will require hard decisions as well as some further help from outside.
"4. There is general realization neither technical assistance nor economic development programs meet immediate need which is to prevent further inflation with resultant Communist exploitation of country's difficulties.
"5. Indonesian leaders recognize future independence of Indonesia inevitably rests upon presence in Pacific. Subandrio and Nasution have been explicit on this point. Foreign Minister, at least in conversations with me, has been gradually de-emphasizing foreign policy of non-alignment and putting greater stress on new and second major element of good neighbor policy.
"6. Indonesians want more positive assurance of continuing US support in military and economic field for long-range planning purpose." (Department of State, Central Files, 756D.5–MSP/8–1159) See Supplement.

The Department of State sent Jones a tentative reply on August 12, informing him that the matter was receiving serious thought in the Department, and a substantive reply would be sent as soon as possible. (Telegram 169 to Djakarta, August 12; Department of State, Central Files, 756D.56/8–1159) See Document 222.

417

218. Telegram From the Department of State to the Embassy in Indonesia

Washington, August 21, 1959, 2:35 p.m.

209. Joint State–Defense message (rptd CINCPAC 31). Your 114 paragraph 3,[1] and CINCPAC's 110128Z August.[2]

1. You authorized inform Nasution, Djuanda and other GOI officials as appropriate that subject to availability of funds US planning to continue Govt to Govt sale of military equipment and services to Indonesia in FY–1960. It should be emphasized to GOI that this is not a commitment on part of US at this time. US unable at the moment give GOI indication of scope and size possible FY–1960 program since this dependent on number of factors including pending Congressional action on Mutual Security legislation. FYI. Care should be taken not to imply possible FY–1960 program would be at or above level FY–1959 program. End FYI.

2. In informing GOI of plans continue military sales you should state that such sales would be under provisions of the military sales agreement of August 13, 1958 and US understanding of the meaning thereof.

3. You may advise GOI that we presently studying Indonesian requests (CHMILTAG's 100407Z June and 090030Z July[3] and reftel) and will inform GOI as soon as we in position discuss specific program for FY–1960. At your discretion stress to GOI importance of cooperation between MILTAG and Indonesian military authorities in developing mutually agreed program requirements with appropriate priorities.

4. Please notify Dept, Hague, London, Canberra when you have informed GOI of foregoing.

Source: Department of State, Central Files, 756D.5–MSP/7–859. Secret; Niact. Drafted by Wenzel and Moore on August 14; cleared with W/MSC, EUR, and Defense; and approved by Parsons. Repeated to CINCPAC, The Hague, London, and Canberra.

[1] Paragraph 3 of telegram 114, July 18, reads: "Best move now would be advice to GOI that we intend sustain and if possible increase judiciously, the military aid program already begun. Indonesian leaders understand our fiscal procedures, that we cannot predict or anticipate congressional action. Therefore, they would be satisfied, in the interim, by an indication of our hopes and proposals for continued aid in FY 1960. Early enunciation of a specific program is, of course, very important." (Ibid., 756D.5–MSP/7–1859) See Supplement.

[2] Dated August 11 this telegram contained CINCPAC's tentative recommendations for a fiscal year 1960 program of military assistance for Indonesia. (Washington National Records Center, OASD/ISA Files: FRC 63 A 1672, 091.3 Indonesia)

[3] Neither found.

For The Hague

Promptly upon receipt info that GOI informed of foregoing, Chargé should in routine manner draw attention Secretary General FO to fact that Amb. Jones telling Indonesians that we are planning continue military aid to Indonesia in FY–1960. Chargé should convey substance numbered paragraph 1 above excepting FYI section. If and when specific FY–1960 program formulated Dutch will be informed as usual of program's nature.

If question is raised you should make clear that this is merely continuation of present limited program within context of our overall policy toward Indonesia.

You should also inform Dutch that Amb. Jones is telling Indonesians that possible FY–60 sales military equipment would be under provisions of military sales agreement of August 13, 1958 and US understanding of meaning thereof per numbered paragraph 2 above.

We will inform Dutch here of FY–1960 plans.

For Canberra and London

We will inform Australians and British here of FY–1960 plans.

Herter

---

219. Telegram From the Embassy in Indonesia to the Department of State

Djakarta, August 22, 1959, 3 p.m.

354. CINCPAC also for POLAD. I had first serious talk with President I have had for some time but for a change it was I who did most of talking. I had assumed President would make major pitch for US assistance in current crisis, but only request he made was specific one for delivery one Lockheed C–130 in January (Embtel 353).[1]

Source: Department of State, Central Files, 756D.5622/8–2259. Confidential. Transmitted in two sections and also sent to CINCPAC.

[1] Telegram 353, August 22, reads in part as follows: "President Sukarno made specific request to me this morning for delivery in January 1960 of one Lockheed C–130 under contract signed August 21. Sukarno said this would be urgently needed at that time to effect deliveries of new rice crop to areas of Indonesia which could not readily be reached by normal channels distibution." Jones informed the Department that the aircraft would be employed to reach isolated distressed areas and suggested that such use of a U.S. airplane "would have beneficial effect for US as well as GOI." He recommended that a "strong effort be made on political grounds to meet President's request." (*Ibid.*) See Supplement.

After exchange of courtesies and discussion Lockheed matter President ordered coffee and then waited for me to take lead in conversation.

I opened by saying I hoped he would not mind if I talked as friend rather than as Ambassador because some of the things I wanted to say had not been discussed with my government and were in context internal affairs rather than external. I referred to deteriorating economic situation in Indonesia, mentioning specific commodity price increases resulting from inflationary pressures. I had been talking with great many people at all levels and I thought he might be interested in receiving my impressions.

I was convinced that people of country recognized as he did that some hard decision had to be made to solve economic problems and people were looking to President Sukarno for leadership. There seemed to be general acceptance among people with whom I had talked that unpopular measures were necessary and I thought Indonesians were ready for such measures once they were explained to them. I said in my opinion there was only one man who could explain such program to people and that was himself. As an illustration of what I meant I cited necessity for increasing taxes. This, I emphasized, was unpopular action in any country but if it was necessary to improve condition of people and was explained to them as something from which they would reap benefit, and if it were necessary for good of country, I was confident people would accept it—indeed welcome it.

President nodded his head at this point and said he agreed. He wanted me to be more specific, however.

I cited through Java that he had to pay four rupiahs a liter for gasoline throughout west and central Java. This was almost four times legal price of gasoline and this was experience not only of Americans but Indonesians. Americans had no objection to paying this price for gasoline which was far lower than they paid at home, I remarked, but it was hard on Indonesian people. Some Indonesian leaders were kidding themselves that legal price of gasoline was real price of gasoline and what people paid. This simply was not true. Meanwhile I emphasized who was getting benefit of this high price—not government, not people, not even producer, only the black market operator who contributed no service. The government could take advantage of situation by increasing prices to point where black market operators would be discouraged and government take additional in taxes.

President interjected observation that he was not convinced this would solve black market situation—he believed black market situation could only be solved by additional supply.

I said of course this was true, but he could induce additional supply through price increase. I pointed out experience in Germany and other countries and emphasized that producers and distributors who are not making money on commodities were not only reluctant to sell at losing price but obviously had no interest in additional investment in facilities to insure widespread distribution. I said I was convinced from my own experience that not only could black market commodities situation be solved by this process but that formula could be developed which would (a) benefit Indonesian Government and (b) do so without imposing additional burden on Indonesian people; rather result would be lessening of burden. I observed that this was large subject to deal with in short time (I had been advised that President had only half hour reserved for me this morning), but that I knew cabinet was meeting all day tomorrow to discuss some of these problems and that was reason I had ventured to raise subject at this time. When his government had reached conclusion as to program, I should be glad to sit down and discuss whole situation with him or appropriate Ministers and to listen to any suggestions they might have as to how we might be of help.

Possibly indicative of President's new state of mind was immediate rejoinder—"I am not interested in programs," he said. "We have had too many programs. I am interested in action." I said I could not agree more and that that was what I had meant.

I pointed out that of course program for solution of all Indonesia's economic problems involved many aspects and one of these was source of capital for development. I said that I had been very glad to see that he had apparently opened door a little wider to private foreign investment in his recent speech on August 17.[2]

President confirmed this. He said he preferred governmental credits but he was willing to have private capital come in. I then said I thought Indonesia would have to depend upon private foreign capital if it was to develop its resources as rapidly as it hoped to do. Many people in Indonesia feared foreign capital. This fear was without foundation. I cited history of development of US and vital role foreign capital had played in this development, pointing out that following our own revolution substantial percentage of our economy was owned and controlled by foreigners. Important point there, I stressed, was that percentage of foreign private investment in America had gone down to about three percent through years but that actual amount of foreign capital invested in America had continued to increase ever since our revolution. What had happened was that America had grown around core of foreign capital which enabled US to get start. Indonesia could do same.

---

[2] The Embassy reported on Sukarno's independence day speech of August 17 in telegram 316 from Djakarta, August 17. (Department of State, Central Files, 856D.424/8–1759)

President appeared very much impressed by this point which apparently had never reached him before. He nodded his head slowly and thoughtfully.

I was not saying this to him in selfish desire to see more American investment in Indonesia, I said. There was ample investment opportunity for American capital in America and other countries. I was making point solely because I felt it was in Indonesia's interest to attract and utilize source of capital which could help them solve problems faster than they could solve them otherwise.

(President then said he was very much interested in what I had to say and would like to have another talk with me in which we would further develop subject.)

In closing conversation I thanked President for his invitation to go with him to Atjeh and Kalimantan (Embtel 351)[3] and said I was looking forward to this very much. I also mentioned that as he knew I had given dinners recently in honor of First Minister and Foreign Minister and would like very much to give luncheon or dinner in honor of President/ Prime Minister of Kerdja cabinet. President said he appreciated invitation and would be very glad to accept. I could work out further details with Doctor Tamzil.

Jones

---

[3] Telegram 351, August 21, reported that on the previous day Tamzil called Jones to extend invitation from Sukarno to join him in a 12-day trip to Atjeh and Kalimantan, commencing September 1. Jones replied that he appreciated the invitation and accepted with pleasure. (Ibid., 756D.11/8–2259)

---

220. Editorial Note

On August 24 the Indonesian Government adopted a series of monetary reforms, including devaluation of the rupiah, freezing of bank accounts, and the reduction of government employee salaries. Mein summarized these reforms in a memorandum of August 31 for Parsons. "As for the longer-range effects of these measures," he observed, "we can expect both deflationary and inflationary results." (Department of State, Central Files, 656D.13/8–3159) See Supplement. The Department of State's classified periodical, *Current Economic Developments*, provided a more detailed analysis of the reforms. "These measures," it noted, "may prove beneficial if they are followed by other economic reforms which add up to a meaningful stabilization program. The measures provide some indication that the Government at last has decided to move to correct the rapidly worsening economic conditions, even to the extent of making politically unpopular decisions. The real test will be the Government's willingness and ability to institute and implement these and other necessary measures to deal with the serious inflation." (Issue No. 580, September 15, 1959, pages 9–12; Department of State, *Current Economic Developments:* Lot 70 D 467) See Supplement.

221.   Memorandum of Conversation

Washington, August 25, 1959.

SUBJECT

>   Suggested United States-United Kingdom Talks Regarding Possible Indonesian Attack on West New Guinea

PARTICIPANTS

>   The Viscount Hood, Chargé d'Affaires, British Embassy
>   Mr. Merchant, Deputy Under Secretary, G
>   Mr. Rewinkel, Deputy Director, BNA

During the course of a conversation on other subjects Lord Hood referred to a conversation in Geneva on July 15 between Secretary Herter and Foreign Secretary Selwyn Lloyd when Mr. Lloyd suggested that it might be useful for the United States and the United Kingdom to consider together what steps they might take in the event of an Indonesian attack on West New Guinea.[1] Lord Hood recalled that both our Governments have assured the Dutch of support in the event of an attack but that the nature of such support had not been spelled out other than to suggest that it might well be political and in the field of logistics. Selwyn Lloyd wondered whether we might not consider having talks, either in

---

Source: Department of State, Central Files, 656C.56D/8–2259. Secret. Drafted by Milton C. Rewinkel, Deputy Director of the Office of British Commonwealth and Northern European Affairs, and cleared in draft by Merchant.

[1] See Document 214.

Washington or elsewhere, on what the United States and the United Kingdom might be prepared to do. Lloyd felt, however, that such talks should be held without the Dutch.

Mr. Merchant stated that we would look into the matter. He commented that the Dutch have been pressing us to hold talks with them but that we have thus far resisted. He said we felt the Dutch have somewhat exaggerated fears concerning the possibility of an Indonesian attack. At the same time we feel that the Indonesians seem to have been taking seriously what we have been saying to them and that the evolution of the Indonesia Government, particularly as regards its general attitude towards the West, has been encouraging. Mr. Merchant stated in conclusion that we would consider the British suggestion and be in further touch.

222. Telegram From the Department of State to the Embassy in Indonesia

Washington, August 26, 1959, 8:20 p.m.

238. For Ambassador from Parsons. This message coordinated with other areas Dept and with other Departments and agencies as necessary and appropriate. Further reply to your 305[1] will follow.

1. Your 276,[2] 305 and 332.[3] As you appreciate we cannot authorize you make any commitments in response anticipated GOI request for expanded economic and/or military assistance. Should such request be received you may however reply that you have instructions to say US will give request most prompt careful consideration in light limits imposed by available funds and other commitments. When discussing

---

Source: Department of State, Central Files, 756D.5–MSP/8–1159. Secret. Drafted by Moore on August 22; cleared with SPA, FE, FN, U/MSC, ED, L/MSA, WE, ICA, Defense, and Treasury; and approved by Parsons. Repeated to CINCPAC for POLAD.

[1] In telegram 305, August 14, Jones reported that a "somewhat tentative approach" regarding the extent of additional U.S. economic aid to Indonesia came from Subandrio in a meeting the previous day. During a discussion of the economic and financial problems facing Indonesia, the Foreign Minister pointed out that communications was one of the principal bottlenecks and asked that the United States give serious consideration to ways in which it might help Indonesia in this field. (Ibid., 756D.5–MSP/8–1459) See Supplement.

[2] See Document 217.

[3] Telegram 332, August 19, reported that General Nasution had sent word that day through the U.S. Army Attaché that he desired to confer with Ambassador Jones on August 24 regarding equipment requirements for the Indonesian Army and economic and financial matters. (Department of State, Central Files, 756D.56/8–1959)

matter with Indonesians you will wish bear in mind limitations indicated in FYI paragraph no. 6 below. We prefer that you await approach from GOI rather than taking initiative.

2. Re line you would propose take with Indonesians, we believe it unnecessary and possibly undesirable make conclusion new mutual security agreements absolute condition for possible expanded assistance. In any case conclusion new agreements no guarantee expanded aid since fund stringencies not affected by nature inter-governmental arrangements. Typically US does not conclude single mutual security agreement with cooperating country but rather two separate agreements covering respectively economic and technical assistance on one hand and military assistance on other.

a. Existing US-Indonesian economic and technical assistance agreement of Oct. 16, 1950,[4] provides adequate legal basis for furnishing economic aid in conformity existing legislation and requirements of policy.

b. Standard military assistance agreement, such as that with Pakistan for example and as distinct from special type agreement concluded with Indonesia Aug. 13, 1958, could facilitate provision military aid and in some ways would be advantageous to us, e.g., enabling us to place adequate mission in Indonesia to work with Indonesian services. Notwithstanding advantages derivable from standard military assistance agreement however it important keep in mind that such agreement would require GOI give assurances contained section 142(a) Mutual Security Act of 1954 as amended (Yugoslavia has in past given such assurances), including expressed willingness to make full contribution to "defensive strength of the free world." Present method of providing military aid to Indonesia does not require GOI give such assurances, as you know. While present method of providing military aid without standard military assistance agreement is somewhat cumbersome since it requires separate Presidential Determination for each program, we can continue operating this basis. While under this method amount of military aid to any country limited by law to $30 million in any one fiscal year, obvious limited fund availabilities and our current policy objectives are such that elimination this ceiling unlikely to affect dimension military assistance.

3. Naturally we would welcome a standard military assistance agreement with Indo. if one could be concluded without jeopardizing our hard won gains in Indo. over past year. Existence of agreement would provide gratifying sign of growing Indo. orientation toward free world. On other hand, if Executive Branch so decided, we could under

---

[4] For text of the Agreement, signed at Djakarta, see 7 UST (pt. 2) 2241.

existing arrangements and within limits funds available expand or broaden our assistance to Indonesia. We reluctant therefore to run any risk of damaging relations with Indonesia by possibly premature effort conclude standard military agreement.

4. We believe there are three possible risks involved in proposing standard military assistance agreement at this time: (a) We might get adverse reaction from our friends in present government who might then become suspicious of our motives; (b) We would risk creating impression on part GOI that greatly expanded assistance would result from agreement when there is no assurance this would be case; (c) Should we succeed in concluding a standard military assistance agreement we might make difficult the domestic political position of this relatively favorable government to the point of rendering it impotent or even of causing its fall. I know you too have these factors in mind and will weigh them in deciding whether to broach subject of standard military assistance agreement.

5. Recapitulating foregoing paragraphs you authorized as follows:

a. In reply to possible GOI request for expanded assistance you may state your instructions are to say that US will give request most prompt careful consideration in light limits imposed by availability funds and other commitments. When discussing matter with Indos you will wish bear in mind limitations indicated in FYI paragraph no. 6 below.

b. In reply such request you may at your discretion raise question of standard military assistance agreement, keeping in mind we have legal authority even in absence such agreement to respond within limits available funds, our commitments elsewhere and our estimate of requirements Indonesian situation.

6. Begin FYI. There follows outline present Washington thinking re likely US response to Indonesian aid requests that may be received:

a. Re economic aid we unlikely be receptive at this time to request for large scale economic development assistance such as Asahan power project. This does not preclude continuing development loans for sound projects through US Govt lending institutions.

Expansion of technical assistance at this time seems not indicated. Believe size of present technical assistance program about maximum which can be supported technically from here. Also believe expansion would be difficult in view limitations imposed by general situation in Indonesia. Indonesia's absorptive capacity limited by poor administrative machinery, travel restrictions, lack of adequate number of suitable trainees. Other administrative difficulties encountered in operation technical assistance mission in Indonesia are inadequate housing, schooling and local currency support. Notwithstanding limitations and difficulties cited this paragraph, we would be sympathetic to proposal for rearrangement present technical assistance program to place greater emphasis on technical assistance designed to equip Indonesia better to cope with these very limitations and conditions which (1) contribute to continued stagnation her economy and (2) reduce her ability fully to realize benefits of foreign aid. For example, increased emphasis on technical assistance designed to effect improvement in Indonesian fiscal management and development activities would seem logical in present situation.

As you point out in your 276, there is immediate need for effective attack on inflation. In view these circumstances we would expect GOI might well request balance of payments loan assistance. While Dept would give careful consideration request this nature if accompanied by adequate justification and by evidence that GOI instituting stabilization program showing promise of effectiveness, Congressional cuts have reduced our ability meet global requirements for this type assistance in FY–60, and, in general, we would have to approach this kind of assistance most cautiously. Certainly little support could be aroused here for this type of assistance to Indonesia from US or other free world sources in absence serious stabilization effort by GOI.

b.   Re military assistance, under present circumstances we see no justification for increased level. Our continuing primary aim remains the strengthening of Indonesian armed forces for maintenance internal security and self defense. As we see it currently, emphasis in military assistance programs would be placed on Army equipment and training, with smaller segments to provide Navy and Air Force with training and with equipment not competitive with that supplied by Communist bloc.

Long range planning for possible future military assistance to Indonesia now under inter-Departmental consideration. End FYI.

We are sending you separately info on our arrangements in Burma.[5]

I would appreciate any reactions you may care to give me on thinking set forth above.[6]

Dillon

---

[5] Reference is to the agreement relating to the sale of military equipment, materials, and services to Burma, signed at Rangoon on June 24, 1958. For text, see 9 UST 1069.

[6] Jones met with Nasution on August 31. Nasution presented specific proposals for additional U.S. assistance to ease the military burdens on Indonesia's civilian economy. Jones informed Nasution that the United States would receive his request and give it prompt consideration and assured him that the United States would continue military assistance at a level yet to be determined. (Telegram 440 from Djakarta, August 31; Department of State, Central Files, 756D.5–MSP/8–3159) See Supplement.

223.   Despatch From the Embassy in the Netherlands to the Department of State

No. 173   The Hague, September 3, 1959.

REF

>   Djakarta's D–904 and D–905, May 26, 1959,[1] and D–925, June 1, 1959;[2]
>   Canberra's D–2, July 1, 1959;[3] and Emb D–60, July 27, 1959[4]

SUBJECT

>   West New Guinea: Comments on Dutch Attitudes with Particular Reference to
>   Embassy Djakarta's Proposal re Settlement of West New Guinea Question

The proposals made in Embassy Djakarta's reference despatches on this subject have been read here with particular interest. We, too, have long felt that some clarification of the U.S. position regarding West New Guinea would benefit U.S. efforts in dealing with the complex of U.S.-Dutch-Indo problems with which we have all been preoccupied during the last two years. The Ambassador has suggested on a number of occasions (e.g., Embtel 1157,[5] rptd Djakarta 149, Canberra 74; and Embtel 1466,[6] rptd Djakarta 225, Canberra 134, et seq.) that this problem be reexamined.

The following additional comments (a synthesis of information and views from the sections of the Embassy concerned and from the Consulates General) are now offered by the Embassy in the hope that they will be helpful when the Department undertakes a new study of the U.S. position regarding West New Guinea. The first section below summarizes the Dutch position on this subject; the second section contains comment

---

Source: Department of State, Central Files, 656.56D13/9–359. Secret.

[1] Documents 202 and 203.

[2] See the source note, Document 203.

[3] Entitled "Australian Policy Toward a Solution in West New Guinea." (Department of State, Central Files, 656.56D13/7–159)

[4] Despatch 60 reported that it was important that the Department clarify U.S. policy toward the West New Guinea problem. (*Ibid.*, 656.56D13/7–2759)

[5] See footnote 4, Document 171.

[6] In telegram 1466, March 10, Young reported that he continued to hope that "ways and means will be found" to help the Netherlands purchase equipment for the defense of West New Guinea. "So far as I know," Young commented, "US and majority of its allies in NATO, SEATO, and UN have never contradicted Dutch view that these powers prefer that West New Guinea remain under Dutch control. This has merely added force to Dutch determination to hold on, for it is unlikely that without strong US pressure, Dutch would voluntarily abandon part of Dutch realm. If US believes Dutch retention West New Guinea is not desirable or necessary, I suggest that this ought to be made known soonest to all concerned." (Department of State, Central Files, 756D.5–MSP/3–1059)

on this position in relation to Embassy Djakarta's analysis and suggestions; and the third section contains this Embassy's conclusions regarding the further development of the Dutch position on West New Guinea and the possibilities of ultimately finding some constructive solution of it.

[Here follows a section summarizing the Dutch position on the West New Guinea dispute; see Supplement.]

Comments on Embassy Djakarta's Suggestions

We fully understand and appreciate the difficulties, inhibitions and obstacles that the West New Guinea problem places in the path of our policy in Indonesia. We recognize also, as Embassy Djakarta has pointed out, that the emotional, political and other aspects of the Indonesian attitude on this subject, no matter how contrived or unrealistic they may be, are nevertheless facts of life which must be accepted and taken into account in determining our position on the New Guinea question in relation to U.S. interests. This same maxim applies, of course, in the case of the Dutch attitude.

After reviewing that attitude, we believe it is clear, first, that the proposal made by Embassy Djakarta would not be sufficiently attractive from the Dutch point of view to persuade them to change their position, and, second, that our initiative, as proposed by Embassy Djakarta, would have far more serious consequences—and not alone for U.S.-Dutch relations—than has been foreseen in the reference despatches.

In essence, Embassy Djakarta proposes that a UN trusteeship over West New Guinea be established for five years after which the area would go to Indonesia; meanwhile, an agreement would be negotiated between the Netherlands under which the Dutch would receive adequate compensation for the Dutch assets seized by the Indonesians and the progressive removal of discriminatory restrictions on Dutch enterprises in Indonesia. However, such an arrangement is not likely to be viewed by the Dutch as an adequate motive for reversing their position on West New Guinea. So far as they are concerned, their people have been expelled from Indonesia and Dutch investments and enterprises have been "stolen". They feel strongly that they have a right to receive adequate compensation for their "stolen" assets *without* giving up anything more. Moreover, the Dutch have long since made it unmistakably clear that they believe that Indonesians, in attempting to join the question of compensation to their claim to West New Guinea, are engaging in nothing short of blackmail. Consequently, to make a settlement with the Indonesians under which they would simply receive what they would regard as doubtful promises of payment for "stolen property," would hardly appear to the Dutch as a persuasive reason for agreeing to give up West New Guinea as well. After all, they were not prepared to give it up in the hope of saving the Dutch businesses in Indonesia which were taken over; and we see nothing to indicate that, now that this has occurred, there is any likelihood of their giving it up in the hope of ultimately salvaging something in the way of compensation to which they feel they are already legitimately entitled.

The Dutch stand in this respect constitutes, in our judgment, a classic case in which characteristic Dutch business shrewdness in protecting its own financial interests was obliged to give way to political and moral considerations which, in this "Calvinistic" country, have been considered of greater and more basic importance in shaping national policy. Being forced to make such a policy choice, however, has, if anything, intensified the emotional reaction of the Dutch—the sense of moral outrage—over the expulsion of Dutch nationals from Indonesia, Indonesian treatment of Dutch business interests in Indonesia and the continuing Indonesian campaign linking compensation with their claim to West New Guinea. In these circumstances, therefore, any attempt to persuade the Dutch to accept a settlement along the lines of Embassy Djakarta's proposals would, in our opinion, be hotly rejected and Dutch protests against such attempts would doubtless find a sympathetic ear among some of our principal allies.

In presenting its suggestions for a settlement of the New Guinea question, Embassy Djakarta has anticipated that it "would probably lead to a degree of strain in Dutch-American relations." We already possess, it seems to us, some standard of measurement by which we may judge just what this degree of strain might be. During the last two years we have enjoyed, in our opinion, the best possible opportunity to observe the strength of Dutch feeling on this subject—namely, their reaction to our military aid program in Indonesia. And this reaction related merely to the *potential* danger to West New Guinea which the Dutch fear our arms aid to Indonesia constitutes. But even this reaction brought us perilously close to full-blown and dangerous disagreement bilaterally and within NATO—a possibility that is still far from being dead. If we should decide to participate in promoting any settlement at this time which envisages turning over West New Guinea to Indonesia, we can only say that the Dutch reaction would be immediate, public, violent and not confined to bilateral channels. It is clear from the foregoing section and depth of feeling from which the Dutch position on West New Guinea springs. Any move on our part which would lead to their displacement in New Guinea would be bitterly and violently resented as an attack on those basic Dutch principles discussed above. Such a move would also rekindle all the latent Dutch bitterness against the U.S. (and presumably the UK) in connection with our policy at the time Indonesia obtained its independence. It is well to recall, in this connection, that the more senior positions in many government ministries here are held by "old Indonesia hands," men who remember the good old days when they held top posts in the Dutch East Indies—and who remember also the days when they lost the jobs they had enjoyed so much. It is no exaggeration to suggest that we would be strongly attacked for trying to kick the Dutch out of West New Guinea as we helped to kick them out of Indonesia. After the treatment they have had at Indonesian hands, there would be little doubt in the Dutch mind that they were being abandoned by the U.S. and their interests sacrificed to Indonesian interests as the expedient price of U.S. policy in that area.

While such a move on our part would certainly have serious consequences for our bilateral relations with the Netherlands, one cannot ignore the repercussions it would also have elsewhere. While the Department is in a better position to judge this point, it seems to us that any U.S. action along the lines Embassy Djakarta suggests would certainly have great significance for the British, French, Belgian and Portuguese Governments which are also burdened with their own delicate colonial problems, Furthermore, all these countries are members of NATO and any action, as suggested in the case of one of our staunchest NATO allies, could not fail, we believe, to cause important repercussions within the Western alliance, which is, however one wishes to qualify it, still basic to our major foreign policy objectives.

One cannot ignore, either, the impact which the suggested course of action can be expected to have on Australia and on our relations with that country. Embassy Canberra's reference despatch has already given indications of this probability. While the Australians have expressed their willingness to accept any disposition of West New Guinea mutually agreed by the Dutch and Indonesians, this appears here to have far more the ring of a platitude than it does of any modification, however slight, in their existing bipartisan policy on this subject. There is surely nothing known here to indicate that the Australians want or expect the Dutch to dispose of West New Guinea—to the Indonesians or anyone else except, perhaps, in due course the Papuans. On the contrary, there seems every reason to believe that the Australians fully expect and anxiously want the Dutch to retain sovereignty over West New Guinea. Their anxiety in this respect has now reached the point where it is sometimes difficult for us to determine which of these two is more ardently seeking the other's support. As this Embassy has reported, Dutch-Australian cooperation in New Guinea has been increasing (Emb D–315, Sept. 26, 1958,[7] and D–405, Oct. 31, 1958[8]) and Prime Minister Menzies'

[7] Not printed. (*Ibid.,* 656.56D13/9–2658)
[8] Not printed. (*Ibid.,* 656.56D13/10–3158)

recent visit here on June 29 confirmed the fact that the Dutch and Australians are making every effort to expand their cooperation at all levels and in all areas involved in the administration and development of New Guinea as a whole. (Emb D–17, July 8, 1959)[9] In his public statement at the time, Mr. Menzies said, "We agreed that, with the ultimate idea of bringing the indigenous populations to a state of self-government, we should each pursue active policies of improving education, health and communications and the exploration of national resources." These endeavors, the Embassy understands from the Foreign Office, are to be carried out with increased cooperation between the Dutch and Australian administrators. From these and other indications it seems clear that, in principle and in practice, the policy interests of the Dutch and Australians in New Guinea are becoming so intertwined as to be inseparable in considering any settlement of the future status of West New Guinea.

Conclusions

Much as we may agree with Embassy Djakarta regarding the desirability of finding a solution for the West New Guinea question, we do not, in view of all the foregoing, see it as a problem of manageable proportions about which the U.S. can do anything constructive in the immediately foreseeable future. Passions have been aroused on both sides and it is as unrealistic, in our opinion, to expect the Dutch to turn over West Guinea to the Indonesians as to expect the Indonesians to restore Dutch properties in Indonesia to their Dutch owners. Consequently, unless we should find that our interests dictate that we should try to force a Dutch-Indonesian settlement of the New Guinea question, we see a period of quiet, during which passions may cool, as the minimum necessary prerequisite to any moves which might have a chance of success in leading to an ultimate settlement of this highly charged issue.

By this comment, however, we do not intend to suggest that the U.S. should do nothing. It is still our belief that the U.S. should make a clear determination of its own best interests in this matter and the position those interests dictate as regards future policy objectives.

For instance, it is our assumption that the U.S. recognizes Dutch sovereignty over Netherlands New Guinea; at least we are not aware that the U.S. has ever challenged it. But is this assumption correct and is it based on any legal finding? It seems to us that one possible course of action to explore, in this connection, is whether U.S. interests would be best served by trying to persuade the Indonesians to give up their opposition to placing the West New Guinea issue before the International Court of Justice or before the Permanent Court of Arbitration. If the In-

---

[9] Not printed. (*Ibid.*, 033.4356/7–859)

donesians continue to feel that the Dutch are acting illegally in not turning West New Guinea over to them, and if the U.S. believes that a solution to the West New Guinea issue must be found, why, then, should we not urge that it be sought through these recognized and established organs of international law?

If, on the other hand, the U.S. accepts the Indonesian view that theirs is primarily a political and not a legal claim to West New Guinea, this would, we believe, require a different approach in assessing the U.S. position. In addition to a legal finding on the question of whether we recognize Dutch sovereignty over Netherlands New Guinea, another fundamental starting point, we think, would then be a U.S. determination of the strategic value in Southeast Asia of New Guinea as a whole and Netherlands New Guinea in particular. This determination would seem to be essential before any decision could be made on the political question of whether the U.S. wishes the Dutch to retain control over West New Guinea. Once this political question is decided, it seems to us that the U.S. would then be in a position to begin thinking in concrete terms about what action it should take in relation to the West New Guinea question. It is quite possible, of course, that even after a thorough-going review, the U.S. might decide to make no change in its present policy of trying to skate between the opposing views of the Dutch and Indonesians without becoming involved in the dispute at all. This is, after all, as much a policy as deciding to support the Dutch or the Indonesians.

Whatever the outcome, however, this Embassy still believes there are basic questions which require answers, even if, for the time being, they do not change our policy or actions. We are hopeful that the despatches under reference, as well as this one, will prompt a study to produce those answers.

Herbert P. Fales
Chargé d'Affaires ad interim

224.   Memorandum From the Director of the Office of Southwest Pacific Affairs (Mein) to the Assistant Secretary of State for Far Eastern Affairs (Parsons)

Washington, September 10, 1959.

SUBJECT

    Situation in Indonesia

Summary

Indonesia's first "guided democracy" government took office July 10, 1959, under Sukarno's premiership (Tab 1).[1] The period since then has been one of organization and consolidation, with (a) Sukarno appointing various subsidiary governmental organs, (b) the Army continuing to expand its role in the government and (c) plans being made to carry out the government's general program (improved supply of basic necessities, better internal security, and continuation of the struggle against all forms of imperialism).

The political parties remain uneasy about the implications of "guided democracy," particularly so since in the new government not only ministers but senior civil servants as well have been directed to sever their ties with parties. The parties are disturbed also by the Army's strengthened role in the government, although non-Communist parties generally prefer this to greater Communist influence. Apart from the anti-Sukarno Masjumi and Socialist (PSI) parties, which are completely excluded from the executive branch, the Communist Party (PKI) is the one most adversely affected by "guided democracy" thus far. The party's role in the government is minimal, while the openly anti-Communist Army is strongly represented. Moreover, it seems plain that Sukarno is using the Army as a counterweight to Communist power.

The most significant action taken by the new government to date was the announcement on August 24 of drastic monetary reforms calculated to curb Indonesia's serious inflation (Tab 2).[2] The ultimate effect of the monetary reforms, which have at least temporarily upset business activity, cannot yet be assessed. The public reaction seems to be one more of bewilderment than resentment, although the government will reap great public disfavor if it does not find means promptly to release frozen funds needed by employers to pay wages. The monetary re-

---

    Source: Department of State, Central Files, 756D.11/9–1059. Secret. Drafted by Moore and cleared with O'Sullivan, Green, and Mary S. Olmsted.

[1] No tabs were attached to the source text. Tab A is printed as Document 215.

[2] See Document 220.

forms, though introduced without consultation with the IMF, may have useful results if followed-up by the tightened fiscal management Sukarno has promised.

An earlier assessment of this government as relatively favorable to U.S. interests on the basis of its composition, remains valid. Several ministers have told us the U.S. should welcome this government as highly favorable to U.S. interests, and we expect requests from the Indonesians for expanded military and economic aid. Within reasons, such expanded aid may well be in our interest, but it is unlikely that we need formulate our attitude towards increased aid on the assumption that this government represents the "last chance" for U.S. influence in Indonesia, as a number of Indonesian leaders have hinted is the case.

[Here follows a detailed discussion of these points; see Supplement.]

225. Telegram From the Embassy in Indonesia to the Department of State

Djakarta, September 21, 1959, noon.

637. CINCPAC also for POLAD. Circular 149.[1] To a striking degree my overall analysis of US objectives and US programs for 1961 parallels that contained in Embassy telegram 697[2] of August 22, 1958, in which I commented on 1960 programs. In that telegram I indicated that I thought our programs necessarily were inadequate, and this continues to be true for largely the same reasons. In Embassy telegram 1835[3] of December 5, 1958 I gave my thinking as to the kind of economic aid program which would be adequate. Our objectives, although we clearly are nearer to their realization than a year ago, remain the same—to secure Indonesia from Communist domination through assisting it in the achievement of political and economic stability.

Source: Department of State, Central Files, 756D.5–MSP/9–2159. Secret. Transmitted in two sections and also sent to CINCPAC.

[1] Circular telegram 149, which was sent to all U.S. Chiefs of Mission on August 19, requested a "succinct, overall analysis of U.S. objectives and role U.S. (both MSP and other) and non-U.S. programs in FY 1961 in achieving them." (Ibid., 120.171/8–1959)

[2] Not printed. (Ibid., 756D.5–MSP/8–2258) See Supplement.

[3] Not printed. (Department of State, Central Files, 856D.00/12–558) See Supplement.

By and large our problems have shifted in degree and emphasis rather than kind during the last year. Steady economic deterioration during that period has been offset to some extent by improvement in the political situation. The latter has been furthered by consolidation of executive power, with concomitant reduction of power in the hands of political parties and parliament where the high water mark of communism in Indonesia has been reached.

While it is not possible to demonstrate that provision of substantial aid to the Indonesian army was entirely responsible for the increased power and intensified pro-Western posture of Indonesian army leaders, there can be no doubt that our aid had considerable influence. Besides giving army leaders new confidence and providing them with means of effective internal security, our aid has helped widen the growing breach between army and PKI. As President Sukarno and the army have drawn closer together, long-run prospect for a head-on clash between Sukarno and PKI, which would greatly assist ultimate achievement of our objectives, has been strengthened. Continued military aid at substantially the current level or slightly higher will be needed to maintain the momentum we have achieved.

Evidence that our program, particularly our military aid efforts, have been aimed in the right direction is to be found in character of present government in which leftist influence has been entirely eliminated from inner cabinet, while anti-Communist influence, largely represented by army, has been expanded and strengthened. There is reason to believe present shape of government more nearly in line with specifications of General Nasution than wishes of President Sukarno, who holds to view Communists should be required share in responsibility for government.

Concurrently our economic assistance, even though on a minor scale in terms of problems, has had considerable influence in improving the political climate. As a minimum it has made friends and has helped train Indonesians in many key governmental positions, influencing their orientation toward west. It has also given important development assistance in certain sections of economy such as Gresik cement, power plants, and assistance to ports, railroads, et cetera.

Greatest danger to US interests here is that improvement in political climate may be nullified by failure GOI to solve grave economic problems. While recent monetary measures demonstrated present government capable taking unpopular measures unlike predecessors, resulting situation fraught with new dangers, and so far there is no evidence of coordinated plan for dealing with these.

Thus well before 1961 we may be called upon urgently to rescue Indonesian economy from nationalistic folly, and it will be in our interest to do so even though we will be in good position to say "I told you so."

In meantime our program on economic front must be kept as flexible as our inherent limitations permit. We are not yet in position to move into kind of relationship with Indonesia which would permit most effective use of our resources, and this makes it imperative that whatever we do has maximum benefit. On some occasions in the past, due chiefly to Indonesian domestic political pressures, our assistance programs have become somewhat more diffused than they should have been and in some cases benefits have been partly offset by imposition of unnecessary rupiah costs on a government facing grave inflationary danger, without return of any immediate economic benefit. In future our economic aid should be confined to three general categories: (1) development; (2) technical and professional training or direct technical support of development projects; and (3) fire brigade projects which have overriding political impact or which meet grave immediate crises such as stabilization. I have listed these in order of dollar magnitude. Order of importance could fluctuate with circumstances.

Since all US programs in Indonesia to date have been primarily political in motivation, problems of coordination have been relatively slight, easily managed at political level. Fair degree of coordination exists with UN programs, Colombo Plan, activities friendly nations, our practice being withdraw from any field which other friendly programs prepared finance. Largest non-US programs of course financed by Sino-Soviet Bloc, many of them contributing usefully to economic stability in Indonesia but carrying with them grave political danger to US and Indonesian interests.

Coordination between USIS, ICA programs and between USIS political programs close, effective. USIS continues contribute useful short and long-range psychological support all US programs. Prospect improving for increasingly aggressive information activity more closely coordinated with indigenous elements such as Indonesian Army.

In summary we are dealing here with a situation so fluid that the primary requirement for advancing US interests is flexibility. It would be unwise at this critical point Indonesian history to commit our course to any particular economic, psychological programs. At optimum our effort should be to keep a boxer stance with our weight balanced on both feet so as best to deal with a fast-changing situation. I realize that this picture is not wholly realistic in reference to US budgetary planning requirements, but it is toward this posture that we should work.

For example, if Indonesian monetary and economic stabilization program recently undertaken is to succeed, further steps will have to be taken and these necessarily will include commodity support for program. In addition to PL 480 possibilities, I believe additional credits for raw materials, spare parts and capital goods to keep production going will be required. Thus I would recommend that in addition to aid programs already approved or under current consideration approximately $50 million be listed for this purpose under "possible requirements" for Indonesian 1961 program. Whether this amount will actually be required will depend upon developments within next weeks or months but it is self-evident rapid action regarding any such support request would be key to success of operation.

Meanwhile our efforts here will be devoted to concentration of aid programs both economic and military on areas of immediate impact eliminating dispersion.

Jones

226.   Memorandum of Conversation

Washington, September 29, 1959.

SUBJECT

    U.S.-Dutch-Indonesian Relations

PARTICIPANTS

For the Netherlands	*For the United States*
Dr. Joseph Luns, Foreign Minister [1]	The Secretary
Dr. J. H. van Roijen, Ambassador	Ambassador Philip Young
Mr. Emil Schiff, Minister	SPA—Mr. Mein
	WE—Mr. McBride
	WE—Mr. Chadbourn

Mr. Luns said he had told Mr. Wilcox the day before that he expected that Indonesia would bring up the West New Guinea issues next year in the United Nations General Assembly.[2] He hoped the United States would support the Dutch position on this matter. He went on to

---

Source: Department of State, Central Files, 656.56D13/9–2959. Secret. Drafted by Chadbourn. Approved in S on October 9.

[1] Luns was in Washington for a series of discussions with U.S. officials on matters of mutual concern, September 28–29. He met with Parsons, Murphy, and Wilcox on September 28. A memorandum of the former conversation is *ibid.*, 756D.00/9–2859; the other conversations are summarized in telegram 454 to The Hague, September 29. (*Ibid.*, 611.56/9–2959)

[2] See Document 267.

say that the Dutch position on this question was the same as the French position on Algeria (i.e., the United Nations is not competent to change the territorial status of a member state). If, however, an Indonesian resolution were passed in the United Nations, the Dutch would simply disregard it.

Mr. Luns then reviewed for the Secretary the history of his talks with Secretary Dulles in regard to a possible Indonesian attack on West New Guinea. He had told Mr. Dulles a year ago that the Dutch were very concerned about Indonesian plans to attack West New Guinea. As a result Mr. Dulles had spoken in very clear terms to Mr. Subandrio about this question, stressing the point that the United States was against the use of force in the settlement of such issues. This had had the desired effect on the Indonesians. Mr. Luns then expressed his gratification that this political deterrent had been successful in restraining Indonesia from any West New Guinea ventures, although he still felt that this was in the nature of a postponement rather than a change in objectives.

Mr. Luns then said he would like to have a reaffirmation of U.S. policy in regard to the possible use of force by Indonesia against West New Guinea. He read a copy of the public statement of October 7, 1958 (see memorandum of conversation, Oct. 7 [8], 1958)[3] and asked whether this remained our policy, to which the Secretary replied in the affirmative. Mr. Luns went on to say that there were two aspects or elements to this problem of West New Guinea, the first being the application of the deterrent in time of peace. The second element was the question of what assistance the U.S. was prepared to give the Netherlands in the event an attack actually occurred. He then read the Dutch version of the private assurances Mr. Dulles had given Ambassador van Roijen during their conversation on October 7, 1958: (The verbatim Dutch text is as follows: "We are not in a position to make advance statements. I expect that if that occurs we would give you logistical support and find other ways to help. You could count on the same pattern as we have shown in other parts of the world. We acted as you know very vigorously in Lebanon and in the Formosa Straits.")

Mr. Luns then urged that the U.S. take prompt action should an attack occur. Even though the Dutch have virtually nothing left in Indonesia, certain Indonesian leaders still continued to threaten the Dutch. As an example, he cited the fact that Subandrio had recently told the Dutch Chargé in Djakarta that the presence of a Dutch naval ship in Indonesian territorial waters would be a casus belli. The Indonesians apparently now define these waters to cover all inter-island waters. It was this type of Indonesian statement that continued to disturb the Dutch. He felt the

---

[3] See Document 159.

situation needed careful watching. The confiscation of Dutch properties in Indonesia, of course, was a sore point for the Dutch. Many of the refugees were now in West New Guinea, resulting in the presence of 18,000 Dutchmen in West New Guinea. Mr. Luns thought Indonesia was now going downhill rapidly, one of the principal reasons therefor being the fact that they will not accept any technical assistance from the Dutch because the Dutch are their whipping boys. This increasingly chaotic situation augmented the danger of Indonesia falling to the Communists. He expressed the complete agreement of his government with the U.S. objective of keeping Indonesia from falling to the Communists. It was a great pity that all this was going on because, in his opinion, there was no basic hostility of the Indonesian people to the Dutch as people as evidenced by the fact that not a single Dutchman had been murdered or hurt in the past few years in Indonesia. It was all caused by the hatred held by the top Indonesian leadership. The Secretary asked Mr. Luns what he thought of the alleged differences between Sukarno on the one hand and Djuanda and Nasution on the other. Mr. Luns replied that Nasution was the best element in the top leadership. Since all of them were very close friends, however, one could not expect that Nasution would ever make any move against Sukarno.

Reverting to the Dulles statements and specifically to the mention of logistical support therein, Mr. Luns asked if we could study ways to help. (It is assumed that Mr. Luns was referring to joint military planning and planning for logistical support.) The Secretary explained that the difficulty in maintaining absolute secrecy in these matters posed a serious problem. Mr. Luns replied strongly that, of course, there would never be any publicity on such a matter. In the case of the "shopping list" for instance, no public mention of the real intended use of the equipment had been made, or ever would be, other than to say that the equipment was intended for "general use." Mr. Luns asked the Secretary for his help in obtaining the items the Dutch have requested on the shopping list. A discussion ensued in which it was agreed that progress on the shopping list had been made, and that the Department of Defense was trying its best to meet the Dutch requirements. The problem had narrowed itself down to questions of specifications and cost; it was the helicopters that were so expensive. It was also brought out that the items on the list were replacements for deteriorating equipment used in the defense of West New Guinea. Mr. Luns said that without our help the Dutch would have to reduce their commitments to NATO in order to maintain the present minimum level of security forces in West New Guinea. This minimum defense posture was designed to boost the morale of the 18,000 Dutchmen on the island as well as the native Papuans, and to discourage an Indonesian attempt at infiltration.

The conversation then turned to an unrelated matter and at this point the Secretary was interrupted by a telephone call. When the Secretary resumed the conversation, Mr. Luns reaffirmed his understanding that the two elements of U.S. policy regarding a possible attack on West New Guinea as expressed by Mr. Dulles on October 7, 1958, remained unchanged. As he understood our thinking, however, the U.S. reserved its position as regards advance planning. The Secretary replied that we were obliged to reserve on this point. Ambassador Young made the point that the fact the Dutch had given us all available information on their military establishment in West New Guinea was in a sense a kind of joint planning and would facilitate any U.S. planning in the future. It was important, he went on, for the Dutch to keep us currently informed on all military aspects of this situation.

The discussion of other matters is being reported in separate memoranda of conversations.[4]

---

[4] The discussion on Indonesia was summarized in telegram 461 to The Hague, September 30. (Department of State, Central Files, 611.56/9–3059) In a 6-page letter of October 2 to Chargé Fales, Ambassador Young summarized his impressions of the Luns visit, indicating that the visit had been quite successful even though very little of a concrete nature had been accomplished. (*Ibid.*, WE Files: Lot 63 D 221, Luns Visit 1959)

---

227.   Editorial Note

On October 29 at the 422d meeting of the National Security Council, Allen Dulles discussed developments in Indonesia during his intelligence briefing:

"Mr. Dulles summarized a recent report from the U.S. Embassy in Djakarta on the talk that Ambassador Jones had recently had with Foreign Minister Subandrio following Subandrio's visit to Peiping. Subandrio had been treated with an arrogance and brutality that had left him staggered. He had come back suggesting that Indonesia should revise its foreign policy as it related to Communist China. He could not understand why the Chinese had been as crude as they had been. They had threatened Indonesia with economic warfare and other unspecified measures. Discussions at the technical level had also been heated. Subandrio stated that, when he had reported his views to the Indonesian Cabinet, Sukarno had supported his position. Mr. Dulles indicated, however, that he was doubtful whether Sukarno would have gone this far. In his view it was more likely that Sukarno had simply told Subandrio that he had 'done a good job.' This affair was in line with the blustering line which Communist China was taking in many fields. Only yesterday they had bombarded the Offshore Islands with more shells (227) than at any time since last March." (Memorandum of discussion by Robert Johnson, October 29; Eisenhower Library, Whitman File, NSC Records)

The reference may be to Jones' conversation with Subandrio on October 24. A memorandum of that conversation, by Jones, is in Department of State, SPA Files: Lot 62 D 409, Communist China. It reads in part as follows: "At the outset of our discussion which lasted two hours Subandrio broke out into an excited tirade against the Chinese Communists. He was obviously upset, hurt and deeply resentful of the Chinese Communists' attitude as well as frightened by their arrogance and direct threats."

---

228. Memorandum of Conversation

Washington, November 4, 1959.

SUBJECT

    Indonesia

PARTICIPANTS

United States	Australia
The Secretary	Mr. R.G. Casey, Minister for
Mr. Parsons, Assistant Secretary for	External Affairs
Far Eastern Affairs	Ambassador Beale
Mr. Mein, Director, Office of	Mr. Loveday, Counselor
Southwest Pacific Affairs	

Minister Casey said that the Australian DMI, Col. Macadie, when in Indonesia recently, was approached first by Col. Sukendro and later by General Nasution and asked if he would accept the task of convincing the rebels of the necessity of giving up the struggle. Col. Macadie's reply on a personal basis to General Nasution served to postpone a decision. Minister Casey handed the Secretary a copy of a memorandum on the

---

Source: Department of State, Central Files, 756D.00/11–459. Top Secret. Drafted by Mein. Approved by S November 10.

approach as well as a copy of an assessment prepared in Canberra. He said that the conclusion of the paper was that it would not be a good thing for Australia to get mixed up in this. (Copy of memoranda attached.)[1]

Minister Casey said that his personal view, based to a certain extent on instinct and after consideration of the matter, was that Australia should not get involved because: (a) Australia does not want the rebels to fold up even if they are not conducting an intensive campaign at the present time; they are the only people in revolt in Indonesia and if they should fold up, there would be no other revolution there; and (b) it would mean Australia involvement in Indonesian domestic affairs which would be misunderstood and might even play into the hands of the Communists. He indicated also that he thought it was in Australia's interest that the rebellion continue since as long as it serves to keep Indonesian attention on domestic affairs, there is less likelihood of the Indonesians turning against West New Guinea. The Secretary commented that there appeared to be a conflict of interests in the Indonesian approach, since if the rebels fold up, the reasons given by the Indonesians for the purchase of large quantities of military equipment would disappear.

Mr. Casey asked if we had any information on the current status of the rebellion. He was given a brief picture of the present situation in Sumatra and in North Celebes as well as of the reported surrender of Darul Islam elements in the Celebes.

Mr. Casey reiterated his statement at the ANZUS meeting that the UK, at his urging, recently agreed to put off a decision on an Indonesian request for the purchase of barges until after the elections.[2] He said that the matter has been discussed again and that the UK has agreed to postpone a decision until after the visit of Prime Minister Menzies to Indonesia in early December. He said that he had heard rumors also of an Indonesian desire to purchase small vessels in the UK. Mr. Casey said he would be in London next week and expected to discuss these matters further with the British.

The Minister asked whether we had any new information on supplies from the Soviet Bloc to Indonesia. He was informed that although we had fairly accurate information on what the Soviet Bloc had supplied, there was no indication of any new arrangements.

Mr. Casey asked whether we had as yet delivered any C–130B's to Indonesia. He was informed that this was a commercial transaction to be

---

[1] Neither printed, but see the attachment to Document 229.

[2] Reference is to the meeting of the ANZUS Council in Washington on October 26; see vol. XVI, pp. 156–169.

financed entirely by the Indonesian Government and that deliveries were not scheduled until sometime in the fall of 1960. He was told that the Indonesian Government, however, is attempting to get delivery of one of the planes in January and that this request is now under active consideration.

The Minister said that Australia continues to be concerned over developments in Indonesia and is grateful for the deterrents applied by the United States in the past and would appreciate any further action the United States can take in this respect.

229.   Memorandum of Conversation

Washington, November 17, 1959.

SUBJECT

Indonesia

PARTICIPANTS

Mr. Booker, Minister, Australian Embassy
Mr. Mein, Director, Office of Southwest Pacific Affairs

Mr. Mein gave Mr. Booker a copy of the attached paper commenting on the Australian paper on "Negotiations with Dissidents" which Minister Casey had handed to the Secretary on November 4, 1959.[1] Mr. Booker expressed his appreciation for receiving the Department's comments.

Source: Department of State, Central Files, 756D.00/11–1759. Top Secret. Drafted by Mein.

[1] See Document 228.

Attachment [2]

COMMENTS ON AUSTRALIAN PAPER ON
"NEGOTIATIONS WITH DISSIDENTS"
Handed to the Secretary by Minister Casey on November 4, 1959

1.   United States Position

It is the policy of the United States Government to encourage a reconciliation between the rebels and the Central Government. We feel that such reconciliation, however, should take place only on the basis of mutually acceptable terms. We would hope that such terms would not mean complete surrender by the dissidents as demanded at this time by the Government. The dissidents still represent an anti-Communist force which cannot be ignored by the Central Government in determining its policies and which could be used as a rallying point should the Communists take over in Java. We would hope, therefore, that any negotiations for settlement of the rebellion would result in attainment of some of the original objectives of the dissidents and in strengthening the anti-Communist forces in Indonesia. The following are some of the reasons for this policy:

a)   Continued P.R.R.I. activity is of primary interest to the Communists since they thrive on chaos. They have been taking full advantage of the political differences resulting from the rebellion as well as of the deteriorating economic situation in the country.

b)   Continuation of the rebellion will serve only to weaken further the economy. The expense of the rebellion is reported to be about one-half of the total budget, which is a considerable drain of funds. This cost is being met primarily through the issue of new bank notes, resulting in growing inflation. This trend will negate any beneficial effects which might have resulted from the August 24 monetary measures. On the other hand, re-establishment of the Government's authority in North and Central Sumatra and North Celebes, which areas are important foreign exchange earners, would assist the Government in improving its foreign exchange position.

c)   Further deterioration in the economy will only increase the amount of foreign aid which eventually might be necessary to put Indonesia back on its feet, and since we presumably would be one of the major sources of such aid, it would be in our interest that the economic situation not deteriorate further.

---

[2] Top Secret. Drafted by Mein and Wenzel.

d) A settlement of the rebellion would permit the Government to devote all of its resources, manpower and energy to other serious problems now facing Indonesia which must be resolved before the country can move forward.

e) A reconciliation with the rebels would facilitate the return to active participation in the political scene of men like Hatta and would serve to remove one of the irritants among the non-Communist political parties. A settlement would create a climate for non-Communist and anti-Communist elements to join forces against the PKI.

f) Continuation of the rebellion would tend to increase Indonesia's suspicions of foreign assistance to the rebels. The rebels are in very serious trouble and their continuing ability to carry on for any length of time would only be interpreted by the Government as an indication that they were being assisted from outside. This suspicion would be directed primarily at us, the Republic of China and the Philippines, making our relations with Indonesia more difficult.

g) Settlement of the rebellion would not weaken the position of Nasution and the Army but on the contrary would permit him to concentrate his efforts on the PKI. Inability on his part to settle the rebellion might in fact weaken his position in the long run. It does not necessarily follow that the state of emergency would be rescinded following a settlement of the rebellion but even if this were to be the case, we would not perceive any diminishing of effective Army control over the country, particularly in the outlying regions. The Army's influence in the formulation of Government policy—e.g., the postponement of national elections—would also continue.

The settlement of the rebellion would have to have at least the tacit approval of Sukarno. However, given the evidences of the Army's ability to influence Sukarno in the past (e.g., the formation of the new Government last July, the Attorney General affair),[3] we do not believe that it is beyond the realm of possibility that Sukarno would acquiesce to some sort of settlement. The Australian view that Sukarno would feel that a settlement would precipitate a major breach between himself and the PKI is, we believe, invalid. It might be pointed out that Sukarno has approved the current Army-inspired drive against the Chinese retailers in Indonesia, which action has caused considerable unrest in the PKI.

---

[3] Reference is to Attorney General Gatot Tarunimihardja's proposed investigation of illegal barter transactions by the Indonesian Army. As a result of Army pressure, Gatot was dismissed from his post in November 1959. The Embassy reported this affair to the Department in despatch 44 from Djakarta, November 30. (Department of State, Central Files, 756D.00/11–3059) See Supplement.

Sukarno's antipathy toward the rebel movement is predicated, on the contrary, on his feeling that the rebels have betrayed the revolution.

h) A settlement would diminish the military strength of the P.R.R.I. although the rebel movement would likely retain some psychological influence. However, as the Australians have pointed out, the P.R.R.I. position is likely to diminish in any event over the next two or three years. On the other hand, a settlement would eliminate or at least substantially reduce the conflict between the two leading anti-Communist forces in Indonesia.

i) We do not believe that a settlement of the rebellion would substantially increase the danger of an Indonesian attack against West New Guinea. By far the most significant deterrent to such action has been statements by the United States and the UK to the Indonesian Government setting forth our strong opposition to any use of force against this territory. This political deterrent would remain effective even if the rebellion were settled.

Summary of United States Position

To sum up the foregoing comments briefly, a major United States policy guidance is to encourage reconciliation between the rebels and the Indonesian Government. The emergence of the Indonesian Army in the past 18 months as the major anti-Communist force in that country and a number of Army inspired and directed actions during this period have been successful in curtailing and in obstructing Communist political activities in Indonesia. While the growth of the Communist machine has certainly been slowed and possibly halted in some areas, in all likelihood none of its essential parts has been damaged. It appears probable that the Army can continue to contain the PKI at least in the short run. However, given the serious continuing political and economic problems created in large part by the rebellion, it does not appear possible for the Army and the Government to take any major steps against the PKI until these problems are resolved or at least diminished. Thus, in the long run the prospects of achieving United States objectives in Indonesia do not appear to be bright unless and until greater political and economic stability is brought about in that country. In other words, there can be little hope for a permanent reduction of the power of the Communist party unless the chaotic internal situation on which Communism thrives is eliminated. The most significant step which could be taken in this direction at the present time would be a reconciliation of opposing non- or anti-Communist elements, specifically the Army and the P.R.R.I. What we would lose in the diminishing of the power position of one anti-Communist element (the P.R.R.I.) would certainly be more than an equivalent gain in the consolidation and strengthening of anti-Communist forces to meet the PKI threat.

2.   *Australian Intercession*

Whether they should accede to Nasution's request is a matter for the Australians themselves to decide. While negotiations between the Indonesian Government and the P.R.R.I. would seem to us to be a matter for the Indonesians themselves, it might be pointed out that such negotiations have taken place off and on over the past several months with no apparent success. The latest attempt to achieve a reconciliation is evidenced by Lt. Col. Sukendro's trip to Singapore and Europe to discuss possible terms with rebel representatives. Although the results cannot be predicted, intercession by a third party could possibly pave the way to a settlement. We would perceive no objection to the Australians exploring this matter further if they should so decide. We agree, however, that if the matter is pursued the dissidents should not be pressed to accept the terms at present offered by the Central Government, since this would amount to a surrender and would only undermine the confidence of the P.R.R.I. leaders and other potential rebels in Western support. One problem which might be faced if the Australians should determine to intercede is that the rebel group outside Indonesia which the Australians would approach might not necessarily represent all the rebels still in Indonesia and consequently any terms worked out would not necessarily be accepted by all elements within the P.R.R.I.

(Discussed with Mr. Krebs and the Agency and cleared in draft by Mr. Parsons.)

---

230.   **Telegram From the Embassy in Indonesia to the Department of State**

Djakarta, November 17, 1959, 7 p.m.

1217. CINCPAC also for POLAD. Codel Pilcher.[1] Called on Sukarno November 17 and had frank spirited exchange of views. Subjects discussed included relations with Red China and Chinese in Indo-

---

Source: Department of State, Central Files, 033.1100–PI/11–1759. Confidential. Repeated to Canberra, London, The Hague, and CINCPAC.

[1] Representative John L. Pilcher (D.–Georgia) was in Indonesia as the head of a Congressional delegation visiting Asia. Additional documentation on the Pilcher delegation is *ibid.*, 033.1100–PI.

nesia, Eisenhower visit to Asia,[2] West Irian and Indonesia association's future.

Asked by Judd[3] his present views on Red China, Sukarno said he very impressed by many things there, e.g., cleanliness; absence flies and sparrows and great construction works. On other hand, he was opposed dictatorship and felt Red Chinese used "the whip," in which he did not believe. Asked whether Chinese people happy under regime, Sukarno said he could only judge by what had seen. In his own limited experience, crowds greeting him were smiling and enthusiastic. When it was suggested that this represented effective organization rather than genuine feelings, Sukarno replied "you can bring out crowds against their will but you cannot prearrange a smile," with which Judd disagreed. He noted same mobilization of people to kill flies and birds had built great wall. Masses can be coerced into slavery as in Tibet. Sukarno said Tibet reports so contradictory he unable to make up mind as to truth. Said, in any case, China should be admitted UN since it unthinkable discuss Tibet question, without Chinese participations. More than 600 million people were left out thereby. Judd pointed out Chinese Communists could not be admitted without amendment UN charter. Ambassador noted China had in past and could again be called in on specific issues such as Tibet without being granted membership.

When asked about possibility putting West Irian under temporary UN trusteeship with expectation it eventually becoming part of Indonesia, Sukarno noted that East Irian was being turned into an Australian colony under so-called trusteeship and refused agree this type solution. Later asked that US give "one simple sentence in support on the justice of Indonesia's claim to West Irian." Said when in US he had talked to American "little people" who had unanimously supported Indonesia's claim to Irian. Only few leaders, he said, prevented US from supporting Indonesia. Perhaps, he chided, this was "left over text book British colonial thinking."

Sukarno added that US like tight rope walker trying to balance its support of West in Europe with support Asian nations in East. He said such policy was, in reality, impossible.

Turning to the forthcoming Eisenhower Asian visit, Sukarno demanded know why President not coming to Indonesia. He said he often invited him and that Indonesia was really very close India. Judd noted that US Government considers Far East to begin at Burma and therefore this visit not to Far East area. Expressed certainty that if President

---

[2] President Eisenhower was scheduled to depart on December 3 on a trip to 11 countries, including India, Pakistan, and Afghanistan.

[3] Representative Walter H. Judd (R.–Minnesota), a member of the Pilcher delegation.

planned trip to Far East, Indonesia would be among countries visited. Noted Eisenhower could not visit one Far East country without visiting several, e.g., Philippines, Thailand, Korea and Japan.

Sukarno emphasized Indonesia's economic future lay in leftist middle road. Categorically denied being communist.

Codel stressed that with patience and mutual understanding, US and Indonesia could continue friendship. Sukarno agreed Indonesia required understanding its problems and allowance time to work out own solutions. Suggested 50 years required solve these problems and during that time, nationalism would be dominant force Indonesia as well as other undeveloped nations.

Jones

231.   Telegram From the Embassy in Indonesia to the Department of State

Djakarta, November 18, 1959, 6 p.m.

1228. CINCPAC also for POLAD. Embtels 1132,[1] 1195,[2] 1217.[3] For Assistant Secretary Parsons from Ambassador. It would be of tremendous advantage to me in advancing US position here if I could suggest to President Sukarno that President Eisenhower planning visit Far East in spring, and if he does come, Indonesia would definitely be included in his schedule.

Embassy officers have reported conversations that indicate failure President Eisenhower schedule trip to Indonesia has been discussed

Source: Department of State, Central Files, 711.11–EI/11–1859. Confidential. Also sent to CINCPAC.

[1] Telegram 1132, November 9, informed the Department that if President Eisenhower visited India and Pakistan without coming to Indonesia, in view of Sukarno's repeated personal invitations, there would be a bad reaction in Indonesia. Jones reminded the Department of Sukarno's philosophy that international relations are basically a matter of personal relations. (*Ibid.*, 711.11–EI/11–959) See Supplement.

[2] In telegram 1195, November 16, Jones pointed out that the first question Sukarno raised during a 50-minute meeting with a visiting Congressional delegation headed by Senator J. Allen Frear, Jr. (D.–Delaware), was why Eisenhower was not coming to Indonesia. (Department of State, Central Files, 711.11–EI/11–1659) See Supplement.

[3] Document 230.

top-level government circles and among politically articulate people. There is feeling of puzzlement, disappointment, and sense being snubbed.

As Department aware in connection visit USS *St Paul*,[4] congressional visits, and other recent events, there has been increasingly favorable attitude toward America and willingness consider American points view. On other hand Indonesian leaders rapidly awakening danger of powerful and ruthless China. Striking disclosures and sharp charges last few days and continuing campaign eliminate rural alien retailers indicate probability continued uneasy, if not outright antagonistic, relationship Indonesia and PRC.

Under these circumstances now favorable time make dramatic gesture, and none would be more effective than indication Eisenhower ultimately to visit Indonesia.

As reference telegrams have reported, President Sukarno has already raised this question directly with me several times in last week.[5] His question indicated puzzlement and disappointment. Our answers have not been convincing to him and others who set great store by such visits, and so I expect question to remain and to be directed again by Sukarno when opportunity arises.

I would appreciate early guidance this subject, since imminence President's India visit bound stimulate further inquiry. I strongly recommend that announcement of intention to visit Indonesia be made as soon as possible.[6]

---

[4] The cruiser U.S.S. *St. Paul* visited Indonesia November 2–5.

[5] In telegram 1253 from Djakarta, November 20, Jones informed the Department that Sukarno had again raised his dissatisfaction with the failure of President Eisenhower to visit Indonesia. Sukarno said "that when the White House announcement of the trip was made he had gotten out a lantern and examined every word to see if there was anything in it for Indonesia but without any success." (Department of State, Central Files, 711.11–EI/11–2059)

[6] In telegram 800 to Djakarta, November 27, Parsons explained to Jones why it would not be possible for Eisenhower to visit Indonesia. (*Ibid.*, 711.11–EI/11–2159) See Supplement.

232.   **Letter From the Assistant Secretary of Defense for International Security Affairs (Irwin) to the Assistant Secretary of State for Far Eastern Affairs (Parsons)**

Washington, November 18, 1959.

DEAR MR. PARSONS: Reference is made to your letter dated 8 September 1959 concerning the development of a long-range plan for Indonesia.[1]

During the past months CINCPAC has developed a long-range plan of military assistance for Indonesia based upon a five-year requirement. The plan, as recommended by CINCPAC, envisages increasing the capability of the Indonesian Armed Forces to maintain internal security and combat Communist activities, as well as insure the continued effective contribution by the military to the development of a stable and independent Indonesia.

The program objectives for each military service provide for:

a. *Army:* A program objective initially to develop a small, well-equipped mobile force for employment in maintaining or restoring control areas threatened or seized by Communist inspired subversion, insurgency or uprising and to re-equip selected units with U.S. equipment, recognizing that the Indonesians will continue to maintain additional units with currently available equipment. Initial equipment offered should consist primarily of light weapons, ammunition, communications and minimum transportation items to avoid dissipation of available funds on non-essential or luxury items.

b. *Navy:* Naval program objectives provide for the qualitative improvement of the Indonesian Navy. The coastal patrol capabilities should be enhanced by the selective replacement of non-effective craft and modernization of others. A modest amphibious lift and logistic support capability, as required for internal security, should be provided. A harbor defense, mine counter measures and air/sea ASW capability to prevent submarine intrusion should be provided on a long-range basis. Technical and matériel assistance for the improvement of Indonesian naval schools and facilities should be provided to the maximum extent possible.

c. *Air Force:* A program objective to develop U.S. oriented and equipped Indonesian Air Force capable of providing a modest airlift and air support for Indonesian forces, limited reconnaissance and air defense capability and an air sea rescue capability for both military and civilian requirements.

With respect to the current program, the United States approved two separate military aid programs for Indonesia, based on Presidential

---

Source: Department of State, Central Files, 756D.5–MSP/11–1859. Secret.
[1] Not found.

Determinations made in 1958 and 1959 which provided a total of $22 million. Shipments under the first increment of the program ($7 million) were essentially completed by December 1958. Army shipments under the second increment ($15 million) will be completed during the first quarter of FY 1960, and it is expected that the Navy program will be completed by the end of FY 1960. The Air Force portion of the program which totals $2.2 million was submitted by the Department of the Air Force to the field for review and refinement. Review of the USAF program was temporarily delayed at the request of Indonesian Air Force (AURI) officials pending the return of AURI representatives touring USAF installations in the U.S. for the purpose of orientation on USAF methods, equipment and training. Indications from the U.S. Military Technical Advisory Group (MILTAG) in Djakarta are that AURI has not confirmed the acceptability of the items recommended by the Department of the Air Force. The equipment which is primarily of a communications and electronics nature will provide, for the first time, good communications for four airfields.

The programs of military aid approved during the past year contributed significantly to improve U.S.-Indonesian relations. Developments in Indonesia indicate the wisdom of continuing a program of military aid to Indonesia during Fiscal Year 1960 in consonance with the long-range plan developed by CINCPAC.

Based upon the fact that Ambassador Jones has informed the Minister of Defense and other Government of Indonesia officials that "subject to the availability of funds, the U.S. is planning to continue the government-to-government sale of military equipment and services to Indonesia in FY 1960," it is deemed appropriate that action be initiated at this time to develop a firm program of military aid for FY 1960.

The proposed FY 1960 program currently being developed will include items such as selected artillery items, small arms, ammunition, vehicles, communications, electronics, engineering and medical equipment, small vessels, helicopters and air sea rescue equipment, Air Force supporting equipment, services, training (including training teams) and training equipment and aids.

It is assumed that the assistance and services proposed herein will be offered to Indonesia on the same basis as that previously rendered (i.e., token payment in either dollars or local currency) and therefore will be tantamount to grant assistance as far as the United States is concerned.

Accordingly, it is recommended that the Department of State initiate action requesting the President, pursuant to Section 451(a) of the Mutual Security Act of 1954, as amended, to make the necessary determination which will authorize the provision of military assistance and services in FY 1960 to Indonesia, from funds appropriated by Section

101(b) of Public Law 80–76,[2] as amended, in the amount not to exceed $20 million, with expenditures therefrom to be charged to the appropriation made available under Section 451(b) of the Mutual Security Act of 1954, as amended.

The foregoing program would be separate from and additional to a program of training of Indonesian Armed Forces personnel in FY 1960 not to exceed $1.5 million. It is also understood that a request for Presidential Determination pursuant to Section 451(a) of the Mutual Security Act of 1954, as amended, covering world-wide training and including $1.5 million for Indonesia is now in process.

Sincerely yours,

John N. Irwin II

---

[2] Reference is to the Second Deficiency Appropriation Act of 1947, passed on May 26, 1947; for text, see 61 Stat. 106.

---

233.   Telegram From the Department of State to the Embassy in Indonesia

Washington, December 7, 1959, 1:58 p.m.

843. Joint State/Defense message. Ref: (a) Deptel 209,[1] rptd The Hague 282, Canberra 57, London 1414, (b) Deptel 692,[2] rptd CINCPAC unn.

1) FYI. President December 3 made determination pursuant Section 451(a) Mutual Security Act that up to $20 million of FY–60 funds

---

Source: Department of State, Central Files, 756D.5–MSP/12–759. Secret; Priority. Drafted by Wenzel, cleared in draft with ISA, and approved by Steeves. Repeated to CINCPAC, The Hague, London, Paris, and Canberra.

[1] Document 218.

[2] Telegram 692, November 6, explained that an FY 1961 military assistance program for Indonesia had not yet been formulated, but the Department of Defense had recommended a program level of approximately $20 million. The telegram also noted that the Mutual Security Coordinator recently approved an FY 1960 military assistance program for Indonesia not to exceed $20 million. (Department of State, Central Files, 756D.5–MSP/10– 3059) See Supplement.

may be used to furnish additional military assistance to Indonesia. (Training program of up to $1.5 million is in addition to foregoing ceiling.) As you were informed (ref b) exact program level within this ceiling will be determined when refined program formulated. Due tight level MAP funds only $15 million thus far approved for programming purposes. End FYI.

2) You authorized inform Nasution, Djuanda and other GOI officials as appropriate that U.S. now prepared furnish additional military equipment and services to Indonesian armed forces in FY–1960 under terms and conditions August 13, 1958 sales agreement. It anticipated that terms of sale to be offered will be along lines terms currently being negotiated for FY–1959 program.

3) FYI. While composition FY–1960 program not yet worked out, it expected that program will include matériel and training for all three armed services with emphasis on Army although definitive breakdown of program between three services has not yet been made. If Embassy deems it desirable, substance paragraph 2 may also be passed to Indonesian Navy and Air Force officials. Dollar ceiling or dollar amount approved for programming (para 1) should however not be divulged to Indonesians. End FYI.

4) Additional instructions re formulation definitive FY–1960 program will be forthcoming soonest.

5) *For The Hague and USRO:*

You should convey in routine manner substance paragraph 2 to FonOff and POLAD respectively indicating additional information re program's nature and magnitude will be forthcoming when specific program formulated.

6) *For Canberra and London:*

Australians and British will be informed here.

Herter

234. National Intelligence Estimate

NIE 65–2–59   Washington, December 8, 1959.

THE PROSPECTS FOR INDONESIA

The Problem

To analyze the present situation and trends in Indonesia and to estimate probable developments over the next two years.

Conclusions

1. The economic deterioration of Indonesia continues and the internal political situation holds little prospect for stability and progress. President Sukarno, the army, and the Indonesian Communist Party (PKI) remain the major political forces. Sukarno remains the dominant political figure and has, by becoming Prime Minister, for the first time committed his personal prestige to the government's performance. However, we do not believe he will give the continuous and effective leadership the situation calls for. (Paras. 28–29)

2. The army, under General Nasution, has greatly increased its role in politics and national administration and has taken some steps to restrict Communist activities. The PKI will probably find it increasingly difficult to follow its past policy of full support of Sukarno and the government, in view of Sukarno's efforts to reduce the power of political parties, army harassment, and the current tension between Indonesia and Communist China. (Paras. 30–32)

3. We do not believe that there will be any drastic rearrangement of political forces during the next year or so. Sukarno will probably remain the key figure. The army will probably maintain a strong position in national political and economic affairs. The antagonism between the army and the Communists will probably become more acute. However, we believe that both the army and the Communists will seek to avoid a showdown, and that Sukarno will be careful to avoid creating situations which might provoke one. (Paras. 28–32)

4. The military stalemate in the rebellion in Sumatra and Celebes will probably continue and a negotiated settlement appears unlikely. (Para. 38)

Source: Department of State, INR–NIE Files. Secret. According to a note on the cover sheet, this NIE was prepared by the CIA and the intelligence organizations of the Departments of State, the Army, Navy, Air Force, and the Joint Staff. All members of the IAC concurred with this estimate on December 8, except the representatives of the AEC and the FBI, who abstained on the grounds that the subject was outside their jurisdiction.

5. Indonesia will almost certainly adhere to its policy of nonalignment. Relations with the Dutch will remain near the breaking point; an attempt to seize West New Guinea by force is unlikely. Relations with most of the Communist Bloc will probably remain cordial. However, the present strain in relations with Communist China could become acute if Peiping continues its intransigent and overbearing attitude on the overseas Chinese issue and pursues its intervention into what Indonesians consider an internal affair. Indonesian relations with the US and the West will probably improve within the limits of a neutralist policy with an anticolonial twist. (Paras. 42–45)

6. We believe Indonesia's numerous and interlocking political, economic, administrative, and internal security problems are likely to persist and possibly intensify but without bringing the country to the point of collapse or disintegration during the period of this estimate. However, there are a number of possible developments which could precipitate a major crisis, particularly the death of Sukarno, a disruption of the power balance maintained by Sukarno between the army and the PKI, or a serious economic reverse, such as a drastic decline in the price of Indonesia's export commodities. (Para. 27)

[Here follow an analysis of the current situation in Indonesia, an analysis of the outlook, and a 3-page appendix analyzing the Indonesian military establishment; see Supplement.]

---

235. Editorial Note

On December 16 at the 429th meeting of the National Security Council, Allen Dulles brought up the subject of recent Indonesian developments during his customary intelligence briefing:

"Turning to Indonesia, Mr. Dulles reported that relations between that country and Communist China had now hit bottom because of the Indonesian policy of re-settling Chinese retailers, most of whom are oriented toward Communist rather than Nationalist China. The dispute, which has been gathering momentum since last summer, is based on an Indonesian decree banning alien retail merchants in rural areas and requiring their re-settlement in towns. When such merchants cannot be absorbed in towns, they are placed in what the Chinese Communists call concentration camps. This decree is a part of the Indonesian campaign of economic nationalism against the Dutch, the Nationalist Chinese, and the Communist Chinese in Indonesia. The Chinese Communists have been demanding repeal of the Indonesian decree, but the Indonesians have refused the Chinese demand. Communist China has ordered the Chinese to resist the Indonesian orders. In a protest of December 9, Communist China renewed its accusation of "intolerant treatment" of the Chinese and proposed implementation of the Indonesian-Communist China Nationality Treaty. Indonesia rejected the Communist Chinese protest and indicated that implementation of the Nationality Treaty would not affect the ban on retail merchants. Sukarno is said to be affronted by Chinese Communist meddling in Indonesia and has issued instructions that the Chinese are to be 'given hell.' The Communist Chinese apparently believe that this issue is a critical one in the contest between Taiwan and Mainland China for the loyalty of the overseas Chinese. Communist China has threatened economic retaliation against Indonesia, possibly including withholding of thirty million dollars in trade credits. To ensure that any Chinese exiles from Indonesia will go to the mainland, Communist China has been giving great publicity to the welcome given to Chinese who return there. Indonesia is perplexed as to how to meet this problem.

"Mr. Dulles also reported that Sukarno had decided to continue martial law in Indonesia, a decision which had put the Communist Party on the spot, since the Party opposes martial law but wishes to support Sukarno. The economic situation in Indonesia is deteriorating due to the continued existence of revolutionary forces on Sumatra. These rebels are badly armed, are short of ammunition, and their financial situation is deteriorating rapidly. [2 lines of source text not declassified] Mr. Dulles felt that even though the economic situation in Indonesia was gloomy, a political collapse was unlikely, and that Indonesia was more friendly to us at present than it had ever been.

"The Vice President asked whether Indonesia recognized Communist China. Mr. Dulles answered in the affirmative, adding that the Chinese Communist Ambassador in Indonesia had been active and indiscreet in this controversy. The Vice President said that one argument for non-recognition of Communist China was the effect recognition would have on countries with overseas Chinese. He wondered how one could appraise the effect of possible U.S. recognition on this problem. He wondered whether the situation would be more or less difficult for Indonesia if it had not recognized Communist China. Mr. Dulles felt the situation would be less difficult for Indonesia if it had not recognized the Chinese Communists, because then the latter would not have the same opportunity to protest and intervene. For example, South Vietnam had had an anti-Chinese program, but had not had the same problems as Indonesia because it had not recognized Communist China. The Vice President felt that when a country like Indonesia recognized Communist China, the result was to orient more overseas Chinese toward Communist China. Mr. Dulles agreed. The Vice President asked whether the Nationalist Chinese were already out of business in Indonesia and Mr. Dulles replied in the affirmative. Mr. Allen said he had recently had a letter from our Ambassador to Indonesia which indicated that the time was ripe for a sharp change in the nature of U.S. programs in that country. The Ambassador felt that we could now engage in anti-Communist propaganda in our USIS out-put in Indonesia." (Memorandum of discussion by Marion Boggs, December 16; Eisenhower Library, Whitman File, NSC Records)

For documentation on the dual nationality treaty and its implementation, see RIIA, *Documents on International Affairs, 1960*, pages 493–499. The referenced letter from Howard P. Jones to George V. Allen, Director of USIA, has not been found.

---

236. Memorandum From the Assistant Secretary of State for Far Eastern Affairs (Parsons) to Acting Secretary of State Dillon

Washington, December 31, 1959.

SUBJECT

Recent Developments in Indonesia

Notwithstanding the persistent instability stemming from Indonesia's precarious economic situation and still sputtering rebellion, there has been perceptible if not precisely measurable progress during the past six months towards the achievement of United States policy objectives in Indonesia. In the main, the important recent developments described below reflect this improvement:

Strained Indonesian-Chinese Communist relations. As a result of its efforts to exclude Indonesia's economically powerful Chinese minority from certain areas of domestic economic life, the Indonesian Government has received repeated threatening protests from Communist China. Asserting that these protests constitute interference in its internal affairs, Indonesia has stood its ground and gone ahead with the anti-Chinese measures. Although Indonesia seems anxious to maintain good relations with Communist China, the incident has already served United States interests in the sense that the arrogant, aggressive nature

---

Source: Department of State, Central Files, 611.56D/12–3159. Secret. Drafted by Moore and cleared with Mein and Steeves. According to a handwritten note on the source text Dillon saw this memorandum.

of the Chinese Communist regime has been clearly exposed to the Indonesians.

Restrictions on Communist activity. Although the Communist Party (PKI) remains one of the principal political forces in the country, Indonesian authorities—chiefly the Army—have continued in recent months gradually to curtail propaganda and political activity by the domestic Communist apparatus. The extraordinary powers employed to this end since early 1958 were scheduled to expire December 17, 1959, but President Sukarno significantly acted on December 16 to extend them indefinitely. He decreed continuation of the so-called State of War (which has prevailed since December 1957), under which he will administer what amounts to martial law throughout the country. The anti-Communist Army leadership, which is heavily represented in the present government, is expected to continue to play the principal role in implementing martial law.

Improved relations with Indonesian Navy and Air Force. Although aid to the Army will be emphasized in the United States program for military assistance to Indonesia in FY 1960, as in FY 1959, the program will also take into account our improving relations with the other armed forces. Relations with the Navy, which was until recently rather reserved in its dealings with us, have improved considerably. In the words of our Ambassador in Djakarta, the Navy has recently indicated an apparent inclination to enter into ". . . all-out cooperation with the United States on somewhat the same basis as the Indonesian Army."[1] This assessment finds substantial confirmation in the view of the British Far East naval commander, as reported by our Naval Attaché in Singapore in mid-December, that ". . . never at any time before has ALRI (Indonesian Navy) been closer to the Western camp."[2] The Indonesian Air Force, while less responsive than the Navy, is showing increased interest in United States material and training.

Australian Prime Minister's Visit to Indonesia. Prime Minister Menzies spent about two weeks in Indonesia earlier this month. The visit was successful on two counts: (1) Menzies had a number of frank discussions with Indonesian leaders including Sukarno, and seems to have developed good personal rapport with the latter (in a Djakarta press conference Menzies said he was greatly impressed by Sukarno and thought him a man of remarkable personality); (2) Sukarno stated publicly that Indonesia had no intention of using force in the West New Guinea dispute (renunciation of force has been stated Indonesian policy

---

[1] As reported in telegram 1468 from Djakarta, December 11. (*Ibid.,* 756D.5622/12–1159) See Supplement.

[2] Ellipses in this paragraph are in the source text.

since February 1959 but Sukarno has never before personally stated this policy).

Trial of American flier. The trial by military court of Allen L. Pope, a United States citizen shot down and captured in May 1958 while flying a bomber for the Indonesian rebels, began December 28 in Djakarta. After the first day's sitting it was recessed until January 2. In an effort to capitalize on widespread public interest in the trial and resentment against Pope, Djakarta's Communist press is trying to stimulate popular demand for the death penalty for Pope. Pope's capture in 1958 intensified then extensive Indonesian suspicion that the United States Government was at least indirectly encouraging the rebels. The current Communist press campaign also hints at supposed United States Government involvement in Pope's activities. However, there has been no indication thus far that the prosecution will make any such accusations in connection with the trial.

237.   Letter From Acting Secretary of State Dillon to Secretary of Defense Gates

Washington, January 7, 1960.

DEAR TOM: I should like to draw your attention to an urgent Netherlands request that the United States assist in maintaining Dutch defensive forces in West New Guinea by making available four C–47 aircraft which the Dutch recently have declared as excess to their requirements in the Netherlands. These planes, which are now physically in the Netherlands, were furnished under MAP.

As you know, the Netherlands has made strong representations for United States assistance in maintaining Dutch defensive forces in West New Guinea. In his letter of March 22, 1959 to Dutch Defense Minister Staf,[1] Mr. Quarles stated that the United States had given the Defense Minister's request most careful attention and that he should like to assure the Dutch "of our willingness to assist you where possible in the purchase of the equipment you need for non-NATO defensive purpose." In subsequent conversations in The Hague and in Washington, officials of the Departments of State and Defense have assured the Dutch that we desire to assist them by facilitating the sale of United

---

Source: Department of State, Central Files, 756.5622/1–760. Secret. Drafted by Cromwell of WE and James R. Fowler of U/MSC and cleared with SPA, RA, FE, U/MSC, and WE.

[1] Not found.

462 Foreign Relations, 1958–1960, Volume XVII

States surplus or excess military equipment. The Department of State would not, of course, propose the transfer of United States military equipment for Dutch non-NATO use unless purchased by the Dutch.

The Dutch have stated that they wish to transfer the four C–47 aircraft to West New Guinea in January, 1960. The urgency derives from the fact that the crash of the fourth Mariner patrol aircraft of the single squadron which the Dutch have in New Guinea has caused the indefinite grounding of all these aircraft. Under these circumstances, Defense Minister Visser has explained to our Ambassdor that he believes it imperative that some replacement aircraft be available for service in West New Guinea as soon as possible.[2] While the four C–47's cannot constitute more than a temporary stopgap measure pending the replacement of the obsolete Mariners by a squadron of serviceable patrol aircraft, the Dutch have stated that the latest crash has aroused Dutch public opinion and has created an acute political situation for the Netherlands Government. According to Ambassador Young the Dutch consider that their national interests in this area are in danger and that they must, without delay, take remedial steps.

Department of State staff have been informally advised by your staff that requirements exist elsewhere in the MAP program for C–47 aircraft. I would like to know, therefore, whether the Department of Defense has planned to use the excess C–47's from the Netherlands to meet these other MAP requirements or whether they would be available for sale to the Dutch to meet the urgent political problem outlined above. In the event that present planning envisages use of these aircraft for other MAP requirements, then it would appear that we are faced with a question of relative priorities as between the Dutch requirement in New Guinea and other MAP needs. In order that this matter can be resolved quickly, I should appreciate your urgent consideration of this problem and an early reply identifying the other MAP requirements for these aircraft together with the views of the Department of Defense as to the military implications and importance of utilizing the C–47's now declared excess by the Dutch for these other requirements as compared to selling them to the Dutch for use in New Guinea.[3]

Sincerely yours,

Douglas Dillon[4]

---

[2] Ambassador Young summarized this conversation in telegraph 898 from The Hague, January 4. (Department of State, Central Files, 756.5622/1–460)

[3] On January 8 Deputy Assistant Secretary of Defense Knight informed Ambassador van Roijen that the United States was prepared to offer the four aircraft for sale to the Netherlands. On February 1, the four C–47s were turned over to the Netherlands at the cost of $70,000 apiece. (Memorandum from Mein to Parsons, February 17; *ibid.*, SPA Files: Lot 63 D 436, Briefing File) See Supplement.

[4] Printed from a copy that bears this stamped signature.

238.   Memorandum From the Commander in Chief, Pacific (Felt) to the Joint Chiefs of Staff

Washington, January 12, 1960.

SUBJECT

U.S. Relationships with the Indonesian Armed Services (C)

1.   Following are CINCPAC's views concerning relationships between the United States and Indonesian armed services. This report is based on a report by Lieutenant Colonel Harry C. McKenzie, former Chief, Air Force Section, Military Technical Advisory Group (MILTAG), Djakarta.

a.   During the past year, the U.S. program of military aid to Indonesia has had a salutary effect in the Indonesian Army. United States and Indonesian Army personnel now mingle in an atmosphere of friendship and mutual respect as opposed to the reserve and suspicion which prevailed in 1958. The Army high command now appears to be staunchly pro-American and firmly opposed to the Communists, international as well as local. A similar, although less pronounced, trend is noticeable in the Navy. In spite of generous assistance from the Soviet Bloc, the orientation of the Navy appears definitely to be swinging toward the United States. These trends are believed to have been influenced to a considerable degree by the U.S. military assistance program and by the honesty and sincerity of U.S. Embassy and MILTAG personnel in their dealings with their Indonesian counterparts.

b.   In the Air Force, however, the program has met with little or no success. During the year, offers of assistance to the Air Force have included training for 100 students; one and one half million dollars worth of communications equipment; technical assistance in the area of search and rescue; and visits of Air Force personnel to USAF installations in the United States. No part of any of these offers has been accepted to date and not one letter or official communication concerning them has been received by MILTAG.

c.   The Indonesian Air Force is believed to be seasoned heavily with Communists and the three most influential leaders, the Chief of Staff, the Deputy Chief of Staff, and the Intelligence Chief are notorious

Source: Washington National Records Center, OASD/ISA Records: FRC 64 A 2170, 092 Indonesia. Secret.

sympathizers, if not card-carrying Communists. They do not recognize MILTAG and have worked actively to have that group, and particularly the USAF representative, discredited. Discussions with their representatives concerning aid offers have been clouded with vacillations, misinterpretations and other dilatory tactics obviously designed to render progress impossible. There is no reason to believe that relationships between the USAF and the Indonesian Air Force will improve as long as the current leadership remains in command of the latter.

d.   As a result of the lessons learned in a year of fruitless efforts on the part of the USAF representative in MILTAG, Chief MILTAG, with the concurrence of the Embassy, has recommended that, subsequent to the recent expiration of the USAF representative's tour, his billet be left vacant until such time as the Indonesian Air Force leaders indicate a desire to promote closer relations with the USAF or to avail themselves of U.S. aid offers. It is the consensus here and in Djakarta that by leaving the space vacant, Indonesian Air Force leaders may be more amenable to U.S. advice and assistance, should they come to fear that the US. aid program may become closed to them. Further, it is believed that the possibilities of a rapprochement with the Indonesian Air Force will be more favorable by keeping the space available than by eliminating the position entirely.

H. D. Felt[1]

---

[1] Printed from a copy that bears this stamped signature.

239.   Telegram From the Embassy in Indonesia to the Department of State

Djakarta, February 19, 1960, 10 p.m.

2289. CINCPAC also for POLAD. Embtels 2226,[1] 2199,[2] 2281.[3] Subandrio asked me today to get in touch with him wherever he was if during Khrushchev's visit[4] I received any news as to possibility Dutch being willing consider bilateral negotiations, clearly indicating any information this sort would strengthen his hand in dealing with Russians.

Also said that "as usual" communiqué to be issued at end of visit would certainly include reference to West Irian. I endeavored to discourage this, emphasizing desirability playing in as low key as possible if he had any real hopes of getting Dutch to conference table.

If there is any chance of US inducing Netherlands to give Indonesians some indication of willingness to meet at conference table, I feel strongly now is time for us to make the effort. I can think of no démarche that would mean more to anti-Communist forces in Indonesia at this time. Removal of highly emotional West Irian issue from field of current Soviet play would be single most important contribution that could be made to support our friends here. Dutch interests too lie in maintenance Indonesia as part of free world. Recognizing emotion is not exclusive property of Indonesians in dealing with Foreign Affairs, I would nevertheless hope right kind of appeal to Dutch might bear fruit.

Source: Department of State, Central Files, 656.9813/2–1960. Confidential; Niact. Also sent to CINCPAC and repeated to The Hague.

[1] Reference is most likely to telegram 2266 from Djakarta, February 18, which reported that within the past 24 hours the Embassy had received an indication that Sukarno planned to obtain major political, economic, and military assistance from Khrushchev in return for political concessions favorable to the PKI. Accordingly Jones was seeking an appointment with Subandrio "to inform him grave concern because of impairment to US-Indonesian relations which likely to flow from deal of type reported." (Ibid., 861.0098/2–1860) See Supplement.

[2] Telegram 2199 from Djakarta, February 13, inquired about the Netherlands readiness to enter into bilateral talks on outstanding issues with West New Guinea. (Department of State, Central Files, 656.9813/2–1360) See Supplement.

[3] Telegram 2281 from Djakarta, February 19, reported that General Jani, Deputy Army Chief of Staff, had recently informed the Army Attaché that Nasution planned to discuss with Sukarno before February 22 the Army's opposition to a "big deal" with the Soviets. (Department of State, Central Files, 861.0098/2–1960) See Supplement.

[4] Soviet Premier Khrushchev visited Indonesia February 18–March 1 as part of a trip to Asia, which included stops in India, Burma, and Afghanistan.

Even a clear limit [*sic*] that Dutch attitude or our own might some day change would be of help.[5]

Jones

---

[5] Telegram 2279 from Djakarta, February 19, reported further on Jones' conversation with Subandrio during which Subandrio tried to reassure Jones that the United States had nothing to fear in the way of a deal between the Indonesians and the Soviets. (Department of State, Central Files, 861.0098/2–1960) See Supplement.

Chargé Fales reported from The Hague in telegraph 1111, February 20, that he believed there were "no presently foreseeable prospects inducing Netherlands take steps, public or private, to change its well known position on West New Guinea issue." (Department of State, Central Files, 656.9813/2–2060) See Supplement.

---

240. Memorandum of Conversation

Washington, February 19, 1960.

SUBJECT

    Defense of West New Guinea

PARTICIPANTS

For the Netherlands	*For the United States*
Mr. Theo Bot, State Secretary for Netherlands New Guinea Affairs [1]	WE—Mr. McBride
Mr. E. Schiff, Chargé d'Affaires	WE—Mr. Cameron
Mr. P. de Lavalette, First Secretary	WE—Mr. Chadbourn
Mr. J. Huydecoper, First Secretary	WE—Mr. Cromwell

Mr. Bot said that he wished to emphasize two major points. First, while Dutch-Australian technical and administrative cooperation was

---

Source: Department of State, Central Files, 756C.5/2–1960. Secret. Drafted by W. Kennedy Cromwell of WE.

[1] Bot arrived in the United States on February 19 for a 2-day visit on his return from an inspection tour of West New Guinea and Australian New Guinea. Briefing papers for Bot's visit were transmitted to Parsons under cover of a memorandum from Mein, dated February 17. (*Ibid.*, SPA Files: Lot 63 D 436, Briefing File) See Supplement. Prior to this meeting Bot met with Deputy Under Secretary Hare and Acting Assistant Secretary of State for International Organization Affairs Woodruff Wallner. The three meetings were summarized in a February 20 letter from Philip Chadbourn of WE to Ambassador Young. Chadbourn noted that the meeting with Hare was largely nonsubstantive; it "turned out to be a National Geographic travelogue about life and things in New Guinea." (Department of State, SPA Files: Lot 63 D 106, Indonesia) A memorandum of the conversation between Wallner and Bot, February 19, is *ibid.*, Central Files, 033.56C11/2–1960. See Supplement.

satisfactory, the Australians would cooperate no further in political and military matters until there were clear indications that the U.S. would approve. Therefore, Mr. Bot continued, the best plan of action would be for the Dutch to issue a clear statement of their purpose and intents in New Guinea, this statement to be supported unequivocally and publicly by the U.S., the U.K., and Australia. Such actions would clear the air and would put to rest any possible gnawing doubts in the minds of the Dutch now in West New Guinea.

Second, Mr. Bot said that West New Guinea had inadequate defenses, but that the Australian section was probably in even worse shape. In this connection, he mentioned that while Australian New Guinea was covered by ANZUS and SEATO guarantees, no such treaty protection was presently given to Dutch New Guinea. He believed it essential, therefore, that secret joint U.S.-Australian-Dutch military planning be undertaken and also that the U.S. issue a secret protocol guaranteeing to defend West New Guinea.

---

241.   Telegram From the Department of State to the Embassy in Indonesia

Washington, February 21, 1960, 1:32 p.m.

1382. Ur 2290[1] and previous.

1.   Dept greatly appreciates your full reporting re possible Sukarno–Khrushchev deal and related matters. Realize difficulty sifting fact from rumor in connection these rapid developments with their serious implications for U.S. interests Indonesia, but will appreciate receiving your continuing assessment situation which we following closely.

2.   FYI. Re your suggestions Dept consider encouraging anti-Communist elements GOI by moves in West Irian policy field no possibility

---

Source: Department of State, Central Files, 861.0098/2–1960. Secret; Priority. Drafted by Moore and approved by Parsons. Repeated to The Hague, CINCPAC, and Moscow.

[1] Telegram 2290, February 19, reported that during a meeting that morning between Djuanda and military members of the cabinet, an agreement was reached, according to Sukendro, on the following limitations on Sukarno's dealings with Khrushchev: 1) a maximum of $100 million in new economic aid could be accepted; 2) no military aid could be accepted; and 3) no bases could be provided to the Communist bloc. (*Ibid.*, 861.0098/2–1960) See Supplement.

this could be done. Re seeking persuade Dutch make gesture to negotiate, our present assessment is that Dutch Govt unlikely be receptive suggestion from any quarter that bilateral talks with Indonesians be undertaken. Moreover timing for such suggestion coming from U.S. would be particularly unfortunate since Dutch feelings towards U.S. currently inflamed over recent refusal KLM landing rights U.S. west coast. In connection this refusal Dutch press dredging up variety of Dutch grudges against U.S. including supposed U.S. sabotage Dutch position in Indonesia after Second World War. In any case we would have reservations re advisability our making any moves such as foregoing even if they possible, since they likely appear hasty, fearful improvisations to counter effects Khrushchev visit. End FYI.

3. If Sukarno intends proceed with reported deal and possesses domestic political strength to carry it through, there seems little or nothing U.S. can or should try do deter him. Only promises of successfully deterring him would seem lie in determined, unified initiative on part those Indonesian political elements which oppose deal and which prepared resist Sukarno this matter with or without U.S. support and encouragement.

Herter

---

242. Telegram From the Embassy in Indonesia to the Department of State

Djakarta, March 4, 1960, 4 p.m.

2479. CINCPAC also for POLAD. First Minister Djuanda told me today "Indonesia remains where it was before" as result of Khrushchev visit, and specifically denied rumors that inclusion of Commies in Cabinet was in offing. He indicated no more Cabinet changes of any kind were likely before President Sukarno departure about April 1 for trip abroad.[1]

Source: Department of State, Central Files, 798.00/3–460. Confidential. Repeated to The Hague, Moscow, Canberra, and CINCPAC.

[1] Sukarno was scheduled to depart Indonesia on April 1 on a 2-month trip to the Middle East, Eastern Europe, Africa, Portugal, Cuba, Mexico, and Japan (via San Francisco).

Echoing the remarks of every prominent Indonesian I have talked with since Khrushchev visit, Djuanda said it pity Eisenhower unable to come here provide political balance. Most likely his reception would be much warmer than Khrushchev's. Mistake was not Indonesia's, he added significantly.

Djuanda added that he was absolutely certain that Sukarno has changed his own position not at all as result of visit but acknowledged the President "has a way of expressing himself, particularly in acting as host" which was likely to create a wrong impression among outsiders.

Subject of Khrushchev visit was raised by Djuanda who asked me for my appraisal of it. I told him I felt it was so far a propaganda victory for Khrushchev but that I recognized GOI had taken precautions to prevent PKI from undue exploitation or enhancement their own position. What impact would really be, I said, would depend on future implementation of Soviet credit, particularly whether this led to closer involvement as result of increased trade relations, presence of technicians greater dependence generally. I added that visit also seemed indicate USSR reasserting its dominant position here as opposed to ChiComs, in effect Khrushchev telling latter they had bungled and should now stand aside.

Djuanda expressed agreement with last comment, saying that visit "must have been unpleasant" for Chinese.

On other points I made he said he doubted PKI could gain much from visit, although party undoubtedly would continue to point to increased Indo-Soviet economic cooperation as evidence of greatness of communism.

As for closer involvement with Soviet Union, Djuanda conceded that danger of having foreign technicians was always present. To speak plainly, he said, there was also problem in having American technicians in Indo. Their ideas of free enterprise undoubtedly made impression on youthful minds. From point of view of those attempting to establish their own identity, these all were outside pressures which affected the situation.

After pointing out obvious differences respective objectives USSR, I asked Djuanda whether it was true that Sukarno did not hit it off well with Khrushchev. He smiled and replied, "more or less." In some ways, he added, he had found himself closer to Khrushchev than Sukarno had since the Soviet Premier was more of a "businessman" who had worked his way up from the bottom and was of a practical bent.

"Did Khrushchev then contribute some ideas that might make a lasting impression," I inquired.

"I hope so," Djuanda replied. "He wanted us to concentrate very hard on a few essential things and let less important matters go until later. This is what I also want."

Jones

243. Memorandum From the Director of the Office of Southwest Pacific Affairs (Mein) to the Assistant Secretary of State for Far Eastern Affairs (Parsons)

Washington, March 7, 1960.

SUBJECT

Suspension of Indonesian Parliament

Sukarno suspended parliament March 5, decreeing an end to its "responsibilities and labors." This action was not wholly unexpected, since it has been widely assumed that the government could not allow parliament to reject the 1960 budget, which parliament appeared about to do. Moreover, it has been rumored since June 1959, when the 1945 constitution was reinstated, that the existing parliament might be dissolved, since guided democracy frankly contemplated at a minimum the dilution of the elected parliament with appointive, "functional" representatives.

Sukarno's decree promised early "renewal" of parliament. This renewal will probably consist of (1) appointment by Sukarno of a new parliament containing functional representatives or (2) appointment of the planned People's Consultative Congress, a kind of super-parliament expected to contain ideological, functional and regional representatives and envisaged as the incarnation of Indonesian sovereignty. However he chooses to handle the renewal question, Sukarno is virtually certain to create a "legislative" body that will see eye to eye with the government.

The suspension of parliament is, as noted above, a logical and not unexpected step in the development of guided democracy, a philoso-

---

Source: Department of State, SPA Files: Lot 63 D 436, Parliament. Confidential. Drafted by Moore.

phy inspired in large part by a desire to end the ineffectual bickering which has marked parliamentary government in Indonesia. Guided democracy is openly anti-party, and even before its suspension parliament had been shorn of most of its statutory power (Sukarno made it clear he acknowledged no responsibility to parliament, only to the People's Consultative Congress). Thus, the principal effect of the March 5 decree is to deprive parliament—already without significant control over governmental affairs—of its opportunity to influence public opinion through its debating sessions.

Although the suspension of parliament hurts all the parties, it probably hurts the Communist Party (PKI) most of all, since that party has been making the most effective use of parliament as a propaganda medium. Sukarno probably was not motivated by any desire thus to curb the PKI, but his action will have the whole-hearted support of the Army leadership in part for this reason. The Army apparently supports the measure without reservation and will now provide, more exclusively than ever, the power to insure implementation of the government's measures.

Implications for United States interests. Since it practically completes the process of concentrating power in the executive, Sukarno's decree seems to take Indonesia further away from the sort of democratic system we would like to see there. However, for the time being the stability of the Indonesian Government—so long as that government is non-Communist—is more important to us than the maintenance of traditional forms of parliamentary democracy, particular so since parliamentary regimes in Indonesia helped to create the near political anarchy that has been a major threat to our interests.

244.   Editorial Note

On March 10 at the 436th meeting of the National Security Council, Allen Dulles discussed Khrushchev's recent trip to Asia during his intelligence briefing:

"Mr. Dulles then reported on Khrushchev's recent trip to Asia. He said the overall response to Khrushchev's appearances did not live up to expectations. Khrushchev received his greatest welcome in Kabul, but it was forced and without enthusiasm. His reception was only moderate in Soerabaja. Throughout the trip Khrushchev was glum and irritable; and particularly in Indonesia he succeeded in irritating his hosts by boasting of Soviet accomplishments, by criticizing the local way of doing things and by such activities as impromptu lectures on Soviet farming methods. A personality clash was quite evident in Indonesia between Sukarno and Khrushchev. On one occasion Sukarno is reported by Subandrio to have said 'I did not invite Khrushchev here to be insulted. You take over.' Khrushchev was alleged to have told the Indonesians that they were not true socialists and that the Indonesian Government needed to exercise more compulsion against the people, a suggestion which Sukarno rejected. However, despite these clashes, the Indonesian leaders seemed to be somewhat impressed by Khrushchev, so that his visit must be scored as a mild success. Mr. Dulles said that in Afghanistan the signing of a cultural agreement with the USSR had been postponed six times before it was finally signed. At Khrushchev's departure Daud appeared uneasy and Khrushchev himself spoke only of the weather, except to say to the King 'Don't be worried; all these difficulties will be straightened out.' The joint Soviet-Afghan communiqué gives some support to Soviet propaganda. In this connection Mr. Dulles noted that Moscow is now claiming that Khrushchev will represent the peoples of Asia at the Summit Meeting. During Khrushchev's visit to India a $375 million aid agreement for assistance to the Third Indian Five Year Plan and to the Indian Atomic Energy Program was signed. Indonesia also accepted assistance from the USSR in the amount of $250 million. Apparently Khrushchev was prepared to offer Indonesia $400–$500 million in addition to the $126 million extended several years ago, only $27 million of which has been used. Indonesia has decided to spread its $250 million credit over seven years and to use it in connection with the $2 billion Five Year Indonesian Economic Development Plan to be implemented from 1961 to 1965. There were reports that Indonesia would also receive a cruiser, submarines and bombers from the USSR. Afghan had accepted Soviet economic aid, including 50,000 tons of wheat. While in Afghan Khrushchev had endorsed a plebiscite for Pushtoonistan. The plebiscite idea had been picked up in the West and applied to Berlin. Concluding his discussion of Khrushchev's trip, Mr.

Dulles reported that throughout the trip recent aggressive acts by the Chinese Communists had apparently loomed large in Khrushchev's thinking. At any rate, Khrushchev had returned again and again in conversation to the Chinese Communists and had stopped in Calcutta on his way home to confer with Nehru on Chou En-lai's acceptance of the Indian invitation to discuss the Sino-Indian border problem. There was evidence, in other words, that Communist China and the USSR were at odds with each other on Asian policies. The Chinese Communist radio had been silent during Khrushchev's trip, but had belatedly endorsed it after it was over.

"Mr. Dillon said that according to his information Indonesia did not want to conclude a new aid agreement with the Soviet Union because of its unused balance of aid previously extended. However, when Khrushchev made it clear that he would offer unlimited amounts of assistance to Indonesia, Sukarno had decided he could not refuse these offers for domestic political reasons. The Indonesians had tried to calculate the maximum Soviet aid they could use without getting too deeply involved with the Soviets and had arrived at a figure of $35 million annually. Sukarno had multiplied this figure by seven and requested $250 million in aid. According to Subandrio, Khrushchev and Sukarno spent only about three minutes concluding this aid agreement." (Memorandum of discussion, March 14; Eisenhower Library, Whitman File, NSC Records)

---

245. Despatch From the Embassy in Indonesia to the Department of State

No. 819   Djakarta, March 14, 1960.

SUBJECT
President Sukarno and His Impact on the Current Indonesian Scene

Summary

Throughout his fifteen years as head of the Indonesian state, President Sukarno's formal authority and his ostensible domination of the government have never been as great as at present. Since assuming his current extraordinary powers in July, 1959, however, he has demonstrated a complete lack of capability to utilize them rationally toward the solution of Indonesia's burgeoning problems. To an increasing extent government is being carried on by others, with Sukarno falling back

Source: Department of State, Central Files, 798.11/3–1460. Secret.

into the negative role of a wielder of vetoes and an obstacle to be by-passed. More and more his attention is deviating from responsible ad-ministration toward concentration on the comparatively sterile process of political maneuver.

Sukarno's reaction to the frustrations of his position has been one of increasing irrationality and emotional extremism, sharpened by physi-cal deterioration. Having alienated progressively larger segments of In-donesian leadership, he now finds support only among the masses—whom he still controls—and among the members of an unreliable pal-ace clique. His status is menaced by a growing polarization of forces around the Army and the Indonesian Communist Party (PKI), both of whom see him as an obstruction to be ultimately shelved although nei-ther is as yet in a position to offer a direct challenge. Such a challenge may emerge whenever either side feels itself strong enough to act or, alternately, if it feels its position is seriously jeopardized. In any case, should Sukarno lose the support of the masses through a continuing in-ability to stem the economic decline, through moral revulsion to expo-sure of his peccadillos after a temporary topping from power (as in cases of Farouk and Peron), or through other developments, his day will be over.

Sukarno's growing irrationality poses a problem to American inter-ests in Indonesia, one which may become more severe as he is driven by the economic crisis to greater extremes of talk and action. In meeting this prospect, it is essential to American policy that it be recognized that he is but one factor in the Indonesian scene. He is not Indonesia, even though he continues to be the most potent symbol of Indonesian nationalism. *End Summary.*

[Here follows the remainder of the despatch; see Supplement.]

---

246.   Memorandum From the Director of the Office of Southwest Pacific Affairs (Mein) to the Deputy Assistant Secretary of State for Far Eastern Affairs (Steeves)

Washington, March 29, 1960.

SUBJECT

Political Tension in Indonesia

General

The political atmosphere is probably more tense than at any time since the rebellion broke out in early 1958. Our Embassy and Consulates

---

Source: Department of State, SPA Files: Lot 63 D 436, Briefing File. Secret. Drafted by Moore.

in Indonesia have reported their own observations and the comments of Indonesian leaders to this effect. Hatta, for example, recently told the Ambassador that it was not impossible for "something" to happen during Sukarno's forthcoming trip abroad.[1] The rising tension has been manifested for months in rumors of political plots and recently in several serious incidents of violence.

Rumored plots include these: (1) a Murba Party "pro-Sukarno" plot to free the President from Army influence; (2) an anti-Nasution plot among Army officers fomented by Sukarno; (3) a plot by Nasution to seize power in a coup; (4) a pro-PRRI plot by Menadonese elements intending to eliminate both Sukarno and Nasution. At least one version of the latter plot links it with the strafing of Sukarno's palace by an Air Force officer of Menadonese origin.[2] Another violent incident—the attack on the Bandung cavalry training center—has also been linked in some rumors with the Menadonese plot. The rich variety of reported plots and outbursts of violence highlight the jittery temper of the current political scene and the difficulty of forecasting the course of events.

Political Maneuvering

The present non-party Government rests on an uneasy balancing of major Indonesian political forces, among which there seem to be increasingly sharp cleavages. For instance, a so-called *Democratic League* of conservative groups has been formed with the avowed aim of preventing a further increase in PKI influence. On March 24, the League issued a statement, signed by prominents of the Catholic, Christian, Masjumi, PSI, IPKI and NU parties (although the NU leaders signed as individuals and were not identified with the party), calling on the Government (in effect Sukarno) not to appoint a "yes-man" parliament but to find a "democratic and constitutional" solution to the problem created by Sukarno's recent suspension of the elected parliament.

Sukarno ignored the League's advice and announced the composition of the new parliament on March 27, declaring that 130 seats would go to political parties, 131 seats to functional groups. Since he indicated

---

[1] Hatta made this remark to Jones during a conversation they had on March 26. (Telegram 2739 from Djakarta, March 26; *ibid.*, Central Files, 798.2/3–2660) See Supplement.

[2] On March 9 an Indonesian Air Force jet aircraft strafed the President's palace in Djakarta with machinegun fire. No one was injured. (Telegraph 2537 from Djakarta, March 9; *ibid.*, 798.00/3–960) See Supplement. In telegram 1530 to Djakarta, March 10, the Department authorized Jones to convey to Sukarno Eisenhower's personal satisfaction that he and the members of his family were safe following the strafing attack. (Department of State, Central Files, 798.00/3–1060) See Supplement. Jones conveyed Eisenhower's message to Sukarno during a meeting with the Indonesian President on March 11. (Telegraph 2581 from Djakarta, March 11; Department of State, Central Files, 798.5–MSP/3–1160) See Supplement.

that several of the member groups of the *Democratic League* would occupy seats in the new parliament, and since it appears that those groups will accept the proffered seats, there seems little likelihood that the League will prove to be a cohesive, effective political force. However, it represents an encouraging if hesitant sign of anti-Communist cooperation.

According to Sukarno's announcement, the PNI, NU and PKI will dominate the political party segment of the new parliament. Preliminary reports of Sukarno's intended appointments to the parliament suggest that the relative position of the extreme leftists will be enhanced by comparison with the old parliament. Our Embassy reports that Nasution will find it difficult to accept this shift without sacrificing (1) the principle of opposing increased PKI influence and (2) the budding Democratic League, which is said to have had his covert endorsement.

Whether or not Nasution cares for the composition of the new parliament, however, he may conclude that (1) the influence of the PKI has not been dangerously increased and/or (2) a direct conflict between himself and Sukarno, in which he might well be bested at this time, would not advance the anti-Communist cause. In any case, the real meaning of the new parliament's composition in terms of the existing political power balance is not clear, despite an apparent gain for the leftists on paper. The armed forces will be substantially represented in the parliament, and the non-Communist elements therein, if acting together, would presumably enjoy a comfortable majority. Finally, it is not yet clear that the parliament will be other than a relatively powerless advisory body to the centralized executive—in which the Army leadership still occupies a key place.

The suspension and re-constitution of parliament is not an isolated incident but part of the process of giving institutional forms to the vague guided democracy concept. Thus, although tension has reached a high point over the parliamentary change, an uneasy political atmosphere has prevailed since the process of implementing guided democracy began in 1959. Just as the concept of guided democracy has never been made clear, the course its development would follow has not been predictable. Uncertainty has engendered doubt as to their fate on the part of individuals and groups, especially political parties, with a consequent nervous jockeying among them for position and favor. In addition to these selfish concerns over power and patronage relationships, there has been—and still is—sincere worry in the minds of some that guided democracy may lead to dictatorship. Others disapprove Sukarno's evident intention to develop guided democracy in keeping with the "unity in *gotong royong*" principle—which he seems to interpret as requiring significant PKI participation in governmental affairs. Whatever misgivings about the nature and course of guided democracy there may be, however, this unclear concept is rapidly being converted into a wobbly institutional system within the framework of which Indonesia's political development and struggles are likely to take place for some time to come.

Conclusions

1. *A major governmental change could occur in the near future but the odds appear to be against it.* There may well be minor changes and regroupings as Indonesia continues to feel its restless way to hoped-for institutional stability under guided democracy, but the outlook seems to be for (a) Sukarno to maintain his pre-eminence while subject to various influences limiting his complete freedom of action and (b) continuation of the delicate political power balance existing among Sukarno, the Army and the PKI. Should a major change occur, it is most likely to involve a move led by Nasution and backed by a variety of elements which oppose some or all present policies, particularly those related to the development of guided democracy, to economic affairs and to the rebellion. In making such a move, Nasution would probably try to win Sukarno's support or at least his acquiescence with a view to associating the popular Sukarno symbol with a new government or new policy line. Nasution would likely try to effect major changes without Sukarno's acquiescence only in response to (a) what he deemed a critical threat to his personal power position or (b) very strong pressure from military and civilian elements which are disposed openly to challenge some of Sukarno's present policies. On balance, it appears unlikely that Nasution will make any major move in the near future, with or without Sukarno's acquiescence, because (a) he probably does not believe his power position has been sufficiently undermined to require desperate action on his part and (b) the elements on which he would have to depend for support are neither united among themselves, nor clearly determined to act, nor uniformly ready to follow Nasution's lead, particularly if to do so would involve them in an open clash with Sukarno.

2. *The outlook for basic United States interests is not appreciably changed by recent events.* Thus far we have found the development of guided democracy tolerable if nerve-wracking. Philosophically we may deplore the drift from parliamentary to authoritarian government, but there is little we could do to arrest this drift. In any case, the end result may well serve some of our short-run objectives, such as the avoidance of a Communist takeover and progress towards greater stability. Meantime, we have good relations with the Indonesian Government, including Sukarno personally, and we have close contact and influence with important non- and anti-Communist elements within and outside the Government. We can draw some encouragement from (a) the fact that

such elements are still influential in the Government, and from (b) recent signs, however tentative, that anti-Communist forces are more disposed than heretofore to make common cause.

247.   Telegram From the Embassy in Indonesia to the Department of State

Djakarta, April 14, 1960, 5 p.m.

2913. CINCPAC also for POLAD. Paris for POLTO. Pass Ambassador Jones upon arrival.[1] Deptel 1731 repeating The Hague 1315 to Department.[2] Embassy foresees likelihood serious repercussions from forthcoming naval visit *Karel Doorman*[3] and reinforcement Biak with Hawker Hunter squadron. Both will be occurring at time acute internal stresses here, with distinct possibility that climactic showdown between Sukarno forces and opponents may be underway by then. Past few months have seen increasing indications that unchecked economic deterioration and growing frustration over failure drastic Sukarno moves of past year to ease country's political problems are combining bring about situation in which further decisive changes seem inescapable sooner or later. Next 6 to 9 months most likely to be crucial period, although climax could come much sooner. Direction this change will take obviously of vital importance US interests.

Source: Department of State, Central Files, 790.5856/4–1460. Secret; Priority. Transmitted in two sections. Also sent to CINCPAC and repeated to The Hague, Canberra, Paris, and London.

[1] Jones was on home leave and scheduled to arrive in Washington on April 19 for consultations.

[2] Telegram 1315 from The Hague, April 8, reads in part as follows: "As Department aware, none of us here had any advance information re Dutch plans. I can only conclude that Dutch are so seriously worried over state New Guinea defenses, that they wished avoid protracted discussions and possibly adverse results of advance consultations." (Department of State, Central Files, 790.5856/4–860)

[3] On March 31 the Netherlands Navy Information Service announced that the aircraft carrier *Karel Doorman* and two destroyers would be making a flag-showing tour of the Far East, including a stop in West New Guinea , between May and December. (Telegraph 1278 from The Hague, March 31; *ibid.*, 790.5856/3–3160) The Netherlands informed the NATO Standing Group, in a letter dated March 30, that because of urgent national commitments in the Far East it was compelled to withdraw the *Karel Doorman* and two destroyers from the NATO Command area temporarily. (Telegram 1385 to The Hague, April 4; *ibid.*) The Netherlands informed the North Atlantic Council of their decision in a meeting on April 6. (Polto 2026 from Paris, April 6; *ibid.*, 790.5856/4–660)

Fact that Dutch carrier will be in West New Guinea water or en route during this period will be serious irritant in situation. Universal hypersensitivity Indonesians all political complexions toward West New Guinea issue will be further sharpened by what virtually all will interpret as aggressive Dutch act. Army, anti-Sukarno parties, other forces pressing for reversal present Sukarno policies will be placed at disadvantage in closely-balanced struggle by long-standing personal identification Sukarno with this highly emotional issue.

May reach serious proportions if Sukarno, feeling position endangered utilizes *Karel Doorman* presence and reinforcement Biak to embark on fiery West Irian liberation drive confound foes and divert country from internal issues. Although has [at?] minimum, genuine apprehensions certain to be created at all levels by *Karel Doorman* visit, it could well tip balance his favor, force opposition either fall in weakly behind him or be branded pro-Dutch. Even without Sukarno seizure of issue, visit will add strong measure irrational xenophobia, greatly enhance suspicion of west at time when balance vote highly precarious.

Danger also exists intrusion *Karel Doorman* into what Indonesians claim as own inland waters could spark serious incident. In this connection, should be recalled Foreign Minister Subandrio specifically warned former Dutch Chargé Hasselmann that entry Dutch naval vessel "Indonesian waters" would be regarded "causus belli." (Deptel 426[4] repeated The Hague 401.) Although Indonesians do not at present press their claim to sovereignty over these waters so far as other nations' ships are concerned they may well attempt to do so in case of Dutch.

While likelihood GOI knowingly precipitating incident probably not too great (although not inconceivable as desperate Sukarno gesture hold own position), somewhat greater possibility unpremeditated incident resulting from chance encounter. March 5 Air Force pilot attack on palace evidence individual members armed forces capable such gestures.

Further result forthcoming Dutch moves may be intensification Indonesian determination speed buildup own armed forces, greater pressure on US and other western countries supply arms including "offensive arms." Temptation accept Soviet bloc arms also likely increase, particularly since Khrushchev visit showed that Soviets eager provide.

In this respect, must be recognized many Indonesians genuinely believe Dutch capable launching aggression against country.

In view foregoing, Embassy believes forthcoming Dutch actions dangerous US interests and, according best Embassy estimate, they are

---

[4] [*text not declassified*]

unnecessary from military point of view. Dutch assertion these actions necessary counteract Indonesian "master plan" seize West New Guinea through infiltration seems highly exaggerated. Without questioning accuracy actual cases infiltration reported by Dutch (The Hague despatch 728)[5] who attempt utilize them as evidence "master plan" appears thorough misreading conditions in country in which central authority outlying areas as tenuous as Indonesia. Also flies in face repeated assurances highest Indo officials, including Sukarno and Subandrio, that only peaceful methods obtain West New Guinea will be utilized. Latest such assurance given by deputy ACS Jani April 12 (Embtel 2891,[6] repeated The Hague 89 Canberra 61) in unequivocal terms.

Even if these assurances completely discounted, logic of current situation makes it improbable Indonesia intends armed move against West New Guinea in near future. Army admittedly strained to limit overcoming PRRI-Permesta rebellion, DI depredations, with Nasution stating publicly rebel defeat not expected for 2–3 years. Granting highly unlikely assumption Indonesia willing jeopardize world standing by West New Guinea aggression, seems clear that for years to come they will not have uncommitted forces do so.

Re "master plan" which Dutch claim Indonesians now implementing (memo conversation Huydecoper–Mein March 24),[7] Embassy has found no evidence its existence. Not impossible such plan drafted at one time as emotional exercise, but if so, it probably resting in file cabinet with rest Indonesia's plethora unrealized and abandoned plans.

Dutch decision take such unsettling actions on basis such apparently slim evidence and at time when they, too, must be aware delicate internal situation here raises question as to actual motives. Embassy hopes Dutch not counting on taking what appears deliberately provocative act in expectation such act will create incident, force US take sides in West New Guinea dispute. If Dutch decision in any way calculated influence possible UNGA action in event West New Guinea issue submitted next session, would seem entirely counter-productive; most likely result will be solidification lukewarm Afro-Asian support behind Indo-

---

[5] Dated March 31. (Department of State, Central Files, 656C.98/3–3160) See Supplement.

[6] Dated April 13. (Department of State, Central Files, 656.9813/4–1360) See Supplement.

[7] In a meeting with Mein on March 24, Huydecoper left an undated 3-page paper on "Indonesian threats to the Netherlands New Guinea," indicating that it was the paper referred to during the van Roijen–Steeves meeting of March 10. Huydecoper said that he would be prepared to discuss the Dutch paper or to answer any questions that it might prompt. Memorandum of conversation, March 29. (Department of State, Central Files, 656C.98/3–2460)

nesia, attraction new support Indonesian position, creation wider rift between Afro-Asians and West.

Embassy realizes little, if any, possibility Dutch can be induced give up plans *Karel Doorman* visit, Biak reinforcement. Hopes, however, that Dutch can be made aware serious nature their actions on Indonesian developments. While good deal damage our mutual objectives in Indonesia unavoidable under circumstances, explosive possibilities of situation could be minimized to some extent if Dutch exercised more effective control over publicity given plan, refrained from further public announcements and comment. (See Embtel 2822,[8] repeated information Hague 88 for Acting Foreign Minister Leimena comment re Dutch handling publicity aspects visit.) Of utmost importance, Dutch should not under any circumstances bring vessel to Indonesian Archipelago waters. Despite legal right traverse Java Sea or East Indonesian waters, attempt do so certain to be taken here as virtually direct aggression.[9]

Henderson

---

[8] Telegram 2822, April 5, reported a conversation between Henderson and Acting Foreign Minister Leimena regarding the Netherlands announcement of the planned *Karel Doorman* visit. (*Ibid.*, 656.9813/4–560) See Supplement.

[9] Telegram 1398 from The Hague, April 29, was based on the "combined efforts of Attachés, Embassy and MAAG officers," and offered information and recommendations regarding the proposed *Karel Doorman* cruise and the planned strengthening of West New Guinea's defenses. (Department of State, Central Files, 790.5856/4–2960) See Supplement.

---

248. Memorandum From the Assistant Secretary of State for Far Eastern Affairs (Parsons) to the Assistant Secretary of State for European Affairs (Kohler)

Washington, April 15, 1960.

SUBJECT

Projected Visit of Dutch Naval Vessels to West New Guinea

From the point of view of our relations with Indonesia which, as you know, have improved considerably over the past two years, I am

---

Source: Department of State, Central Files, 790.5856/4–1560. Secret. Drafted by Wenzel and cleared with Mein and Steeves. Copies of this memorandum were sent to Dillon and Merchant.

concerned by the recently announced Dutch Government plans to send the aircraft carrier *Karel Doorman* and two DDE's on a six-month "flag-showing" visit this year to Southeast Asia, including West New Guinea. The Dutch political decision to refrain from giving the United States advance notice of this decision (described in The Hague's telegram 1315, Tab A)[1] is particularly disturbing, especially in view of their insistence that we keep them and the NAC informed of our plans and programs in Indonesia.

The proposed *Doorman* tour would present serious problems for us in our relations with Indonesia. The announcement of the tour has been attacked violently in the Indonesian press and Indonesian Government spokesmen have publicly condemned this projected Dutch show of force in the West New Guinea area. On April 11 the Indonesian Minister Counselor, under instructions of his government, raised with the Department the question of the *Karel Doorman* cruise which he termed belligerent and provocative and detrimental to the peace of the area and to Indonesian-Free World relations (Tab B).[2] The minister asked whether the United States could not moderate the Dutch attitude. It seems clear that the *Doorman* visit could seriously undercut the efforts the United States has been making to dampen Indonesian chauvinism with respect to the West New Guinea issue.

The démarche of April 11 represents the third time the Indonesian Embassy has approached the Department in the past two months to express serious concern over what the Indonesians term a Dutch military "build-up" in the West New Guinea area. On February 10 the Indonesians raised the question of the sale of four Dakotas to the Dutch for use in West New Guinea;[3] and on March 23 the Indonesians questioned us on possible Dutch plans to purchase Neptune aircraft here to replace obsolete aircraft in West New Guinea.[4] The main themes running through these Indonesian démarches were that this Dutch military "build-up" could only serve to heighten tensions in the area and that the United States could and should do something to deter the Dutch from this course of action. The Indonesians have shown particular interest in whether or not the United States had concurred in the use of any MAP equipment by the Dutch in West New Guinea.

---

[1] See footnote 2, Document 247. No tabs were attached to the source text.

[2] Memorandum of conversation, April 11. (Department of State, Central Files, 790.5856/4–1160) See Supplement.

[3] A memorandum of this conversation is in Department of State, Central Files, 790.5856/2–1060.

[4] A memorandum of this conversation, March 23, is *ibid.*, 790.5856/3–2360.

What concerns me above all about the proposed *Karel Doorman* tour is, of course, the Dutch intention to retain MAP-furnished carrier aircraft aboard the ship during the Southeast Asia visit. Whether or not it is legally and technically feasible for the Dutch to do this under the existing NATO and MAP agreements, the use of MAP-furnished aircraft by the Dutch in West New Guinea, albeit for a limited period of time, could seriously jeopardize our friendly relations with Indonesia and be generally embarrassing to us in our relations with other Asian countries. If they do not already know, the Indonesians will almost certainly become aware of the presence of MAP aircraft aboard the *Karel Doorman* and we will be open to the charge of bolstering the Dutch military posture in West New Guinea through the use of United States-owned aircraft. Needless to say, such a situation would be exploited thoroughly by the Communists in the area.

You will recall that in connection with the recent Dutch procurement of four United States Dakotas for use in West New Guinea, the Department took the position (Mr. Dillon's letter of January 7, 1960 to Mr. Gates)[5] that "The Department of State would not, of course, propose the transfer of United States military equipment for Dutch non-NATO use unless purchased by the Dutch." In that case we in fact took pains to sell the Dakotas to the Dutch, after they had been declared surplus, and we were thus able to inform the Indonesians that there was no question of our concurring in the use of MAP equipment in the West New Guinea area. Despite the temporary aspect of the *Doorman* mission, it appears that we are faced with the same basic questions—i.e., whether or not we would concur in the transfer of MAP equipment for use in West New Guinea by the Dutch defense forces.

Since we will have to reply shortly to this latest Indonesian démarche, and since I assume that EUR is currently considering how the Department should appropriately react to the Dutch plans for the *Karel Doorman* cruise, I would appreciate an opportunity for EUR–FE consultation on this question.[6]

---

[5] Document 237.

[6] Kohler replied to Parsons in an April 15 memorandum. (Department of State, SPA Files: Lot 63 D 436, 322—West New Guinea Problem) See Supplement.

249. Editorial Note

In an April 21 memorandum to Under Secretary of State Dillon, Assistant Secretary Parsons recommended that the United States provide the Indonesian Navy with an engineering survey at Ambon, the principal Indonesian administrative and military base in the Moluccas. The reason for Parsons' recommendation was Indonesia's acceptance during Khrushchev's recent visit of a $5 million credit and technical help with construction of an oceanographic and marine science institute at Ambon. Parsons' memorandum noted the danger of Soviet assistance acting as a precursor to Soviet aid to the Indonesian Navy. The institute could provide the Soviet Union an opportunity to do scientific and probably intelligence work over which the United States would be unable to maintain surveillance. By helping in reconstructing the modest naval base at Ambon, the United States could keep a close watch on Soviet activities there and strengthen the Indonesia Navy's hand in resisting pressure for further Soviet assistance. In addition to recommending the engineering survey within the 1960 fiscal year Military Assistance Program, Parsons also asked for authorization to inform Australian and Netherlands officials of the decision. (Department of State, SPA Files: Lot 63 D 436, Supplies and Equipment for Armed Forces) See Supplement.

Dillon approved both recommendations on May 3. His stamped approval is on a copy of this memorandum in Department of State, WE Files: Lot 63 D 136, Indonesia Miscellaneous. On May 16 John Mein, Director of the Office of Southeast Asian Affairs, explained to Australian officials the U.S. decision to aid the Indonesian Navy with its base facilities at Ambon. (Memorandum of conversation, May 16; *ibid.*, Central Files, 798.56311/5–1660) See Supplement. During a conversation on May 17 Deputy Under Secretary of State for Political Affairs Raymond Hare outlined the U.S. position on Ambon to Ambassador van Roijen. (Telegram 1674 to The Hague, May 19; Department of State, Central Files, 656.9813/5–1960) See Supplement.

250. Editorial Note

On April 28 at the 442d meeting of the National Security Council, Allen Dulles discussed developments in Indonesia during his intelligence briefing:

"Mr. Dulles reported that in Indonesia the Army, in Sukarno's absence, was supporting an anti-Sukarno campaign. Mr. Dulles, however, doubted that Nasution would make any move toward taking over the government from Sukarno even though Nasution is undoubtedly quite disturbed at the situation in Indonesia. Mr. Dulles said that one of the salient features of the Indonesian situation was the fact that the economy was slowly deteriorating." (Memorandum of discussion by Boggs, April 28; Eisenhower Library, Whitman File, NSC Records)

---

251.   Memorandum of Conversation

Istanbul, May 3, 1960, 7:15 p.m.

SUBJECT

Dutch Military Reinforcements for West New Guinea

PARTICIPANTS

For the Netherlands	*For the United States*
Dr. Joseph Luns, Foreign Minister	The Secretary
Dr. H.R. van Houten, State Secretary	EUR—Mr. Kohler
for Foreign Affairs	EUR/RA—Mr. Fessenden

Foreign Minister Luns opened the conversation by reviewing for the Secretary the history of Dutch actions in West New Guinea from the time of the 1949 Round Table Conference. Emphasizing the inadequacy of the Dutch defense forces in West New Guinea, Mr. Luns said that the Dutch Government had no choice but to dispatch the *Karel Doorman* and to send additional military and air force equipment and personnel.

Under these circumstances, the Dutch were concerned at what Mr. Luns termed the US lack of response and sympathy for the Dutch action. The Dutch did not like but were now resigned to United States policy toward Indonesia. Dutch acceptance of American military and economic support of the Indonesian Government did not mean, Mr. Luns said, that the US could ignore the interests of its ally in New Guinea. He recalled his conversation with Secretary Dulles in October, 1958,[1] and the Dutch belief at that time that Indonesia planned to attack West New Guinea in March, 1959. Mr. Luns said that Mr. Dulles had assured him

---

Source: Department of State, Central Files, 656C.98/5–360. Secret. Approved by S on May 16. Secretary of State Herter and Foreign Minister Luns were in Istanbul for the NATO Council meeting May 1–4.
[1] See Document 159.

that the last thing the US wanted was to see the Netherlands turn over West New Guinea to the Indonesians. Mr. Luns said that the United States had been convinced then of the danger of such an attack and that Secretary Dulles' stern talk with Indonesian Foreign Minister Subandrio had deterred the Indonesians from taking overt action.

At the present time, Mr. Luns continued, there was absolute evidence of an Indonesian plan to take over West New Guinea by means of infiltration and subversion. The Dutch had clear evidence of six recent infiltrations by small bands of Indonesians, two of which had occurred in 1960. These infiltrations and subversive activities, in conjunction with the lack of Dutch defense forces, were undermining the morale of both the indigenous Papuans and the 15,000 Dutch resident in New Guinea.

Mr. Luns remarked that because the US had given the Dutch no military guarantee for New Guinea and because the territory was not covered by any regional security treaty, the Dutch had no recourse but to divert national forces to meet the imminent threat of Indonesian aggression.

Mr. Luns said that he had discussed the WNG problem with Mr. Selwyn Lloyd and that he had emphasized the Dutch concern over the British sale of 1500 parachutes to Indonesia. [2-1/2 lines of source text not declassified] He noted that Foreign Minister Wigny had made a full statement on the Congo. Mr. Luns said that he had, however, been dissuaded from making such an exposition by Mr. van Houten.

Mr. Luns said that the Dutch Government was particularly disturbed by the reaction of a Departmental officer who had said that the Dutch action in reinforcing West New Guinea defenses was provocative and that the Dutch were "asking for trouble." The officer reportedly had gone on to say that the Dutch were over-reacting and were over-excited because of the "barking of a few Indonesians."[2]

The Dutch Foreign Minister appealed for a firmer US stand on the principle of the Dutch presence in West New Guinea. He remarked that both the UK and Australia had been firm on this point and the Dutch saw no reason why the US could not strengthen its position regarding Dutch sovereignty. He also asked that the US approach the Indonesians to set forth in clear fashion the limits beyond which the Indonesians could not go and to repeat Secretary Dulles' warning against the use of force.

The Secretary replied that we had taken every opportunity, including reiteration at the time of each arms sale, to spell out to the Indonesian Government that the arms being sold them were to be used for internal security and legitimate self-defense. We had also repeatedly warned the

[2] No record of this conversation has been found.

Indonesians against the use of force. In view of the recent Indonesian propaganda regarding WNG, the Secretary said that he did not believe that the Dutch announcement of military reinforcements was inflammatory. With respect to Mr. Luns' report of the comments of a Departmental officer, the Secretary said that these reported remarks should not be considered the policy of the United States Government. The Secretary assured Mr. Luns that we would again clearly state our position to the Indonesian Government and said that there had been absolutely no change in our West New Guinea policy which Secretary Dulles had stated to Mr. Luns in late 1958.

Mr. Luns said that he was very gratified to receive the Secretary's reaffirmation of US policy. He asked whether he could summarize the US position at the moment by saying that the United States follows the situation with an open mind and an awareness of the dangers of the phased plan of the Indonesians for obtaining West New Guinea. The Secretary did not reply directly to this question but asked the best means by which the Department could obtain the latest Dutch intelligence information. Mr. Luns replied that this could best be effected through the Central Intelligence Agency.

---

252. Special National Intelligence Estimate

SNIE 65–60   Washington, May 3, 1960.

THE SHORT-TERM OUTLOOK IN INDONESIA

The Problem

To estimate the likelihood and consequences of a coup in Indonesia during the next two or three months.[1]

Source: Department of State, INR–NIE Files. Secret. According to a note on the cover sheet, this SNIE was prepared by the CIA and the intelligence organizations of the Departments of State, the Army, the Navy, the Air Force, and the Joint Staff. All members of the IAC concurred with the estimate on May 3, except representatives of the AEC and the FBI, who abstained on the grounds that the subject was outside their jurisdiction.

Parsons recommended in an April 21 memorandum to Cumming that a Special National Intelligence Estimate on Indonesia be prepared in "view of the current political tension in Indonesia and the seeming possibility that a move to depose the present government might occur." Parsons believed that the estimate should be prepared within a week "to be of maximum usefulness." (Ibid., SPA Files: Lot 64 D 469, Memoranda, Jan/June 1960)

[1] In telegram 3052, April 28, the Embassy offered its analysis of Indonesian internal developments. (Ibid., Central Files, 798.00/4–2860) See Supplement.

Conclusions

1. Political power in Indonesia has become increasingly polarized between the Army and the Indonesian Communist Party (PKI). The economy is in a sad state and popular discontent, particularly in urban areas, is increasing. Sukarno, after nearly a year of complete formal power, has made no constructive move to solve the country's problems. He has taken some steps which tend to weaken Nasution's position and to increase the political potential of the PKI. An increasing number of political leaders, and some military leaders as well, believe that Sukarno's power must be greatly reduced or eliminated if Indonesia's economic and political decline is to be halted and an eventual Communist takeover averted. (Paras. 6, 8–11, 16)

2. Since Sukarno's departure for a world tour on 1 April, Nasution has almost certainly been seeking to organize public support and backing from military and political leaders. He probably hopes to build enough strength to prevent a diminution of the Army's position and to force Sukarno to accept restrictions on his monopoly of political power and a parliamentary formula which would bolster the anti-Communist elements in the government. He may also be attempting, in this process, to ascertain the backing he would have for a move to seize power. (Paras. 21–23)

3. Nasution may find that he has created a situation, wittingly or unwittingly, in which he will have to move to seize power or face dismissal. Thus the odds favoring a coup attempt by Nasution during the next two or three months have probably gone up, but we believe that the chances are still less than even that a coup will take place. In any event, relations between Sukarno and Nasution will probably be marked by growing suspicion and tension.[2] (Paras. 22–23)

4. If Nasution should attempt a coup in the near future with the support of most of the Army, we believe that he would probably succeed. (Para. 26)

5. In the absence of firm and unified opposition from Army and political leaders, President Sukarno will probably proceed to reorganize his cabinet, giving stronger representation to the Nationalist Party (PNI) and the Nahdatul Ulama (NU). He may also include one or two PKI members. Although Sukarno will continue to rely upon the Army to

---

[2] The Assistant Chief of Staff for Intelligence, Department of the Army, believes that since Sukarno's departure 1 April 1960 on a world tour, there have been evidences of political maneuvering, primarily below the Nasution level. Conflicting reports have been received regarding prospects for a move by Nasution with Army support to seize power. The Assistant Chief of Staff for Intelligence, Department of the Army, believes that while the temptation to take direct political action may exist, such a move by Nasution is unlikely at this time. [Footnote in the source text.]

counterbalance the PKI and to play an important administrative role, he will seek to diminish the Army's political influence and will probably attempt to curtail Nasution's power. (Para. 27)

[Here follows the Discussion section; see Supplement.]

---

253. Telegram From the Embassy in Indonesia to the Department of State

Djakarta, May 9, 1960, 3 p.m.

3180. CINCPAC for POLAD. Paris for USRO. Polto 3 sent Department Polto 2227, sent The Hague Polto 88, sent London Polto 482.[1]

Assume reference cited in reference Polto telegram is Djakarta's 3107[2] to Department rather than Djakarta's 3071.

Embassy fully appreciates difficulties which attempt obtain NATO statement might create, recognizes that most which may be obtainable might be Dutch unilateral statement plus selection of non-provocative route for naval visit.

Embassy does not believe there is anything to gain by private statement to Indonesians as to US confidence in peaceful intentions of Dutch. Most serious aspect of problem is not, of course, assuaging fear within GOI that Dutch may be planning aggression. Real problem is to minimize opportunity for Indonesian Communists to exploit issue to their own advantage and to detriment of other major political elements within Indonesia which just now are in process of uniting against them for first time. Issue is creating diversion for Communists just when they most need one. Foregoing does not mean that fear of Dutch aggression is entirely artificial. Indonesians won independence in 1950 only after

---

Source: Department of State, Central Files, 656.9813/5–960. Confidential. Also sent to CINCPAC and repeated to The Hague, London, and Paris.

[1] This telegram of May 5 recommended that, from NATO's point of view, any statement to the Indonesians should, in view of the likelihood of its becoming public, be limited to the following two points: "(1) Dutch, as NATO members, retain sovereign right to withdraw forces from NATO area, and (2) US has confidence in Dutch commitments re peaceful settlement disputes as UN member and NATO member just as it has confidence in Indonesian assurances." (Ibid., 790.5856/5–560)

[2] Telegram 3107, May 3, reviewed the Netherlands position in the West New Guinea dispute. (Ibid., 656.9813/5–360) See Supplement.

years of bloody fighting with the Dutch. Dutch are proposing to send naval force to West Irian which will for time being change entire balance of military power in Indonesian area. Dutch force apparently superior in fire power to both Indonesian Navy, Indonesian Air Force which possesses no carriers and only squadron or so of operational jets which have no base near enough to do battle in eastern reaches of country. Embassy's impression is projected cruise force would in fact comprise naval, air power which may well rival or surpass anything Dutch could have brought to bear during fighting phase of Indonesian revolution. Any US statement to Indonesians that need have no worry in this situation likely to be ignored at best or more likely treated as evidence of partiality to Dutch in West Irian disputes.

Henderson

254. Telegram From the Department of State to the Embassy in Indonesia

Washington, May 14, 1960, 3:54 p.m.

1975. Deptel 1976.[1] Dept believes mounting Dutch-Indonesian tension over projected *Karel Doorman* cruise and augmentation Dutch armed forces West New Guinea could lead to developments prejudicial to U.S. interests and policies in area. We concerned particularly that (1) as result some incautious act by either party Dutch-Indonesian armed incident might occur and (2) continuation existing tension may further stimulate Indonesian domestic political developments inimical to our objectives in Indonesia.

In view foregoing and in view our overall desire keep West New Guinea dispute quiet in interest our relations with both Netherlands and Indonesia, we propose try moderate Dutch and Indonesian attitudes and actions in present situation. To this end you instructed seek earliest possible appointment with Acting FonMin Leimena and tell him following:

Source: Department of State, Central Files, 790.5856/5–1460. Secret; Niact. Drafted by Moore and approved by Steeves. Repeated to The Hague, Canberra, CINCPAC for POLAD, London, and Paris for Herter. Secretary of State Herter was in Paris for the Heads of Government and Chiefs of State meeting May 15–19.

[1] Printed as telegram 1640 to The Hague, Document 255.

1. In response his informal plea to you and Indo Embassy Washington approach to Dept U.S. prepared discuss with Dutch implications of *Doorman* cruise and reinforcement West New Guinea defenses. Begin FYI. You should make sure Leimena understands that U.S. deems it impracticable seek cancellation these Dutch actions and therefore will not attempt persuade Dutch to cancel them. As set forth below we will seek Dutch steps short of cancellation to minimize unfavorable impact. End FYI.

2. We believe likelihood our conversations with Dutch having useful results would be greatly enhanced were GOI now to restate publicly and formally its existing policy of not resorting to force to resolve the West New Guinea dispute. We strongly hope GOI will find it feasible promptly to issue such policy restatement.

3. We would also hope GOI will take all feasible steps to moderate Indonesian official and public reaction to projected Dutch actions, with a view especially to preventing recurrence acts such as vandalism at Dutch Embassy Djakarta, which can only serve inflame issue and reduce Dutch receptiveness to our suggestions re calming current furor.

4. It is our continued understanding, concerning which we would appreciate renewed GOI assurances, that military equipment obtained by Indonesia from U.S. will be used for internal security and legitimate self defense only, not in any attempt resolve West New Guinea dispute by force.

Report niact results your conversation with Leimena.[2]

Henderson

---

[2] Henderson met with Leimena at his home on May 15 and outlined the four points contained in this telegram. He reported on this meeting in telegram 3251 from Djakarta, May 15. (Department of State, Central Files, 790.5856/5–1560) See Supplement.

---

255. Telegram From the Department of State to the Embassy in the Netherlands

Washington, May 14, 1960, 3:55 p.m.

1640. Begin FYI. Secretary approved May 11 following courses of action in an attempt to moderate both Indonesian and Dutch actions in

---

Source: Department of State, Central Files, 790.5856/5–1460. Secret; Niact. Drafted by Robert M. Beaudry of WE, cleared with ISA and U/MSC, and approved by Ivan White. Also sent to Djakarta, CINCPAC, London, Paris for the Secretary, and Canberra.

connection with forthcoming cruise of *Karel Doorman* to West New Guinea.[1]

1. Advise Indonesian government that we are prepared discuss implications of *Doorman* cruise with Dutch and seek public restatement of Indonesia's policy of no resort to force for resolution WNG dispute. Also we will express hope Indonesian government could take steps moderate official and public reaction this matter with view especially prevent recurrence acts such as vandalism at Dutch Embassy Djakarta.

2. Call in Dutch Ambassador discuss military reinforcements WNG and *Doorman* cruise. We will inform Dutch of conversations with Indonesians outlined above emphasizing anxiety U.S. avoid possibility of incident. We would suggest that Dutch might place the matter in better perspective by issuing public statement (a) affirming Dutch government's adherence to principle of peaceful settlement international disputes and maintenance Dutch obligations under the UN Charter, (b) underlining the defensive nature and purpose of matériel being sent to WNG, and (c) emphasizing flag-showing nature *Doorman* cruise including proposed route vessel will follow.[2]

3. Inform Dutch Ambassador that we would propose tell Indonesians of our discussions with Dutch after issuance Dutch public statement.

4. Discuss substance our approach in advance with UK and Australian embassies here.[3]

Execution this policy planned as follows:

Embassy Djakarta being instructed approach GOI as outlined above. Parsons who will be with Sukarno party Puerto Rico weekend May 14–15 will seek opportunity make parallel approach Subandrio. Hare will see Ambassador van Roijen p.m. May 17. Consultations UK and Australian embassies here as indicated, above.

At same time we discuss with Dutch Ambassador question of *Doorman* cruise and reinforcement West New Guinea defenses we will tell him of aid U.S. has decided to give Indonesian Navy with rehabilitation modest base facilities at Ambon. This matter unrelated to Dutch actions West New Guinea but timing of separate U.S. Govt. decisions on the two

---

[1] On May 11 Herter initialed his approval of this course of action and that in Document 254 on a memorandum from Kohler and Parsons recommending this action. (Department of State, FE Files: Lot 62 D 26, Indonesia 1960)

[2] In telegram 1466 from The Hague, May 16, Ambassador Young outlined the reasons why he opposed this course of action. (Department of State, Central Files, 798.11/5–1660) See Supplement.

[3] In separate conversations on May 16 Mein informed representatives of the British and Australian Embassies of the U.S. response to the *Karel Doorman* trip. (Memoranda of conversations by Mein; Department of State, Central Files, 790.5856/5–1660)

matters has been such that we believe best discuss both at one time with Dutch. For info all addressees. U.S. decision to help with Ambon base facilities taken in response to strong, specific request from Indonesian Navy Chief of Staff and with view facilitating U.S. surveillance Russian activity at Ambon oceanographic institute. This point will be made with Dutch in explaining our decision re Ambon. Only early U.S. action at Ambon will be engineering survey financed under FY–60 military assistance program for Indonesia. Our intention, which will be conveyed to GOI after we tell Dutch, is to follow through with construction of modest facilities in succeeding fiscal years subject of course to availability of funds and overall MAP programming requirements.

Dept will inform Australians and British as well as Dutch of our intentions re Ambon. End FYI.[4]

Dillon

---

[4] In telegram 1674 to The Hague, May 19, the Department of State informed Young that after seriously considering his views, it decided to approach the Dutch as outlined above. The Department described in detail a meeting among Hare, Parsons, and van Roijen on May 17 in which Hare made the démarche. (*Ibid.*, 656.9813/5–1960) See Supplement.

---

256. Telegram From the Embassy in Indonesia to the Department of State

Djakarta, May 18, 1960, 11 a.m.

3281. CINCPAC for POLAD, Paris for Secretary. Verbatim text. Embassy telegram 3251.[1] Chargé summoned to home of Acting Foreign Minister Leimena morning May 18 to be given aide-mémoire by Leimena text of which follows:

"Following are comments given by Dr. J. Leimena, Acting Minister of Foreign Affairs and Deputy First Minister of the Republic of Indonesia on the information furnished orally and summarized in an aide-

---

Source: Department of State, Central Files, 790.5856/5–1860. Confidential; Niact. Repeated to The Hague, London, Canberra, Paris, and CINCPAC.

[1] See footnote 2, Document 254.

mémoire of the US Embassy, Djakarta, dated May 16, by Mr. John W. Henderson, Chargé d'Affaires A.I. of the Embassy of the United States of America in Djakarta:

"1. The Government of the Republic of Indonesia appreciates the attention given by the Government of the United States of America to the question of the dispatch of the Dutch aircraft carrier *Karel Doorman* and other Dutch warships, miliary equipment and combat troops to West Irian. While realizing fully the significance of the efforts of the United States in this regard, it would have been more satisfactory to the Indonesian Government, if the United States could see its way clear to attempt to seek cancellation of the projected Dutch action, inasmuch as the dispatch of above-mentioned Dutch warships and the Dutch military buildup in West Irian constitute a provocation to the Indonesian people.

"2. The Indonesian Government has reiterated time and again that the Indonesian policy in relation to the West Irian dispute is a peaceful one. This peaceful policy has been restated recently by Dr. Subandrio in the course of his visit to Cuba when he was accompanying President Soekarno.

"3. The Indonesian Government would like to point out that expression of public opinion in the press and in resolutions adopted by various layers of the Indonesian community and demonstrations is a direct consequence of the Dutch provocative actions. In the meantime the Indonesian Government has taken all normal and also special precautionary measures with a view to controlling outbursts of excesses. The United States Government is undoubtedly aware of the fact that no disorderly demonstrations have taken place notwithstanding that an explosive situation continues to exist.

"4. The understanding of the United States Government that military equipment which is obtained by Indonesia from the United States will be used for internal security and legitimate self-defense only, and not in any attempt to resolve the West Irian dispute by force, is correct."

Comments follow.

Henderson

257.   Telegram From the Department of State to the Embassy in Indonesia

Washington, May 18, 1960, 6:12 p.m.

2006. Re The Hague's 1460 to Department[1] being repeated Djakarta. During Puerto Rico visit Parsons had no discussion with Sukarno on *Karel Doorman* or related matters although soon after arrival he had opportunity tell Ambassador Moekarto that he had certain points of interest to make to Subandrio at convenient time. One such point was appropriateness of timely Indonesian reaffirmation non-use of force policy West Irian dispute. Moekarto subsequently told Parsons Subandrio would like have talk with him on plane enroute New York on 16th.

In resultant talk on 16th Parsons made four points covered Deptel 1975[2] repeated to The Hague 1639. In addition he referred to intimations he had seen that US had prior agreement with Dutch and supported *Karel Doorman* trip. He said these intimations totally unfounded and so far as he knew Dutch had given us no advance information of their intent dispatch vessel to Far East.

Subandrio's reaction to four points was responsive and understanding, but he made no commitments. Actually it would have been surprising if Subandrio had done so because Parsons told him Chargé in Djakarta was making démarche to Government there and also Subandrio had indicated *Karel Doorman* one of subjects he wished to raise with Acting Secretary in Washington on 19th.[3]

Subandrio made it clear that he did not regard renewed request for public reaffirmation of non-use of force policy as indicative of US lack of faith in Indonesian promises. He said he quite understood value of such

---

Source: Department of State, Central Files, 798.11/5–1460. Confidential. Drafted and approved by Parsons. Repeated to The Hague.

[1] In telegram 1460, May 14, Young suggested that Parsons should use the greatest caution in his talks with Sukarno in Puerto Rico, and that Jones should exercise the same caution in his talks with the Indonesian President in San Francisco. (*Ibid.*) See Supplement.

In an April 25 memorandum to the President Herter noted that Sukarno planned to make informal stopovers in Puerto Rico (May 14–16) and San Francisco (May 22–23) as part of his worldwide tour. He recommended that Eisenhower designate a personal representative to greet Sukarno in Puerto Rico and deliver a personal letter from Eisenhower welcoming Sukarno to the United States. Eisenhower approved Herter's recommendation and designated Assistant Secretary Parsons to greet Sukarno in Puerto Rico on May 14. He also approved, with minor changes, a draft letter to the Indonesian President, which Parsons delivered on May 14. (Department of State, Central Files, 798.11/4–2560) See Supplement.

[2] Document 254.

[3] Indonesian Foreign Minister Subandrio was scheduled to meet with Acting Secretary Dillon in Washington on May 19.

reaffirmation in connection with forthcoming US efforts with Dutch. Surprisingly he did not mention his remarks in Cuba of which Parsons then had no knowledge. In course of discussion he did indicate puzzlement and concern over Dutch motivation in sending ship at time when it bound to cause sharp repercussions in Indonesia. If it was Dutch intention provoke incident and force showdown, Indonesia of course would be ready. He hoped this would not be case and Parsons assured him that he did not think Dutch had any such intention.

Dillon

---

258. Memorandum of Conversation

Washington, May 19, 1960.

SUBJECT

> Indonesian Situation; Indonesian-Netherlands Relations

PARTICIPANTS

> Dr. Subandrio, Foreign Minister of Indonesia
>
> The Acting Secretary, Mr. Dillon
> Mr. Parsons, Assistant Secretary for Far Eastern Affairs
> Mr. Mein, Director, Office of Southwest Pacific Affairs

The Minister said he was glad to have this opportunity to visit Washington since there were no special problems between us. He said that although we may have trouble at times understanding developments in Indonesia and we may wonder whether any progress is being made, he thought that from the Indonesian viewpoint they continue to make gradual progress. He said there had been a gradual economic decline resulting from changes which have occurred and also from the actions against the Dutch and Chinese but that they are prepared to accept these conditions.

Source: Department of State, Central Files, 033.9811/5–1960. Secret. Drafted by Mein on May 24. Approved in U on June 6. Dillon was briefed for this meeting with Subandio in a memorandum from Parsons dated May 18. (Ibid., SPA Files: Lot 63 D 436, Briefing File) For memoranda of conversation between Subandrio and Dillon, Parsons, and Mein, and between Sukarno and Governor Brown of California and Jones, see the Supplement.

The Minister said that in the political field they have certain ideas which they want to work out. There is no longer a political vacuum as existed between 1950 and 1957 and they now have certain basic conceptions of what is necessary for the people. He said they were aware of the Communist problem and danger, but the handling of the situation took a certain amount of maneuvering. The Minister said that as a result of the trip and of developments in Indonesia, President Sukarno is aware that this is not the time to play politics. The Minister referred to the dissolution and formation of Parliament as not being very significant. As to Parliament, he said, "we do not attach much importance" anyway since if the Parliament as appointed does not work out, the President and Nasution can always dissolve it again. This procedure, however, will enable them to extend the interval before the next elections, which he thought desirable. This would (1) permit the development of new personalities in the parties which have been dominated by the old leaders who gained prominence in the revolution, and (2) give time to the non-Communist parties to organize themselves so as to establish a balance between the Communists, who are the best organized and financed party in Indonesia, and the non-Communist parties, and (3) would also permit the creation by Sukarno of a national feeling in Indonesia in case anything happens to him and which he believes none of the old leaders can accomplish at the present time. The Minister said that whether this would require more than one stage is not clear, but that is the basis for the National Front. No one, he said, including the armed forces, wants any outside domination and the new situation will permit Indonesia to absorb and digest any foreign ideas.

The Minister referred to the actions taken by the Indonesian Government against the alien Chinese and stated that he was standing firm in this matter. If the problem is not solved now, he said, it probably cannot be solved. He was apparently quite shaken by a statement made to him in Peiping last October when the Chinese threatened to send a warship to protect the Chinese in Indonesia.

Another problem, he said, which is not of direct U.S.-Indonesian interest, is that of the relations between Indonesia and the Netherlands. He said that if asked why the Indonesians are so upset by the forthcoming visit of the *Karel Doorman*, it is not the mere sending of a ship but more the policy statement issued by the Netherlands Government referring to the aggressive acts of Indonesia. He said that Indonesia has given us and others repeated assurances that they do not intend to use force for the settlement of this problem, but that if asked now, he cannot make a public statement along these lines because the Dutch have put him on the defensive. There are some military groups in Indonesia that do want a showdown on the West New Guinea problem, but Sukarno and others do not want this. He said he did not know what the United States could do in this situation but he thought that if the *Karel Doorman* were not sent, it would be of great help not only to Indonesia but also to the general situation in the area. He said that the Dutch have referred to "infiltrations" of West New Guinea by Indonesians (which he did not deny), but he said that if there should be an uprising in West New Guinea, it would not be the result of such infiltrations but rather action by local forces. He said that not only in West New Guinea but also in the other Dutch colonies there are local groups who would like to see a change in the status of the area. Contributing to this desire on the part of some local groups, of course, is the progress which has been made in Indonesia as compared to West New Guinea. The Minister said that the Government had replied to our Aide-Mémoire[1] and had restated its assurances, but a public statement at this time would be impossible since it would appear to have been made under U.S. pressure.

The Acting Secretary said that we were very pleased with the Aide-Mémoire given us by the Indonesian Government in Djakarta, which was very helpful even if it could not be made public. The Acting Secretary said that we had had preliminary talks with the Dutch. He did not think there was much chance of cancellation by the Dutch since they had announced the trip. The Dutch had made it quite clear that they had no aggressive intentions and that the measure was purely defensive. Although the first announcement was unfortunate, there is a chance that they will make their position clear by a further statement. The general policy of the Dutch is to be defensive and not to aggravate the situation, and we are trying to do what we can to ameliorate the situation. The Minister asked whether there was any chance of the Dutch correcting the statement. The Acting Secretary said he did not think there was much chance of this, but that we hoped that further statements would clarify the matter.

The Minister said he was being pressed by some quarters in Djakarta to break diplomatic relations with the Netherlands. In his opinion this is not desirable since among the other consequences would be action against the remaining Dutch interests in Indonesia, against Shell, etc., which would set in a chain reaction. He reiterated that in this case it is not only that Indonesia would appreciate the assistance to Indonesia in having the trip cancelled but that cancellation would be of help to the situation in the area. He said that in all fairness, however, he must state that preparations were under way for severing diplomatic relations but he sincerely hoped this would not be necessary. Again the Minister emphasized that some restatement on the part of the Dutch would be helpful since it is not so much the sending of the vessels as the tenor of the

---

[1] See Document 256.

statement made by the Dutch that has been harmful. The timing of the visit is also bad, especially in view of the actions which the Government was taking against the Chinese and the effect this was having on the Communist Party. He asked again whether from the U.S. viewpoint there would not be any chance of correcting the statement. The Acting Secretary reiterated that he did not think so but he hoped that further statements would be helpful and would tend to play down the issue. The Minister said he also hoped this would be the case and he also hoped that Mr. Luns would have some influence in the situation and be able to improve the climate, since he had not been present at the time the statement was made.

259.   Special National Intelligence Estimate

SNIE 65–2–60   Washington, May 24, 1960.

THE WEST NEW GUINEA PROBLEM

The Problem

To estimate probable developments in the West New Guinea situation over the next six months or so.

Conclusions

1. We believe that Indonesia will not attempt an armed attack against West New Guinea during the next six months at least. Indonesia will probably continue to seek its objectives in New Guinea by international political pressure and by attempts to subvert the Papuans and Indonesians in West New Guinea. (Paras. 10–11, A–9)

2. Dutch reinforcement of its New Guinea defenses and the planned flag-showing cruise by the aircraft carrier *Karel Doorman* will evoke an intense emotional and nationalistic response in Indonesia. However, we

Source: Department of State, INR–NIE Files. Secret. The CIA and the intelligence organizations of the Departments of State, the Army, the Navy, the Air Force, and the Joint Staff participated in the preparation of this estimate. All members of the USIB concurred with the estimate on May 24, except representatives of the AEC and the FBI, who abstained on the grounds that the subject was outside their jurisdiction.

believe that neither the Dutch nor the Indonesians will attempt to provoke an armed conflict. Although we believe that a deliberate military action is unlikely during the period of this estimate, we cannot exclude the possibility of military incidents, such as an irrational attack against Dutch naval units or settlements in New Guinea or an accidental armed clash. (Paras. 12–14)

3. The furor over Dutch action will almost certainly work to the advantage of both Sukarno and the Communists. It will enable Sukarno to rally opinion behind him and divert attention from Indonesia's internal problems. The PKI will be able to consolidate further its claim as a nationalist movement and Sukarno's most loyal supporter. Any efforts of General Nasution and the army to combine with anti-Communist elements against Sukarno's tendency to increase Communist participation in the government will be seriously undermined. (Para. 15)

[Here follow a 3-page Discussion section, an annex on Dutch and Indonesia military capabilities in the area, and a map; see Supplement.]

---

260. Telegram From the Embassy in Indonesia to the Department of State

Djakarta, May 25, 1960, 8 p.m.

3373. Department pass ACSI, CINCPAC for POLAD. Colonel Sukendro, political deputy to General Nasution, told Chargé May 25 he had "full mandate" from Nasution to attempt arrange through US Government "informal understanding" with Dutch concerning *Karel Doorman* cruise, reinforcement West Guinea.

Assertion of authority from General Nasution came in response to Chargé's direct question.

Proposal was made after Chargé had put hypothetical questions to Sukendro as to whether public statement by Dutch giving assurance of peaceful intent, minimizing quantity and quality of proposed reinforcements, and showing route from Indonesian territorial waters, would be helpful in dealing with internal political problem.

Source: Department of State, Central Files, 790.5856/5–2560. Top Secret; Niact. Repeated to The Hague and CINCPAC.

Sukendro, speaking with care through interpreter whom he had brought to meeting called at his initiative, replied that such statement would indeed help but at this juncture it would be better for Dutch to pass such assurances privately to Indonesian Army (he specified that it should not be transmitted to GOI through other channels). Army then could make use of information internally at proper time, would let Dutch know when public statement would be helpful and would let US know when assurances could be passed officially, to GOI by US. Much depended, Sukendro said, on way in which any public statement was made as well as on timing. If these considerations not fully understood, Dutch statement would be more harmful than helpful by giving Communists new leverage for reviving issue.

Sukendro said Communist plan had been to drum up issue until Sukarno returned, then hand it to him as ready-made means of uniting country, preventing "political confrontation" set for that time. "Now," Sukendro said, "that has been cut off." Asked how it had been cut off, Sukendro replied that during recent demonstrations 72 Communist leaders had been arrested. Remainder so discouraged they had at least temporarily abandoned efforts to stir up public. Whether they could break out with new campaign upon return of President, he could not say. He reasoned, however, that public statement by Dutch now would deprive Army of effective anti-Communist weapon which they would have if Dutch assurances given only to them and in private.

Chargé pointed out that he required to deal with GOI on official level on behalf of US Government; Sukendro was asking that US deal with Nasution directly as an intermediary with Dutch Government. Was there no one in Dutch Mission with whom Sukendro could talk about such arrangement? Sukendro replied that he would do so if it developed that it would be worth his while. He expressed doubt that much could be accomplished in such manner, said he would prefer US participation.

It was at this point Chargé asked for assurance that General Nasution had authorized such approach. Sukendro unhesitatingly replied in the affirmative, elaborating that authorization had been given in framework of anti-Communist political effort.[1]

Chargé said US Government had great confidence in the integrity and ability of General Nasution. If he asked us to assist him, US undoubtedly would do its best to help. Chargé asked Sukendro to inform General Nasution that his request would be promptly transmitted to US

---

[1] In telegram 3374, May 26, Henderson commented further on his meeting with Sukendro. (*Ibid.*, 790.5856/5–2660) See Supplement.

Government for consideration; Chargé would let Sukendro know if reply received.

It appeared obvious to Chargé that Sukendro wants as much information as possible before President Sukarno returns. Letter from President previous day indicated he would try to be back by his birthday, June 6, but he was tired and wanted to rest few days in Tokyo, Sukendro said. [2]

Henderson

---

[2] In telegram 3397, May 29, the Embassy suggested that the contents of telegram 3373 gave the United States a "strong card to play in reassuring Luns re Indonesian intentions. Obviously if Nasution seeking 'informal understanding' with Dutch he would not likely at same time be planning attack on New Guinea." The Embassy recommended that the Department pass this information to the Netherlands in strict confidence. (Department of State, Central Files, 790.5856/5–2960)

---

261. Memorandum of Conversation

Washington, May 26, 1960.

SUBJECT

U.S.-Dutch-Indonesian Relations

PARTICIPANTS

Dr. J.H. van Roijen, Dutch Ambassador
Mr. E.L.C. Schiff, Minister, Dutch Embassy

G—Mr. Hare
WE—Mr. Chadbourn

After speaking about another subject, which is being reported separately,[1] Mr. Hare referred to his conversation with the Ambassador on May 17 regarding the cruise of the *Karel Doorman* and other Dutch meas-

---

Source: Department of State, Central Files, 601.5698/5–2660. Secret. Drafted by Chadbourn.

[1] Van Roijen stated that he had received instructions from his government to tell the Department of State that it was concerned that Eisenhower might visit Indonesia as part of his projected Far East visit. If Eisenhower visited Indonesia, it would be interpreted "as a slap in the Dutch face." The Netherlands would feel constrained to reexamine its policy towards the United States and the result might even be a reorientation of that policy. (Memorandum of conversation, May 26; *ibid.*, 0711.11–EI/5–2660) See Supplement.

ures for the defense of West New Guinea (Deptel 1674 to The Hague).[2] In accordance with the Ambassador's request he had asked Acting Secretary Dillon to emphasize to Mr. Subandrio that the U.S. knows that the Dutch have absolutely no desire to create an incident or force a showdown over West New Guinea. Mr. Hare wanted the Ambassador to know that Mr. Dillon had stated that the Dutch had made it quite clear they had no aggressive intentions and that their actions were purely defensive (Deptel 2022 to Djakarta).[3]

After expressing his appreciation for this action, Ambassador van Roijen said that his Embassy had just received the Dutch Government's reaction to American plans to help build a naval facility at Ambon. While the Dutch could not say they were pleased with this development, it appeared to be an irrevocable step and there seemed to be little the Dutch could do about it other than accept it. The Ambassador went on to say that his Government hoped we would agree to pass on to the Dutch, on a confidential basis, any information we picked up at Ambon about Russian activities there as well as any information bearing on the security of West New Guinea. Mr. Hare agreed to this proposal and instructed Mr. Chadbourn to see that this was carried out.

---

[2] See footnote 4, Document 255.
[3] Not printed.

---

262. Telegram From the Embassy in the Netherlands to the Department of State

The Hague, May 27, 1960, 11 p.m.

1524. Paris also for USRO, Thurston and Finn.

1. Foreign Minister Luns requested that I call on him at 5:00 p.m. May 27. 40-minute discussion ensued with Luns and Doctor N. S. Blom, Government Commissioner for Indonesian Affairs, Ministry Foreign Affairs.

2. Luns opened conversation by stating he had just conferred with British, French, and Australian Ambassadors in joint session. He had, however, requested me to come by myself as he had an additional matter to discuss. Luns also stated that he had been conferring with Prime

---

Source: Department of State, Central Files, 656.9813/5–2760. Secret; Niact. Transmitted in two sections and repeated to Djakarta, Paris, Canberra, London, Kuala Lumpur, New Delhi, and CINCPAC for POLAD.

Minister Rahman of Malay Federation and expects to consult with him further this evening. Tomorrow Luns will have conversations with Indian Ambassador, [3-1/2 *lines of source text not declassified*]. (Embassy happens to know that Australian Ambassador is in London and was represented at meeting by Chargé H.W. Bullock.)

3. Luns was as deeply upset as I have ever seen him, and I believe very sincerely disturbed by what he described as "a serious emergency situation relating to Indonesia." He said he had every reason to believe that Indonesia was preparing for attack on West New Guinea which could possibly take place middle of next week. Luns said he was urging UK, France, Australia and USA in strongest possible terms to make immediate representations to Indonesian Government against any military operation or threat of military operation. Luns would like to see us tell Indonesia in no uncertain terms exactly what we would do if Indonesians launched an attack, and he was most insistent that substance this conversation be relayed to Seventh Fleet. Luns went on at some length insisting that his intelligence sources were reliable and corroborated by variety press items. As an example, he handed me a Reuter's despatch, datelined Djakarta May 26, relating to a 24-hour alert for Indonesian military units on islands near West New Guinea and implying that Dutch were responsible for unidentified aircraft seen over these islands; also, another article with Djakarta dateline May 27 emphasizing Indonesian military units brought maximum state of readiness; cancellation of all officer leaves in east Indonesian territory; and reports of unidentified aircraft repeatedly seen over east Indonesia. Luns then said that these articles and other public statements should in themselves be sufficient justification for US to make representations to Indonesians against possible military action.

4. Luns also said that, in addition to Indonesian Army units stationed on nearby islands Indonesians already had some MiGs, bombers, landing craft, as well as quite a large number naval units in area. In response to my questions, Luns thought that military action, if it did come, would be in nature of "major minor attack." By this he meant a sizeable landing of Indonesian troops with landing craft and naval and air support. Luns also at same time emphasized weakness of present Dutch forces in New Guinea area and fact that meagre forces already there necessarily had to be widely deployed to maintain morale of local population.

5. Department will note that Luns reference to timing of such contemplated military action generally coincides with sailing of *Karel Doorman* and escort vessels from Holland (Embtel sent Department 1522,[1]

---

[1] Telegram 1522, May 27, transmitted a translation of the communiqué issued by the Netherlands about the *Karel Doorman* cruise. The communiqué noted that the aircraft carrier, escorted by two destroyers and a tanker, would depart the Netherlands on May 31. (*Ibid.*)

Canberra 73, Djakarta 95, Paris 236). Luns flatly stated that he believes Indonesia is ready to declare war on Holland and feels this supported by his conversation with Malay Prime Minister. According Luns, Malay Prime Minister stated that Sukarno will be out very shortly and that new Indonesian regime will move against New Guinea. Luns corroborated fact that Japan and Philippines had been approached with request they bar their territorial waters to *Doorman,* and Japanese had advised Luns they regarded this request as "silly." He said he not heard from Filipinos.

6. Luns had come directly from special Cabinet session this afternoon at which all military Chiefs of Staff were present to discuss this emergency situation. According Luns, various courses of action were contemplated, but for moment they decided on following:

(A) Immediately advise the countries mentioned above and urge them to put up strong political deterrent;
(B) Continue with *Karel Doorman* voyage and strengthening of New Guinea Defense Forces;
(C) Alert and have ready for immediate transfer to New Guinea reinforcements of 600 marines—300 from Curacao and 300 from Netherlands—who would be shipped out unarmed by KLM aircraft (already alerted) first of next week, if necessary;
(D) Call for special session of Security Council first part of next week if deemed advisable. Luns admitted course of action (D) would only be invoked reluctantly.

7. Reverting to his talks with Malay Prime Minister, Luns said he was conferring with him at 7:00 tonight to discuss a joint communiqué to be issued May 28. Luns read me rough draft of this communiqué which specifically stated that Prime Minister Rahman supported Dutch statements that Netherlands had no aggressive intent concerning Indonesia and that he felt Dutch had every right and justification in taking measures which they now contemplate.[2] Luns also has scheduled meeting with *New York Times* correspondent Gilroy at 11:00 a.m., May 28 to give him statement reiterating fact that Dutch have no aggressive intent.[3] Luns feels that joint communiqué with Malay Prime Minister, his interview with Gilroy, and announcement of *Karel Doorman* cruise route tonight should do much to alleviate Indonesian fears and reduce tensions.

8. There is no doubt about fact that Prime Minister De Quay, Cabinet, and Chiefs of Staff regard present situation as very tense and do not discount possibility of Indonesian military action in immediate future.

---

[2] This communiqué, issued on May 28, is summarized in an October 18 memorandum by Tanguy. (*Ibid.*, SPA Files: Lot 63 D 436, West New Guinea Problem)

[3] For text of this story by Harry Gilroy, reporting his interview with Luns, see *The New York Times*, May 27, 1960, p. 2.

Dutch Government has issued very specific instructions through its various channels to all personnel, military and civilian, in West Guinea against doing anything which could be construed as provocative in nature or even interpreted as anti-Indonesia. I questioned Luns at some length why he felt that Indonesia could run risk of being labelled an aggressor by initiating kind of action he was worried about. Although Luns denies that unidentified planes over Indonesian islands near New Guinea were Dutch, he is afraid Indonesians will make this charge or a similar one a basis for claiming Dutch to be the aggressor and thus provide grounds for retaliation. I told Luns so far as I knew, these planes were not U–2's.[4]

Young

---

[4] In telegram 1523 from The Hague, May 27, Young commented that most of the substance of Luns' remarks were based on a recent [text not declassified] message, which was already available, to the Department dealing with the Indonesian military threat against West New Guinea. "Department, therefore," he noted, "is in position to make its own assessment reliability basic information." (Department of State, Central Files, 656.9813/5–2760)

In telegram 1525 from The Hague, May 28, Young reported that during his conversation with Luns the previous day the Foreign Minister also referred to the possibility of Eisenhower being invited to visit Indonesia on his Far Eastern tour. "He asked me to make 'strongest possible representations' to Department," Young noted, "that this would be regarded as 'a very distinct slap in face' and a deliberate action against a tried, true and trusted ally. Luns said that Dutch reaction would be violent." (Ibid., 711.11–EI/5–2860) See Supplement.

---

263.   **Memorandum of Telephone Conversation Between Secretary of State Herter and President Eisenhower**

Washington, May 28, 1960, 12:05 p.m.

The President telephoned from Gettysburg to say that he had been very annoyed over the Dutch declaration,[1] and wanted to discuss this with the Secretary. The President said he couldn't go to Indonesia since he is committed to be in Japan on June 19, but he thought we should let the Dutch Ambassador know that we are very annoyed at one country

---

Source: Eisenhower Library, Herter Papers, Telephone Conversations. No classification marking.
[1] See footnote 1, Document 261.

saying what the President can do in another independent country, and that we don't think this is in accordance with good diplomatic conduct.

The Secretary said he agreed with the President; that this was the second time van Roijen had been out of bounds—having gotten out of bounds with Secretary Dulles a couple of years ago— and the Secretary agreed his knuckles should be rapped.

The President said when this was reported to him by John Eisenhower or General Goodpaster, they had said the Ambassador was very embarrassed but had indicated he was under very specific orders from his Government after a complete Cabinet meeting. The President said we ought to let the Dutch Government know this is now an independent country and that it is not within the bounds of decency and diplomatic usage to say this will strike at the basis of friendly relations between our two countries, which the President said was as extreme as anything he could think of.

The Secretary said the reason the Dutch are so touchy is that they are sending a warship to West New Guinea and also sending some reinforcements out there and the Indonesians have reacted quite violently, so the Dutch are extremely touchy at the moment.

The President said it would have been one thing if the Dutch had said "please, as a friend, don't go to Indonesia," but the President said it was something else again for them to say this is striking at the very basis of our friendly relations. The President said if our relations are this fragile and weak, maybe we had better take a good look at the whole picture.

The Secretary said he agreed we should make this very clear to the Dutch.

The President said he had sent word to the State Department that he could not visit Indonesia, not because of the Dutch declaration but because of the time element. The President said he thought the Secretary should tell the Dutch that while the time element alone made it impossible for the President to go to Indonesia, the President joins with the Government in thinking this is in very bad taste and uncalled for— something of this kind. The President said he has always admired the Dutch extremely and used to enjoy visiting their country, but he was not going to see them get away with saying that an incident of this kind or his doing something he has a right to do strikes at the basis of our friendly relations.

The President said he won't leave here before the 11th or 12th of June and there may be an extra day in Anchorage. The President said if he gave two or three days in the Philippines, where he lived so long, had even 24 hours in Taipei, and one day on a cruiser or somewhere as a day of rest, that was all there was time for.

The Secretary said we could say the President's domestic schedule had been arranged to take out this set period of time and could not be changed.

264. Telegram From the Department of State to the Embassy in the Netherlands

Washington, May 29, 1960, 2:26 p.m.

1732. Your 1523[1] and 1524.[2] Request you see Luns soonest possible and tell him following which also being conveyed Dutch Embassy here May 29:

1. Current US intelligence does not indicate likelihood imminent Indonesian attack West New Guinea. Special May 24 estimate this subject[3] prepared by US intelligence community concludes among other things "We believe that Indonesia will not attempt an armed attack against West New Guinea during the next six months at least." The estimate does not exclude possibility minor armed clash incident to *Doorman* cruise, but now that inoffensive route for cruise has been established and publicized this possibility seems substantially reduced. Begin FYI. [*less than 1 line of source text not declassified*] report mentioned your 1524 received after preparation foregoing estimate but reviewed by intelligence areas Dept [*less than 1 line of source text not declassified*] and deemed not to alter the estimate. End FYI.

2. In support our own intelligence estimate we have received recently and passed orally to Dutch through their Ambassador in Washington written Indonesian Govt assurances that Indonesian policy of not resorting to force in West New Guinea dispute remains valid and that Indonesia will not use military equipment obtained from US to attempt resolve dispute by force. We have no reason disbelieve these assurances especially in view of public reiteration basic Indonesian policy this matter May 13, in Havana by Indonesian Foreign Minister Subandrio.

Source: Department of State, Central Files, 656.9813/5–2760. Top Secret; Niact. Drafted by Moore and Cameron and approved by White. Also sent to Djakarta and repeated to CINCPAC for POLAD.

[1] See footnote 4, Document 262.

[2] Document 262.

[3] Document 259.

3. In light Indonesian assurances cited foregoing paragraph and recent helpful Dutch moves (publication inoffensive route of *Doorman* voyage, Dutch Information Service release which seems designed lessen tension and alleviate Indonesian anxiety) we believe there good reason hope for lessening of tension in situation rather than exacerbation of dispute by Indonesian military action. Draw as appropriate on Djakarta's 3396 to Department,[4] 145 The Hague, especially references to lessening public excitement this issue and fact Dutch announcements contributing this development.

4. You are also authorized to pass on to Luns on highly confidential basis approach made by high Indonesian army source to Embassy Djakarta reported in Djakarta's 3373 to Department,[5] 141 The Hague, 627 to CINCPAC; Djakarta's 3374 to Department,[6] 142 The Hague, 628 to CINCPAC; Djakarta's 3397 to Department,[7] 146 The Hague, being repeated CINCPAC. We consider this further evidence Indonesian desire moderate current suspicions. If a direct channel between Dutch and Indonesian army leaders could be established it might provide Dutch additional and direct assurances of Indonesian army intentions. Inform Luns that we will tell above-mentioned Indonesian army source that we have spoken to Dutch on this matter and that further initiative must come from Indonesians. We do not intend act as go-between in this matter, but would be willing pass message from Dutch back to Indonesian army source if Dutch so desire. We shall also tell Indonesian army source that for such contact to be fruitful, Indonesian army should be in position rationalize to Dutch reported moves such as alert in Eastern islands and leave cancellations.

5. For Djakarta: In view your tel 3396 and the maneuvers suggested above which involve your return to Sukendro, tend to agree with you that request for any further assurances at this juncture may be counter productive. You are authorized tell Sukendro of our approach to Luns para 4 above, emphasizing to him as we are to Dutch that beyond initial contact we wish to remove ourselves as go-between.

6. Notwithstanding our estimate of situation and doubtful reliability report of possible Indonesian attack, we understand Dutch concerns in matter and therefore we are further investigating report of Indonesian intentions which Luns has given us. We would hope that any moves of political or military nature which Dutch may feel obligated

---

[4] Telegram 3396, May 29, informed the Department that the Embassy had no indication that any Indonesian attack on West Irian was either imminent or contemplated at any time in the future. (Department of State, Central Files, 656.9813/5–2960)

[5] Document 260.

[6] See footnote 1, Document 260.

[7] See footnote 2, Document 260.

take in preparation for eventuality of possible Indonesian attack, would be discreet and not likely provoke further Indonesian reaction which would enhance possibility of incident through incautious move by one side or other. We strongly agree with Luns' hope that Dutch will not find it necessary bring matter into Security Council.

Begin FYI. Department informed by Australian Embassy Washington that Australian Government approached by Dutch along lines Luns' approach to you. Australian official reaction is that Dutch unduly alarmed since Australian intelligence like ours does not substantiate Dutch report of imminent Indonesian military action. Australians reason that Indonesian actions such as 24-hour alert consistent with publicly announced intention reinforce east Indonesia areas and need not reflect any aggressive intentions. Australians note further that similar Dutch alarm in early 1959 proved unfounded and that current Dutch alarm apparently arises from unspecified intelligence report. Australians believe Dutch approach may be effort exploit current SEATO conference[8] by forcing discussion of West New Guinea dispute therein. In light foregoing analysis Australian Government believes "greatest pressure" on Indonesians requested by Dutch would be justified only on "much stronger evidence." Therefore Australian Government has merely authorized its Ambassador Djakarta at his discretion to question GOI regarding military preparations in East Indonesia with view subtlety putting Indonesia on notice that their activities under scrutiny. Australians planning reply to Luns giving him their intelligent estimate but assuring him that Australian Government studying matter closely and urgently.

We informed that British also approached by Dutch along same lines and that British reaction similar to Australian. British have reportedly already passed their views to Dutch at London and The Hague. End FYI.

Herter

---

[8] The sixth meeting of the SEATO Council of Ministers was scheduled for May 31–June 2 in Washington.

265. Telegram From the Embassy in the Netherlands to the
Department of State

The Hague, May 31, 1960, 6 p.m.

1538. Department pass CINCPAC for POLAD. Reference Deptel
1732,[1] repeated Djakarta 2075.

1. As planned (Embtel 1528,[2] repeated Djakarta 99) I had 45-min-
ute talk this morning with Prime Minister De Quay, who is also acting
Foreign Minister in Luns' absence. I covered all points contained in reftel, as instructed, but did not refer to any Indonesian source by name. De
Quay confirmed that same had been covered in his report from Ambassador van Roijen, although latter was not nearly as specific. De Quay
was pleased that we would continue our investigations of question Indonesian threat to New Guinea and appreciated fact that we understand
Dutch concern in this matter (paragraph 6 reftel). He commented that he
too regards taking matter to Security Council as last resort. He said if
Dutch took problem up in Security Council they should probably do so
only once and he felt case was not strong enough to do so now.

However, he did not rule out possibility of doing so later. De Quay
also emphasized fact that Dutch are doing everything possible to minimize tension and avoid any act or incident which might be considered
provocative.

2. When I had finished my summary, De Quay stated he would
like to give me his interpretation and thinking, especially re approach
made by Indonesian army to US. De Quay added he was sending message today to van Roijen outlining his thinking on this matter.

3. De Quay said that his analysis of this situation leads him to conclusion that there may very well be some real danger of an Indonesian
landing operation, if not a larger attack on New Guinea, and that Dutch
worries in this respect are substantiated by Indonesian army approach
to US. De Quay feels that Sukarno is pretty far left, although he may not
be communist in name or fact; that Sukarno definitely is going to play
ball to some extent with communists as well as with leftist political leaders and groups in Indonesia; and that eventually, if Sukarno remains in
power, he will align Indonesia to much greater extent than he has so far

---

Source: Department of State, Central Files, 656.9813/5–3160. Top Secret; Niact.
Transmitted in two sections.

[1] Document 264.

[2] In telegram 1528, May 30, Young reported that he was scheduled to meet with
Prime Minister De Quay at 11 a.m. on May 31. (Department of State, Central Files, 656.
9813/5–3060)

with communist bloc. De Quay sees General Nasution as counter-balance, an anti-communist who wishes to continue to play ball with US and West. De Quay feels that Nasution will not and cannot afford to break with Sukarno, at least at this time, and that Sukarno can still pull together and command great personal following among Indonesians. Thus, De Quay sees two basically conflicting approaches and personalities in Sukarno and Nasution, but he believes that, if Sukarno directed Nasution to make military threat or landing on one of off-shore islands of Netherlands New Guinea, Nasution would still obey orders and do it. Thus, De Quay interprets Indonesian army approach in Djakarta as method whereby Nasution is attempting to augment pressure from US and others on Sukarno to refrain from any military adventure in New Guinea. According to De Quay, all these pressures would keep Sukarno from engaging in such military adventure and would thus keep Nasution in position where he would not have to receive such an order for military operation against Western interests. De Quay therefore reasons that Indonesian army approach to US substantiates fact that there is danger of a military operation ordered by Sukarno to which Nasution might not subscribe, but which he would have to support. In this connection, De Quay noted that it was Sukarno and not Nasution who had directly ordered present build-up and other military measures in East Indonesian territory.

4. De Quay stated flatly that of course Dutch Government could not talk with Nasution, his representative, or Indonesian army. Dutch Government could only talk with Indonesian Government and that, therefore, any such conversations directly between Dutch Government and Indonesian army were out of question.

5. De Quay went on to say that he had talked with British Ambassador Sir Paul Mason who had reflected to De Quay British feeling that there was no imminent threat of military action against WNG. Mason informed De Quay that British Government had made representations to Indonesian Government urging that nothing be done of provocative nature by Indonesians and stating that of course Dutch had no aggressive intent against Indonesia. De Quay again pointed out that he felt such representations were most useful as deterrent and hoped that US would continue to make such representations in view of what he considers to be continuing danger as outlined in paragraph three above.

6. De Quay said that in his conversations with Malayan Prime Minister on May 28, Malayan Prime Minister had little use for Sukarno and felt very strongly that Sukarno would line up with communists. Malayan Prime Minister also told De Quay that Sukarno would continue to play Western assistance against Eastern assistance as long as he possibly could and that there was no question but what Sukarno would

line up with East in event of any show-down, although trying to maintain air of independent neutrality in meantime.

7. De Quay urged that US make further representations to Indonesian Government in accordance with Dutch Government's request given me by Luns (paragraph 2, Embtel 1524,[3] repeated Djakarta 96). I pointed out to De Quay that this had been done again very recently and, in fact, we had received written aide-mémoire from Indonesian Government as recently as May 18[4] affirming its assurances re West New Guinea. This information had been given to Ambassador van Roijen and Luns was fully familiar with it. In view of this and many times before it that we had gone to Indonesian Government on same matter, I had some feeling that such approaches could lose their effectiveness by being pushed too hard. After further conversation, De Quay said he fully understood our position and that certainly he agreed that we should not push on this matter so hard and so often that it became meaningless. Thus, although he was reconciled to fact we were not anxious to make any representations to Indonesian Government at this time, he still felt we should point out our concern to Indonesians based on press notices of Indonesian military build-up in Eastern territory, for these moves could only increase tension at time when everyone wished to reduce it.

8. De Quay referred to fact that *Karel Doorman* had already sailed May 30 on its cruise and again emphasized route which he considered to be as non-provocative as possible. I noted reports in Dutch press that *Doorman* had sailed day earlier than originally scheduled; De Quay replied with chuckle that it had, and indicated he was waiting to see if anything might happen today as result of it. This was undoubtedly a reference to Luns point (paragraph 5, Embtel 1524) that Indonesians would engage in some kind of provocative action at time *Karel Doorman* sailed, and the implication by De Quay was that *Doorman's* schedule was moved up one day on purpose just to throw off any possible Indonesian timing. (While *Doorman* actually sailed from Rotterdam May 30, it is off-shore and will not leave Dutch waters until today.)

9. Djakarta's 3402 to Department[5] received after my talk with De Quay. Message garbled and not clear what additional "informal understanding" Indonesians seek. As De Quay is cabling his comments to van

---

[3] Document 262.

[4] See Document 256.

[5] In telegram 3402, May 31, Henderson reported on a conversation he had with Sukendro the previous day. The Chargé noted that the "informal understanding" that the Indonesian Army sought from the Dutch went beyond the *Karel Doorman* incident. "From Sukendro's point of view," Henderson stated, "he is now in position of waiting for message from Dutch through us at which time he now understands it will be necessary for him to take initiative for direct contact if exchange is to be continued." (Department of State, Central Files, 790.5856/5–3160) See Supplement.

Roijen, and if Department has further information re this "informal understanding" and its potential coverage, it may wish take subject up with van Roijen if Department still wishes pursue effort find some way to establish informal contact between Indonesian army and Dutch.

Young

266. Memorandum of Conversation

Washington, June 2, 1960.

SUBJECT

Possibility of the President's Visiting Indonesia [1]

PARTICIPANTS

Dr. J.H. van Roijen, Ambassador of the Netherlands
Mr. J.L.R. Huydecoper, First Secretary, Dutch Embassy

M—Mr. Merchant
M—Mr. Long
WE—Mr. Chadbourn

After discussing various other matters, [2] Mr. Merchant referred to the Ambassador's démarche on May 26 concerning the possibility of the President's visiting Indonesia. In the first place, Mr. Merchant said, the decision not to go to Indonesia. had been made prior to the Ambassador's talk with Mr. Hare on May 26. Because of time limitations the President would not make any visits south of the Philippines.

Source: Department of State, Central Files, 711.11–EI/6–260. Secret. Drafted by Chadbourn. Approved in M on June 9.

[1] In a memorandum to Secretary Herter, May 30, Assistant Secretary Kohler recommended that the Secretary call in the Netherlands Ambassador to review recent developments in U.S.-Dutch relations and to inform the Dutch that the tone of their recent démarche concerning the possibility of an Eisenhower visit to Indonesia was "inappropriate." (*Ibid.*, WE Files: Lot 63 D, 106, Indonesia) See Supplement. Herter was unable to see van Roijen, because of SEATO obligations that week. He asked Merchant to talk with him along the lines of the Kohler memorandum of May 30. (Memorandum from John A. Calhoun of S/S to Merchant, May 30; Department of State, WE Files: Lot 63 D 106, Indonesia) See Supplement.

[2] Memorandum of conversation, June 2, not printed. (Department of State, Central Files, 656.9813/6–260) See Supplement.

Mr. Merchant then referred to Mr. Hare's statement to the Ambassador to the effect that the liberty of action of the President could not be bound, even hypothetically. Mr. Merchant said that had the Dutch come to us as a friend and asked us to consider their point of view, it would have been readily understandable. But we do not find it possible to accept a hypothetical condition being placed on the movements of the President to other countries with which we maintain friendly relations. Moreover, we found the Ambassador's démarche, made under instructions, to be excessive in tone and not in keeping with the maintenance of good relations between our two countries. The use of phrases such as a reevaluation or reorientation of Dutch policy vis-à-vis the U.S. was most disturbing to us. The President's reaction had been comparable and the effect of the Ambassador's démarche had not been a happy one.

The Ambassador appeared to receive these remarks with equanimity and said that he had wanted to speak in all frankness in order that we be left with no doubt as to the violence of Dutch reaction should the President have decided to go to Indonesia. He was afraid that Dutch sentiments in this matter might be overlooked in the United States. He thought it was accurate to compare Dutch reaction to a Presidential visit to Sukarno in Indonesia to U.S. reaction should Prince Bernhard visit Cuba, thereby giving the impression that the Netherlands endorses Castro's anti-U.S. actions. The Ambassador said that he had wanted to impress on us the seriousness of this matter to the Dutch. He said that his government had wanted us to know that the Dutch can not be taken for granted. In closing, he said that he would pass on to his government the Secretary's and the President's reactions as outlined to him by Mr. Merchant.[3]

---

[3] At 7:10 p.m. that evening, Goodpaster called Herter. The Secretary said that the President had spoken to him about Dutch representation in connection with Indonesia, and that Mr. Merchant had seen the Dutch Ambassador and had "read the riot act to him." (Eisenhower Library, Herter Papers, Telephone Conversations) The following day, the President met with Herter and Merchant and discussed Merchant's meeting with van Roijen:

"Mr. Herter then told the President that Mr. Merchant had 'taken down' the Dutch Ambassador quite severely. The Ambassador had taken it well although he had not liked it. The reported action of the Dutch government in threatening to reexamine their relations with the U.S. and NATO in the event the President visited Indonesia was done by the government (i.e., the Foreign Office) and not by the Dutch Cabinet. The President warmly approved Mr. Merchant's action and said the Dutch government should know that the decision not to visit Indonesia was made some days before the Ambassador had given this word." (Memorandum of conversation, June 3; Eisenhower Library, Whitman File, Miscellaneous Material)

267.   Memorandum From the Assistant Secretary of State for International Organization Affairs (Wilcox) to the Under Secretary of State for Political Affairs (Merchant)

Washington, June 29, 1960.

SUBJECT

    Possible move to inscribe Netherlands New Guinea item at 15th GA; meeting in your office, 3:00 Thursday, June 29, 1960

Discussion:

1. It is possible that Indonesia will request the inscription of the Netherlands New Guinea item in the agenda of the 15th General Assembly. Although there are no definite indications that the Indonesians have made a decision to this effect, growing internal political pressures, the increased voting strength of the anti-colonials in the GA, and the reinforcement of Dutch military units in Netherlands New Guinea could stimulate them to do so.

On April 21 Netherlands Ambassador van Roijen informed me that The Hague would like the United States to consider instructing our Embassies in a few key Afro-Asian capitals to discourage discreetly the inscription of the New Guinea item.[1] On May 4, Netherlands Minister Schiff specified to a Department officer that the Dutch hope was that we would instruct some of our Embassies to respond in a negative vein if asked their views about the advisability of inscription and another UN debate on Netherlands New Guinea.[2]

From the United States viewpoint, inscription of the West New Guinea item would be undesirable for several reasons. Debate of this issue at the General Assembly would further exacerbate an already tense situation and further increase the disruptive influence of this issue. Moreover, if a resolution desired by the Indonesians should be adopted, the GOI might consider that even an implicit GA endorsement of its claim to West New Guinea afforded justification for vigorous action to oust the Dutch. Another likely unfavorable consequence is that the Dutch might abandon their efforts to prepare the Papuans for self-determination, and/or grant them independence precipitously and prematurely.

    Source: Department of State, Central Files, 320/6-2960. Confidential. Drafted by William B. Buffum and Stephen E. Palmer, Jr. of UNP and cleared by EUR, NEA, and AF.

    [1] An April 21 memorandum of conversation is *ibid.*, 320/4–2160. See Supplement.

    [2] A memorandum of this conversation is in Department of State, Central Files, 656.9813/5–460.

It appears to be in our interest, therefore, to do what we can in a reasonable and quiet way to discourage an Indonesian decision to seek inscription. We believe that this objective can best be served at least for the time being by instructing our Embassy in Djakarta very discreetly to discourage the Indonesians from raising the New Guinea question in the General Assembly again.

We are uncertain whether US approaches in key Afro-Asian capitals would materially affect the responses of these governments to any Indonesian initiative, and we prefer to defer such approaches at this time. Moreover, such approaches would entail added risks of misunderstanding by the Indonesians.

2. The meeting in your office was necessitated by the fact that agreement on the attached instruction could not be obtained at the bureau level. FE opposes the sending of such instructions, and is preparing its dissenting comments. This impasse is symptomatic of a fundamental cleavage of opinion within the Department with respect to the New Guinea issue. Inasmuch as this issue is again active and may be debated at the 15th General Assembly, it is imperative that a thorough reevaluation of our policy towards the West New Guinea question be undertaken on an urgent basis. This might be done by S/P.

I believe it likely that a study will show that some of the basic premises on which our neutral policy on the West New Guinea issue was based have changed and that a complete review of our policy is therefore required. It is clear, for example, that in the expanded General Assembly, our previous position of neutrality can no longer insure that a resolution on New Guinea will not be passed. For example, a simple resolution recommending negotiations between Indonesia and the Dutch would probably muster the necessary 2/3 majority. This, of course, would be taken as a defeat for the Dutch. Admittedly, a major handicap in determining the implications of GA action on West New Guinea is the complete lack of a long-range US policy decision on the ultimate disposition of that territory. This, in turn, means we cannot at present devise or execute tactics that will give us maximum maneuverability and influence.

Recommendations: [3]

1. That you approve the attached telegram to Djakarta, instructing the Embassy to discourage discreetly the idea of inscription of the West New Guinea item in the agenda of the 15th General Assembly. [4]

---

[3] A note at this point on the source text reads: "See FE memo of dissent." In a June 30 memorandum to Merchant, Steeves outlined FE's position on Wilcox's memorandum of June 29. (*Ibid.*, SPA Files: Lot 64 D 469, Memoranda) See Supplement.

[4] Sent as circular telegram 32 to Djakarta, July 7. (Department of State, Central Files, 656.9813/7–760) See Supplement.

2. That you authorize me to inform the Netherlands Chargé of the action taken, on the understanding that this is for the confidential information of his Government only.[5]

3. That you instruct that a re-evaluation of our policy on the West New Guinea issue be undertaken on an urgent basis.[6]

---

[5] Wilcox did this on July 8. (Memorandum of conversation, July 8; Department of State, Central Files, 756C.00/7–860) See Supplement.

[6] A meeting on the West New Guinea problem was held on July 1 during which it was agreed that a re-evaluation of present policy on West New Guinea was urgently needed. Merchant summarized this meeting and asked S/P to undertake such a study in a July 2 memorandum to Gerard Smith. (Department of State, Central Files, 711.56C/7–260)

---

268.   Memorandum of Conversation

Washington, July 5, 1960.

SUBJECT

    U.S.-British "Understanding" Regarding West New Guinea

PARTICIPANTS

    Mr. Ledward, Counselor, British Embassy
    Mr. Steeves, Deputy Assistant Secretary for Far Eastern Affairs
    Mr. Bell, Director, Office of Southwest Pacific Affairs

Mr. Steeves briefly reviewed the Dutch approaches to us in October–December 1958 with respect to the support which the Dutch might expect from us in the event of armed conflict between the Indonesian and the Dutch over West New Guinea. Mr. Steeves said that our position has not changed since Secretary Dulles told the Dutch that we would help to the limit of our legal authority in the event of Indonesian aggression, but that he could make no prior commitment without Presidential approval and he doubted that the President would give his approval without Congressional sanction.[1]

Mr. Steeves stated that in our view there was no "understanding" with respect to any British-U.S. action in the event of aggressive action

---

Source: Department of State, Central Files, 656.9813/7–560. Secret. Drafted by Bell on July 8.

[1] See Documents 159 and 168.

by the Indonesians against West New Guinea, but that we were of course prepared to discuss the subject further if the British so desired. Mr. Steeves explained that because so many factors now unknown might be attendant at the time of a hypothetical Indonesian attack, it would seem difficult to hold meaningful bilateral consultation on specific steps.[2]

---

[2] On July 15 Ledward again called on Steeves to discuss the alleged U.S.-U.K. understanding regarding West New Guinea. He noted that during a June 15 meeting in London between Foreign Secretary Lloyd and Foreign Minister Luns, Luns requested assurances of assistance in the event of a Netherlands-Indonesian armed conflict over West New Guinea. Steeves replied that the U.S. position was the same as that outlined to Ledward in their earlier conversation of July 5: "That we were willing to continue discussions with the UK and Australia but that we could not go any further with the Dutch than Secretary of State Dulles had in 1958." (Memorandum of conversation by Bell, July 15; Department of State, Central Files, 656.98/7–1560)

---

269.   Telegram From the Embassy in Indonesia to the Department of State

Djakarta, July 6, 1960, noon.

47. CINCPAC for POLAD. Deptels 2258,[1] 2265.[2] Embassy has deferred action on informing AURI pending further instructions.

Embassy notes purpose of deferment is to give CINCPAC time to submit comments and recommendations. Presumably these recommendations foreshadowed in CINCPAC message to CHMILTAG 292008Z.[3]

CINCPAC reasoning again raises issue which Embassy had believed long since settled, i.e., whether Marshal Suryadarma's pro-Com-

---

Source: Department of State, Central Files, 798.5622/7–660. Secret. Transmitted in two sections. Also sent to CINCPAC.

[1] Telegram 2258, June 28, a joint State–Defense message, authorized Jones to inform the Indonesian Air Force that, subject to the availability of funds in Fiscal Year 1961, the United States was prepared to consider its request to procure 50 T–34 aircraft. (Ibid., 798.5622/6–2860) See Supplement.

[2] Telegram 2265, June 29, reads as follows: "If you have not already done so, you should refrain from approaching AURI re T–34 trainers until further instructed. Delay designed afford CINCPAC further opportunity study matter and submit his comments and recommendations." (Department of State, Central Files, 798.5622/6–2960)

[3] Not found.

munist proclivities, if any, or his complete unreliability as an anti-Communist force should be a major factor in determining the level or kinds of assistance to Indonesian Air Force. Although Embassy recognizes other political considerations involved in question of long-range bombers, for example, our views of Suryadarma should not mislead us as to the more basic reasons why aid to AURI can advance our interests here.

The question is not whether or not Indonesian Air Force will have trainers. We do not have power to withhold trainers but only to help prescribe where they must be obtained.

Therefore our decision is whether AURI is to obtain trainers from us with possible increase in pro-Western orientation or from bloc with increased hostility to West as result our efforts to confine aid purely to those items which we think best.

Even more important consideration, however, is need to counter Communist charges that US working with Nasution against President, other elements of GOI who desire neutral course. At this time when President Sukarno is in mood of deep distrust toward us it even more important than ever we avoid appearance of internal political meddling by favoring one or two services to exclusion of another. If Suryadarma gains stature because of this policy, Embassy regards such development as unfortunate by-product but not of sufficient importance to justify change in policy. Certainly Marshal Suryadarma's prestige will rise just as high if he obtains his trainers from Soviet bloc as if he obtained them from us. It is true that Sukarno considers AURI military counter-weight to Nasution, but again, bloc trainers in Suryadarma's hands likely to accentuate this capacity to a greater degree than if trainers, technical back-stopping come from US.

On other hand, so long as we can answer Sukarno by pointing out we are not discriminating between the various forces at his disposal, we reduce danger of Communist-backed Sukarno move against Nasution.

While it might be contended we should give Air Force something less useful to it than training aircraft, we cannot long hope to maintain any sort of relationship with AURI if we insist on right to determine what is good for it. In any case, almost any substitute items would add just as much to Suryadarma strength and prestige as would trainers.

Embassy extremely reluctant seek General Nasution's views on this sensitive subject at this time. Although we are close to Nasution in many ways neither he nor we have ever put cards on table to extent of permitting him to have voice in determining kind of material furnished Air Force. This would presuppose understanding between us which had best remain unspoken for now. Further, even though Nasution as Minister of Defense theoretically controls Suryadarma, all concerned are perfectly aware this not in fact true relationship. Should Suryadarma or President Sukarno learn we had discussed question with Nasution, harm to US interests would be incalculable.

Therefore Embassy considers US should make own unaided judgment as to whether trainer planes of type and quantity desired would significantly add to capability of Air Force to resist Nasution and how much weight this consideration should be given.

Embassy for its part has great difficulty in understanding how training planes could possibly effect power balance should Nasution decide to move against Sukarno and AURI.

It would seem that arguments advanced against trainers would inveigh against any assistance at all.

MILTAG, ARMA concur this estimate. Although AIRA temporarily absent from Djakarta, Chargé believes foregoing reflects his views also.

Embassy will comment other aspects Deptel 2258 after final confirmation of instructions.

In that connection meanwhile, however, one effective means of helping meet CINCPAC objective would be fund trainers over and above amounts already programmed by MILTAG for Army and Navy.[4]

Henderson

---

[4] In telegram 57 to Djakarta, July 11, the Department of State indicated that it concurred completely with the Embassy's reasoning as set forth in telegram 47 as well as its recommendation that U.S. officials should not consult with Nasution on the T–34 project. (Department of State, Central Files, 798.5622/7–660) See Supplement.

The Embassy re assessed the orientation of the Indonesian Air Force as no longer Communist-oriented in despatch 161, August 26, entitled "Current Political Trends in the Indonesian Air Force and Possible Relationship Thereto of U.S. Aid." (Department of State, Central Files, 798.00/8–2660)

---

270.   Telegram From the Embassy in Indonesia to the Department of State

Djakarta, August 1, 1960, 6 p.m.

287. CINCPAC FOR POLAD. More acute phase confrontation between PKI and Indonesian Government inevitable within next months,

---

Source: Department of State, Central Files, 798.00/8–160. Confidential. Also sent to CINCPAC.

Foreign Minister Subandrio predicted during my call this morning. Recent action by army in arresting and interrogating PKI leaders had been taken with Sukarno's specific approval, and repercussions of such action bound continue, Subandrio said.

PKI was divided into two schools of thought, one believed objectives could best be realized by giving lip service to Sukarno, other was convinced time had come to oppose Sukarno openly. Latter group had prevailed in issuance of statement attacking government.

Sukarno was Marxist but no Communist and PKI hopes of bringing him into Communist camp had been dashed by recent events, Subandrio explained. Communists continued to fish in troubled waters, Subandrio said. Only area in which they had been successful was stirring up Sukarno's suspicions that US objective was to get rid of him. (Embassy telegram 3616)[1]

Sukarno had been practically convinced that (1) failure President Eisenhower to visit Indonesia; (2) trip of *Karel Doorman;* (3) attacks on him in US publications; and (4) Admiral Burke's Hollandia statement were all part of package and tied in with much advertised coup d'état which never came off. Sukarno believed even if State Department had not been advised of *Karel Doorman* adventure that Pentagon had given advance nod of approval.

Subandrio inquired how my interview with Sukarno went Sunday (Embassy telegram 283)[2] and asked me whether I had been able to convince the President that his suspicions were unjustified. I replied frankly that I did not know; but that President was most cordial throughout and appeared to accept points I had made. I went over same ground then reviewed our support program with Subandrio and asked him how President could think we were gunning for him when we were supporting his government to this extent. I emphasized situation was quite different today from that prior to adoption 1945 Constitution in that this

---

[1] In telegram 3616, June 18, Henderson summarized a conversation he had that day with Subandrio, during which the Foreign Minister noted that President Sukarno continued to have the feeling, "rightly or wrongly," that the United States was seeking to change the regime in Indonesia and wanted to remove him from power. Subandrio stated that although he attempted to reason with Sukarno, pointing out that the United States was only concerned that Sukarno might take Indonesia to the Communist side, the President clung to the belief that the United States was working against him. (*Ibid.,* 611.98/6–1860) See Supplement.

[2] In telegram 283, August 1, Jones summarized a half-hour courtesy visit that he had with Sukarno on Sunday morning, July 31. Jones assured the Indonesian President that the American people were showing considerably greater interest and understanding of Indonesia's problems. He also pointed out that, regardless of the results of the upcoming national election in the United States, there would be no fundamental change in U.S. policies or attitudes toward Asia in general or Indonesia in particular. (*Ibid.,* 611.98/8–160) See Supplement.

was now Sukarno's government. Were US unwilling support Sukarno we would have withdrawn our support at time he took over complete responsibility for government. I again denied that US had been consulted in connection with *Karel Doorman* plans and said I was certain that Subandrio's own consultations in Washington must have led him to conviction this was true. As for Admiral Burke's statement, Foreign Minister who had seen full text must realize this was slip of tongue which occasionally happens to all of us and did not represent US intention to establish base in West New Guinea.

Subandrio in agreeing said he hoped that I would make these same points when I next saw Sukarno.

I asked what Subandrio thought President had in mind in wanting to have serious talk prior to August 17. Foreign Minister laughed, said presumably Sukarno wanted to warn me of all the terrible things he might say in his independence day speech. Turning serious, he said he did not know but that it could be on the subject of West Irian. Pressures were beginning to mount and Sukarno might well have something new to say on this subject. The movement of *Karel Doorman* to West New Guinea had aroused flare of Indonesian nationalism and demands for action were well-nigh irresistible. What action would be taken he could not say as no decisions had been made.

Jones

---

271. Telegram From the Embassy in Indonesia to the Department of State

Djakarta, August 1, 1960, 7 p.m.

289. Reference: Embassy telegram 288.[1] Since my return, I have heard repeated rumors that Sukarno would make dramatic move against Shell [a?] feature of August 17 address. I raised this question

---

Source: Department of State, Central Files, 898.2553/8–160. Confidential. Repeated to The Hague and London.

[1] In telegram 288, August 1, the Embassy reported that a normally reliable labor source revealed that the Indonesian Government had decided to nationalize the Shell Oil Company on August 17. (*Ibid.*) See Supplement.

with Foreign Minister this morning, pointing out (a) unfortunate repercussions on US-Indonesia relations that would inevitably accompany
movement against an international corporation which is 23 percent
American-owned; (b) unfortunate effect such action would have on
Indonesia's international standing; and (c) immediate alarm that would
develop from among other countries' fear that this was first step in na-
tionalizing of oil industry in Indonesia.

I said I could not conceive that GOI would be so lacking in appreciation of its own interests as to take such action but I recognized strong
national tide running.

I hoped Foreign Minister could reassure me on point.

Subandrio denied firmly any consideration being given to nationalization of oil industry generally but he admitted there was group
within Cabinet which wanted to move against Shell because of its Dutch
ownership. He indicated move, if it were made, would probably be
against Dutch shareholders in Shell, thus confirming possibility reported by Djuanda to me eight months ago.

If objective were to attack Dutch portion of Shell interests, how did
GOI plan to accomplish this? I queried, pointing out practicable and legal obstacles to action against a group of shareholders within an international corporation, situs of which was outside Indonesia. Subandrio
admitted this was problem which had not been solved and that final decision as to what would be done and how it would be done had yet to be
made. He could not, however, discount possibility entirely that some
step would be taken against mixed enterprises which contained Dutch
capital; there would be no action whatever, he emphasized, against foreign investment generally.[2]

Subandrio said he would note my comments and see to it that
Sukarno and others who were considering this problem took full cognizance of points made.[3]

Jones

---

[2] In telegram 223 to Djakarta, August 10, the Department of State instructed
Ambassador Jones to discuss the possible nationalization of Shell with Sukarno and
Djuanda before August 17, suggesting that nationalization of Shell might have a serious
effect on U.S. interests in Shell and would seem an adverse portent for U.S. oil companies
and other U.S. enterprises operating in Indonesia. (Department of State, Central Files,
898.2553/8–1060)

[3] In telegram 418 from Djakarta, August 15, Jones stated that the U.S.-British position
on the Shell nationalization question had been made amply clear to the Indonesians.
"When all is said and done, however," Jones added, "our strongest ally in this matter is
Indonesian army and as Department aware, army has gone to bat vigorously on this matter. At this stage, any further pressure on our part is likely to be resented as unwarranted
interference and stimulate 'I'll show'em' attitude of which Sukarno quite capable." (Ibid.,
898.2553/8–160) See Supplement.

272.   Memorandum of Conversation

Washington, August 24, 1960, 9:15 a.m.

SUBJECT

Farewell Call on the President by Ambassador Moekarto

PARTICIPANTS

The President
His Excellency Moekarto Notowidigdo, Ambassador of Indonesia
J. Graham Parsons, Assistant Secretary of State for Far Eastern Affairs

Ambassador Moekarto said that he had been here seven years as Ambassador and two years as Indonesia's representative to the United Nations. He said he greatly enjoyed his stay and had learned much which would be of benefit to him in his later service to his country. He and his family were most grateful for the hospitality and courtesy they had everywhere received. The President expressed his gratification and asked if the Ambassador's successor had arrived. Mr. Moekarto replied that he was today requesting agrément for Madame Supeni who for ten years has been Chairman of the Foreign Relations Committee of the Indonesian Parliament. He said that she is an outstanding and able woman. He added that also in his country women had equal status with men and as a matter of fact there were perhaps greater numbers of women in Parliament and in public life there than here. The President referred to the several women he had sent as Ambassadors during his Administration and said that he would particularly like to meet Madame Supeni. He specifically requested that when she came the State Department arrange for him to set aside more than the usual time for her initial call.

Ambassador Moekarto said that he wanted to bring up particularly the subject of the length of time students from Indonesia could stay in this country. At independence his country was left without trained people in all fields and it was so to speak "technically underdeveloped." Indonesia had benefited from and was grateful for United States technical assistance in the amount of about ten million dollars a year and many hundreds had come to this country to learn. He wished, however, that they could stay long enough to come to understand our institutions and

---

Source: Department of State, Central Files, 601. 9811/8–2460. Confidential. Approved by the White House on August 26. Herter briefed Eisenhower for this meeting in a memorandum dated August 12. (Ibid., 601.9811/8–1260) See Supplement. Moekarto's farewell call on Secretary Herter on August 10 was summarized in telegram 225 to Djakarta, August 10. (Department of State, Central Files, 601.9811/8–1060) See Supplement.

our way of life so they could contribute more usefully in the future. Mr. Dulles before his death had written him expressing enthusiasm for the thought of finding some way for students to stay for not six months to a year but for a longer term, say four to six years. The Ambassador realized that there were difficulties for us but hoped that some way could be found to make longer stays possible. He thought it would be a good "intellectual investment" for the United States.

After asking how many students come here each year, the President said that he could see some justification for varying the length of stay of people in different categories. For instance, those who were learning a profession needed to stay a longer time, whereas an agricultural expert who in fact lived with people interested in agriculture during his training could learn about this country and its ways more quickly. He said he agreed with what the Ambassador had said as to the value of a longer stay for students in the United States and he hoped that something could be done.

The Ambassador then raised the West Irian question which he described as a delicate political issue. The recent Dutch action in sending the carrier *Karel Doorman* to West Irian had greatly aroused Indonesian concern and it was feared that some action by the *Karel Doorman* might set off a conflagration.[1] The Ambassador briefly described the Indonesian case on West Irian and mentioned that the matter had been taken up in the United Nations but Indonesia had not secured a two-thirds majority. He hoped that the United States could help in preventing a clash and in securing a favorable resolution of this issue on which his people felt most strongly.

The President said that while he had not been to West Irian he had been to other outlying and undeveloped areas in the Far East and he found it difficult to understand why the feeling which had arisen over West Irian was so strong. He did not know why the area was important although he understood there was bauxite there and, the Ambassador added, oil. The President had talked to Ambassador Young who had told him that Dutch feeling on the issue was almost incandescent.[2] Perhaps the Dutch had the feeling of being kicked out with the help of oth-

---

[1] During his independence day speech on August 17 President Sukarno announced the severance of diplomatic relations with the Netherlands. He stated that this step was being taken in response to the dispatch of the *Karel Doorman* to West New Guinea. In telegram 439 from Djakarta, August 17, the Embassy informed the Department of Sukarno's action, indicating that aside from the remarks concerning the breaking of relations with the Netherlands the speech did not depart very much from the draft text that the Department had already received. There was no mention in the speech of the nationalization of Shell, as earlier speculated, or any other specific moves against Netherlands interests. (Department of State, Central Files, 656.98/8–1760) See Supplement.

[2] No record of this conversation has been found.

ers and perhaps they regarded this issue as symbolic as though, so to speak, it kept the Dutch flag flying and added to their prestige a little. He would however talk to the State Department, to Secretary Herter in fact, and get the best possible briefing to see if there was anything we could do.[3] He thought, however, that in this situation it was hard to be "a friend of the court" and be caught in the middle.

In taking his leave the Ambassador expressed his good wishes to the President for the future. The President in replying particularly asked that the Ambassador give his warm regards to President Sukarno whose visit here and whose young son he remembered well.

---

[3] See Document 276.

---

273.   Telegram From the Department of State to the Embassy in Japan

Washington, August 27, 1960, 4 p.m.

392. Ref: (a) Djakarta's 494[1] rptd info Tokyo 8, The Hague 37. (b) Tokyo's 620[2] rptd info Djakarta 7, The Hague 4. (c) Djakarta's 511[3] rptd info Tokyo 9, The Hague 39, CINCPAC 71.

In light serious crisis building up over *Karel Doorman*, anticipate Japanese Government may approach us following up Oda talk with

---

Source: Department of State, Central Files, 790.5856/8–2560. Confidential; Priority. Drafted by Robert L. Sneider of NA and Wenzel of SPA, cleared with WE and SPA, and approved by Parsons. Repeated to Djakarta, The Hague, and CINCPAC.

[1] Telegram 494, August 24, reported on a conversation between Jones and Ruslan Abdulgani, Acting Chairman of the National Advisory Council, regarding a planned visit of the *Karel Doorman* to Yokohama September 8–12. Abdulgani asked whether the United States could influence Japan to cancel the visit. (*Ibid.*, 790.5856/8-2460) See Supplement.

[2] In telegram 620, August 25, MacArthur reported that the Embassy felt it would "be grave error" to try and influence the Japanese to cancel the *Karel Doorman* visit. MacArthur continued: "not only is *Karel Doorman* incident directly related to West New Guinea issue on which we have maintained strict neutrality, but at same time Netherlands is staunch NATO ally. It would seem unthinkable for us to undermine Netherlands on issue where our policy is one of neutrality." (Department of State, Central Files, 790.5856/8–2460)

In telegram 246 from The Hague, August 26, Young agreed with MacArthur's reluctance to approach Japanese about the *Karel Doorman* visit and added "that his comments apply with equal force and validity to any suggestion that we approach Dutch re *Doorman* visit to Japan or its return to West Guinea." (*Ibid.*, 790.5856/8–2660)

[3] In telegram 511, August 25, Jones informed Parsons that a "serious crisis" was building in Indonesia over the *Karel Doorman*'s return to West New Guinea following its Japan visit. Jones feared the crisis would jeopardize U.S. interests in Indonesia unless allayed. (*Ibid.*, 790.5856/8–2560) See Supplement.

Jones. We recognize Japanese Government caught between conflicting pressures on one hand of maintaining its interests in Indonesia and blocking Indonesian shift toward Communist Bloc and on other hand avoiding antagonizing Dutch to detriment of desires most recently expressed by Kosaka for expansion West European trade. Possibility that Japanese Government may re-assess its position in view planned return *Karel Doorman* to West New Guinea and may be inclined seek our support to extricate itself from present dilemma. We concur completely with Embassy Tokyo judgement that we should avoid intervening directly in this problem and particularly having Japanese Government shift responsibility for decision to us.

Accordingly in response any inquiries from Japanese Government you should make clear our view that decision re *Karel Doorman* visit is one for Japanese Government itself to make. In this event you authorized give Japanese Government substance of Indonesian reactions to *Karel Doorman* cruise and evaluation current Indonesian situation as set forth reftel (c). Department will take same line if approached by Japanese here.

For Djakarta. You authorized take same line with Oda if he should approach you again this subject. You further authorized inform Abdulgani Department confirms position you have taken that in view US policy on West New Guinea issue, US could not take steps influence Japan to cancel *Karel Doorman* visit.

For Tokyo. Foregoing drafted prior receipt Tokyo's 650[4] which being given urgent consideration.[5]

Dillon

---

[4] Telegram 650, August 27, summarized a conversation between MacArthur and Japanese Vice Foreign Minister Hisamoto Yamada concerning the *Karel Doorman* visit. During this meeting Yamada reported that the Japanese Government has asked the Netherlands Government to review its request regarding the *Karel Doorman* visit, indicating that it hoped that the Netherlands would take the initiative in postponing or canceling its plan. (Department of State, Central Files, 790.5856/8–2760) See Supplement.

[5] In telegram 659 from Tokyo, August 28, MacArthur reported that Yamada met with the Netherlands Ambassador and told him that if the *Karel Doorman* returned to the Netherlands from Japan without revisiting West Irian then the Japanese would permit the visit to Japan. If the Netherlands insisted that the vessel must return there, however, Japan would insist that the visit be canceled. (Department of State, Central Files, 790.5856/8–2860) See Supplement. In telegram 256 from The Hague, August 28, Young expressed his agreement with MacArthur's comments and stated that Yamada's proposal to the Netherlands Ambassador in Japan "represents reasonable solution of this difficult problem." (Department of State, Central Files, 790.5856/8–2860) See Supplement.

Telegram 678 from Tokyo, August 30, reported that according to Yamada the Netherlands Government had decided that the *Karel Doorman* would visit Japan as scheduled and not return to West New Guinea but proceed homeward to the Netherlands. (Department of State Central Files, 790.5856/8–3060)

274.   Telegram From the Embassy in Indonesia to the Department
of State

Djakarta, August 31, 1960, 8 p.m.

616. CINCPAC also for POLAD. Furor over *Karel Doorman* visit Japan may have tended obscure highly important long-awaited confrontation between Army and Indo Communist Party (PKI). On balance, greatest significance *Karel Doorman* affair may prove to be extent to which it has affected and will continue affect this confrontation:

PKI has been openly challenged by series unprecedented Army moves past few weeks, culminating outright banning of Party major areas Sumatra, Kalimantan and Sulawesi. These moves, taken in overt defiance repeated Sukarno calls for national unity, already appear reached stage at which Army drawback difficult without considerable risk discrediting present leadership and opening way subsequent replacement. Army fully aware serious challenge to Sukarno inherent in actions already taken but determined not withdraw them. While somewhat less clear whether Army willing push on toward showdown, ARMA sources state Nasution still determined extend PKI ban to East and West Java in near future, despite Sukarno's wishes.

Open conflict between Sukarno's two chief sources support will inevitably pose severe threat to his control over country. If current confrontation progresses to point he no longer able play one off against other President will be faced most serious political dilemma recent years whether acquiesce Army weakening of PKI and risk eventually finding self dependent on Army sufferance, or throw in lot with PKI at risk provoking complete Army take-over or, at least, loss central control over outer islands. Sukarno real pro in political intrigue, however, may yet find means divert Army challenge. *Karel Doorman* affair has until now been one of chief diversionary weapons in Sukarno arsenal, which as shown by Parliamentary resolution August 31 (Embtel 615)[1] he continuing exploit to hilt; remains be seen whether proposed modification vessel's schedule if implement [*sic*] The Hague telegram 268,[2] may be sufficient blunt his exploitation issue, although it might help.

Source: Department of State, Central Files, 798.00/8–3160. Secret; Priority. Transmitted in two sections. Also sent to CINCPAC and repeated to Manila, The Hague, London, Tokyo, Canberra, Hong Kong, and Singapore.

[1] Dated August 31. (*Ibid.*, 790.5856/8–3160)

[2] In telegram 615, August 30, Young reported that during a conversation the previous day with Luns the Foreign Minister informed him that the *Karel Doorman*'s visit to Japan would take place according to the original time schedule, namely, between September 8 and 12. (*Ibid.*, 790.5856/8–3060)

President apparently endeavoring regain initiative while avoiding head-on clash with Army. As reported Embtel 589,[3] he agreed at Bogor not demand revocation bans on PKI to date but insisted no further bans be imposed without approval Supreme War Administration. From other sources understand Djuanda and Nasution, not President, are to be responsible for such approval.

Real test of Army determination force showdown with PKI thus shaping up in Java. Should Army carry through, will be indication Army convinced time ripe and own strength sufficient make bid assume predominant position in power structure, may well mark beginning of end current Sukarno domination national policy. On other hand, Army retreat now would probably be fatal present leadership, give PKI major boost. If Sukarno able engineer form of stand-still agreement (toward which he apparently striving), momentum behind current Army drive will be lost, situation may revert to former precarious balance.

But begins to look as though Army were playing for keeps. For first time in years, PKI faced with serious assault on position, by only force in country strong enough offer successful challenge. This, of course, is goal toward which US has long been working. Final showdown still to come, however, and may yet be put off by Sukarno maneuvering.

This connection, ARMA informed by General Jani August 31 that commanders areas where PKI banned met with Sukarno that morning, strongly defended actions. President later asked Nasution arrange meeting with all ministers, governors, regional commanders, heads armed forces between September 8 and 12 for complete airing matter. Jani said all on Army side would be briefed prior meeting "not be frightened" Sukarno opening statements, believed none would back down. Meantime, according Jani, Army will extend ban on PKI prior scheduled meeting.

Meeting appears Sukarno device gain time further maneuvers while ostensibly acceding strong Nasution position. Sukarno, at his best on platform, undoubtedly hopes use meeting reassert his authority. Nasution according Jani aware of this, will take measures intended prevent weakening Army unity.

Jones

---

[3] Dated July 30. (*Ibid.*, 798.00/7–3060)

September–December 1960: Visits of President Sukarno and Army Chief of Staff Nasution to the United States; U.S. Reexamination of Policy Toward Indonesia and the West Irian-West New Guinea Dispute

275. Telegram From the Embassy in the Netherlands to the Department of State

The Hague, September 3, 1960, 6 p.m.

297. Paris also for USRO. Department pass CINCPAC for POLAD.

1. Foreign Minister Luns advised me this noon, September 3, when he came to lunch alone at Embassy residence, that Japanese had cancelled *Karel Doorman* visit.[1]

2. Luns said that Japanese Foreign Minister had telephoned Japanese Ambassador The Hague this morning asking latter to see Luns immediately and request Dutch to cancel visit of Dutch Naval unit. In event that Dutch did not cancel visit, Japanese Foreign Minister stated his government would then have to "remit visit to some future date." Luns said that this did not mean end of September or any other foreseeable date in immediate future and amounted to outright cancellation.

3. Luns refused cancel visit and evidently gave Japanese Ambassador full-blown lecture on state of Japanese Government, danger of being blackmailed by robbers like Sukarno, lack of free-world support by Japanese, and other pertinent and related subjects.

4. Dutch Foreign Office will put out communiqué this afternoon, September 3, which will state that visit cancelled by Japanese specifically due to Indonesian pressures. Luns stated decision would be made later today re any action which may be taken by Netherlands Government as result Japanese cancellation. Luns thinking at lunch time was that he would withdraw Dutch Ambassador from Tokyo. Response my inquiry whether this meant break in diplomatic relations or just ex-

---

Source: Department of State, Central Files, 790.5856/9–360. Secret; Niact. Repeated to Tokyo, Djakarta, and Paris.

[1] Sukarno met with Japanese Ambassador Takia Oda at Bogor Palace on September 1 and requested that the Japanese Government cancel the *Karel Doorman* visit. Oda informed Jones the following day that, as a result of Sukarno's representations, he had recommended to his government that the visit be canceled. (Telegram 643 from Djakarta, September 2; *ibid.,* 790.5856/9–260)

tended consultations, Luns replied "probably extended consultations or something like it."

5.   Luns attitude, and he reflects that of Netherlands Government, was most bitter against Japanese, almost to point of being violent. Luns was greatly upset personally at Japanese attitude, which of course he regards as lack of support for entire free world. He finds it hard to believe that Japanese could be so blackmailed by Indonesians.

6.   Luns made strong emotional plea for US support of Dutch position and fervently hoped US would make some statement which would at least concur in Dutch attitude and expressed disappointment in Japanese action. During course of lunch, Luns repeated this plea several times in different forms, even going so far as insisting that US must condemn Japanese for this decision and support its friend and ally, the Netherlands. Luns asked specifically that I transmit his request, which I promised to do. But, at same time, I reminded him of long-standing US position, and my conclusion is that he will not be surprised if US does not respond to his appeal.

7.   Luns said that *Doorman* would go to Noumea on September 17 and that this would be announced.[2]

Young

---

[2] In telegram 330 to The Hague, September 4, the Department informed the Embassy that "we cannot comply with Luns request that we issue statement expressing disappointment at Japanese action cancelling visit." (*Ibid.*, 790.5856/9–360) See Supplement.

Circular telegram 374, September 8, gave the Department of State's assessment of the Japanese decision to withdraw its invitation for the *Karel Doorman* to visit Japanese ports. (Department of State, Central Files, 790.5856/9–860) See Supplement.

276.   Memorandum Prepared for President Eisenhower

Washington, September 9, 1960.

THE WEST NEW GUINEA PROBLEM

History of the Dispute

The dispute between the Netherlands and Indonesia over West New Guinea began in 1946 during the inconclusive negotiations which preceded the first major outbreak of hostilities between Holland and its rebellious colony. At that time the Dutch, over Indonesian protest, excluded the Residency of New Guinea from the discussions, and when the Dutch and Indonesians sat down at The Hague in 1949 to conclude an agreement granting Indonesia its independence, sovereignty over the area emerged as one of the principal points of difference.

To avoid a breakdown of negotiations, both parties agreed to a temporizing treaty provision which noted that the two powers had been unable to reconcile their views on the status of New Guinea and provided that the status quo, i.e., Netherlands control, should be maintained until the differences were resolved, and stipulated that within a year from the signing of the treaty the "political status" of Western New Guinea should be decided by negotiation.

During the negotiations which took place in 1950 and 1951, it became apparent that these views could not be reconciled and early in 1952, by a constitutional amendment, the Netherlands Government designated West New Guinea as a part of the Netherlands Realm, and from that time took the position that Dutch sovereignty over the area was no longer subject to negotiation. The Indonesian Government has refused to accept this action and has attempted unsuccessfully, both by direct approaches and through resolutions in the General Assembly in the United Nations, to persuade the Netherlands to re-open the subject.

The problem has become an emotion-charged issue both in the Netherlands and in Indonesia. Both governments have taken positions from which they cannot retreat without severe loss of prestige. In Indo-

---

Source: Eisenhower Library, Whitman File, Dulles–Herter Series. Secret. Drafted by Underhill and Wenzel and cleared with Emmons, Parsons, Kohler (in draft), Wilcox, Hare, and Bromley Smith. Transmitted to the White House on September 9, under cover of a memorandum from Stoessel to Goodpaster. Stoessel's covering memorandum reads as follows: "During Indonesian Ambassador Mukarto's farewell call on the President August 24, the President said he would ask the Department for a briefing on U.S. policy regarding the West New Guinea dispute between the Netherlands and Indonesia. In transmitting the memorandum of that conversation for your approval on August 25, we indicated we would send you such a briefing. It is enclosed. It has been approved by the Secretary."

nesia the issue has taken the proportions of a national crusade and has been intensively exploited by extremist elements especially the powerful Communist Party seeking to worsen relations between Indonesia and the Free World.

A variety of arguments are brought forth by each side. The Dutch maintain that they have a moral responsibility to civilize the stone-age Papuan tribes and to give them at some time the right of self determination. They hold that there are no ties, ethnic, cultural or religious between the Malay Javanese and the Melanesian Papuan, and that to turn over New Guinea to Indonesia would only be substituting one form of colonialism for another.

The Indonesians maintain that they are the legitimate heirs of the entire area of the former Dutch East Indies, and that the Netherlands is clinging to a portion of its former Far Eastern empire for out-moded colonialist motives. They point out that many ethnic groups are represented in Indonesia, that there is a strong Melanesian strain in Indonesians from the eastern islands, and that the Papuans have unquestionably more in common with them than they have with the Dutch.

The Australians, while earnestly striving to maintain close and friendly relations with the Indonesians, have strongly supported the Dutch position since they feel that a West New Guinea in Asian hands would threaten the military security of their country. The Japanese invasion of New Guinea during World War II is still fresh in Australian minds.

West New Guinea itself would appear hardly worth the bitter emotions raised on its account. While extensive in area, it is made up of dense jungle, snow-capped mountains, and impenetrable mangrove swamps. Except for petroleum in minor quantities, raw materials in exploitable quantities have not been found. The colony is an economic liability to the Mother country and is likely to continue so for the indefinite future. The approximately 700,000 natives of the area are among the most primitive on the face of the earth, less than half having been brought under nominal Dutch jurisdiction.

United States Position

From the outset, the United States has maintained an impartial position in this dispute between two countries with which we have friendly relations. The United States is, however, opposed to any resort to the use of force to settle the West New Guinea issue and has recently reiterated this view to both parties. Indonesia as well as the Netherlands has pledged not to use force. The United States position on this question is set forth within the current statement of United States policy on Indonesia, NSC 5901 dated January 16, 1959,[1] adopted by the National Security Council on January 29, 1959 and approved by the President on February 3, 1959. Paragraph 36 of NSC 5901 provides the following Major Policy Guidance on this question: "While for the present maintaining neutrality in the West New Guinea dispute in our relations with other governments, explore within the U.S. Government solutions to this problem compatible with over-all U.S. objectives, for possible discussion with other interested governments."

For the past several weeks the Policy Planning Staff of the Department of State has been engaged in an intensive study of the West New Guinea problem and the United States policy in this respect. The results of this study will be available in the very near future.[2]

---

[1] Document 177.
[2] See Document 289.

---

277. Telegram From the Embassy in Indonesia to the Department of State

Djakarta, September 16, 1960, 4 p.m.

819. For Assistant Secretary Parsons from Ambassador. Embtel 801.[1] With prospect of move reported reference telegram fat now in fire and Department faces decision that may well determine course events Indonesia a long time to come. I have endeavored weigh all factors this

---

Source: Department of State, Central Files, 798.11/9–1660. Secret; Priority.

[1] Telegram 801, September 16, reads:

"[less than 1 line of source text not declassified] Subandrio has received instructions from Sukarno to make direct approach to US Government to request official invitation for President to visit Washington while he is in US.

"Meanwhile, ARMA was approached last night by officer representing General Jani urging that Sukarno be issued such invitation. Army apparently feels Nasution would be on spot if he is received in Washington when head of state is ignored.

"Embassy comments follow." (Ibid.)

Sukarno was scheduled to be in New York for an address before the U.N. General Assembly on September 29. General Nasution, who was planning to travel with Sukarno, was scheduled to leave New York on the evening of September 29 and spend 2 days in Washington meeting with U.S. officials.

decision and reached conclusion that unless Sukarno received in Washington there is danger serious weakening US power keep Indonesia out of Soviet orbit.

I am fully aware justifiable reluctance Department support placation leader whose irresponsibility has justly earned him label as first class international irritant. You are also aware my concern implications his open support of PKI. My recommendation, however, is based on following:

There is no early prospect of Sukarno being removed from the scene. The Army, sole force capable of achieving this, has no such intention. Lesson of September 12 meeting as reported Embtel 778[2] is that Nasution still considers Sukarno essential and for this or other reasons will make no move to oust him. Instead Nasution effort will be directed at harnessing President. In absence any indication that Army intends actual move against Sukarno foreseeable future, I believe essential we attempt remove already deep-seated suspicion of Sukarno that US has supported Army campaign against him and is gunning for him. If Sukarno not accorded official recognition US Government, his conviction US hostile intentions will be confirmed. Moreover, not unlikely some in Army would also regard cold shoulder as deliberate affront national prestige and thus would move closer to Sukarno. I need not elaborate popular furor Sukarno could create over alleged US antipathy.

In sum, I consider it almost certain that failure to receive Sukarno Washington, following on heels of what he already considers snub in President Eisenhower's failure to come to Indonesia on occasion his Philippine visit, could result in serious dimunition if not neutralization our influence Indonesia. Needless to say, decrease US influence almost certain result in perhaps disproportionate increase influence Soviet bloc.

I recommend that I be authorized to extend invitation to Sukarno to make informal visit was [U.S.] for purpose making call on President Eisenhower.

Jones

---

[2] Telegram 778, September 14, reported on an Army conference on September 12 that was addressed by Sukarno. "Sukarno's obvious failure to win over army leaders in spite of all-out effort," the Embassy observed, "has certainly diminished his stature." The Embassy also pointed out that the distance between Sukarno and the Army had probably further widened, with the regional commanders more than ever on the opposite side from Sukarno with regard to the PKI issue. (*Ibid.*, 798.00/9–1460) See Supplement.

278.   **Telegram From the Embassy in Indonesia to the Department of State**

Djakarta, September 17, 1960, 6 p.m.

834. Embassy telegram 801.[1] In considering recommendations referenced telegram may be helpful for Department have Embassy views assessment of possible alternative methods handling Sukarno visit and estimated impact thereof.

Sukarno trip looming as major event in both internal and external scene here. President obviously jolted by recent Army challenge to authority, running scared. As result, is pulling out all stops to focus nationwide Communist-Moslem unity, muffle Army-PKI confrontation, divert populace from ever-increasing woes, recreate image national and world leader, and not least flatter own ego. Obviously views trip as combination happy climax to less happy developments past six months, panacea for national ills and personal frustrations. May even see his future closely tied to it. There is, of course, unreality in all this, but is very real to him.

As Department aware, Sukarno has moved away from US in past six months, harbors fixation based on what he considers ample evidence that US out to get him. This, carefully nurtured by PKI propaganda and large-scale and effective Soviet blandishments, has been further reinforced by obvious fact his chief internal foes clearly lean towards West. If this fixation confirmed by cold shoulder in US on UN visit (and his definition cold shoulder will be particularly sensitive in present frame of mind), we may well face his open hostility for long time to come.

There might conceivably be advantages to cold shoulder treatment if we conclude time has arrived write off Sukarno. Little doubt that his star has declined in past year; his unending intrigues have kept country in state constant turmoil, have been major factor in preventing progress toward reasonable politico-economic posture; his guided democracy increasingly shaping up as open totalitarian system. These facts recognized by growing number other leaders who, if not yet ready abandon him, are at least deeply disturbed.

This particularly significant in case of Army, which Embassy continues believe is only force now in sight with capabilities reversing present deterioration. Recent events—Army drive against PKI, Nasution moderating influence in question nationalization foreign oil companies,

---

Source: Department of State, Central Files, 798.11/9–1760. Secret; Priority. Transmitted in two sections. Also sent to USUN and CINCPAC for POLAD.

[1] See footnote 1, Document 277.

even apparently inconclusive outcome September 12 conference—encouraging in this respect, but Army still long way from mastery situation. Army has moved hesitantly in past, as conference compromise shows, still cannot be fully counted on move resolutely against Sukarno unless direct conflict over PKI develops.

In this extremely delicate contest, conceivable that expression US coldness toward Sukarno would tip balance, bring about Nasution–Sukarno conflict, provide final push to dislodge President or neutralize him.

Element of risk, however, is very great. Should move fail bring prompt results, should Sukarno subsequently remain in power for even relatively short time, he might well lash out in fear and anger and succeed in pulling country so far toward Soviet bloc that it would be impossible retrieve short of military means. Concurrently, he might erect impenetrable barrier against further cooperation from West, either deliberately or in rage, by seizure foreign oil companies, estates, et cetera. His attempts implement these possible moves might themselves trigger Army reaction, thereto realizing postulated goal. On other hand, Army would be at severe disadvantage in any dispute involving apparent defense foreign interests, particularly with spellbinder Sukarno in opposition. (Viz., Army passivity when Sukarno brought country to verge break in relations with Japan over *Karel Doorman* visit.) Should Army fail at this stage, US would virtually have lost Indonesia.

On balance, risk involved in foregoing course seems too extreme, chances of success too slim and adverse impact of failure disastrous. By entirely cutting off US from Sukarno, pinning all hopes on Army, we would surrender virtually all opportunities maintain our influence in likely even Army–Sukarno contest continues indecisive series skirmishes for prolonged period. Even more dangerous, we would be placing selves in all but hopeless position should (as is not impossible) Sukarno succeed in bringing Army at least temporarily to heel.

Alternative course, that of giving Sukarno welcome in Washington, also raises possible disadvantages. As long as President follows present policies, it clearly not in our interest support any action likely improve their chances. In this sense, special treatment might give appearance of endorsement Sukarno's recent actions, enhance his prestige, might even spur him into stepping up pace in belief nothing to worry about from US. Also Army, other foes Sukarno extremism might be disillusioned by spectacle US friendly hand for Sukarno, lose heart in struggle. Unfortunate impact on Southeast Asia SEATO allies, other Western-oriented neighbors, who no friend Sukarno NATO associates also a consideration.

Embassy doubts that possible unfavorable side-effects US friendly reception Sukarno would be of major nature. Sukarno always creature of emotions, operating on basis impulse; signs US friendliness far less likely produce rigidity in present course than impulsive softening or even deviation from course. Much of which Embassy convinced motivated not by true ideology but by suspicion of West and Soviet cultivation his ego. His susceptibility such gesture probably particularly great at this time; all indications point to his having feeling somewhat akin desperation in wake buffeting recently experienced at hands Army (Embassy telegram 778).[2] Re possible reaction his internal opponents to warm treatment in US, fact must be recognized that even opponents here hold ambivalent view toward President, seeing him not only as current menace but (to perhaps dwindling but still appreciable extent) as major symbol nation and revolution. Thus Sukarno's reception in Washington more likely be taken as homage Indonesia rather than person of President. Perhaps more important, any moderation anti-Western bias in Sukarno make up would make easier their task of changing his policies (which, even to most vociferous of opponents) save rebels (does not necessarily imply his physical removal from Palace).

Further element for consideration is probable content Sukarno speech at UNGA which certain to be unpalatable at many points to Western positions and may give unfortunate impression Indonesian identity with bloc. As Sukarno not accustomed freezing text speeches until last minute, content unlikely be fixed until just before delivery. Accordingly, may be deeply influenced by advanced indications nature reception in US.[3]

Jones

---

[2] See footnote 2, Document 277.

[3] In telegrams 872 (September 21) and 911 (September 23) from Djakarta, Jones again urged the Department to offer an official invitation to Sukarno to visit Washington. (Department of State, Central Files, 798.11/9–2160 and 798.11/9–2360) The Department responded in telegrams 460 (September 22) and 468 to Djakarta (September 23) that President Eisenhower could not yet make any commitment to see Sukarno. (Ibid., 798.11/9–2160 and 798.11/9–2360)

279. Memorandum of Conversation

SecDel/MC/90   New York, September 23, 1960, 4–4:45 p.m.

SECRETARY'S DELEGATION TO THE FIFTEENTH SESSION OF THE UNITED NATIONS GENERAL ASSEMBLY
New York, September 19–24, 1960

PARTICIPANTS

U.S.	*Netherlands*
The Secretary	Mr. Joseph Luns, Foreign Minister
Amb. Philip Young	of the Netherlands,
Foy D. Kohler	Mr. C.W.A. Schurmann,
	Netherlands Ambassador to the
	U.N.

SUBJECT

Foreign Minister Luns' call on the Secretary

[Here follows discussion of other subjects.]

Mr. Luns then brought up the subject of West New Guinea. He emphasized that the Netherlands had always been ready to accept a UN trusteeship for West New Guinea under which the UN could supervise the sincerity of the Dutch in carrying out their pledge to prepare the territory for self determination. Speaking of Dutch-Indonesian relations, he said that Sukarno now had nothing left with which to hit the Dutch—the round table agreements had been repudiated, all Dutch property had been seized, Dutch citizens had been thrown out, no Dutch planes or ships were allowed to touch Indonesia, there are no diplomatic relations. He wanted to stress, and he had stressed in his talk with Assistant Secretary Parsons,[1] that despite some difference between us on the evaluation of intelligence, there still remained a real danger of Indonesian aggression. It was not inconceivable, for example, that the Indonesians could fake an attack and attribute it to the Dutch, allege that there was an uprising in West New Guinea and claim that Indonesia was going to aid this uprising, possibly with "volunteers." The question was—what would we do then in the event of direct or indirect aggression. Going to the UN was not a policy but rather a long procedure. The US should decide concretely what it would do in such a case. In reply to a

---

Source: Department of State, Secretary's Memoranda of Conversation: Lot 64 D 199. Confidential. Approved by Herter on October 6. The meeting was held at the Waldorf Towers.

[1] Not printed. (Memorandum of conversation, September 15; *ibid.*, Central Files, 798.00/9–1560) See Supplement.

question from the Secretary, Mr. Luns said that he was going to stay in New York until after Sukarno's arrival and speech in the general debate and that he would speak after that before returning to The Hague. Continuing, he said that he had talked with the Secretary General of the UN who believes that it would be impossible to get any UN action in advance of actual aggression since the Dutch would not be able to prove a military danger. The Secretary General had also agreed that if the Dutch should come to the UN for a UN observer, there was a possibility that some of the Afro-Asian nations would bring up proposals which would result in an invitation to the Dutch to get out. Mr. Luns then raised the question as to whether Sukarno would be seeing President Eisenhower and suggested that in that event the President could perhaps say something in the nature of a warning.

In reply the Secretary said that the President had decided to see Chiefs of State and Heads of Government in New York but to receive no Foreign Ministers. Mr. Luns then referred to the President's reception of Lord Home,[2] which the Secretary explained as being due to the fact that Lord Home was new and that the British had particularly desired that he have a chance to meet the President without engaging in substantive discussion.

Reverting to the New Guinea question, Mr. Luns acknowledged the U.S. political deterrent had so far been effective but stressed that he was raising the question of a military decision. Obviously, the Netherlands was not going to fight a Pacific war alone. It was clear that the Indonesians now had sufficient troops, matériel and transport to enable them to move in on West New Guinea overnight and be established there the next day as a fait d'accompli. He said that when the Netherlands had announced that they were sending one battalion to reinforce West New Guinea, Sukarno had raged to Subandrio that the Dutch must have got hold of Indonesian plans, probably through the Indonesian Foreign Ministry. Subandrio had denied this possibility, saying that the Ministry's only copy was in his own safe. Mr. Luns said that he had talked about this question with Gates[3] and Allen Dulles. He pled for a U.S. decision and action to get the Indonesians to lay off any aggression. In this

---

[2] British Foreign Secretary.

[3] Luns met with Secretary of Defense Gates on September 19 concerning primarily NATO and defense matters. At the conclusion of the meeting Luns "stated that he had one more personal request. He said that the Dutch had some feeling that the Indonesians might attack Dutch New Guinea. He asked that the Secretary personally look into the matter. He thought that the U.S. should reaffirm to Indonesia its general opposition to the use of force to solve issues between nations and its specific opposition to the use of force by Indonesia against New Guinea. There was an inference that if Indonesia attacked New Guinea, the U.S. should assist the Netherlands at least logistically." (Memorandum of conversation, September 30; Department of State, Central Files, 033.5611/9–1960)

connection, he reiterated that the Netherlands would be prepared to accept a representative of the UN Secretary General or anything of the kind.

There ensued some discussion as to the date of Sukarno's arrival in New York. The Secretary had thought he would arrive on October 7 but the Dutch thought Monday, September 26 (later inquiry at the Department indicated an arrival date of September 28). Mr. Luns then reiterated that his Government thought it important that he see the President briefly. Amb. Young supported Mr. Luns in this connection, citing the importance of the Dutch role in connection with the DeGaulle proposals[4] and the fact that under the Dutch governmental system the Foreign Minister was in all respects, as regards the handling of foreign relations, independent of the Dutch Prime Minister. Mr. Luns emphasized that he would be able to see the President very privately and the matter would be kept entirely secret as it had on a similar call a few years ago. The Secretary made no commitment.

Prior to Mr. Luns' departure, the Secretary said he wanted to express the very sincere gratitude the U.S. feels for the unfailing support which the Dutch have always given us, despite a few unfortunate difficulties in our relationship, both in NATO and in the UN.

---

[4] Reference is to French President Charles de Gaulle's proposals for closer European cooperation within the framework of his Council of Nations.

---

280.   Telegram From the Embassy in Indonesia to the Department of State

Djakarta, September 26, 1960, 8 p.m.

941. CINCPAC also for POLAD. For Assistant Secretary Parsons from Ambassador. Now that army has apparently reached point where it has to play for keeps on the PKI issue or lose its hold on situation here, Nasution may expect assurances additional US Government support during Washington visit[1] although he may for obvious reasons find it

---

Source: Department of State, Central Files, 798.00/9–2660. Top Secret; Priority. Transmitted in two sections and also sent to CINCPAC.

[1] Jones discussed Nasution's upcoming visit to the United States with the General on September 19. (Telegram 841 from Djakarta; September 19; *ibid.*, 033.9811/9–1960) See Supplement.

most difficult to raise this question himself. I consider it essential, therefore, that opportunity be created by our side for such expression. At this point, Nasution needs to know unequivocally where we stand and we in turn could profit by frank exchange of views bound to ensue under circumstances in which initiative is ours.

Nasution will certainly want answers to two questions: (1) To what extent can he count on increasing support from US as he continues to carry out present program to curb power and influence of PKI; (2) In event of irreconcilable conflict with Sukarno developing, what backing can Nasution anticipate from US?

From my talks with him, I am convinced that Nasution's objective is to steer Sukarno into anti-PKI position but that he has no present intention of getting rid of Sukarno, believing latter's political leadership still important to nation. In other words, Nasution believes he can convert or if he can not convert he can control Sukarno. Thus answer to first question will be vital to him.

Nasution is realist, however, and knows that point may be reached when break between himself and Sukarno will develop. He is marshalling his forces, hoping his obvious strength will lead Sukarno to avoid open conflict. But he must prepare for possibility of break and consequently must have an answer to question number two.

Nasution is not only fighting our battle within Indo; he is fighting internal foe who has tremendous external resources. Soviets have let it be known that $250 million aid is by no means upper limit of what they are prepared to do in economic development, and [*less than 1 line of source text not declassified*] Martadinata's return from Moscow with $200 million for navy and $100 million for AURI in his pocket, illustrates that in military area, Soviets are willing to bid high price to neutralize influence US and alter direction in which Nasution has been steering nation. Nasution has got to know something about resources he may be able to count on.

Problem of course is to provide Nasution kind of assurances he needs without either (A) putting him on spot of apparently being disloyal his President or (B) forcing Sukarno into Soviet camp should he hear, as he probably would hear, of assurances given Nasution.

To avoid above pitfalls, we could, I believe, inform Nasution in general terms that US is prepared to provide substantial increase in military and economic support to an Indonesian government which would adopt a sound program for establishment of political and economic stability in country. Sound program might be defined to include: (A) continuing curb on power PKI; (B) adoption financial economic stabilization program; (C) settlement of rebellion; (D) adoption program economic development designed improve standard of living.

We could further inform Nasution without soliciting reply that should army as a result of all-out conflict with PKI find itself in control of Indonesia, he could count on immediate large scale military and economic support by US Government. No reference should be made to Sukarno.

I appreciate that important question any commitment new US aid would be estimate foreign policy orientation new regime, although I do not think this should be determining. While not impossible, I believe we cannot expect army-dominated regime adopt pro-west alignment, at least in short run, because of strong nationalist feelings, sensitivity toward colonialism and imperialism which will continue be nurtured by West New Guinea problem. Army controlled regime would probably be to right of Sukarno on foreign policy but adhere to "independent" line. Crucial difference, however, would be removal PKI influence, which may be expected to result in increased wariness, if not actual coolness, toward Soviet bloc. However, Soviet bloc may still find room for maneuver this situation which my opinion underscores necessity US making clear its intention support Nasution on basis of mutual objectives.

If we make démarche along above lines, I consider it of utmost importance for Sukarno to be received at White House. For Nasution to be given red carpet treatment at Cabinet level while Sukarno is overlooked would light fires of resentment in breast Indonesian President which would unquestionably start him on road undermining Nasution. Further, if word as to assurances given Nasution reached Sukarno's ears, his suspicions that this was directed against himself would appear far less well-founded if he already had received royal welcome.

In the skirmish of September 12, army program was slowed down, yet it seems clear that real power is more and more coming into Nasution's hands. At this stage, I think it vital that he be given strong assurances of support without Sukarno removal from scene being made condition precedent. In nutshell any US tactic at this point should be to support Nasution without antagonizing Sukarno.

Jones

281. Memorandum From the Assistant Secretary of State for Far Eastern Affairs (Parsons) to the Under Secretary of State for Political Affairs (Merchant)

Washington, September 27, 1960.

SUBJECT

Support for the Indonesian Army in the Event of a Showdown between Nasution and Sukarno or Nasution and the Communists

Minister of Defense and Chief of Staff, General Abdul Haris Nasution, will be in Washington September 28 and 29 and will see the Secretary of Defense and others in the Defense Department. We have requested an appointment for him with Secretary Herter. As you are aware, the Army is the strongest element in Indonesia opposed to the growth of Communist influence in the country. Army leaders have recently banned Communist activities in certain areas of Indonesia and have forced Sukarno to agree to placing a ban on all political activity until November 30. It is possible that this situation may result in a final confrontation between the Army and Sukarno on the Communist issue sometime during the coming months. Until now Nasution has followed a moderate course despite some pressure within the Army to take drastic action. We believe that before Nasution would act, he would want assurances from us that we would support him if he found himself in need of military or economic aid in a struggle to reduce the influence of the Communists in Indonesia and eliminate Sukarno as an effective force in the country.

I request that I be authorized to give the necessary assurances to Nasution along with the following line: I would inform General Nasution that we are aware of and heartened by recent actions which the Army has taken to curb Communist power. We are also aware of the fact that this is an internal Indonesian matter. We are heartened because we profoundly believe that Communist efforts to gain power in all countries are incompatible to the true independence of those countries. In contrast to the Communists, it is American policy in Indonesia and elsewhere to desire the true independence of the country. We know from our experience elsewhere that sometimes when there is strong opposition to a strong Communist party in a given country there can be a showdown. In such circumstances if there is a crisis and those who oppose the Communists and who work for the true independence of the country

---

Source: Department of State, Central Files, 798.00/9–2760. Secret. Drafted by Bell on September 26.

want to know where the United States stands, they can be sure that the United States stands with them. If American help is wanted in the form of military or economic assistance, the United States in such circumstances does its best to be helpful and quickly. It is not possible to foresee in advance what type of aid might be needed or could be provided. In any event, we would like General Nasution to feel that the United States would wish to be helpful to Indonesia too in such circumstances, and if there should be a request for help of the kind we have already provided, such as small arms and vehicles, or rice to meet a food emergency, he could be sure we would do our best to meet his request.

I would further tell General Nasution that we are not asking for any comment from him but merely wish to assure him that in the event of such a contingency we will back him up; but that if he does have any suggestions, we will take them into consideration in our planning for such a contingency.

If you agree with this approach,[1] I will make copies of this memorandum available to the Secretary, the Secretary of Defense and others in the Pentagon who will be talking with General Nasution.[2]

---

[1] Merchant initialed his approval of this recommendation on September 27. Another copy of this memorandum bears the following handwritten comment by Avery F. Peterson, dated September 28: "Jeff. As mentioned, Mr. Dillon wholly endorsed this, thought in fact it should be stronger, and that mention should be made of our concern over closure of last non-Sukarno newspaper. Said this *was* contingency planning." (*Ibid.*, FE Files: Lot 62 D 26, Indonesia 1960)

[2] Parsons telephoned Secretary of Defense Gates on September 28 and informed him that Merchant and Dillon had approved his talking with Nasution in order to reassure the Indonesian General that he could rely upon the United States "to give him quick and effective support if required." A memorandum of this conversation by Parsons reads: "I said that inasmuch as this was a potential commitment of supplies and funds I thought we should touch base with him. Mr. Gates expressed full agreement with this line and asked if he should say anything. I said that it would be helpful if he could reflect a favorable attitude toward the General and his present requirements if reasonable from the military point of view. I cautioned him on the necessity of not embarrassing General Nasution with the political figures which may be around him." (*Ibid.*, WE Files: Lot 63 D 106, Indonesia)

282.   Telegram From the Department of State to the Embassy in
       Indonesia

Washington, September 30, 1960, 4:08 p.m.

515. Embtels 941[1] and 972.[2] General Nasution accompanied by
Colonels Yusuf and Kusmardjo called on Parsons afternoon 29th. Major
Benson his escort officer only other American present.

At invitation of General Nasution Parsons said he glad give him indication American reactions to recent events. He said that US was aware
of and heartened by recent Army actions curb communist activities in
outlying parts of Indonesia. We were aware also that this was internal
matter. We were heartened because of our belief that communist activities not compatible with true independence or nationalism although
they sought to use nationalism in their drive for world domination under control of Moscow. In contrast American policy has always sought
to support independence of free world countries including Indonesia
because we believed that a world of free nations organized each according to their own national genius was in best long-term interests of
United States. Moreover we support not only political but economic independence for newly developing countries.

Parsons continued that if strong opposition to a strong communist
party, a situation which he thought existed in Indonesia, should at some
time give rise to a crisis and a confrontation it might be that anti-
communists would wish to know where US stood. He wished to say after consulting various superiors in US Government that if such situation
occurred in Indonesia General Nasution could be sure that US would
wish to support those who oppose communists. If US was asked to help
in such situation US would do its best to help quickly and effectively
and would try to meet any reasonable request. It should be remembered
that US was not like communist countries which could pledge their aid
without even thinking of their own people because US had to persuade
its people that their money should be used to assist foreign countries.
Nevertheless if confrontation occurred and new situation resulted General Nasution could be assured that we would feel strongly that we
should help him if requested. Parsons added that he did not ask General

Source: Department of State, Central Files, 033.9811/9–3060. Secret; Priority; Limit
Distribution. Drafted and approved by Parsons. Repeated to USUN and CINCPAC for
POLAD.

[1] Document 280.

[2] In telegram 972, September 28, Ambassador Jones discussed the upcoming visit of
Sukarno to the United States. "I believe we have unusual opportunity with both Sukarno
and Subandrio in US," he noted in part, "to straighten out erroneous perspective Sukarno
now holds toward US." (Department of State, Central Files, 611.98/9–2860)

Nasution to comment on foregoing statement as he merely wished him to know that this was our attitude. He added that if the US was giving aid to a government which was striving for political and economic stability and was taking steps to curb PKI to settle rebellion and to introduce appropriate financial economic development measures it would be that much easier for this government to work vigorously to meet Indonesian needs.

Parsons also said that he understood that there had been statements made although not at top level in Indonesian Government which suggested that US did not wish true independence for Indonesia because it feared that Indonesia would then adversely influence SEATO countries and might stifle US economic interests in Indonesia. He said nothing could be further from truth and that far from fearing strong Indonesia we desired this. Americans like most non-communist peoples desired to concentrate on their own affairs and live at peace and sooner other countries obtained full independence sooner burden American aid programs could be reduced. If Indonesia became stronger under guidance of those who concerned to prevent communist domination of Indonesia he was certain Indonesian influence with other countries including SEATO allies would not be harmful. It should be noted this connection that US fully respected Indonesian neutrality policy as it also respected neutrality policy of Burma and Cambodia. As for American enterprise Parsons felt that continuance American enterprise must be justified on grounds benefits to Indonesian economy too and he felt that if they were allowed to operate under reasonable arrangements in Indonesia benefits to Indonesian economy would be obvious and would be recognized. If American enterprises on the other hand were bad for Indonesia, which he did not believe, and Indonesians decided they did not want them then in that case they would simply have to withdraw. Point was however that contrary to what he understood had been said in Indonesia recently US was not interested in a weaker Indonesia for any narrow purpose of its own but rather desired strong and truly independent Indonesia.

In reply General Nasution gave lengthy exposition of manner in which Army was working quietly in all regions and in all functional groups as well as in political front to obtain practical control so as to thwart communists. Only place they had real roots was central eastern Java where decade ago Defense Minister who was communist had trained cadres down to village level. He said to understand Indonesian situation correctly it must be realized that frontal clash not likely and not wanted. On contrary process he described would continue. He also showed his pleasure at obvious indications of confidence in and support for him and Army. Parsons said that he had not meant to imply that he thought frontal clash about to occur or that he advocated such a course;

he merely wished to have General Nasution know what our attitude would be if unexpected situation developed. General Nasution said he appreciated this.

Parsons at no time mentioned Sukarno in above context. Nasution referred to him as "father" rather than "commander" and explained how Sukarno had no organization and instead of being man of action was man whom all parties and groups sought to persuade and influence in order obtain his support. It was clear Nasution was thinking in terms Sukarno's continued usefulness as "father image" and there was no hint of any thought of eliminating him from scene.[3]

Herter

---

[3] During their conversation, Parsons also discussed the West New Guinea dispute with Nasution. He stated that a resort to violence would weaken both parties and expressed the hope that none would be used. Parsons also informed Nasution that the U.S. Government had approved in principle the grant of 300 million rupiahs, derived from P.L. 480 sales, to Indonesia for barracks construction. (Telegrams 522 and 523 to Djakarta, September 30; *ibid.*, 033.9811/9–3060 and 798.56/9–2660) See Supplement for both.

---

283. Memorandum of Conversation

Washington, September 30, 1960.

SUBJECT

Call on the Secretary by General Nasution

PARTICIPANTS

Gen. Abdul Haris Nasution, Minister of Defense and Chief of Staff, Indonesia
Gen. Gatot Subroto, Vice Chief of Staff Indonesian Army
Col. Andi Jusuf
Lt. Col. Kusmardjo Subroto
Col. R.M.S. Soerjosoerarso, Military Attaché, Indonesian Embassy

The Secretary
J. Graham Parsons, Assistant Secretary for Far Eastern Affairs
Major George Benson, Escort Officer, DOD

Source: Department of State, Secretary's Memoranda of Conversation: Lot 64 D 199. Secret. Drafted by Parsons on October 1 and approved in S on October 5.

General Nasution said he was having a busy, useful visit to the United States. Several years ago our relations had not been quite as understanding but now they were much better and particularly with the military including CINCPAC. He referred to his talk with Mr. Parsons yesterday and said that he thought our understanding of each other's situation was good. He appreciated what had been said to him in that talk which had continued so long that he was almost late for the reception at the Indonesian Embassy.

The Secretary asked about the Indonesian contingent proceeding to the Congo (this subject is covered by telegram sent to Djakarta and Leopoldville).[1]

The Secretary asked about this year's harvest in Indonesia and was told that the figures indicated a somewhat better crop. Nasution hoped that the goal of self-sufficiency could be reached in a few years but in this field too Indonesia was hampered by a lack of transport. Surplus areas had a hard time, not being adequately served so that their produce could be transported. He mentioned at some length the lack of communications and transport which also hampered the Army in its efforts to carry out security missions which were sometimes delayed as much as four months or more. In this context he said that the rebels operating against the Government had been reduced from over 100,000 to about 20,000 and he hoped that the situation can be cleaned up, at the end of which it would be necessary to terminate the war emergency powers. General Nasution expressed appreciation for our military aid program and for the responsiveness of CINCPAC to certain of his needs.

At the opening of the conversation and again at the close the Secretary expressed his pleasure that General Nasution and his colleagues had been able to come here and his own pleasure at being able to meet the General. He paid him a warm compliment on his successful conduct of his difficult position as top military commander in Indonesia.[2]

---

[1] Reference is to telegram 525 to Djakarta (also sent to Léopoldville), September 30. (*Ibid.*, Central Files, 033,9811/9–3060) See Supplement.

[2] During his visit to Washington, Nasution also met at the Pentagon with Assistant Secretary of Defense Irwin. An informal memorandum of that conversation, drafted by Colonel W.S. McCrea of ISA, was sent to the Embassy in Indonesia under cover of a December 29 letter from Emmons to Henderson. (Department of State, SPA Files: Lot 63 D 436, 350.3–N) See Supplement.

284. Memorandum of Conversation

Secdel/MC/98   New York, October 5, 1960, 9:30 a.m.

SECRETARY'S DELEGATION TO THE FIFTEENTH SESSION OF
THE UNITED NATIONS GENERAL ASSEMBLY
New York, September 19–October 8, 1960

PARTICIPANTS

U.S.	Indonesia
The Secretary	President Sukarno
Mr. James Bell	

SUBJECT

US-Indonesian Relations; UN Matters

The Secretary called on Sukarno at 9:30 this morning. Sukarno opened the conversation by requesting a better understanding of Indonesia by the United States. When the Secretary told the President that he felt we were more sympathetic and understanding than the President realized, Sukarno immediately turned to the question of West New Guinea saying that we could best demonstrate our friendship for Indonesia by coming out directly on the Indonesian side in their dispute with the Netherlands. Sukarno said he consistently told the Indonesian people that Indonesia was very friendly toward the United States, but that they could not understand our position on this issue. The Secretary asked why Indonesia did not take the matter to the International Court of Justice and Sukarno replied that there was no question that West New Guinea was a part of the Netherlands Indies and that there was nothing to be adjudicated. He said that this was a matter of principle. The Secretary then pointed out that while we did not support Indonesia, neither do we support the Netherlands and that we were maintaining our policy of impartiality. He also referred to our desire to maintain friendship with both Indonesia and the Netherlands, particularly as the Netherlands was an ally. Sukarno said that we seem to tie NATO in with this issue, and that we should not—that we should have a real Asian policy, not complicated by NATO.

President Sukarno then asked the Secretary to please convey his regards to President Eisenhower. Sukarno recalled the visit of Vice Presi-

---

Source: Department of State, Secretary's Memoranda of Conversation: Lot 64 D 199. Confidential. Drafted by Bell on October 10 and approved by S the same day. The meeting was held at the Waldorf Astoria. Steeves briefed Herter for this meeting in a memorandum of October 1. (*Ibid.*, FE Files: Lot 62 D 26, Indonesia 1960) See Supplement.

dent Nixon to Indonesia[1] and said that he hoped the Secretary would also give his best regards to the Vice President.

Sukarno referred to a newspaper report that Kasavubu[2] had refused to accept the Indonesian troops sent to the Congo.[3] Secretary said that he understood Kasavubu had made such a declaration some days ago but had subsequently reversed himself.

The Secretary referred to the Five Power Resolution on a possible meeting between President Eisenhower and Khrushchev[4] and informed President Sukarno that an amendment would be offered making the resolution more general in nature. President Sukarno asked if the amendment would be our answer to the resolution and the Secretary replied that it would represent our position on the matter. He then explained some of the reasons why the meeting would not be possible at this time under the present circumstances. He said that the personal attacks on the President did not deter him from meeting with Mr. Khrushchev and then repeated for Sukarno's benefit some of the comments that Khrushchev had made about President Eisenhower. The Secretary pointed out that President Eisenhower could not undertake conversations which would commit a new administration particularly as a new President would be elected in about five weeks. Despite these circumstances the Secretary said that he had hoped he would hear from Gromyko but that he had not.

President Sukarno invited the Secretary to be his guest in Indonesia while he was in office or after his retirement. The Secretary said he appreciated the invitation and would certainly like to have an opportunity to see Indonesia, but was afraid that such a trip would not be possible.

The rest of the conversation was largely an exchange of pleasantries.

---

[1] Nixon visited Indonesia in October 1953 as part of a larger trip to the Far East and South Asia.

[2] Joseph Kasavubu, President of the Congo.

[3] Indonesian troops were being considered as part of the U.N. peacekeeping force in the Congo; for related documentation, see vol. XIV, pp. 251 ff.

[4] On September 29 a draft resolution calling on Eisenhower and Khrushchev to meet was presented to the U.N. General Assembly by Sukarno, Nehru, Nasser, President Joseph Broz Tito of Yugoslavia, and President Kwame Nkrumah of Ghana. (U.N. doc. A/4522)

285.   Memorandum From Acting Secretary of State Dillon to President Eisenhower

Washington, October 5, 1960.

SUBJECT

President Sukarno's Call on You at 10:30 A.M., Thursday, October 6[1]

At your invitation, President Sukarno of Indonesia will pay a call on you at 10:30 a.m., Thursday, October 6. I and Mr. John M. Steeves, Acting Assistant Secretary for Far Eastern Affairs, will be present with President Sukarno. The following material has been prepared for your use during this meeting.

1.   *Sukarno's Suspicions of the United States*

Discussion. During the past several months we have received a number of disquieting reports which suggest that the Indonesian Government believes that the United States does not wish true independence for Indonesia since the United States fears that Indonesia would then adversely influence our SEATO allies and since a strong Indonesia might stifle United States economic interest in that country. There are clear indications also that Sukarno suspects that the United States is attempting to undermine his personal position and to replace him with Indonesian leaders more sympathetic with United States policies. The reasons behind Sukarno's reported attitudes are complex. He is, as you know, a vain and sensitive individual who responds markedly to personal attention. He probably believes that the Communist Bloc has been more sympathetic to Indonesia's problems than has been the United States and to justify this attitude he would cite the visits of Khrushchev to Indonesia, the massive offers of economic and military assistance extended by the Bloc to Indonesia over the past three years and the Bloc's unwavering support of the Indonesian position in that country's dispute with the Netherlands over West New Guinea. On the other hand, Sukarno has been severely disappointed over your inability to visit In-

---

Source: Department of State, Central Files, 798.11/10–560. Secret. Drafted by Wenzel; cleared in draft with Blue of WE. A signed copy of this memorandum is in the Eisenhower Library, Whitman File, Eisenhower Diaries; Eisenhower's initials are on that copy, indicating that he read it.

[1] President Eisenhower approved this meeting with Sukarno during a meeting with Dillon on October 5. According to a memorandum of that conversation, by John Eisenhower, October 5, "Mr. Dillon then expressed concern over the feelings of President Sukarno of Indonesia who is reportedly leaving tomorrow. Sukarno brought Nasution along with him and Nasution has been to Washington and seen everyone. We do, of course, like to deal with Nasution, but fear that if Sukarno feels slighted, it will go hard with Nasution in Indonesia." (*Ibid.*)

donesia. Disappointment has also been voiced by the Indonesian Government over the lack of support from the United States for Indonesia in the West New Guinea issue. In addition, the Indonesians have also sometimes expressed less than complete satisfaction with American aid which they have characterized as slow and grudgingly given as compared with Communist Bloc assistance.

Sukarno is the key to the course of political events in Indonesia and will likely remain so for some time. The current political situation in Indonesia can be described as an intense three-way power struggle with the Indonesian Army pitted against the Communist Party and President Sukarno playing a balancing role between these two antagonistic forces. In his efforts to forge a new government structure to cope with Indonesia's desire for economic progress, Sukarno has accepted the Communist Party as an element whose participation he believes is important for the achievement of this objective. Thus Sukarno's attitude toward the Communists has inhibited efforts by the Indonesian Army to curb the Party's activities.

Part of Sukarno's suspicions of the United States probably derive from our military assistance to the anti-Communist Indonesian Army which we have extended since 1958. This program may have generated a fear in Sukarno's mind that we are building up and encouraging the Indonesian Army to oust him. General Nasution, the Army Chief of Staff and leader of Indonesia's anti-Communist forces, has, incidentally, just completed a successful visit to Washington during which he was cordially received by several high level United States officials including the Secretaries of State and Defense.

In view of the foregoing, we deem it imperative that we do everything possible to allay these suspicions on Sukarno's part.

Recommendations

A. That, in the course of your conversation with Sukarno, you emphasize that the United States fully respects Indonesia's policy of nonalignment and that the United States wishes nothing more than a strong and truly independent Indonesia. We sympathize greatly with Indonesia's efforts to achieve economic and social progress; our assistance programs are designed, within the means available to us, to encourage Indonesia in achieving these goals.

B. That you express your sincere regret that you have been unable to respond to Sukarno's numerous and gracious invitations to visit Indonesia during your term of office.

2.   *The West New Guinea Issue*

President Sukarno is likely to raise the West New Guinea issue in some context during his conversation. Attached at Tab A is a briefing paper on this subject which was recently prepared by the Department for your background information.[2]

Recommendation

That you express the hope that there will be a peaceful and mutually satisfactory solution to this problem between two countries with both of which we maintain friendly relations.

Douglas Dillon[3]

---

[2] Document 276.

[3] Printed from a copy that bears this stamped signature.

---

286. Memorandum of Conversation

Washington, October 6, 1960, 10:30 a.m.

SUBJECT

    Call of President Sukarno on the President

PARTICIPANTS

    The President
    Acting Secretary of State Douglas Dillon
    Acting Assistant Secretary of State John M. Steeves
    Brig. Gen. Goodpaster, The White House
    President Sukarno of Indonesia
    Foreign Minister Subandrio of Indonesia

After the formal exchange of greetings President Eisenhower recalled that the last time they had met was during President Sukarno's official visit to the United States.[1]

Source: Department of State, Central Files, 798.11/10–660. Secret. Drafted by Steeves and approved in U on October 13 and by the White House on November 22. Another memorandum of this conversation, drafted by Goodpaster, October 12, is in Eisenhower Library, Whitman File, Eisenhower Diaries. See Supplement. Jones summarized this meeting in *Indonesia: The Possible Dream*, pp. 183–184. Steeves commented on the Sukarno visit in a letter to Jones, October 10. (Department of State, FE Files: Lot 62 D 26, Indonesia)

[1] Regarding Sukarno's official visit to the United States in May 1956, see *Foreign Relations, 1955–1957*, vol. XI, pp. 267–273.

President Sukarno remarked that the passage of five years found them both older but he congratulated President Eisenhower on his healthful appearance. This was in response to the President's remark that he had undergone three rather severe illnesses since they last met.

The President took the initiative in raising the matter of the resolution sponsored by the five neutral powers in the United Nations, of which Indonesia was one. The President assured Sukarno that he did not question their motive, in fact he was 100% in accord with the objective they were trying to serve. He dwelt on the theme that the armaments race and general tension was leading to a most unsatisfactory situation and that anyone who desired peace and tranquillity could not help but be disturbed by this growing confrontation. The President explained to Sukarno why the gesture of merely getting together with Khrushchev was futile and in our view productive of further tension rather than a lessening of it. He said that over the weekend he had given very serious thought as to what his own personal attitude ought to be and what stance the United States should take. He realized that Khrushchev disliked him intensely personally. Khrushchev had acted with extreme rudeness, but even with all of this if there was anything that could be served by the President humbling himself and setting aside his personal feelings, he of course should be very happy to do it. At this point in the conversation Sukarno told the President that the neutrals of course had withdrawn their resolution last night at the United Nations because they were not receptive to the amendments suggested by Australia. Sukarno said he felt that a meeting between the two if it had accomplished nothing else would break the ice.

The President went on to explain the situation after the U–2 incident and the meeting in Paris. He made reference to the fact that the revelation that we were conducting such operations as the U–2 was not any great new news to the Soviets. This was one of the facts of life that had been recognized between the two powers for some time, but even with this knowledge if Khrushchev felt that this U–2 incident prevented their getting together and necessitated the cancellation of his visit to Russia that he could have said so in Moscow. He did not need to come to Paris in order to make his position clear. It was therefore obvious that Khrushchev was determined to make as much propaganda as possible out of the breakup in Paris. He knew, for instance, that it would be impossible for the President of the United States to meet his demands for an apology. The President also remarked to Sukarno that the accident of the location of the United Nations placed Khrushchev in the United States but that this fact had no practical bearing on their getting together. If it had not been for the United Nations meeting there would of course be no possibility of Khrushchev being invited to the United States. Khrushchev's being in the United States therefore seemed to appear to many as a natural opportunity to get together which really was not true. He was as "distant" as though he were still in Moscow. The President returned to the point of assuring Sukarno that it was only the firm conviction that nothing would be accomplished which caused him to reject the idea of a meeting and that he wanted Sukarno to understand it.

Sukarno maintained his viewpoint that they should and that part of the conversation ended.

The President then turned to ask Sukarno about Indonesia and how they were getting along. Sukarno said they were making progress. He said, for instance, in 1955 they were producing about 5-1/2 million tons of rice, now it is seven million. In 1955 they were importing a million tons of rice, now it is 250,000 tons. He said that his planning people tell him that by 1965 they should be self-sufficient, this despite the fact that their population is now 92 million as against 72 million when they gained independence. In response to a question about their literacy, he pointed out that at the inception of independence illiteracy was 94%, it is now 40%, by 1965 it would be zero. He gave some other interesting statistics on education. In 1949 there were only three-quarters of a million students mostly in the elementary grades, now there are eight million students in schools, with a very large growth in their high schools during this period. He made personal reference to the fact that when he was studying engineering he was one of eleven students in the university grades or in higher technical studies. Today they have 55,000 in the universities. The President asked Sukarno about the USS *Hope* which was on its way to Indonesia. Sukarno said they would certainly welcome it and he would take the opportunity to visit it. In talking of Indonesia's health problem with specific reference to malaria, he said that Indonesia had probably made the most progress of any country in southern Asia in abolishing malaria and that by 1965 they hoped to have it eliminated.

Turning to economics Sukarno explained their eight-year plan which was to cost 250 billion rupiahs. There was some difficulty translating this into dollars due to the uncertain value of the rupiah. He said that by 1965 they would have their own blast furnaces. Sukarno reminded the President that the United States had its initial problems too and that they were therefore not particularly discouraged with the many problems they face now. The President humorously responded, what do you mean "used to have our problems, we have plenty now". He recalled that a philosopher had said that "when the human family successfully eliminates its difficulties it will die". He referred to Gibbon's *History of the Rise and Fall of the Roman Empire* and said that Rome fell because it had seemingly eliminated its problems. It became soft and thus deteriorated.

Sukarno said he was most disappointed that the President had never visited Indonesia. The President very tactfully pointed out that in both of the trips which he made into various parts of Asia the problem turned out to be one of time, that in a large country like Indonesia he could not stop for a mere courtesy call as he had done in some small countries but that he felt it would be insulting to come to Indonesia unless he could have stayed a week. He told Sukarno that he was most anxious to come and that next year he was going to be a private citizen, and if Indonesia would give him a visa he would think very seriously of coming to Indonesia, Australia and New Zealand, an area he was most anxious to visit. Sukarno smilingly turned to Subandrio and told him to make sure that the President got his visa.

The President told Sukarno he wanted to return to the discussion of the United Nations. He specifically mentioned the Congo. He said that prior to Sukarno's arrival, during his two trips to the United Nations, he had talked to African leaders. He had, for instance, been very impressed by Olympio[2] and he had also talked with Bourguiba's son. He explained to Sukarno that a situation such as we faced in the Congo simply had to be handled by the United Nations and that those contributing forces to the security force must ensure that they were subject to the United Nations command. Sukarno said that he accepted this completely and reminded the President that a battalion of Indonesian troops had just landed in the Congo and that they had been taken there by an American carrier. It was quite obvious that Sukarno was not willing to accept our interpretation of what was going on in the Congo and he asked the President if he had talked to Nkrumah, Sekou Toure[3] and Kanza,[4] the representative from the Congo. He made no reference to his support of Lumumba[5] but at least agreed that the United Nations must be supported for this was the only way. The President assured him that the United States was staying strictly out of the internal complications, but merely wanted the Congolese to be able to settle their own internal affairs without outside interference.

The President asked Sukarno if they had their own airlines and he said that the Garuda Airlines were the Indonesian national airlines; however for long trips he preferred Pan American. For this trip he had chartered a jet 707. The President recounted the early days of Pan American and the clippers that crossed the Pacific taking five days instead of a few hours now.

Sukarno asked the President where he was going to live when he retired. He said Gettysburg but he knew that having travelled and been

---

[2] Sylvanus E. Olympio, Prime Minister of Togo.
[3] President of Guinea.
[4] Thomas Kanza, the Congo's Minister-designate to the United Nations.
[5] Patrice Lumumba, Prime Minister of the Congo.

as busy as he had been that he must still think of being very active. He thought he might write a book, travel a few months every year and do a bit of painting. Someone suggested some lectures, but he said emphatically he had done enough talking and this did not interest him. Sukarno responded that he too had been approached about lecturing in universities after his presidential days. He said he wasn't interested.

The visit closed with the President showing Sukarno his paintings in his room and inviting in the entourage accompanying Sukarno. Prior to inviting the group in, pictures were taken.

287.   Memorandum of Conversation

Washington, October 7, 1960, 11:25 a.m.–12:05 p.m.

SUBJECT

Conversation With Luns

PARTICIPANTS

The President
Joseph Luns, Foreign Minister of the Netherlands
Dr. J.H. van Roijen, Ambassador of the Netherlands
Foy D. Kohler, Assistant Secretary
Philip Young, US Ambassador to the Netherlands
General Goodpaster

(The President received Foreign Minister Luns privately on the understanding that no public reference would be made to the meeting until after Mr. Luns returned to The Hague in mid-October.)

After the opening exchange of amenities and in response to a reference by the President to his reception of Indonesian President Sukarno yesterday,[1] Mr. Luns launched into a presentation of the Dutch concern about the situation of West New Guinea. In this connection he said that Sukarno, having tried four times unsuccessfully to secure a UN resolu-

Source: Eisenhower Library, Whitman File, Eisenhower Diaries. Secret; Limit Distribution. Drafted by Kohler and approved by the White House on October 12. Another copy of this memorandum of conversation is in Department of State, Central Files, 033.5611/10–760. Briefing papers for Luns' visit are *ibid.*, WE Files: Lot 63 D 221, Luns Visit 1960, and WE Files: Lot 63 D 136, Netherlands Miscellaneous.

[1] See Document 286.

tion on the question, had been saying that it was now clear the New Guinea issue could only be settled by a "surgical operation." Mr. Luns said the Dutch could not mount a substantial military effort in WNG and that the only thing which could surely stop Sukarno from aggressive action would be a US warning that it would act against such aggression. After Mr. Luns' exposition, the President asked Mr. Luns why the WNG problem had not been settled at the time of the "shotgun separation" of the Netherlands and Indonesia. Mr. Luns replied that WNG had always been separate from Indonesia. They were different races of peoples. At the Round Table Conference the Dutch had said that the Papuans were not yet in a position to make a choice. The matter was to be reconsidered in a year but in that year Indonesia had by force changed the Indonesian Union into a unitary state thus destroying the basis on which a solution had been contemplated. Since that time Sukarno had been using the Dutch as a whipping boy over the issue of WNG. Dutch nationals had been ousted, property confiscated, debts repudiated, diplomatic relations terminated. Now no instrument was left to Sukarno except the use of force. Mr. Luns reiterated the fear he had expressed to Secretary Herter in his interview on September 23 that Sukarno would stage an alleged Dutch attack on Indonesia to justify moving into West New Guinea.[2] At that point Sukarno would have Soviet support. A major crisis would develop which would also seriously affect NATO. Ambassador van Roijen supplemented Mr. Luns' statement by pointing out that Indonesia had no rights whatsoever to WNG; in fact the Dutch had proposed that this question of alleged rights and obligations be taken to the International Court of Justice but the Indonesians had refused.

The President then inquired as to the feelings of the Indonesian people about Sukarno's claims to WNG. Mr. Luns replied that the Indonesian government was a dictatorship. The people were in fact uninformed but they supported Sukarno on the basis of his political power. He went on to say that the threat to the Australian position in eastern New Guinea, if Indonesia took over WNG, would be very serious. The President replied that he recognized this and was concerned. He had made these inquiries in order to know more about the problem. He had the impression that WNG was much more an expense to the Dutch than an asset. Mr. Luns confirmed that this was the case. However, he said, the Dutch have a responsibility toward the Papuans to uphold the same principle of self-determination under which Indonesia itself had become independent. The President then asked what would happen if the West New Guineans themselves wanted to unite with the eastern part of the Island. Mr. Luns replied that this would be all right. What the Dutch

---

[2] See Document 279.

were now doing, he said, was preparing the Papuans to make a choice. It was possible that they would choose union with Australian New Guinea or that they would seek links either with the Dutch or with the Australians or with both.

The President then inquired about the state of the population in West New Guinea, particularly as respects literacy. Mr. Luns replied that there were about 500 schools including a number of high schools. The first Papuans were now ready for university studies. The Papuans were increasingly being brought into the governmental administration and the Dutch goal was to make the administration 95% Papuan at the earliest possible moment. He then repeated that the population of WNG was no kin to the Indonesians. The President asked whether they were a type of Polynesian as found in the other Pacific Islands. Mr. Luns replied affirmatively and went on to say that he had had a long talk with Prime Minister Nehru about this problem. Nehru had admitted that the Dutch were on the right track but he did not know whether this would be reflected in the Indian position in the UN. He then reiterated his fear that Sukarno would launch trumped up charges as a prelude to military intervention. He hoped that Sukarno could be discreetly warned against any such action. Ambassador Young commented that Secretary Dulles had delivered a rather sharp warning to the Indonesians in 1958 which had been effective at that time.

The President then said he had asked about the literacy situation because in his talk with Sukarno yesterday Sukarno had said that at the time of Indonesian independence 94% of the population was illiterate but that this figure had now been reduced to 40% and that the Indonesians expected to reduce it to zero by 1965. Sukarno had said that there were 15,000 new schools in Indonesia. Mr. Luns said this was a typically false statement. Sukarno himself was an example of the educational system the Dutch had developed in Indonesia and was a graduate of the University of Batavia. The President said that Sukarno had admitted this but alleged there were only eleven such graduates. Mr. Luns retorted that in his speech to the United Nations Sukarno had actually equated "democracy" with "unanimity" also. In Indonesia itself he had destroyed the free press. Mr. Luns repeated that this was a grave problem to which he would ask the President to give earnest consideration. The President replied that he would discuss the matter with Secretary Herter and that Mr. Luns could be sure that he would not forget.[3]

[Here follows discussion of other matters.]

---

[3] Tosec 71 to New York, October 12, reported on an October 10 conversation between Kohler and van Roijen regarding U.S. warnings to the Indonesians on the use of force in West New Guinea. (Department of State, Central Files, 656.9813/10–1260) See Supplement.

288.   Memorandum of Conversation

SecDel/MC/136   New York, October 12, 1960, 11:30 a.m.

SECRETARY'S DELEGATION TO THE FIFTEENTH SESSION OF
THE UNITED NATIONS GENERAL ASSEMBLY, NEW YORK

PARTICIPANTS

US	Foreign
The Secretary	H.E. Foreign Minister Soebandrio,
Mr. Henri Sokolove (FE) (Reporting	Indonesia
Officer)	Minister Nugroho, Indonesian
	Embassy, Washington

SUBJECT

Use of Force re West New Guinea

Secretary Herter opened the conversation by saying that he was glad that President Eisenhower and President Sukarno had met in Washington and had a good conversation.[1] Dr. Soebandrio agreed with the Secretary's sentiments.

Then the Secretary said that he had been disturbed by a phrase which had appeared in President Sukarno's speech before the General Assembly. The President in speaking of West Irian had used the phrase "surgical operation." The Secretary asked if this implied the use of force in the settlement of the West Irian dispute.

Dr. Soebandrio said that the problem of West Irian had existed for many years. He hoped that the Netherlands would ultimately agree to a peaceful solution of this problem. Indonesia had promised Australia that there would be no use of force in solving the problem of West Irian. However, the Dutch seemed bent on reinforcing their military in West Irian and in carrying out military reconnaissance in a provocative way. If the Dutch continue these activities it will provoke a section of the army interested in a military revenge on the Dutch and other elements in Indonesia which would not be above promoting a military conflict over West Irian. President Sukarno is trying to suppress such warlike sentiments.

Secretary Herter pointed out that the U.S. has wanted to be meticulous in assuring that U.S. arms which were being made available to In-

---

Source: Department of State, Secretary's Memoranda of Conversation: Lot 64 D 199. Secret. Drafted by Sokolove of FE and approved by S on October 19. This conversation was held at the Waldorf Towers.

[1] See Document 286.

donesia would not be used in any military conflict with the Dutch. At this point Dr. Soebandrio again referred to the Dutch activities mentioned above and Secretary Herter emphasized that he wanted to be sure that U.S. arms will not be used unless there is some provocation. Soebandrio said that Indonesia bears the possible use of NATO arms by the Dutch in this conflict; and he asked Secretary Herter to please do whatever he could to calm the Dutch. To this the Secretary replied that we have done everything we could to calm the Dutch and he repeated that we do not want to have our arms used for conflict in this dispute. Dr. Soebandrio brought this part of the conversation to a close by referring to the fact that the *Karel Doorman* seems to have disappeared. He mentioned that the cruise of the *Karel Doorman* hurt relations with Japan and he underscored the fact that the Indonesians are very sensitive about this dispute. At this point both the Secretary and the Minister agreed that the West Irian dispute gave the communists a subject on which to stir up trouble which is in accord with their general policy.

Referring to the discussion on the use of force, Dr. Soebandrio asked the Secretary for suggestions on how to solve the West Irian problem. The Secretary said that the U.S. had always hoped that the problem would be solved when the Indonesians and the Dutch set down to develop an amicable and peaceful plan. To this Soebandrio countered that the Indonesians had introduced a resolution into the United Nations calling on the Dutch to negotiate; but the resolution had failed. The Secretary then suggested that since the Dutch had turned over certain islands to the Republic of Indonesia and retained certain others, without arousing any complaint from the GOI, he wondered whether the case of West Irian could not be settled by the International Court of Justice. To this Soebandrio countered that the dispute is really a political one rather than a juridical one. Secretary Herter asked if it really is political. He expressed the belief that it is a good case for the ICJ to handle. Then he said that he understood that by using the word "political" Dr. Soebandrio was in fact drawing attention to the domestic emotion involved in the dispute.

Dr. Soebandrio, still pursuing the problem, explained that ethnic differences between various sections of Indonesia are as great as between West Irian and Indonesia. However, he felt that the Dutch were becoming more tolerant and that there was a trend "to get rid of West Irian." There was the matter of Dutch public opinion, but Dr. Soebandrio felt the Dutch public opinion would eventually permit the Dutch government to get rid of West Irian if it could find a suitable formula. He expressed the hope that the U.S. could sound out the Dutch on a solution to the dispute. Both Secretary Herter and Dr. Soebandrio discussed briefly the Luns proposal on West Irian at the U.N. and concluded that while it was unclear, he was suggesting some sort of trusteeship arrangement. Dr. Soebandrio seemed to feel that this would be a possible step in the direction of permitting the Dutch people ultimately to accept the transfer of West Irian to Indonesia.

Concluding the discussion, Secretary Herter stated that we have been counselors of moderation regarding West New Guinea.[2]

---

[2] In telegram 521 to The Hague, October 13, the Department informed the Embassy of this discussion. (Department of State, Central Files, 320/10–1360)

---

289.   Editorial Note

On October 12 the Director of the Policy Planning Staff, Gerard C. Smith, transmitted a paper entitled "The Problem of West New Guinea (West Irian)" in response to a request on July 2 by Under Secretary of State, Livingston T. Merchant, for such a study. The paper included a 12-page discussion of the problem which was defined as follows: "to determine whether the US position on the Netherlands-Indonesia controversy over West New Guinea, which is now one of neutrality, should be modified and, if so, how." In addition to the discussion section, there were 5 pages of conclusions and 1 of recommendations. The recommendations read as follows:

"1. We should refuse to participate in any joint trusteeship or condominium over West New Guinea, such as the Dutch evidently considered proposing.

"2. We should endeavor to promote a direct UN trusteeship for West New Guinea, under article 81 of the Charter, advancing for that purpose such of the considerations, set forth herein, as may be appropriate in discussions with the respective parties.

"3. Considering the requirements of tactics, the necessarily close and enduring concern of Australia with matters involving both West New Guinea and Indonesia, and our own relationships with the various parties, the preferable sequence of our approaches, in promoting such a solution, would appear to be: (a) Australia; (b) the Netherlands and Indonesia, simultaneously and through carefully selected intermediaries, provided the Australians so agree. Frank and strictly bilateral US-Australian talks, resulting in an understanding, should improve chances that further discussions with the other interested parties would be fruitful.

"4. We should, if the suggestions outlined under recommendation No. 2 meet significant resistance, explore any alternative plans which any of the interested parties may have under consideration, in order to ascertain whether they seem to merit US support; if not, we should consider whether to make the fact and nature of our démarches known to the world public, and whether to attempt to mobilize opinion in favor of a trusteeship exercised directly by the UN." (Department of State, S/P Files: Lot 67 D 548, Indonesia) See Supplement.

On October 27 Merchant forwarded the entire study to Secretary of State Herter. Merchant's covering memorandum to the Secretary reads:

"Following a series of intra-Departmental meetings on West New Guinea last summer, I requested S/P to undertake a study reevaluating our present policy. This S/P study (attached at Tab A) was completed on October 12. It is excellent, and I recommend that you read it. Mr. Kohler (EUR) and Mr. Steeves (FE) concur in its conclusions and recommendations, as do I.

"EUR and FE also recommend that no action should be attempted at the present session of the General Assembly beyond a secret unilateral approach to the Australians to be made as soon as possible. I, likewise, endorse this recommendation and recommend your approval of the recommendations of the report and this timing of action with respect to them."

Herter initialed his approval of Merchant's recommendations on October 28. (Department of State, Central Files, 656.9813/10–2760)

---

290.   Telegram From the Department of State to the Embassy in Indonesia

Washington, November 5, 1960, 4:29 p.m.

722. Ref: (a) ALUSNA Djakarta 300932Z September,[1] (b) ALUSNA Djakarta 010312Z November,[2] (c) Your 997.[3] We are naturally most con-

---

Source: Department of State, Central Files, 798.5–MSP/10–1160. Secret. Drafted by Wenzel, cleared with U/MSC and in substance with OSD/ISA/FE, and approved by Steeves. Repeated to CINCPAC.

[1] In this telegram, September 30, Lieutenant Colonel Henry A. McCartney, Naval Attaché in Djakarta, reported on several recent meetings with members of the Indonesian Navy, which included discussion of a Soviet offer of a 10-year loan of $20 million. (Ibid., 798.56/10–360) See Supplement.

[2] In this November 1 telegram, the Naval Attaché reported that the conditions of the Soviet loan to the Indonesian Navy had been resolved within the Indonesia Government. (Department of State, Central Files, 798.5621/11–160)

[3] In telegram 997, September 30, Ambassador Jones commented on telegram 300932Z (see footnote 1, above). "If in fact strong element Navy leadership here desires to keep Navy out of Soviet clutches," he noted in part, "it seems clear to me it is in US interest to help, even if this help means promising them some equipment we would rather they did not have." (Ibid., 798.5/9–3060) See Supplement.

cerned over emerging details new Soviet credit for equipment and training Indonesian Navy (ALRI). If current intelligence correct (ref a), staggering loan offer totaling over $400 million represents supreme Soviet effort bring ALRI under complete Soviet influence in coming years. As you have pointed out (ref c), if Soviet program implemented as planned, this will be the likely result.

Amount of leverage we can bring to bear on this situation however appears limited. As you know, any long-term commitment on our part furnish equipment to ALRI would involve certain political and legal considerations and, in case of providing major ships, prior Congressional authority would be required. Even if these problems were surmountable, expansion ALRI program significantly beyond present level would likely present difficult funding problem. Given current level MS appropriations and world wide requirements, it is improbable we could satisfy ALRI (even if we desired do so) if new Soviet program is indication ALRI desires.

Perhaps best basis for approach to GOI would be suggestion on our part that GOI seriously consider implications new Soviet loan from point of view its own self-interest. Unless objection perceived, request you seek early opportunity for frank discussion Soviet loan with Djuanda, Nasution and other officials as desirable, pointing out obvious dangers to Indonesia's independence inherent in massive Soviet program for ALRI. Useful peg for discussions with Djuanda might be your recent conversation (Embtel 1100)[4] during which he expressed concern over GOI financial position and stated "he was watching GOI commitments very carefully to avoid over-extension" (guidance re payment for MAP will be forthcoming shortly). If Djuanda is seriously concerned about GOI finances, it is not easily comprehensible how he could agree to huge Soviet loan for naval equipment, much of which of dubious benefit to Indonesia. You might also remind Djuanda of our actions in the past to help alleviate GOI financial difficulties (through PL–480 sales, acceptance of token rupiah payment for MAP, etc.) and point out our distress that fiscal benefits to GOI derived from such assistance could be completely negated by multi-million purchase of Soviet naval equipment.[5]

Herter

---

[4] Dated October 11. (Department of State, Central Files, 798.5–MSP/10–1160) See Supplement.

[5] In telegram 092316Z from the Naval Attaché in Djakarta to the Chief of Naval Operations, November 10, the Attaché noted that there was a growing awareness, as expressed in telegram 722, that the Soviets were determined to win the Indonesian Navy to their side. (Department of State, Central Files, 798.5621/11–960) See Supplement.

291. Telegram From Embassy in Indonesia to the Department of
State

Djakarta, December 3, 1960, noon.

1591. Parsons from Ambassador. View conflicting reports as to reshuffle of GOI Cabinet in which several Ministries would go to PKI, you
may wish to have my own assessment on developing situation.

There is no doubt but what we have been witnessing a closer rapprochement between Sukarno and Soviet bloc in last six months as well
as clear predilection on his part to protect PKI. Factors in these developments may be summarized as follows:

1. Regardless of every effort we have made to convince Sukarno to
contrary, he clearly is still suffering from misapprehension US is gunning for him. Major element in this is vast conceit which led him to interpret President Eisenhower's failure to visit Indonesia when he went to
Manila as personal snub.

2. Massive Soviet effort in economic and military aid now totalling
minimum of $750 million currently with much more to come if Soviets
can induce Army to accept help.

3. Khrushchev's playing up of Sukarno as leader Afro-Asian bloc
and potential head third force in world. This cynical but effective pan-
dering to Sukarno vanity is set off in his mind against what he considers
US lack of responsiveness if not actual antagonism to himself.

4. Sukarno's concept of western colonialism and imperialism combined with his wholly Socialist a la Indo ideas which lead him to swal-
low line without gagging.

5. Last but not least, indeed probably most important, is unanimous and vocal Soviet bloc support for Indos claim to WNG.

It now appears Sukarno has struck balance and come up with dual
answer of closer association Indo with Soviet bloc externally and natural
corollary of inclusion PKI in government here. This of course is no new
thing: Sukarno has been aiming in this direction a long time. Our policy
has been directed toward building up deterrents to hold him in check.

Principal deterrent of course has been power and anti-Communist
posture of General Nasution and Indo Army. We can still hope that this
deterrent will be effective. But I would not be discharging my responsibility if I did not provide Department with warning that Nasution may
not be able to stand up to Sukarno as issue is being developed and may

Source: Department of State, Central Files, 798.00/12–360. Secret; Priority.

be presented. Sukarno's bringing Nasakom concept under tent of Pantjasila (five principles on which Indo political philosophy based) (Embtel 1500)[1] means that, specious as such reasoning is, Nasution may be presented with simple proposition, if you are against Nasakom, you are against the Pantjasila. Sukarno may do it with mirrors or Javanese mysticism, but Nasution may be hard put to find his way through morass of mumbo jumbo and explain to people his refusal to go along. In open confrontation Sukarno he has not only to have power, but must be on the right side of issue as Indos see it.

[*less than 1 line of source text not declassified*] reports [*less than 1 line of source text not declassified*] indicate decision to include PKI in Cabinet may be announced within next week or ten days. As against this, we have positive statements from Nasution, Djuanda, Subandrio, Leimena, Jani and others who should be in position to know that what we fear and what is so widely rumored will not happen. Indeed Jani says Nasution firmer than ever this point (see ARMA CX 317).[2] I am by no means giving up hope, therefore, but I don't like the smell of things. I have asked for appointment with Sukarno in endeavor to draw him out on his current thinking. I also plan see Nasution when he returns from Sumatra.

On one thing, everyone here is agreed: That if Army is united it has power to do what it will. As I have repeatedly stated, I am convinced Nasution can and will stand up to Sukarno on this issue if issue is clear cut. But if it is foggy or if incidents in connection WNG enable Sukarno to rally country on super-charged nationalistic issue, then there is real question whether Nasution can isolate issue of communism with sufficient clarity to block Bung in what he wants to do.

Jones

---

[1] In telegram 1500, November 26, the Embassy reported that Sukarno's image of Nasakom, the unity of nationalist, religious, and Communist elements, was becoming increasingly firm. (*Ibid.*, 798.00/11–2660) See Supplement.

[2] Not found.

292. Telegram From the Department of State to the Embassy in Indonesia

Washington, December 6, 1960, 8:03 p.m.

871. Djakarta's 1568[1] and 1573,[2] The Hague's 698.[3] Department agrees desirability not let doors partially opened by Tunku close without U.S. effort encourage further discussion of issue which serving useful purpose of exposing views various interested parties and of focusing attention on liabilities inherent prolonged failure find satisfactory solution.

Believe our interest best furthered now by quiet and private expression our desire that the Tunku's mission not be abandoned. Accordingly, unless Chiefs of Mission perceive objection, following action should be taken:

For Kuala Lumpur: Ambassador should seek appointment with Tunku to reiterate our pleasure at his high-minded effort and to urge that his disappointment and chagrin at Subandrio's rejection of UN inspection commission not cause him to cease efforts, as Subandrio remarks not outright rejection Tunku's basic concept of trusteeship toward which Indonesians have indicated some flexibility. You may wish point out that Subandrio's subsequent statement that he has not yet received report from Tunku also suggests Indonesians do not wish close matter finally. If you think desirable, you may add your under-

---

Source: Department of State, Central Files, 656.9813/12–260. Secret; Limit Distribution. Drafted by Lindquist and approved by Parsons. Also sent to Kuala Lumpur and The Hague and repeated to Canberra and London.

[1] Telegram 1568, December 1, reads as follows:

"Now that first round over in Tunku mediation effort WNG believe something to be gained by US encouragement both sides maintain open mind toward further efforts. My understanding Dutch and Indo positions is tolerance for further mediation tenuous at best. Open US encouragement might tend moderate impact of pressures on both sides reject further mediation. Important, from US point of view, would also be possibility, through such action, of escaping from box Sukarno has put us in as unwilling assist settle WNG issue. I would appreciate Department's view." (*Ibid.*, 656.9813/12–160)

[2] In telegram 1573, December 2, the Embassy reported that Subandrio informed Jones on November 30 that he regretted the necessity of issuing a statement that dismissed the Tunku's proposal for sending a U.N. mission to West New Guinea. Subandrio stated that Indonesia dismissed the Tunku's mediation efforts because of mounting tensions with the Netherlands over West New Guinea. In addition, Indonesian officials believed that he did not sufficiently understand their position on West New Guinea and had conducted "public diplomacy" on the issue. (*Ibid.*, 656.9813/12–260) See Supplement.

[3] In telegram 698, December 2, Young stated that the Netherlands was prepared to discuss its problems with Indonesia at any time and any place, as long as the Indonesians realized they were not prepared to give up sovereignty over West New Guinea. Young failed to see how the United States could openly encourage mediation on West New Guinea, without jeopardizing its policy of neutrality. (Department of State, Central Files, 656.9813/12–260) See Supplement.

standing our Ambassador Djakarta suggesting Indonesian Govt keep channel open to Tunku. In event Tunku adamant his current usefulness at end, you should urge him not make final, despairing public statement, rather, that quiet withdrawal would avoid bitterness and provide springboard for future efforts should circumstances warrant. Essential you avoid any comment on substance various proposals, stressing merely our desire keep communications channel open.

For Djakarta: Ambassador should seek early opportunity suggest discreetly to Djuanda or Subandrio that abrupt alienation Tunku not in best interests Indonesia, that conciliatory gesture now would gratify fellow Asian who clearly concerned welfare of area. You may, in your discretion, observe that Subandrio statement in Singapore may be interpreted by other Asian nations, unfamiliar with intricacies WNG issue, as unreasonable attitude toward UN, that further exchange with Tunku might provide opportunity reach more understandable position.

For The Hague: Ambassador should take appropriate opportunity convey to Luns our satisfaction cordial Dutch reception Tunku, commenting this connection that we hope sincere effort by Asian leader can, with continued Dutch cooperation and openmindedness, lead to reduced tension and Cold War exploitation this issue.[4]

Herter

---

[4] In telegram 1683 from Djakarta, December 10, the Embassy indicated that it welcomed the Department's suggestions in telegram 871 and concurred with the Department's desire to keep the Tunku's mediation effort going. (Department of State, Central Files, 656.9813/12–1060) See Supplement.

In telegram 286 from Kuala Lumpur, December 12, Ambassador Byington reported that he spoke with the Malayan Prime Minister as instructed, and the Tunku's immediate reaction "was one of skepticism." He also expressed his feelings of unhappiness with both the Netherlanders and the Indonesians. (Department of State, Central Files, 656.9813/12–1260) See Supplement.

293. National Security Council Report

NSC 6023   Washington, December 19, 1960.

DRAFT STATEMENT OF U.S. POLICY ON INDONESIA

General Considerations

1. The chief danger confronting U.S. policy with respect to Indonesia is that a combination of domestic instability, burgeoning Sino-Soviet Bloc economic and military aid, and substantial local Communist strength may lead to a Communist takeover or to a policy increasingly friendly toward the Sino-Soviet Bloc on the part of whatever regime is in power. The size and importance of Indonesia, together with its strategic position in relation to Australia and Free Asia, and the serious consequences of its loss to Communist control, dictate a vigorous U.S. effort to prevent these contingencies.

2. Basically, any non-Communist Indonesian regime likely to come to power will desire to follow a "neutralist" policy, seeking aid on its own terms from both the Free World and the Bloc and balancing each off against the other. It is unlikely that any foreseeable non-Communist regime will depart from this basic policy, even though there is growing concern among Indonesians, including the Army, over the magnitude of Communist strength and the extent of aid accepted from the Bloc. Many Indonesian leaders remain suspicious of Western motives. These leaders, preoccupied with colonialism, focus their criticism on the Western European attitude toward nationalist movements in Africa and Asia, and especially toward the West New Guinea issue. Formal political commitments to either the Free World or the Soviet Bloc would constitute in their minds unacceptable abridgement of their international freedom of action; and regional military security pacts are opposed on the grounds that they increase rather than reduce international tension.

3. Indonesia has certain advantages and points of strength. It shares no common boundary with a Communist state. Although the Indonesians have an extremely low per capita cash income, a salubrious climate and fertile soil make the crushing poverty and starvation characteristic of some Asian nations rare in Indonesia. A predominantly subsistence economy cushions most Indonesians from adverse commercial and financial developments. While there is severe over-population on Java and much "shared poverty," absentee landlordism and glaring in-

---

Source: Department of State, S/S–NSC Files: Lot 63 D 351, NSC 6023 Series. Secret. Transmitted to the NSC on January 21, 1961, under cover of a memorandum from the Executive Secretary of the NSC. Approved by the President on January 2.

equalities in land distribution are almost unknown. Western concepts of individual freedom and democratic government find some parallel in the democratic structure of the Indonesian village and the Indonesian tradition of compromise and collective decision-making.

4. On the other hand, Indonesia was ill-prepared to face the problems and assume the responsibilities of independence. The educational policy of the colonial regime prevented the development of an indigenous civil service and a corps of trained professional men. Dutch economic policy militated against the growth of an Indonesian entrepreneurial class. The Dutch policy of regarding all political activity as subversive prevented the acquisition of a healthy political experience and a knowledge and understanding of political techniques; rather, a pattern of negativism, opportunism and irresponsible obstructionism has emerged. Finally, Dutch administrative policies tended to preserve and accentuate regional and ethnic differences.

5. The Indonesian Community Party (PKI)[1] is relatively well-organized, well-financed, and well-led. It is unique among Indonesian political parties in its discipline, unity of purpose, and command of the techniques of political action. It also dominates the Indonesian labor movement through its labor federation, SOBSI, and its electoral strength is particularly concentrated in central and east Java. The PKI, which has capitalized on internecine quarrels, venality, and incompetence in the non-Communist parties, demonstrated in 1957 and 1958 local elections its steadily increasing popular support. If the election scheduled originally for 1959 had been held, the PKI would probably have emerged as the largest party in Indonesia and would have been in a strong position to use this as a base to demand cabinet representation. However, it now appears that elections may be postponed until 1962. The party has established itself in a strong psychological position by refraining from overt extra-legal activities and strongly supporting Sukarno's policies and political concepts, most effectively with respect to the issues of the rebellion of 1958 and the sovereignty of West New Guinea. Recently, in an effort to discredit the present non-Communist government while sustaining superficially undiminished support for Sukarno, the PKI has directed stinging criticism at the effectiveness of government methods of achieving policy goals. At the same time, it is free of any responsibility for government failures and inadequacies since it has not been formally represented in any cabinet. Since the return to the executive-president type 1945 Constitution in mid-1959, PKI representation has been appointed to the Supreme Advisory Council, the National Planning Coun-

---

[1] There are no completely reliable figures on PKI membership, but it probably numbers at least 1,500,000. PKI claims that it is Indonesia's largest party are probably correct. [Footnote in the source text.]

cil, the "re-tooled" Parliament and the People's Consultative Congress, thus reflecting President Sukarno's conviction that all major elements of Indonesian society should have a voice in policy formation. Of the nation's highest level executive and deliberative organs, only the cabinet has thus far remained free of Communist membership. In the circumstances now prevailing, in which Sukarno is vigorously urging cooperation between nationalist, religious and Communist elements, the possibility that the PKI may be able to secure one or more cabinet posts must be recognized. Open measures of repression against the PKI, although frequently undertaken by the Army, are difficult to justify on internal political grounds, and expose their perpetrators to charges of truckling to Western pressure. At present the PKI probably lacks the resources to seize power by overt force, and postponement of the elections may delay a bid for power via the polls. However, there is a serious and continuing danger that Indonesia may fall to Communism through Government inadequacy, Communist subversion, legal political means, or, as a last resort, by violence.

6. PKI efforts have been complemented in the external field by the Sino-Soviet Bloc, which since September 1956 has offered to Indonesia approximately one billion dollars in military and economic credits. Arms and military equipment not available from Free World sources, which have pursued a policy of limited assistance to Indonesia in the military sphere, have been obtained by use of these Soviet Bloc credits. Additionally, the PKI has benefited from consistent and vigorous Soviet Bloc support of Indonesia's claim to West New Guinea and from the support, diplomatic and propaganda, offered by the Bloc during the 1958 rebellion.

7. The anti-Communist political groups in Indonesia have clearly lost ground in the recent past. However, in the past year many non-Communist leaders and political parties have demonstrated a greater realization of the Communist danger facing their country and appear more willing than before to cooperate among themselves and with the Army to give Indonesia a more effective government and check the growth of Communist strength and influence. The most recent example of this encouraging development was the establishment in mid-1960 of the Democratic League, a loose political coalition comprising Christian, Moslem, Nationalist and Socialist elements. Formation of the League was made possible by the presence of discreet Army support and, although the successes of the League were limited, the basis for future further cooperation was established. Despite this more recent tendency to cooperate among the anti- and non-Communist parties, they remain severely divided by factional strife and ideological considerations and hampered by indecisiveness and poor organization. As a result of recent Presidential action, both the Masjumi and Socialist parties have been

disbanded and, although their members continue to exert influence in anti-Communist circles as individuals, the magnitude of formal opposition to the PKI nonetheless has been significantly reduced as a result of these parties' demise. These non-Communist elements, however, continue to comprise a significant element of Indonesian society which is seeking to steer a course designed to avoid authoritarian rule in Indonesia by Sukarno, the military or the Communists. They exercise a stabilizing influence on political developments in Indonesia and, to a somewhat lesser extent, on Indonesian foreign policy expressions. In present-day Indonesia, however, a basic necessity for development of this anti-Communist potential to more effective proportions is strong military backing.

8.   The Indonesian political stage continues to be dominated by the President, the Army and the PKI. In the past two years the Army, under the leadership of General Nasution, has sharpened its awareness of Communist policy and has sought to curb wherever possible the more flagrant of the PKI acts to undermine the effectiveness of the government. In these developments, the Army has had the cooperation of First Minister Djuanda and the prominent anti-Communist elements mentioned above. The most striking development in Indonesia in the past one and a half years has been the rapid consolidation of the organs of political expression into the hands of President Sukarno. Since promulgation by decree of the present constitution of July 5, 1959, and the formation of a new cabinet in which Sukarno assumed for himself the post of Prime Minister, other top level government policy-forming organs, such as the Parliament, the Supreme Advisory Council, the National Planning Council and the People's Consultative Congress, have been either re-vamped or established on the President's terms, including appointments made personally by the President. Sukarno thus is now in a position to impose his policies on the nation through a legalistic facade of his own making. All of the government organs mentioned above, with the exception of the cabinet, contain Communist representation and thus are consonant with Sukarno's concept of "Gotong Rojong— mutual cooperation" as a means of developing his unique theory of guided democracy. Sukarno remains Indonesia's most prominent political element. He retains his position due to a number of factors. The first of these is the role that he played in the Indonesian revolution and the symbol that his person constitutes as an embodiment of the Indonesian state. He retains the respect of the Javanese masses and to a lesser extent that of common Indonesians in the outer islands. Another reason for Sukarno's position is his extraordinary, almost mystic, ability as a political practitioner. In a nation with many contending internal forces, Sukarno alone continues to be a meeting point for the conflicting ideologies and through his balancing, maneuvering, encouraging and reject-

ing he has made himself politically indispensable. Still another reason for Sukarno's prominence, a reason related to his personal popularity, is that all of the diverse political elements in the nation hope to exploit his personal stature to achieve their own ends, and one of his political techniques is that the door is never quite closed to the possibility that this or that group might be able to achieve this aim. Despite Sukarno's position, he keenly feels the lack of a strong organized mass political base loyal to him personally. Unlike other national leaders in Asia, Sukarno is neither the titular nor actual head of a political party machine. Several previous attempts to establish such a political organization, such as through the medium of the National Front for the Liberation of West Irian, have not been successful. A current campaign to develop such a political base for Sukarno may be found in the plans now being formulated for the establishment of a national political front, in which will be represented the various political and power forces of the nation. It appears that technical formation of the front may be delegated to the Army, and it may be anticipated that this will sharpen to a degree the struggle for power between Sukarno and the anti-Communist Army leadership. Although a substantial segment of the educated elite of Indonesia questions Sukarno's ability to provide constructive leadership for Indonesia, his ability as a balancer of forces, his position vis-à-vis the masses, and the lack of attainable alternatives combine to further his indispensability. He is a living national monument, a political fact of life which must be lived with.

9. The Indonesian Army is the largest element of the Indonesian armed forces. The Army and the predominantly non-Communist orientation of its officer corps represent the principal obstacles to the continued growth of Communist strength in Indonesia. This situation derives to a considerable degree from the favorable impressions made on the several hundred Indonesian officers trained in U.S. service schools, many of whom now hold responsible positions. These officers have accepted U.S. organization, equipment, and training methods and, upon return to their homeland, have exerted a strong influence in orienting the Army toward the West and toward the United States in particular.

10. Under the leadership of the anti-Communist General Nasution, the Army has assumed an increasingly powerful position in the political arena including a growing policy-making role. The Army is likely to continue to exercise considerable authority in civil affairs barring an open break between Sukarno and Nasution. The Army's increased power has in part resulted from two factors: the considerable authority it is permitted under the present "state of emergency," and the prestige accruing from its success in suppressing the regional revolt. The Army's objective is to steer a middle-of-the-road course designed to implement both in domestic and international terms Indonesia's neutralist position

in the cold war, a fundamental concept widely approved even among those Indonesians most apprehensive over the advances of the PKI. In these terms, the Army will continue to suppress and frustrate PKI aims, recognizing them as inimical to the welfare of the nation. At the same time, the Army will not accede to the demands of the extreme Moslem right which favors a theocratic state and a large measure of local autonomy. Although Navy and Air Force leaders have in the past had relatively minor influence in national affairs, their role in this respect now is increasing and they may be expected in the future to demand a more prominent part in policy decisions. Unlike the Army, which has preferred to obtain matériel support mostly from Free World sources, the Air Force in the past and more recently the Navy have turned to the Soviet Bloc for large scale assistance in procuring military hardware. There is strong evidence, however, that the decisions to obtain Soviet Bloc equipment have in part been made with some misgivings and have resulted in the recent past from an inability to obtain such items in desired quantities from the Free World.

11. Until recent years the Indonesian armed forces were equipped with weapons, aircraft and ships of varied origin and type, including Dutch, British, United States and Japanese, primarily of World War II vintage or earlier. Spurred on by the impending rebellion and the fear of a would-be Dutch attack in late 1957, the Indonesian Government began to make major purchases of military equipment abroad. Because the United States and other Free World countries were generally unwilling to sell military equipment to Indonesia at that time, approaches were made to the Soviet Bloc and an Indonesian military procurement mission was dispatched to Bloc countries. Since that time Indonesia has procured over $200 million of Bloc military equipment on long term credit terms, primarily for the Air Force (jet fighters and bombers, transports and trainers) and the Navy (patrol craft, destroyers and submarines). Army purchases of Bloc equipment (mostly standard hardware) have been relatively modest. The Indonesian Navy is currently negotiating an additional credit purchase agreement with the Soviet Union which would cover a number of heavy warships, submarines, patrol and service vessels and training reportedly totaling approximately $300 million. In view of Indonesia's "active and independent" policy and the generous Bloc offers, continuing Indonesian purchases of military equipment from the Bloc can be expected.

12. In view of the emerging importance of the military as a stabilizing and anti-Communist force in Indonesia, the United States since mid-1958 has been furnishing modest quantities of military equipment to Indonesia in response to long-standing Indonesian requests. Since Indonesia is unwilling because of its policy of non-alignment to conclude a standard military assistance agreement with the United States, this as-

sistance has been provided under a sales agreement concluded on August 13, 1958, whereby military equipment has been delivered to Indonesia for its internal security and self-defense in return for token payment in local currency. The necessary Presidential Determinations under the appropriate section of the Mutual Security Act of 1954, as amended, have been obtained to provide military programs for Indonesia not to exceed $22 million in FY 1959, $20 million in FY 1960 and $21 million in FY 1961. The large part of the U.S. equipment furnished has gone to the Indonesian Army since we regard this service as the best vehicle for maintaining a measure of stability and anti-Communist alertness in Indonesia. Smaller amounts of equipment have been furnished to the Navy and the Air Force to minimize inter-service jealousies and to avoid spotlighting the Army as an instrument of U.S. policy. U.S. assistance is believed to have contributed in part to the growing anti-Communist posture of the Army, and assistance to the Navy has helped in some measures to enhance U.S. ties with that service. U.S. relations with the leftist Air Force leadership continue to leave much to be desired although recent Air Force inquiries about U.S. equipment may possibly indicate a greater receptivity toward the procurement of U.S. military items. Taking into account the uncertainties of the Indonesian situation, U.S. military assistance to Indonesia is limited and selective and subject to continuing review in light of developments in that country. The United States also takes into account the concerns expressed by the Netherlands and Australia about a military build-up in Indonesia and the possibility of Indonesian armed action against West New Guinea. In this connection, Indonesia has now furnished the United States with written assurances that U.S.-furnished equipment will not be used against West New Guinea. In addition to the United States, other Free World countries including the United Kingdom, France, West Germany and Japan have sold substantial quantities of military equipment to Indonesia since 1958.

13. U.S. policy has for a number of years called for the provision of both technical assistance and economic aid to Indonesia. Since 1950 U.S. assistance to Indonesia in the economic sphere has totaled approximately $372 million and may be divided into three categories:

a. The grant-aid U.S. technical cooperation program has concentrated on the important problem of developing technical, professional, and managerial skills, with major emphasis on education. In addition to technical assistance furnished in a number of fields in Indonesia such as agricultural, public health, etc., over 2,000 Indonesians have been brought to the United States under the auspices of the International Cooperation Administration for various types of technical training;

b. U.S. lending agencies (Export-Import Bank, Development Loan Fund, International Cooperation Administration) have since 1950 extended a number of long-term loans to Indonesia for various economic development projects;

c. Since 1956 the United States has concluded three Public Law 480 agreements with Indonesia under which surplus agricultural commodities have been sold to Indonesia for local currency. The major part of the sales proceeds are being loaned or granted to Indonesia for economic development projects.

In the past few years Indonesia has become increasingly receptive to U.S. economic assistance and is now actively seeking such assistance. While generally quite satisfied with the substance of U.S. assistance, Indonesia has occasionally expressed dissatisfaction with the lengthy and complicated negotiations involved in U.S. aid transactions. Indonesia also receives various types of technical and economic assistance from Free World nations through the Colombo Plan. In addition, Indonesia is receiving war reparations from Japan through an agreement concluded in 1958. Since 1956, the Soviet Bloc has offered Indonesia almost a half billion dollars in economic assistance. Bloc offers have taken the form of announcements of willingness to make available large sums in the form of long-term, low interest rate credits without any indication of the specific uses of the funds. These announcements are exploited vigorously for their propaganda value, although the subsequent negotiations over the use of the funds have sometimes been considerably protracted. The initial Soviet offer in 1956 was not accepted by the Indonesians until 1958. Actual expenditures under the Bloc economic credits have to date totalled only about $80 million. Bloc equipment furnished under the programs has not always been satisfactory, although deliveries have been prompt once country decisions were made as to the nature of the goods to be imported. Considerable numbers of Bloc technicians are employed in Indonesia on these projects.

14. The Indonesian Government fiscal and financial situation, although recovered slightly from the depths suffered approximately one year ago, remains a matter of major concern. In the past three years, additional heavy burdens have been imposed on the already unstable economy by a series of developments: the outer island rebellion of 1958 which, although no longer a military threat to the central government, continues in the form of acts of economic attrition such as large-scale smuggling of rubber and copra and inciting of turmoil in the countryside which prevents the development of productive agriculture; the anti-Dutch campaign during which Dutch-owned assets were seized by the Government and thousands of Dutch nationals, many of them technicians, departed from Indonesia; and the decree effective January 1, 1960, forbidding aliens, most of whom were Chinese, to transact retail business in rural areas. Added to the above is the demonstrated inability of the Indonesian Government to develop and pursue a realistic attainable economic or fiscal plan. Such planning as has been accomplished

has failed to meet economic needs. The Indonesian masses, especially those outside metropolitan areas, live on a subsistence economy and are relatively unaffected by this situation, but the absence of economic development and the inability of the Indonesian Government to provide needed public services, such as schools, hospitals, roads and inter-island communications, have contributed to dissatisfaction and political unrest. These conditions have been exploited by the Communist Party, particularly on the overcrowded island of Java, to win popular support. Ultimately, actions to defeat Communism in Indonesia must, if they are to have any hope of success, be supplementary to long-range effective programs to improve the living standards of the masses and to demonstrate capacity for progress in solving Indonesia's serious economic and social problems.

15. The shortage of trained professional men, administrators, and technicians is an underlying obstacle to progress in the solution of Indonesia's manifold political, economic and social problems. The Indonesian Government is making strenuous efforts to remedy this deficiency, and this is one field in which U.S. assistance can pay great long-range dividends.

16. In the 1958 rebellion, the regional leaders and their rebel forces in the outer islands were no match for the government forces in regular military operations. However, the rebels are proving to be effective guerrilla fighters and are seriously harassing the government forces and hampering the re-establishment of effective civil authority in North and Central Sumatra and North Celebes. Although the rebels lack the military capability and the political following to re-establish their control of major populated areas, they have some local support and can continue guerrilla warfare for a prolonged period, creating serious economic and political problems for the central government. Although most responsible Indonesian elements will agree privately that the final solution to the 1958 rebellion lies not in military action but in political and economic concessions and reform, an unyielding attitude of President Sukarno makes it politically impossible for this realization to be stated publicly. There are recently indications, however, that secret negotiations between the Army and the rebels have taken place and that some measure of settlement ultimately may be achieved. Since Sumatra, Borneo and Celebes produce a major portion of Indonesian export earnings, they are of great significance to the Indonesian economy. Regional distrust of the central government, however, is likely to continue.

17. The unresolved dispute between Indonesia and the Netherlands over West New Guinea has become in Indonesia a major liability not only to the United States and its European allies, but also to moderate elements in Indonesia favoring a rapprochement with the Netherlands and closer ties with the Free World. It has poisoned

Dutch-Indonesian relations, and undermined Indonesia's otherwise excellent relations with Australia. Internationally the Soviet Bloc, by strongly supporting Indonesia's position in the dispute, has on frequent occasions successfully exploited Indonesia's basic policy on neutralism in the cold war by defining issues so as to practically force Indonesia's support as a matter of principle. Domestically, the PKI has used its strong support of the Indonesian position as a major implement of policy. Sukarno is again agitating the New Guinea issue, and the new Indonesian military purchases plus other evidence suggest that the Indonesians will adopt a more activist and threatening posture toward New Guinea, though overt military intervention still seems unlikely.

18. The United States cannot expect to reap the full benefits of aid to Indonesia while at the same time appearing to oppose Indonesian aspirations on the one international issue which has aroused great nationalist emotion in Indonesia and is a personal idée fixe with Sukarno. Not to support Indonesia on this issue is to leave this key gambit to the Communist Bloc. On the other hand, a reversal of U.S. policy would create grave complications with the Netherlands and Australia, with unforeseeable results. However, it should be recognized that U.S. support of Indonesia on the West New Guinea issue probably would not deflect Indonesia from pursuing a basically neutralist course.

19. Our present policy has been followed because of the serious adverse consequences which would ensue if the United States supported either the Dutch or the Indonesian position. The former would drastically reduce if not eliminate U.S. influence in Indonesia, deal a serious blow to pro-U.S. elements and be exploited by the Soviet Bloc and the PKI as proof of U.S. hostility to the aspirations of the peoples of Asia and Africa. To support Indonesia, on the other hand, would have an equally serious damaging effect both on our bilateral relations with the Netherlands and Australia and in our working relationships with the former in NATO and the latter in ANZUS. At the same time, this unresolved issue is a major deterrent to successful pursuit of U.S. objectives in Indonesia, and an armed clash between the disputants, which remains a possibility, could seriously undermine the achievement of these objectives. Accordingly, we believe it desirable to explore possible arrangements, utilizing the United Nations, of achieving a cooling-off period or of otherwise isolating the issue from cold war exploitation.

20. U.S. ability to influence Indonesian policy and government actions is limited by Indonesian:

a. Resistance to guidance and direction from any foreign source.
b. Reluctance to undertake ties and associations which would appear to bind Indonesia politically and militarily to the West.
c. Continuing suspicion that the United States may be motivated more by a desire to combat Communism in Indonesia than to assist in the establishment of a strong Indonesian state.

d. Preoccupation with colonialism, both as it relates to its own West New Guinea issue and to other current issues between Western European nations and dependent or newly independent states in Asia and Africa and the position which the United States has taken on these issues.

e. Resentment over alleged U.S moral and material assistance to the rebels.

f. Irritation, frustration, and doubt of U.S. intentions occasioned by the length of time required by the United States in the provision of military and economic assistance.

21. U.S. ability to influence Indonesian policy and actions is strengthened by the following factors:

a. The predominantly Western cultural orientation of the Indonesian governing elite and the moral and intellectual commitment of this elite to the principles of democratic, representative, government.

b. A strong desire for economic assistance, military supplies and equipment, and higher education and professional training from the United States and other Free World countries.

c. The fact that approximately 90 percent of Indonesia's trade is with the Free World.

d. The teaching of English as the first foreign language in Indonesian schools.

e. Western orientation of the Army, which results in part from training accorded Indonesian officers in U.S. service schools.

f. Difficulties, sometimes causing severe strain in relations between Indonesia and Communist China, which arise from differing policies toward Indonesia's Chinese population.

Objectives

Short-range

22. Prevention of Communist control of Indonesia, or vital parts thereof, by overt armed attack, subversion, economic domination, or other means.

Long-range

23. The establishment of a politically stable, economically viable nation, friendly to the Free World, with the will and ability to resist Communism from within and without, and the denial of its human and natural resources and strategic positions to the Sino-Soviet Bloc.

Major Policy Guidance

24. Employ all feasible means, including, in accordance with constitutional processes, the use of U.S. armed force if necessary and appropriate to prevent Indonesia or vital parts thereof from falling under Communist control by overt armed attacked, subversion, economic domination, or other means; concerting action with other nations as appropriate.

25. While seeking an ultimate pro-Free World orientation, accept Indonesia's neutralist policy, as necessary, even though the present regime maintains diplomatic, trade and cultural relations with the Sino-Soviet Bloc and is receiving Bloc military equipment and economic assistance; but endeavor to ensure that these relations are reasonably balanced by relations with the Free World.

26. Seek by official and personal relations, as well as through the general character of U.S. relations with Indonesia, to encourage Sukarno to regard the United States as a friend of Indonesia, to direct this influence into constructive channels, and to restrict and contain the harmful aspects of his influence on Indonesian political and economic development.

27. Encourage reconciliation between the rebels and the central government, and cooperation among non-Communist political and military leaders, as well as between political parties, in order to stimulate the development of a more effective non-Communist political force.

28. Maintain and strengthen existing U.S. ties with the Indonesian police and military establishment; and increase their capability to maintain internal security and combat Communist activity in Indonesia by providing appropriate arms, equipment, and training, on a limited but continuing basis. To the maximum extent practicable, U.S. training of personnel of the Indonesian armed forces should be expanded and efforts made to curtail Sino-Soviet Bloc training programs.

29. Demonstrate interest in and concern for economic development in Indonesia while avoiding actions which might be interpreted as an attempt to control or take responsibility for Indonesian economic development. To this end:

a. Encourage Indonesia to take steps such as the following to further its economic development:

(1) Improve its basic economic and fiscal policies, including the budgeting of government expenditures and a tax structure and administration which will increase government revenues.

(2) Control inflation and gradually eliminate inflationary pressures.

(3) Create a favorable climate for private investment.

(4) Reduce corruption.

(5) Expand technical, administrative, and entrepreneurial skills among Indonesian nationals.

(6) Foster diversification of the economy without neglecting stable exports.

(7) Maintain and increase close friendly commercial relations with the United States and other Free World nations.

b. Support loans to Indonesia by international organizations where consistent with relevant U.S. loan policies.

c. Encourage other Free World nations to continue measures designed to contribute to Indonesia's economic development.

    d. Continue to provide appropriate economic and technical assistance to Indonesia.
    e. Continue to provide U.S. loans for economic development which are consistent with relevant U.S. loan policies.

    30. Encourage Indonesia to improve administration and planning by modernizing laws and administrative procedures.

    31. Seek to broaden Indonesian understanding of the United States and the Free World and to convince Indonesia that closer cooperation with the Free World is desirable, by:

    a. Encouraging and assisting Indonesians to travel and study in the United States and other Free World countries.
    b. Strengthened programs for training of Indonesians.
    c. Making full use of U.S. private organizations to assist educational, cultural, medical, and scientific activities in Indonesia.
    d. Identifying the United States with willingness to assist peoples struggling with problems of independence, and emphasizing the U.S. tradition of anti-colonialism.

    32. Encourage the development of closer relations between Indonesia and other nations of Free Asia, particularly Australia, Japan, the Philippines and the Federation of Malaya, and seek opportunities for improvement in relations between Indonesia and the Netherlands.

    33. Give priority treatment to requests for assistance in programs and projects which offer opportunities to isolate the PKI, drive it into positions to open opposition to the Indonesian Government, thereby creating grounds for repressive measures politically justifiable in terms of Indonesian national self-interest.

    34. Encourage government officials and other national leaders to oppose Communist activities, to understand the relations of these activities to international Communism, to realize the danger of Communist China, and to foster such understanding and opposition throughout the Indonesian populace.

    35. Encourage the development of non- and anti-Communist labor, peasant, business and similar organizations.

    36. While for the present maintaining neutrality in the West New Guinea dispute in our relations with other governments, explore within the U.S. Government and with other interested governments solutions to this problem compatible with over-all U.S. objectives, possibly through the UN.[2]

---

[2] The NSC Planning Board prepared an 8-page financial appendix to NSC 6023, which was transmitted to the NSC and added to the policy paper on January 10, 1961. (Memorandum from Lay to the National Security Council, January 10, 1961; Department of State, S/S–NSC Files: Lot 62 D 1, NSC 6023 Series) See Supplement.

294. Memorandum From Secretary of State Herter to President Eisenhower

Washington, December 21, 1960.

SUBJECT

Approach to President Sukarno re Commutation of Death Sentence Imposed on Allen Pope[1]

In making a determination on December 9, 1960 permitting FY 1961 military assistance to Indonesia of up to $21 million without regard to the requirements of certain provisions of the Mutual Security Act of 1954, as amended,[2] you expressed the desire that at an appropriate time President Sukarno be informed of your interest in the commutation of the death sentence imposed on Allen Lawrence Pope, the American flyer who was shot down and captured in May 1958 while allegedly aiding a rebel movement in Indonesia. You indicated that such an approach to President Sukarno be in addition to instructions then contemplated and thereafter issued to the American Ambassador. Such instructions, in effect, were for the Ambassador to tell President Sukarno that there has been brought to your attention a telegram from Mrs. Pope, the flyer's wife, asking for your assistance, and to inform Sukarno that you have expressed an interest in the case.

Source: Eisenhower Library, Whitman File, Dulles–Herter Series. Secret. Parsons transmitted a draft of this memorandum to Herter on December 10, under cover of a memorandum in which Parsons explained that Mrs. Allen Pope had sent a telegram to President Eisenhower on December 8, asking him to intercede with President Sukarno to spare her husband's life. Herter approved the draft memorandum to the President without change. (Department of State, FE Files: Lot 62 D 26, Indonesia 1960) See Supplement. A note on the source text by Goodpaster indicates that this memorandum was "reported" to Eisenhower on December 22.

[1] Extensive documentation on the Pope case is in Department of State, Central Files, 298.1122 Pope.

[2] On December 7 Herter sent Eisenhower a memorandum, requesting a Presidential determination permitting the use of up to $21 million in funds for military equipment and materials to Indonesia for fiscal year 1961. (Ibid., 798.5–MSP/12–760) See Supplement. President Eisenhower approved the request on December 9, and the Department informed the Embassy in Indonesia in telegram 920, December 14. The Department instructed the Embassy to inform appropriate Indonesian officials that the United States was prepared to furnish additional military equipment and training to the Indonesian Army, Navy, and Air Force in fiscal year 1961 under the terms of the military sales agreement of August 13, 1958. (Department of State, Central Files, 798.5–MSP/12–1460) See Supplement.

On December 22, Ambassador Jones met with Air Marshal Suryadarma and informed him that the requested T–34 aircraft, approved in the Presidential Determination of December 9, would soon be delivered. Suryadarma expressed his appreciation. (Telegram 1821 from Djakarta, December 22; Department of State, Central Files, 798.5–MSP/12–2260) See Supplement.

I have considered this matter very carefully and have concluded that, for the following reasons, such an approach at this time may not be in the best interests either of Mr. Pope or United States policy in Indonesia:

1. The approach already authorized, couched more in non-political humanitarian terms, expresses your interest in a personal manner likely to be best understood and appreciated by President Sukarno.
2. A subsequent approach related, even with utmost subtlety, to our Military Assistance Program with Indonesia might be strongly resented by Sukarno as an unacceptable implicit condition to United States assistance. There is a real danger that he might reject not only the plea on behalf of Mr. Pope but United States assistance as well. United States military assistance has been directed toward strengthening, in particular, the Indonesian Army, which is western-oriented. The point which is most important in considering the merits of this approach is that our military aid program has steadily enhanced our position with these anti-Communist elements as a counter to the instability of the President. Sukarno might actually welcome an issue of this emotional nature to justify the refusal of United States aid to his forces and turn completely to the Soviets.
3. Mr. Pope has not exhausted legal avenues for amelioration of his death sentence available to him under Indonesian law. Although the Appellate Court has confirmed the death penalty imposed by the lower court, he has a right either to appeal to the Supreme Court or to petition the President of Indonesia for executive clemency. An appeal to the Supreme Court would not act as a bar to a subsequent plea for executive clemency. On the basis of a report from our Ambassador, it appears that Mr. Pope intends to perfect an appeal to the Supreme Court. President Sukarno may respond to a further approach in your name now by saying that he is powerless in the matter until a formal appeal for executive clemency is made to him in accordance with Indonesian law. An approach now might lessen the effectiveness of such action as we might wish to take at a later date.

On the basis of your Determination with respect to the Military Assistance Program for Indonesia for Fiscal Year 1961, the Department has now conveyed the substance of this program to our Ambassador in Djakarta with an authorization enabling him, in turn, to pass this information to the Indonesian authorities. Because certain factors made it important from the point of view of our policy objectives to pass this information without delay to the Indonesian Government, the Department took this action on the basis of the authorization provided by your Determination rather than hold such action in abeyance.[3]

In view of the considerations outlined in the foregoing paragraphs, I strongly concur with your opinion that the Military Assistance Program for Indonesia should not be made in any sense a quid pro quo with respect to the Pope case. Furthermore, I recommend that under present

---

[3] See footnote 2 above.

circumstances, and for the foreseeable future, such further action as we may take with respect to Mr. Pope not be related in any manner to the operation of the Military Assistance Program in Indonesia.

Christian A. Herter

---

295.   Telegram From the Embassy in Indonesia to the Department of State

Djakarta, December 27, 1960, 4 p.m.

1861. Department pass CNO for DNI. CINCPAC also for POLAD. Reference: (A) Deptel 722;[1] (B) Deptel 789;[2] (C) Embtel 1699;[3] (D) Deptel 938.[4] It has become perfectly clear that USSR reached conclusion at time of Khrushchev visit last February there was real chance of Communist success in Indonesia provided sufficient price were paid. It equally apparent that Soviets prepared give Indos anything they ask for, respective of its economic or military soundness so long as position of Sukarno and PKI strengthened vis-à-vis other Indo elements and GOI is made increasingly dependent on Soviet bloc thereby.

Source: Department of State, Central Files, 798.5–MSP/12–2760. Secret. Transmitted in two sections and also sent to CINCPAC.

[1] Document 290.

[2] Telegram 789, November 23, indicated that although the Department doubted it could bring any leverage to bear in countering the current Soviet loan offer for naval equipment, it would appreciate detailed recommendations from the Embassy regarding steps the United States might take to counter the Soviet program. (Department of State, Central Files, 798.5/9–3060) See Supplement.

[3] Telegram 1699, December 12 (also sent to CINCPAC for Admiral Felt), reported Jones' concern that U.S. unwillingness to support ALRI base development at Ratai Bay might be an invitation for the Soviets to provide the support required. (Department of State, Central Files, 798.5–MSP/12–1260) See Supplement.

Admiral Felt replied in telegram 160337Z from CINCPAC to CNO, December 15, that the considerations advanced in favor of supporting ALRI's proposal for U.S. support of its base development program at Ratai were essentially political in nature. (Department of State, WE Files: Lot 63 D 106, Indonesia) See Supplement.

[4] In telegram 938, December 27, the Department requested any comments that the Embassy might have on Department telegrams 722 and 789 in "view of imminent departure high-level GOI team for Soviet Union in connection new Soviet assistance program for ALRI and AURI." (Department of State, Central Files, 798.5–MSP/12–2760)

This policy implemented first in economic field; it is now turn of military, and there is no way in which we can prevent Soviets offering massive assistance without concern as to whether offensive capabilities, sensitivities of NATO or peace of area might be involved.

This new policy of Soviet Union has left us, broadly speaking, only three main alternatives:

1. To match or surpass Soviet offers, thus enabling Sukarno to play one of power blocs off against the other and entering into a race which would involve monumental expenditure over an indefinite period of time.
2. To decide Indo was not worth saving for the free world or could not in any event be saved, abandoning Indo to the Communist bloc.
3. To continue a moderate program of economic and military assistance sufficient to bolster the political position of our friends within Indonesia and to enable those who are willing to stand on principle to do so without being submerged by the overwhelming temptation of and pressures engendered by Soviet offers.

To Embassy it is obvious that only third alternative is practicable and offers any hope of protecting US national interest in Southeast Asia.

Embassy has sought to point out at every opportunity that the problem confronting the US is not whether Indonesia will some day have an army, navy and air force befitting the great power it intends to become, but only the direction from which help will be derived in achieving this military strength.

It is unrealistic to expect Indos to reject offers of bombers, long-range artillery, paratroop equip, capital ships and other offensive weapons merely because these come from a Communist country. Certainly the army, navy and perhaps even air force would prefer to avoid contagion of communism if there were free world alternatives. There are none at present.

In this situation all we can hope to do is prevent the Soviet drive from destroying the influence of our friends utterly. This means that we must be prepared to offer positive program contributing to goals Indos seek without being led into excessive support of those things we regard as unnecessary frills or purely offensive in character. At same time, if we insist upon being too squeamish on either ground, we invite still further Soviet offers.

Since navy is most critical immediate problem, Embassy has given most attention to countering Soviet effort in this field.

Embassy, MILTAG and Attachés have considered what means might serve counter Soviet program and remain within limitations established reference B. In connection this objective, timely arrival information re FY 1961 program (Deptel 920)[5] was helpful and it has been transmitted to officials concerned. In addition I have of course taken every opportunity point out to Indos danger of reliance on bloc military aid, but difficult impress them when US unwilling provide what they want. Case in point is Ratai Bay (Embtel 1699).

There is no likelihood entirely heading off acceptance Soviet's offer to navy in view Sukarno's desire preserve balance he considers essential to his active independent foreign policy and his desire for prestige ships. Furthermore, Indonesian naval leaders are determined to get on with their program of building a navy suitable to their archipelago nation. However, it is noteworthy that they have (as have army and initially AURI) consistently turned first to US for their needs and have accepted Soviet offer only as second alternative.

Embassy believes naval leaders would respond favorably to reasonable proposal which would serve as alternative to acceptance all vessels Soviet Union has offered. Such proposal would have to be designed assist them in beginning to develop a navy adequate to achievable national objectives, which include not only coast guard and inter-island shipping, but also internal security and self defense. In Indonesia US cannot, as it may be able do in some countries heavily dependent upon US assistance, establish mission for navy, but can perhaps lead ALRI in direction consistent with US objectives.

One positive way of doing this would be offer to assist ALRI by: (1) designing around surplus US navy electronics patrol/escort vessel particularly suited to ALRI maritime problems, (2) continuing to supply ships and equipment under grant aid, (3) assisting in mutual security military sales thru extension modest line of credit, (4) planning and supporting patrol operation base development program which would most effectively support ALRI operation and growth. Support this program with material and equipment not locally available under both sale and grant aid, (5) training ALRI personnel in both fleet operation and in logistical support activities. In this connection equipment for fleet training schools and assistance in supply and logistics essential for development of sound navy. Greater use of MTTS will not only serve military purposes but also materially aid US in gaining sympathy ALRI personnel. Indonesians could purchase patrol/escort vessel described above in sufficient numbers from Japan or elsewhere for far less than outlay for Soviet equipment. Time required to carry out such program, which would take several years, would afford time for experience to temper exaggerated expectations this youthful navy. If so, in spite of Sukarno, possibility exists not all ships offered by USSR would actually be pur-

---

[5] See footnote 2, Document 294.

chased, although he will undoubtedly see that cruiser and submarines are accepted.

In absence more positive approach as outlined above we will be left with alternative of providing as much training as possible to ALRI, in order offset to some extent Soviet training and indoctrination efforts. I am not sanguine about effect of such effort as emphasis on training officers for Soviet vessels will inevitably reduce numbers available for US training. Furthermore, content US training does not compare with intensive POL indoctrination naval trainees will receive in Soviet Union.

As for relationship to other armed forces of any program we may propose to ALRI, army is most important element there and we must therefore continue allot to it major share aid program so long as required. Any significant change in level aid to ALRI or AURI must not be at expense army program. Re AURI, indications are it beginning come our way to some extent (Embtel 1812)[6] and if we continue to be responsive we may eventually be able gradually reduce its previous heavy reliance upon bloc equipment.[7]

Jones

---

[6] Reference to telegram 1812 is apparently incorrect, since it deals with another subject.

[7] In telegram 1874 from Djakarta, December 28, Ambassador Jones referred to CINCPAC telegram 160337Z (see footnote 3 above). He indicated his agreement with Felt's view that the wisdom of assistance to the Indonesian Navy could not be measured entirely by ordinary military standards. (Department of State, Central Files, 798.5–MSP/12–2860) See Supplement.

296. Memorandum of Discussion at the 472d Meeting of the National Security Council

Washington, December 29, 1960.

[Here follow a paragraph listing the participants at the meeting and agenda items 1 and 2.]

3. *U.S. Policy on Indonesia* (NSC 5901;[1] Memo for NSC from Executive Secretary, same subject, dated June 24, 1960;[2] NSC Action No. 2215–c; SNIE 65–60;[3] NIE 65–2–59;[4] NSC 6023;[5] Memo for NSC from Executive Secretary, same subject, dated December 28, 1960[6])

Mr. Gray presented NSC 6023 to the Council. (A copy of Mr. Gray's Briefing Note is filed in the Minutes of the Meeting and another copy is attached to this Memorandum).[7]

In the course of his briefing Mr. Gray dwelt on the West New Guinea problem and asked Mr. Merchant to comment on the pros and cons of our policy on this issue, on available alternatives to present U.S. policy, and on possible solutions to the problem.

Mr. Merchant said West New Guinea represented a case where the national interests of the Netherlands and Indonesia were in direct conflict. It would be difficult to exaggerate the amount of emotion engendered in each country by this question. Powerful arguments could be adduced for the support of either the Dutch or the Indonesian position but, on balance, the Department of State believed that the West New

---

Source: Eisenhower Library, Whitman File, NSC Records. Top Secret. Prepared by Boggs.

[1] Document 177.

[2] This June 24 memorandum from Lay noted that the OCB Working Group on Indonesia had recommended, in accordance with NSC Action No. 2215–c of April 9 and in view of developments that transpired since the adoption of NSC 5901, that consideration be given to making editorial revisions in the General Considerations section of NSC 5901. (Department of State, S/S–NSC Files: Lot 63 D 351, NSC 5901—Memoranda) NSC Action No. 2215–c outlined procedures for updating NSC papers. (*Ibid.*, S/S–NSC (Miscellaneous) Files: Lot 66 D 95, Records of Action by the National Security Council)

[3] Document 252.

[4] Document 234.

[5] NSC 6023, a draft statement of policy on Indonesia (Document 293), was transmitted to the NSC on December 19, under cover of a note from James Lay. (Department of State, S/S–NSC Files: Lot 63 D 351, NSC 6023 Series) It was discussed at the December 29 meeting of the NSC and approved by the President without change on January 2.

[6] This memorandum from Lay enclosed the views of the JCS on NSC 6023. In a memorandum of December 27 from General Lemnitzer to Secretary of Defense Gates, the JCS indicated that they considered the revised draft statement of policy to be acceptable from a military point of view. (*Ibid.*)

[7] Not printed; see Supplement.

Guinea case was similar to the Kashmir case in that the U.S. must adopt a neutral attitude and endeavor to persuade both parties to "de-fuse" the issue. The Netherlands was our loyal ally in NATO. Indonesia was an important country in Southeast Asia and although it tended at times to move toward the Communist Bloc, it would probably move faster in that direction if we supported the Dutch. Another factor in this situation was the impression Indonesia had created in the Afro-Asian anti-colonial bloc, an impression that the Western countries, including the U.S., were "colonial powers." Mr. Merchant then noted that the U.S. had already begun extraordinarily secret conversations with the Australians, looking toward a solution which might eliminate Indonesia's irritation with the Dutch and reconcile the Dutch to the situation in Indonesia.

Secretary Gates said defense officials in the Netherlands were convinced that the Indonesians sooner or later would attack West New Guinea. He wondered what the U.S. would do in such an eventuality. Mr. Merchant said the U.S. had many times warned Indonesia against taking military action. Recently we had written pledges from Indonesia that it would not use U.S. equipment for aggressive purposes against West New Guinea. Mr. Dulles felt one difficulty in West New Guinea lay in the fact that we have no U.S. official constantly in the area and are hence not in a good position to get early intelligence of a major military move.

The President wondered who would be the aggressor in the event of a clash over West New Guinea. We would want to arrive at an accurate identification of the aggressor. However, the Soviets and the Communist Chinese would have a canned answer to the question of who is the aggressor. The President added that the Dutch hope West New Guinea has some value but he was unable to entertain such a hope. Mr. Merchant said West New Guinea was mostly a national fetish, a symbol of the old Dutch Empire. He added that Ambassador Jones and Mrs. Pope had had a favorable interview with Sukarno yesterday.

Mr. Dulles said that one of the fliers for the Indonesian rebel forces had recently redefected to the Sukarno government. If he confesses to his activities in the rebellion, Pope's case may be prejudiced. Secretary Gates wondered whether we could get Pope out of Indonesia. Mr. Dulles said the matter was under study. However, if we made an attempt in this direction and failed, Pope's case for clemency would be destroyed.

The President felt it was necessary to devise better ways of finding trustworthy people for government service. He was thinking about the redefector mentioned by Mr. Dulles. Such a person should not have enough information so that his confession upon redefection would be damaging. The Martin–Mitchell case[8] indicated that we did not succeed in keeping unreliable people out of sensitive jobs. The President wondered whether we were sufficiently aware of the problem and whether we were compartmentalizing the information we provided some individuals to avoid their having too wide a knowledge.

Mr. Gray then concluded the discussion of Indonesia by reading the last half of Page 3 and all of Page 4 of his Briefing Note.

The National Security Council:

a.   Discussed the draft statement of policy on the subject contained in NSC 6023; in the light of the views of the Joint Chiefs of Staff thereon, transmitted by the reference memorandum of December 28, 1960.

b.   Adopted the statement of policy in NSC 6023; and directed the NSC Planning Board to add a revised Financial Appendix thereto.

Note: NSC 6023, as adopted by the action in b above, subsequently approved by the President; and referred together with the Financial Appendix for implementation by all appropriate Executive departments and agencies of the U.S. Government, and to the Operations Coordinating Board as the coordinating agency.

[Here follows the remainder of the memorandum.]

Marion W. Boggs

---

[8] Bernon F. Mitchell and William H. Martin were two crytography experts at the National Security Agency who defected to the Soviet Union in August 1960.

Index

Abdul Rahman, Tunku ibni Al-Marhum, 504-505, 512-513, 569-570
Abdulgani, Ruslan, 48, 527n, 528
Afghanistan, 233, 472
Afro-Asian Bloc, 33
Afro-Asian Conference, Cairo, 29
Aidit, Dipa N., 93, 175
Air Coordinating Committee, 357
Air Force, Department of the, 453
Algeria, 288, 335, 439
All-Indonesian Veterans Conference, 103
Allen, George V., 330, 459
Allison, John M., 5, 6, 10, 12, 13-14, 48, 71n
Alphand, Hervé, 236
Ambon, 484, 492-493, 503
American Sales Company, 134, 142
Amory, Robert, 230
Anderson, Dillon, 350
Anderson, Robert, 53
ANZAM, 325
ANZUS, 18, 26
    Council Meetings:
    Washington, Oct. *1958*, 273n, 283-290
    Washington, Oct. *1959*, 443
    New Guinea dispute, 67, 340, 467, 580
Arellano, Lt. Gen. Alfonso, 206
Argentina, 388
Army, U.S. Department of the, 160, 177
Arneson, Harold D., 167n
Arnold, Edwin H., 58-60
Atjeh, 105
Australia (*see also Australia and Australian subheadings under other subjects*), 66, 296, 556
    Communist control of Indonesia, 171, 194
    Indonesia, relations with, 96, 287, 303, 340, 343, 349, 397, 583
    Netherlands, relations with, 431-432
    notification of U.S. aid to Indonesia, 256, 299-300, 304, 419, 455, 484
    United States, relations with, 278, 330, 431, 580

Australian Broadcasting Company, 107

Baird, Julian B., 227, 306-307
Bambu Runtjing, 102
Bandung Charter, 352
Baraduc, Jacques, 236
Barclay, Roderick E., 138
Barlian, Lt. Col., 20, 80, 118
Barnes, Robert G., 15n, 297n
Barnes, Maj. Gen. Verdi B., 230
Bauxite, 526
Beale, Howard, 107-108, 191-193, 279-281, 442
Beaudry, Robert M., 491n
Becker, Loftus E., 27, 53n, 54, 91n
Belgium, 28, 431
Bell, James D., 518, 519n, 545n, 551
Benes, Eduard, 78
Benson, Ezra Taft, 382n
Benson, Maj. George, 314, 547
Berding, Andrew H., 236
Berlin, 325, 472
Berlin, Col. Jack, 51, 53, 60, 117-119
Bernau, Phyllis D., 44n, 45n, 46n, 52, 108n, 114n, 121n, 166n, 218
Bernhard, Prince, 292, 515
Biak, 348
Bishop, Maj. Gen. William H.A., 219
Blitz stories, 6, 13n, 14, 48, 305
Blue, William L., 553n
Boggs, Marion W., 459, 485, 590
Bohlen, Charles E., 63, 140, 256
Booker, Malcolm R., 107, 191, 279, 444
Borneo, 11, 23, 81, 176, 299, 308, 339, 529, 579
Bot, Theo, 466-467
Bourguiba, Habib Kamel, 558
Brazil, 388
Bridges, Styles, 269
Brook, Norman, 219
Brown, Edmund G., 496n
Buffum, William B., 516n
Bullock, H.W., 504
Burger, J.A.W., 295n
Burgess, W. Randolph, 138, 379-381, 392
Burke, Adm. Arleigh A., 15, 89n, 99n, 188-189, 204, 522-523
Celebes revolt, 167, 202, 244

Burke, Adm. Arleigh A.—Continued
    U.S. military aid to Indonesia,
        117-119, 125, 168, 230-231, 256,
        298, 329, 566n
    U.S. military intervention in
        Indonesia, 45-46, 55
Burma, 83n, 112, 233, 397, 416, 427, 548
Byers, Lt. Gen. Clovis E., 230-231
Byington, Homer S., 570n

Cabell, Charles B., 20n, 91n, 167n, 187n,
    283
Caccia, Harold, 91-92, 99-100, 108n, 125,
    172, 219, 412
Calhoun, John A., 514n
California-Texas Oil Company
    (CALTEX), 54-60, 83, 87, 377-378
Cambodia, 95, 548
Cameron, Turner C., Jr., 27n, 122, 169,
    206, 211, 264n, 366n, 466, 508n
Canada, 279, 387
Cary, Maj. Gen. Joseph B., 230
Casey, Richard G., 26, 67, 303, 442-445
    New Guinea dispute, 279-281, 283,
        287-290, 349
    U.S. military aid to Indonesia, 271n,
        272n, 273, 274n
Castro, Fidel, 515
Celebes:
    Darul Islam rebellion, 105
    revolt in, 11, 69, 80, 86, 93, 121-122,
        148, 456
        British-U.S. talks, U.S. cease-fire
            proposal, 172-173
        capture of U.S. airman (see also
            Pope, Allen L.), 187n, 211
        cease-fire proposal, 163, 172-177,
            180, 195
        China, Republic of, military aid to,
            126-127, 131-137, 139-141, 172,
            176, 182, 184n, 185, 212, 220,
            237, 238-239, 322-323, 446
        China, Republic of, military
            intervention, 182, 184n,
            194-195, 202-204
        guerrilla warfare, 228-229, 259,
            326-327, 339, 579
        Korea, Republic of, military aid to,
            237
        Menado, fall to government of, 228,
            232, 235
        Morotai seizure by rebels, 86, 130,
            148, 194

Celebes—Continued
    revolt in—Continued
        Netherlands military aid to, 12
        Philippine military aid for, 172,
            176, 185, 212, 220-221, 237, 238,
            446
        rebel bombing, 183, 187, 189n,
            220-221, 237-238, 241-247, 249
        Sumatra rebels, rivalry with,
            400-401
        U.S. military aid to, 126, 131-137
        U.S. nationals as combatants in,
            128n, 131n
        U.S. position, 90-91, 160-162, 180,
            191-192, 211
Central Intelligence Agency (CIA), 16,
    45n, 487
Chadbourn, Philip H., 438, 466, 502-503,
    514
Chalid, Idham, 48, 79, 176, 391
Charter of the Struggle to Save the
    State, 35
Chiang Kai-min, 135
Chiang Kai-shek, 194-195, 202-204, 244,
    281
China, People's Republic of (see also
    China, People's Republic of
    subheadings under other subjects), 1,
    76, 115, 306, 397, 469, 473
    Australian recognition of, 272-273
    Indonesia, relations with, 303, 343,
        396-398, 441-442, 451, 456-460,
        497, 581
    Netherlands policy on, 281-282
    New Zealand recognition of, 272
    U.N. membership, 449
China, Republic of (see also China,
    Republic of subheadings under other
    subjects), 24, 135, 194, 398
Chinese offshore islands, 281, 442
Civil Air Transport (CAT), 109
Clark Field, 140, 142, 148
Cochran, H. Merle, 39
Cole, Col. William R., 98, 149, 160, 176-
    178, 216, 221, 235, 264, 402n, 521
Collins, Gen. J. Lawton, 350n
Collins, Brig. Gen. Richard, 19n, 488n
Colombo Plan, 397, 437, 578
    meeting, Seattle, Nov. 1958, 301n,
        304n
Colonialism, 32, 324, 335, 341, 399, 534,
    567, 572, 581

Communism. *See under* Indonesia.
Congo, Republic of the (Leopoldville), 486, 550, 552, 558
Congress, U.S., 201, 205*n*, 286
  Mutual Security Act of *1954*, 15, 298, 425
  Mutual Security Act of *1955*, 15
  Mutual Security Act of *1958*, 256, 305, 316, 338, 453-454, 577, 584
  Mutual Security Act of *1959*, 411*n*, 418
  P.L. *80-76*, 454
  P.L. *480*, 95, 182, 207, 217, 304-305, 309, 390, 549*n*, 566, 578
  Second Deficiency Appropriation Act of *1947*, 454
Copper, 66
Copra, 578
Cottrell, Sterling J., 36-37, 39*n*, 43-44, 48, 50-53, 55-58
Council of Nations, 542
Couve de Murville, Maurice, 236-237
Covert activities, 2-3, 38, 109-110
Cromwell, W. Kennedy, III, 461*n*, 466
Cuba, 411, 515
Cumming, Hugh S., Jr., 4, 125, 16*n*, 19*n*, 47, 91*n*, 99*n*, 222-224, 253*n*, 255, 396
Cutler, Robert, 16*n*, 19*n*, 30, 34*n*, 46, 55
Cyprus, 335
Czechoslovakia, 10, 13-14, 78, 246

Dale, William N., 219, 220*n*
Daridan, Jean, 236
Darul Islam, 20, 23, 93, 105, 371, 400, 443, 480
Daud Khan, Sardar Mohammed, 472
de Gaulle, Charles, 542
de Lavalette, P., 466
Dean, Patrick, 219
Defense, U.S. Department of, 16, 328, 424*n*
  U.S. military aid to Indonesia, 120*n*, 255, 293, 362-363, 367-368, 454*n*, 519*n*
Denny, Adm. Michael M., 219
Development Loan Fund (DLF), 304, 309, 373, 577
Diefenbaker, John, 279
Dien Bien Phu, 103, 397
Dillon, C. Douglas, 15*n*, 256*n*, 316*n*, 378*n*, 459, 481*n*, 546*n*
  Indonesian-U.S. relations, 371, 495*n*, 553-555

Dillon, C. Douglas—Continued
  Karel Doorman cruise, 496, 498, 503
  political situation in Indonesia, 376, 405, 413
  U.S. economic aid to Indonesia, 355, 358*n*, 372-373
  U.S. military aid to Indonesia, 292, 298, 484
  U.S. military aid to the Netherlands, 461-462, 483
Djakarta Charter, 391
Djambek, Col., 20, 35, 37
Djatikusumo, Gen., 251*n*
Djogkjakarta, Sultan of, 8, 35, 400
  cabinet role for, 175, 178-179, 184, 224, 226, 229
  Sumatra revolt, 21, 36
  visit to Washington, Feb. *1958*, 27
Djuanda, Kartawidjaja, 3, 61, 96*n*, 186, 371*n*, 417, 440, 524
  anti-Americanism, 134, 268, 270*n*
  Celebes revolt, 162, 172-177, 180, 239*n*, 241
  communism, 84-86, 127-128, 164-165, 222, 233, 468-470, 530
  military opposition to, 186, 240-241, 250-251, 574
  Indonesian-U.S. relations, 139-140, 183, 190*n*, 227-228, 300, 469
  New Guinea dispute, 153, 154*n*, 257, 570
  political situation in Indonesia, 92, 182-184, 225, 283, 337, 409, 413, 415, 568
  prime minister role for, 84, 353
  Soviet military aid to Indonesia, 12, 88, 566
  Sumatra revolt, 38, 70, 82, 118
    bombing of oil facilities, 53, 56, 58-60
    China, Republic of, military aid for, 126, 131-135
    Padang group ultimatum, 20-21, 35
  U.S. economic aid to Indonesia, 372-373
  U.S. military aid to Indonesia, 159, 277, 417, 455
    augmented program, 309*n*, 310*n*
    New Guinea, ban on use in, 260-263, 354-355
    visits to Washington, proposed, 200, 276

Douglas, James H., 203
Doyle, Vice Adm. Austin K., 202-204
Draper Committee, 350*n*
Draper, William H., 350*n*
Drumright, Everett F., 194-195, 202-204, 239
Dudley, Rear Adm., 230
Dulles, Allen W., 3-4, 24*n*, 92*n*, 99, 167*n*, 219-220, 457-459
  Celebes revolt, 80-81, 130, 187, 228-229, 326-327
  communism, 148-149, 472-473
  New Guinea dispute, Indonesian military intervention in, 289, 332, 439, 541, 591
  political situation in Indonesia, 114-116, 326, 360, 484-485
  Soviet bloc military aid to Indonesia, 11, 327
  Sumatra revolt, 14, 19-24, 26-27, 38, 52, 54-55, 65, 80-81, 86, 97, 100-101, 114, 121-122, 125, 326-327
  U.S. military aid to Indonesia, 125, 255-256
  U.S. military intervention in Indonesia, 44-45, 108-109
Dulles, John Foster, 19*n*, 24*n*, 167*n*, 201*n*, 253*n*, 298*n*, 299*n*, 390-391
  Celebes revolt, 90, 162, 172-173, 138, 187*n*, 191-192, 194, 202, 242, 244, 329
  China, People's Republic of, 281
  communism, 61, 164-166, 232-234
  economic situation in Indonesia, 234
  French-U.S. talks, 236-237
  Indonesian-U.S. relations, 48, 178, 218, 301-302, 526
    U.S. statement of friendship, 189-190, 192, 195-196
  Netherlands-Indonesian relations, 27-29, 122-124, 282, 302, 305
  Netherlands-U.S. relations, 507
  New Guinea dispute, 283-284, 292, 327-328, 485-486
    Australian position, 279-281, 327-328
    Indonesian military intervention in, 153-154, 169-171, 286-288, 294-296, 344-346, 412, 518, 519*n*, 561
  political situation in Indonesia, 36-37, 163-164, 222, 283

Dulles, John Foster—Continued
  Southeast Asia, 219-220
  Sumatra revolt, 38, 52-54, 60*n*, 63-64, 67, 71-72, 79, 88, 90-91, 97, 107-108, 110, 114, 121, 125, 138, 329
    British-U.S. talks, 91-92, 99-100
  U.S. economic aid to Indonesia, 303-304, 356
  U.S. military aid to Indonesia, 120, 125, 255-256, 263, 313
    augmented program, 300, 303, 316, 318*n*
  Netherlands position, 206-212, 284-285, 297
  U.S. military intervention in Indonesia, 44-45, 46*n*, 49, 108-110
  U.S. policy toward Indonesia, 1, 4, 252, 329

Earman, J.S., 19*n*
East Indonesian Republic movement, 23
Economic Cooperation Administration (ECA), 229
Egypt, 12, 28-29, 71, 282
Eisenhower, Dwight D., 19*n*, 81, 114, 296, 330, 526, 556-557, 558-559, 591-592
  Celebes revolt, 128*n*, 130, 326
  communism, 149, 203, 220*n*
  Indonesian-U.S. relations, 189, 201, 381, 475*n*, 495*n*, 525-527, 551, 584
  New Guinea dispute, 291-292, 533*n*, 559-561, 591
  Sukarno U.S. visits, 527, 539*n*, 541, 553, 555-559
  Sumatra revolt, 38, 55, 100-101, 125, 229, 326
  U.S. military aid to Indonesia, 263, 345*n*, 350
  U.S. military intervention in Indonesia, 49, 65, 108-110
  U.S. policy toward Indonesia, 329, 571*n*
  visits:
    China, Republic of, June *1960*, 507
    Indonesia, invitation, 373*n*, 449-451, 469, 502*n*, 506-508, 514-515, 522, 536, 553-554, 557-558, 567
    Japan, June *1960*, 506
    Philippines, June *1960*, 507, 514, 536
    South Asia, Dec. *1959*, 449-451
Eisenhower, Maj. John S.D., 507, 553*n*

Elbrick, C. Burke, 27, 122, 138, 219, 236, 264*n*, 265*n*, 299*n*
Emmons, Arthur B., III, 533*n*, 550*n*
Export-Import Bank, 228, 254, 299, 304-305, 307, 309, 321, 355-358, 577

Fales, Herbert P., 433, 441*n*, 466*n*
Far East, 33, 42*n*, 232
Farland, Joseph S., 230
Farley, Philip J., 107, 236
Farouk, King, 474
Felt, Adm. Harry D., 351-352, 362, 367, 463-464, 586*n*, 589*n*
Fessenden, Russell, 485
Finn, Richard B., 14, 230, 503
FitzGerald, Dennis A., 255
Five-Power Resolution, 552, 556-557
Foreign Ministers Meeting, Geneva, July–Aug. *1959*, 410
Fowler, James R., 461*n*
Fox, Lt. Gen. Alonzo P., 230
France (*see also* France and French subheadings under other subjects), 28, 78, 122, 288
Frear, J. Allen, Jr., 450*n*
Frost, Rear Adm. Laurence H., 19*n*, 89*n*, 150, 157-159, 162

Gani, A.K., 69
Garcia, Carlos P., 63-64, 244
Garuda Airlines, 254, 299, 304, 355-356, 558
Gates, Thomas S., Jr., 408*n*, 461, 483, 541, 546, 554, 590*n*, 591
Germany, Federal Republic of, 28
Gilroy, Harry, 505
Gleason, S. Everett, 14, 20*n*, 27, 38, 49, 55, 65, 81, 86, 101, 122, 130, 149, 229, 230, 326*n*
Goodpaster, Brig. Gen. Andrew J., Jr., 108, 291, 507, 515*n*, 555, 559, 584*n*
Graham, Frank, 75
Gray, Gordon, 327-328, 330, 590, 592
Green, Marshall, 219, 395*n*, 413*n*, 434*n*
Greene, Joseph N., 63*n*
Gromyko, Andrei A., 552
Guided democracy, 1, 196, 326, 434, 470-471
    Constitution of *1945*, 352-354, 376
    definition of, 74, 78
    mutual cooperation (*gotong rojong*), 574
    U.S. position, 36-37, 198

Hadi, 246
Hammarskjöld, Dag, 541-542
Hanafi, A.M., 75, 98, 175, 184, 224-227, 231, 246, 375
Hardi, 140
Hare, Raymond A., 466*n*, 484, 493*n*, 502-503, 514-515, 533*n*
Harr, Karl, 407
Hatta, Mohammad, 29, 76, 84, 92, 400
    all-party conference, 79-80, 82
    communism, 84-86, 127-128
    political role for, 7, 8, 54, 68, 82*n*, 118, 140, 184, 446
    political situation in Indonesia, 5, 64-65, 74, 83-86, 96, 217, 475
    Sumatra revolt, 21, 35-36, 38, 43, 112, 117, 175
Helmahera, 130
Henderson, John W., 383, 389, 419, 522*n*, 550*n*
    Karel Doorman cruise, 478-481, 489-491, 500-502, 513*n*
Henderson, Loy W., 10, 13, 71, 90*n*, 91*n*
Hensley, Stewart, 225-226
Herter, Christian A., 16*n*, 91*n*, 167*n*, 185*n*, 316*n*, 490*n*, 525*n*, 533*n*, 550, 552
    Celebes revolt, 90-91, 442-443
    Indonesian-U.S. relations, 495*n*, 551, 554, 584-586
    Karel Doorman cruise, 491, 492*n*, 493, 498-499
    nationalization of Netherlands property, 366*n*, 410-411
    Netherlands-U.S. relations, 506-508, 514*n*, 515
    New Guinea dispute, 485-487, 527, 540-542, 565
    Indonesian military intervention in, 154*n*, 438-441, 560-564
    political situation in Indonesia, 149, 352
    Sumatra revolt, 3, 35, 38, 60*n*, 90-91, 97, 442-443
    U.S. military aid to Indonesia, 117, 125, 253*n*, 255, 361, 362*n*, 486-487
    U.S. military intervention in Indonesia, 45-46, 65, 108
Hidajat, 374
Hirsch, R.S., 134
Ho Chi Minh, 359-360
Hoffman, Paul, 229

Home, Alexander Frederick Douglas, 541
Hood, Vicount Samuel, 91, 99, 172, 219, 423
Houghton, Amory, 236
Houten, Hans R. van, 485-486
Howe, Fisher, 4
Hoyer Millar, Frederick, 360
Huks, 205
Hungary, 165, 233
Hussein, Lt. Col. Ahmad, 20, 35, 37-38, 68, 93, 105
Huydecoper, Jonkheer J.L.R., 466, 480

Ibnu, Col. Sutowo, 149, 235
Imperialism, 567
India (see also India and Indian subheadings under other subjects), 77, 83n, 103, 112, 165, 233, 279, 472, 473, 561
Indonesia (see also Indonesia and Indonesian subheadings under other subjects):
    agreements with the United States:
        Civil Aviation Agreement, proposed, 254
        Cochran–Subardjo Agreement, 39
        Constabulary Agreement of Aug. 1950, 39
        Economic and Technical Assistance Agreement, Oct. 1950, 425
        Military Assistance Agreement, Aug. 1958, 260-263, 417, 419, 425, 576-577
    agriculture, 550, 557
    arms embargo, Netherlands call for, 297
    Australia, relations with, 96, 303, 340, 343, 349, 397, 583
    Australian-British-U.S. working party on, 5, 25-26
    Australian-U.S. talks, 191-193, 442-444
    British military aid to, 137, 231, 297, 313, 333, 344-345, 360, 393, 443, 486, 577
    capture of U.S. airman. See under Celebes, revolt in; see Pope, Allen L.
    China, People's Republic of:
        economic aid, 89
        military threat of, 103, 302-303, 365
        relations with, 303, 343, 396-398, 441-442, 451, 456-460, 497, 581

Indonesia—Continued
    China, Republic of, military aid to, 221
    communism (see also Communist Party of Indonesia (PKI) below), 6-9, 6, 75-781, 127-130, 246-247
    Communist Party of Indonesia (PKI), 8, 73-74, 79, 87, 93, 336, 471, 475-476, 500
        arrest of leaders, 501, 521-522
        banning of, 95, 529-530, 545
        cabinet participation, 103, 573
        Constitution of 1945, 352-354, 374-376, 391, 402-407, 408, 409-410, 414, 522, 572
        Constitution of 1950, 409, 414
        elections, 1, 8, 129, 283, 572
        electoral strength of, 1, 61, 77-78, 128, 223, 258-259, 284
        infiltration of military by, 33, 84-85, 148-149
        military opposition to, 158-159, 163, 172-174, 176-179, 181, 196-199, 203-205, 213-214, 222-224, 249-251, 261-262, 415, 436, 460, 536n, 537-538, 542-543, 544-549, 567-568, 574-576
    Muslims in, 77
    New Guinea dispute, 196, 224, 386
    opposition role for, 217, 434
    outer island revolts, 22, 24, 183, 447, 572
    Philippine position, 64
    resettlement of Chinese retailers, 499
    threats against U.S. interests, 175, 223
    U.S. position, 232-234, 268, 343, 357, 572
    Communist takeover of, 18, 33, 91n, 92, 164-166, 171, 194, 201-202, 329, 573
    Constitution of 1945, 391, 402, 403-404, 406
    corruption in, 84
    coup of Oct. 1952, 8
    coup plots, 474-475, 487-489
    Czech economic and military aid to, 11, 20n, 81, 90, 123, 254, 289, 338
    economic situation, 157, 247, 234, 259, 327, 339, 403, 416, 420-421, 496, 557, 578-579, 582-583
    education, 557, 561

Indonesia—Continued
  Egyptian military aid to, 95, 123
  elections:
    1957, 1, 8, 400, 572
    1959, 197, 258, 278, 283-284, 572
    People's Consultative Congress,
      353
  ethnic groups:
    Atjehnese, 23, 119, 372, 400
    Bataks, 101, 105
    Chinese, 126, 303, 365, 396, 448-449,
      451, 457-458, 497, 499, 578
    Javanese, 115, 534
    Menadoese, 475
    Moluccans, 23, 308
  foreign investment in, 421-422
  four-power military planning for, 125
  French military aid to, 231, 577
  French-U.S. talks, 236-237
  Germany, Federal Republic of,
    military aid to, 297, 577
  Ibu Sukarno Children's TB Hospital,
    254, 275
  Indian military aid to, 44
  interservice rivalry, 264, 314-316, 416
  Italian military aid to, 25-26, 41-42
  Japan, relations with, 343, 397, 528,
    531n, 538, 563, 578, 583
  Japanese economic and military aid
    to, 12, 181, 186, 577, 589
  Korea, Republic of, relations with,
    221, 359, 398
  literacy in, 557, 561
  Madiun coup, 1948, 102, 136, 157-158,
    196, 246
  Malaya, relations with, 343, 583
  martial law in, 458, 460
  military capabilities of, 348
  monetary reform, 85, 422-423,
    434-436, 543
  Nahdatul Ulama, see NU under
    political parties below
  nationalization of Netherlands
    property in, 5, 7, 27-30, 282, 384,
    386-387, 578
  negotiations with rebels:
    Australian intercession in, 442-444,
      448
    British position, 327

Indonesia—Continued
  Netherlands, relations with (see also
    nationalization of Netherlands
    property above), 73
  compensation agreement proposal,
    384, 386-387
  diplomatic break, 9, 498, 526, 540
  financial obligations, 11, 384
  Indonesian position, 497-499
  KPM shipping line, 88, 96
  New Guinea dispute, 340
  U.S. position, 343, 583
  Netherlands refugees, 6, 9, 123
  Netherlands ships, purchase of, 373
  Netherlands-U.S. talks, 6-9, 122-124
  neutralism, 76, 335, 342, 548, 554,
    569n, 571, 582
  Oct. 17 Affair, 102-104, 106
  oil industry, nationalization of, 305,
    523-524, 526n, 537
  partition of, 139-140
  Philippine-U.S. talks on, 63-64, 67n
  Philippines, relations with, 50, 96,
    343, 583
  Polish economic and military aid to,
    11, 289, 338
  political parties (see also Communist
    Party of Indonesia above), 78,
    336-337, 456-457
    Association of Defenders of
      Indonesian Independence
      (IPKI), 102, 104-105, 475
    Democratic League, 475-476, 573
    Masjumi, 20, 64, 85, 102-103, 105,
      129, 197, 217, 391, 415, 434,
      475, 573-574
    Murba, 375, 475
    Nationalist Party (PNI), 20-23, 82,
      87, 128-129, 197, 213, 217, 223,
      403-404, 406, 476, 488
    NU (Nahdatul Ulama), 23, 82, 105,
      175-176, 183, 197, 217, 224, 391,
      402, 406, 475-476, 488
    Socialist Party (PSI), 20, 129, 391,
      434, 475, 573-574
  political situation:
    all-party conference, 79-80, 82
    banning of political activity, 406,
      545

Indonesia—Continued
  political situation—Continued
    British position, 100
    cabinet reorganization, 217, 232
    coalition government proposal, 1
    demonstrations, banning of, 181
    Netherlands position, 411-412
    formation of new government,
      413-415, 434-435, 475-477
    Islamic influence, 402
    Karya Cabinet, 415
    military, political role of, 93-94,
      149-152, 337-338
    National Business Cabinet, 35
    National Front, 497
    non-Communist government,
      formation of, 17-18, 88, 163-164
    oil legislation, 377, 378n
    parliament, suspension of, 470-471
    People's Consultative Congress,
      353, 573-574
    Sukarno role, 60-63
  rebellion of 1958, see Celebes, revolt
    in; Sumatra, revolt in
  Revolutionary Government of the
    Republic of Indonesia (PRRI),
    19-20, 23-24, 94, 371, 400, 445,
    447, 480
  Sino-Soviet bloc economic and
    miltary aid to, 89-90, 327, 437,
    443, 567, 573, 578
  Soviet economic aid to, 11, 89, 465n,
    467-469, 472-473
    marine science institute, 484, 493,
      503
  Soviet military aid to, 132, 160, 285,
    586-589
    aircraft, 94, 194, 289, 338, 543, 576
    ships, 12, 81, 543, 565-566, 576
  Soviet Union, relations with, 62, 381,
    468-470
  State of Danger Law, 409-410
  strategic importance of, 66-67
  Swedish military aid to, 365, 369
  transport and communications
    difficulties, 550
  United States, relations with, 3, 48,
    73-80, 306-307, 398-400, 553-554
    anti-Americanism, 134, 265-271
    Netherlands-U.S. relations as
      complicating factor, 302, 310
    improvement of, 300, 342, 351, 371

Indonesia—Continued
  United States, relations
    with—Continued
    New Guinea dispute, 36-37,
      350-351
    U.S. statement of friendship, 183,
      189-190, 192, 195-196
    U.S. weapons demonstration, 143,
      148, 150, 188-189, 206, 215
    U.S. contingency planning for, 15-19
    U.S. economic aid to, 338-339,
      372-373, 435-458, 577-578
      civil aviation, 156, 164, 299, 304,
        307, 309, 355-358
      Economic Development Program, 2
      education and health, 254, 579
      electric projects, 181, 186, 254, 299,
        304, 307, 309, 426, 436
      export licences, 200, 254, 299,
        303-304
      fertilizer plants, 299, 304-305, 357
      rice, 25, 95, 124, 182, 190-191, 196,
        200, 299, 304-305
      rice-for-cotton switch, 113, 207-208
      technical assistance, 2, 197-198
      training programs, 164
      transportation, 156, 164, 181, 186,
        214, 235, 254, 299, 304, 436
    U.S. military aid to, 15, 39-40, 95,
      255-258, 284-285, 338, 358,
      576-577
      Air Force rejection of, 464-465
      aircraft, 303, 313, 368-370, 394,
        419-420, 443-444, 519-521, 584n
      augmented program, 300, 303, 309,
        311-312, 316-318, 345-347, 355n
      Australian position, 271-274,
        297-298
      Bailey bridges, 256, 311-312,
        316-317
      barracks construction, 228, 254,
        257, 549n
      benefits from giving of, 277-278,
        435-436, 565n
      British position, 137
      delay in delivery of, 329, 341
      Netherlands position, 5, 7, 206-212,
        313, 345-347
      engineering surveys, 484, 492-493,
        503
      export licenses for, 361-362, 368-370
      increases in, 230-231, 292-294

Indonesia—Continued
  U.S. military aid to—Continued
    Indonesian position, 159, 181, 197,
      262-263, 376
    infantry units, equipping of, 312,
      314-318, 350
    long-range planning for, 310-312,
      452-455
    military assistance agreements,
      417-418, 424-427
    NATO, effect on, 379-381, 392-393,
      395
    New Guinea, ban on use in,
      192-193, 260-261, 265-266, 268n,
      273, 281, 354-355, 486-487
    police equipment, 39
    public opinion on, 269-270
    request for, 117-118, 125
    token package, 30, 33-34, 155-156,
      163-164, 168, 197, 253, 262-263
    troop training, 39, 118, 254, 257,
      341, 453-455, 582
  U.S. military intervention in, 2, 49, 52,
    54-55, 65, 99, 138
  U.S. policy toward, 25-26, 252,
    334-344, 400-401, 571-583
  Western military aid to, Netherlands
    position, 28-29, 40-42
  Yugoslav military aid to, 11, 89, 338
Information Media Guarantee
  Agreement (IMG), 254
Ingraham, Edward C., 382n, 383n
International Cooperation
  Administration (ICA), 39, 264, 373,
  424n, 437, 577
International Court of Justice (ICJ), 9,
  432, 551, 560, 563
International Monetary Fund (IMF), 435
Iran, 28-29, 210, 282
Iraq, 241-243
Irian, West. See New Guinea dispute;
  West New Guinea.
Irwin, John N., II, 91n, 99n, 167n, 253n,
  550n
  U.S. military aid to Indonesia, 120n,
    125, 255-256, 292-294, 298,
    362-363, 367, 452-454
Islam, 76, 115
Islamic states, 151, 405, 407, 576
Israel, 288, 295
Italy, 78

Jandrey, Fred W., 42n, 169, 206, 211,
  294, 303n
Jani, Gen., 98, 257, 314, 465, 480, 530,
  535n, 568
Japan (see also Japan and Japanese
  subheadings under other subjects), 5,
  24, 28, 343, 386-387, 397, 528,
  531-532, 538, 563, 578, 583
Jarvis, Francis, 356n
Java, 2, 23, 32, 340, 404, 579
  Communist Party of Indonesia (PKI),
    8, 529
  Communist takeover of, 18, 24-25,
    445
  Darul Islam revolt, 105
Johnson, Robert H., 46-47, 442
Joint Chiefs of Staff (JCS), 89n, 94-95, 99,
  351
  outer islands revolts, 14, 167
  U.S. military aid to Indonesia, 120,
    156, 168, 216n, 292n, 329, 463
  U.S. policy toward Indonesia, 30-34,
    327n, 590n, 592
Jones, Howard P., 198, 496n, 56n
  anti-Americanism in Indonesia,
    267-271
  Australian-British-U.S. talks, 25-26
  Celebes revolt, 160-162, 177-179,
    220-221, 241-245
  China, Republic of, military aid to,
    126-127, 131-137, 245n, 322-323
  U.S. cease-fire proposal, 173-177,
    180
  China, People's Republic of, 441-442,
    449
  Chinese minority in Indonesia, 303
  Communists in Indonesia, 232,
    245-248, 459
    banning of PKI, 529-530
    cabinet role for, 353, 354n, 567-568
    military opposition to, 127-130,
      158-159, 181-184, 204-205,
      240-241, 249-251, 261-262,
      542-544
  Development Loan Fund, 373n
  Netherlands-Indonesian relations, 96,
    305n
  Netherlands-U.S. relations, 171n,
    323-325
  economic situation in Indonesia, 234,
    420-421

Jones, Howard P.—Continued
  Eisenhower Indonesia visit, proposal,
    450-451
  Indonesian-U.S. relations, 73-74,
    139-140, 200-201, 227-228,
    274-276, 301n
  improvements in, 300, 350-351, 392
  Sukarto U.S. visit, 535-539
  U.S. statement of friendship,
    189-190, 192
  interservice rivalry in Indonesian
    military, 264, 314-316
  Karel Doorman cruise, 478, 521-523,
    527n, 528
  New Guinea dispute, 248, 323-325,
    465-468
  Indonesian military intervention in,
    153-154, 332, 412n
  Indonesian renunciation of force in,
    209, 495n
  U.S. neutrality in, 358-360, 383n
  oil, 378, 523-524
  political situation in Indonesia, 60-63,
    82-86, 149-152, 216, 224-226,
    374-375, 402-405, 414-416
  Pope case, 218, 225, 591
  Soviet-Indonesian relations, 468-470,
    586-589
  Sukarno U.S. visit, 547n, 555n
  Sumatra revolt, 35-36, 57-60, 92-94,
    98, 235
  China, Republic of, military aid,
    126-127, 131-137
  U.S. recognition of rebel regime,
    71-72, 79-80
  U.S. economic aid to Indonesia, 95,
    191, 309, 320-322, 358, 435-438
  U.S. military aid to Indonesia,
    111-113, 119, 257-258, 269,
    277-278, 309-310, 424, 435-436,
    565n
  aircraft, 419-420, 443-444, 519n,
    584n
  military assistance agreement, 417,
    419
  New Guinea, ban on use in, 281,
    354-355
  token package, 256, 262-263
  U.S. military aid to the Netherlands,
    352n
Jones, John Wesley, 4-5, 15n
Jones, Mary Lou, 275, 320
Joxe, Louis, 236

Judd, Walter H., 449
Juliana, Queen, 292
Jusuf, Col. Andi, 161, 257, 547, 549

Kalimantan. See Borneo.
Kanza, Thomas, 558
Karel Doorman cruise:
  Australian-U.S. talks, 492-493
  British-U.S. talks, 492-493
  Netherlands position, 503-506,
    511-514
  Netherlands-Indonesian relations,
    breaking of, 526
  Indonesian military response to, 500,
    504-505, 508-510
  Indonesian position, 489-490, 493-494,
    497-503, 522-523
  Japan visit, 505, 527-529, 531-532, 538,
    563
  Malayan position, 504-505
  New Caledonia visit, 532
  Philippines visit, 505
  U.S. position, 499-500
  West New Guinea, 478-483, 485,
    490-493
Kasavubu, Joseph, 552
Kashmir, 77, 591
Kawilarang, Gen., 105, 161-162, 184n
Ketel, David H., 6, 8, 27, 40, 42, 169-170,
    206, 211, 294, 318
Khrushchev, Nikita S., 381, 567
  Five-Power Resolution, 552, 556-557
  visit to Indonesia, 465, 467-469, 479,
    484, 553, 586
Kidder, Randolph A., 236
Kleffens, Eelco van, 42n
KLM Airlines, 468
Knight, James L., 97
Knight, Robert, 362, 367, 374, 462n
Knowland, William F., 269
Kohler, Foy D., 347n, 381, 395n, 483n,
    492n, 514n, 533n, 540, 559, 561n
  New Guinea dispute, 481, 485, 565
Korea, Republic of, 24, 221, 359, 398
Korean war, 102-103
Kosaka, Zentaro, 528, 531
KPM shipping line, 88, 96, 373
Krebs, Max V., 16n, 448
Kuomintang, 396
Kusmardjo, Col. Subroto, 547
Kusumasumantri, Iwa, 104

Labor issues, 278, 336, 343, 583

Laloy, Jean, 236
Laos, 95
Laskey, Denis, 138
Lawrence, David, 97
Lay, James S., 47, 327n, 334n, 571n,
    583n, 590n
Lebanon, 245, 271, 295, 439
Ledward (U.K.), 518, 519n
Leimena, Johannes, 481, 490-491, 493,
    568
Lemnitzer, Gen. Lyman L., 590n
Lev, Daniel S., 352n
Lewis, Geoffrey, W., 410
Lewis, Maj. Gen. Millard, 19n
Libby, Vice Adm. Ruthen E., 230
Lindquist, Robert S., 569n
Lloyd, Selwyn, 25, 67, 138, 166n,
    331-333, 412, 423-424, 486, 519n
Lockheed, 356-357
Looram, Matthew J., Jr., 236
Loveday, H.M., 442
Lubis, Col. Zulkifli, 20, 35, 37, 101, 106,
    151, 188
Lumumba, Patrice, 558
Luns, Joseph, 122, 281-282, 329, 570
    Netherlands refugees, 123, 366
    Karel Doorman cruise, 499, 502n, 503-
        506, 508-511, 513, 529n, 531-532
    New Guinea dispute, 123, 291-292,
        485-487
    Indonesian military intervention in,
        153-154, 169-171, 286-288,
        294-296, 318-319, 320n, 331-334,
        364-365, 410-411, 440-441, 519n,
        559-561
    U.N. role in, 438-439, 540-542,
        559-560, 563-654
    political situation in Indonesia,
        411-412
    U.S. military aid to Indonesia, 206,
        208, 260-261, 264-266, 278n,
        284-285, 313, 345-347
    U.S. military aid to the Netherlands,
        411
    West New Guinea, civil unrest in, 124
Lyon, Cecil B., 236

MacArthur, Douglas II, 527n, 528n
MacDermot, F.F., 113n, 131, 137, 152,
    162, 211
Macmillan, Harold, 125, 219-220, 360
Magsaysay, Ramon, 205
Malaka, Tan, 102

Malaria, 557
Malaya, 24, 95, 246, 343, 388, 570, 583
Mann, Thomas C., 297n
Mao Tse-tung, 9
Marshall Plan, 78, 399
Marsudi, Maj., 216
Martin, William H., 592
Masaryk, Jan, 78
Mason, Paul, 503, 512
Mcbride, Philip, 271, 274
Mcbride, Robert H., 318n, 368n, 438n,
    466
McCartney, Lt. Col. Henry A., 314n,
    565n, 566n
McClelland, Roswell, 230
McCrea, Col. W.S, 550n
McElroy, Neil H., 120, 155
McIntyre, Laurence R., 113n, 131, 162,
    211, 251, 355
McKenzie, Lt. Col. Harry C., 463
Mein, John Gordon, 1n, 4, 10, 13-14,
    15n, 16n, 91n, 163n, 164n, 167n,
    172n, 185n, 191n, 200n, 201n, 217n,
    232, 252n, 301n, 304n, 305n, 361n,
    392n, 405n, 407n, 411n, 413n, 445n,
    459n, 462n, 466n, 481n
    economic situation in Indonesia, 422,
        496
    foreign policy of Indonesia, 395
    Karel Doorman cruise, 492n
    Nasution biography, 101-106
    NATO arms sales agreements, 40, 42
    Netherlands-Indonesian relations, 4-6
    New Guinea dispute, 279, 318, 364,
        438, 480
    outer island revolts, 107, 442, 444
    political situation in Indonesia, 196,
        199, 390, 409-410, 416n, 434-435,
        470-471, 474-478
    U.S. military aid to Indonesia, 125,
        255, 300, 484
    U.S. military intervention in
        Indonesia, 116
Menzies, Robert G., 271-274, 331, 349,
    374, 431-432, 460-461
Merchant, Livingston T., 316n, 410,
    481n, 514-515, 545, 546n
    New Guinea dispute, 318-320,
        423-424, 516, 517n, 518n, 564-565,
        590-591
    U.S. military aid to Indonesia, 361n,
        368-370, 381, 394

Mexico, 387-388
Middle East, 95, 243-244, 249, 251n
Military Assistance Advisory Group
   (MAAG), 293, 481n
Military Assistance Program (MAP),
   294, 455, 462, 482-483, 566
Miller, Dudley W., 283n, 300
MILTAG, 367, 418, 453, 463-464, 521,
   587
Minnehasa (see also Celebes), 139
Mitchell, Bernon F., 592
Moluccas, 23, 484
Moore, Robert W., 361n, 367n, 376n,
   405n, 407n, 409n, 411n, 413n, 418n,
   424n, 434n, 459n, 467n, 470n, 474n,
   490n, 508n
Morotai, 86, 130, 148, 194
Moslem Youth Group (GPII), 23
Mukarto, Nodowidigdo, 196, 390
   communism, 196, 217-218, 228
   Indonesian-U.S. relations, 197-199,
      227, 525-527, 533n
   New Guinea dispute, 196, 495
   U.S. economic aid to Indonesia, 321,
      357
Munro, Leslie, 116-117
Murphy, Robert D., 14-15, 19n, 25, 39n,
   66, 125, 230-231, 297n, 352n, 405n,
   407, 408n, 413n, 438n
Musa, 136
Mutual Defense Assistance Program,
   262n

Nainggolan, Maj. W.F., 98
Nasakom, 568, 573
Nash, Walter, 116-117, 125, 283, 289
Nasser, Gamal Abdul, 9, 12, 76, 237,
   281, 302
Nasution, Maj. Gen. Abdul Haris, 94,
   101-106, 197, 397
   Celebes revolt, 161-162, 173-174,
      176-177, 221n, 243, 442
   communism, 85, 128, 446
   coup plots, 475, 488-489
   economic situation in Indonesia, 417
   interservice rivalry in Indonesian
      military, 264, 416
   Japanese economic aid, 186
   Karel Doorman cruise, 500-501
   military opposition to communism,
      250-251, 543-544
      appointment of political officers,
         240-241

Nasution, Maj. Gen. Abdul
   Haris—Continued
   military opposition to
      communism—Continued
      banning of PKI, 529-530
      outer islands revolts, effect on, 172,
         179
      U.S. position, 164-166, 213-214, 222,
         284, 542-549
   Netherlands view of, 7, 440, 512
   political role of, 118-120, 337-338, 371,
      402, 413, 415, 436, 485
   political situation in Indonesia, 226,
      284, 374-375, 406, 476-477
   Soviet military aid to Indonesia, 566
   State of Danger Law, 409-410
   Sukarno-military split, 268, 276, 535n,
      536
   Sumatra revolt, 21, 35-36, 68, 112, 442
   U.S. economic aid to Indonesia, 235
   U.S. military aid to Indonesia, 231,
      233-234, 255, 257-258, 260, 263,
      309n, 311-312, 317, 417, 424n,
      427n, 455, 520-521
   U.S. support for, 167-168
   visits:
      Washington, Oct. 1960, 542,
         545-550, 553n, 554
      Washington, proposed, 113, 200,
         216, 276
National Advisory Council (NAC)
   Document No. 88, 356
National Council, 1, 7, 35, 85
National Front for the Liberation of
   West Irian, 575
National Intelligence Estimate NIE
   65-2-59, 456-457, 590
National Security Council (NSC):
   actions:
      No. 1788, 3, 31, 327
      No. 2215, 590
   documents:
      NSC 5518, 2, 30, 47, 327
      NSC 5901, 327, 329-330, 334-344,
         535, 590n
      NSC 6023, 571-583, 590, 592
   Special Committee Report on
      Indonesia, 2-3, 31, 47, 327
   meetings:
      350th (Jan. 6, 1958), 11
      352d (Jan. 22, 1958), 14
      353d (Jan. 30, 1958), 20n

National Security Council—Continued
meetings—Continued
354th (Feb. 6, 1958), 26-27
355th (Feb. 13, 1958), 38
356th (Feb. 27, 1958), 49
357th (Mar. 6, 1958), 54
358th (Mar. 13, 1958), 65
359th (Mar. 20, 1958), 80-81
360th (Mar. 27, 1958), 86
362d (Apr. 14, 1958), 100-101
363d (Apr. 24, 1948), 121-122
364th (May 1, 1958), 130
365th (May 8, 1958), 148-149
370th (June 26, 1958), 228-229
395th (Jan. 29, 1959), 326-330
422d (Oct. 29, 1959), 441-442
429th (Dec. 16, 1959), 457-459
436th (Mar. 10, 1960), 472-473
442d (Apr. 28, 1960), 484-485
472d (Dec. 29, 1960), 590-592
Natsir, Mohammed, 8, 85, 151
Nehru, Jawaharlal, 165, 233, 246, 279, 473, 552n, 561
Netherlands (see also Karel Doorman cruise; Netherlands subheadings under other subjects), 28, 570
Australia, relations with, 431-432
Netherlands Information Service, 509
First Chamber of Parliament, 170
Indonesia, relations with, see Netherlands, relations with under Indonesia
Indonesian refugees in, 123
Japan, relations with, 28, 528, 531-532
Labor Party, 295
political situation, 388, 563
United Kingdom, relations with, 328
United States, relations with, 77, 293, 323-325, 330, 406, 542
Eisenhower visit to Indonesia, 502n, 506-508, 514-515
New Guinea dispute, 4-5, 278, 323-325, 430-431, 467-468, 580
U.S. military aid to, 332, 351-352, 394, 411, 428n, 440, 461-462, 482
U.S. military aid to Indonesia, notification of, 256, 260-261, 264-266, 299-300, 304, 345-347, 362, 368-370, 380, 392-395, 419, 455, 484
Netherlands East Indies Army, 102, 104
Netherlands Indies, 551

neutralism, 76, 306, 335, 342, 417, 457, 520, 569
New Guinea, 66-67, 366, 466n, 467, 560-561
New Guinea dispute (see also Karel Doorman cruise), 4-5, 36-37, 224, 247-248, 335, 431, 533-534
Australian position, 280, 327, 349, 360, 411, 486, 534, 560
Australian-U.S. relations, 278
Australian-U.S. talks on, 67, 564-565, 591
Biak, reinforcement of, 478-479, 481
British-Netherlands talks on, 519n
British position, 328, 431, 486
British-U.S. talks, 344-345, 518-519
cold war context for, 283-284, 324
cooling-off period, proposal for, 96, 248, 580
decolonization, 323-325
Indonesian claims to West New Guinea, 76, 432-433
Indonesian military intervention in, 192-193, 347-348, 364-365, 457, 541, 562-564
Australian position, 320n, 510
British position, 313n, 320n, 344, 412n, 423-424, 510, 512
Netherlands position, 169-171, 282, 294-296, 410-411, 559-561
planning for, 412, 440-441, 467
U.S. actions in the event of, 286-288, 294-296
U.S. position, 169-171, 300, 345, 380, 412n, 518, 519n
Indonesian renunciation of force in, 209, 257, 302, 408, 460-461, 495-496, 508, 590-591
International Court of Justice role in, 9, 432, 551, 560, 563
Karel Doorman, visits by, 478-483, 485, 489-493
Malayan position, 569-570
Netherlands, 123, 278, 327-328, 516-517, 563
Indonesia, talks with, 465-468, 563, 569n
internal opposition in, 324, 328, 344
United States, relations with, 67, 318-320, 331-334
North Atlantic Treaty Organization, 41, 207, 379-381, 388, 440, 489n

New Guinea dispute—Continued
    Philippine position, 280
    PKI position, 196
    Soviet position, 37, 560, 567, 573
    Sukarno role in, 61-62
    U.N. resolutions, Indonesian, 438,
        559-560
    U.N. role in, 516-517, 580
    U.N. trusteeship, 384-389, 540,
        563-565, 569-570
        Burger motion, 295
        five-year proposal, 428-433
    U.S. position, 77, 323-325, 327, 340,
        344, 358-359, 382-384, 499-500,
        517-518, 534-535, 564-565,
        579-580, 590-591
    Vietnam, Democratic Republic,
        position, 359
Nixon, Richard M., 381, 458-459,
    551-552
Nkrumah, Kwame, 552
Noor, 76
North Atlantic Council (NAC), 40-42,
    153, 265, 333, 478n
    21st Ministerial Meeting,
        Copenhagen, May 1958, 138,
        169-170
    22d Ministerial Meeting, Paris, Dec.
        1958, 313
    25th Ministerial Meeting, Istanbul,
        May 1960, 485n
North Atlantic Treaty Organization
    (NATO), 366n, 538
    arm sales agreements, 40-42
    Heads of Government meeting, Paris,
        Dec., 1957, 25, 291
    Karel Doorman cruise, 489
    Netherlands role in, 515n, 542n, 580
    New Guinea dispute, 67, 207, 411,
        340, 379-381, 388, 392-393, 395,
        428n, 431, 440, 478n, 551, 560
Nugroho, 562

O'Connor, Jeremiah J., 408n, 416n
Oda, Takia, 527-528, 531n
O'Donnell, Adm. Edward J., 367, 374
Oil, 66, 290, 523-524, 526
Okinawa, 325
Olmsted, Mary S., 356n, 377n, 434n
Olympio, Sylvanus E., 558
Operations Coordinating Board (OCB),
    19n

O'Sullivan, James L., 6, 25n, 232n, 376n,
    434n
Outer islands (see also individual islands),
    1, 2, 19-20, 404, 445-447

Pak Yu, 203
Pakistan, 77, 416, 425
Paku Alam, 321
Palmer, Stephen E., Jr., 376n, 516n
Pan-American Airlines, 558
Pantjasila, 75-76, 151-152, 196, 247, 249,
    301, 375, 568
Papuans, 366, 385, 431, 440, 486, 499,
    516, 534, 560-561
Parsons, J. Graham, 91n, 163n, 164n,
    200n, 207, 252n, 266n, 269n, 297n,
    301n, 303n, 316n, 352n, 361n, 391,
    392n, 395n, 416n, 418n, 448,
    459-460, 462n, 466n, 467n, 527n,
    533n, 569n, 584n
    communism, 542, 545-549, 567
    Constitution of 1945, 390, 407-410
    coup plots, 487n
    economic situation in Indonesia, 422,
        496
    Eisenhower Indonesia visit, proposal,
        450, 451n
    Indonesian-U.S. relations, 525, 535,
        549-550
    Karel Doorman cruise, 481-483, 492,
        493n
    New Guinea dispute, 495, 540
    outer islands revolts, 52, 71, 442
    political situation in Indonesia, 54,
        283, 413-414, 434, 470
    U.S. military aid to Indonesia, 125,
        255, 424-427, 452, 484
Pate, Gen. Randolph M., 230
People's Consultative Congress,
    470-471
Perbepsi, 103
Permanent Court of Arbitration, 432
Permesta, 480
Peron, Juan, 474
Peterson, Avery F., 546
Philippines, 24, 66, 264, 388
    Communist control of Indonesia, 91n,
        171, 194
    Indonesia, relations with, 50, 96, 343,
        583
Phillips, Col., 230
Picher, Lt. Gen. Oliver S., 230

Pilcher, John L., 448
Plimsoll, James, 279
Pope, Allen L., 187n, 211, 214, 216, 218,
    225, 239, 242, 278, 461, 584-586, 591
Porter, Dwight J., 138
Portugal, 431
Post, Rear Adm. William S., Jr., 292n
Prawiranegara, Sjafruddin, 8, 38, 85, 97,
    188
Prijono, 75, 375
PRRI. See Revolutionary Government of
    the Republic of Indonesia (PRRI)
    under Indonesia.
Pushtoonistan, 472

Quarles, Donald A., 328, 461
de Quay, Jan E., 406, 505, 511-513

Raymond, John M., 218
Reams, Robert B., 16n, 91n, 167n
Reinhardt, George F., 99, 138, 219, 230
Rewinkel, Milton C., 423
Rhee, Syngman, 281, 359
Rice, 85, 89, 95, 182, 207, 304-305, 557
Richards, Arthur L., 19n, 35n
Riley, Vice Adm. Herbert, 204, 240,
    241n
Robbins, Capt., 255
Roberts, Frank, 138
Robertson, Walter S., 5, 10, 13, 19n, 39n,
    53n, 91n, 99n, 113n, 163n, 164n,
    167n, 185n, 217, 230-231, 232n,
    266n, 267, 287, 301n, 364, 390-395
    Celebes revolt, 160, 187n, 220
    China, Republic of, military aid to
        rebels, 194, 202, 323n
    U.S. cease-fire proposal, 172-173,
        184n
    communism, 61, 91, 181-184, 204,
        205n
    Communist takeover of Indonesia,
        90, 91n, 201-202
    foreign policy of Indonesia, 395
    guided democracy, 352-354, 376
    Indonesian-U.S. relations, 73, 136-137,
        200n, 201-202, 274, 392
    Nasution biography, 101
    NATO arms sales agreement, 40-42
    New Guinea dispute, 154n, 169, 171,
        279, 281, 294, 364-366
    political situation in Indonesia, 217,
        405-406
    Sukarno, political role, 6-9, 276n

Robertson, Walter S.—Continued
    Sumatra revolt, 16-17, 54, 63-64,
        70-71, 98
    U.S. economic aid to Indonesia, 321n,
        355-358
    U.S. military aid to Indonesia, 15,
        111-113, 125, 255-256, 269-270,
        281, 284-285, 379
        aircraft, 361-362, 368-370
        augmented program, 300, 316-318
        barracks construction, 228, 252
        Netherlands position, 206, 210-212,
            297-298, 299n
        long-range planning for, 362,
            367-368
    U.S. military intervention in
        Indonesia, 108, 116-117
    U.S. policy on Indonesia, 1-3, 252
Rockwell, Stewart, 230
Roem, Mohammed, 8, 82
Roijen, Jan H. van, 122
    Netherlands refugees, 6, 9
    Netherlands-U.S. relations, 506-507,
        514-515
    Karel Doorman cruise, 492, 493n, 511,
        513-514
    nationalization of Netherlands
        property in Indonesia, 27-30
    New Guinea dispute:
        Indonesian military intervention in,
            169-171, 294-296, 318-320, 364,
            480n, 561n, 559-560
        U.N. role in, 438, 516-517
        U.S. economic aid to Indonesia, 124
        U.S. military aid to Indonesia,
            206-212, 347n, 368-370, 484,
            502-503
        U.S. military aid to the Netherlands,
            462n
Round Table Conference, 1949, 485
Royal Netherlands/Shell, 377-378
Rubber, 66, 360, 578
Rukmito, Col., 132
Rumbold, Anthony, 138
Saleh, 75
Samba, Maj., 238
Sarbini, Col., 416
Sarit, Field Marshal Thanarat, 326
Sartono, 20
Schiff, Emil L.C., 438, 466, 502, 516
Schow, Maj. Gen. Robert A., 19n
Schurmann, Carl W.A., 540

Scott, Robert H., 100
Sebald, William J., 271-274
Sebilleau, Pierre, 236
Senate Foreign Relations Committee,
    136, 358*n*
Serrano, Felixberto M., 63-64, 140, 280
Shell Oil Co., 377-378, 523-524, 526*n*
Shuman, Perry, 216, 221
Silawangi Division, 23
Simatupang, Gen. T.B., 105, 397
Simbolon, Col., 8, 20, 35, 37, 105
Singapore, 46, 171, 271, 397, 448, 570
Smith, Bromley, 533*n*
Smith, Gerard C., 230, 518*n*, 564
Smith, H. Alexander, 358-359
Sneider, Robert L., 527*n*
SOBSI, 336, 572
Soerjosoerarso, Col. R.M.S., 549
Sokolove, Henri, 562
Southeast Asia, 33, 66, 219-220
Southeast Asia Treaty Organization
    (SEATO), 33, 95, 132, 233, 306, 538
  British membership, 398
  Council meetings:
    Manila, Mar. *1958*, 60*n*, 63, 125
    Washington, May–June *1960*, 510
    Wellington, Apr. *1959*, 371*n*
  French membership, 398
  Indonesian position, 83, 87, 104, 398,
    548
  New Guinea dispute, 67, 428*n*, 467
  Sumatra revolt, 44, 50
Soviet Union, 1, 12, 233, 306
  China, People's Republic of, relations
    with, 469, 473
  Indonesia, relations with, 11, 62, 381,
    468-470
Special National Intelligence Estimates:
  SNIE *65–58*, 258-259, 327
  SNIE *65–59*, 347-348
  SNIE *65–60*, 487-489, 590
  SNIE *65–2–60*, 499-500
Sprague, Mansfield D., 25, 66-67, 230,
    256*n*
Stabler, Wells, 284*n*, 294, 301*n*, 318, 364,
    368*n*
Staf, Cornelis, 292, 351*n*, 461
Stalin Peace Prize, 75
Standard Vacuum Oil Co. (STANVAC),
    51-53, 60, 87, 117, 305, 371, 377-378
State of Danger Law, 409-410

Steeves, John M., 454*n*, 459*n*, 474, 480*n*,
    481*n*, 490*n*, 517*n*, 518-519, 551*n*,
    553, 555, 565
Stewart, Allen, 230
Stoessel, Walter J., 533*n*
Stroh, Adm. Robert J., 255-256
Stump, Adm. Felix B., 5, 19*n*, 108,
    204-206, 213
  Celebes revolt, 202-203, 244-245
  Indonesian-U.S. relations, 148, 150,
    158, 188-189, 206, 215
  U.S. military aid to Indonesia, 216*n*,
    255
Subandrio:
  anti-Americanism, 270*n*
  cabinet role for, 413
  Celebes revolt, 126, 220-221, 237,
    241-243, 244*n*
  China, People's Republic of, 302-303,
    396
  communism, 127-130, 172-274, 222,
    251, 264-265
  Netherlands refugees, 9
  Netherlands view of, 412
  economic situation in Indonesia, 496
  foreign policy of Indonesia, 417
  Indonesian-U.S. relations, 36-37,
    73-74, 139, 183, 189*n*, 190*n*, 227,
    241*n*, 277, 300, 301, 371, 399,
    535*n*, 558
  Japanese economic aid, 186
  Karel Doorman cruise, 479, 492,
    497-499, 503
  nationalization of Netherlands
    property in Indonesia, 302,
    305-306
  New Guinea dispute, 465, 466*n*,
    569-570
  Indonesian military intervention in,
    153-154, 345-346, 412*n*, 439,
    541, 562-564
  renunciation of the use of force,
    209, 495-496, 508
  oil industry, nationalization of, 524
  political situation in Indonesia, 60-63,
    224-225, 374-375, 390-392, 406,
    497, 568
  resettlement of Chinese retailers, 497,
    499
  Southeast Asia Treaty Organization,
    88

Subandrio—Continued
Soviet Union, 472
Sumatra revolt, 43-44, 50, 53, 55-58,
62, 70-72, 126
U.S. economic aid to Indonesia, 191,
214, 322, 424n
U.S. military aid to Indonesia, 39n,
197, 260-261
visits:
Australia, Feb. 1959, 303, 347, 349,
351, 355, 396
China, People's Republic of, 1959,
441
Cuba, May 1960, 494, 496, 508
South Asia-Mideast, Jan.–Feb. 1958,
11
Washington, Oct. 1957, 61n
Washington, June 1959, 200,
304-306, 390n
Washington, May 1960, 495-499,
523
Washington, Oct. 1960, 555
Subardjo, Achmad, 39
Subijakto, Adm., 158, 263, 375
Subroto, Gen. Gatot, 8, 149, 184n, 188,
205, 314, 549
Subroto, Lt. Col. Kusmardjo, 549
Subyakto, Adm. See Subijakto, Adm.
Sudirman, Gen., 151
Suez Canal, 28
Sukanto, 83, 86, 400
Sukardjo, Lt. Col., 98
Sukarno, 84, 106, 280-281, 326, 359-360,
371n, 373-374, 505, 512-513
anti-Americanism of, 265-271
assassination attempt on, 6, 35
Celebes revolt, 195, 241-243, 245
China, People's Republic of, 9,
441-442, 448-449
communism, 92-93, 75, 114-115,
127-129, 164, 168, 172-175, 179,
205, 229, 232-234, 246-247,
249-251, 259, 436, 522, 529, 536
Communist influence on, 3, 61-62,
196-198, 213, 220, 284, 301, 415
coup plots, 475, 488-489
economic situation in Indonesia,
420-421, 557
Eisenhower Indonesia visit, proposal,
522, 557-558
Five-Power U.N. resolution, 556
foreign investment, 421-422
Indonesian views of, 61-63

Sukarno—Continued
Indonesian-U.S. relations, 4, 48, 74-80,
190n, 227, 271, 275, 300, 306-307,
342, 350-351, 551, 553, 582, 591
invitation for Eisenhower visit,
449-451
Karel Doorman cruise, 478-480,
522-523
martial law, 458, 460
Middle East, 249
military, relations with, 484-485, 549
nationalization of Netherlands
property, 305
Netherlands view of, 412, 440,
511-512
Netherlands-Indonesian relations,
526n
neutralism, 520
New Guinea dispute, 73, 247-248,
261-263, 358-359, 460-461, 559-560
Indonesian military intervention in,
153, 380, 541, 562, 580
oil, nationalization of, 523-524
outer islands revolts, 327, 446
Pantjasila, 75-76
political role of, 74, 275-276, 402-410
political situation in Indonesia, 1, 283,
436, 470-471
all-party conference, 79-80, 82
banning of political activity, 529,
545
Constitution of 1945, 352-353,
375-376, 391-392
formation of new government, 96,
224-226, 413-415, 475-477
popular support for, 118, 159, 308
Soviet military aid to Indonesia, 465n,
467-469, 472-473, 586-589
Soviet view of, 90
Sumatra revolt, 20-22, 26, 35-36, 38,
43, 49, 54, 68-69, 98, 107-108
U.N. speech, 535n, 539
U.S. economic aid to Indonesia, 13,
191, 321-322, 357
U.S. military aid to Indonesia,
111-112, 125, 231, 261-263, 277,
309-310, 419-420, 443-444
U.S. view of, 3, 5, 201, 223, 236-237,
337, 456-457, 473-474, 574-575
visits:
Asia, Europe, Latin America,
Apr.–June 1959, 352, 359n,
402n, 468, 488, 492, 494

Sukarno—Continued
  visits—Continued
    Latin America, 7
    Los Angeles, June 1959, 359,
      381-382, 391-392
    Sino-Soviet bloc, Aug.–Oct. 1956,
      76
    South Asia-Mideast, Jan.–Feb. 1958,
      6-7, 11
    United States, May 1956, 75n, 76,
      527, 555
    Washington, Oct. 1960, 535-539,
      541-542, 547n, 553-559, 562
Sukarno, Madame, 178
Sukendro, Col., 98, 149, 176-179,
    188-189, 205, 403-404
  Karel Doorman cruise, 500-502, 513n
  outer islands revolts, 442, 448
  U.S. military aid to Indonesia,
    157-159, 214-216, 315n
Sukiman, 262
Sulawesi. See Celebes.
Sumatra, 16, 339, 529
  revolt in, 11
    airdrops of U.S. arms, 70-71, 97,
      226
    Australian position, 107-108
    belligerent status for rebel regime,
      67, 71-72, 79-80, 88, 99-100, 110
    bombing by government forces,
      45-46
    bombing of oil facilities, 51-53,
      55-60
    British-U.S. talks, 5, 18, 91-92,
      99-100
    Celebes rebels, rivalry with,
      400-401
    China, Republic of, military aid, 71,
      87, 71, 126-127, 131-137, 446
    economic sabotage, 235, 240
    establishment of rival government,
      14-15, 19-20, 23-24, 38, 94
    evacuation of foreign nationals,
      55-60
    failure of, 114, 121-122, 130, 148,
      236
    government attacks, 49, 54, 65,
      100-101
    guerrilla warfare, 229, 259, 326-327,
      339, 579
    Indonesian position, 174
    Indonesian-U.S. talks on, 43-44
    Islamic nations position, 23

Sumatra—Continued
  revolt in—Continued
    NATO arms sales to Indonesia, 42n
    Netherlands position, 29
    Padang group ultimatum, 19-24,
      26-27, 35, 38
    Philippine position, 63-64
    SEATO involvement in, 44, 50
    Soviet position, 24, 50
    stalemate, 80-81, 456
    territorial gains by government
      forces, 68-69, 86-87, 92-94
    U.S. position, 16-17, 90-91, 111-112,
      211
  rubber estates, security of, 371
  secession of, 99, 110
  U.S. economic aid for, 214, 299
Sumual, Lt. Col., 20, 80, 121, 163, 174
Sunardjo, 224
Sunario, Maj., 188, 205, 221, 396
Supeni, 525
Supreme War Administration, 530
Suryadarma, Marshal, 263, 312, 314,
    374n, 416, 519-521, 584n
Suwirjo, 174
Suwito, 51, 53, 56, 237-238
Sweden, 103
Switzerland, 103
Syria, 71

Taiwan (see also China, Republic of), 325
Taiwan Straits crisis, 396, 439
Tamzil, 320, 359, 422
Tanguy, 505
Tarunimihardja, Gatot, 446n
Taylor, Gen. Maxwell D., 113, 120, 200,
    230-231, 300
Thailand, 24, 95
Thurston, 503
Tibet, 397, 449
Timberman, Maj. Gen. Thomas S., 230
Time magazine, 278
Tin, 66, 360
Tito, Joseph Broz, 309, 552n
Tobing, Ferdinand Lumban, 175, 184,
    224
Toure, Sekou, 558
Treasury, U.S. Department of the, 424n
Triebel, Rear Adm. C.O., 30, 34n, 230
Turkey, 387
Tuthill, John W., 236
Twining, Gen. Nathan F., 14, 155-156,
    167, 230

U–2 incident, 556
Ulmer, Alfred C., Jr., 91*n*, 167*n*, 255
Underhill, Francis T., Jr., 15*n*, 39*n*, 53*n*,
   101*n*, 217*n*, 297*n*, 395, 396*n*, 533*n*
United Kingdom (*see also British
   subheadings under other subjects*),
   328, 333, 419
United Nations, 24, 33, 161, 354*n*, 561,
   564
   General Assembly, 480, 516-517, 533,
      540, 551, 562
   Sukarno speech, 535*n*, 539
   West New Guinea trusteeship
      proposal, 384-385, 387-389,
      569-570
   Indonesian peacekeeping troops, 550,
      552, 558
   New Guinea dispute, 280, 286, 324,
      334*n*, 340-341, 384-385, 387-389,
      428*n*, 438, 449, 563, 569-570, 583
   Security Council, 287, 320, 505,
      510-511
United Press, 169-171
United States Information Agency
   (USIA), 330
United States Information Service
   (USIS), 437, 459

van Roijen. *See* Roijen.
Vietnam, Republic of, 24, 458
Vittrup, Maj. Gen. Russell L., 260,
   262-263, 270, 277-278
Voorst, S.G.M. van, 27, 40-42, 206-207,
   211, 265*n*, 278*n*

Wallner, Woodruff, 466
Wan Tan Nea, 135
Warouw, Col., 105, 157, 174, 221, 239*n*
Waugh, Samuel C., 356, 358
Wells, Bartlett, 255
Wenzel, Robert H., 35*n*, 53*n*, 301*n*, 303*n*,
   304*n*, 316*n*, 352*n*, 355*n*, 392*n*, 418*n*,
   445*n*, 454*n*, 481*n*, 527*n*, 533*n*, 553*n*,
   565*n*

West New Guinea, 289-290, 292, 561
   Australian administration of, 341
   civil unrest in, 124
   decolonization of, 323-325
   Netherlands refugees in, 440
   independence for, 516
   Indonesian claims to, 76, 432-433
   strategic value of, 66-67, 325
   U.N. trusteeship for, 324, 340-341,
      563-564
   unification with Australian sector,
      366, 560-561
   U.S. administration of, proposal for,
      324, 564
   U.S. Navy visits to, 331-332
Wheeler, Maj. Gen. Earle G., 230
White, G.D.L., 116
White, Ivan, 491*n*, 508*n*
White, Paul Lincoln, 57, 70, 126
White, Gen. Thomas D., 230
Wilcox, Francis O., 438, 516-518, 533*n*
Wilkinson, 377, 378*n*
Wilopo, 8, 82, 197, 217
Wisner, Frank, 125, 255
World Court. *See* International Court of
   Justice (ICJ).

Yamada, Hisamoto, 528*n*
Yeh, George Kung-Chao, 142, 148,
   194-195, 203-204, 239
Young, Philip, 122, 282, 291, 406, 466*n*,
   542
   Karel Doorman cruise, 492*n*, 493*n*,
      503-505, 511-514, 527*n*, 528*n*,
      529*n*, 531-532
   New Guinea dispute, 294, 331-334,
      438, 526, 540, 559, 561, 569*n*
   U.S. military aid to Indonesia, 278*n*,
      345-347
   U.S. military aid to the Netherlands,
      351*n*, 352*n*, 462
Yu Ta Wei, 202-204
Yugoslavia, 165, 233, 372, 425
Yusuf, Col. *See* Jusuf, Col. Andi.

ISBN 0-16-041836-4

90000

DATE DUE			
			Printed in USA